American Foreign Policy

4TH EDITION

American Foreign Policy

Past, Present, Future

Glenn P. Hastedt

James Madison University

PRENTICE HALL , Upper Saddle River, New Jersey 07458

Library of Congress Cataloging-in-Publication Data

Hastedt, Glenn P. (date)
    American foreign policy : past, present, future / Glenn P. Hastedt.—4th ed.
      p.   cm.
    Includes bibliographical references.
    ISBN 0-13-083579-X (alk. paper)
    1. United States—Foreign relations.   2. United States—Foreign relations—1945–
    3. United States—Foreign relations administration.   I. Title.
    E183.7.H27   1999
    327.73—dc21   99-21622
                                                                   CIP

Editorial director: Charlyce Jones Owen
Editor in chief: Nancy Roberts
Senior acquisitions editor: Beth Gillett Mejia
Editorial/production supervision and
   interior design: Barbara Reilly
Copyeditor: Sylvia Moore
Editorial assistant: Brian Prybella
Production assistant: Kathleen Sleys
Prepress and manufacturing buyer: Ben Smith
Marketing manager: Christopher De John
Cover design: Bruce Kenselaar

This book was set in 10/11 ITC New Baskerville by Stratford
Publishing Services, Inc., and was printed and bound by Courier
Companies, Inc. The cover was printed by Phoenix Color Corp.

Printed in the United States of America
10 9 8 7 6 5 4 3 2 1

ISBN 0-13-083579-X

Prentice-Hall International (UK) Limited, *London*
Prentice-Hall of Australia Pty. Limited, *Sydney*
Prentice-Hall Canada Inc., *Toronto*
Prentice-Hall Hispanoamericana, S.A., *Mexico*
Prentice-Hall of India Private Limited, *New Delhi*
Prentice-Hall of Japan, Inc., *Tokyo*
Pearson Education Asia Pte. Ltd., *Singapore*
Editora Prentice-Hall do Brasil, Ltda., *Rio de Janeiro*

*To Cathy,
Sarah,
and Matthew*

Contents

PART II
THE HISTORICAL CONTEXT OF AMERICAN FOREIGN POLICY

CHAPTER 3

The American National Style   30

CHAPTER 4

Post-Vietnam U.S. Foreign Policy   48

PART V
POLICY TOOLS

CHAPTER 13

Diplomacy   *284*

CHAPTER 14

Covert Action   *304*

Preface

Much has happened in the world since *American Foreign Policy: Past, Present, Future* first appeared. Cautious speculation about whether the cold war had ended has been replaced by a certainty that the cold war is behind us. This belief has led to a change in the nature of the political debate over the proper conduct and content of American foreign policy. As a nation we seem less interested in debating the merits of past foreign policy initiatives and more interested in discovering how best to maneuver through the contours of an evolving post–cold war era. In part, this is a matter of necessity. As old problems lose their sense of urgency and are replaced by new ones, policies long considered to be in the national interest become less compelling. The post–cold war era holds out both promises and challenges, and this duality is at the center of disagreements over how to proceed. For many, the post–cold war era offers the prospect of realizing goals and objectives long held to be unattainable because of the demands of national security considerations. It is a moment to be seized and acted upon. For others, little has changed and the game of world politics remains the same. Bold initiatives to build a new world order are to be shunned in favor of policies designed to preserve American hegemony or maintain a favorable balance of power.

The uncertainty over how to proceed, and debates over the proper distribution of power in formulating policy, make this an exciting time to study American foreign policy. The fourth edition of *American Foreign Policy* builds upon the three previous editions and incorporates new material in the hope of providing students with a solid foundation for examining American foreign policy as it operates under these changing conditions. As with the previous editions, this edition does not argue for a right answer to any of the questions it presents. I see the purpose of a textbook as establishing a foundation on which instructors can build through the selection of additional reading materials and lectures. Its sole theme is that if we are to confront the future successfully, we must first understand the past and be clear about how the policy-making process operates.

Conceptually, the basic structure of the book remains the same, but the organizational scheme is somewhat different. Part I examines the global context of American foreign policy. Two chapters look at the global setting and the emerging foreign policy agenda. Part II examines the historical context of American foreign policy. Chapters in this section deal with post-Vietnam foreign policy and learning from the past. Part III examines the foreign affairs government. It includes chapters on the domestic context of American foreign policy, the Constitution and foreign affairs, and the political institutions that play leading roles in the making of American foreign policy. Part IV looks at the process by which foreign policy is made. One chapter examines models of policy making and the other presents a series of case studies. Part V presents an overview of the policy tools at the disposal of policy makers. A focus on policy tools rather than problems is used because this type of discussion can be readily directed at whatever current foreign policy problems sit atop the agenda. Part VI concludes the discussion of American foreign policy with a survey of alternative futures. Each future is discussed in terms of (1) the major threat to American security interests, (2) the responsibility of the United States to other countries, and (3) the responsibility of the United States to the global community.

The major addition to this fourth edition is a new second chapter on the emerging foreign policy agenda. This chapter expands the discussion of foreign policy issues that was in the first chapter of previous editions and gives it more emphasis. The goal is to help students see the ways in which the post–cold war agenda of American foreign policy is changing and yet not lose sight of those issues that have traditionally been of concern to policy makers. Other significant changes include a discussion of presidential decision making on Bosnia; new material on diplomacy, arms control, and military policy; and a section on Congress that examines the impact of region and party.

I would like to thank Jay Ovisovitch for his comments on the chapter surveying post-Vietnam foreign policy. I would also like to thank those instructors who used the earlier editions for the suggestions they sent me on how to improve this edition. I am also grateful to Steven W. Hook of Kent State University, Roy Licklider of Rutgers University, and B. David Meyers of University of North Carolinia-Greensboro for their insightful comments. As always, any errors of interpretation or fact are mine alone.

Finally, as with the first three editions of *American Foreign Policy: Past, Present, Future,* this edition is dedicated to Cathy, Sarah, and Matthew.

Glenn P. Hastedt

American
Foreign
Policy

1 The Global Setting of American Foreign Policy

WHY THE INTERNATIONAL SYSTEM MATTERS

One of the cornerstone documents of cold war American foreign policy was National Security Council Document 68 (NSC-68). The product of a review of America's initial efforts to implement a policy of containment against the Soviet Union, NSC-68 asserted that the purpose of American foreign policy is to "foster a world environment in which the American system can flourish." Today, one-half century later, with both the cold war and the Soviet Union no longer in existence, few would disagree with its characterization of the purpose of American foreign policy.

Far less consensus exists on the nature of the contemporary "world environment" and how it affects the "flourishing" of the American system. In truth, this has always been the case. Americans have seldom been united in their thinking about the nature of the international system or how it affects their lives. Isolationists routinely see the world as threatening to American values and try to construct barriers to U.S. involvement in international ventures. Internationalists see involvement in world affairs as crucial to the flourishing of the American system but often find themselves in disagreement over when, how, and where to become involved.

Globalization

The current debate over the potential benefits and dangers of globalization provides us with a window on the debate over America's relationship to the world at the turn of the century. Globalization is a summary term that speaks to the "intrusive and intense economic interaction" currently taking place in the international economy among "a large and growing number of entities outside government control," which has been brought on by rapid advances in communication and information technologies and government policies designed to reduce barriers to the free flow of goods and capital across national boundaries. Globalization is, at the same time, credited with promoting prosperity and growth for the U.S. economy while it is held accountable for the loss of jobs and increasing income disparities.

Richard Haass and Robert Litan assert that "globalization is a reality, not a choice."[1] The problem facing the United States is not whether to participate in a globalized economy but how to participate. Focusing on the economic costs and benefits of globalization, they argue against erecting economic barriers whose purpose it would be to insulate the American economy from the forces of globalization. Instead, they urge that ways be found to better manage America's participation in a globalized economy.

Security specialists also see dangers in globalization. They note that "with this advent of this burgeoning free trade in technical ideas and the people who think about them, we have entered a new era in the history of [nuclear] proliferation." These dangers extend beyond the domain of highly sophisticated weapons technologies. Michael Klare notes that small arms and light weapons now play a central role in many ethnic and sectarian conflicts.[2] In fact, they have become weapons of choice. These weapons are easily produced and readily obtained in the global marketplace. The Israeli Uzi submachine gun is in the inventory of 39 states and the Belgian FAL assault rifle has been manufactured in such diverse states as Argentina, Australia, Canada, Mexico, Israel, and South Africa.

The potential impact of globalization extends far beyond realms of military security and economic prosperity. Benjamin Barber fears that the emerging global consumer culture which is accompanying economic globalization is indifferent to the existence of democracy in the United States and around the world.[3] Alan Tonelson is also fearful of the non-economic consequences of globalization.[4] He sees the globalization of production as threatening America's future as a cohesive and successful society.

What Type of International System Exists Today?

While it is a striking feature of the contemporary international system, globalization is not its sole defining characteristic. Some observers stress the continued importance of underlying structural constants in assessing the ways in which the international system provides opportunities and challenges to policy makers. Others emphasize the importance of post–World War II trends. More recently some scholars have begun to catalog the emerging characteristics of the post–cold war era. In the remainder of this chapter we examine each of these aspects of the contemporary international system in order to clarify the global setting of American foreign policy.

THE INTERNATIONAL SYSTEM: STRUCTURAL CONSTANTS

Decentralization

The first enduring feature of the international system is its decentralized nature. Unlike in highly developed domestic political systems, there exist no central political institutions to make laws or see to their enforcement. Additionally, there is no common political culture in which to anchor an agreed-upon set of norms governing the behavior of states. The combined result is a highly competitive international system in which there is a constant expectation of violence and very little expectation that either international law or appeals to moral principles will greatly influence the resolution of an issue.

Decentralization does not mean that the international system operates in a state of anarchy. Ordered anarchy would be a more apt characterization. For while enforceable laws and common values are absent, rules do exist that lend a measure of predictability and certainty to international transactions.[5] They do so by indicating the limits of permissible behavior and the directions to follow in settling disputes. Rules are less permanent than laws, are more general in nature, and tend to be normative statements rather than commands. Different international systems operate according to different rules and therefore place different opportunities and challenges before policy makers. Neutrality, for example, is generally held to be permissible according to the rules of loose bipolarity but impossible under the rules of tight bipolarity.

Self-Help System

The second structural constant grows out of the first: The international system is a self-help system. States must rely on only themselves to accomplish their foreign policy goals. To do otherwise runs the risk of manipulation or betrayal at the hands of another state. It is important to stress that great powers as well as smaller powers need to heed the admonition to avoid excessive dependence on others. One of the points stressed by opponents within the Reagan administration to using Israel as a go-between in its plan to sell weapons to Iran in hopes of gaining the release of American hostages in Lebanon was that Israeli and U.S. national interests were not identical and that in some cases they were in direct conflict.[6]

The self-help principle challenges policy makers to bring goals and power resources into balance. Pursuing more goals than one has the resources to accomplish or squandering resources on secondary objectives saps the vitality of the state and makes it unable to respond effectively to future challenges. Vietnam is argued by many to be a classic example of the inability to balance goals and resources and its crippling consequences. American policy makers entered into the Vietnam conflict with little understanding of the history of the region or of the Vietnamese struggle for independence. Once involved, U.S. policy produced steady increases in the level of the U.S. commitment to the war, but it did not bring the United States any closer to victory. Instead the reverse occurred. The longer the United States was there and the greater the level of this commitment, the more elusive victory became. Perhaps most frustrating was the inability to devise a workable exit scenario. The Vietnam experience continues to cast a long shadow over U.S. foreign policy. Many conservatives agree that the Vietnam syndrome has prevented the United States from acquiring either the capability or the will to protect its vital interests in the Persian Gulf, Angola, or Central America.

A Stratified System

The third structural constant is the stratified nature of the international system. The equality of states embedded in the concept of sovereignty is a legal myth. The principle of sovereignty dates back to the Treaty of Westphalia and the beginnings of the modern state system in 1648. It holds that no legal authority exists above the state except that which the state voluntarily accepts. The reality of international politics is quite different, and sovereignty is a matter of degree rather than an absolute condition. States are "born unequal."[7] The resources they draw on for their power are distributed unequally across the globe. As such, the ability of states to accomplish their foreign policy objectives (as well as their very choice of objectives) will vary from state to state.

Two key areas of disagreement among recent administrations have been over how great a degree of power inequality exists in the international system and the identity of the power centers. Reagan's foreign policy was based on the assumption that the international system is essentially bipolar. The Soviet Union and the United States were held to be the two central actors involved in a global power struggle. Furthermore, it was a struggle in which incompatible ideologies were a powerful force in affecting foreign policy decisions. The Carter, Ford, and Nixon administrations all saw power distributed more broadly, and ideology was seen as less of an important factor for the operation of the international system. The Nixon and Ford foreign policies stressed the ability to coexist with Russia (the policy of détente) and alluded to using other powers as counterweights to Russia (the "China card"). The early Carter administration also felt that the United States could coexist with the Soviet Union. Its foreign policy differed from its predecessors' in its emphasis on human rights and economic issues. This switch in concerns brought with it a shift in the identification of power centers away from the Soviet Union and toward Western Europe, Japan, and key third world states. With the invasion of Afghanistan, Carter's priorities changed, and once again the Soviet threat became the primary foreign policy problem for the United States.

The dramatic easing of cold war hostilities that took place early in the Bush administration left unchanged the stratified nature of world politics. What it did was change the identity of the key world powers and the likely arenas of conflict; consequently, the Soviet military threat is being replaced by Japanese and German economic power.

THE INTERNATIONAL SYSTEM: POSTWAR TRENDS

Diffusion of Power

Although the basic structure of the international system has endured over time, the system itself is not unchanging. Four post–World War II trends are especially notable: a diffusion of power, issue proliferation, actor proliferation, and regional diversity. Power is the ability to achieve objectives. It is typically viewed as something one possesses, a commodity to be acquired, stored, and manipulated. But power must also be viewed as a relational concept. What is ultimately at issue is not how much power a state has, but how much power it has in a specific issue compared to those it is dealing with.

The postwar era has seen a steady diffusion of power. This in turn has created a frustrating gap between the ends and means of U.S. and Soviet foreign policy. Other states are increasingly able to resist their leadership or significantly add to the costs they must pay in order to achieve their goals. The only partially successful United States–led 1980 Olympic boycott and Soviet pipeline embargo are mirrored in the Soviet Union's inability to manipulate the International Congresses of Communist Parties to condemn Chinese "heresies," and its difficulty in finding a workable policy to deal with events in Poland.

It is not so much that the quantity of power possessed by the Soviet Union and the United States has declined. U.S. and Soviet dominance in the field of nuclear weapons remains unchallenged. The same holds true for conventional weapons. In absolute terms these two economies still rank among the world's greatest. What has changed is the utility of certain types of power, the issues being contested, and the ability of other states to exploit points of sensitivity and vulnerability. Bargaining and negotiation have replaced command and dominance as the central feature of the relationship between the superpowers and other states.

The causes for the diffusion of power can be found both in the specifics of American (and Soviet) foreign policy and in the more universal cycles of hegemonic decline. Robert Gilpin, after examining the decline of empires throughout history, asserts that we can identify a cycle of hegemonic decline.[8] As the cycle progresses, a combination of the burdens of imperial leadership, increased emphasis on the consumption of goods and services, and the international diffusion of technology conspire to sap the strength of the imperial state and bring about its decline.

The specific successes and failures of postwar American foreign policy have also contributed to this diffusion of power. The impact of foreign policy failures is relatively easy to anticipate. In the wake of defeat follows the search for scapegoats, a disillusionment with the task undertaken, and a desire to avoid similar situations. Vietnam stands out as the most significant military failure, and it is held by many to have been responsible for destroying the postwar domestic consensus on the purpose of American power.

Economic failures have also contributed to the diffusion of power. Economic sanctions directed against Castro in the sixties failed to bring down his regime and only made him more dependent on Soviet support. Repeated efforts at bringing about economic and social development in the third world such as Truman's Point Four Program and Kennedy's Alliance for Progress have also failed. The continued existence of widespread poverty has proven to be a fertile breeding ground for anti-U.S. nationalist and revolutionary forces.

Even American foreign policy successes have hastened the decline of U.S. dominance. The reconstruction of the Japanese and Western European economies ranks as two truly remarkable achievements. In a sense U.S. foreign policy has almost been too successful here. These economies are now major economic rivals of the U.S. economy and often outperform it. The North Atlantic Treaty Organization (NATO) is another success that has had a dual impact. Its creation in 1949 did succeed in erecting a military shield for Western Europe and in stopping any further Soviet expansion into Europe. At the same time NATO offered U.S. European allies, most notably the French, the opportunity to pursue their own foreign policy objectives, often at the expense of U.S. interests.

Issue Proliferation

The second area of evolutionary change is issue proliferation. More is involved here than simply an increase in the number of issues on the foreign policy agenda. Their character has also changed as the line between foreign and domestic policy has become increasingly blurred. Not long ago one could speak of a clear-cut foreign affairs issue hierarchy. At the top were a relatively small number of high-politics problems involving questions of national security, territorial integrity, and political independence. At the bottom were the numerically more prevalent low-politics issues of commerce, energy, environment, etc. Although largely intuitive, the line between high and low politics was well established. The positions occupied by issues in this hierarchy were also relatively fixed. This allowed policy makers to develop a familiarity with the issues before them and the options open to them. Today this is no longer the case.

The high-politics category has become crowded. The oil crisis and fear of resource scarcity elevated economic issues to the status of national security issues. Economic recession and high unemployment have made the existence of an open international system a question of high politics. There is now also a great deal of movement within the high–low ranking system. Under Carter human rights for a time became a pivotal concern for the United States. Under the Reagan administration it returned to a low-politics position when the emphasis shifted to international terrorism.

The high–low politics distinction was implicitly based on the existence of a prior distinction between foreign and domestic policy. This distinction has become increasingly difficult to maintain. How, for example, do we classify attempts to get Japan to agree to export restrictions on goods shipped to the United States or the negotiations over the damage done in Canada by acid rain originating in U.S.–based industries? The term increasingly used to characterize these and other issues that contain significant domestic and international dimensions is *intermestic* (*inter* from international and *mestic* from domestic).[9] Intermestic, however, says nothing about the importance of the issue that is the central distinction to the high–low policy continuum. It deals with an entirely different dimension: the relative importance of foreign and domestic considerations in searching for a solution. Issue proliferation has thus brought with it added complexity. Policy makers must judge not only the ranking of an issue but also the extent of its domestic impact. They then must be prepared to constantly reevaluate their thinking in light of changing circumstances. Tables 1–1 and 1–2 illustrate how the high–low scale and the foreign–domestic scale can be used to classify issues and show how issues have changed position over time.

Actor Proliferation

The third evolutionary feature of the international system is actor proliferation. On the one hand, actor proliferation has taken the form of an expansion in the number of states. In 1982, the United States had diplomatic relations

TABLE 1–1   Illustrative Distribution of Issues in Late 1960s

FOREIGN POLICY "IMPORTANCE"		100% Domestic	50/50 Intermestic	100% Foreign Policy
High			Vietnam War	Nuclear strategy
				Arms control
			Recognizing China	Covert actions
				Foreign Aid
				Test Ban Treaty
			Tariffs	
				Energy
				Grain sales
		Interest rates		Routine diplomatic
		Environmental		negotiations
		standards		
Low				

RELATIVE IMPORTANCE OF FOREIGN
AND DOMESTIC CONSIDERATIONS
TO RESOLUTION OF ISSUE

TABLE 1–2   Illustrative Distribution of Issues in Early 1980s

FOREIGN POLICY "IMPORTANCE"		100% Domestic		50/50 Intermestic	100% Foreign Policy
High		Arms control/ Nuclear freeze	MX		
		Panama Canal Treaty	Covert action		Human rights— Carter
		Energy policy Tariffs/Quotas	Foreign aid		International terrorism— Reagan
		Grain sales			
			China/Taiwan		
		Interest rates			Human rights— Reagan
		Environmental standards			Routine diplomatic negotiations
Low					

RELATIVE IMPORTANCE OF FOREIGN
AND DOMESTIC CONSIDERATIONS
TO RESOLUTION OF ISSUE

with 150 states. This compares to 130 in 1970, 74 in 1950, and 58 in 1930. This expansion in the number of states has brought with it a corresponding expansion in the number of views that can be found on any given problem. Quite often these views are based on different starting premises and assumptions than those held by the United States. The Law of the Sea Conference illustrates the impact that the proliferation of states has had on U.S. foreign policy. The very number of states participating presented great obstacles to achieving an agreement. So too did the diversity of views expressed, as well as the intensity with which they were held. The decision-making rules for the proposed International Seabed Authority that would oversee seabed mineral exploration emerged as a major point of contention. The United States insisted on some form of weighted voting. It refused to participate in a system where it could be outvoted by an alliance of small states. In the end, these problems produced a situation where on April 30, 1982, the United States was the only Western industrialized state that refused to sign the treaty. One hundred and thirty states voted to sign it and thereby concluded a process of negotiation and discussion begun in 1967.

Although the growth in the number of states has nearly run its course, continued growth is taking place in a second area: nonstate actors. States have never been the only actors in world politics. Yet it is only comparatively recently that nonstate actors have appeared in sufficient numbers and possessed control over enough resources to be significant actors in world politics. Three categories of nonstate actors may be identified. They are Intergovernmental Organizations (IGOs) such as the United Nations, NATO, and the Organization of American States; Nongovernmental Organizations (NGOs) such as General Motors, the International Red Cross, the Catholic Church, and the Palestine Liberation Organization; and subnational actors such as the Central Intelligence Agency (CIA), Defense Department, New York City, and Texas.

Statistically, the growth in the number of nonstate actors has been explosive.[10] On the eve of World War I, there were only 49 IGOs and 170 NGOs. In 1940 the numbers had grown to over 80 IGOs and about 500 NGOs. By the mid-1970s, there were approximately 300 IGOs and 2,400 NGOs. Of the NGOs existing in 1966, 501 were founded after 1950 and 251 after 1960. The emergence of nonstate actors as a significant force in world politics is generally tied to the inability of the state to adequately respond to the demands citizens place on it. In some cases they have emerged as byproducts of state efforts to meet these demands. In others they have emerged as challenges to the state for the loyalties of its citizens.

Actor proliferation has also altered in three ways the context within which American foreign policy decisions are made. First, the presence and actions of nonstate actors have altered the language used in thinking about foreign policy problems. The language of the cold war now competes with the imagery of interdependence for the attention of policy makers. Second, nonstate actors often serve as potential instruments of foreign policy. There are major advantages to using a nonstate actor to advance state objectives. By not being identified as part of a state, their actions may be better received by other actors. Decisions made by the International Monetary Fund or World Bank tend to be more readily accepted by third world states than if they had come directly from the United States. The third impact nonstate actors have on U.S. foreign policy is that they often limit the options open to policy makers. Their ability to resist and frustrate state initiatives necessitates that policy makers consider courses of action that they otherwise would likely reject. The Palestine Liberation Organization serves as just such a complicating and limiting factor in attempts to construct a viable Middle East peace plan.

Regional Diversity

As a superpower, the United States not only is concerned with the structure and operation of the international system as a whole but is also concerned with the operation of its subsystems. Three subsystems are especially important to the United States. Each presents the United States with different management problems and thus requires a different solution.[11] It should be stressed that U.S. policy makers have not always viewed the world from this perspective, nor do they uniformly do so today. For much of the cold war era, the international system was viewed as an undifferentiated whole in which competition with the Soviet Union was the key management problem. The first is the Western system which is made up of the advanced industrial states of the United States, Canada, Western Europe, and Japan. The principal problem in the Western system is managing interdependence. All acknowledge that the central institutions of the Western system accomplished their major objectives. NATO and a series of bilateral alliances have brought military security. Free trade and regional trading agreements such as the European Community have provided economic growth and prosperity. At issue today is the distribution of costs and benefits. U.S. leadership and initiative once so eagerly sought by its allies is now often resisted. For its part the United States has begun to question the costs of leadership and seeks to have its allies pick up a larger share of the defense burden. A similar situation holds for economic relations. Many in the United States are no longer willing to underwrite a free-trade system or to accept economic discrimination in the name of alliance unity, whereas U.S. allies have become increasingly disenchanted with U.S. economic policies.

The second subsystem is the North–South system. A quite different set of perspectives governs interactions in this system from that in the Western system. In place of expectations of sharing and mutual gain, the South perceives exploitation. The fundamental management problem in the North–South system is coping with military and economic dependence. Where solutions to the problems of interdependence lie in the fine tuning of existing international organizations and practices, solutions to the problems of dependence require constructing a new system that the South is willing to accept as legitimate.

The third subsystem of concern to the United States is the East–West system. The fundamental management problem here is one of reintegration. With the beginning of the cold war, a split developed in the international system, dividing it into two antagonist and largely self-contained parts. The past three decades have seen efforts at establishing rules of conduct to bridge this gap. Arms agreements have been the primary vehicle for moving the two sides from military competition to military cooperation. Beginning with the Limited

Test Ban Treaty in 1962, a series of arms control and arms limitation agreements were signed between the United States and the Soviet Union, culminating in the signing of SALT II. Since then the situation has deteriorated, and the gap between the two sides has intensified. The need for economic reintegration was made clear by the massive Soviet grain purchase of 1972, which had the unexpected effect of sending the price of grain skyrocketing in the United States. Pressures for economic reintegration also emanated from the Soviet desire for Western technology, the deepening Soviet involvement in the international oil market, and Western interest in exporting goods to the Soviet Union. These pressures have not yet become strong enough to produce meaningful reintegration.

THE INTERNATIONAL SYSTEM: EMERGING CHARACTERISTICS OF THE POST–COLD WAR WORLD

In time it will be possible to speak of the last decade of the twentieth century as something other than the "post–cold war era." It will acquire an identity of its own, just as the late 1940s are no longer referred to as the post–World War II era but are seen as part of the cold war. That time, however, is not here yet. Instead of being able to catalog a set of qualities that will give this period its own defining characteristics, we are left to speculate about which of the features that now seem so prominent will endure and shape future foreign policy decisions. Commentators on American foreign policy have taken two different paths in trying to conceptualize what it is about the current international system that we ought to study most. The first seeks to answer this question by providing us with an overarching set of symbols or metaphors to use in evaluating contemporary events and deciphering where they may take us. The second approach is more modest and focuses on highlighting the forces now at work which either were not present prior to the end of the cold war or were obscured by the all-encompassing nature of that conflict.

John Lewis Gaddis has put forward two of the most frequently invoked sets of images. Where the cold war was defined by the struggle between two superpowers and their alliance partners, Gaddis suggests that we might think about the current international system as being composed of a struggle between two underlying sets of forces tugging in opposite directions.[12] On the one hand are forces of integration that act to bring together peoples and countries. Opposed to it are the forces of fragmentation that work to resurrect old sources of friction and rivalry as well as create new ones. Gaddis notes that it is unclear which set of forces the United States ought to embrace in its foreign policy. Integrationist forces, he cautions, can be disruptive and do not offer automatic protection against unwanted events and trends. In fact, they may help bring them about and thus be part of the problem. Gaddis offers the AIDS pandemic as an example. The freer movement of peoples across international borders is certainly one of the most integrative forces at work in the world today. Yet it also is a major obstacle to dealing with AIDS and a source of friction among states.

Forces of integration and fragmentation are not new to the post–cold war era. Their potential for changing the landscape of world politics in fundamental ways is suggested by another metaphor employed by Gaddis. Borrowing from the field of geology, Gaddis asserts that we might think in terms of "tectonic motion."[13] Geologists describe the earth's crust as composed of giant tectonic plates that press up against one another and are subject to tremendous pressures. Normally these pressures produce only the slightest amount of movement. However, under certain circumstances they can result in large-scale movements (that is, earthquakes, volcanic explosions) that literally reshape continents and alter their climates. From this perspective the challenge facing policy makers is to better understand the nature of tectonic motion so that they will not be as surprised by the end of the post–cold war era as they were by the end of the cold war.

Just what are these potentially volatile integrative and/or fragmenting forces? An extensive list of candidates exists to choose from. While the listing and importance attached to each varies from commentator to commentator, it is possible to identify six forces which have received special attention in the post–cold war era.

The Proliferation of Weapons of Mass Destruction. A fundamental reality of the nuclear age is that the knowledge needed to build a nuclear weapon is readily available to those who want it. Two trends now merge with this reality to create a scenario in which a large number of states may soon possess an "at-the-ready" nuclear arsenal, one that can be assembled in a matter of hours or days.[14] One of these trends is the increasing ease with which nuclear weapons facilities can be constructed due to advances in technology. "Every year . . . the size of key facilities is getting smaller, as is the required number of scientists and technicians . . . the amount of electrical power consumed . . . and the time for each step in the nuclear weapons development process." The second trend is the diffusion of long-range delivery systems and advances in mobile tactical ballistic missile systems. On the one hand, this represents an extension of the ongoing process of power diffusion that was discussed above. On the other hand, it appears to hold the potential for radically transforming the basic structure of world politics that makes it an unprecedented occurrence. Morton Kaplan first spoke to the international system-transforming capabilities inherent in the widespread proliferation of such weapons in the late 1960s in his pioneering work on international systems theory.[15] He argued that each international system operated according to a unique set of rules determined by the distribution of power. Kaplan continued that the range of possible international systems that might come into existence was not limited by those which we had already experienced (that is, bipolar and multipolar). One such new international system was a unit veto system which could result from 10 to 20 countries having a usable nuclear capability. The result would be a situation where the great powers pursued largely isolationist foreign policies and where there were few alliances, as each state relied on the threat of nuclear retaliation to protect its interests.

The Emergence of New Forms of Power. Historically the debate over how best to realize one's foreign policy objectives has been cast in terms of the relative utility of military power versus economic power. This debate continues in the post–cold war era, with many arguing that military power now has been supplanted once and for all by economic power as the instrument of choice by policy makers. This is not the first time that an obituary has been written for military power. Similar assessments about the lessened value of military power and the increased importance of economic power were made after Vietnam and during the OPEC-led oil price hikes of the early 1970s. What is new is that commentators are beginning to talk about a new form of power. Joseph Nye refers to it as "soft power." Soft power is not rooted in control of land, an abundance of natural resources, large populations, or inventories of weapons. It draws its strength primarily from human resources.[16] These are resources which the United States is rich in; they provide it with the ability to exert a leadership role in world affairs at a time when its other power resources may be in decline compared to other states. The system-transforming potential of soft power stems from the fact that in order to use it effectively policy makers must embrace a new view of leadership and think about power relationships differently. Soft power is not power that can be used to command or force other states to act in a prescribed fashion. Rather, it is power to lead by example and to foster cooperation. "It is the ability to structure a situation so that other countries develop preferences consistent with our goals."

Political Fission.   This too could be seen as a continuation of a previously discussed trend, that of actor proliferation. Yet it is also more than that. Political fission promises to increase the number of actors in a quite different fashion and with very different consequences. In the past it was hoped that world politics might be transformed through the creation of peaceful "webs of interdependence" among these newly emerging actors. Today new actors are being created as a result of the inability of individuals and governments to act in concert with one another. This is most notable at the state level where nationalism has emerged as a powerful divisive force. Karin Von Hippel has identified 78 different nationalist claims that had not been resolved by mid-1994 and that hold the potential for splitting states.[17] That number could easily increase. Today over 180 states with in excess of 8,000 distinct ethnic cultures belong to the United Nations. Political fission also is evident at the international level.[18] The potential significance of political fission does not lie in the end of the state as the fundamental unit of world politics. The state remains the model for those seeking to destroy it. Rather, it lies in the "incoherence" of world politics, as neither states nor international organizations will possess the political resources necessary to bring about and sustain collaborative problem-solving efforts.

The Emergence of New Ideas.   John Mueller has argued that ideas are the primary driving force in world politics. In his view, the cold war came about because of a clash in ideas. It ended not because of a redistribution of military power resources or a change in the strength of national economies, but because of changes in those ideas. Mueller concludes that scholars have been wrong to think that only war can bring about a change in the structure of the international system. "The system can be transformed by a mere change of ideas."[19] This is exactly what happened between 1988 and 1991 as the Soviet Union changed its world view from that of a zero-sum game to a positive-sum game. "Previously we [the Soviet Union] reasoned: the worse for the adversary, the better for us . . . but today this is no longer true." The two ideas which have commanded the most attention in the post–cold war era are democracy and the obsolescence of war among the major powers. Both are seen by their advocates as having system-transforming potential through the curbs they place on the resort to violence.

Advances in Communication Technology.   Writing in 1971, Swedish scholar Johan Galtung argued that in the future the advanced states of the world would no longer continue to exert their imperialistic control over less developed areas through the physical presence of troops as they did in the past or through the use of economic instruments such as multinational corporations and international financial and trade bodies as they were currently doing.[20] Instead, they would rely on instant communications where "parties who want to communicate with each other will set up ad hoc communication networks . . . guided by enormous data-banks and idea-banks that permit participants to find their opposite numbers." Live-time coverage of the 1991 attempted Soviet coup, the 1989 student demonstrations on Tiananmen Square, and the Persian Gulf War are testimony to Galtung's insight into the direction in which communications technologies were moving. What is still unclear is the exact role modern communication technologies will play in world politics. Will they allow leaders in one country to shape events abroad (as they did during the Soviet coup attempt and the Gulf War when U.S. leaders were able to judge for themselves what was happening and shape their policies accordingly)? Or will they exert an independent force pushing leaders into action where they otherwise might have remained silent (such as in the Tiananmen Square demonstrations when Chinese student protesters held up English language signs to television cameras)? Will policy be improved by the added information which this revolution in communication technology brings to the policy process or will policy suffer as officials struggle to have an answer ready for an aroused public on the six o'clock news?

The Ethnicization of International Relations.   During the cold war, scholars and practitioners developed a vocabulary to organize their thinking about world politics: East versus West; North versus South; client state; buffer state; and neutral state.[21] Often these terms obscured reality as much as they highlighted its vital characteristics. Still, they provided a point of departure for making policy. With the end of the cold war these concepts have lost much of their relevance. They no longer identify the major fault lines of international relations. A new vocabulary must be created. By the mid-1990s a consensus has developed that at the center of this new vocabulary must be ethnic conflict. Not only are ethnic conflicts becoming internationalized but an ethnicization of international relations is taking place. Increasingly states and international organizations are defining their foreign policies in terms of ethnic sympathies or finding that ethnic considerations weigh heavily in the choices before them. The choices themselves are changing as new forms of conflict management develop. Cold war peacekeeping efforts have been replaced by peacemaking; UN trusteeship of colonial territories has been replaced by UN efforts to save failed or failing states; deterrence, it is argued by some, must be replaced by a strategy of reassurance.

PLAN OF THE TEXT

In this chapter we have examined the ways in which the international system affects U.S. foreign policy and how policy makers have struggled with defining the American national interest. The global setting is one of four influences that serve as background factors in the making of U.S. foreign policy. The other three are past foreign policy undertakings, the American national style, and our ability to learn from the past. Understanding U.S. foreign policy requires us to be sensitive to these more general influences as well as to be aware of how U.S. foreign policy is made and the instruments available to policy makers. The discussion of the foreign policy process begins with an examination of the domestic context within which policy makers operate and then proceeds to examine the major institutional actors in the making of American foreign policy. Next, we turn our attention to policy-making models and case studies to help us better understand how these political forces interact. The following section introduces us to five policy instruments that are of special importance for understanding U.S. foreign policy: diplomacy, economics, covert action, military power, and arms control. The text concludes by presenting eight alternative future paths which American foreign policy might travel down. Within this broad framework of broad-based background factors and more narrowly focused process- and instrument-oriented constraints, no attempt is made to identify a correct interpretation of events or course of action. Instead, a balanced discussion of alternative viewpoints is presented and questions are put forward in the hope of challenging readers to think critically about how U.S. foreign policy can build on its past and present in order to better confront the future. Before completing our overview of the background factors that influence American foreign policy we turn our attention in the next chapter to a discussion of the concepts of foreign policy and the national interest.

NOTES

1. Richard Haass and Robert Litan, "Globalization and Its Discontents: Navigating the Dangers of an Entangled World," *Foreign Affairs* 77 (1998), 2–6.
2. Michael Klare, "The New Arms Race," *Current History* 96 (April, 1997), 173–78.
3. Benjamin Barber, "Democracy at Risk," *World Policy Journal* 15 (1998), 29–41.
4. Alan Tonelson, "Globalization: The Great American Non-Debate," *Current History* 96 (November, 1997), 353–59.
5. For a discussion see Raymond Cohen, *International Politics: Rules of the Game* (New York: Longman, 1981).
6. *The New York Times, The Tower Commission Report* (New York: Bantam, 1987), p. 137.
7. Robert Tucker, *The Inequality of Nations* (New York: Basic Books, 1977).
8. Robert Gilpin, *War and Change in World Politics* (New York: Cambridge University Press, 1981). For a dissenting view on the decline of U.S. power, see Bruce Russett, "The Mysterious Case of Vanishing Hegemony; or, Is Mark Twain Really Dead," *International Organization,* 39 (1985). 207–32.

9. Bayliss Manning, "The Congress, the Executive and Intermestic Affairs: Three Proposals," *Foreign Affairs*, 56 (1977), 306–24.

10. For discussions of the growth of nonstate actors, see Werner Feld, *International Relations, A Transnational Approach* (Sherman Oaks, Calif.: Alfred, 1979); and Harold K. Jacobson, *Networks of Interdependence* (New York: Knopf, 1979).

11. The three subsystems as well as the management problems they present are taken from Joan Edleman Spero, *The Politics of International Economic Relations*, 3rd ed. (New York: St. Martin's, 1985), pp. 13–19.

12. John Lewis Gaddis, "Toward the Post–Cold War World," *Foreign Affairs*, 70 (1991), 102–22.

13. "Tectonics, History, and the End of the Cold War," in John Lewis Gaddis, *The United States and the End of the Cold War: Implications, Reconsiderations, Provocations* (New York: Oxford University Press, 1992), 155–67.

14. Roger C. Molander and Peter A. Wilson, "On Dealing with the Prospect of Nuclear Chaos," *The Washington Quarterly*, 17 (1994), 19–39.

15. Morton A. Kaplan, "The Systems Approach to International Relations," in Morton A. Kaplan (ed.), *New Approaches to International Relations* (New York: St. Martin's: 1968).

16. Joseph S. Nye, Jr., "Soft Power," *Foreign Policy*, 80 (1990).

17. Karin Von Hippel, "The Resurgence of Nationalism and Its International Implications," *The Washington Quarterly*, 17 (1994), 185–200.

18. On the problems associated with this see Gerald Helman and Steven Ratner, "Saving Failed States," *Foreign Policy*, 89 (1992/93), 3–20; and Morton H. Halperin and David J. Scheffer, *Self-Determination in the New World Order* (Washington, D.C.: Carnegie Endowment for International Peace, 1992).

19. John Mueller, *Quiet Cataclysm* (New York: HarperCollins, 1995), p. 35.

20. Johan Galtung, "A Structural Theory of Imperialism," *Journal of Peace Research*, 2 (1971), 91–98.

21. See Stephen P. Cohen, "U.S. Security in a Separatist Season," *Bulletin of Atomic Scientists* (July/August, 1992), pp. 28–32; and Rodolfo Stavenhagen, "Ethnic Conflicts and Their Impact on International Society," *International Social Science Journal*, 127 (1991), 117–32.

2 The Emerging Foreign Policy Agenda

FOREIGN POLICY PROBLEMS

Foreign policy is about choices. It is about the goals and values people want to realize and the types of threats they wish to be protected against. Foreign policy is also about costs. It is about how much people are willing to pay in order to achieve their goals and what types of sacrifices they are willing to make. For over 40 years, questions of values, threats, costs, and sacrifice were framed with reference to one overriding problem: the Soviet threat. The American people saw the Soviet Union as a global challenger that threatened virtually all aspects of American society. The appropriate response was containment. Over time, the Soviet Union became an enemy that most Americans felt quite comfortable dealing with. By and large, it acted in predictable ways that made the task of containment seem quite manageable.

All of that has changed. With the breakup of the Soviet Union and the end of the cold war, American foreign policy has lost its "magnetic north pole."[1] An aura of uncertainty now hangs over its content and conduct. New questions have joined (and in some cases replaced) those which dominated the foreign policy agenda of the cold war era. Answers that once seemed obvious and were valued for their insight and clarity are now the subject of intense debate.

The outcome of the current debate is uncertain. It is unclear what goals Americans will want to pursue in their foreign policy in the twenty-first century. It is unclear how they will define and rank threats to the American national interest or what level of protection they will desire. In addition, no one can tell with certainty how much they will be willing to pay or what sacrifices they will be willing to endure in order to realize these goals or to be protected from these threats.

A starting point for thinking about goals, threats, costs, and sacrifice is the realization that there is no such thing as a standard or typical foreign policy problem. Presidents discover two truths very quickly. First, foreign policy problems come in many shapes and sizes and they often defy simple categorization. At a minimum, most foreign policy problems contain within them a bundle of distinct policy problems or issues that intersect in complicated ways. This makes deciding on how to approach a problem difficult because of uncertainty over just what the problem is or how attacking one aspect of the problem will affect its other dimensions. Second, foreign policy problems are seldom ever "solved." As George Shultz, President Ronald Reagan's Secretary of State, noted, policy making does not involve confronting "one damn thing after another . . . it involves confronting the same damn thing over and over."[2]

The problem of AIDS (acquired immunodeficiency syndrome) illustrates both these points.[3] Because there is currently no cure for AIDS the great temptation is to treat it as a health problem. For all of the human suffering associated with AIDS, at least from a foreign policy perspective, it is much more. AIDS is an economic problem. The World Bank asserts that the spread of AIDS is in part responsible for the slowed growth rate experienced by the economies of sub-Saharan states. AIDS is also a multifaceted security problem. Large numbers of HIV-infected personnel within a military establishment reduce its ability to carry out assigned tasks. The presence of large numbers of HIV-infected individuals in neighboring states is a potential source of tension as leaders seek to shield their states from its spread or export the AIDS problem to other states through forced deportation programs. Finally, AIDS can be viewed as a human rights problem. Fears exist that cultural norms and public laws will place women and children who have contracted AIDS in a disadvantaged position in seeking help or treatment.

Thinking about Foreign Policy Problems

In addition to recognizing that foreign policy problems often represent bundles of issues rather than discrete policy areas, it is important to realize that foreign policy problems also differ in terms of their history and origin.

Some foreign policy problems are inherited from previous administrations. The key dilemma faced by presidents here is whether to continue the course and endorse the policy line of their predecessors or move in a new direction. Bush inherited Reagan's policy of support for the Contras in Nicaragua and ineffective opposition to Noriega in Panama, and he moved quickly to distance himself from those policies. Carter inherited a nearly complete SALT II arms control agreement from Ford and turned his back on it. Clinton inherited a military presence in Somalia from Bush. While Bush's postelection decision to send U.S. troops did not tie Clinton's hands or foreordain the policy shift from humanitarian aid to nation-building, it did leave him with fewer options than had they not been there on inauguration day.

Some foreign policy problems are new, the product of unfolding events beyond one's borders that earlier administrations never had to confront. With no track record of successes and failures against which to weigh their choices, presidents are left only with the informed judgment of their advisers and their own political instincts to guide them in selecting policy options. The momentous events in Eastern Europe that the Bush administration faced in 1989 and 1990 certainly qualify in this regard. Other than in the Eisenhower administration, when calls for "rolling back the iron curtain" were commonplace (but never put into action), it is difficult to remember when the United States even had a foreign policy toward Eastern Europe. The same situation confronted the Bush administration in Russia, where it was forced to respond to the dissolution of America's cold war enemy followed by requests from it for foreign aid. Active support for the Irish peace process and promoting North

Atlantic Treaty Organization (NATO) enlargement are two new issues that the Clinton administration successfully addressed.

Other foreign policy problems can largely be attributed to perceived or actual failings in an administration's own foreign policy. The problem here can be either a specific policy or the administration's handling of foreign policy issues in general. At the heart of many of the criticisms leveled at the Carter and Clinton administrations is their inconsistency and lack of decisiveness in dealing with a broad array of foreign policy problems. The Reagan and Bush administrations suffered more from charges that they mishandled specific foreign policy items. For the Reagan administration it was Iran–Contra. Bush was plagued by his inability to fashion a policy toward China that satisfied both human rights advocates and those who saw China as an economic and strategic ally.

A fourth category of foreign policy problems consists of issues confronted by previous administrations and forgotten about because they were considered solved. For the Bush and Clinton administrations the specter of massive refugee flows from Cuba and Haiti were one such problem. Refugee flows from these two states to the United States had been a recurring phenomenon since the first exodus following Castro's seizure of power and had occurred most recently during the Reagan administration. President Clinton was forced to confront an even more ominous "solved" problem in 1998 when India and Pakistan detonated nuclear weapons, thereby reintroducing the problem of nuclear proliferation on the foreign policy agenda.

A last type of foreign policy problem we can identify consists of problems rooted in long-term structural features of the international system. These issues may or may not have been addressed by previous administrations. The Bush administration's policy dilemma on whether to allow Japan to build a new generation jet fighter (the FSX) with U.S. help is an example of this type of foreign policy problem. The plan was for the United States and Japan to jointly develop a new fighter modeled on the F-16, with Japan bearing the cost of planning and producing the plane. At issue was the relative importance of economic and military security considerations. Advocates of the sale viewed it in geopolitical terms: With the FSX, Japan would be able to take a greater role in the defense of Pacific sea lanes. Opponents of the deal argued that it provided Japan with access to areas of technology in which the United States held a lead and that in doing so the FSX deal would further undermine U.S. economic strength and technological competitiveness. In the end, a compromise was struck. Viewed in more abstract terms, the FSX deal illustrates the policy dilemma faced by Great Powers in decline. As Paul Kennedy puts it in his *The Rise and Fall of the Great Powers,* over time the uneven pattern of economic growth and global productivity works against the ability of Great Powers to maintain their position of international dominance.[4] Succumbing to "imperial overreach," they are unable to balance their short-run military security needs with the long-term need to build and maintain an economic base that is capable of generating increasing levels of productivity and income. Instead, the former is emphasized to the neglect of the latter.

To repeat a point made earlier, foreign policy problems do not come in neat packages. They also do not have neat histories. Some foreign policy problems may contain elements from several of the above categories as they make their way to the White House. For the Clinton administration, Bosnia was one such problem. Dubbed "the problem from Hell" by Secretary of State Warren Christopher, fighting between the Serbs, Croats, and Bosnians in what once was Yugoslavia has its roots in what may be one of the most intractable problems in world politics: the incompatibility between ethnic boundaries and political boundaries and the desire of peoples to bring them into line—something only done at the expense of other peoples. Bosnia was also an inherited problem for the Clinton administration, one it drew attention to in the 1992 presidential campaign when candidate Bill Clinton attacked Bush's largely passive policy as unwise and immoral. It became a problem for President Clinton when his administration was unable to convince NATO allies of the wisdom of the U.S. position or even to clearly articulate a consistent position. Finally, Bosnia represents the rebirth of a problem long forgotten. Ethnic tensions are nothing new to this part of Europe. They played important roles in the onset of World War I and the history of World War II. They faded from view with the establishment of communist rule and the emergence of Tito as a strong ruler. Never far beneath the surface, these ethnic tensions reemerged after Tito's death and the subsequent fall of communism in Russia and Eastern Europe.

THE NATIONAL INTEREST

One unifying thread that runs through these and other types of foreign policy problems is a common vocabulary and set of symbols. The first challenge facing a student of American foreign policy is to become comfortable with its terminology. The experience is often a frustrating one because authors using the same term frequently attach different meanings to it. For example, take the calls from commentators positioned all across the political spectrum for the United States to pursue a foreign policy of "maturity." This plea is based both on a reading of the past and on expectations about the future. Looking to the future, they see problems confronting U.S. foreign policy makers that are not likely to lend themselves to clear-cut alternatives or easy choices. Looking to the past, there is the feeling that U.S. foreign policy has not been all that it could be, that its content has fallen short of our needs and expectations. Commentators are in far less agreement on what constitutes a mature foreign policy. For some *maturity* means greater consistency, for others it means coming to terms with the nature of world politics, and for still others it means a greater attachment to principle.

Debates such as the one over the meaning of *maturity* involve far more than just disagreements over facts and details. They are struggles to control the language of U.S. foreign policy, to set its reference points, assumptions, and symbolism. By looking at the way in which terms are being used, we can learn much about the nature of American foreign policy and the process by which it is made and implemented.[5] The key term whose definition must be controlled if U.S. foreign policy is to be moved in one direction or another is *the national interest*. National interest is the concept used by writers to characterize the objectives of state policy in foreign affairs. Box 2–1 illustrates the complex process of stating goals and values—and hints at the changing political complexion of

BOX 2–1   Series of Presidential Statements Shows Change in Marines' Mission

Excerpts from President Reagan's Statements
on the Marines' Mission in Beirut

Aug. 24, 1982, from a letter to the House speaker and Senate president pro tem:

U.S. military personnel will assist the government of Lebanon in carrying out its responsibilities concerning the withdrawal of Palestinian personnel under safe and orderly conditions. The presence of our forces will in this way facilitate the restoration of Lebanese government sovereignty and authority in the Beirut area.

This step will not, by itself, resolve the situation in Lebanon, let alone the problems which have plagued the region for more than 30 years. But I believe that it will improve the prospects for realizing our objectives in Lebanon:

A permanent cessation of hostilities;

Establishment of a strong, representative central government;

Withdrawal of all foreign forces;

Restoration of control by the Lebanese government throughout the country;

and establishment for conditions under which Lebanon no longer can be used as a launching point for attacks against Israel.

Sept. 1, 1982, from a speech to the nation:

. . . I'm happy to announce that the U.S. Marine contingent helping to supervise the evacuation has accomplished its mission. Our young men should be out of Lebanon within two weeks.

Sept. 29, 1982, from a letter to the speaker and the president pro tem:

I want to emphasize that . . . there is no intention or expectation that U.S. armed forces [will become involved in hostilities. They are in Lebanon at the formal] request of the government of Lebanon, and our agreement with the government of Lebanon expressly rules out any combat responsibilities for the U.S. forces. All armed elements in the area have given assurance that they will refrain from hostilities and will not interfere with the activities of the multinational force. Although isolated acts of violence can never be ruled out, all appropriate precautions have been taken to ensure the safety of U.S. military personnel during their temporary deployment in Lebanon.

Nov. 11, 1982, from a news conference:

I can't give you a close-out date on [how long the Marines will remain in Lebanon]. But I can tell you that we're trying to push as fast as we can on the two things that must happen. And that is the ability of the Lebanese government to heal the wounds and bring their people together and have control. But also it hinges on getting the three foreign factions—the PLO, the Syrians, and the Israelis—out of Lebanon. And we are pushing on that as fast as we can.

May 17, 1983, from a news conference:

> The multinational forces are there to help the new government of Lebanon maintain order until it can organize its military and its police and assume control over its own borders and its own internal security. So it could be that the multinational forces will be there for quite a period.

Sept. 21, 1983, from a meeting with regional news media:

> . . . The multinational force is there to help in this achieving of stability and control by Lebanon, and I think the mission still goes on. But from the very first, I said we will never send our men any place where they will not be allowed to defend themselves if they come under attack, and that recently has happened, and they have been defending themselves.

Oct. 24, 1983, from a meeting with regional news media:

> If Lebanon ends up under the tyranny of forces hostile to the West, not only will our strategic position in the eastern Mediterranean be threatened, but also the stability of the entire Middle East, including the vast resource areas of the Arabian peninsula.
>
> To the extent that the prospect for future stability is heavily influenced by the presence of our forces, it is central to our credibility on a global scale.

Source: Compiled by staff researcher Carin Pratt, *The Washington Post*, October 25, 1983. © 1983 *The Washington Post*. Reprinted with permission.

the foreign policy debate—in the U.S. rationale for sending peacekeeping forces to Lebanon in the Reagan administration.

The need to send U.S. Marines to Lebanon had its roots in the June 1982 Israeli invasion of that country and the political and military chaos that followed in its wake. Along with the invasion of Grenada, the placement of U.S. warships in the Persian Gulf, and the Iran–Contra affair, this action was one of the most controversial of Reagan's presidency. It raised questions about both the process of U.S. foreign policy making (Was it necessary to invoke the War Powers Act?) and the objectives of U.S. foreign policy (What was our Middle East foreign policy and what were we trying to accomplish by sending troops to Lebanon?). As with the Persian Gulf naval deployment that precipitated the inadvertent downing of an Iranian civil airliner, tragedy also visited the Marine peacekeeping mission in Lebanon. On October 23, 1983, terrorists sent a car loaded with explosives into the Marine compound, killing 241 U.S. soldiers. Not quite four months later, in February 1984, President Reagan announced the withdrawal of the remaining 1,600 Marines from Lebanon. The problem of defining the U.S. national interest is not unique to the Reagan administration. Compare its effort with that of the Clinton administration on Bosnia presented in Box 2–2.

The range of goals and values policy makers may choose to pursue is virtually endless. The same is not true for the resources at their disposal. The limits here are quite real and specific. And since all goals are costly, decisions must

BOX 2–2   Christopher on Bosnia

Jan. 13, confirmation hearing, Senate Foreign Relations Committee:

I believe the future of Europe is at stake in Bosnia. Already the problems in Bosnia and the rest of the former Yugoslavia are ricocheting around the Balkans and Europe. . . . Failure to introduce sufficient military force into the Bosnian equation will, I fear, prolong the agony and allow the conflict there to grow and threaten our national security interests.

Feb. 10, introducing Bosnia Diplomatic Initiative, State Department:

The continuing destruction of a new United Nations member challenges the principle that internationally recognized borders should not be altered by force. . . . Bold tyrants and fearful minorities are watching to see whether ethnic cleansing is a policy the world will tolerate. If we hope to promote the spread of freedom, if we hope to encourage the emergence of peaceful ethnic democracies, our answer must be a resounding 'no.'

March 10, hearing, House Appropriations Subcommittee:

The case is no less than the prevention of a conflagration that could envelop all of southeastern Europe and perhaps rage beyond, as it sometimes has from that area, to consume a substantial portion of the world. . . . That's why the United States is interested, that's why we're wanting to take an active role there.

June 1, "MacNeil/Lehrer Newshour":

Bosnia is a human tragedy, a humanitarian—just a gross—grotesque humanitarian situation. But it is not [like] a confrontation between the United States and Russia. It does not affect our vital national interests except as we're concerned about humanitarian matters and except as we're trying to contain it.

July 21, news conference, State Department:

That's a tragic, tragic situation in Bosnia, make no mistake about that. It's the world's most difficult diplomatic problem, I believe. It defies any simple solution. The United States is doing all it can consistent with our national interest.

Aug. 11, "MacNeil/Lehrer Newshour":

So I think we'll continue to do all we can in the national interest, but we've concluded that it is in our national interest to prevent the strangulation of Sarajevo, in conjunction with our allies.

Source: The Washington Post, August 19, 1993. © 1993 The Washington Post. Reprinted with permission.

constantly be made about what goals and values to emphasize and which ones to neglect. The lack of fit between goals and resources results in the concept of national interest being used in two quite different ways. Some employ the concept to describe the goals and values being pursued in a state's foreign policy. No a priori definition of national interest is assumed to exist, and the U.S. national interest is whatever U.S. policy makers are willing to make sacrifices to achieve. Others use the concept in a normative sense, seeking to have added emphasis given to values and goals which in their view are currently being slighted by policy makers.

Keeping in mind the distinction between normative and descriptive uses of national interest is the first step in understanding the language and nature of the debate about American foreign policy. The second step is to realize that definitions of national interest can be made at varying levels of abstraction. At a high level of abstraction, national interest is employed with reference to questions of national purpose, national identity, and national survival. At a medium level of abstraction, it is used in relation to matters of priorities and broad policy assumptions. The concept of national interest used at the lowest level of abstraction centers on day-to-day problem-solving concerns: strategies, tactics, and operational assumptions. Table 2–1 presents three foreign policy

TABLE 2–1   Definitions of National Interest at Three Levels of Abstraction

	Issue Area		
Level of Abstraction	International Economic Policy	Nature of Soviet Threat	U.S.–Latin American Relations
High	U.S. liberal principles prosper in an open international economic order.	Soviet threat is global.	Manifest destiny: U.S. has special responsibility to lead in region.
Medium	Protectionism must remain an exception to the rule.	Soviets are expansionist.	U.S. (capitalist) pattern of development is most appropriate for Latin America.
	MNC produce growth and development for all states in the international system.	U.S. can rely on client states to protect its regional interests.	U.S. has special defense responsibilities in region.
Low	Participate in GATT.	Support for the shah.	Caribbean Basin Initiative.
	Reject Law of Sea Treaty.	Arms sales.	Isolate Cuba.
	Tie foreign aid to state's willingness to adopt pro-capitalist economic strategies.	Pershing II missile placed in Europe.	Invade Grenada when request for help is received. NAFTA

problem areas for the United States (international economic policy, the Soviet threat, and U.S.–Latin American relations) and illustrates how keeping track of levels of abstraction helps to order and relate competing conceptualizations of national interest to one another.

THE EVOLVING FOREIGN POLICY AGENDA

One of the most hotly debated questions among observers of world politics is the extent to which the future will resemble the past. Are we entering a new era in world politics or will we see the reappearance of old habits of thought and action that shaped foreign policy decisions? There are many ways of approaching this question. One is to examine the ways in which the foreign policy agenda of today differs from that of the past. In this section we examine five policy areas for signs of continuity and change.

Economic Development: From Producing Growth to Managing Capital Flows

The initial cold war economic development concerns centered on bringing about the rapid recovery of the European and (to a lesser extent) Japanese economies. The Marshall Plan helped to accomplish this goal, and U.S. attention shifted to the third world. Now the concern became one of bringing about economic growth to minimize the attractiveness of communism to these newly sovereign states. The development strategy put forward by the United States emphasized the benefits of foreign investment and envisioned these states as emulating the American experience.

Over time, it became apparent that American-style growth was not going to be the reality for third world states, and a backlash developed. Cries were heard for the creation of a new international economic order, one that would be more responsive to the concerns of third world states and would allow them to control their own economic resources and destinies. Questions were raised about the benefits of foreign aid and using large scale government spending programs to stimulate growth in third world states. The latter part of the cold war saw the emergence of competing economic development models. Two of the most prominent advocated a strategy of sustainable development, which sought to balance growth and environmental considerations, and export-led growth strategies, which saw the road to economic growth as based on a fuller participation in the international trading and investing system.

The debate over the merits of foreign aid and competing development strategies is still very much with us, but a new problem now also preoccupies policy makers: how to manage international financial flows. A first glimmer of the problem was seen in 1995 when Mexico needed help from the United States to restore investor confidence in the value of the peso. It emerged with full force in 1997–1998. What started as a currency problem for Thailand exploded into a full scale global crisis in little more than one year as Malaysia, Indonesia, the Philippines, Hong Kong, Japan, and Taiwan all found their currencies under attack from speculators and investors who feared for the stability and health of these economies. Around the world small and large stock markets alike, those in Brazil, Russia, the United States, and Europe, also came under pressure. The Clinton administration and the International Monetary Fund (IMF) have tried to fashion a response. Both their efforts have met with criticism. The American efforts have been handicapped by disagreements between the administration and congressional Republicans over the terms for making additional funds available to affected states. The IMF was slow to abandon lending policies that were originally designed as solutions to deal with the international debt problem of the 1980s.

Covert Action: From Targeting Communists to Targeting International Crime Organizations

The 1947 National Security Act established the Central Intelligence Agency (CIA). Among its tasks were the following: (1) to advise the National Security Council on intelligence matters, (2) to correlate and evaluate intelligence, and (3) to perform other functions and duties relating to national security intelligence. This last responsibility has served as the legal foundation on which CIA covert action has been conducted. The principal target of CIA covert action during the cold war was the Soviet Union and its allies around the world. Its first covert action campaigns were conducted in Europe to help make sure that communists would not win elections in Italy and other Western democracies. Unsuccessful attempts were also made to foment unrest within the rapidly solidifying communist bloc. As the attention of American foreign policy shifted to the third world so too did covert action programs. Governments and leaders unfriendly to the United States were targeted in Asia, the Middle East, Africa, and Latin America.

In the process, the CIA became the most controversial of all U.S. government bureaucracies. For some the CIA had become a "rogue elephant" out of control and pursuing policies of its own making and for its own benefit. For others, the CIA remained a vital instrument of foreign policy that needed to be reinvigorated if the United States was to win the cold war. The latter perspective was embraced by the Reagan administration, and under it the CIA and covert action became key players in foreign policy in Nicaragua and Afghanistan.

With the end of the cold war, the CIA strikes many observers as an organization in search of a mission. Its intelligence functions are challenged by CNN and other media sources that can provide policy makers with "real time" intelligence. Its covert action abilities require an enemy against whom they will be directed. International crime organizations are seen as that enemy. Traditional law enforcement techniques are seen as incapable of dealing with the threat posed by these organizations. In 1998, President Clinton unveiled an International Crime Control Strategy which identifies the major international crime threats to the United States as drug trafficking, nuclear smuggling, the transfer of sensitive U.S. technology to rogue states, and trafficking in women and children. The five major international crime organizations generally are regarded to be the Italian Mafia, the Russian mobs, the Japanese Yakuza, the Chinese triads, and the Colombian cartels.

Military Strategy: From Interstate War to Peacemaking and (Perhaps) Cyber-Warfare

Regardless of whether it was conceived of in nuclear or conventional terms, early cold war military planners thought in terms of interstate wars. The North Atlantic Treaty Organization (NATO) was designed to prevent a Russian attack on Western Europe; a treaty was signed with Japan to provide it with security against an external enemy; and U.S. forces fought a war in Korea which began when North Korean forces crossed into South Korea. Vietnam forced the American military to operate in a very different context. Rather than fight an enemy's army in direct combat, U.S. soldiers in Vietnam for the most part confronted a faceless enemy that blended in with the civilian population and did not engage in frontal assaults but relied upon guerrilla tactics.

Both interstate wars and guerrilla wars are still very much with us and continue to preoccupy American strategists. The Persian Gulf War is a post–cold war example of the former, while Afghanistan provides an example of the latter. They do not, however, capture the essence of the conflict situations in which U.S. forces now find themselves operating. In Somalia, Bosnia, and Haiti, peacemaking—not defeating the enemy—has become the primary task. The key questions are no longer who started the war, which side is the aggressor, or who are our allies. The challenges confronting U.S. forces in peacemaking operations consist of protecting themselves from attack, mediating between combatants who are not fully resigned to ending the war, building trust among people, protecting human rights, and supervising the reconstruction of the political and economic fabric of a society. These are tasks which contain a significant military element but also go far beyond what professional soldiers have been trained to do in the past.

An important development in the military's thinking about how to conduct warfare in the post–cold war era is its increased reliance upon information and communication technology. The Internet, sophisticated telecommunications equipment, high-speed computers, and intelligence-gathering satellites provide the military with a wealth of information it can bring to bear against an adversary. However, they also constitute points of vulnerability that can be attacked or manipulated. This is equally true for the United States when it is on the offensive as when it is on the defensive. In 1996, Director of Central Intelligence John Deutch identified information warfare as the second most pressing national security problem facing the United States. He and others called for the development of a national strategy to manage this information infrastructure.

Arms Control: From Limiting Nuclear Weapons to Controlling the Spread of Weapons of Mass Destruction

The centerpiece of the cold war arms control agenda was stopping the spread of nuclear weapons. The initial concern of U.S. policy makers was with the desire of our European allies to enter the nuclear club. After Great Britain and France became nuclear powers, U.S. security guarantees prevented others from following suit. Attention then shifted to stopping third world states from going nuclear. The United States was joined in this endeavor by the Soviet Union, whose leaders shared a fear of the destabilizing consequences of global nuclear proliferation. U.S. and Soviet officials also entered into a lengthy series of talks among themselves that were designed to place restraints on the level and intensity of nuclear competition between the two nations. These negotiations were often surrounded in political controversy and culminated in the SALT and START agreements.

The breakup of the Soviet Union and the end of the cold war appeared to transform the nuclear problem. No longer was the primary concern the motives and actions of would-be nuclear states. It was now the loss of control over the Soviet nuclear inventory and the possibility that Russian scientists might sell nuclear secrets to the highest bidders. These dangers still exist, but in 1998 they were superseded by a revival of traditional proliferation concerns when India and Pakistan detonated nuclear devices.

Nuclear weapons are not the only weapons of mass destruction today. Also prominent in the minds of defense planners are the "poor man's nukes": chemical and biological weapons. So concerned is the Defense Department about the potential use of chemical and biological weapons against U.S. forces that it has ordered 1.4 million active troops and one million reservists and civilians to be vaccinated against anthrax. A partial list of states that possess chemical and biological weapons includes China, India, Iran, Iraq, Libya, North Korea, Pakistan, and Syria. The military value of chemical and biological weapons is widely questioned, and a strong international consensus exists against their use. Still, fears exist that such weapons may prove attractive to terrorist organizations. A precedent for such a use exists. In 1995, members of the Aum Shinrikyo (Supreme Truth) cult released deadly poison gas into the Tokyo subway system, killing 12 and injuring more than 5,000 people.

Human Rights: From Political Rights to Social and Economic Rights?

American thinking on human rights has traditionally approached the subject from a perspective that stresses the protection and advancement of legal and political rights. The primary threat to these rights comes from the actions of governments, and the proper way of protecting these rights is through laws and free elections. Woodrow Wilson's Fourteen Points and Franklin Roosevelt's Four Freedoms are powerful foreign policy expressions of this perspective.

During the cold war, American foreign policy was slow to embrace human rights as a high-priority issue. National security concerns easily dominated the agenda. A break with this pattern occurred during the Carter administration, which not only tried to put human rights at the center of its foreign policy but also adopted a more expansive definition of human rights that included a concern for oppressive social and economic conditions. Ronald Reagan's administration rejected this interpretation of human rights and adopted one that stressed political rights and defined communist rule as the fundamental threat to them.

Some twenty years later, controversy continues to surround the proper definition of human rights and its proper place in American foreign policy. The emphasis on building democracy, and the intense political reaction to scenes from Tiananmen Square shows the continued centrality of political and legal rights in American thinking. The unwillingness of the Bush and Clinton administrations to sacrifice strategic and economic interests for human rights concerns also shows the continued reluctance of policy makers to elevate human rights to the top of the foreign policy agenda. At the same time, U.S.–Chinese human rights relations also point to a possible return to a Carter-type definition of human rights violations as concerns for child labor practices, family planning policies, and use of prison labor are now heard with increased frequency in discussions of how China violates human rights.

SUMMARY AND THE FUTURE

There is nothing simple about foreign policy problems. They arrive on the policy agenda from quite varied routes. They constitute bundles of issues that can be separated in any number of ways. And their presence may prove to be short-lived or become a permanent fixture. How foreign policy problems are dealt with is also not a simple matter. There is nothing automatic about how the "communist challenge" is defined or what "promoting democracy" means. Problem definition is heavily influenced by the language of the political debate over the purposes of American foreign policy. The most powerful weapon in this debate is the concept of "the national interest." We can learn much about who controls the policy making process by studying efforts to give content and direction to this phrase.

The changes we have cataloged above are not an exhaustive list of how the foreign policy agenda of today differs from the past. The international trade agenda was long dominated by a concern for promoting global free trade and opening up markets to American goods. To some extent it still is, but now there is also a concern for managing regional trading blocs and protecting American markets from the predatory actions of foreign firms. The most important intelligence estimates used to focus on the military capabilities of the Soviet Union. Today, many call for the CIA to concentrate its efforts on providing economic intelligence to policy makers. In the 1970s, the primary natural resource issue was controlling oil. As the Persian Gulf War made clear, this is still of paramount concern to many, but there is now also growing concern about such disparate natural resource problems as access to water, biodiversity, and global warming.

We can expect the foreign policy agenda to continue to evolve, for issues to be added and subtracted, to disappear and reappear. What we cannot tell with equal certainty is what the exact composition of that agenda will look like. This will be determined by the interaction of several forces. Primary among them will be the strategic vision of the future adopted by policy makers and the domestic politics that will determine the identity of the players and the resources they will be able to bring to bear on foreign policy problems. The pull of the past will also play a significant role in determining the future of American foreign policy and it is to this we turn in the next chapters.

NOTES

1. James Schlesinger, "Quest for a Post–Cold War Foreign Policy," *Foreign Affairs,* 72 (1992/93), 17–28.
2. Jim Hoagland, "Why Clinton Improvises," *The Washington Post,* September 25, 1994.
3. This section draws from Dennis C. Weeks, "The AIDS Pandemic in Africa," *Current History* (May 1992), 208–13; and Kimberly A. Hamilton, "The HIV and AIDS Pandemic as a Foreign Policy Concern," *The Washington Quarterly,* 17 (1993), 201–15.
4. Paul Kennedy, *The Rise and Fall of the Great Powers* (New York: Random House, 1987).
5. John P. Lovell, "The Idiom of National Security," *JPMS* 11 (1983), 35–51.

The American National Style

To the casual observer, one of the most startling qualities of U.S. foreign policy is how suddenly it can change direction. Equally startling can be the depth of the change. In 1976 détente went from being the foreign policy trademark of two administrations to a nonterm in Ford's failed bid to be elected president. Human rights arrived on the scene as the centerpiece of U.S. foreign policy during the Carter administration. Four years later it too was gone, replaced by anticommunist rhetoric reminiscent of the 1950s and 1960s. Or consider Nixon's stunning announcement of July 15, 1971, that he would visit the People's Republic of China. For over two decades the United States had refused to recognize the existence of the mainland communist government. Without warning foreign policy changed, surprising both U.S. friends and enemies in the process. American policy makers now spoke of "playing the China card" instead of trying to promote China's international isolation. Close observers of U.S. foreign policy see a different picture. Looking beyond these and other sudden changes in direction, they see a high degree of continuity in the attitudes towards world affairs and methods of acting that have guided the making of U.S. foreign policy.

The importance of ideas as a force in foreign policy decision making stems from both their immediate and long-term impacts.[1] In the short run, shared ideas help policy makers and citizens cope with the inherent uncertainty involved in selecting between competing policy lines. Consistency with the principles of free trade or isolationism may not produce the "correct" policy, but these criteria do provide a basis for the selection or rejection of one. Ideas also become institutionalized as organizations and laws are designed around them. Because organizations and laws are slow to change, they become an anchor for any future reform debate. Once in place, political constituencies will coalesce around policies rooted in these ideas and lobby for their continued existence. As a result, ideas continue to exert an influence on policy long after they have lost their vitality and after those who espoused them have passed from the scene. Viewed over the long term, the result of this interplay of policies and ideas is a layering pattern in which policies reflecting different sets of ideas and pulling in different directions are combined, with little overall coherence.

This pattern is very much evident in the area of American commercial policy. Judith Goldstein observes that conventional attempts to explain American trade policies by reference to the weight of societal interest groups or the demands of the international system fail to account for their actual evolution.[2] Only by looking at the "political salience of economic theories" can one explain America's movement from a protectionist cycle that began in the early nineteenth century and culminated in the highly protective tariffs of the 1930s to a free trade cycle that now contains elements of free trade and fair trade.

The national security policy arena provides an even clearer picture of the influence of the impact of shared ideas and ways of acting on American foreign policy. Throughout most of the cold war period, these ideas and actions were embodied in the concept of containment. The first public statement of containment came in an article in *Foreign Affairs* authored by George Kennan. In it he argued:

> Soviet pressure against the free institutions of the western world is something that can be contained by the adroit and vigilant application of counter-force at a series of constantly shifting geographical and political points, corresponding to the shifts and maneuvers of Soviet policy but which cannot be charmed or talked out of existence.[3]

The logic of containment became embodied in a wide range of U.S. foreign policy initiatives. The Truman Doctrine, which pledged U.S. support to all states coming under pressure from international communism, was faithful to it. So too were early U.S. foreign aid programs intended to rebuild the economies of Western Europe (the Marshall Plan) and bring economic development to the third world (the Point Four Program). It was U.S. military policy, however, that became the primary vehicle for implementing containment in the form of a series of encircling alliances around the Soviet perimeter: NATO, the Southeast Asia Treaty Organization (SEATO), and the Central Treaty Organization (CENTO). What disagreements existed within policymaking circles were largely over the tactics and strategies to be used and not the ends of U.S. foreign policy. Such disputes were possible in part because in his article Kennan did not specify the means of containment. He would later become a critic of containment, arguing that his ideas had been misinterpreted and misapplied. Kennan specifically objected to the heavy reliance on military force and the perceived need to practice containment everywhere and anywhere that communist expansion was encountered.

Even the Nixon administration's much heralded shift to a policy of détente could be comfortably fit into the larger strategy of containment. Détente was designed to protect U.S. influence as much as possible in an era of lessened power abroad and increased isolationist feeling at home. Confrontation and crisis management were now too expensive to be the primary means for stopping Soviet expansion. Détente sought to accomplish this end by creating a framework of limited cooperation within the context of an international order that recognized the legitimacy of both U.S. and Soviet core security goals.[4]

This long-term continuity in U.S. foreign policy goes back beyond the period of containment. It stretches back to the very beginnings of the United States. In this chapter we examine the foundations of the American national style of foreign policy. First, we look at the tendency for U.S. foreign policy to fluctuate between isolationism and internationalism. Second, we examine the patterns of thought and action that provide the building blocks for both of these general foreign policy orientations. Finally, we look to the post–cold war era.

ISOLATIONISM VERSUS INTERNATIONALISM

U.S. foreign policy is frequently discussed in terms of a tension between two opposing general foreign policy orientations: isolationism and internationalism. From the isolationist perspective American national interests are best served by "quitting the world" or at a minimum maintaining a healthy sense of detachment from events elsewhere. It draws its inspiration from Washington's farewell address in which he urged Americans to "steer clear of permanent alliances with any portion of the foreign world" and asserted that "Europe has a set of primary interests which to us have none or very remote relations."[5] Among the major foreign policy decisions rooted in the principles of isolationism are the Monroe Doctrine, the refusal to join the League of Nations, the neutrality legislation of the 1930s, and, more loosely, the fear of future Vietnams. The internationalist perspective sees protecting and promoting American national interests as requiring an activist foreign policy. Internationalists hold that the United States cannot escape the world. Events abroad inevitably impinge upon U.S. interests and any policy based on the denial of their relevance is self-defeating. The global depression of the 1930s, Hitler's rise to power, the outbreak of World War II, and the constant outward thrust of post–World War II communism are proof to the internationalists that Washington's advice is no longer relevant. Such widely divergent undertakings as membership in the United Nations and NATO, the Marshall Plan, the Alliance for Progress, CIA covert action, the Helsinki Human Rights Agreement, and involvement in Korea and Vietnam can be traced to the internationalist perspective on world affairs.

The oscillation between isolationism and internationalism has not been haphazard. An underlying logic appears to guide the movement from one to the other. Frank Klingberg identifies five periods of U.S. foreign policy of approximately 25 to 30 years' duration.[6] Each combines an introvert (isolationist) and extrovert (internationalist) phase.

	Introvert	Extrovert
1.	1776–1798	1798–1824
2.	1824–1844	1844–1871
3.	1871–1891	1891–1918
4.	1918–1940	1940–1966/67
5.	1966/67–	

Klingberg suggests that in each period U.S. policy makers were forced to confront a major foreign policy problem. In period 1 it was independence; in period 2 issues involving manifest destiny were dominant; in period 3 it was the process of becoming an industrial power. The crisis of world democracy dominated period 4, and today the need to create a stable world order lies at the heart of the challenges facing U.S. foreign policy. In each period the dominant cycle (introversion or extroversion) imposes limits on the types of solutions that can be considered by policy makers and predisposes the public to accept certain courses of action. Klingberg also sees the cyclical movement between isolationism and internationalism as being spiral in nature. Each movement toward internationalism is deeper than the one before it, and each reversal to isolationism is less complete than the one preceding it. Updating Klingberg's chart by adding 25 years to his last introvert phase would yield the prediction that, by the mid-1980s, the United States should once again be embarking on a new extrovert phase. The activist foreign policies adopted by the Reagan administration and continued by Bush suggest this is in fact the case. Though reluctant to commit U.S. forces to Bosnia, the Clinton administration also is solidly internationalist in outlook. It took great pains in its first two years in office to blunt calls for a more isolationist foreign policy. Continuing Klingberg's analysis even further into the future suggests that the next introvert phase should begin to set in around 2014.[7]

Disagreement exists over the mechanism triggering a shift from one phase to the next. Klingberg suggests a number of possibilities: the failure of a long-term policy, the arrival of a new generation of policy makers, the onset of a critical problem requiring a solution incompatible with the dominant mood, and the corruption or distortion of an ongoing line of action. Dexter Perkins suggests that shifts in foreign policy orientations may be tied to the business cycle.[8] He finds that in periods of economic recovery after a period of stagnation and decline, U.S. foreign policy takes on a belligerent tone. The more stable the economy, the more moderate is U.S. foreign policy. In a similar vein Robert Dallek sees the periodic outward thrust of U.S. foreign policy as a product of domestic frustrations and disappointments.[9] Foreign policy successes are sought as a sign that the American dream is still valid and capable of producing victories.

Whatever the specific trigger, the movement from isolationism to internationalism and back again is made possible because both general foreign policy orientations are very much a part of the American national style. One does not represent the American approach to world affairs, and the other its denial. They are two different ways in which the patterns of American foreign policy, its fundamental building blocks, come together.[10] Both are united in the conviction that the institutions and ideals brought forward by the American experience need protection. The approaches differ on how best to provide for their continued growth and development. Isolationism seeks to accomplish this end by insulating the American experience from corrupting foreign influences. Internationalism seeks to protect them by creating a more hospitable global environment. For both, world affairs gain meaning and importance (or irrelevance) primarily in terms of how they affect the American historical experience and American ideals.

SOURCES OF THE AMERICAN NATIONAL STYLE

The sources of the American national style are found in the conditions under which earlier generations of American policy makers operated and the ideas that guided their thinking.[11] Few nations can look back on as favorable a set of conditions in which to grow and develop. The vast size of the United States brought with it an abundance of natural resources on which to build a prosperous economy. Between the mid-1600s and the mid-1800s, America grew from a series of isolated settlements into an economic power rivaling its European counterparts. Just as important for the development of the American national style is the fact that this growth took place without any master plan. Individual self-reliance, flexibility, and improvisation were the cardinal virtues in developing America. Guided by these principles, the United States has become a "how-to-do-it" society whose energies are largely directed to the problem at hand and whose long-range concerns receive scant attention.[12]

It also needs to be noted that this growth occurred in an era of unparalleled global harmony. With the exception of the Crimean War, from the Congress of Vienna in 1815 until the outbreak of World War I in 1914, the Great Powers of Europe were largely at peace with one another. Closer to home, the defense of its continental borders never required the creation of a large standing army or navy. For more than a century, America's peace and security required very little effort on its part. Peace and security seemed to come naturally, and they were widely accepted as the normal condition of world affairs. The links between American security and developments abroad went unnoticed. Democracy, rather than the strength of the British navy or the European balance of power, was seen as the source of American security.

The faith in the power of democracy reflects the extent to which American political thought is rooted in the eighteenth-century view of human nature. Most important to the development of the ideas that have guided U.S. policy makers is the work of John Locke, who argued that people are rational beings capable of determining their own best interests. The best government was held to be that which governed least. To Locke the historical record indicated that the exercise of power inevitably led to its abuse and corrupted the natural harmony existing among individuals. Conflicts between individuals could be settled without the application of concentrated state power. The wastefulness and destructiveness of war disqualified it as a means of conflict resolution. Negotiation, reason, and discussion are sufficient to overcome misperceptions and reconcile conflicting interests.

In contrast to war, trade is seen as a force promoting the peaceful settlement of disputes. The dynamics of the marketplace bind individuals together in mutually profitable exchanges. The power of the marketplace and the power of governments are seen as being in direct competition with one another. The greater the power of one over society, the less the power of the other. Since commerce creates a vested interest in peace, logic again points to limiting government powers. The American historical experience seemed to offer vivid proof of the correctness of the liberal outlook on human affairs. Had not the United States been largely at peace with the world? When it went to war had it not been provoked? Had it not enjoyed an unprecedented record of economic growth and prosperity? Was not its past free of the class conflicts that had rocked European society?

It is only a short step from answering yes to these questions to a belief in the uniqueness of the American experience and the existence of an American mission. It is a step Americans traditionally have taken. American "exceptionalism"[13] is taken to demand a leadership role in world affairs. During isolationist periods leadership takes the form of standing apart from international politics and leading by example. In internationalist periods it is revealed in attempts to transform the international system. In either case it is American values that determine the goals sought and the American experience that provides the criteria for judging success and failure.

Before proceeding, a caveat is in order. This is not the only way to characterize the American historical experience, value system, or national style.[14] For some, the United States has been antirevolutionary, seeking to prevent social change and third world revolutionary movements that might threaten its dominant position in world affairs. This view is often found in the writings of revisionist historians who find U.S. foreign policy to be imperial in nature and rooted in the expansionist needs of capitalism. Others see U.S. foreign policy as racist, as evidenced by its immigration policy which systematically discriminated against the Chinese and other non-Western Europeans; its hesitancy to support international human rights conventions; and its attitude toward the suitability of Hawaii, Puerto Rico, and the Philippines for either statehood or independence. Finally, some would argue that what we have called internationalism is better defined as interventionism: a tendency to intervene in the affairs of other states to a degree far beyond that which is required by any reasonable definition of U.S. national interest. In this view there is no competing theme of isolationism but only an opposition to specific cases of intervention (such as Vietnam) on pragmatic or tactical grounds.

PATTERNS

Unilateralism

Three patterns of thought and action provide the building blocks from which the American national style emerges. The first pattern is unilateralism, or a predisposition to act alone in addressing foreign policy problems.[15] Unilateralism does not dictate a specific course of action. Isolationism, neutrality, activism, and interventionism are all consistent with its basic orientation to world affairs. The unilateralist thrust of U.S. foreign policy represents a rejection of the balance-of-power approach for providing national security. This approach, second nature to European diplomats, is alien to the American experience. Security could largely be taken for granted, and collaborative efforts were unnecessary. The willingness to apply the American approach to security on a global basis also reflects the American sense of exceptionalism and is often perceived by others to be an insensitive and egoistic nationalism.

The best known statement of the unilateralist position is the Monroe Doctrine. With the end of the Napoleonic Wars, concern arose that Spain might attempt to reestablish its control over the newly independent Latin American republics. Great Britain approached the United States over the possibility of a joint declaration to prevent this from happening. The United States rejected the British proposal, only to turn around and make a unilateral declaration to the same end: The United States would not tolerate European intervention in the Western Hemisphere, and in return it pledged not to interfere in European affairs. In 1904 the Roosevelt Corollary to the Monroe Doctrine was put forward. Spurred into action by the inability of the Dominican Republic to pay its foreign lenders, President Theodore Roosevelt sent in U.S. forces. The Roosevelt Corollary established the United States as the self-proclaimed policeman of the Western Hemisphere. It would play that role many times. The years 1904 to 1934 saw the United States send eight expeditionary forces to Latin America, conduct five military occupations ranging in duration from a few months to 19 years, and take over customs collections duties twice. The legacy of the Monroe Doctrine continues into the post–World War II era. The CIA-sponsored overthrows of the Arbenz government in Guatemala and the Allende government in Chile, U.S. behavior in the Bay of Pigs and the Cuban missile crisis, the 1965 invasion of the Dominican Republic, the 1983 invasion of Grenada, and the 1989 invasion of Panama testify to the continued influence of unilateralism on U.S. behavior in the Western Hemisphere.

The nature of the American participation in World War I and the subsequent U.S. refusal to join the League of Nations also reflect the unilateralist impulse. Official World War I documents identify the victors as the Allied and Associated Powers. The only Associated Power of note was the United States. For U.S. policy makers this was more than just a mere symbolic separation from its European allies. Woodrow Wilson engaged in personal negotiations with Germany over ending the war without consulting the allies over the terms of a possible truce. The United States was also the only major victorious power not to join the League of Nations. While this abstention is often attributed to isolationism, Robert Tucker argues that the U.S. refusal represented a triumph of unilateralism.[16] Membership would have committed the United States to a collective security system that could have obliged it to undertake multilateral military action in the name of stopping international aggression.

The impact of unilateralist thinking also comes through clearly in the neutrality legislation of the 1930s. These acts placed an embargo on the sale of arms to warring states. Because arms sales were seen as the most likely method of U.S. entry into a war, they had to be prohibited regardless of the consequences that the embargo might have on events elsewhere. The post–World War II shift from isolationism to internationalism did not bring about an abandonment of unilateralism; it only placed a multilateral façade over it. Control over NATO's nuclear forces remains firmly in the hands of the United States. The presence of the UN flag in Korea and references to SEATO treaty commitments in Vietnam could scarcely conceal the totally U.S. nature of these two wars. Within the United Nations the veto power protects U.S. vital interests from the intrusion of other powers, and the system of weighted voting used in international financial organizations guarantees the United States a preponderant voice in their deliberations. And last, where its will has been successfully challenged, the United States has withdrawn from the organization as it did in 1984 when it pulled out of the United Nations Educational, Scientific, and Cultural Organization (UNESCO).

The American penchant for unilateralism was never far beneath the surface in its dealings with allies during the later years of the cold war or in the first years of the post–cold war era. Nowhere was this perhaps more evident than in the Reagan administration's secret effort to sell arms to Iran in return for the freedom of American hostages in Lebanon at a time when its public stance was one of pressuring allies not to negotiate with terrorists. Unilateralism was also evident in its approach to summitry. James Schlesinger argues that at the Reykjavik summit meeting with Mikhail Gorbachev, "The administration suddenly jettisoned 25 years of deterrence doctrine . . . without warning, consultation with Congress or its allies."[17] President Bush embraced unilateralism in assembling a global coalition against Saddam Hussein. It was the United States which decided when to launch air strikes; it was the United States which decided when to begin ground operations; it was the United States which ended the ground war; and it was the United States which declared the coalition's objectives to have been met. A vivid reminder of the continued pull of unilateralist thinking in the post–cold war era came early in the Clinton administration when as a price for congressional approval of the GATT agreement, Clinton agreed to insert an "escape hatch" into the treaty which would allow the United States to withdraw if the World Trade Organization's arbitration process consistently violated U.S. rights.

Moral Pragmatism

The second pattern to American foreign policy is moral pragmatism.[18] The American sense of morality involves two elements. The first is that state behavior can be judged by moral standards. The second is that American morality provides the universal standard for making those judgments. By definition American actions are taken to be morally correct and justifiable. Justifying the invasion of Panama as necessary to protect democracy is a case in point. Flawed policy initiatives are routinely attributed to leadership deficiencies or breakdowns in organizational behavior and not to the values that guided that action. In the aftermath of World War I, the Nye Committee investigated charges that the United States had been led into war by banking interests, and the McCarthy investigations followed the "loss of China." General William Westmoreland, commander of U.S. forces in Vietnam from 1964 to 1968, was accused by the CBS news program "60 Minutes" of having lied about enemy troop levels.

American pragmatism takes the form of an engineering approach to foreign policy problem solving.[19] U.S. involvement is typically put in terms of "setting things right." It is assumed that a right answer does exist and that it is the American answer. Moreover, the answer to the problem (be it Lebanon, Nicaragua, the defense of Europe, economic growth in the third world, arms control) is seen as being permanent in nature. Problems arise when others do not see the problem in similar terms. To some this has been especially evident in U.S.-Soviet arms control talks. According to Freeman Dyson, the American approach to strategic thinking "treats nuclear war as a mathematical exercise," and its basic concepts (deterrence, sufficiency, and retaliation) are supposed to "guarantee" continued U.S. security.[20] Operating on the basis of a very different historical experience, the Soviets have developed concepts (victory, superiority, and offensive action) that "are goals to be striven for, not conditions to be guaranteed." To the Soviets uncertainty remained inherent in the nature of warfare, for which no engineering solution exists.

The preferred American method for uncovering the solution is to break the problem into smaller ones the same way an engineer would take a blueprint and break it down into smaller tasks. An organizational or mechanical solution is then devised for each of the subproblems. In the process it is not unusual to lose sight of the political context of the larger problem being addressed. When this happens, the result can be the substitution of means for ends, improvisation, or the reliance on canned formulas to solve the problem.

Both the Monroe Doctrine and its Roosevelt Corollary show the influence of moral pragmatism. Cecil Crabb argues that "the major purpose of the Monroe Doctrine was to preserve the fundamental distinction between old and new world political systems."[21] This goal and its premises went unquestioned. Attention instead focused on how to accomplish this end. The option seized did not reflect the realities of international politics. The Monroe Doctrine was a success because it reflected both British and American interests and because of the power of the British navy. It did not succeed because of American power. Roosevelt justified his corollary to the Monroe Doctrine on the grounds that if nations near the United States could not keep order within their own borders, then the United States had a moral obligation to intervene. Once again the question was largely defined as an engineering problem, how best to intervene.

The neutrality legislation of the 1930s provides an example of moral pragmatism at work in a quite different setting. Here the concern was not with asserting U.S. influence but with detaching the United States from world affairs. As first put forward, the legislation was easy to implement but paid little attention to the political realities of the day. Weapons were not to be sold to either side. Yet refusing to sell weapons to either participant guaranteed victory to the stronger side and invited its aggression. The neutrality legislation was repeatedly amended in an effort to close the gap between technique and political reality. In 1937 the president was given the authority to distinguish between civil strife and war. In 1939 it permitted the cash-and-carry purchase of weapons by belligerents. This allowed the United States to sell weapons to Great Britain but made a mockery of the neutrality principle. The overreliance on formulas by the United States in the post–World War II era has frequently been commented on. Among the most prominent have been (1) opposition to aggression, (2) containment of communism, and (3) defense of free nations. All three have been criticized for being moral abstractions, failing to provide concrete guidance on how to tailor goals to the situation at hand, select the proper approach to solve the problem, or weigh the costs and benefits of a course of action.[22] One author argues that the anticommunist impulse in particular has been used to sanction almost any course of action no matter how immoral if it brings about the greater goal of stopping communism.[23] Right wing dictators have been supported as the lesser of two evils, governments overthrown, states invaded, international law violated, and the rights of American citizens compromised in the pursuit of this end. The potential dangers of rooting U.S. foreign policy on a foundation of moral pragmatism came through quite clearly in the Iran–Contra fiasco. Convinced of the moral correctness of the goal of freeing American hostages in Lebanon, the Reagan administration proceeded to sell arms to Iran and then diverted monies gained through these sales to the U.S.-backed Contras fighting the Sandinista government in Nicaragua. The reliance on engineering solutions and formulas to solve problems also reached excess here, as witnessed by National Security Council (NSC) staffer Lieutenant Colonel Oliver North's equation for achieving the release of the

American hostages, part of which read: 1 707 w/300 TOWs = 1 AMCIT (American citizen).

Certainly, compared to the Carter and Reagan administration's foreign policies, Bush's lacked a strong sense of moral purpose. It was almost all pragmatism with no vision. And his administration was roundly criticized for it. Yet, in carrying out his most ambitious foreign policy initiative, the war against Iraq, Bush demonstrated a penchant for moral pragmatism. Saddam Hussein was defined as the embodiment of evil and a threat to American national interests. The justness of the American cause was unquestioned. Attention focused solely on how to accomplish the stated goal of bringing about a removal of Iraqi forces from Kuwait with a minimum loss of American lives. The centerpiece of the chosen solution was air power and, as Elliot Cohen observes, "reliance on air power has set the American way of war apart from all others . . . it plays to the machine-mindedness of American civilization."[24]

Legalism

The third pattern to U.S. foreign policy is legalism. It grows out of the rejection of the balance of power as a means for preserving national security and the liberal view that people are rational beings who abhor war and favor the peaceful settlement of disputes.[25] A central task of U.S. foreign policy, therefore, is to create a global system of institutions and rules that will allow states to settle their disputes without recourse to war. The primary institutional embodiments of the legalist perspective are the League of Nations and the United Nations. Also relevant are the host of post–World War II international economic organizations that the United States joined (that is, the World Bank, International Monetary Fund, and General Agreement on Tariffs and Trade). Just as commerce between individuals binds them together, international trade is assumed to bind states together and reduce the likelihood of war.

The rule-making thrust to legalism is found in the repeated use of the pledge system as an instrument of foreign policy.[26] In creating a pledge system, the United States puts forward a statement of principle and then asks other states to adhere to it either by signing a treaty or by pledging their support for the principle. Noticeably absent is any meaningful enforcement mechanism. The Open Door Notes exemplify this strategy for world affairs problem solving. In the Notes the United States unilaterally proclaimed its opposition to spheres of influence in China and asked other powers to do likewise, but it did not specify any sanctions against a state that reneged on its pledge. The Washington Naval Disarmament Conference of 1922 and the 1928 Kellogg–Briand Pact are also part of the pledge system. The Washington Naval Disarmament Conference sought to prevent war by establishing a fixed power ratio for certain categories of warships. The agreement failed to include inspection or enforcement provisions. Its restraining qualities were soon overtaken by a naval arms race in areas left uncovered by the agreement and by a general heightening of international tensions. The Kellogg–Briand Pact sought to outlaw war as an instrument of foreign policy. Yet true to its unilateralist impulse, the United States stated that signing the pact would not prevent it from enforcing the Monroe Doctrine or obligate it to participate in sanctions against other states. The SALT I and SALT II agreements follow in the tradition of the pledge system. They specify in broad terms the nuclear inventories that the Soviet Union and the United States are permitted to have without creating any enforcement provisions.

A variation of the pledge system has become a prominent feature of U.S. bilateral and multilateral trade policy. Confronted with an intransigent Japan in 1993, U.S. negotiators settled for a "framework" agreement that specified how future agreements would seek to resolve issues of trade imbalances and barriers to trade without detailing the particulars of the agreement. On the multilateral level, agreements were signed in 1994 that pledged the United States and 33 other Western Hemisphere states to create a free trade zone by 2005 and that pledged the United States and 17 Pacific Basin countries to create their own free trade zone by 2020. In neither case were organizational blueprints or detailed schedules for creating these free trade areas presented.

Legalism has also placed a heavy burden on U.S. foreign policy. In rejecting power politics as an approach for providing for U.S. national security, policy makers have denied themselves use of the "reasons-of-state" argument as a justification for their actions. Instead, they have sought to clothe their actions in terms of legal principles. Post–World War II examples include fighting the Korean War under the UN flag, seeking the Organization of American States' approval for a blockade during the Cuban missile crisis, and citing a request by the Organization of Eastern Caribbean States as part of the justification for going into Grenada. This pattern has continued in the post–cold war era. Bush obtained UN endorsement for his military campaign against Iraq, and Clinton did the same for his use of force in Haiti.

CONSEQUENCES OF THE AMERICAN NATIONAL STYLE

As we suggested earlier, these three patterns come together to support both isolationism and internationalism. They also produce four consequences for the overall conduct of U.S. foreign policy regardless of which general foreign policy orientation is dominant. The first consequence is a tendency to "win the war and lose the peace," a phrase used by some commentators to describe the net result of U.S. aid to the anti-Soviet rebels in Afghanistan. As Robert Osgood wrote in 1957:

> The United States has demonstrated an impressive ability to defeat the enemy. Yet . . . it has been unable to deter war; it has been unprepared to fight war; it has failed to gain the objectives it fought for; and its settlements have not brought satisfactory peace.[27]

This condition stems from the American tendency to see war and peace as polar opposites. War is a social aberration while peace is the normal state of affairs. Strategies and tactics appropriate for one arena have no place in the other. The two categories must be kept separate to prevent the calculations of war from corrupting the principles of peace. In times of peace reason, discussion, and trade are relied on to accomplish foreign policy objectives. In times of war power is the appropriate tool. The absence of a conceptual link between war and peace means that war cannot serve as an instrument of statecraft and that war plans will be drawn up in a political vacuum. The objective of war is to defeat the enemy as swiftly as possible. Only when that is accomplished can one return to the concerns of peace. The closing stages of World War II illustrate the problem inherent in the war–peace dichotomy. Should U.S. forces have pushed as far as possible eastward for the political purpose of denying the Red Army control over as much territory as possible, or should they have stopped as soon as the purely military objectives of the offensive were realized and not risked the lives of U.S. soldiers on nonmilitary goals? The latter course of action was selected, and the cold war East–West boundary in Europe reflects this choice.

The second consequence is the existence of a double standard in judging the behavior of states. Convinced of its righteousness and the universality of its values, and predisposed to act unilaterally, the United States has often engaged in actions that it condemns when practiced by other states. The United States can be trusted with testing and developing nuclear weapons, but other states, especially third world states, cannot. Soviet interventions into Afghanistan and Czechoslovakia are condemned as imperialism while U.S. interventions into the Dominican Republic, Grenada, and Panama are held to be morally defensible. The United States urges its allies not to sell weapons to terrorists or those who support them while at the same time the United States is selling weapons to Iran in the hopes of securing the release of U.S. hostages in Lebanon. The reverse condition also holds. Activities considered by most states to be a normal part of world affairs have been highly controversial in the United States. The clandestine collection of information and covert attempts to influence developments in other states are cases in point. Both are longstanding instruments of foreign policy. Yet the United States has always exhibited a reluctance to employ them for fear of their potentially corrupting effect on American freedoms.

The third consequence is an ambivalence toward diplomacy. In the abstract, diplomacy is valued as part of the process by which states peacefully resolve their disputes. Along with international law and international organizations, diplomacy occupies a central place in liberal thinking about the proper forums for conducting foreign relations. The product of diplomacy, however, is viewed with great skepticism. If the U.S. position is the morally correct one, how can it compromise (something vital to the success of diplomacy) without rejecting its own sense of mission and the principles it stands for? As John Spanier notes, under these conditions compromise is indistinguishable from appeasement.[28] It does not matter whether the other party to the negotiations is a twentieth-century communist state or an eighteenth- or nineteenth-century European state. In either case the fruits of diplomacy have been looked upon with suspicion. We do not have to look further into the past than the SALT talks to see evidence of this ambivalence. Pressures within the United States for stopping the arms race are considerable. Yet the products of arms control talks with the Soviet Union have been met with distrust and hostility: Has the United States accepted a position of inferiority? Did it give away too much? How can the Soviets be trusted?

The fourth consequence is impatience. Optimistic at the start of an undertaking and convinced of the correctness of its position in both a moral and a technical sense, Americans tend to want quick results. They become impatient when positive results are not soon forthcoming. A common reaction is to turn away in frustration. The next time a similar situation presents itself and U.S. action is needed, none may be taken. Calls for no more Vietnams and opposition to sending U.S. forces into Central America reflect this sense of frustration. So too did the demand to get U.S. Marines out of Lebanon following the terrorist attacks on the U.S. compound. The desire for quick and visible results is seen by many as creating a bias for the use of the military as an instrument of foreign policy. Neither diplomacy nor economic power offers quick results. Both are slow working and work best when used out of the public eye. A vicious circle thus can be created. The demand for quick results leads to a reliance on military power, but the rigid distinction between war and peace makes it difficult to use that power effectively. Its use may be marked by a double standard or, as Osgood observed, may simply fail to meet its political objectives. If that is the case, then diplomacy may be turned to. Yet here again the results are likely to be slow in forthcoming, and the settlement will be looked upon with skepticism. Frustration will set in and dominate U.S. foreign policy until a consensus exists supporting new foreign policy initiatives.

All four of these consequences were fully evident in the Persian Gulf War. A dominant criticism of Bush's handling of the Persian Gulf War was that he ended it too soon, producing a situation in which once again the United States had won a war but found itself saddled with an unsatisfactory peace. Instead of stopping the ground attack at the symbolic 100-hours point, many contend that he should have allowed U.S. forces to press ahead, destroying more of Iraq's military capability and even removing Saddam Hussein from power. Failure to do this produced a situation in which a defeated Iraq was able to mount repeated challenges to the United States and the world community in the months that followed the conclusion of hostilities. A double standard for judging state behavior was also evident. The Bush administration had no trouble identifying Iraqi violations of international law or encroachments on human rights. Yet it was quick to deny that in carrying out its "precision bombing" attacks on Iraq it had engaged in questionable behavior according to Western just law doctrines or that it had not acted morally in failing to come to the defense of the Kurds when Iraqi forces turned against them after the war was over. Diplomatic activity during the Gulf War was directed almost wholly at keeping the allies united in their opposition to Iraq. Having defined Saddam Hussein as evil, there was little reason for the Bush administration to engage in a diplomatic dialogue with him, and it was skeptical of efforts by Gorbachev and others to negotiate an end to the conflict. Finally, American impatience led to abandoning economic sanctions in favor of military action. And, as noted above, the optimism that came with the application of air power soon led to disenchantment with its results. That disenchantment was all but inevitable according to Cohen because faith in the mystique of air power obscured the reality that warfare is inherently messy and brutal, and that the use of massive amounts of air power invites primitive but effective forms of revenge.[29]

As subsequent dealings with Iraq have shown, disenchantment with air power does not mean that the U.S. will abandon it as an instrument of foreign policy. The Clinton administration repeatedly turned to air strikes (including bombings in December, 1998 just prior to Ramadan) against Saddam Hussein in an effort to curb his pursuit of weapons of mass destruction and to punish Iraq for aggressive acts.

A REVIVAL OF WILSONIANISM?

What then of the post–cold war era? Will the American national style continue to exert its influence over the content and conduct of American foreign policy? For those who answer in the affirmative, the clearest expression of the continued influence of the American national style on American foreign policy lies in the renewed interest in Wilsonianism brought on by the end of the cold war. A standard ingredient in post mortems of Wilson's foreign policy was that it was naively idealistic. The implication was that it was a fundamentally flawed vision which offered little guidance to future generations of American foreign policy makers. This is no longer the case. Many now concede that the Wilsonian vision was ill-suited to the first decades of the twentieth century but assert that it is quite relevant to the conditions of the post–cold war era. Rather than characterizing Wilson as an idealist, many see him as a vindicated visionary.[30]

Proponents of neo-Wilsonianism as the basis for post–cold war American foreign policy center their attention on his Fourteen Points. Presented in a speech Wilson delivered before Congress in 1918, the Fourteen Points constituted an outline for constructing a new world order. The first five points would lay the foundation for a new, "open" era of international politics. Point 1 called for "open covenants of peace, openly arrived at . . . diplomacy shall proceed always frankly and in the public view." Point 2 called for freedom of the seas. Point 3 urged "the removal, so far as possible, of all economic barriers and the establishment of an equality of trade conditions among all the nations consenting to the peace." Disarmament was the subject of Point 4, which called for reducing national armaments "to the lowest point consistent with domestic safety." Point 5 called for an end to colonialism. Points 6 through 13 addressed the problems of national self-determination and drawing national boundaries in Europe, which Wilson considered critical for the establishment of a secure and lasting peace. Point 14 asserted that "a general association of nations must be formed under specific covenants for the purpose of affording mutual guarantees of political independence and territorial integrity to great and small states alike."

That Wilson's proposals did not fare well at the Paris Peace Conference and that the United States did not vote to join the League of Nations are acknowledged as great failures but are no longer treated uniformly as signs that the ideas Wilson espoused were defective. Many now echo historian and Wilson biographer Arthur S. Link's conclusion that Wilson possessed a "higher realism" in his handling of foreign affairs.[31] Link characterizes Wilson as a quick learner in foreign policy matters who took personal control over foreign policy making because of the incompetence of those in high-ranking State Department positions. He was a man who recognized the need for give and take in treaty negotiations. He was all of this while remaining loyal to his fundamental Christian principles and belief in democracy.

Those advocating a neo-Wilsonian foreign policy have not gone unchallenged. Some opponents have reexamined the Wilsonian legacy and asked: "Are we all not Wilsonians?" while others have asserted that advocates of a neo-Wilsonian foreign policy have drawn too narrow a picture of Wilsonianism.

Robert Tucker asks the first question.[32] Rare is the modern president, he observes, who does not claim to be a Wilsonian. Some argue that the Reagan Doctrine could be seen as the ultimate embodiment of the Wilsonian legacy, given its commitment to expand democracy, and that Reagan was the "most Wilsonian of presidents since Wilson's time."[33] This overextension of the Wilsonian label leads Tucker to reexamine the roots of Wilsonian thought. He concludes that Wilson's approach to foreign policy shares much in common with Jefferson, who is cited by many as an early advocate of isolationism. They both rejected amoral European-style diplomacy and sought to replace it with a new diplomacy that rested on the will of the people. They were united in the belief that American interests could only be safeguarded by a reformed international system. Tucker asserts that only force could bring this condition about. Rejecting this course of action led Jefferson to embrace isolationism. For Wilson, it came to mean creating a global concert of powers that would bring such a reformed international system into existence. Where the Wilsonian vision encountered problems was in the relationship between ends and means. Could a reformed international system be created with only limited costs and demands being placed on the United States? If not, then the Wilsonian vision of a democratic world could only be purchased at an excessive price and one which threatened to undermine the very American values it was designed to foster. It is these questions of the relationship between means and ends and force and peace which Tucker sees as representing the core challenge facing the Wilsonian vision today.

David Fromkin raises the second question posed above: What is Wilsonianism?[34] He concludes that it is a mistake to equate Wilsonianism with collective security. At a minimum, attention must be given to several other aspects of Wilson's thinking. Foremost among these is his belief in a strong presidency. Wilson saw the president's control of foreign policy as "very absolute." He believed that the Senate had no choice but to ratify any treaty submitted to it by the president regardless of any doubts about its wisdom or the secrecy with which it may have been negotiated. Also critical to any definition of Wilsonianism, Fromkin argues, is a close examination of the relationship between words and deeds in Wilson's decision making. Fromkin sees a pattern in which Wilsonian principles followed his actions rather than preceding them. As a consequence, Wilsonian principles served to rationalize policy made for very different reasons, rather than direct it. He freely changed sides on an issue or applied standards unevenly. Fromkin concludes that Wilsonianism can only be taken to mean "a certain way of talking and thinking about international relations in terms of concepts that are inspiring and high minded but impractical application provides no guidance."

Alternatives to a Wilsonian post–cold war American foreign policy have also been proposed. George Kennan suggests that the writings and policies of John Quincy Adams offer an appropriate place to think about how to respond to the challenges of Iraq, Lebanon, Somalia, Haiti, and Bosnia. According to Adams, American foreign policy should be based on the principle that the United States was "the well-wisher to the freedom and independence of all" but "the champion and vindicator only of her own."[35] Adams was putting forward an argument for non-intervention into the affairs of others and advocating a foreign policy that was to be based on the "power of example." To go further, he warns, would involve the United States in "wars of interest and intrigue, of individual avarice, envy, and ambition."

SUMMARY AND THE FUTURE

What of the future? Will the American national style remain the same, or will it change? Can it be allowed to remain the same, or must it change? The American national style is not frozen in place. In the eyes of one observer, legalism has already lost much of its influence.[36] Change might come about as a result of the increased presence of women, blacks, and Hispanics in the policy-making process.[37] Their histories read quite differently from those presented in the standardized accounts of the American past, and they may bring to the policy process a very different style of acting and thinking about solutions of foreign policy problems. Change might also come about as the result of major crises in the operation of the international or domestic order. The onset of such crises increases societal receptivity to new ideas and creates a window of opportunity for these ideas to seize a place on the political agenda.[38] In a sense, this is exactly what happened after the end of the cold war. Realism, the dominant paradigm for practicing world politics during the cold war, seemed ill-suited for the emerging conditions of post–cold war international relations. This stimulated a search for an alternative world view and a renewed interest in Wilsonianism.

By definition the American national style is neither good nor bad. It is simply a descriptive statement about how policy makers tend to think about foreign policy problems. The historical record suggests that the American national style has been a source of strength and weakness. Its impact is often largely determined by the context within which policy makers operate. The very aspect of the American national style which is a source of strength in one case has proven to be a source of weakness in another. The Truman administration experienced the success of the Marshall Plan and the failure of the Point Four Program. The Kennedy administration successfully managed the Cuban missile crisis and precipitated the Bay of Pigs fiasco. The fit between American national style and future policy problems is thus uncertain. Much rests on both the nature of those problems and the ability of U.S. policy makers to learn from the past.

A degree of caution must be employed in relying on a national style approach to foreign policy analysis. The patterns we have discussed cannot be seen as dictating the details of U.S. foreign policy. Too many other factors are at work for this to be the case. What they do appear capable of doing is placing boundaries on what type of action will be considered permissible or appropriate for the United States to undertake. Foreign policy initiatives that do not build on these policies (détente) or that are seen as excessive applications of them (the Iran–Contra policy) are unlikely to receive sustained support by the American public.

NOTES

1. Judith Goldstein, *Ideas, Interests, and American Trade Policy* (Ithaca, N.Y.: Cornell University Press, 1993), 1–18.

2. Ibid.

3. George Kennan, "The Sources of Soviet Conduct," *Foreign Affairs*, 25 (1947), 576.

4. For convenient discussions of containment and détente, see John Spanier, *American Foreign Policy Since WW II*, 10th ed. (New York: Holt, Rinehart & Winston, 1985), pp. 23–29, 189–200, 304–6, and 316–21; Charles W. Kegley, Jr., and Eugene R. Wittkopf, *American Foreign Policy: Pattern and Process*, 2nd ed. (New York: St. Martin's, 1982), pp. 48–69; and Henry T. Nash, *American Foreign Policy: A Search for Security*, 3rd ed. (Homewood, Ill.: Dorsey, 1985), pp. 44–48 and 249–50.

5. Quoted in Howard Bliss and M. Glen Johnson, *Beyond the Water's Edge: American Foreign Policy* (Philadelphia: Lippincott, 1975), pp. 52–53.

6. Frank Klingberg, "Cyclical Trends in American Foreign Policy Moods and Their Policy Implications," in Charles W. Kegley, Jr., and Patrick J. McGowan (eds.), *Challenges to America: United States Foreign Policy in the 1980s* (Beverly Hills: Sage, 1979), pp. 37–55.

7. Frank L. Klingberg, "Cyclical Trends in Foreign Policy Revisited in 1990," *International Studies Notes*, 15 (1990), 54–58.

8. Dexter Perkins, *The American Approach to Foreign Policy* (Cambridge, Mass.: Harvard University Press, 1962), p. 154.

9. Robert Dallek, *The American Style of Foreign Policy, Cultural Politics and Foreign Affairs* (New York: New American Library, 1983).

10. Max Lerner, cited in Cecil Crabb, Jr., *American Foregin Policy in the Nuclear Age*, 4th ed. (New York: Harper & Row, 1983), p. 47; and Richard Ullman, "The 'Foreign World' and Ourselves: Washington, Wilson and the Democratic Dilemma," *Foreign Policy*, 21 (1975/76), 97–125.

11. For a discussion of these points, see Stanley Hoffmann, *Gulliver's Troubles, or the Setting of American Foreign Policy* (New York: McGraw-Hill, 1968); John Spanier, *American Foreign Policy Since WW II*, 9th ed. (New York: Holt, Rinehart & Winston, 1983); Perkins, *The American Approach to Foreign Policy;* and Amos Jordan and William J. Taylor, Jr., *American National Security, Policy and Process* (Baltimore, Md.: Johns Hopkins University Press, 1981).

12. Kenneth Keniston, quoted in Bliss and Johnson, *Beyond the Water's Edge*, p. 110.

13. Stanley Hoffmann, "Foreign Policy Transition: Requiem," *Foreign Policy*, 42 (1980/81), 3–26.

14. For a discussion of alternative interpretations of U.S. foreign policy and national style, see Kegley and Wittkopf, *American Foreign Policy*, pp. 69–81.

15. For a discussion of unilateralism, see Gene Rainey, *Patterns of American Foreign Policy* (Boston: Allyn & Bacon, 1975), pp. 19–43.

16. Robert Tucker, *The Radical Left and American Foreign Policy* (Baltimore, Md.: Johns Hopkins University Press, 1971), p. 34.

17. James Schlesinger, "Reykjavik and Revelations: A Turn of the Tide?" *Foreign Affairs*, 65 (1987), 431.

18. For a discussion of American foreign policy highlighting these themes, see Arthur Schlesinger, Jr., "Foreign Policy and the American Character," *Foreign Affairs*, 62 (1983), 1–16.

19. Hoffmann, *Gulliver's Troubles*, p. 150.

20. Freeman Dyson, "On Russians and Their Views of Nuclear Strategy," in Charles W. Kegley, Jr., and Eugene R. Wittkopf (eds.), *The Nuclear Reader: Strategy, Weapons, War* (New York: St. Martin's, 1985), pp. 97–99.

21. Crabb, *American Foreign Policy*, pp. 36–37.

22. Hoffmann, *Gulliver's Troubles*, pp. 141–143; and Frederick Hartmann, *The Relations Among Nations*, 6th ed. (New York: Macmillan, 1983), pp. 421–26.

23. David Watt, "As a European Saw It," *Foreign Affairs*, 62 (1983), 530–31.

24. Elliot A. Cohen, "The Mystique of U.S. Air Power," *Foreign Affairs*, 73 (1994), 109–24.

25. For a critical discussion of the impact of legalism, see George Kennan, *American Diplomacy, 1900–1950* (New York: Mentor, 1951).

26. Rainey, *Patterns of American Foreign Policy*, p. 36.

27. Robert E. Osgood, *Limited War: The Challenge to American Strategy* (Chicago: University of Chicago Press, 1957), p. 29.

28. Spanier, *American Foreign Policy Since WW II*, 10th ed., p. 11.

29. Cohen, "The Mystique of U.S. Air Power," p. 124.

30. See Charles W. Kegley, Jr., "The Neoidealist Moment in International Studies? Realist Myths and the New International Realities," *International Studies Quarterly*, 37 (1993), 131–46.

31. Arthur S. Link, *The Higher Realism of Woodrow Wilson* (Nashville, Tenn.: Vanderbilt University Press, 1971).

32. Robert W. Tucker, "The Triumph of Wilsonianism?" *World Policy Journal* 10 (1993), 83–100.

33. Ibid.; and Tony Smith, "Making the World Safe for Democracy," *The Washington Quarterly*, 16 (1993), 92–102.

34. David Fromkin, "What Is Wilsonianism?" *World Policy Journal*, 11 (1994), 100–12.

35. George Kennan, "On American Principles," *Foreign Affairs*, 74 (1995), 116–26.

36. Rainey, *Patterns of American Foreign Policy*, p. 386.

37. Kenneth Longmyer, "Black American Demands," *Foreign Policy*, 60 (1985), 3–16; and Bill Richardson, "Hispanic Concerns," *Foreign Policy*, 60 (1985), 30–39.

38. Goldstein, *Ideas, Interests, and American Trade Policy*.

CHAPTER

 Post-Vietnam
U.S. Foreign Policy

James Woolsey, President Clinton's first Director of Central Intelligence, described the passage from the cold war to the post–cold war era as one where "we have slain a large dragon" and now find ourselves living "in a jungle filled with a bewildering variety of poisonous snakes." That dragon was not killed in one fell swoop. Nor did the snakes suddenly emerge from behind the dense underbrush. We passed through a transition period in which the defining features of the cold war gradually gave way to the emerging characteristics of the post–cold war era. It was a period in which there were both a dragon and snakes. In this chapter we will highlight the major features of this transition period. We will begin our survey with American foreign policy as it emerged from the Vietnam War and carry it into the first years of the Clinton administration. For the sake of convenience, we will organize our discussion around presidential administrations. We will examine their major political-military foreign policy undertakings and their major international economic policy initiatives, and we will present a sampling of opinion regarding their stewardship of American foreign policy.

THE NIXON (AND FORD) ADMINISTRATIONS: LEAVING VIETNAM AND ENTERING DÉTENTE

In 1971, four years before the Vietnam War ended with the surrender of the U.S.-backed South Vietnamese government in 1975, President Nixon proclaimed the need for a "new and stable framework for international relations."[1] The policy of containment whose logic led to the United States involvement in Vietnam was discredited. It had been conceived in the late 1940s as a strategy for countering aggressive Russian foreign policy initiatives by bolstering threatened governments and repelling communist military advances. The defense of the status quo became its primary objective. Over time an additional element, "falling dominoes," was added to containment. It became an article of faith among American policy makers that any Russian/communist territorial gain, no matter how insignificant, represented a threat to American security because it could be the first in a row of falling dominoes that could ultimately bring down a vital ally. Vietnam was perceived by many in the United States as just such a first domino. As we will detail in the next chapter, the Vietnam War was a true watershed in American foreign policy. The inability of American forces to defeat North

Vietnam and the unwillingness of the American public to bear the costs of an indefinite military operation led to a major rethinking about the proper goals of American foreign policy.

The centerpiece of President Nixon's strategy for building a "new and stable framework for international relations" was a policy of détente with America's two cold war adversaries, Russia and China, and a more balanced partnership with American allies. Gerald Ford did little to change that in his term in office other than to ban the word "détente" from the Republican political vocabulary during his 1976 bid for the presidency.

Much of the intellectual energy behind Nixon's strategy came from Henry Kissinger, who first served as Nixon's National Security Adviser and then became his Secretary of State. To Kissinger, a principal source of unrest in world politics came from the presence of revolutionary states whose interests lay in overturning the status quo rather than working to protect it. Détente was intended to bring about a relaxation of tensions between the United States and its major cold war adversaries so that they might enter into the management of the international system as co-partners. Only when the legitimacy of the international system was accepted by all the major powers could there be stability. The decline in American military power necessitated that the economic power be used as a carrot and stick to induce the desired Soviet behavior in the political-military arena. Finally, the central feature to the management of a stable international system was the successful operation of a balance of power. For Nixon and Kissinger that entailed an ability and willingness to play off China and Russia against each other as well as practice "linkage politics."

The basis for U.S.–Soviet détente was laid at the May 1972 Moscow Summit conference between Nixon and Soviet President Leonid Brezhnev. This summit is best known for the Strategic Arms Limitation Agreement (SALT I), which sought to slow the arms race and stabilize the U.S.–Soviet nuclear balance by placing qualitative and quantitative limits on the offensive strategic weapons. Also signed was a statement of political principles pledging both parties to conduct their foreign policies on the basis of peaceful coexistence, forgo efforts of one party to obtain unilateral advantages at the expense of the other, and recognize that their security interests are governed by the principle of equality.

Establishing a basis for détente with China was complicated by the lack of diplomatic relations between the two states. Ever since 1949 when Mao Zedong's forces had driven the pro-Western forces of Jiang Jieshi (Chiang Kai-Shek) out of China on to the island of Taiwan, the United States had steadfastly refused to recognize Mao's government as the official government of China. Nixon moved to break through the decades of formal silence by announcing to a surprised American people that he would be going to China. The major document emerging from that historic trip was the 1972 Shanghai Communiqué. It pledged both the United States and China to normalize relations and pursue antihegemonic policies in the Asia-Pacific region.

These foundations proved to be too weak to support a new international framework. Détente with the Soviet Union floundered because the two countries never understood it to mean the same thing. For the Soviet Union détente was a means to break out of containment and place U.S.–Soviet competition on a different—more equal—basis. For the United States détente was a necessary concession intended to preserve America's global influence at lessened cost. Matters quickly came to a head in the third world. Much to Russia's dismay, the United States intervened in the 1973 Arab-Israeli War in a way that all but eliminated Russian influence in the region for a decade. American leaders soon felt betrayed by continued Russian assistance to African Marxist movements in Angola, Mozambique, and the Horn of Africa. Normalization of Chinese-American relations never moved far beyond the symbolic stage. Domestic politics restricted both Nixon and Ford's ability to make the necessary political compromises. During the last part of Nixon's administration, Watergate dominated his political attention. President Ford found himself in a tough primary campaign against the more conservative Ronald Reagan.

Still another part of Nixon's new and stable political framework involved a change in relations between the United States and its allies. The Nixon Doctrine, officially announced in 1969 while the United States was still very much involved in the Vietnam War, stated that America's allies could no longer count on the United States to send troops abroad to defend them. American aid would be restricted to the transfer of money, equipment, and technology. Saudi Arabia and Iran were two prime beneficiaries of the Nixon Doctrine. The United States funneled large amounts of military equipment in their direction in an effort to create surrogate powers whom the United States could count upon to resist the spread of Soviet influence to the Middle East.

Like détente, the Nixon Doctrine proved to be less than an effective foundation for a new world order. The perceived need for loyal allies in the third world blinded American policy makers to the scale of human rights abuses in these countries and the growing isolation of their rulers from the larger society. Nowhere would this become more visible than in Iran, where between 1973 and 1978 the Shah had purchased some $19 billion worth of American-made weapons. The permanence of his rule was never seriously questioned by high-ranking American policy makers. Not only was his fall unexpected but the specter of Iranian militants in power would haunt more than one president. The Nixon Doctrine also failed because of the inability of the Nixon administration to exercise the required degree of self-restraint. Faced with the prospect of communist governments in Chile and Angola, the Nixon administration neither left these states to fend for themselves nor turned to surrogate powers to prevent this from happening. Instead, it turned to covert action. The resulting efforts to unseat President Salvador Allende in Chile and oppose the Popular Movement for the Liberation of Angola (MPLA) were major policy failures and became stimuli for congressional efforts to place curbs on the presidential conduct of foreign policy.

Kissinger recognized that "international political stability required international economic stability."[2] Yet Nixon's plans for creating a new and stable international system were all but silent on this point. Benign neglect best characterized his administration's international economic policies.

American policy makers had been instrumental in creating the three key international economic institutions of the post–World War II era: the International Monetary Fund (IMF), the International Bank for Reconstruction and Development (the World Bank), and the General Agreement on Tariffs and

Trade (GATT). Collectively they composed what came to be known as the Bretton Woods system. Each addressed a different aspect of the international economic puzzle. The IMF sought to ensure monetary stability so that states, individuals, and corporations would have the confidence to engage in international economic transactions. GATT sought to reduce barriers to trade in order to maximize the opportunities for such transactions. Finally, the World Bank made funds available to help create economic infrastructures that would allow states to participate effectively in an international economic system of free trade.

By the time Nixon became president in 1969, the Bretton Woods system was showing signs of fatigue and collapse. This was most evident with regard to international monetary transactions. The IMF was established to govern a system of fixed exchange rates in which currencies would be valued in terms of gold and could be exchanged for gold on demand. Any significant changes in the value of a country's currency would have to be approved by the IMF. The system never worked as anticipated due to the postwar weakness of European economies and an insufficient supply of gold. It quickly became evident that only one currency, the U.S. dollar, could serve as the basis for international trade. The challenge facing policy makers in the late 1940s and for most of the 1950s was getting enough U.S. dollars into foreign hands to spark a revival in world trade. Answers were found in foreign aid programs such as the Marshall Plan and military expenditures through NATO and the Korean War.

As the 1960s began it was clear that the United States no longer needed to encourage an outflow of U.S. dollars. This outflow had reached dangerous proportions and had become the central management problem in the international monetary system. That foreign holdings of U.S. dollars now exceeded the U.S. gold reserves was indicative of how severe the problem had become. Further compounding the problem was the fact that the dollar had become overvalued due to the inflation brought on by Vietnam and the corrective steps taken by other states to adjust their exchange rates in the face of U.S. inaction.

International pressure on the dollar reached a breaking point in August 1971. Nixon announced that the United States was devaluing the dollar (that is, increasing the dollar price of gold), suspending the convertibility of dollars into gold, and imposing an across-the-board 10 percent surtax on imported goods. According to most observers, Nixon's actions marked the end of the Bretton Woods system. The ten leading industrial nations met at the Smithsonian in Washington in December in an effort to piece back together a management structure. Although Nixon hailed the accord, the agreement amounted to little more than after-the-fact crisis management. Even those efforts proved to be inadequate as in March 1973 the United States once again moved to devalue the dollar and announced that it would allow the value of the dollar to "float." No longer would the United States set and defend an exchange rate. Market forces would determine the dollar's worth. The practical effect of this move was to pass on to other states more of the costs of managing the international monetary system.

Before the year ended additional strains would be placed on the international monetary system by the response of the Organization of Petroleum Exporting States (OPEC) to the Western intervention and Arab defeat in the

October Yom Kippur War. Frustrated with the continued Israeli occupation of Arab lands as a result of the 1967 war and seeing no prospect for changing the status quo through diplomacy, Egypt and Syria surprised Israel with a stunning first blow. After one week of fighting Israeli forces gained the upper hand and now it was the Arab states which were in danger of suffering a massive defeat. Last minute U.S. and Soviet intervention brought the war to an end after seventeen days but only after President Nixon put U.S. nuclear forces on a heightened alert status. Acting in unison, OPEC states first embargoed the sale of oil to the industrialized world and then raised its price to new unheard-of levels. By and large, ad hoc consultations were relied upon to manage the effects of the OPEC-engineered price hikes. It was only in late 1975 under the prodding of the Germans and French that the United States agreed to a formal conference to address management problems. That conference, which took place in Jamaica in 1976, failed to bring about any meaningful reform.

Nixon's Foreign Policy Evaluated

Both conservatives and liberals criticized Nixon's foreign policy. Each objected to the status quo–oriented nature of détente and its lack of a clear overriding moral purpose. Liberal critics argued that Nixon's foreign policy was anachronistic. It was irrelevant to the conditions of the post-Vietnam era. The main issues on the international agenda were questions of hunger, poverty, and global inequalities of wealth. These were issues that cried out for policy innovation and international cooperation. To these critics, Vietnam had proven the futility of trying to hold back demands for political and social reform with military power. They were equally skeptical of the ability of American economic power as manifested in foreign aid and the overseas operation of American companies to move international society forward. What was required was a fundamental reorientation of American foreign policy and a recommitment to traditional American values.

Conservative critics took exception to Nixon's willingness to accept the Soviet Union as a full partner in the family of nations. To them, the Soviet Union was still the enemy. To enter into a working relationship with it was tantamount to ideological surrender, implying that fundamental similarities existed between the two states that made cooperation possible. This denied the uniquely revolutionary nature of communist systems and the ultimate objectives of their foreign policy. Nothing about the behavior of the Soviet Union (or China) had changed. What had changed was the American perception of their actions.

A third line of criticism directed at détente focused on its lack of intellectual rigor and problems in its execution. Robert Tucker identified several flaws.[3] First, there was a contradiction between the recognition of the limits of power implied by détente and the overall continuity in roles and interests in American foreign policy. Second, Tucker asked, was there any reason to assume, as détente did, that America's allies would be relatively passive, its adversaries reasonably restrained, and the third world stable and undemanding? Détente required that all of these conditions be met in order to succeed. Third, the Nixon administration's obsession with secret methods undermined the domestic base of support for its policy. Fourth, there was little evidence to suggest that economic carrots and sticks had influenced Soviet foreign policy in the past. Why was it assumed that this would be the case now? Tucker concludes that despite public rhetoric to the contrary, détente was more of a "holding operation than a settled strategy."

THE CARTER ADMINISTRATION:
AMERICAN FOREIGN POLICY WITH A PURPOSE:
PROMOTING HUMAN RIGHTS

In a pattern that was to be repeated four years later, President Jimmy Carter entered office pledging to lay the basis for a new American foreign policy. Where the Nixon-Ford-Kissinger foreign policy had stressed realpolitik and balance-of-power considerations, Carter promised a foreign policy that was "democratic, . . . based on fundamental values, and that uses power and influence . . . for humane purposes." This was to be done by focusing American foreign policy on promoting human rights and solving regional problems rather than on simply countering the Soviet Union's every move.

At the very onset of his administration, Carter proclaimed that "our commitment to human rights must be absolute."[4] Carter did not venture into completely uncharted territory in advocating that human rights be a central element in American foreign policy. As Arthur Schlesinger, Jr., has noted, "Americans have agreed since 1776 that the United States must be the beacon of human rights to an unregenerate world."[5] There also existed a political base on which to build such a policy because Congress had begun to force the human rights issue on reluctant presidents. Congress began requiring the State Department to attest to the acceptability of a country's human rights record as a precondition for the granting of foreign aid. Amendments, such as the Jackson-Vanik Amendment, which made the granting of most favored nation status to the Soviet Union dependent on changes in its emigration policy for Soviet Jews, were attached to bills sharply curtailing the president's freedom to make foreign policy. Eventually even the Nixon administration moved to embrace human rights by its participation in the Conference on Security and Cooperation in Europe which produced the Helsinki Accords in August 1975. This agreement made Soviet and Eastern European human rights practices a permanent item on the diplomatic agenda. Carter did, however, move American human rights policy forward. His vision of human rights was more expansive than that held by previous administrations. Where traditionally the United States had thought about human rights in terms of civil and political rights, the Carter administration added a concern for economic and social rights.

Looking back four years later it was evident that this commitment, however genuine, was not always translated into policy. For every act taken in the name of promoting human rights, there seemed to be a counterexample where human rights concerns were sacrificed in the interests of protecting American economic and strategic interests. The Carter administration sought to portray these lapses as indicative of its willingness to be flexible and take a case-by-case approach in deciding upon what course of action to take. To his critics it translated into inconsistency. On the plus side of the ledger the administration claimed that foreign military sales programs were reduced to South Korea, Indonesia, and Zaire. Economic aid programs to Nicaragua, Afghanistan, Ethiopia, El Salvador, the Philippines, Paraguay, Uruguay, Chile, the Central African Empire, and Guinea were postponed, reduced, or eliminated. Countries such as India, Sri Lanka, Botswana, Peru, and the Dominican Republic were also rewarded with increased assistance levels for improving their human rights record. The administration abstained or voted no on human rights grounds to 117 loan requests made to international lending organizations. Critics, however, pointed to situations where either nothing was done or far more could have been done: China, South Korea, the Philippines, Zaire, Iran, Panama, and Indonesia.

In Latin America the first regional issue addressed by Carter was the status of the Panama Canal. The United States and Panama had been involved in difficult negotiations over the future of the Panama Canal for over two decades. Carter moved quickly to bring these negotiations to a conclusion, and in September 1977 two treaties were signed. The Panama Canal Treaty immediately voided all existing treaty arrangements and gave the United States the right to run the Panama Canal until December 31, 1999. At that time control over the Panama Canal would be transferred to Panama. The terms of the second treaty, the Treaty Concerning the Permanent Neutrality and Operation of the Panama Canal, would come into effect in 2000. It authorized the United States and Panama to take "whatever action it deems necessary" to ensure that the canal would "remain secure and open to peaceful transit by vessels of all nations on the terms of entire equality." These treaties provoked intense debate in Congress. It was only after a major lobbying campaign and the acceptance of congressionally authored amendments that the treaties were approved by the Senate and then only by the slimmest of margins.

Carter was less successful in engineering a successful endgame to the political unrest brewing in Central America. In Nicaragua a long-time U.S. ally, Anastasio Somoza, was under increasing pressure from a broad-based group of opposition forces led by the Sandinista National Liberation Front. In a marked departure from policies followed by previous administrations, Carter chose not to support the besieged dictator. He sought to convince Somoza to enter into negotiations with his opponents. Unwilling to do so, Somoza fled the country in 1979. The Carter administration recognized the new Sandinista government and provided it with economic aid in order to "create stability out of revolution." Relations between the United States and the Sandinistas soon soured, and the final installment of this $75 million aid package was suspended by Carter in his final days in office due to reports of rising Soviet influence there. Carter also authorized a secret intelligence finding that permitted the CIA to support anti-Sandinista forces within Nicaragua. Concerns now grew about Sandinista support for Marxist insurgents in neighboring El Salvador.

Further from home, Carter's regionalist approach scored a major diplomatic triumph when in September 1978 he played host to a meeting between Egyptian President Anwar Sadat and Israeli Prime Minister Menachem Begin at the presidential retreat at Camp David. After decades of war between the

Arabs and Israelis, an unexpected peace opening had occurred in November 1977. Sadat announced that he would be willing to go to Israel to discuss a peace agreement. That trip and months of follow-up negotiations made little headway. In a bold move to break this deadlock, Carter invited both leaders to Camp David where they agreed upon a framework for a "just, comprehensive, and durable settlement of the Middle East conflict." Carter's Middle East policy was not without controversy. Sadat's bold initiative was in large measure brought about by an earlier misstep in American foreign policy. Carter wished to convene a Middle East summit conference in Geneva which would be co-chaired by the United States and the Soviet Union. This would have effectively brought the Soviet Union back into the region as a major player after years of exile due to Nixon's policies during and after the 1973 Yom Kippur War. Sadat feared that a superpower-imposed agenda would be detrimental to Egypt's interests, and he therefore moved to seize the diplomatic initiative. Some also found shortcomings in the Camp David agreement. First, it was silent on the question of a Palestinian homeland. Second, it brought with it a hefty price tag in terms of U.S. foreign aid that would now begin to flow to Egypt and Israel. Economic and military aid was seen as necessary in order to ensure that these "islands of stability" in the Middle East did not deviate from the path toward peace.

Lessening the central role that the Soviet Union played in American foreign policy deliberations proved to be easier said than done. In large measure this was due to the fact that the Carter administration needed Soviet cooperation in order to realize some of its more ambitious foreign policy goals. Arms control was a case in point. Carter inherited from Ford a virtually completed strategic arms control proposal, the 1974 Vladivostok Accords. Only two issues remained outstanding: the Soviet backfire bomber, which was thought by some to possess the capability of striking the United States from the Soviet Union, and the American cruise missile, which was small in size and could be mounted on a wide variety of delivery platforms, thus creating potentially significant verification problems.

Carter chose not to take the Vladivostok agreement as a starting point for a SALT II treaty. Instead he proposed a treaty which would make radical reductions in each side's strategic arsenal and would limit their ability to modernize strategic weapon systems. Already resenting the implication that the Soviet Union should not be the central focal point of U.S. foreign policy, and distrustful of Carter for his human rights rhetoric and criticism of its treatment of political dissidents, the Soviet Union balked. It saw Carter's proposal as an attempt to restore American nuclear superiority and demanded that negotiations proceed on the basis of the Vladivostok Accords. It would take two and one-half years of difficult negotiations before a SALT II agreement would be reached. Signed by Carter and Brezhnev in Vienna in 1979, and submitted to the Senate for ratification that summer, SALT II was never voted on. It became a victim of the Soviet invasion of Afghanistan and the subsequent hardening of U.S.–Soviet relations.

Two other factors contributed to the inability of Carter to make U.S. foreign policy less centered on the Soviet Union. First, important forces in the Carter administration continued to view the Soviet Union as an important object of attention. Foremost among these was National Security Adviser Zbigniew Brzezinski. He disagreed with the Nixon-Kissinger view that the Soviet Union could be made into a partner with a vested interest in preserving the global status quo. To Brzezinski, the Soviet Union's legitimacy had to be challenged ideologically and its internal weaknesses exposed and exploited. Advocacy of human rights became a policy instrument that was useful for this purpose. Second, as we previously noted, in the Soviet view détente did not mean the end to competition. Thus, it continued its military buildup and its policy of supporting Marxist revolutionary movements in Africa and Latin America.

It was support for pro-Russian Marxist forces in Afghanistan that brought about a return to cold war relations between the United States and the Soviet Union. The roots of the 1979 Soviet invasion can be traced back to a 1973 coup d'état in which the king of Afghanistan was deposed. Within a short period of time the new government came under attack from the Maoist and pro-Soviet factions of the Marxist People's Democratic Party. In April 1978 the Maoist Khalq faction led a successful coup which ended in the signing of a 20-year treaty of friendship between the two countries. The new government sought to impose a radical series of economic and social reforms on the Afghan people. The government ignored Soviet recommendations to slow down the pace of reform. Unwilling to see an ally fall, the Soviet Union stepped up its shipment of military equipment and sent in combat personnel. In September 1979 a rival Maoist faction seized power. It too refused to heed Moscow's advice and followed an even more radical reform program. Once again the Soviet Union increased its military presence in Afghanistan. In December, confronted with an increasingly chaotic situation and the pending triumph of Islamic rebel forces, Russia sent an invasion force of more than 50,000 soldiers into Afghanistan and brought Babrak Karmal, head of the pro-Soviet Parcham faction, back from exile to serve as the new president.

Carter denounced the Soviet invasion. He halted the SALT II ratification process, suspended the sale of high technology to the Soviet Union, imposed a grain embargo, and called for the establishment of a Rapid Deployment Force. Carter also issued a warning, which came to be referred to as the Carter Doctrine, in his 1980 State of the Union address. He stated that any "attempt by outside force to gain control of the Persian Gulf region will be quickly repelled by any means necessary including military force."

The harsh tone of Carter's response reflected more than just his disillusionment with the Soviet Union. It also reflected his administration's frustrations in dealing with the new rulers of Iran, who one month before the Soviet invasion of Afghanistan had seized the American embassy and taken American hostages. With only a slight period of interruption, Iran had been ruled from 1941 until 1979 by one of America's most loyal third world allies, Mohammed Reza Shah Pahlavi. That interruption came in 1953 when the Shah was forced into exile as Iranian nationalists seized power. He was restored to the throne largely through the efforts of a CIA-inspired coup. Over time the corruption and repression of the Shah's rule reached the point where he became dependent upon the military and his ruthless secret police, the SAVAK, to stay in power. Even this proved to be insufficient as the 1970s drew to a close and Iranians took to the streets demanding reform.

The Carter administration was caught off guard by the Shah's rapidly mounting political troubles. It had become an article of faith that the Shah would remain in power and that Iran would be pro-West. After first backing the Shah, the Carter administration unsuccessfully urged him to negotiate with his opponents. The most important opposition leader was the Ayatollah Khomeini, who was in exile in France and returned to Iran on January 31, 1980, to take over the reins of government. The Shah had left Iran in the middle of the month. The Carter administration first weighed letting him come to the United States but reconsidered due to fear of the reaction it might provoke in Iran. In October, at the urging of Kissinger, Brzezinski, and David Rockefeller, who headed Chase Manhattan Bank, and over the objection of the U.S. embassy in Iran, Carter agreed to let the Shah come to the United States in order to receive potentially life-saving medical care. Two weeks later the embassy was seized and demands were issued for the return of the Shah to Iran to stand trial.

Carter's response to the hostage crisis was to apply economic sanctions in the hope of securing the hostages' release. This strategy failed to bring about their quick release. Neither did a military rescue mission conducted in April 1980. Instead, Carter's handling of the crisis fed a fervent election-year debate both about his stewardship of American foreign policy and the overall direction that it should take. The hostages would be released on Ronald Reagan's inauguration day, after spending 444 days in captivity.

The Carter administration also faced challenges along a broad array of international economic issues. Among the most prominent were slowed economic growth, mounting protectionist pressures, galloping inflation, a besieged dollar, and skyrocketing oil prices. The primary thrust of Carter's international economic policy lay in efforts to establish multilateral management systems. Annual economic summits attended by leaders from the most advanced economies were one device Carter tried to use for this purpose. Great expectations were attached to a 1978 plan by which the German and Japanese economies would follow expansionist policies that would pull the remainder of the world's economies out of their economic doldrums. The "locomotive theory" was derailed, however, by rising doubts about the value of the dollar. These were fed by the inability of the United States to pursue economic policies at home that seemed capable of combating inflation, and by dramatic increases in the price of oil due to rising demand for oil and the political unrest in Iran.

Multilateral economic management was also pursued in the area of international trade at the Tokyo Round GATT talks. Begun in 1973 and concluded in 1979, these talks were conducted in a very different setting from that which surrounded the Kennedy Round GATT negotiations of the 1960s. Then states felt capable of striking bold bargains that would open up the world economy to freer trade in industrial goods. The atmosphere during the Tokyo Round was marked by caution, and the ultimate success of these talks was not taken for granted. In spite of the difficulties encountered, the Tokyo Round talks did produce some notable successes. The problem of nontariff barriers to trade was addressed for the first time. Codes were established in such areas as dumping, government procurement, licensing, subsidies, and countervailing duties.

While marking a significant advance, these codes were not endorsed by all the parties to Tokyo Round talks, thus allowing countries legally to continue to engage in discriminatory trade practices. International trade in agricultural goods also remained largely beyond the reach of GATT regulations. These deficiencies were sufficiently glaring that in 1983 the Reagan administration began lobbying for a new round of trade talks. These negotiations, known as the Uruguay Round, would begin in 1986.

Carter's Foreign Policy Evaluated

Echoing a familiar theme, Stanley Hoffmann characterized Carter's foreign policy as "the hell of good intentions." It suffered, he concluded, from "an almost total addiction to erratic tactics."[6] The Carter administration changed course repeatedly on a constant stream of issues: the status of U.S. troops in South Korea, the neutron bomb, the transfer of high technology to the Soviet Union, relations with Somalia, and the Middle East. According to Hoffmann, while personal and institutional factors contributed to these inconsistencies, the critical factor was his administration's strategic incoherence. Most notable here was the mistaken belief that it could package world affairs into two categories: one involving military relations with the Soviet Union, the other involving everything else. Still, Hoffmann found much good in Carter's foreign policy. It addressed long-term problems ignored by previous administrations, such as conventional arms control and the law of the seas; its human rights policy increased American prestige in the world; and it understood that the conditions for American influence over world affairs were changing. Robert Tucker was less kind in his critique. Labeling it a failure, Tucker asserts that the root cause of Carter's problems lay in his administration's vision of the world, a vision that was futuristic to the point of being irrelevant for policy. Only near the end did his administration face up to the central problem confronting American foreign policy: the rapid growth in Soviet military power. Moreover, it was a vision that Tucker found to be "immoderately optimistic." Citing human rights as a prime example, he asserts that the Carter administration had little sense that its policy departures might come with a hefty price tag. Given this flawed, "immature" view of the world, Tucker argues that the Carter administration had no right to be either surprised or outraged by the Soviet Union's invasion of Afghanistan. Surprise was unwarranted because evidence of increased Soviet aggressiveness and the American unwillingness to use its military power to counter it were clear in the mid-1970s. Outrage was unwarranted because the Soviet Union never promised to play by the American interpretation of détente.

Jeane Kirkpatrick, who would serve as ambassador to the United Nations in the Reagan administration, put forward a critique that resonated well with conservative Republicans.[7] She argued that Carter's human rights policy was fundamentally flawed because it did not recognize the differences between right wing governments and left wing totalitarian ones such as in the Soviet Union. Right wing governments could make a transition to democracy, and their violations of human rights generally were done in the name of national security and stopped short of depriving citizens of their basic freedoms. Totalitarian governments could not make the transition to democracy, she argued. Their violations of human rights were far more destructive and carried out on principle.

A final perspective on the Carter administration's foreign policy is provided by David Skidmore.[8] He argued that Carter's initial foreign policy was neither confused nor incoherent. It was also not a product of his personal moralism. Rather, Carter's troubles stemmed from the domestic response to his strategy of adjustment. By maximizing his political flexibility, Carter had severely limited his ability to draw on the doctrines and symbols that presidents traditionally relied upon to build a foreign policy consensus. In the end, Carter was forced to turn back to such well-established techniques of gaining public support as relying upon anticommunist symbols, overstating threats and overselling solutions, and developing "doctrines" to provide a unifying focus for his foreign policy. He did so too late to save his presidency and further postponed the time at which the aims of American foreign policy are adjusted to correspond with its decline in power.

THE REAGAN ADMINISTRATION: A RENEWED COLD WAR

Reagan and his foreign policy team possessed a world view that was fundamentally at odds with the thrust of Carter's foreign policy. Early in his first term, Reagan characterized the Soviet Union as an "evil empire," charging that "the only morality they recognize is what [which] will further their cause: meaning they reserve unto themselves the right to commit any crime; to lie; to cheat." This language was intended to convey to the Soviet Union and the rest of the world that where Nixon and Carter had sought to establish a working relationship with Soviet leaders by using "carrots and sticks" (and then mostly carrots), his administration would rely primarily on the stick.

From the Reagan administration's perspective, a prerequisite for such a policy shift was to rebuild America's military power. To that end, Reagan called for spending $1.6 trillion over five years to revamp the American military establishment. Among the projects to be funded were the construction of 100 B-1 bombers, development of a neutron bomb, renewing the production of poison gas for use in chemical warfare, the deployment of the MX missile, and an upgrading of the Rapid Deployment Force. Modernizing America's strategic forces (those forces capable of carrying nuclear weapons to the Soviet Union, that is, nuclear submarines, intercontinental ballistic missiles, and the manned bomber) was held to be particularly important because "a window of vulnerability" had opened in the U.S.–Soviet strategic balance. Without these new weapons, the Reagan administration charged that Soviet nuclear forces could threaten and intimidate the United States and its allies.

Consistent with its new hard-line approach, the Reagan administration also changed the tone of U.S. arms control policy. Where Nixon and Carter had voiced their suspicions regarding Soviet violations of SALT II and the Anti-Ballistic Missile (ABM) Treaty in diplomatic channels, the Reagan administration went public with its misgivings. Among the most significant allegations it leveled at the Soviet Union were that it was developing a new class of strategic missiles (the SS-25), that it had constructed a battle management ABM radar facility at Krasnoyarsk, and that it was illegally hiding (encrypting) information from its missile and warhead testing programs. These highly public accusations of cheating were coupled with a toughening in the language used to characterize the U.S.–Soviet strategic relationship. References to nuclear war-fighting capabilities and the ability to prevail in a protracted nuclear conflict were frequently voiced by Reagan administration officials. For example, Secretary of State Alexander Haig in his confirmation hearings spoke of the possible need to fire a nuclear shot across the Soviet bow to deter it from invading Europe.

Perhaps the most visible symbolic stick employed by the Reagan administration against the Soviet Union was the Strategic Defense Initiative (SDI) or "Star Wars." Announced as a long-term research plan in a speech in March 1983, President Reagan called upon the scientific community to devise a system that would allow the United States to "intercept and destroy their [Soviet] strategic missiles before they reach our soil or that of our allies." The exact details of the Star Wars system were not spelled out in the speech but attention soon focused on the creation of a layered defense scheme that would be heavily dependent upon space-based weapons systems. Its ultimate success would hinge upon still-to-be-developed weapons and communication technologies. To its supporters, Reagan's SDI program offered hope of finding a way out of the uncomfortable reality of the nuclear age: that one's security was dependent upon the ability to carry out a retaliatory nuclear strike because there was no way to prevent that strike from taking place. To its opponents, SDI was dangerous because it promised to unleash a new arms race between the United States and the Soviet Union as each sought to develop offensive weapons capable of penetrating a Star Wars shield.

The Reagan administration's willingness to engage in a strategy of verbal confrontation with the Soviet Union created a great deal of unease among America's European allies. Never having warmed to Carter, whom they saw as inexperienced in world affairs, they now faced another American administration that did not appreciate the European perspective on security matters and that seemed at war with itself when it came to making policy decisions. An early sign of difficulty came when the Reagan administration attempted to orchestrate an embargo on the sale of natural gas pipeline technology to the Soviet Union. The Europeans saw the proposed technology-now-for-energy-later swap as a means of lessening their dependence on Middle East imports. The Reagan administration saw it as a harbinger of greater Russian influence in Western Europe and a way for the Soviet Union to improve its current economic situation. The Europeans were upset not only because the Reagan administration was unsympathetic to their view but because at the same time it was dropping Carter's grain embargo, an act sure to improve the state of Russia's economy.

Further problems between the United States and its European allies arose around the negotiation of an Intermediate Nuclear Forces (INF) Treaty. The origins of this problem date to the Carter administration and the perceived need to respond to the Soviet development of the SS-20. The large-scale deployment of this missile threatened to upset the balance of power in

Europe. The two options available were to negotiate an arms control agreement to prevent this from happening or to counter it by introducing a comparable weapons system. The Europeans feared the first option because it might result in the "decoupling" of Europe from the United States. NATO security guarantees were considered credible because of the belief that there was no way to keep a nuclear war in Europe from spreading to the United States. This new generation of missiles suggested that it might be possible, and European leaders were reluctant to endorse such a course of action. The political climate in 1979 made it impossible for the United States to sign an arms control agreement with the Soviet Union as the Europeans would have preferred. In the end a compromise, "dual-track" strategy was agreed upon. NATO would begin the deployment of Pershing II missiles and cruise missiles in 1983 if no arms control agreement had been reached.

The belligerent posture of the Reagan administration toward the Soviet Union all but guaranteed that this would not be the case. In both Europe and the United States vocal peace movements sprang up fearful that U.S. policies would bring about a nuclear confrontation between the superpowers. In 1981 the Reagan administration tried to counter these voices by calling for acceptance of a "zero option" in the INF talks: The United States would not deploy its Pershing II and cruise missiles as scheduled if the Soviet Union would remove their already deployed SS-20s. The Soviet Union rejected the proposal from the outset. Talks broke off in 1983 with no agreement, and the highly controversial deployment began. No further movement on the INF front occurred until 1985 when a new round of arms control negotiations began and Mikhail Gorbachev assumed power in the Soviet Union. To the surprise of the Reagan administration, Gorbachev embraced the zero option concept for intermediate range nuclear forces, and in 1987 an INF Treaty was signed at a Reagan-Gorbachev summit conference in Washington, D.C.

Reagan and Gorbachev became regular partners at summit conferences, meeting five times in the last four years of the Reagan administration. The nature of these meetings and their outcomes were quite varied, ranging from working sessions with no formal agenda to ones characterized by serious arms control negotiations. It was their second summit meeting in Reykjavik, Iceland which provoked the most controversy. Approached with insufficient preparation, the Reagan administration was caught off guard by Gorbachev's proposal that both the United States and the Soviet Union eliminate all offensive strategic weapons. Reagan accepted the proposal only to back off later when Gorbachev insisted that the United States forgo any out-of-laboratory testing of its SDI program as part of the deal. The proposal—and its acceptance—were controversial because had the deal gone through it would have meant abandoning 25 years of deterrence doctrine without any consultation with Congress or allies. Moreover, it was only Reagan's personal attachment to a weapons system most believed could never work that prevented this from happening.

The Reagan administration also brought about a reorientation of American foreign policy toward third world states. Where Carter had sought to deal with these issues largely within a regional context, Reagan placed them squarely within the context of expansionist Soviet foreign policy. The initial focal point of attention was Central America where a civil war in El Salvador quickly was cited as a "textbook case" of communist aggression. Large-scale fighting had begun in 1979 when reform-minded elements of the military seized power and installed José Duarte as president. This set off a wave of right wing violence that targeted radical and reformist political groups. Centrist and leftist forces then united to form the Revolutionary Democratic Front to oppose Duarte, who was unable to control this rising tide of violence. The Reagan administration contended that a large part of the problem in El Salvador was due to Russian and Cuban military support for leftist rebel forces that was being funneled through Nicaragua. In a move to cut off the supply of weapons, Reagan signed a presidential finding in March 1981 authorizing the CIA to organize and fund moderate opponents of the Sandinistas. These forces became known as the Contras, and the administration's staunch support for them became one of the most controversial elements of Reagan's foreign policy.

That controversy had many dimensions and would culminate in a 1984 congressional budget resolution cutting off all funding for the Contras. One issue involved how to judge the activities of the Contras. Human rights groups complained at length about their brutality. Noting that this "after all, was war," CIA officials acknowledged in congressional testimony that the Contras had assassinated judges, doctors, and other supporters of the Sandinista regime. Reagan in a 1983 address stated that the Contras were "freedom fighters" and the "moral equivalent of the founding fathers." Closely related to this was the question of their military effectiveness. With a leadership recruited largely from the National Guard forces that had been loyal to the deposed dictator Somoza, the Contras never developed into a force that could lay claim to the loyalty of the Nicaraguan people. Nor did they ever demonstrate a sustained ability to carry out military maneuvers effectively. A third issue involved their ultimate purpose. The Reagan administration repeatedly claimed that the objective was not to overthrow the Sandinista government, only to make it respect international law and stop its support for revolutionary forces elsewhere in Central America. Congress was far less enthusiastic in its support for the Contras. It was also suspicious of their ultimate motives and passed legislation forbidding the use of U.S. funds to overthrow the Sandinista government. Fourth, controversy existed over how far the United States should go to support the Contras. The Reagan administration was embarrassed by the revelation that the CIA had helped produce a manual instructing the Contras on assassination methods. In addition, it was roundly castigated by Congress for mining Nicaraguan harbors without fully informing congressional intelligence oversight committees.

The Reagan administration's unwillingness to drop its support for the Contras in spite of their military failures and in the face of congressional opposition became one of the driving forces in the Iran–Contra scandal that would engulf the Reagan administration in its second term. The other driving force was the continued specter of Middle East terrorism. An ill-fated attempt by the Israelis to rid Lebanon of terrorists in 1982 led to the establishment of a multinational peacekeeping force in that country. U.S. Marines formed a significant part of that force. At first their presence was welcomed, but gradually the Marines became identified with the pro-Israeli side of the civil war that was taking place in Lebanon. This led to a steady wave of terrorist attacks directed against Americans: In 1983, 241 Marines were killed when terrorists attacked their barracks in Beirut; in 1984 three Americans, one of whom was the CIA station chief, were abducted; and in 1985 four more Americans were taken hostage.

In the Reagan administration's view, the central force behind these anti-American terrorist activities was the Iranian government of Ayatollah Khomeini. Bringing about a change in this government was seen as a key to ending Middle East terrorism. The standing Reagan administration policy for dealing with terrorists was one of nonnegotiation. However, in this case Reagan's personal obsession with the fate of the American hostages led those around him to explore alternative means for bringing about their release. One proposal put forward was to aid the political stature of Iranian moderates by lifting the arms embargo against Iran and selling it weapons. It was hoped that Iran would respond to this move by arranging for the release of the American hostages.

The two concerns were combined into one policy when the decision was made to take the monies raised by the sale of these weapons and use it to support the Contras. The operation was run from the White House by Lieutenant Colonel Oliver North. President Reagan denied any knowledge of the link between the transfer of weapons, the release of the hostages, and funding for the Contras. A total profit of $16 million was realized from the arms sales, but the Contras only received about $3.8 million. Congress had been kept in the dark about the operation, in violation of existing laws, and when it became public a major confrontation ensued between the two branches.

The Reagan administration's support for the Contras was part of a larger strategy known as the Reagan Doctrine. It was designed to move the United States beyond a policy of containment to one where support would also be given to groups trying to overthrow ruling communist governments. In addition to Central America, the Reagan Doctrine was very much evident in U.S. foreign policy toward Afghanistan. The original Soviet military plan called for the Afghan army to pacify the Afghan population following the 1979 invasion. Wholesale defections negated this strategy and required the introduction of large numbers of Soviet forces who now had to bear the primary responsibility for fighting the guerrillas or Mujahadin. Initially the Soviet Union sought to conduct a conventional military campaign against the Mujahadin. After sustaining initial losses, the Mujahadin countered by retreating into the mountains and out of reach of Soviet forces. By the early 1980s Soviet leaders had become disillusioned with the military stalemate and the continued political infighting among the Afghan communists.

An important factor standing in the way of any negotiated exit from their "Vietnam" was the military support being received by the Mujahadin from the United States. In 1984 the Reagan administration was underwriting the Mujahadin to the tune of $120 million. In 1987 this figure had increased to $630 million, bringing the total value of U.S. military aid to that point to $2.1 billion. It would be 1988 before a negotiated end to the Soviet presence in Afghanistan was agreed upon through a series of bilateral agreements reached between Afghanistan and Pakistan, and between the United States and the Soviet Union.

In general, the Reagan administration addressed international economic problems only when it felt forced to do so. This was not surprising. Not only was Reagan an advocate of keeping the government out of economic decision making, thereby allowing the market to run its natural course, but the return to cold war themes all but guaranteed that international economic problems would not receive a high priority. One area in which the Reagan administration did act forcefully was U.S.–Japanese trade. Persistently large trade imbalances (with the United States importing far more from Japan than it is able to sell there) brought forward complaints about Japanese unfair trade practices and a steady torrent of calls from Congress that Japan take steps to narrow the gap or be punished for its unwillingness to do so. Twice in his first term Reagan forced Japan to "voluntarily" place restraints on its exports to the United States. The first occurred in his first year in office and involved automobiles. The second came just prior to his reelection and involved textiles. These ceilings remained in place for his entire term as president and were joined by restraints on steel and machine tool exports to the United States.

Japan was not the only target of the Reagan administration's anger in the area of trade. China, Mexico, Canada, South Korea, Brazil, Singapore, and the Netherlands, along with others, were targeted for retaliation. So extensive were the Reagan administration's efforts that the percentage of goods coming into protected American markets rose from 12 percent to 24 percent. The ultimate expression of American anger at what it perceived to be the unfair trade practices of others was the Omnibus Trade and Competitive Act of 1988. Its key provision was known as "Super 301." This clause required the president to identify unfair trading states, establish a timetable for negotiating a settlement to the dispute, and identify possible retaliatory steps that the United States might take.

Against its will, the Reagan administration was also forced to act to forestall a worsening of the international debt crisis. In August 1982, Mexico announced that it would be unable to make the annual payment on its $80 billion debt. The implications of this announcement were staggering. Nine leading American banks had up to two and one-half times their total capital and assets in loans to third world countries. Along with Mexico, Brazil and Argentina owed approximately 40 percent of the debt held by American banks. If these countries defaulted, these banks would collapse and the entire international economic system would be threatened. The initial response to this problem involved a combination of IMF-imposed austerity programs, new bridge loans by the United States, and stretched-out commercial repayment schedules.

By 1985 it became apparent that an impasse had been reached and that more needed to be done if sustained growth was going to take place in the third world. The Baker Plan, named after Secretary of the Treasury James Baker, was the Reagan administration's proposed solution. In return for speeding up their domestic reforms and further opening their economies to foreign investment, third world states were to receive additional funds from commercial banks so that they could grow out of the crisis. The World Bank would also target the 15 most indebted states with increased loans in order to encourage commercial banks to work with them in solving their debt problems. Finally, creditor states such as the United States would open up their markets to third world goods in order to provide greater export opportunities. The Baker Plan proved to be inadequate to the task, largely due to the inability to attract funding on the necessary scale. As the Reagan administration ended it was widely agreed that "debt fatigue" had set in on the part of all of those involved and that a new start at solving the problem would have to be taken by the incoming Bush administration.

Reagan's Foreign Policy Evaluated

As one might expect, Reagan's handling of foreign policy brought forward a wide range of opinion. Michael Mandelbaum argued that in the final analysis Reagan was a "lucky president."[9] He stated that Reagan's success in managing U.S. foreign policy had little to do with his own efforts. The primary reasons for success were "the result of forces and trends outside the control of the United States and of measures undertaken by others and occasionally even opposed by Mr. Reagan." Foremost among these others was Jimmy Carter. According to Mandelbaum, the essence of luck is timing, and good timing was evident all around him: The Soviet Union was gripped by a leadership crisis for most of his term in office; its economy was experiencing a severe downturn; arms control agreements restrained it militarily; the Middle East was quiet politically due to Carter's Camp David agreement; international oil markets were favorable to the West. This combination of circumstances minimized his missteps and allowed Reagan to pursue a status quo foreign policy that experienced few geopolitical setbacks.

Many critics on the political right were dismayed by the final resting place of Reagan's foreign policy. It looked suspiciously like "Carterism without Carter." The radical reorientation of American foreign policy that had been promised did not come about. Gone was much of the combative rhetoric and distrust of communists that marked his first years in office. Gone too was the willingness to stand by America's third world allies. Arms control was once again a fixture on the agenda. President Reagan had traveled to China. With U.S. blessing President Marcos of the Philippines was removed from office in large measure because of his human rights violations and antidemocratic policies. And, in its last days in office, the Reagan administration had taken steps toward establishing a formal diplomatic dialogue with the Palestine Liberation Organization.

Robert Tucker suggests that all these critics overstate their case and miss the mark.[10] While Reagan may have been lucky, he also skillfully realized his primary foreign policy goals: reversing the decline in American power, restoring the credibility of its power as a force in world politics, and stopping the expansion of Soviet influence. Tucker acknowledged the essential continuity of the Carter and Reagan administrations. But to him, it was not a matter of a Reagan about-face. Instead, it reflected the underlying influence of cultural and geopolitical factors on the selection of policy. Tucker sees Reagan's failure as residing in his inability or unwillingness to make a sustained effort to rebuild the domestic foreign policy consensus that was shattered by Vietnam. Most critically, Reagan failed to get the American people to understand that the pursuit of foreign policy goals deemed to be in the national interest requires sacrifice. "From the very outset, the great appeal of the president's policies was that they demanded so little of the public while promising so much." The defense buildup was paid for with a budget deficit. The invasion of Grenada was swift. Retaliatory strikes against Qaddafi for his support of international terrorism brought no retaliation. When costs were encountered, such as the attack on the Marines in Lebanon, the policy initiative was quickly terminated. Tucker feared that future presidents would find this new consensus with its emphasis on low-cost successes to be too fragile a foundation on which to build a foreign policy.

THE BUSH ADMINISTRATION: LEAVING THE COLD WAR AND ENTERING A NEW WORLD

By temperament and experience George Bush was the polar opposite of Ronald Reagan. Where Reagan was an ideologue with little personal experience in world affairs, Bush was a pragmatist who had served as Director of Central Intelligence, Ambassador to China, and Ambassador to the United Nations. What Bush promised the American people in his 1988 election campaign was continuity in overall policy without the excesses and missteps that hounded the Reagan administration. That he often was able to deliver on this promise came to be judged both as a sign of weakness and a sign of strength in his handling of foreign policy. This was because his presidency coincided with an era of immense change in world politics: the passing of the cold war.

Bush first moved to tie up two loose ends of Reagan's Central American foreign policy. He terminated the controversy over Nicaragua by entering into an agreement with Congress over funding for the Contras. Congress would approve nonmilitary aid for the Contras through the elections scheduled for 1990 and the Bush administration would not request any lethal aid. It would also use diplomatic and economic leverage to bring about peaceful change in Nicaragua. Moreover, any one of the committees with oversight jurisdiction in this area could cut off the flow of aid. The Sandinistas had agreed to internationally supervised elections in the hopes of gaining international legitimacy and breaking American opposition to their rule. The Bush plan was put forward fully expecting a Sandinista victory. To its surprise, the Sandinistas were voted out of office as the anti-Sandinista candidate, Violeta Barrios de Chamorro, won by an impressive margin.

Panama presented Bush with a very different problem. Rather than dealing with "the enemy," Bush was confronted with a former ally who once had served as a CIA agent and was now a liability openly defying the United States. During the Reagan administration, officials increasingly became concerned with the flow of drugs from Latin America to the United States. Panamanian ruler General Manuel Noriega was a major player in this game. As early as 1985 the Reagan administration had warned Noriega about its concerns over the political situation in Panama and reports about his involvement in drug trafficking and money laundering. Little was done to change the situation until 1988 when, after being unable to agree on the wisdom of using military force against Panama, the Reagan administration imposed economic sanctions. It also negotiated a deal whereby Noriega would step down and the United States would drop a grand jury indictment against him for drug trafficking. The deal collapsed in May, and in July Reagan agreed to a covert action that might have resulted in Noriega's assassination. The plan was never carried out, due to objections from the Senate intelligence committee, and a more modest one was put in its place.

Matters came to a head in 1989. First, in May Noriega annulled the Panamanian election won by his opponent, leading Bush to recall the U.S. ambassador. Then, in October, a failed U.S.-supported coup attempt led to strong criticism of Bush's handling of his Noriega problem. Finally, in December, less than one week after the Panamanian National Assembly unanimously voted Noriega to be "maximum leader" and declared Panama to be in a "state of war" with the United States, 13,000 U.S. troops were committed to removing Noriega and his forces from power. The invasion was condemned by the Organization of American States but justified by Bush as consistent with American rights under the Panama Canal treaties and as necessary to protect American lives.

Reagan also left Bush unfinished business in the area of strategic arms control. During his campaign against Carter, Reagan had characterized the SALT framework as fatally flawed. In 1981, when the Reagan administration moved to reopen arms control talks with the Soviet Union, they were rechristened the Strategic Arms Reduction Talks (START). No headway was made in these negotiations until the 1986 Reykjavik Summit when an agreement in principle was reached to reduce all strategic nuclear weapons by 50 percent over a five-year period. This breakthrough proved to be somewhat illusory, for it was not until July 1991 that Bush and Gorbachev signed the START I Treaty. START I was submitted to the Senate for ratification in November of that year. According to its terms, the United States and the Soviet Union would be limited to 1,600 delivery vehicles and 6,000 strategic explosive nuclear devices. There were also sublimits for the delivery vehicles that these warheads could be placed on. Deeper cuts were agreed to in 1992 when Bush and Boris Yeltsin agreed upon a START II Treaty. Strategic inventories were reduced to 3,500 for the United States and 2,997 for the Soviet Union. In addition, both sides agreed to eliminate all multiple independently targeted reentry vehicles (MIRVs) from their ICBMS.

Unforeseen political developments in the Soviet Union stalled the START process. The forces unleashed by Gorbachev in his reform drive had succeeded in doing far more than transform the Soviet political system. They also altered its political borders and dispersed its nuclear arsenal. Where the United States once faced one nuclear enemy, it now faced four: Russia, Belarus, Kazakhstan, and Ukraine. Several months of negotiations produced a Protocol to the START I Treaty signed in May 1992 wherein all three new nuclear states pledged to destroy their nuclear arsenals by 1999. With this completed, the U.S. Senate ratified START I in October 1992. Political tension between these states and Russia, however, continued to slow progress in the area of arms control. Deadlines for the destruction of weapons were not met, and further progress was often made conditional on prior steps being taken by one or all of the others.

The foreign policy problems emanating from Gorbachev's reform efforts came at the Bush administration in a series of unrelenting waves. The first came in December 1988 just weeks prior to his inauguration. In a speech to the United Nations Gorbachev unilaterally announced that the Soviet Union would reduce by 500,000 the number of its soldiers stationed in Europe. Next came Poland and Hungary. In 1989 Solidarity, the trade union movement which had emerged in the early 1980s as the focal point for opposition to the communist system in Poland, was legalized and free elections were held. Solidarity won a stunning victory and the new Polish government pledged to implement market-based economic reforms. Communist rule ended in Hungary in 1990. Officially disbanded in 1989, a renamed communist party was badly beaten in free elections held in March and April 1990.

Even more astonishing was the next wave. In August and September 1989 large numbers of East Germans began fleeing their country. This exodus was accompanied by widespread demonstrations calling for democratic reform. The pressures generated by these events were so great that they brought down the regime of long-time communist party head Erich Honecker. Then, in November, in a move that many cite as the symbolic ending of the cold war, the Berlin Wall came down. That same month West German Chancellor Helmut Kohl proposed creating a confederation that would unite the two Germanies. In February of the following year the new East German prime minister offered his own reunification plan. A meeting of the four "occupying powers" (France, Great Britain, Russia, and the United States) and the two Germanies—the two plus four talks—in May led to agreement on a framework for reuniting Germany. In October 1990 East and West Germany were formally reunited into one country.

The next waves came from the Soviet Union itself. In March 1990 Lithuania, a Baltic state forcibly made part of the Soviet Union in 1940, declared its independence. Gorbachev called the move "illegitimate and invalid." In a move designed to blunt the drive of other republics to leave the Soviet Union and shore up his political base, Russia and the nine republics agreed in April 1991 to a new union treaty that would give them more autonomy. One day before this treaty was to take place, civilian and military hard-line opponents of Gorbachev calling themselves the "State Committee for the State of Emergency," attempted to seize power. Russian President Boris Yeltsin rallied forces inside and outside the government to thwart the coup. Although Gorbachev was returned to power his political powers were greatly weakened and pressures were intensified for independence. As the year ended Russia, Belarus, and Ukraine announced that the Soviet Union no longer existed. In its place they unveiled a new Commonwealth of Independent States (CIS) open to all Soviet republics. Georgia and the Baltic republics of Lithuania, Estonia, and Latvia chose not to join.

A final wave that moved in on the Bush administration had its origins in Yugoslavia. With the cold war now over and lacking a leader of the stature of Tito to hold it together, Yugoslavia began to unravel in 1991. The year began with the Serb-dominated Yugoslav government sending troops into that country's six republics in order to disarm "illegal armed units." Croatia responded by placing its police and territorial self-defense forces on maximum alert. In

June Croatia and Slovenia declared their independence but held off from actually seceding. By summer's end Yugoslav (Serbian) federal forces launched a major offensive into Croatia in the name of protecting ethnic Serbian guerrillas operating there. Serbia rejected a European Community (EC)–sponsored peace plan, which led Germany to formally recognize the independence of Croatia and Slovenia in December. This was followed in February 1992 by a UN Security Council vote to send peacekeeping forces to Croatia to enforce a tense cease-fire. The fighting did not end. Instead, it shifted to Bosnia-Herzegovina, whose independence had also just been recognized by the EC and the United States.

Both individually and collectively these events presented the Bush administration with an unprecedented series of foreign policy challenges. They involved these fundamental questions: To what extent should (or could) the United States act to support these first steps to democracy and market-based economies? To what extent should the United States work for German reunification? What was the future role of NATO? How quickly should the United States move to recognize the sovereignty of these breakaway republics? Where did the political boundaries of Europe begin?

The Bush administration followed a "wait and see" policy in responding to most of these developments. At the Paris Economic Summit in July 1989 Bush made it clear that he was willing to allow Western European states to play the lead role in promoting peaceful change in Eastern Europe. With the United States preoccupied with the Persian Gulf War, Western Europe also assumed the lead role in responding to the dissolution of Yugoslavia two years later. Although the Bush administration did not try to stop German reunification, it did not play a major role in the endgame. Final details were worked out between Kohl and Gorbachev. Torn by doubts about Gorbachev's true agenda and the long-term prospects for his political survival, the administration responded cautiously to calls for economic assistance. It postponed action to make agricultural credits available to Russia and moved slowly on the question of giving it most favored nation status. Early in the administration National Security Adviser Brent Scowcroft wondered publicly about whether the true purpose behind Gorbachev's policies was to weaken the NATO alliance by causing dissension among its members.[11] Yet at the same time the administration was hesitant to abandon Gorbachev as his political difficulties mounted. For example, it refused to impose economic sanctions on Russia for attempting to stop Lithuania from becoming independent.

The Bush administration's indecision in how to respond to the unprecedented also characterized its policy toward China. Following the death of former communist party leader Hu Yaobang in April 1989, thousands of student protesters took to the streets in Shanghai, Beijing, and other cities demanding prodemocracy reforms and calling for the current party leadership to resign. Over the next months the protests escalated, with as many as one million demonstrators crowding on to Beijing's Tiananmen Square. On June 4, Chinese troops attacked the demonstrators on Tiananmen Square, killing hundreds. Martial law was declared. Before it was lifted in January 1990 an often violent crackdown on prodemocracy forces inside and outside the government was carried out.

President Bush responded to the Tiananmen Square massacre by impos-ing economic sanctions against China, including suspending arms sales. In the weeks that followed, the Bush administration suspended all high-level contacts between the two governments and called for international organizations to postpone consideration of Chinese loan applications. By the end of the year, however, the administration had lost much of its enthusiasm for punishing China for its human rights violations. Concern shifted to protecting what it saw as American long-term strategic and economic interests in the region, interests that might be damaged if it were unable to carry out normal diplomatic rela-tions with China. Accordingly, the Bush administration vetoed a bill that would permit Chinese citizens to prolong their legal stay in the United States, lifted a congressional ban on loans to firms doing business with China, and announced the sale of three communication satellites to it. It was also revealed that the Bush administration sent National Security Adviser Scowcroft and Under Secretary of State Lawrence Eagleburger to China secretly in July to talk with Chinese leaders.

The defining moment of the Bush administration's foreign policy was the Persian Gulf War.[12] Convinced that Saddam Hussein was engaged in noth-ing but saber-rattling bravado, George Bush and other world leaders were stunned by the successful August 2, 1990 Iraqi invasion of Kuwait. Charging that Hussein's act was one of "blatant aggression," Bush issued an executive order freezing Iraqi and Kuwaiti assets in the United States and cutting off trade with Iraq. He stated that U.S. military intervention was not under con-sideration, but he soon backed off from the statement. The administration's attention quickly turned to Saudi Arabia, which it feared might be Iraq's next target. Four days after the invasion, in response to a request from Saudi King Fahd, Bush ordered 2,300 U.S. paratroopers, AWACS, and B-52 and F-11 air-craft to guard Saudi oil fields as part of Operation Desert Shield. The number of U.S. forces sent to Saudi Arabia reached 100,000 before the end of August and climbed over the 200,000 mark in November with predictions of up to 400,000 by early 1991.

Iraq's conquest of Kuwait was declared "null and void" by the UN Secu-rity Council. That body also imposed mandatory economic sanctions on Iraq and authorized the United States to use its ships in the region to uphold the embargo. On November 29, it authorized states "to use all means necessary" to end Iraq's occupation of Kuwait. The UN resolution gave Iraq until January 15, 1991 to do so. The Bush administration conducted a major diplomatic campaign to put together a global coalition and make such a resolution possi-ble. In addition to addressing the UN General Assembly, Bush met with Gor-bachev in Helsinki and went to the Middle East to meet with King Fahd and Egyptian President Mubarak. He met with Syrian President Assad in Geneva. Secretary of State James Baker traveled to Europe, the Middle East, and the Soviet Union. He also met with Chinese leaders in Cairo.

1991 began with talks between Baker and Iraqi Foreign Minister Tariq Aziz. Since the invasion, Iraq had alternated between issuing bellicose warn-ings about its resolve and willingness to fight a holy war and more peaceful ges-tures that indicated a possible willingness to seek a peaceful solution (or divide the alliance), such as releasing hostages and offering to consider a partial withdrawal. The talks produced no headway and Iraq again adopted a hostile posture, indicating that it would strike Israel if attacked. In the United States, Congress began debate over whether to authorize Bush to use force against Iraq or require him to give economic sanctions more time to work. On January 12, both houses voted to give Bush that power. Three days later Bush ordered coalition forces to attack Iraq if the UN deadline was not met and the following day, January 16, Operation Desert Storm was launched to liberate Kuwait.

Amid around-the-clock allied bombing of Iraqi military targets, Iraq made good its threat to attack Israel. Iraqi troops also invaded Saudi Arabia and briefly took possession of a town before being forced to retreat. On February 23, allied forces invaded Iraq and 100 hours later President Bush declared that Kuwait was liberated. At a joint session of Congress on March 6, Bush announced that the war was over.

Tension in the region did not end, however. Saddam Hussein turned his remaining forces against Kurdish forces in northern Iraq and Shiite Muslims in the south. Although the United Nations condemned Hussein's actions, it took no steps to protect his targets and Bush announced that the United States would not act to either support them or bring down his government. Instead, the United States turned its attention to establishing a new security framework in the region and tried to restart the Arab–Israeli peace process. A new problem came into focus by summer. As part of its surrender, Iraq agreed to allow the United Nations to supervise the destruction of its chemical and biological weapons and its ballistic missiles. Not only was Iraq interfering with UN inspection teams, but mounting evidence pointed to the existence of a larger-than-expected Iraqi nuclear capability.

When he was defeated by Bill Clinton in the 1992 election, Bush's post-election foreign policy was expected to be quiet. It was anything but that. Just days after the election, the Bush administration announced that it was imposing a 200 percent tariff on EC exports to the United States in retaliation for EC's refusal to reduce agricultural subsidies that hampered U.S. trade opportunities in Europe. In early December, the United States began consulting with its European allies over ways of stopping Serbian flights over Bosnia-Herzegovina. In early January, Bush and Yeltsin signed the SALT II Treaty. And, of utmost significance to the incoming Clinton administration, on December 4, following a UN vote authorizing the action, Bush ordered U.S. troops to move into Somalia to help deliver food and humanitarian assistance. Operation Restored Hope began with three ships carrying 1,800 troops. U.S. Marines encountered little resistance upon going ashore, but fighting soon broke out and UN Secretary General Boutros-Ghali called upon the United States to disarm Somali rebel forces.

Just as with questions of political-military foreign policy, Bush often proved to be effective in tying up loose ends left him by the Reagan administration in the area of international economics. On debt relief, his administration introduced the Brady Plan. Named after Secretary of the Treasury Nicholas Brady, it signaled redirection in thinking about how to deal with this problem. Recognizing that some debtor states could not pay back their loans in full even with extended payment periods, attention would now be given to reducing the overall level of debt through buybacks, conversion of debt into bonds at lower interest rates, and debt-for-equity swaps. In return for an agreement on the part of creditors to reduce the level of indebtedness, the World Bank and IMF promised to guarantee the remaining amount of interest or principal owed. Although it did not bring an end to the debt crisis, the Brady Plan proved to be an effective tool in transforming it into a manageable problem.

The Bush administration encountered greater difficulties in fashioning a coherent strategy to bring about a new world order in international trade. Pursuing a combination of unilateral, regional, and global policy initiatives, Bush often sent out contradictory signals that undermined American credibility.[13] His primary global initiative was the Uruguay Round GATT talks. Although they were not begun until 1986, these were the first major post–cold war economic negotiations. The United States entered into them with far less economic leverage over other states than in the past and with little inclination to subordinate domestic economic goals to security concerns. It also entered the talks with a list of grievances. Foremost among them was a demand that Europe open its markets to American agricultural products and that third world states open their markets to American service industries. Negotiations broke down in December 1990 when U.S. and EC representatives were unable to agree on a formula for liberalizing agricultural trade. Third world states, which were also interested in promoting greater free trade in agriculture, indicated that without movement on this point they would block progress on questions involving trade on services.

Six months before the Uruguay Round talks stalled, Bush also indicated his interest in establishing a regional trading bloc linking together all the states of the Western Hemisphere. First to be linked together as part of this Enterprise for America Initiative were the economies of Mexico, Canada, and the United States. Two different sets of criticisms emerged in response to this initiative. The first focused on the specific terms of the North American Free Trade Agreement (NAFTA). Concern was expressed by labor and environmental groups that the Bush administration had given inadequate attention to these issues in his rush to get an agreement signed early enough to help him in his campaign against Bill Clinton. The second set of critics focused on what they saw as (1) the questionable merits of organizing the post–cold war international economic system around a series of regional trading blocs and (2) the inherent tension that would be created between the free trade rules of a Uruguay-based global trading system and the favoritism that would have to be a part of a system of regional trading blocs.

Bush's Foreign Policy Evaluated

The hallmark of the Bush administration was its pragmatism. It is not surprising, therefore, that evaluations of it differ largely over the relative value placed on pragmatism versus "vision." In surveying the scene after the Persian Gulf War, David Gergen wrote that the Bush administration was "far more adept at cleaning up the debris of an old world than building the framework of the new."[14] The problem, according to Gergen, was Bush's concentration on short-term goals and a planning horizon that seemed to extend only a year into the future. The cost of Bush's pragmatism was a series of missed opportunities: an opportunity to build a bipartisan consensus for the post–cold war era similar to that which had been put into place after World War II and an opportunity to use the afterglow of victory as a springboard to realize other foreign policy goals. Michael Mandelbaum agreed with Gergen.[15] He argued that while the American national interest was well served when Bush kept the United States in the background as the events in Russia and Eastern Europe played themselves out, the same was not true for the post–cold war agenda. What was needed now was a president with vision and one able to master the intricacies of international economics.

Pragmatism was not without its defenders. William Hyland asserted that it was highly desirable because for the remainder of the twentieth century the international system was likely to be in a state of transition.[16] Under such conditions "no overriding principle articulated in advance will be sufficient to handle the burgeoning diversity of the new international agenda." He continued that one of the most difficult lessons Americans would have to learn was that for many of these emerging issues the United States would be on the sidelines rather than in the center of the fray. Thus, both in terms of its restraint and its style the Bush administration's foreign policy was well suited for its time.

Not all commentators focused their attention on the relative merits of pragmatism. Writing after the Gulf War, Owen Harries presented a different critique.[17] Once an admirer of how Bush handled this crisis, he came to believe that the administration's policy was deeply flawed in three respects. The first mistake was "the immediate, unqualified, and unilateral commitment of American power to achieving the complete, unconditional withdrawal of Iraq from Kuwait." Harries maintains that in doing so the Bush administration lost a great deal of leverage it might have had over other countries in the area of burden sharing. Only after commitments from U.S. allies were secured should Bush have made any commitments. The second mistake was "the opportunistic importance it has attached to the role of the United Nations as the authorizer of policy." Harries sees the short-term benefits of this policy as being outweighed by the long-term consequences of fostering the belief that UN approval is needed for the legitimate use of force. The most serious mistake made by Bush was the "disproportion" of its response. "The very size of the reaction ... ensures that it cannot be a convincing precedent. This kind of behavior is simply not replicable on a regular basis. ..." As such, he feared that future aggressors would not be deterred by Iraq's defeat because they would realize that the United States was unlikely to respond in a similar manner.

THE CLINTON ADMINISTRATION: INTO THE BREACH

Candidate Bill Clinton won the presidency largely on the basis of domestic issues. As president, Clinton planned to continue that emphasis but was prevented from doing so by a series of rapidly unfolding events abroad. American foreign policy in the first months of the Clinton administration was largely reactive in nature. "Damage control" was the order of the day. Efforts at exercising global leadership, either unilaterally or in a collective setting, were sporadic and when undertaken met with little success. Even worse, the vacillation in words and deeds that characterized them reinforced the image of a United States uncertain about its role in the post–cold war international system.

The major international peace initiative under way to end the fighting in Bosnia when Clinton took office was the Vance–Owens plan, which would have split Bosnia into ten semiautonomous provinces united only by a loose central authority. Within the first two months the Clinton administration (1) declared the plan to be "fatally flawed," (2) promised to become actively engaged in its negotiations, and (3) through a policy review indicated a willingness to develop a policy different from that endorsed by Bush. A change in policy would have been consistent with Clinton's campaign promises to lift the UN embargo on weapons to Bosnia and to use American air power. When Clinton's plan was announced in February 1993, it proved to be markedly similar to the Vance–Owens formula. Very quickly, the Clinton administration seemed overwhelmed by the complexity of organizing relief efforts, obtaining allied consent on the use of force, and bringing the warring parties together for peace talks.

Barely two months later, after putting forward his plan, Clinton was proposing a new, stronger policy, one that might involve the use of force. The next day, Secretary of State Warren Christopher assured Congress that the United States would use force only if an exit strategy existed, the public supported such a policy, and it held out the prospect of stabilizing the situation. These were conditions that all recognized would not be easily met. May brought more talk of a united U.S.–Western European position, but negotiations again failed to produce an agreement on U.S. proposals to use force. By July, the Clinton administration was blaming the Europeans for the growing crisis and said it did not have plans for further action. August brought another change in direction, with the Clinton administration outlining conditions for the use of troops in Bosnia to enforce a peace settlement. It also saw three resignations by State Department officials critical of what one termed a "misguided, vacillating, and dangerous" policy.

Delivering humanitarian relief in Somalia also proved to be a complex undertaking. General Colin Powell, chairman of the Joint Chiefs of Staff under Bush, had estimated that the operation would last two to three months. Other Bush administration officials hoped to have the troops home by the end of Bush's term in January 1993. Both forecasts were wide of the mark. The goal was to be humanitarian relief and not nation-building, but once in place U.S. forces found themselves inexorably drawn into the middle of a civil war among rival warlords. The chief U.S. protagonist was General Mohammed Farah Aidid. The United Nations had taken over command of the relief effort in May and Aidid came to view the UN presence (which continued to include U.S. troops) and its efforts to disarm his forces as a direct threat to his political future in Somalia. A June 1993 attack by his forces killed 24 Pakistani peacekeeping soldiers and led to a UN Security Council Resolution calling for the apprehension of those responsible. Shortly thereafter UN authorities in Somalia issued an order for Aidid's arrest. However, after that UN forces rarely ventured out of their compounds, and control of Mogadishu increasingly passed into the hands of Somali fighters.

Closer to home, Haiti presented the Clinton administration with still another set of policy challenges. During his presidential campaign Clinton had criticized Bush for his policy of refusing to allow Haitian boat people to enter the United States without a hearing and promised to change that policy. Fearing that thousands or perhaps hundreds of thousands of Haitians might attempt to come to the United States after Clinton's inauguration, however, the president-elect made it known that he would continue Bush's policy of interdiction and forced return. Clinton quickly came under attack for breaking yet another campaign promise he had made regarding Haiti. Critics asserted that he was not doing enough to restore exiled Haitian President Jean-Bertrand Aristide to power. The democratically elected Aristide had been forced out of office in a September 1991 coup. A resolution to the crisis seemed at hand in July when, under the increasing weight of UN and U.S. economic sanctions, an agreement was reached setting the terms under which Aristide was to reclaim the presidency.

Stung by the mounting criticism of the content and conduct of its foreign policy, the Clinton administration sought to regain conceptual control over the direction of American foreign policy by having high-ranking administration members present an orchestrated series of high-profile public speeches in September 1993. The inaugural speech was delivered by Secretary of State Warren Christopher, who argued that the United States must remain actively engaged in world politics not out of altruism but because there are "real American interests that will suffer if we are seduced by the isolationist myth." He also rejected as a false polarity the notion that the United States must choose between unilateralism and multilateralism in the conduct of its foreign policy. Both are means to the end of protecting American interests and not ends themselves. Christopher went on to note that when multilateralism is the chosen means it will never be under circumstances where the end result is to "subcontract" American foreign policy to another power or person.

Anthony Lake, Assistant to the President for National Security Affairs, presented the second speech. In it he identified democracy and market economics as its core concepts and argued that the successor doctrine to containment should be that of "enlargement." Lake argued that as a strategy, enlargement had four component parts: (1) the strengthening of the community of major market democracies, (2) fostering and consolidating new democracies and market economies, (3) countering aggression by "backlash" states hostile to democracy and markets as well as supporting their liberalization, and (4) working to help democracy and market economics take root in regions of greatest humanitarian concern. Lake also introduced a series of caveats to accompany such a strategy: We must be patient and pragmatic, view democracy broadly, and respect diversity. Viewed from this perspective, Lake argued that many of the current foreign policy debates were overdrawn and that although Bosnia and Somalia were important issues, they were not problems whose handling served to define American foreign policy. The more fundamental issue is the age-old question of whether the United States should be significantly engaged abroad at all.

The third speech was given by Ambassador to the United Nations Madeline Albright. She argued that the Clinton administration was fashioning a new foreign policy framework that would be more diverse and flexible than the old. Diplomacy was identified as America's first choice as a means for solving problems, but Albright quickly noted that there will always be times when words and sanctions are not enough. For this reason modern, versatile, ready, and strong military forces were a continued necessity. Albright argued that it would be wrong to produce a precise list of circumstances under which military action might be taken. She did, however, offer a set of questions which needed to be addressed before military obligations were undertaken as part of a UN peace-keeping effort: (1) Is there a real threat to international peace and security or a humanitarian disaster? (2) Does the proposed peacekeeping mission have clear objectives? (3) Is a cease-fire in place and do all the involved parties agree to a UN presence? (4) Can an endpoint to UN participation be identified? As did Christopher, Albright ended her speech by rejecting calls for isolationism and promised an engaged America.

Taken as a whole these speeches were designed to rebuke or silence two sets of critics. First were those who either saw no unifying purpose to the administration's foreign policy and feared a period of ad hocism or disliked what they saw—namely its emphasis on multilateralism. Second were those who called for the United States to adopt an isolationist position in response to the unfolding of the new world order. The speeches failed to do so because once again events drove the Clinton administration into a reactive decision-making mode that seemed to lack a clear sense of direction.

The situation in Bosnia continued to worsen for the Muslim population. This brought renewed cries from Congress in 1994 to lift the arms embargo against the Bosnians so that they might better defend themselves. Clinton resisted these pressures, citing the damage it would do to America's role as a world leader and its ability to convince allies to back the U.S.-supported embargo against Iraq. It also exposed the deep rift that existed between the United States and its European allies over how to respond to the crisis as they wrestled throughout 1994 over the question of using military force against the Serbian separatists in Bosnia. At year's end the Clinton administration all but admitted defeat and abandoned its two-year effort to get the Europeans to accept the use of air power. On the eve of a NATO summit, it agreed to back the European-favored policy of seeking a diplomatically engineered cease-fire followed by a peace treaty.

Matters took a decided turn for the worse in Somalia. Attacks on U.S. and UN forces continued, casualties mounted, and Aidid eluded capture. The June attack on the Pakistanis had led to the creation of a special American military unit that would be sent to Somalia to capture Aidid or, failing that, to capture a number of his high-ranking aides. This unit was dispatched to Somalia after four U.S. soldiers were killed in an August ambush. The strike took place on October 3, 1994 and resulted in the capture of several of Aidid's aides. However, a U.S. helicopter was shot down in the raid and a rescue effort was mounted. In the 15-hour battle that followed, 18 U.S. soldiers were killed and 84 were wounded.

Coming quickly on the heels of the debacle in Somalia was an embarrassment in Haiti. According to the terms of the July agreement, Aristide was to return to power on October 31. In preparation for this transfer of power, the USS Harlan County arrived in Haiti carrying American and Canadian trainers whose job it was to reform the Haitian security services. They were met by a mob that threatened to attack the troops. At the request of the Pentagon, which said that the U.S. forces were not combat-ready, Clinton ordered the USS Harlan County to leave Haiti. In the wake of this failure, the United States and the United Nations once again turned to economic sanctions in an effort to force the Haitian military to accept Aristide back. Tensions also began to rise between Aristide and the Clinton administration over the content and timing of plans for returning him to power.

By summer 1994 the rising number of Haitians fleeing to the United States and congressional calls for action led the Clinton administration to once again rethink its Haitian policy. Instead of returning fleeing Haitians, they would now send them to "safe havens." There was also open talk about the use of force to end the Haitian crisis. In late July the UN Security Council authorized the use of force in Haiti, and by early September this use of force was referred to by Clinton administration officials as "a certainty." The threatened invasion seemed about to become a reality when an invasion task force was put in place off the Haitian coast on September 18. Then, at the last minute, Clinton dispatched former president Jimmy Carter, Senator Sam Nunn, and General Powell to Haiti to secure a peaceful settlement of the conflict by negotiating the departure of Haitian ruler Lieutenant General Raoul Cedras and his key aides. After receiving a three-hour extension past its original deadline, 30 minutes before the final deadline an agreement was reached. U.S. troops would now land unopposed. The agreement was viewed as a major foreign policy success in Washington, but it did not come without its costs. The Clinton administration succeeded only by accepting Carter's view that Cedras was not a "thug" who had created a "nightmare of bloodshed" but a misunderstood military leader "concerned with his country."

The Clinton administration had barely put the Haitian crisis behind it when it became involved in highly controversial negotiations with North Korea over the fate of that country's nuclear program. In June 1994 North Korea withdrew from the International Atomic Energy Association (IAEA). Its actions marked the sharpest turn yet in an ongoing international dispute over North Korea's widely rumored efforts to develop nuclear weapons. Concerned not only for what the impact of a North Korean nuclear weapons program would have on the security of neighboring states in Asia but also for Israel and Europe should North Korea begin exporting its nuclear weapons, the United States moved in the United Nations to organize international political and economic sanctions against it. At the same time the Clinton administration sought to negotiate an agreement with North Korea that would place international controls over its nuclear program. Under terms of the agreement reached in October 1994, North Korea agreed to freeze its capacity to make nuclear arms and allow international inspections, but it did not have to dismantle its current facilities. For its part, the United States committed itself to ease trade restrictions and make available advanced nuclear technologies. The major gain from Washington's perspective was North Korea's agreement to do more than was necessary according to the Non-Proliferation Treaty (NPT) including the ultimate dismantling of all nuclear facilities built over the past 20 years. The problem as others saw it was that Washington had agreed to give North Korea special status, allowing it to put off for five years meeting full compliance with the provisions of the NPT. This might encourage other renegade nuclear states to bargain for concessions in return for placing limits on, or accepting international inspection of, their nuclear facilities.

Little respite for the Clinton administration in foreign policy matters appeared in 1995. The year began well with the administration negotiating an unlimited extension of the Non-Proliferation Treaty (NPT). In its twenty-fifth year, the NPT was the centerpiece of international efforts to stop the spread of nuclear weapons. The end of the cold war had drawn renewed attention to the dangers posed by nuclear proliferation and many feared that if the NPT agreement was not extended the number of nuclear states might grow rapidly. Because several states objected, the prospects for obtaining international consent to an unlimited extension had been considered problematic. Overcoming their opposition through a combination of behind-the-scenes arm twisting and a public pledge to halt all U.S. nuclear testing (itself a controversial move within the administration), Clinton was able to create a broad-based international consensus behind the treaty's indefinite extension.

By mid-year, however, the Clinton administration was on the receiving end of a series of defeats inflicted by the Republican-controlled Congress. Over Clinton's objections, both houses voted to lift the arms embargo on Bosnia by veto-proof margins. Clinton had argued against doing so on strategic grounds and in the interests of maintaining allied unity. The House then approved spending 25 percent more for a ballistic missile defense system than the administration had requested. At the same time, Senate Republicans voted in favor of a plan to build a nationwide ballistic missile defense system to protect American cities within eight years. Not only was the amount of money controversial, but the entire concept of a ballistic missile defense system raised serious questions about continued adherence to the 1972 ABM Treaty, since many analysts felt that such a system could not be constructed if the terms of the treaty were adhered to.

International trade was high on the Clinton administration's foreign policy agenda for most of its first two years in office. Its major successes came in the area of multilateral agreements. The Bush administration left it two agreements in varying degrees of completion. The first was NAFTA. With the negotiations completed and ratification held up by the 1992 presidential campaign, all that was left for the Clinton administration to do was secure congressional approval. Given the emotions stirred by the NAFTA agreement over its environmental provisions and possible impact on American jobs, this was easier said than done. The Clinton administration was forced to put together a broad-based bipartisan coalition to lobby Congress. This effort paid off with a vote of 288–146 in the House and 76–24 in the Senate. The second multilateral trade initiative Clinton inherited from Bush was a nearly complete Uruguay Round GATT treaty. Negotiations on this treaty were completed in December 1993 and it was submitted to Congress for its approval in September 1994. Opposition from Democrats led by Senator Ernest Hollings (S.C.), who chaired the Commerce Committee, which had partial jurisdiction over the treaty, made it imperative that Clinton obtain Republican support for the GATT treaty. He managed to do so only by making a number of concessions, including giving up his request for "fast track authority" to speed the treaty's passage through Congress and including a provision that permitted the United States to withdraw from the World Trade Organization (WTO) if its sovereignty were to be violated by WTO rulings. Congressional opposition combined with election-year politics forced Clinton to call for a special post–mid-term election session of Congress to vote on and approve the GATT treaty, which it did. The House voted for enabling legislation to implement the GATT treaty by a vote of 288 to 144 while the Senate followed suit with a 76 to 24 vote.

Clinton was less successful in other trade initiatives. Particularly trying were negotiations with China and Japan, where the economic victories were fragile and the political costs high. Conflict with China involved two separate sets of issues. The first centered on the link between China's human rights policies and renewal of its most favored nations (MFN) trading status. Human rights and trade had become linked in the aftermath of the Tiananmen Square riots with improvement in the former being made a condition of obtaining the latter. Bush had moved to separate the two, pointing to the importance of China as a market for U.S. goods and arguing that trade could be a force for improving China's human rights record by increasing its standard of living and opening it up to outside influences. Candidate Clinton had promised to reverse this policy, but as president he came under heavy pressure from business interests to decouple the two issues. In 1993, Clinton sought to find a middle-ground position. He extended MFN status because of China's importance to the world economy but said that future extensions would be tied to improvements in its human rights record. Clinton moved further away from that position in 1994 when he once again extended China's MFN status in spite of its continued failure to improve its human rights record. Also complicating U.S.–China trade relations was China's refusal to crack down on companies engaging in illegal shipment of goods to the United States. At issue were two practices. One involved shipping textiles and clothing to the United States in such a way as to evade U.S. quotas on these products. The other involved the theft of intellectual property and the illegal reproduction of computer software, music, and videos. Accommodations in each of these areas was only reached after the conflict escalated to the point where each side threatened the other with economic sanctions.

The trade dispute with Japan covered familiar territory. As had previous presidents, Clinton wanted Japan to drop trade barriers that were perceived as discriminating against U.S. products and driving up the trade deficit between the two countries. The administration believed it had begun moving Japan in that direction in July 1993 when a G-7 summit conference meeting in Tokyo produced a framework agreement for resolving the problem. Unlike previous U.S.–Japanese agreements this one focused on the actual amounts of foreign products purchased in Japan rather than on the level to which trade barriers were being reduced. However, instead of rectifying the problem this agreement only created an additional point of tension between the two states. By early 1994 little progress had been made and it was apparent that no agreement was likely to be forthcoming. A February 1994 summit conference between Clinton and Japanese Prime Minister Morihiro Hosokawa ended in failure. In August the United States formally accused Japan of "longstanding discrimination" against U.S. products and set in motion a 60-day clock that could culminate in the imposition of sanctions against Japanese imports. Two months later, this cycle of trade negotiations concluded with the announcement of another agreement that would open Japan up to U.S. insurance firms and medical equipment companies and give American telecommunication firms access to Japanese government contracts. The scene was repeated yet again in 1995 when the postponed dispute over automobiles broke into the open only to be resolved at the last minute against a backdrop of an impending trade war between the two states.

The first significant international monetary problem to confront the Clinton administration involved a steep plunge in the value of the Mexican peso. Clinton's request to Congress for $40 billion in loan guarantees encountered strong opposition. Coming on the heels of highly contested votes approving NAFTA and GATT, the need to bail out Mexico revitalized those who had opposed these treaties. They quickly moved to add such political conditions as stepped-up border patrols and a commitment from the Mexican government to raise wages. The prospect of a long lobbying campaign coupled with the perceived need to move quickly and a fear that Mexican officials would reject any aid package too heavily laden with qualifying conditions led Clinton to act on his own authority (but with the support of congressional leaders) to offer Mexico a $20-billion plan. In return, Mexico agreed to put up its oil revenues and pursue an economic austerity plan.

In Clinton's second term foreign policy initiatives outpaced domestic ones. NATO enlargement was agreed to with little opposition in the Senate. This was somewhat surprising since the merits of NATO expansion were a hotly debated topic among academics with many arguing that NATO enlargement was ill-advised. The administration also claimed the Irish peace agreement as a success. While not formally a party to these talks it played an important facilitating role.

Setbacks were also present. The Middle East peace process unraveled and U.S.–Israeli relations grew strained. Fighting in the former Yugoslavia continued and spread into Kosovo, forcing the Clinton administration to threaten NATO air strikes if Serb forces did not withdraw. Earlier, faced with the disturbing possibility that fighting might spread throughout the rest of the Balkans, in 1997 the Clinton administration abandoned its self-imposed year-end deadline for removing U.S. forces from the region and announced that they would continue on indefinitely. U.S. efforts to isolate Iraq encountered rough going in 1998 when it became known that the administration had decided to soften its insistence on international inspections of suspected Iraqi nuclear facilities in hopes of maintaining an international consensus behind economic sanctions.

On the economic front, Clinton was rebuffed in his efforts to obtain fast-track negotiating authority for international trade talks that would enlarge NAFTA. The economic crisis in Asia necessitated that the U.S. and the International Monetary Fund (IMF) work together to try and restore stability and confidence in global financial markets. Their efforts brought forward charges from development specialists that the IMF's lending policies were antiquated and refocused congressional criticism on the willingness of the IMF to support social programs that the Republican congress was philosophically opposed to.

President Clinton's mounting personal and domestic political problems also cast a shadow over American foreign policy. They did so in three ways. First, in an effort to direct attention away from impeachment efforts, Clinton engaged in a series of highly publicized diplomatic initiatives including meetings with Yeltsin and efforts to reinvigorate the Middle East peace process by bringing the key participants to the United States for a summit conference. Clinton also authorized retaliatory air strikes by U.S. planes against Iraq for its provocative actions against British aircraft. Some saw this as overreaction and an attempt to create a crisis atmosphere which would make it harder for his detractors to press their case. Finally, as Clinton's troubles mounted, concern was expressed in foreign capitals about his ability to serve effectively as commander-in-chief and chief diplomat of the United States in his interactions with other countries.

Clinton's Foreign Policy Evaluated

Early evaluations of Clinton's foreign policy were almost uniformly negative. The harshest commentary came from isolationists who argued that America's national interest did not extend beyond safeguarding the immediate physical security of the United States and preserving its system of government.[18] Conservative and liberal internationalist critiques centered their complaints on Clinton's inexperience and repeated policy zig-zags. Inexperience was seen as responsible for overly embracing multilateralism and an expansive definition of American national interests. The frequent and abrupt policy changes were seen as the product of Clinton's personality and managerial style. Together they produced qualities that conservatives found troubling. Paul Wolfowitz, who served in the Reagan and Bush administrations, urged the administration to be more cautious in its support of peacekeeping and more forthcoming in its efforts to build an international consensus that supports basic American interests.[19] He compared the challenge facing Clinton to that encountered by Warren Harding and Harry Truman and raised the question of which Clinton would most come to resemble. Both took office after great historic struggles had been completed and faced the challenge of leading the United States into a new era of world politics. History, notes Wolfowitz, judges their foreign policies very differently. Truman's is applauded while Harding's is cited as a major contributing factor to the collapse of the interwar system.

Evaluations presented by American commentators around the conclusion of the first Clinton administration were hardly more supportive. Incoherent, indecisive, inconsistent, and lacking a clear focus continued to be the most frequently heard characterizations of its foreign policy, with one commentator, Michael Mandelbaum, going so far as to summarize Clinton's first-term foreign policy as being akin to a "supermarket shopping spree, grabbing whatever it takes a fancy to, without worrying about the costs or whether the product is the right brand or is genuinely needed."[20]

The neo-Wilsonian orientation of Clinton's foreign policy also continued to attract criticism. Mandelbaum asserted that what united its flawed policies toward Haiti, Bosnia, and Somalia was a mistaken focus on the social, political, and economic conditions within these states. These three foreign policy problems were not inherited, he maintains, but were the product of the Clinton administration's inability to focus its foreign policy on questions of true national interest.

Foreign evaluations of Clinton's foreign policy during his first term were mixed and often more charitable. *Foreign Policy,* a leading academic journal that focuses on problems in American foreign policy and world politics, asked its regional editors to evaluate Clinton's record from their region's perspective.[21] Those aspects of foreign policy on which the Clinton administration rated highest centered on the conduct of diplomacy: sustaining American hegemony, attracting quality people to the foreign policy bureaucracy, and conducting personal diplomacy. Its lowest grades were received on questions dealing with vision: the ability to make tough choices, balancing rhetoric and action, and developing a coherent strategic outlook. Summary regional rankings were quite consistent, with all respondents grading the Clinton administration at between 5 and 6 on a 10-point scale. In a telling commentary on Clinton's foreign policy agenda, no editor was asked to provide an African perspective.

SUMMARY AND THE FUTURE

A single chapter survey of American foreign policy, even one concerned only with the post-Vietnam era, must be selective and can only hope to paint a broad picture of what has transpired. We have seen how six presidents sought to redefine America's role in the world after Vietnam. A wide variety of answers were put forward, ranging from Carter's effort to infuse American foreign policy with a new sense of purpose to Reagan's embrace of cold war principles and Nixon's efforts to practice realpolitik. Different as they were, all of these answers were put forward in the belief that the nature of world politics remained essentially unchanged. With the end of the cold war this assumption is widely challenged, and the task of articulating a vision of America's role in the post–cold war world fell to the Bush and Clinton administrations. Neither one has been able to do so. Each in its own way has moved from crisis to crisis searching for answers and making up the rules as it goes.

The collective efforts of these six administrations leave a legacy that present and future administrations must work with in constructing their foreign policies. Possible future foreign policies are not limited to those attempted here, and in the concluding chapter we examine a fuller menu of options from which future administrations might draw. For the moment, however, the task is to gain a deeper appreciation of how the past influences the present and future. To do so, in the last chapter we examined the traditional ways in which Americans think about foreign policy as we examined the American national style. In Chapter 5 we will examine in greater detail the cold war, Vietnam, and the Persian Gulf War in order to see what lessons they hold for the future.

NOTES

1. Richard Nixon, *U.S. Foreign Policy for the 1970s: Building for Peace* (Washington, D.C.: U.S. Government Printing Office, 1971), p. 6.
2. Quoted in Thomas G. Paterson, J. Garry Clifford, and Kenneth J. Hagan, *American Foreign Policy: A History Since 1900,* 2nd ed. (Lexington, Mass.: D. C. Heath, 1983), p. 592.
3. Robert Tucker, "America in Decline: The Foreign Policy of Maturity," *Foreign Affairs,* 58 (1980), 449–84.
4. A. Glenn Mower, Jr., *Human Rights and American Foreign Policy: The Carter and Reagan Experiences* (New York: Greenwood Press, 1987).
5. Arthur Schlesinger, Jr., "Human Rights and the American Tradition," *Foreign Affairs,* 57 (1979), 513.

6. Stanley Hoffmann, "Requiem," *Foreign Policy*, 42 (1981), 3–26.

7. Jeane Kirkpatrick, "Human Rights and American Foreign Policy: A Symposium," *Commentary* (November 1981), 42–45.

8. David Skidmore, "Carter and the Failure of Foreign Policy Reform," *Political Science Quarterly*, 104 (1993/94), 699–729.

9. Michael Mandelbaum, "The Luck of the President," *Foreign Affairs*, 64 (1986), 393–413.

10. Robert W. Tucker, "Reagan's Foreign Policy," *Foreign Affairs*, 68 (1989), 1–27.

11. Arnold Horelick, "U.S.-Soviet Relations: Threshold of a New Era," *Foreign Affairs*, 69 (1990), 51–69.

12. In the next chapter we will look more closely at the debate over the lessons this event holds for American foreign policy. Here we will concentrate on presenting an overview of the conflict.

13. C. Michael Aho and Bruce Starks, "The Year the World Economy Turned," *Foreign Affairs*, 70 (1991), 160–78.

14. David Gergen, "Missed Opportunities," *Foreign Affairs*, 71 (1992), 1–20.

15. Michael Mandelbaum, "The Bush Foreign Policy," *Foreign Affairs*, 70 (1991), 5–22.

16. William G. Hyland, "The Case for Pragmatism," *Foreign Affairs*, 71 (1992), 38–52.

17. Owen Harries, "Drift and Mastery, Bush Style," *The National Interest*, 23 (1991) 1–7.

18. Doug Bandow, "Keeping the Troops and Money at Home," *Current History*, 579 (1994), 8–13.

19. Paul Wolfowitz, "Clinton's First Year," *Foreign Affairs*, 73 (1994), 28–43.

20. Michael Mandelbaum, "Foreign Policy as Social Work," *Foreign Affairs*, 75 (1996), 16–32.

21. "Grading the President," *Foreign Policy*, 109 (1997/98), 34–69.

CHAPTER

5 Learning from the Past

If there are to be no more Vietnams (or Munichs, Pearl Harbors, Koreas, Irans), policy makers must learn from past foreign policy failures. Yet, as Richard Betts notes in commenting on the problem of strategic surprise, remarkably little learning from the past takes place.[1] The same mistakes occur over and over. Since the beginning of World War II, "there have been few if any examples of failures by major powers attempting to inflict effective shock in the initiation of war."

We begin this chapter by treating the problem of learning from the past as a generic one and asking how and what policy makers learn: the types of events they learn from, the types of calculations they make, and the lessons they learn. The bulk of the chapter presents three case studies drawing on post–World War II U.S. foreign policy to illustrate these points. The cold war illustrates the problem of learning from the past when interpretations vary greatly. Vietnam shows how policy makers relied on historical analogies in making decisions. Finally, the Persian Gulf War is examined to uncover lessons about the effectiveness of U.S. military strategy in the post–cold war era.

HOW DO POLICY MAKERS LEARN FROM THE PAST?

Policy makers learn by matching the known with the unknown.[2] This is not a passive act. They do not sit back and simply accept data as a given, but actively interact with it.[3] In doing so they are making judgments about what is a piece of evidence (a signal) and what is unimportant (noise). Discriminating between the two is no easy task. Moreover, having identified a piece of data as a signal does not tell the policy maker what to do; it only sets in motion the process of learning. Information received in the Philippines that Pearl Harbor was under attack did not tell policy makers there that they were the next target or what steps to take to defend themselves. Roberta Wohlstetter, in her classic account of the U.S. intelligence failure at Pearl Harbor, identifies 56 separate signals ranging in duration from one day to one month pointing to the Japanese attack. She also notes that prior to the attack there was a good deal of evidence to support all of the wrong interpretations. Wohlstetter suggests that the United States failed to anticipate the Japanese attack on Pearl Harbor, not for a lack of signals, but because there was too much noise. Similar problems of discriminating between noise and signals confront U.S. policy makers in the

Middle East as they seek to secure the release of U.S. hostages and combat terrorism. Who can be believed? Who has the hostages? Are they alive? What threats are real? What type of negotiations or trade might really secure their freedom?

Policy makers discriminate between signals and noise by making a series of assumptions about what motivates the behavior of others or what constitutes the underlying dynamics of a problem confronting them. Consider the intercepted Japanese directive to their U.S. embassy and consulates to burn their codes. In retrospect this is taken as a clear indication that hostilities were imminent. But during the first week of December, the United States ordered all of its consulates in the Far East to burn their codes, and no one took this to be the equivalent of a U.S. declaration of war against Japan.[4]

The assumptions policy makers bring to bear on foreign policy problems are influenced by their long-term experiences and immediate concerns. Long-term experience provides policy makers with a data base against which to evaluate an ongoing pattern of behavior. For Franklin Roosevelt and other U.S. policy makers, personal experiences and their reading of history led to a conclusion that the presence of the U.S. fleet at Pearl Harbor was a deterrent to a Japanese attack. They failed to appreciate that it also made a fine target. For their part, Japanese leaders drew upon their 1904 war opening attack in the Russo–Japanese War as the model for how to deal with a more powerful enemy. Immediate concerns largely determine what we expect to see. Preoccupation with economic difficulties in country X will blind policy makers to evidence that they ordinarily would have recognized as pointing to a military coup. In the 70s U.S. policy makers were surprised by the Turkish invasion of Cyprus and the Portuguese coup, not because these events could not have been foreseen, but because so much attention was riveted on Vietnam.

Once they are in place, perceptual systems are not readily changed. They easily become obsolete and inaccurate. Holding onto one's views in the face of challenges is not necessarily irrational. No firm evidence exists that open-minded policy makers are better equipped to avoid surprises than are closed-minded ones. Some would even argue that a firm conceptual system is a necessary requirement for action, that in its absence one is condemned to indecision in the face of unfolding events. The principle involved here is cognitive consistency.[5] Individuals try to keep their beliefs and values consistent with one another by ignoring some information, actively seeking out other data, and reinterpreting still other information so that it supports the individuals' perception of reality. The result is that instead of being a continuous and rationally structured process, learning is sporadic and constrained. Policy makers do not move steadily from a simplistic understanding of an event to a more complex one as their experience and familiarity with it build. New information and new problems are fit into already well-established perceptual systems. Learning thus rarely produces dramatic changes in priorities or commitments, and changes in behavior tend to be incremental.

A well-documented case of this process at work is John Foster Dulles's perception of the Soviet Union.[6] Dulles was Secretary of State for all but a few months of the Eisenhower administration and had a closed belief system. He saw the Soviet Union as a hostile state and interpreted any data that might indicate a lessening of hostility in such a way that it reinforced his original perceptions. Cooperative Soviet gestures were not a sign of goodwill but the product of Soviet failures and represented only a lull before they would engage in another round of hostilities.

EVENTS POLICY MAKERS LEARN FROM

The sporadic and constrained nature of the learning process means that not all aspects of the past are equally likely to serve as the source of lessons. Two categories of events are turned to most often by policy makers in their search for lessons. The first is the dramatic and highly visible event. Policy makers turn to these events out of the conviction that because they are so dramatic and visible they must contain more information about international politics than do more commonplace happenings. The scars they leave in defeat and the praises sung in victory are so deeply entrenched in the collective memory of society that the individual does not have to experience them personally in order to see them as holding lessons for the present. Events of this magnitude are often referred to as generational events because an entire generation draws upon them for lessons. War is the ultimate dramatic event. A policy maker need not have been involved in the negotiations at Munich to invoke the analogy and point to the dangers of appeasement or in Korea to cite the military and political problems of fighting a limited war.

The corollary to paying a great deal of attention to highly dramatic events is to all but ignore the nonevent. The crisis that almost happened but did not is not learned from. Warnings about the weakness of the Shah of Iran were heard as early as 1961 when members of the Senate Foreign Relations Committee warned the newly installed Kennedy administration that no number of weapons could save him. Mass unrest and corruption, they argued, doomed him to defeat. Senator Hubert Humphrey declared: "This crowd they are dead. They just don't know it. . . . It is just a matter of time."[7] Policy makers will invoke the images of the Marines killed by terrorists in Lebanon in debating policy but will fail to cite the terrorist attacks that were prevented by the timely use of intelligence. Rather than crediting intelligence with having anticipated an attack, they will question whether it was ever to have taken place. The more often the warning is given and no attack occurs, the easier it is for policy makers to dismiss the next warning. The November 27 warning to Pearl Harbor that a Japanese attack was possible was not the first such warning received. An alarming dispatch had been received in October, and no attack had followed. Also, there had been several other warnings issued during the course of 1941 that the Japanese in Honolulu were burning their codes.

The second type of event typically searched for lessons is that which the policy maker experienced firsthand. Especially important are those experiences that took place early in the policy maker's career. The lessons drawn from events experienced firsthand tend to be overgeneralized to the neglect of lessons that might be drawn from the careful analysis of the experiences of others. U.S. thinking about the post–World War II role of the atomic bomb provides an example of the pull of personally experienced events on policy making.[8] The initial decisions were made by the men who had defeated Germany and Japan. In formulating ideas about the uses to which the bomb might be put, they drew heavily upon these experiences. From 1945 to 1950 the Soviet targets identified for destruction by the atomic bomb duplicated those emphasized in the U.S. World War II policy of targeting commercial and industrial centers. To these men the atomic bomb was not a qualitatively new weapon for which a new strategy had to be developed. It was only the latest and most powerful weapon developed to date. It would be left to politicians to put forward the first strategy tailored to the political and technological realities of the postwar era.

Firsthand experiences that occur early in a policy maker's career are especially important because perceptual systems are resistant to change. Individuals are most open to competing images of reality when they confront a situation for the first time. Once selected, a label or category establishes the basis for future comparisons. These early firsthand experiences are not necessarily related to foreign policy problems. They may be ways of thinking about problems that proved successful in the past, positions taken on issues that produced the desired outcome, or strategies used in winning political office.[9] Early firsthand experiences are also of special significance because of the conditions under which policy makers must try to learn from the past. Decisions must be made, and a policy maker's attention is constantly spread over a wide variety of situations demanding his or her attention. Henry Kissinger spoke to these problems in his memoirs when he stated that "policy makers live off the intellectual capital they have brought with them into office; they have no time to build more capital."[10]

TYPES OF CALCULATIONS MADE ABOUT THOSE EVENTS

When an event is recognized as a possible source of lessons, policy makers frequently engage in three types of calculations. First, they pay attention to what happened and seldom to why. The iron curtain descended across Europe; Vietnam fell; the American embassy was attacked, and hostages were taken. Focusing on what happened rather than on why creates a type of tunnel vision that obscures from view the differences between the present situation and earlier ones. What can one conclude from the fact that for the 1968 invasion of Czechoslovakia, the 1979 invasion of Afghanistan, and the 1981 noninvasion of Poland the Soviet Union required three months' preparation time? Betts suggests not very much.[11] Policy makers could not assume that the Soviets would need three months in order to prepare for the next invasion. None of these were extremely urgent cases; they do not preclude more rapid mobilizations or a mobilization starting at a higher stage of readiness.

Second, in examining what happened, policy makers tend to dichotomize the outcome into successes and failures. They tend to forget that most policy initiatives are designed to achieve multiple objectives, that success and failure are rarely ever total, and that neither success nor failure is permanent. Problems are not so much solved as redefined and transformed into new challenges and opportunities.

When a policy is defined as a success, policy makers are especially prone to ignore three considerations in applying it as a lesson: (1) its costs, (2) the possibility that another option would have worked better or produced the same result at less cost, and (3) the role accident, luck, and chance play in affecting the outcome of events. In the 1960s, careful observers felt compelled to warn policy makers not to read into the 1965 invasion of the Dominican Republic a formula for successful invasions elsewhere in Latin America. They cautioned that focusing on the success of the invasion diverted attention from such key issues as general weaknesses of U.S. policy in the Caribbean, the unique aspects of the situation in the Dominican Republic, acts of omission by the United States that brought about the need for an invasion, and the costs the invasion brought in terms of a deepening involvement of the United States in the domestic politics of the Dominican Republic.[12] More recently, what will the lessons of Grenada be? Is it a model for future interventions into Caribbean Basin states, or should it be treated as an invasion of opportunity under circumstances that are unlikely to be repeated? It was a simple plan drawn up in 48 hours. U.S. forces were already on their way to Lebanon and were easily diverted to Grenada. No one was expecting the Reagan administration to commit troops to combat just days after the surprise attack on the Marines in Lebanon. Although it was a clear military success, problems were encountered. The intelligence community underestimated the number of regular Cuban and Grenadian forces on the island with the result that greater resistance than expected was encountered; once on the island the military complained that it lacked adequate maps to get around; and U.S. allies opposed the invasion and openly criticized the United States for its actions.

When defined as a failure, a different set of biases tends to grip policy maker thinking. There is (1) the presumption that an alternative course of action would have worked better and that policy makers should have known this and (2) an unwillingness to admit that success may have been unattainable or that surprise is inevitable. The congressional investigation into Pearl Harbor takes up 39 volumes, and the success of the Japanese attack continues to bring forward a never-ending series of books asserting that U.S. policy makers knew of the attack and permitted it to happen.

Third, to the extent that policy makers do seek to discover explanations, they tend to treat the most visible features of the situation as having had the biggest impact on the outcome of events. Diplomatic and military histories are written in terms of personalities and actors' strategies. Rarely is organizational planning, careful staff preparation, or bureaucratic coordination placed at the center of analysis.

LESSONS LEARNED

Three lessons are most often learned by policy makers from their studies of history. The first is to expect to see more of the same. The Shah was expected to continue in power in 1979 simply because he had ruled for so long. Iran without the Shah seemed inconceivable. The grain shortage of 1973 caught U.S. policy makers by surprise because for policy makers "the grain problem" was always one of too much grain. It did not occur to them that the combination of large-scale Soviet purchases of grain plus global drought would send the price of grain in the United States skyrocketing.

A second lesson learned is to expect continuity in the behavior of other actors. In part this occurs because policy makers are insensitive to the perceived costs of inaction as viewed by another state. The United States made this mistake at Pearl Harbor. U.S. estimates of Japanese behavior were based on the cost of attacking the United States. Insufficient attention was given to the costs that the Japanese would experience if they did nothing and allowed the status quo to continue into the future. For similar reasons the hostile acts or words of allies surprise policy makers more than the hostility of an enemy. Having labeled a state as an ally, policy makers tend to become insensitive to the continuing conflicts of interest between them and the possibility that the ally will act to resolve them.

Third, policy makers learn to avoid policies that failed and to repeat policies that brought success. This would be fine if two conditions did not work against the continued success of a policy. First, successful policies get overused. They are applied to problems and situations for which they were not intended. Second, a successful policy often changes the situation in ways that will frustrate its future use. In the 60s military aid to the Shah may indeed have been responsible for averting the coup predicted by members of the Senate Foreign Relations Committee, but it also changed the situation so that by the late 70s continued military aid became part of the Shah's problem instead of the answer.

What might we expect from current efforts to learn from the past? We can expect to see a lag in the impact of contemporary events on U.S. foreign policy. Individuals are most open to learning from firsthand experiences and generational events early in their adult lives. They reach positions of political power much later, and it is only then that they will be able to incorporate these lessons into policy. An example of this delayed impact of life experiences confronts the United States today in Europe. Observers speak of the "successor generation," the generation of Europeans who have grown up in the peace and prosperity of postwar Europe. They do not remember or appreciate U.S. sacrifices in defeating Hitler or in the rebuilding of Europe. For them the United States is an economic competitor and as much a danger to their security as the Soviet Union. Their political awakening and gradual assumption of political power represents a real challenge to the ability of U.S. policy makers to maintain the cohesion of the Western alliance.

We should also not expect to avoid surprises by improving how we learn from the past. Not only is surprise inevitable, but anticipating events often requires stepping outside of, or going against, historical patterns no matter how well understood they may be.[13] Improving how we learn from the past will aid policy makers in recognizing patterns: the causes of revolution, the nature of crises, the dynamics of resource scarcity. It is of less help in anticipating the unique, the exception to the rule. Knowing that the enemy always does A before B makes the defender extremely vulnerable to the enemy who quite consciously chooses to go right to B. In spite of having warnings of an impending invasion, Joseph Stalin remained convinced that he still had time. Hitler had always issued an ultimatum before attacking, and none had yet been issued. Unfortunately for Stalin, none would be issued.

Finally, we must question whether or not the American political system is conducive to learning from the past. In raising this question, we are shifting our concern from individual learning to organizational learning. Are the lessons learned by policy makers translated into changed behavior on the part of the organizations they direct? Or do these lessons become the victims of bureaucratic negotiations, standard operating procedures, and professional conservatism? John Lovell concludes that it is by no means clear that efforts to learn from the past have had the slightest impact on U.S. foreign policy.[14] We return to this issue in Part II in which the institutions and processes of U.S. foreign policy making are examined.

LEARNING FROM THE PAST: CASE STUDIES

Our attention now shifts to an examination of the cold war, Vietnam, and the Persian Gulf War. The primary concern in looking at the cold war is to illustrate the difficulty of drawing lessons from an event when there is so little agreement about its basic nature. Our focus is on three questions central to the process of learning from an event: When did it begin? Whose fault, if anyone's, was it? Why did it end? We cannot hope to learn from an event if we do not have a clear sense of its dynamics or of our own responsibility for how it unfolded. To err in the first instance will result in mistaking a symptom of a problem for the problem itself. To err in the second instance leads either to an arrogance of power as we overestimate our own importance or to a crippling sense of guilt as we blame ourselves for too much. The purpose of examining Vietnam is twofold. First, Vietnam is used to provide a look at the range of lessons used by policy makers in making decisions. The lessons of the past used by members of the Kennedy and Johnson administrations in arguing for and against various policy options provide the material for this part of the case study. The second reason for looking at Vietnam is to illustrate the range of lessons that American elites have drawn from U.S. involvement. We examine the Persian Gulf War in order to get a better understanding about the reasons for the failure of American efforts at deterrence and compellence. A debate is under way as to which of these two strategies is best suited for the post–cold war era. The Persian Gulf War may hold important insights because it provided the first post–cold war test of these two strategies.

The Cold War

In 1989 academics as well as policy makers in both the Soviet Union and the United States proclaimed an end to the cold war. George Kennan, the father of the containment doctrine around which so much of U.S. cold war foreign policy was built, stated that "whatever reasons there may once have existed for regarding the Soviet Union primarily as a possible, if not probable, military opponent, the time for that sort of thing has clearly passed. . . . [It] should now be regarded essentially as another great power like other great powers."[15]

For all of the scholarship that has been directed at it, the cold war remains for many "the most enigmatic and elusive international conflict of modern time."[16] For our purposes we define it as a period of competition, hostility, and tension between the Western powers and communist bloc states. While frequently intense, it never escalated into direct and open warfare between the two bloc leaders—the Soviet Union and the United States. No single issue or geographic area dominated the conflict. At any one point in time, the U.S.–Soviet cold war interactions were characterized by some combination of political maneuvering, diplomatic wrangling, psychological warfare, ideological competition, economic coercion, arms races, and proxy wars.

Beginnings of the Cold War.   At least four different starting points have been given to the cold war. The conventional starting point is the immediate post–World War II period. World War II is also often employed as a starting point. Less frequently used are the 1917-to-1920 era and the interwar period. Our concern in this section is with evaluating the merits of these competing starting points. Is one position more compelling than the rest? Are they mutually exclusive? Can they be integrated into a composite explanation that is superior to any single explanation? Before taking up these issues, we briefly present the evidence typically cited supporting each of the four starting points.

1917 to 1920   The earliest starting point for the cold war employed with any frequency is the period beginning with the November 1917 revolution and continuing through the ensuing civil war.[17] Table 5–1 presents a chronology of major dates in the history of the cold war. The March 1917 revolution caught all of the revolutionary parties unprepared. The czar was replaced by a provisional government that was backed by the Western Powers because of its pledge to continue Russia's participation in World War I. Within Russia this government walked a tightrope. It occupied an unstable middle ground between leftist revolutionary forces and right wing reactionary groups. On November 7, 1917, its life came to an end when the Bolsheviks seized power. Lenin was unalterably opposed to Russia's continued participation in what he saw to be an imperialist war, and one day after taking control of the government, the Bolshevik party set in motion Russia's withdrawal by issuing a Declaration of Peace calling for an immediate peace without annexations or indemnities. A preliminary armistice was soon signed between Russia and Germany, and then on March 15, 1918, a final peace treaty was signed at Brest-Litovsk.

The Soviet exit from the war coupled with an almost simultaneous German offensive in the West spread panic through the allied leadership. On April 9, 1918, Japan sent troops into the Soviet Union. Great Britain, France, and the United States followed suit. Although a heavy dosage of anti-Bolshevik sentiment influenced the U.S. decision to intervene, the objectives were pictured as quite limited. Militarily, it was to prevent allied war material from falling into German hands and to help the Czech Legion escape from the Soviet Union so that it could continue fighting on the Western Front. A political objective was to check the ongoing expansion of the Japanese presence in Siberia. By this rationale the Western presence in the Soviet Union should have ceased on November 11, 1918, with the ending of World War I, but it did not. American forces did not leave the Soviet Union until early 1920. From the

TABLE 5–1   Chronology of the Cold War: 1917–1950

March 1917	Czar overthrown; provisional government established.
November 1917	Bolshevik Revolution.
March 1918	Treaty of Brest-Litovsk ends Russian participation in war.
April 1918	Japanese troops enter Russia followed by U.S., U.K., and France.
March 1919	COMINTERN established.
June 1919	Versailles Treaty signed.
December 1922	U.S.S.R. is officially established.
November 1933	U.S. recognizes Soviet Union.
September 1938	Munich Agreement.
August 1939	German–Russian Nonaggression Pact.
November 1939	Russia invades Finland.
June 1941	Germany invades Russia.
February 1945	Yalta Conference.
August 1945	Atomic bomb dropped on Hiroshima.
April 1946	Iranian crisis begins.
March 1947	Truman Doctrine announced.
June 1947	Marshall Plan for recovery of Europe outlined.
September 1947	COMINFORM created.
February 1948	Communists seize power in Czechoslovakia.
June 1948	Berlin crisis begins.
April 1949	NATO established.
August 1949	Russia explodes first atomic bomb.
June 1950	North Korea invades South Korea.

end of World War I until their departure, Western troops took part in the Russian civil war lending support to the white (anticommunist) forces.

The Interwar Period.   U.S.–Soviet relations improved little during the interwar period.[18] Two points of tension were carryovers from their 1917-to-1920 encounters. The Soviets continued to feel slighted over the United States' withholding of diplomatic recognition, which did not come until 1933. For its part the United States remained suspicious of communist intentions. The Soviet Union was pursuing a two-track foreign policy. At the official level the Soviet Union sought normal relations with the West. On another level it was seeking to spread revolution and overthrow capitalism. The specific object of U.S. and Western concern was COMINTERN. Created in 1919, it was an international organization of communist parties headquartered in Moscow but theoretically not connected with the Soviet government. Its avowed purpose was to undermine capitalist society from within and to counter the actions of traditional Western European socialist democratic parties.

As World War II approached, new issues emerged that raised the level of distrust and suspicion existing between the Soviet Union and the United States and brought the two powers into ever closer and more continuous contact. One issue was the repeated rejection by the West of Soviet appeals at the League of Nations for a collective security system directed at Hitler. Matters came to a head with the Munich crisis of September 29–30, 1938. Without Soviet or Czech participation, the British and French sought to achieve "peace in our time" by acceding to Hitler's demand that the Sudetenland be incorporated into the Third Reich. In the Soviets' eyes this had the effect of both inviting a German attack on the Soviet Union and providing a gateway to carry it out.

The primary Soviet foreign policy goal since at least 1934 had been to keep the Soviet Union out of war. Stalin now acted with a renewed sense of urgency to accomplish this objective. His efforts culminated in the signing of the Molotov–Ribbentrop Pact on August 31, 1939. Stalin saw himself as having bought two things with the treaty: time to prepare for a possible war with Germany, and territory. Secret protocols to the pact gave the Soviet Union rights to eastern Poland and the Baltic region. The West saw duplicity in the treaty for at the same time that Stalin was negotiating with Hitler, he was also engaged in talks with the West about new security arrangements. Soviet motives and sincerity were further questioned with its November 1939 invasion of Finland. The League of Nations responded to this act of aggression by expelling the Soviet Union. It reacted angrily to this step. Japan, Italy, and Germany had each shown a similar disregard for international law in carrying out their expansionist policies, yet they were not expelled. Instead, they were allowed to withdraw from the League of Nations on their own initiative, an option not made available to the Soviet Union.

World War II. Hitler's surprise attack on the Soviet Union instantly transformed it from an aggressor state into a valuable Western ally. It did little, however, to bring a greater degree of trust to their relationship. Almost immediately, controversy developed over the delay in opening the second front. Promised by Roosevelt in 1942 and again in 1943, the Normandy landing did not take place until June 1944. Western leaders based their case for delay on a lack of invasion barges, the need for careful planning, and the time required to build up the necessary military forces. Soviet leaders saw it differently. They placed greater emphasis on Winston Churchill's declaration that there would be no invasion until Germany was weakened to the point where Western casualties would not be excessive.[19] The Soviets saw in Western delays an attempt to lock Germany and the Soviet Union into a series of battles that would leave them militarily exhausted and the Soviet Union vulnerable to future Western pressures.

From the Western point of view, Soviet unwillingness to commit itself to fighting Japan was a major irritation. The American military lobbied hard for a guarantee of Soviet participation in the war against Japan at the earliest possible date. Without such participation it was estimated that the war in the Pacific would continue 18 to 24 months after the end of fighting in Europe. Soviet assurances were only given at Yalta in 1945 when Stalin pledged to commit Soviet troops no later than 90 days after the defeat of Germany. Of all the war-related controversies, it is the American decision to drop the atomic bomb that has emerged as one of the fundamental points of disagreement between the orthodox and the revisionist interpretations of the cold war. In the orthodox view, the use of the atomic bomb was based on military considerations. Without its use, not only would the war with Japan drag on, but its termination would require an invasion of the home islands at a high cost in American lives. The revisionist interpretation sees in the dropping of the atomic bomb not military necessity but political maneuvering. They see the Japanese military capability as being overstated by the orthodox interpretation. In the revisionist view, the atomic bomb was used to send a signal to the Soviet Union that the United States had "sufficient power to affect the developments in the border regions of the Soviet Union" and that the United States was prepared to take a "firm" stance in negotiations over the shape of the postwar world.[20]

The Post–World War II Era.   Those who date the cold war as beginning in the post–World War II era place the greatest emphasis on events between 1946 and the beginning of the Korean War. It is in this period that the Soviet Union and the United States repeatedly collided over the political-geographic debris of World War II. At Yalta the United States and the Soviet Union had presumably reached an understanding on how the power vacuum in Eastern Europe was to be filled. Roosevelt felt that he had received Stalin's agreement to free elections in which all democratic parties could participate. The systematic exclusion of pro-Western parties from the electoral process in Poland and throughout Eastern Europe struck many in the West as a doublecross. To Stalin it was simple realpolitik. For its security the Soviet Union had to have a defensive corridor on its European border. The Soviet position was that U.S. troops occupied Italy and Japan and determined the nature of those governments. So, too, would Soviet troops determine the nature of the Eastern European governments.

The fate of Eastern Europe was only one of a host of issues that came together in rapid-fire succession to throw a cloud over postwar U.S.–Soviet relations. June 1945 saw a Soviet attempt to pressure Turkey into a revision of the Dardanelles Strait Agreement that would have given the Soviet Union partial administrative control over naval bases as well as the entry point from the Black Sea to the Mediterranean Sea. The year 1946 found the Soviet Union and the United States in conflict over Iran when Soviet troops refused to leave according to the schedule agreed upon at the Tehran Conference. Instead, the Soviet Union attempted to create Soviet-dominated republics out of Iran's northern provinces by first manipulating the Azerbaijanian population and then the Kurdish minority. Soviet pressure was also placed on Greece in 1946 in the form of an expansion and intensification of the ongoing civil war. Cut off from its traditional Eastern European markets and having been devastated by the German occupation, the Greek government was finding it extremely difficult to pursue both economic recovery and defeat the communist insurgency. First British and later American aid played central roles in allowing the Greek government to persevere.

The year 1948 was pivotal in U.S.–Soviet cold war relations. First, the COMINFORM (Communist Information Bureau) was created. Like the COMINTERN before it, the COMINFORM was a vehicle for uniting communist parties under Soviet leadership. The COMINTERN had been disbanded during the war as a sign of good faith, and the creation of this new organization raised new doubts about the Soviet Union's true motives and fueled fears of communist subversion. The susceptibility of Western Europe to communist pressures was recognized by the Western Powers. It had been a primary motivating factor in the creation of the Marshall Plan in 1947, which was designed to spur European economic recovery and political unity, both of which were seen as necessary if the westward expansion of communist influence was to be halted.

Second, there occurred the first of the postwar Berlin crises. The original intention of the allies was that Germany was not to be partitioned but only divided into occupation zones for administrative purposes. By 1948, however, the U.S. and British zones had been merged, and the Western powers were discussing the future of Germany without consulting the Soviets. Differing views over reparations and the overall increase in hostility between the Soviet Union and the West made partition an increasingly likely reality. On June 18, 1948, the Western allies instituted a currency reform in their zones. That evening the Soviet Union, which had already withdrawn from the Allied Control Council which theoretically ruled over all of Germany, informed the Western Powers that they no longer had any right of access to Berlin. The Soviets then cut off all surface traffic from Berlin to the Western zones. Three days later the United States and Britain launched a massive air supply operation to keep West Berlin afloat. Three hundred and twenty-four days later the blockade was lifted, with Germany and Berlin firmly divided into eastern and western zones.

Finally, 1948 saw the downfall of the pro-Soviet but noncommunist Benes government in Czechoslovakia. Alone among the Eastern European states, Czechoslovakia had a tradition of democracy. The first postwar election produced a coalition government in which the communist party controlled the Ministry of the Interior to whom the police report. In February 1948, amid indications that the Czech communist party would not fare well in an upcoming election and on the heels of government efforts to limit the power of the Minister of the Interior, the Czech communist party engineered the downfall of the Benes government. In its aftermath pro-Western political elements were purged, and Czechoslovakia came to resemble the other Soviet-dominated Eastern European satellite states.

The year 1949 brought little relief as tensions continued to mount. In April 1949 the United States and 11 of its Western European and Atlantic allies signed the treaty establishing the North Atlantic Treaty Organization (NATO). Through it the United States pledged itself to the defense of Western Europe. In late 1949 U.S. security interests were dealt a double blow. The Soviet Union unexpectedly detonated an atomic bomb, which ended the American atomic monopoly years before U.S. policy makers had thought possible. Second, there was the "fall of China." It was inconceivable to most Americans that its ally, Jiang Jienshi (Chiang Kai-shek), could be defeated by the communist Ma Zedong. China now had to be added to the Soviet Union as a major communist power to be contained. All of these accumulated tensions spilled into the open in June 1950 when North Korea attacked South Korea. The cold war was now firmly established, and it had a global rather than just a European character to it.

When Did It Begin?   Having reviewed the historical record, the question remains, When did the cold war begin? The best answer may be, "It depends." It depends on what it is about the cold war that you are interested in or hold to be most important. If the overall pattern of U.S.–Soviet interaction is the primary concern, then the post–World War II era is the most appropriate place to date its origins. It is only at this point in time that overall U.S.–Soviet interactions take on the necessary degree of permanence, intensity, and tension to merit the label *cold war.* Prior to World War II, U.S.–Soviet interactions, while often adversarial in nature, were too intermittent and fragmented to produce the intensity or tension that later contacts did. Even during World War II when interactions did become permanent and intense, U.S.–Soviet tensions were always muted by the mutually recognized need to unite against Hitler. Stalin disbanded the COMINTERN and toned down the ideological rhetoric. Roosevelt earnestly sought to allay Soviet fears of Western duplicity and often distanced himself from Churchill's staunch anticommunist positions.

If, however, one sees in the historical record not one but many cold wars, then the post–World War II era is often a less satisfactory starting point.[21] Viewed as a conflict between rival ideologies, the 1917-to-1920 era is the most appropriate starting point. When viewed as a competition for global influence and prestige, the most appropriate starting point may not be until the late 50s or early 60s when Cuba, Africa, Asia, and Latin America became battlegrounds for U.S. and Soviet foreign policy. If one takes the cold war to be primarily an arms race between the superpowers, then the Korean War may be the date to select, for it is with its involvement in Korea that the United States reversed its policy of retrenchment and began to expand its armed forces.

Last, if the European balance of power is used as the focal point, we may have two different starting points. The Soviet Union clearly identified its national security interests with the distribution of power in Europe as early as the 1930s. Only after World War II did the United States act with an appreciation for the importance of Europe to its national security. In fact, it is this mutual recognition of the importance of Europe to their national security that first gave postwar U.S.–Soviet interactions the high degree of permanence, intensity, and tension that brought into existence the concept of a cold war.

Placing Responsibility.   Subject to even more disagreement than when the cold war began is who, if anyone, was responsible for it. According to the orthodox interpretation, responsibility for the cold war is placed on the Soviet Union.[22] The United States is pictured as basically reacting to and trying to check Soviet outward thrusts. Where advocates of the orthodox view see a constant pattern of Soviet expansion combined with an inflexible and Messianic ideology, the revisionists see an insecure and weak Soviet Union.[23] In their view, the United States is primarily responsible for the cold war. Its misreading of Soviet goals (which are held by revisionists to be fundamentally defensive in nature), exaggeration of Soviet military power, and obsession with communism combined to produce a series of policies that left the Soviet Union no choice but to act unilaterally in protecting its national interests.

As examples of unwarranted and overly aggressive U.S. policies, revisionists cite the dropping of the atomic bomb, the abrupt ending of lend-lease, British and U.S. actions in Germany, the handling of the Marshall Plan, the rhetoric of the Truman Doctrine, and the creation of NATO. They also cite the considerable evidence that Stalin was not determined from the outset to establish miniature Stalinist systems in Eastern Europe. The decision to do so was taken only as U.S.–Soviet relations deteriorated and the cold war intensified.

Other schools of thought on the origins of the cold war reject attempts to assign responsibility. Advocates of these interpretations see the United States and Soviet Union as victims of international politics and the nature of the state system. One version holds that a clash between the two states was all but inevitable given what had already transpired in Europe. Louis Halle, for example, asserts that the cold war is the fourth in a series of great wars that have been fought to maintain or restore the European balance of power. He lists the Napoleonic Wars, World War I, and World War II as its predecessors.[24] A second line of argument sees the United States and Soviet Union as having become locked into a conflict spiral. In such a situation the initial moves of each side are calculated to meet a specific end, but the struggle itself soon comes to dominate the players and impose a different logic and set of imperatives upon them. In essence, the conflict begins to feed upon itself, and players lose control over their own actions. Central to the dynamics of a conflict spiral are mutual fear and suspicion.[25] They combine to produce an inherent distrust of the opponent's motives and often distort the meaning of his actions. Breaking out of a conflict spiral is extremely difficult to accomplish. Economic or political exhaustion is one method; war is another. However, neither method is guaranteed to prevent the conflict spiral from starting up again.

Learning from the past requires making sense out of these alternative positions. One way of bringing a sense of order to these competing views is to disaggregate the cold war into various dimensions, as we did in discussing when it began, and raising the question of responsibility for each dimension. A second approach is to recognize that these interpretations are pitched at different levels of analysis. Interpretations that place the behavior of the United States and Soviet Union in the context of a conflict spiral or a struggle over the balance of power rest on a reading of the dynamics of the international systems. Systems-level analysis views foreign policy as an attempt by states to adapt to their geopolitical environment. The process of adaptation is often one that leaves few, if any, alternatives in the eyes of policy makers. The question of responsibility becomes secondary to the needs of adjustment and self-preservation.

Assessing cold war responsibility at this level involves asking types of questions that the orthodox and revisionist do not address. The concern is not with purpose. (Why did the Soviet Union refuse to leave Iran?) It is with identifying factors—including those that policy makers themselves may have been only dimly aware of—that provide the necessary and sufficient conditions for the emergence of a particular orientation toward the international system.[26]

The standard orthodox and revisionist interpretations operate on a strategic level of analysis. At this level, actions are evaluated by placing oneself in the position of the policy maker in an attempt to determine the rationale for his or her action. Typically, the state is viewed as a unified actor, and rationality is assumed. According to Charles Learche, the key to understanding strategic interactions is to identify the state's strategic concept, which he views to be a composite formulation of a state's sense of national purpose, a situational estimate, and its fundamental operating principles.[27] The question of responsibility then becomes one of identifying and judging the appropriateness of the strategic concepts employed by the United States and the Soviet Union.

Finally, cold war responsibility can be assessed at the decision-making level. Interpretations that stress Truman's or Stalin's personality, belief systems, or the impact of bureaucratic factors operate on this level. Responsibility is assigned here for specific actions on the assumption that strategic concepts lend themselves to more than one interpretation when applied to a specific situation. Defense of Greece and Turkey may have been dictated by U.S. strategic principles, but the rationale presented in the Truman Doctrine was not. It bore the imprint of specific personalities, belief systems, and bureaucratic interests.

The real challenge in addressing the question of responsibility is making judgments about how the forces associated with the three levels come together to produce a phenomenon as complex as the cold war. Under what conditions do forces at one level dominate those at another? Is the pattern consistent over time? What points of opportunity are open to policy makers who wish to limit conflict or simply direct events in a certain direction? When is the danger of war or a major escalation greatest?

Why Did the Cold War End?   That the cold war is over seems clear. What is not clear is why it ended. Both practitioners and scholars were caught off guard. Each group had come to treat it as a fact of life and had not anticipated the possibility that it might end. Consequently, neither their policies nor theories were directed at bringing this about or predicting its occurrence.[28] The question of why it ended is important because the answer can be seen as validating the correctness of certain policy lines, thus promoting them as a way of settling future conflicts.

Initial efforts to explain the end of the cold war had a decidedly political coloring. Conservatives attributed it to the success of Reagan's foreign policy of "peace through strength." For them the end of the cold war was a vindication of George Kennan's containment strategy. Kennan had prophesied that should Soviet leaders be confronted by the constant application of counterpressure, not only would their expansionist efforts be thwarted but the Soviet political system would also be transformed. The Reagan administration's combination of military and ideological assertiveness signaled a marked reversal in U.S. foreign policy from the détente era of Nixon and Carter. No longer was the United States interested in making the world safe for communism, according to this line of thought. The administration's disinterest in arms control and its rapid expansion in the size of the defense budget spoke to a new willingness to challenge the Soviet Union militarily. The avowed goal of the Reagan Doctrine was not only to contain the spread of communism but to unseat existing communist governments. Reagan's ideological rhetoric reinforced the point that there would be no compromises with Soviet leaders. The problem facing Soviet leaders in responding to a determined Reagan administration was that decades of neglect and mismanagement had reduced the Soviet economy to the point where it could not provide the basis for an effective counterchallenge.

Liberals saw the end of the cold war differently. They pointed to the importance of Western internationalist ideas. Of particular significance from their point of view were the influences of globalist values and antinuclearism. Both were important because of the lack of foreign policy sophistication on the part of Gorbachev and his key advisers. These ideas provided them with a means of putting their stamp on the foreign policy establishment and a way of advancing their domestic agenda. Globalism introduced these new Soviet leaders to such key concepts as interdependence and ecological sustainability. It also highlighted the role that international organizations such as the United Nations could play in ensuring Russian security. The principal Western proponent of antinuclearism was Ronald Reagan. This aspect of Reagan's thinking often is downplayed by conservatives, but to liberals it was crucial for the end of the cold war. From their perspective it was this part of Reagan's foreign policy agenda that Gorbachev was responding to and not his hard-line military posture. Reagan's antinuclearism gave Gorbachev hope that arms control initiatives would not be dismissed out of hand and that they provided an avenue for redirecting Soviet expenditures so as to further economic reform. Beth Fischer suggests that this more conciliatory side of Reagan's foreign policy emerged some 15 months prior to Gorbachev's coming to power. What remains unclear is why the shift away from its more confrontational policy took place.[29]

More recent efforts to explain the end of the cold war have drawn a much more complex picture. Attention has shifted away from simply identifying those aspects of American foreign policy or American society which challenged Soviet leaders or were found inviting by them to uncovering links between these forces and Soviet domestic politics.[30] One of the arguments made by many who take this approach is to caution against claiming too much credit on behalf of American foreign policy in ending the cold war. For example, Raymond Garthoff argues that "the American role in ending the Cold War was necessary but, naturally, not primary . . . in the final analysis, because the Cold War rested on Marxist-Leninist assumptions of inevitable world conflict, only a Soviet leader could have ended it."[31]

One of the consequences of treating Soviet politics as a key part to understanding why the cold war ended is that it directs attention to the process of learning that Soviet leaders may have engaged in after Brezhnev's death. Among the tentative findings put forward by researchers is that Gorbachev learned inductively through trial and error, and that one of the reasons that he was able to learn was that he was a relatively uncommitted thinker on national security problems and open to new ideas.[32] Also playing an important but even role in the process of learning that took place in both the East and West as the cold war ended were networks of transnational actors (scientists, policy analysts, political leaders) who were able to gain access to the Soviet political system.[33] They then helped put together a "winning coalition" that supported Gorbachev's new thinking in foreign policy.

Vietnam

America's involvement in Vietnam spanned the terms of six presidents. The cost of the war and its level of destruction were enormous: 55,000 American dead; a maximum American troop presence of 541,000 men; a total cost of $150 billion; untold numbers of Vietnamese dead and wounded; 7 million tons of bombs dropped; and 20 million craters left behind. Table 5–2 presents a chronology of major events in the history of the U.S. presence in Vietnam. Our purpose in examining Vietnam is not to establish responsibility but to highlight (1) the types and sources of lessons used by U.S. foreign policy makers in making decisions and (2) the lessons that have emerged from this involvement. This type of evaluation is necessary both to better understand Vietnam and to evaluate assertions that Angola, Nicaragua, or country X is another Vietnam. The need for it is evident in the ignorance of the public and U.S. policy makers about what happened there. A public opinion poll taken March 21–25, 1985, revealed that only three in five Americans knew that the United States supported South Vietnam. In a press conference on February 18, 1982, in response to a question about covert operations in Latin America, President Reagan stated:

> If I recall correctly, . . . North and South Vietnam had been, previous to colonization, two separate countries [and] provisions were made that these two countries could, by the vote of their people together, decide whether they wanted to be one country or not. . . . Ho Chi Minh refused to participate in such an election. . . . John F. Kennedy authorized the sending of a division of Marines. And that was the first move toward combat troops in Vietnam.[34]

Vietnam Chronology.   The first president to have to deal with Vietnam was Truman. Initially, his views on Indochina resembled those held during World War II by Roosevelt, who was sympathetic to Ho Chi Minh's efforts to establish independence for the region and unsympathetic to French attempts to reestablish their prewar position of colonial domination. In 1947 Truman resisted French requests for U.S. aid and urged France to end the war against Ho Chi Minh who, while one of the founders of the French communist party, had proven himself a valuable ally and nationalist in defeating Japan. Truman's views were soon to undergo a stark and rapid transformation. By 1952 the United States was providing France with $30 million in aid to defeat Ho Chi Minh, and in 1953, when his presidency ended, the United States was paying one-third of the French war cost. Ho Chi Minh was also redefined from a nationalist into a communist threat to U.S. security interests. Nothing had changed in Indochina to warrant this new evaluation of the situation. Dramatic events, however, were taking place elsewhere as cold war competition took root. In the process decisions on Indochina came to be viewed in a larger context. France was reluctant to participate in a European Defense System, something the United States saw as vital if Europe was to contain communist expansionist pressures. In a virtual quid pro quo, the United States agreed to underwrite the French war effort in Indochina the same day France announced its intent to participate in plans for the defense of Europe.

The Eisenhower administration began by reaffirming Truman's financial commitment to France and then enlarged upon it. By the end of 1953, U.S. aid rose to $500 million and covered approximately one-half of the cost of the French war effort. For Eisenhower and Secretary of State John Foster Dulles, expenditures of this magnitude were necessary to prevent a Chinese intervention that they both felt was otherwise likely to occur. Unfortunately for the

TABLE 5–2 Chronology of U.S. Involvement in Vietnam

September 1940	France gives Japan right of transit, control over local military facilities, and control over economic resources in return for right to keep nominal sovereignty.
March 1945	Gaullist French forces take over administration of Vietnam from pro-Vichy French troops.
September 1945	Ho Chi Minh declares Vietnam to be independent.
February 1950	U.S. recognizes French-backed Bao Dai government.
March 1954	French forces defeated at Dien Bien Phu.
April 1954	Geneva Peace Talks begin; end in July.
September 1954	SEATO created.
July 1956	No elections held in Vietnam.
October 1961	Taylor–Rostow mission sent to Vietnam; 15,000 advisers sent in as a result.
November 1963	Diem and Kennedy assassinated.
August 1964	Gulf of Tonkin incident.
February 1965	Pleiku barracks attacked; 8 U.S. dead and 60 injured; Operation Rolling Thunder launched in retaliation.
May 1965	Westmoreland requests 80,000 troops.
July 1965	Johnson announces an additional 125,000 troops to be sent to Vietnam.
January 1968	Tet Offensive.
March 1968	Bombing halted; Johnson steps out of presidential race.
April 1970	Cambodia invaded.
March 1972	Major North Vietnamese offensive launched.
April 1972	B-52 bombings of Hanoi and Haiphong.
May 1972	North Vietnamese harbors mined.
December 1972	Peace talks collapse and then resume after heavy bombing.
January 1973	Peace agreement signed.
March 1975	North Vietnamese offensive begins.
April 1975	South Vietnam surrenders.

French, U.S. aid was not enough to secure victory, and Eisenhower was unwilling to go beyond financing a proxy war.

The end came for the French at Dien Bien Phu. With its forces under siege there, France informed the United States that unless it intervened Indochina would fall to the communists. With no aid forthcoming, the process of withdrawal began. France's involvement in Indochina officially came to an end with the signing of the 1954 Geneva Peace Accords. According to this agreement, a "provisional demarcation line" would be established at the seventeenth parallel. Vietminh troops loyal to Ho Chi Minh would regroup north of it, and pro-French Vietnamese forces would regroup south of it. Elections were scheduled for 1956 to determine who would rule over the single country of Vietnam. The Geneva Accords provided the French with the necessary face-saving way out of Indochina. Ho Chi Minh's troops controlled three-quarters of Vietnam and were poised to extend their area of control. All parties to the agreement expected Ho Chi Minh to win the 1956 election easily.

The United States did not sign the Geneva Accords but pledged to "refrain from the threat or use of force to disturb" the settlement. However, only six weeks after its signing, the Southeast Asia Treaty Organization (SEATO) was established as part of an effort to halt the spread of communism in the wake of the French defeat. Signatory states to this collective security pact were Great Britain, France, New Zealand, Pakistan, the Philippines, Thailand, Australia, and the United States. A protocol extended coverage to Laos, Cambodia, and "the free people under the jurisdiction of Vietnam." The Vietminh saw the protocol as a violation of the Geneva Accords because it treated the seventeenth parallel as a political boundary and not as a civil war truce line. Political developments below the seventeenth parallel supported the Vietminh interpretation. In 1955 the United States backed Ngo Dinh Diem, who had declared himself president of the Republic of Vietnam. With U.S. support he argued that since South Vietnam had not signed the Geneva Accords, it did not have to abide by it and hold elections. The year 1956 came and went with no elections. By the time Eisenhower left office, U.S. military aid reached the point where 1,000 U.S. military advisers were stationed in South Vietnam.

When the Kennedy administration first looked at Southeast Asia, its primary concern was Laos, and its goal was to create a neutral state. For many it was also seen as a potential test case of the Soviet Union's ability to work constructively with the United States. The Vietminh had long supported the communist Pathet Lao forces, but the Soviet Union had only begun to do so openly just before Kennedy's inauguration. Should the Vietminh triumph in Vietnam, the fear was that the Soviet Union would be unable to restrain its support for other communist parties in Indochina. Under such conditions the value of Laos as a test case of U.S.–Soviet cooperation would be greatly lessened, and the establishment of a communist government in Laos would become a real possibility.

The landmark decision on Vietnam during the Kennedy administration came in October 1961 with the Taylor–Rostow Report. Receiving contradictory information and advice on how to proceed, Kennedy sent General Maxwell Taylor and Walt Rostow to Vietnam on a fact-finding mission. They reported that South Vietnam could only be saved by the introduction of 8,000 U.S. combat troops. Kennedy rejected this conclusion, but while skeptical of the argument, he did send an additional 15,000 military advisers. Kennedy's handling of the Taylor–Rostow Report is significant for two reasons. First, the decision was typical of those he made on Vietnam. He never gave the advocates of escalation all that they wanted, but neither did he ever say no. Some increase in the level of the American military commitment was always forthcoming. Second, in acting on the Taylor–Rostow Report, Kennedy helped shift the definition of the Vietnam conflict from a political problem to a military one. Until this point Vietnam was seen by the Kennedy administration as a guerrilla war in which control of the population was key. From now on, control of the battlefield was to become the priority item.

Under Johnson, U.S. involvement in the war steadily escalated. Pressures began building in January 1964 when the joint chiefs of staff (JCS) urged him to put aside U.S. self-imposed restraints so that the war might be won more quickly. They especially urged aerial bombing of North Vietnam. In August 1964 this bombing began in retaliation for an incident in the Gulf of Tonkin. The United States stated that two North Vietnamese PT boats fired on the *C. Turner Joy* and *Maddox* in neutral waters. President Johnson also went to Congress for a resolution supporting his use of force against North Vietnam. The Gulf of Tonkin Resolution passed by a unanimous vote in the House and by an 88-to-2 vote in the Senate. It gave the president the authority to "take all necessary measures to repel any armed attack against the forces of the United States and to prevent further aggression." The incident itself is clouded in controversy. Later studies suggest that the incident was staged or that it never occurred. These views hold that Johnson was merely looking for an excuse to begin the bombing.[35] In the eyes of many, the Gulf of Tonkin Resolution became the functional equivalent of a declaration of war.

From that point forward, the war became increasingly Americanized. Operation Rolling Thunder, a sustained and massive bombing campaign, was launched against North Vietnam in retaliation for the February 1965 Vietcong attack on Pleiku. In March 1965 General William Westmoreland requested that two Marine corps be sent to Vietnam. By April the JCS recommended that 50,000 U.S. combat troops be sent. In May this figure was revised upward to 80,000. In June Westmoreland sought 200,000 ground forces and projected a need for 600,000 troops by 1967. U.S. goals were also changing. A Pentagon Papers memorandum put forward the following priorities: 70 percent to avoid a humiliating defeat; 20 percent to keep South Vietnam from China; and 10 percent to permit the people of South Vietnam to enjoy a better, freer way of life.[36]

The Tet Offensive in January 1968 brought yet another challenge to the Johnson administration, and in many ways it was the final challenge. In March 1968 Johnson announced a halt in the bombings against North Vietnam and that he was not a candidate for reelection. The Tet Offensive was a countrywide conventional assault by communist forces on South Vietnam. It penetrated Saigon, all of the provincial capitals, and even the U.S. embassy compound. The U.S. response was massive and expanded bombings of North Vietnam. In the end the communist forces were defeated. As a final thrust to take control of South Vietnam, it had been premature, but it did demonstrate the bankruptcy of U.S. policy. Massive bombings and hundreds of thousands of U.S. combat troops had not brought the United States closer to victory.

Vietnam was for Nixon, as it had been for Kennedy, a secondary issue. Establishing détente was Nixon's primary concern, and this policy could be threatened by any weakness or vacillation in U.S. policy on Vietnam. American commitments to Vietnam had to be met if the Soviet Union and China were to respect the United States in the post-Vietnam era. The strategy selected for accomplishing this was Vietnamization. Gradually, the United States would reduce its combat presence such that by 1972 the South Vietnamese army would be able to hold its own when supported by U.S. air and naval power and economic aid.

The inherent weakness of Vietnamization was that the strategy could succeed only if the North Vietnamese did not attack in the transition period before the South Vietnamese army was ready. Nixon and Kissinger designed a two-pronged approach to lessen the likelihood that this would occur. Cambodia was invaded with the hope of cleaning out North Vietnamese sanctuaries, and the bombing of North Vietnam was increased. Nevertheless, the potential danger became a reality when in the spring of 1972 North Vietnam attacked across the demilitarized zone (DMZ). At this point Nixon was forced to re-Americanize the war in order to prevent the defeat of South Vietnam. Bombing of North Vietnam now reached unprecedented levels, and North Vietnamese ports were mined.

Being carried out against the backdrop of this fighting were the Paris Peace Talks. They had begun in earnest in 1969 but had made little progress. With this escalation of the war Nixon also offered a new peace plan, which included a promise to withdraw all U.S. forces after an Indochina-wide cease-fire and exchange of prisoners of war (POWs). Progress was now forthcoming. Hanoi was finding itself increasingly isolated from the Soviet Union and China, both of whom had become more interested in establishing a working relationship with the United States than in defeating it in Vietnam. It was now South Vietnam that began to object to the peace terms and stalled the negotiating process. In early December the "final talks" broke off without an agreement. On December 18, 1972, the United States ordered the all-out bombing of Hanoi and Haiphong to demonstrate U.S. resolve to both North and South Vietnamese leaders. On December 30 talks resumed, and the bombing was ended. A peace treaty was signed on January 23, 1973.

President Ford was in office when South Vietnam fell in 1975. What had begun as a normal military engagement ended in a rout. On March 12, 1975, the North Vietnamese attacked across the DMZ. On March 25 Hue fell. Five days later Da Nang fell. The United States evacuated on April 29, and on April 30 South Vietnam surrendered unconditionally.

Lessons Used by Policy Makers. In examining the lessons used by policy makers in their decision making on Vietnam, our focus is on the Kennedy and Johnson administrations because it is here that the major escalations in the type and level of the U.S. commitment took place. We can identify two broad types of lessons of the past held by U.S. policy makers. The first are political lessons, and the second are strategic and tactical ones.

The political lessons of the past differed for elected and appointed policy makers only in their details. The bottom line was the same: Personal survival in the upper circles of decision making in Washington required creating an image of toughness. The source of this lesson for elected officials was the "loss" of China. The Republicans had successfully leveled this charge against the Democrats. Kennedy applied the same strategy against Nixon in 1960, accusing the Eisenhower administration of losing Cuba. Politically, Kennedy saw Vietnam as his China. Johnson drew the same lessons as did Kennedy. As Johnson stated many times, he would not be the first president to lose a war. In a similar vein David Halberstam suggests that "Johnson did not take the domino theory seriously; he was far more worried about . . . what this [the fall of Vietnam] would do to him in terms of domestic politics."[37]

The national security managers also drew upon the fall of China for lessons. To this they could add lessons from decision making in the Korean War. In each case the implications were the same. A reputation for toughness was the most highly prized virtue that one could possess.[38] The bureaucratic casualties in the decision-making process on China were those who, even though they were correct, had become identified with the soft side of a policy debate. Those who had been hawkish—but wrong—emerged relatively unscathed from McCarthyism. To a lesser extent Korea produced a similar pattern. Dean Rusk, who had failed to predict the Chinese entry into Korea but was staunchly anti-communist, did not pay a price for being wrong. In 1961 he became Kennedy's Secretary of State.

Standing out among the host of strategic and tactical lessons of the past drawn upon by policy makers on Vietnam was the Munich analogy and the danger of appeasement. Munich had become a symbol for a generation of policy makers.[39] Its impact was so great that even those with no personal contact with the European peace efforts in the late 1930s could draw upon it for insight. Johnson, for example, saw the central lesson of the twentieth century as being that the appetite for aggression is never satisfied. It was Rusk who drew most openly and repeatedly on the Munich analogy. While he recognized that differences existed between the aggressions of Ho Chi Minh and Hitler, the basic point remained the same. "Aggression by any other name was still aggression and . . . must be checked."[40]

Very different were the lessons of the French experience in Indochina. Ernest May states that it was on the mind of every participant in the debate on the Taylor–Rostow Report.[41] Yet it had a negligible impact on American thinking, falling far short of being a generational experience on the order of Munich. Only George Ball actively drew upon this analogy. He had firsthand experience with the French war effort, having served as a lawyer for France during the Geneva negotiations. To him the war was unwinnable, and he warned Kennedy that if he sent the 15,000 combat troops to Vietnam as recommended, the commitment would escalate to 300,000 men.

Ball became concerned with U.S. policy in Vietnam because he feared that it was diverting attention from Europe. This Europeanist orientation to world politics was not unique within the Kennedy–Johnson administrations. McGeorge Bundy was "totally a man of the Atlantic." He was also very much a product of the 1950s and the cold war, so that when he entered the debate on Vietnam, he was an advocate of the U.S. presence. Kennedy's first ambassador to Vietnam, Fritz Nolting, and his top aide, William Trueheart, were also Europeanists who were totally ignorant of Asia and Asian communism. The predominance of Europeanists illustrates the interaction of political and strategic and tactical lessons of the past. A president concerned with making sure Vietnam did not become his China had limited options in making appointments. A residue of doubt continued to hang over the credentials of most Asian experts. While they lacked knowledge about Asian affairs, a president could feel politically safe with Europeanists in key decision-making positions.

The lack of knowledge about Asia on the part of key policy makers comes through in the strategic and tactical lessons they drew from Asian events. In many respects Kennedy was more knowledgeable about Asia than most in his administration. He had taken a special interest in Indochina while in Congress and had read on guerrilla warfare. Yet for all of this his views were not particularly sophisticated. According to Halberstam, they rested more on intuitive feel than on knowledge.[42] The inadequacy of this intuitive feel is evident in Kennedy's favored set of lessons of the past: Magsaysay's struggle against the Huk guerrillas in the Philippines and the British experience in Malaysia. Both contests were of a far different order from what was being contemplated in Vietnam. For example, the Malaysian analogy was flawed in at least five respects according to the U.S. military.

1. Malaysian borders were far more controllable.

2. The racial characteristics of the Chinese insurgents in Malaysia made identification and segregation a relatively simple matter as compared with the situation in Vietnam.

3. The scarcity of food in Malaysia compared to the relative plenty in South Vietnam made the denial of food to the guerrillas a far less usable weapon.

4. More important, in Malaysia the British were in actual command of military operations.

5. Finally, it took the British 12 years to defeat an insurgency that was less strong than the one in South Vietnam.[43]

The professional military also proved unable to draw on Asia for insights into how to fight in Vietnam. Westmoreland was "a conventional man in an unconventional war." Vietcong challenges only brought a request for more and more men and more bombing. They did not produce innovative strategies or tactics. Robert McNamara was no different in this respect. Never challenging the assumptions of policy, he limited himself to translating ideas into workable processes. In the end he was unable "to adapt his values and terms to Vietnam realities."[44] The approach of the chairman of the Joint Chiefs of Staff, General Maxwell Taylor, was not very different. While he spoke of the challenge of brush-fire wars, his cables from Vietnam and the Taylor–Rostow Report indicated that Taylor was not really talking in terms of fighting a guerrilla war. His concern was with the military problem in Vietnam, and he approached it in a very conventional manner. Additional troops were the answer; political reforms were not mentioned. Taylor's analogy was with Korea and not the Philippines or the French experience in Indochina. Looking at Korea, he drew favorable comparisons with battlefield conditions and terrain. Taylor overlooked the differing nature of the two wars. Korea had been a conventional war begun by a border crossing by uniformed troops who fought in large concentrations.[45] This was not Vietnam in 1964.

The lessons drawn by two other policy makers deserve mention. The first is Walt Rostow, who brought to Vietnam decision making a firm set of beliefs on how to win the war and of the necessity of winning it. In his eyes communist intervention had taken place in South Vietnam, breaking the first rule of peaceful coexistence. The boundaries of the two camps were immutable, and any effort to alter them had to be resisted. His solution was air power. Rostow had selected bombing targets during World War II and was convinced that massive bombing would bring North Vietnam to its knees. He was challenged on this point by George Ball, who had been a member of the Strategic Survey Group that studied the impact of the allied bombing of Germany. It concluded that the bombing had been of limited value. Ball concurred in this conclusion and argued that bombing North Vietnam would be equally futile. The second person worth looking at is Lyndon Johnson, who drew heavily upon his experience in Texas politics in formulating his Vietnam strategy. He had opposed the idea of a coup against Diem. That simply was not the way things were done in Texas. "Otto Passman and I, we have our differences, . . . but I don't plan his overthrow."[46] Beyond that, the United States had given its word to Diem, and you don't go back on your word. Johnson also felt that displays of toughness were prerequisites for dealing with the Vietnamese. Here he drew upon analogies to his dealings with Mexicans. "If you don't watch they'll walk right into your yard and take it over . . . but if you say to 'em right at the start, 'Hold on just a minute,' they'll know they are dealing with someone who'll stand up. And after that you can get along just fine."[47]

Lessons Learned.   Vietnam had a tremendous impact on public opinion and elite attitudes. It destroyed the postwar consensus on the ends and means of U.S. foreign policy and left in its place three competing belief systems: cold war internationalism, post–cold war internationalism, and neo-isolationism. That three competing belief systems have merged is an indication that the lessons of Vietnam are not self-evident or easily agreed upon. The identification of three belief systems understates the extent of disagreement on the lessons of Vietnam. In identifying the lessons of Vietnam, we rely on a survey conducted by Ole Holsti and James Rosenau.[48] Respondents were asked to assess the lessons of Vietnam, the sources of failure, and the consequences of that failure. They were also asked to identify their positions on Vietnam when the war first became an issue for them and toward the end of the U.S. involvement. The sample was divided into three parts. The first was made up of a random sampling of names from *Who's Who*. The second group was selected on a quota basis from key groups in society (foreign service officers, clergy, women, labor, media, academics, and politicians). The third group was made up of military personnel.

On the basis of attitudes held at the beginning and end of Vietnam, Holsti and Rosenau identify seven groups holding different notions about the sources, consequences, and lessons of Vietnam. These groups covered the entire range of opinion from consistent critics to consistent supporters and are listed in Table 5-3. Note the distribution of membership in these groups. There is no clustering of opinion at the center as in a normal curve, which would have only a few respondents at each extreme. Fully 30 percent of the sample resides at the extremes, confirming the depth of the impact Vietnam had on American attitudes.

Looking first at the sources of failure, Holsti and Rosenau were able to identify 21 reasons why the United States lost in Vietnam, according to those they polled. The reasons are listed in rank order in Table 5–4. All seven groups held the sources of failure to be many, with all but the ambivalents citing seven or more reasons. The depth of the disagreement is great. Not only are the sources of failure ranked differently by the various groups, but no one explanation appears in all seven groups. Only three appear in six of these groups: the United States' lack of clear-cut goals, the presence of Soviet and Chinese aid, and North Vietnamese dedication.

A more coherent picture emerges when we look at the consequences of Vietnam cited by the seven groups. Their responses are found in rank order in Table 5–5. All three groups of supporters cited international system-related concerns as the most important consequences of Vietnam. The three groups of critics cited Vietnam's domestic impact as most significant. The ambivalents joined with the supporters in identifying international system consequences as most important but altered their ranking. Only one consequence was cited by all seven groups but not with the same relative importance: The United States will limit its conception of its national interest.

The picture becomes cloudy again when turning to the lessons of Vietnam. As indicated in Table 5–6 where they are rank ordered, 34 lessons of Vietnam were cited. No one lesson appears in all seven groups. Only two appear in six groups: Executive-legislative cooperation is vital, and Russia is expansionist.

Three other lessons appear in five groups: Americans have a lack of patience, the United States must avoid graduated escalation, and the United States must honor alliance commitments. Finally, no overlap exists between the 12 lessons identified by the supporters and the six identified by the critics.

The Persian Gulf War[49]

The Persian Gulf War can be divided into four periods. The first begins in early 1990 and ends with Iraq's August 2 invasion of Kuwait. The second encompasses the period between that invasion and the beginning of the bombing campaign in January 1991. The third stage involves the war itself, the

TABLE 5–3   Distribution of Attitudes on U.S. Involvement in Vietnam

Group Label	Number	Percentage
Consistent supporters	363	15.9
Converted supporters	128	5.6
Ambivalent supporters	346	15.2
Ambivalents	128	5.6
Ambivalent critics	63	2.8
Converted critics	867	35.0
Consistent critics	378	16.6

Source: Ole Holsti and James N. Rosenau, "Vietnam, Consensus, and the Belief Systems of American Leaders," World Politics, 32 (1979), p. 8.

TABLE 5–4 Rankings of the "Most Important Sources of Failure" as Cited by Each Group

Supporters	Converted Supporters	Ambivalent Supporters	Ambivalents	Ambivalent Critics	Converted Critics	Critics
American "no-win" approach	American "no-win" approach	Soviet and Chinese aid	Soviet and Chinese aid	Unrealistic U.S. goals	N. Vietnamese dedication	Unrealistic U.S. goals
Restricted air power	Soviet and Chinese aid	American "no-win" approach	N. Vietnamese dedication	Saigon lacked popular support	Saigon lacked popular support	Saigon lacked popular support
Soviet and Chinese aid	Restricted air power	N. Vietnamese dedication	Dissidents hurt U.S. credibility	Misunderstood third world nationalism	Unrealistic U.S. goals	N. Vietnamese dedication
Media hurt war support in U.S.	U.S. had no clear goals	Media hurt war support in U.S.	Media hurt war support in U.S.	N. Vietnamese dedication	Soviet and Chinese aid	Misunderstood third world nationalism
Military advice unheeded	Media hurt war support in U.S.	Dissidents hurt U.S. credibility	Saigon lacked popular support	U.S. had no clear goals	Misunderstood third world nationalism	U.S. ignorance of Vietnam
Dissidents hurt U.S. credibility	Dissidents hurt U.S. credibility	N. Vietnam peace violations	N. Vietnam peace violations	U.S. ignorance of Vietnam	U.S. had no clear goals	U.S. had no clear goals
N. Vietnam peace violations	Military advice unheeded	U.S. had no clear goals		Soviet and Chinese aid	U.S. ignorance of Vietnam	Opposition of world opinion
Congressional interference	N. Vietnam peace violations	Restricted air power		Media hurt war support in U.S.		
U.S. had no clear goals	N. Vietnamese dedication	Saigon lacked popular support				
	Congressional interference					

Note: This table lists all the explanations of "failure" that received at least an average rating of 0.67 (moderately important) on a scale of 1.00 (very important) to 0.00 (not at all important). Explanations are listed in order of decreasing importance for each group.

Source: Ole Holsti and James N. Rosenau, "Vietnam, Consensus, and the Belief Systems of American Leaders," *World Politics,* 32 (1979), p. 21.

TABLE 5–5 Ranking of the "Consequences of Vietnam" Receiving Highest Agreement from Each Group

Supporters	Converted Supporters	Ambivalent Supporters	Ambivalents	Ambivalent Critics	Converted Critics	Critics
Communists will seek other triumphs	Communists will seek other triumphs	Communists will seek other triumphs	U.S. will limit conception of national interest	U.S. economy damaged	Long-term threats neglected	Long-term threats neglected
American credibility damaged	American credibility damaged	American credibility damaged	Communists will seek other triumphs	Long-term threats neglected	U.S. will limit conception of national interest	Lost faith in U.S. government
U.S. will limit conception of national interest	U.S. will limit conception of national interest	U.S. will limit conception of national interest	American credibility damaged	Lost faith in U.S. government	Lost faith in U.S. government	U.S. economy damaged
				American credibility damaged		U.S. will limit conception of national interest
				U.S. will limit conception of national interest		

Note: This table lists all the "consequences of Vietnam" that received at least an average rating of 0.30 on a scale of 1.00 (agree strongly) to −1.00 (disagree strongly). Consequences are listed in order of decreasing importance for each group. This table does not include data for the item stating: "As a result of the Vietnam experience, the U.S. is likely to keep military assistance to anti-Soviet factions in Angola to a minimum." Congressional action had settled that issue before some respondents returned their questionnaires.

Source: Ole Holsti and James N. Rosenau, "Vietnam, Consensus, and the Belief Systems of American Leaders," *World Politics,* 32 (1979), p. 31.

TABLE 5–6 Ranking of the "Lessons of Vietnam" Receiving Highest Agreement from Each Group

Supporters	Converted Supporters	Ambivalent Supporters	Ambivalents	Ambivalent Critics	Converted Critics	Critics
Avoid graduated escalation	U.S.S.R. is expansionist	Avoid graduated escalation	U.S.S.R. is expansionist	Avoid Angola involvement	U.S.S.R. is expansionist	Avoid Angola involvement
U.S.S.R. is expansionist	Avoid graduated escalation	U.S.S.R. is expansionist	Must honor alliance commitments	Third world revolutionaries are nationalistic	Avoid graduated escalation	Press more likely to tell truth on foreign policy
Must honor alliance commitments	Must honor alliance commitments	Domino theory is valid	Exec.-Congress cooperation is vital	Exec.-Congress cooperation is vital	Avoid Angola involvement	Excessive reliance on military advice
Domino theory is valid	Exec.-Congress cooperation is vital	Must honor alliance commitments	Avoid graduated escalation	Americans lack patience	Exec.-Congress cooperation is vital	Rely too much on president to define national interest
Exec.-Congress cooperation is vital	Americans don't understand role of power	Exec.-Congress cooperation is vital	Americans lack patience	Rely too much on president to define national interest	Must honor alliance commitments	Third world revolutionaries are nationalistic
Avoid half-measures militarily	Domino theory is valid	Americans lack patience		U.S.S.R. is expansionist		Scale down international role
Americans don't understand role of power	Americans lack patience	Americans don't understand role of power		U.S. should solve own problems		Enlist UN cooperation

(continued)

TABLE 5–6   Ranking of the "Lessons of Vietnam" Receiving Highest Agreement from Each Group (continued)

Supporters	Converted Supporters	Ambivalent Supporters	Ambivalents	Ambivalent Critics	Converted Critics	Critics
Soviets abuse détente	Avoid half-measures militarily	Americans can't fight limited war		Press more likely to tell truth on foreign policy		
Americans lack patience	Americans can't fight limited war					
Americans can't fight limited war						
Strike at heart of enemy power						
Communist victory antithesis of U.S. interests						

Note: This table lists all "lessons of Vietnam" that received at least an average rating of 0.40 on a scale of 1.00 (agree strongly) to −1.00 (disagree strongly). Lessons are listed in order of decreasing importance for each group.

Source: Ole Holsti and James N. Rosenau, "Vietnam, Consensus, and the Belief Systems of American Leaders," *World Politics*, 32 (1979), p. 51.

five weeks of aerial bombardment and the 100 hours of ground warfare. The fourth and final stage involves the posthostility diplomacy between Iraq and the UN forces as well as Saddam Hussein's military action against the Kurds and Shi'ites. Each holds lessons for the future. We will examine the first two in detail because our concern is with the failure of U.S. deterrence and compellence strategies. If we were concerned with the effectiveness of Patriot missiles or the dangers posed by SCUD-type missiles, our proper focus would be on the third period. If it were on the building of a postwar security system in the Middle East it would be on the fourth period. Table 5–7 shows the chronology of the war.

Period 1: February–August 1990.   On February 15, 1990, Voice of America (VOA) broadcast a story about how democracy was taking hold in countries that were once dictatorships. In the course of doing so. it identified Iraq as a state where the "secret police were still widely present." The Iraqi government complained to U.S. Ambassador April Glaspie that this constituted a "flagrant interference in the internal affairs of Iraq." Glaspie wrote a letter apologizing for the comment, stating that "it is absolutely not United States policy to question the legitimacy of the Government of Iraq nor to interfere in any way in the domestic concerns of the Iraqi people and government." Before the month was out, Saddam Hussein again complained about American foreign policy toward Iraq. At a February 24 meeting of the Arab Cooperation Council in Jordan, he warned other Arab states about "undisciplined and irresponsible behavior" on

TABLE 5–7   Persian Gulf War Chronology

August 2, 1991	Iraqi troops invade Kuwait.
August 6, 1991	UN Security Council imposes economic sanctions.
August 7, 1991	President Bush begins Operation Desert Shield by ordering U.S. troops, aircraft, and warships to Saudi Arabia.
August 9, 1991	UN Security Council declares Iraqi annexation of Kuwait "null and void."
August 10, 1991	The United States begins a naval blockade of Iraq.
August 22, 1991	President Bush announces callup of 40,000 military reservists.
November 29, 1991	UN Security Council passes Resolution 678 authorizing members to "use all necessary means" against Iraq unless it withdraws from Kuwait by January 15, 1992.
January 12, 1992	The Senate votes 52–47 to authorize Bush to use force to carry out UN Resolution 678; the House votes 250–183 supporting a presidential use of force.
January 15, 1992	At 7:00 P.M. EST, the air attack on Baghdad begins.
January 17, 1992	Iraq launches SCUD missiles at Israel.
February 22, 1992	Bush issues Saddam Hussein an ultimatum to leave Kuwait by noon February 23.
February 24, 1992	The ground war begins.
February 27, 1992	President Bush announces that offensive actions will end.

the part of the United States and that Israel might undertake "new stupidities . . . as a result of U.S. encouragement." Moderate Arab states felt threatened by Hussein's comments, which they read as veiled criticisms of their relationships with the United States.

There was little veiled in Hussein's other major pronouncement. He wanted the Gulf states to provide Iraq with $30 billion in aid for doing their bidding in the war against Iran. Should this money not be forthcoming, Hussein promised to "take steps to retaliate." Iraq's economy had been severely damaged by the 1980–1988 Iran–Iraq War. It had cost Iraq over $500 billion and left it with a staggering war debt. $40 billion was owed to other Arab states and a similar amount was owed the West. The key to Iraq's economic recovery lay in oil sales, but the price of oil had been dropping steadily from $20.50 per barrel in January 1990 to $13.00 per barrel in July. Each dollar drop cost Iraq an estimated $1 billion in annual revenues. Not surprisingly, Saddam Hussein blamed overproduction by Kuwait and other OPEC states for this situation.

The next two months saw a flurry of diplomatic activity in the region as Jordan's King Hussein engaged in an unsuccessful round of shuttle diplomacy to heal the rift between Iraq and the other Middle East oil-producing states. In April, Saddam Hussein continued his verbal attacks on the United States and Israel, telling a group of Iraqi military officers that "this is the biggest conspiracy in modern history" and that "we have a duty to defend Iraq." He also implied that he would use chemical weapons against Israel, noting that "we will make the fire eat up half of Israel." In the following days Saddam Hussein sought to soften these remarks. He contacted the Saudis and arranged to meet with their ambassador to the United States, who was told that these remarks had been blown out of proportion and to pass this along to the Bush administration. Saddam Hussein went on to reassure the Saudi official that he had no designs over his neighbors but that he had to "whip them [the Iraqi people] into a sort of frenzy or emotional mobilization . . . so they will be ready for whatever may happen."

The State Department publicly termed Hussein's comments "inflammatory," and an official White House spokesperson labeled them "particularly deplorable and irresponsible." At this point the Bush administration began to contemplate economic sanctions against Iraq. Plans were drawn up to eliminate credits for wheat purchases by Iraq and the import of military and dualuse technologies. They were formally presented for consideration by an April 16 meeting of representatives from interested cabinet offices. There the plan ran into opposition and was dropped: Both the Commerce Department and the National Security Council objected. The White House also opposed the idea because at the time the Bush administration was trying to head off congressional pressures for economic sanctions against Iraq.

A congressional delegation visited Iraq shortly after Saddam Hussein's speech. Headed by Senator Bob Dole, it both threatened and reassured Iraq. Saddam Hussein was warned that a prerequisite for improvements in U.S.–Iraqi relations was a halt in Iraq's efforts to acquire chemical and biological weapons. In private conversations, however, members of the U.S. delegation apparently struck a more conciliatory note, indicating that they saw Saddam Hussein as a man of peace and that both the Bush administration and many in Congress opposed economic sanctions. In Washington, Bush received the Saudi ambassador and, while doubting Saddam Hussein's honesty and true intentions, agreed to obtain a statement from Israel that it had no intention of attacking Iraq. After this was done and communicated to Saddam Hussein, the Bush administration considered the matter closed.

Saddam Hussein, however, soon went back on the verbal offensive. His anger was directed at what he perceived to be the overproduction of oil by OPEC states. At a May summit meeting of Arab states he charged that Kuwait and other quota-busting oil-producing states were "virtually waging an economic war against my country." He also promised that "one day the reckoning will come." In July Saddam Hussein unleashed a new round of attacks against OPEC states for their oil-pricing policies. On July 10, the OPEC oil ministers had agreed to raise the price of oil back to $18 per barrel, but Kuwait qualified its position by stating that it would review and possibly reverse this decision in the fall. For all practical purposes, this was an invitation to oil companies to wait and purchase Kuwaiti oil at a reduced price in the near future. Saddam Hussein responded by laying out the totality of his demands of Kuwait. He demanded $2.4 billion in compensation for oil that was dumped from disputed oil fields, $12 billion in compensation for the loss of revenues resulting from the depressed price of oil brought about by Kuwait's overproduction, Kuwaiti forgiveness of Iraq's $10 billion war debt from the Iran–Iraq War, and a lease on the strategic island of Bubiyan.

In a memorandum to the Arab League Saddam Hussein also charged Kuwait and the United Arab Emirates (UAE) with being part of a "Zionist plot aided by imperialists." At virtually the same time, Iraqi radio broadcast a speech by Saddam Hussein asserting that low oil prices were a "poisoned dagger" pointed at Iraq. In that speech he also threatened to take matters into his own hands if need be, stating that "if words fail to protect us, we will have no choice other than to go into action to reestablish the correct state of affairs and restore our rights."

Accompanying this hostile rhetoric were troop movements by key units in Iraq's Republican Guard toward the Kuwaiti border. While disturbed by this sudden military show of force, U.S. officials concluded that Iraq's purpose was to intimidate Kuwait and not to invade it. They reached this conclusion because of the absence of supply and support units necessary to sustain an invasion and because the number of troops observed was judged to be too small for an invasion of Kuwait. Still, Saddam Hussein's actions seemed to demand a countermove. Kuwait put its small army on alert, and Secretary of Defense Dick Cheney stated that the Bush administration would "take seriously any threat to U.S. interests or U.S. friends in the region." The United States also responded favorably to a request from the UAE for military assistance by providing it with two aerial tankers and quickly arranging for, and making public, a joint naval exercise. The UAE was not entirely pleased with the U.S. response. Wanting reassurance and the military aid, but not wanting to antagonize Saddam Hussein, it had hoped to keep matters secret.

Saddam Hussein's July outburst also set in motion a new round of diplomatic efforts. King Hussein, Yasir Arafat, head of the Palestine Liberation Organization, and Egyptian President Hosni Mubarak all tried to diffuse the growing tension. Ambassador Glaspie also met with Saddam Hussein. Glaspie had been trying to arrange a meeting ever since his July 17 radio address. On July 25 she was summoned to meet with him on such short notice that she was unable to get instructions from the State Department. In her conversation with Saddam Hussein, Glaspie repeated the standard U.S. position. The United States "would not countenance violence or the threat of violence or in fact threat of intimidation." It would "defend our vital interests" and "defend the sovereignty and integrity" of our "friends in the Gulf." The United States wanted better relations with Iraq. And the United States had "no opinion on the Arab–Arab conflicts, like your border disagreement with Kuwait." After this meeting Glaspie cabled Washington that it should back off the public criticism of Saddam Hussein and that his interest in a peaceful settlement of the dispute was sincere.

The United States continued on this diplomatic course right up until the invasion. On July 31, John Kelly, Assistant Secretary of State for Near East and South Asian Affairs, in testimony before a House Foreign Affairs subcommittee, acknowledged that Iraq's military buildup along the Kuwaiti border was troubling and demanded a response. He argued, however, against economic sanctions and in favor of flexibility. When questioned as to how far the United States was prepared to go in defending the sovereignty of allied states, Kelly stated that "we have no defense treaty relationship with any Gulf country" and that "we do not have a treaty commitment which would oblige us to engage U.S. forces."

This same day, Pat Lang, the Defense Intelligence Agency's (DIA) national intelligence officer for the Middle East and South Asia, issued a warning that Iraq would soon go to war. Lang had been watching the Iraqi buildup since the middle of July. In a span of 11 days, he had seen eight divisions move a distance of 300–400 miles, placing some 100,000 soldiers on the Kuwaiti border. Neither the CIA nor DIA fully supported Lang's conclusion. The next day, August 1, additional satellite intelligence had come in, making it clear that an invasion was about to be launched. Its troops were now in a classic air-land assault posture. Both the CIA and DIA now concurred with Lang's assessment that a crossover point had been reached. In his briefing to the Joint Chiefs of Staff and Secretary of Defense Cheney, General Norman Schwarzkopf, who headed the Central Command, stated that there was little or nothing that could be done. The United States only had 10,000 troops in the region and almost all of them were naval forces.

Period 2: August 1990–January 1991.   On August 2, Iraqi troops crossed into Kuwait and within a matter of hours took control of the entire country. On August 4 President Bush spoke out against the invasion, stating that "it would not stand." The next day the United Nations voted to impose economic sanctions against Iraq, and on August 24 it followed with a vote to authorize the use of force to impose those sanctions. Earlier the United Nations had voted to condemn the invasion and called for Iraq's immediate and unconditional withdrawal from Kuwait. In late September, Iraq's Revolutionary Command Council rejected the UN call for withdrawal and promised that any effort to bring this about would result in "the mother of all battles."

Military action was also forthcoming. On August 6, President Bush authorized the Pentagon to implement Operations Plan 90–1002. This was a top-secret contingency plan put together in the 1980s to deal with the prospect of a Middle East war against the Soviet Union or Iran. Because the possibility of an Iraqi attack had not been given high priority, 90–1002 had not been updated. Its central assumption that planners would have 30 days notice prior to the start of fighting to begin deploying forces and moving supplies was not met. Schwarzkopf calculated that implementing 90–1002 would require 17 weeks, 200,000–250,000 troops, and the cooperation of Saudi Arabia or some other Arab state where the United States could set up bases.

Few American or Saudi observers doubted Iraq's ability to seize Saudi territory in the days immediately following the invasion of Kuwait. One wrote that his forces could have reached the Saudi capital of Riyadh in three days. They were in a position to split off its oil-rich eastern province from the rest of Saudi Arabia and in the process destroy the social contract on which the Saudi government was built. What was uncertain was whether the Iraqis knew that they had this potential and, if so, whether they intended to act on it. The danger of an Iraqi attack against Saudi Arabia struck many as particularly grave in the first days of the American deployment. It was only in late August that U.S. military commanders felt that the American military presence had grown to the point that Saddam Hussein would probably no longer consider attacking Saudi Arabia as a viable option.

Not only did the Bush administration find itself debating Saddam Hussein's intentions, but they also disagreed on the ultimate purpose of the American display of force. Answering this question was crucial because without a military goal, a discussion of military options such as that of implementing 90–1002 made little sense. At the first postinvasion meeting of the National Security Council, Bush asserted that "we just can't accept what's happened in Kuwait just because it's too hard to do anything about it." General Powell argued that the United States ought to draw a firm line with Saudi Arabia because that was where real U.S. interests lay. UN Ambassador Thomas Pickering noted that this left Kuwait on the other side of the line.

U.S. diplomatic efforts were now directed at holding the anti-Iraq international coalition together and building support for military action designed to force Iraq out of Kuwait. Russian and French diplomatic initiatives in September and early October suggested a weakening of international resolve. Both put forward terms that were at variance with the UN demand for an Iraqi withdrawal. By early November, however, it was clear that these efforts had failed, and attention turned to laying the diplomatic groundwork for military action. In rapid succession the Chinese agreed not to veto a UN resolution authorizing the use of force, and the British and Russians publicly acknowledged that the use of military force might be necessary.

In need of particular attention was Saudi Arabia. Its cooperation was seen as essential for the success of 90–1002. Intelligence information available to the Bush administration indicated that the Saudi leadership was anything but firm in its resolution to oppose Saddam Hussein. It appeared they were giving consideration to paying Saddam Hussein billions of dollars in oil revenues as a means of deflecting his attention away from their country. One telling point of controversy between the United States and Saudi Arabia was over the composition of a delegation that the Bush administration was sending to brief them. Saudi leaders wanted a low-level team, presumably so that it would be easier for them to delay or say no to U.S. requests for military cooperation, thereby not offending Saddam Hussein. The Bush administration, in contrast, wanted to send (and did send) a high-ranking delegation to make its case and obtain from the Saudis the necessary invitation to set up military bases on their soil.

With international support well on the way to being assured, President Bush announced on November 8 that the size of the U.S. military presence in the Persian Gulf would double. The purpose was to ensure that should they desire to do so, coalition forces could conduct a successful offensive operation. Bush then traveled to the Middle East to meet with Arab leaders to gain their backing for a military push against Iraq. On November 29, the Security Council voted 12–2, with one abstention (China), to set January 15, 1991 as the deadline for Iraq's peaceful exit from Kuwait. If this did not happen, it authorized member states cooperating with Iraq "to use all means necessary" to bring about Iraq's immediate and unconditional withdrawal.

A formidable force under U.S. command was being assembled very rapidly in the Persian Gulf. Over 400,000 U.S. forces would arrive in the Middle East. Coalition air forces would fly 109,876 sorties, drop 88,500 tons of bombs, and shoot down 35 Iraqi airplanes. The size of this force did not preclude a debate in the United States over the ultimate wisdom of going to war.[50] Three prominent former policy makers spoke out against war. Zbigniew Brzezinski, Carter's National Security Adviser, counseled against going to war in congressional testimony saying that "the threat posed by Iraq was far from catastrophic." Admiral William Crow, who was chairman of the Joint Chiefs of Staff under Reagan, stated that, although Iraq must leave Kuwait, "we should give sanctions a fair chance before discarding them." James Schlesinger, who served as Secretary of Defense and Director of the Central Intelligence Agency, cautioned against using force given the unpredictable nature of the region and the possibility that the United States might have to involve itself deeply in Middle East affairs "in the aftermath of a shattering war." Speaking in favor of war, or at least accepting the need for it, was Henry Kissinger, former Secretary of State and National Security Adviser, who feared that if Iraq's aggression went unchecked a domino effect would take place in which moderate governments would collapse amid escalating crises. Also supporting it was Jeane Kirkpatrick, who served as UN Ambassador under Reagan. She argued that Saddam Hussein must be punished in order to "deter future aggression from similar violence and make the world safer for all."

With U.S. war plans being finalized and the time of the attack set, Bush went to Congress to get its approval for the use of force. This move was debated within the administration, but by early January it became clear that Congress intended to take up the question whether or not the Bush administration asked. The debate was framed as a choice between two options: authorizing the president to use force or insisting that economic sanctions be given more time. Economic sanctions were imposed almost immediately. On August 2, the Bush administration froze all Iraqi and Kuwaiti assets; it also moved to prohibit trade and financial dealings with Iraq. Great Britain, France, Russia, and the United Nations all followed suit. In December, William Webster, the CIA's Director, stated that Iraq had lost more than 90 percent of its imports and 97 percent of its exports and had deprived Iraq of $1.5 billion in foreign exchange. He estimated that Iraq's foreign exchange reserves would have been depleted by the spring and that it would not have the financial means to entice potential sanctions-busters to aid it. By the summer he expected only energy-related and some military industries to be fully functioning. Somewhat less optimistically, Webster also concluded that Iraqi ground and air forces could probably remain near their current levels of readiness for up to nine months.

After an often emotional debate, Congress voted on January 12, 1991, to support the president by a vote of 250–183 in the House and 52–47 in the Senate.

At the same time that Congress was debating the wisdom of going to war, the Bush administration was engaged in last-minute diplomatic negotiations with Iraq in Geneva. A January 8 meeting between Secretary of State Baker and Foreign Minister Tariq Aziz ended in deadlock. Aziz stated that the blunt language used by Bush in a letter given to him by Baker that demanded Iraq's withdrawal from Kuwait was "incompatible to the language that should be used in correspondence between heads of state." The following day, Saddam Hussein delivered a radio address in which he claimed that the Iraqi forces were ready for war and confident of victory. A last-minute visit by UN Secretary General Javier Perez de Cuellar also failed, and on January 14, Iraq's National Assembly voted to support Saddam Hussein's refusal to make concessions. The United Nations-set deadline of January 15, 1991, arrived and passed. At about midnight, January 16, coalition aircraft took off from Saudi Arabia to begin the air campaign against Iraq.

Deterrence.   The United States sought to deter two Iraqi actions in the time period chronicled above: an invasion of Kuwait and an invasion of Saudi Arabia. One lesson that we can try to learn from the Persian Gulf War will answer the question: Why did deterrence fail in the first case and succeed in the second? Was it because of inadequacies in deterrence theory or the inability to design and implement an appropriate strategy? The Persian Gulf War is an important test case. If deterrence could not be made to work outside of the context of deterring a Soviet nuclear attack on the United States or one of its key allies, then U.S. security policy would need to be anchored around a different strategic doctrine in the post–cold war era.

Deterrence theory builds upon a straightforward assumption about why states go to war. War is assumed to be the product of a rational decision calculus in which costs and benefits are weighed against each other. Only when the expected benefits of going to war exceed the expected costs of doing so will a state go to war. Once this decision has been made, other states face the prospect of (1) fighting a war to defend themselves, (2) appeasing the would-be aggressor—in essence giving it all or part of what it wants in the hopes of averting war, or (3) convincing the would-be aggressor to alter its plans and accept the status quo. Deterrence strategies are designed to accomplish this last outcome by rearranging the elements of this decision calculus in such a way that costs exceed benefits. To do so they must convincingly communicate both a willingness and an ability to raise the costs to the would-be aggressor should it go forward.

In regard to the first effort at deterrence, a strong case can be made that U.S. policy makers did not come close to implementing a coherent deterrence strategy. The United States neither possessed the capability to raise the costs to Iraq of an invasion of Kuwait (much less defeat any such effort) nor did it clearly communicate its position to Iraq.

From a military perspective the only counter to Saddam Hussein's attacking force was Kuwait's small army and air force. Bush administration officials gave little thought to augmenting this force. The only concrete move in this direction was the training exercise with the UAE and transfer of the two airborne refueling aircraft. Just days before the invasion, a high-ranking civilian defense department official proposed that, as a show of force, the United States move the maritime prepositioned ships from the Indian Ocean to the Persian Gulf. Each ship contained 30 days worth of food, ammunition, and supplies for a Marine unit of 16,000. General Powell objected to the idea and no ships were deployed. In making his case Powell noted that this move implied a commitment to send ground troops, that no one was proposing that the United States do this, and that Kuwait had not asked for such help.

The absence of a credible capability to defeat or punish Iraqi forces made signaling U.S. resolve a difficult task to accomplish. U.S. public pronouncements suggested an administration unsure of what it wanted to do and the image it wished to project. The statements by Ambassador Glaspie, Assistant Secretary of State Kelly, and other Bush administration officials did not point to a "line in the sand" beyond which Iraqi forces could not move with impunity. Instead, they contained expressions of concern mixed with declarations indicating limits to the extent of any potential U.S. involvement. When strong statements were made, they were quickly followed with retractions or modifiers. For example, at one point Secretary of Defense Cheney stated that U.S. defense commitments to Kuwait had not changed since the Iran–Iraq War when the United States had reflagged Kuwaiti tankers. That same day a Pentagon spokesperson stated that Cheney had been quoted "with some degree of liberty by the press." In commenting on the U.S.–UAE naval exercise, the Secretary of the Navy told Congress that U.S. forces had gone on alert status. Later, this statement was retracted.

It seemed that the Bush administration did not think it necessary to convey a credible threat because few believed that Saddam Hussein could seriously think of going to war so soon after the costly Iran–Iraq War of 1980–1988. This was the conclusion of a fall 1989 National Intelligence Estimate. It judged that Saddam Hussein wished to dominate the Gulf but that because of the costs suffered by Iraq in that war he was unlikely to use military force to do so. The conclusion that Iraq would not use force was also shared by most Arab leaders, and this reassuring message was regularly communicated to the Bush White House.

Iraqi aggression against Kuwait was not deterred because deterrence as it is supposed to be practiced was not attempted. The United States had sought to stop Saddam Hussein by engaging in a series of half-measures. An enemy making cost-benefit calculations about the consequences of an aggressive move was not likely to be deterred under these circumstances. An interesting question is raised by this conclusion: Could Saddam Hussein have been deterred if a deterrence strategy had been properly executed? The answer might be "no." If Saddam Hussein's primary motivation for invading Kuwait grew out of economic desperation, then it is possible that he would have pressed forward regardless of the military costs because of the perceived consequences of inaction—continued economic problems that could lead to his overthrow. Deterrence might also have failed due to the image of the United States held by Saddam Hussein. Janice Gross Stein observes that his

> judgment of American intentions was deeply rooted in the political and cultural context which reinforced the long-standing image of the United States as an imperialist power working through its wealthy agents in the Gulf against the interests of Arab states like Iraq.[51]

Because he saw the United States as engaged in a pattern of economic and covert warfare against him, Saddam Hussein may well have framed his choices as "open confrontation and long-term sabotage."

Having failed to deter the invasion of Kuwait, the United States turned its attention to deterring an invasion of Saudi Arabia. Implementing plan 90–1002, the United States moved quickly to place a credible deterrent force in his path. It also moved aggressively on the diplomatic front to garner support for Operation Desert Shield. The overall tactical requirements for a successful deterrence strategy were thus in place. But was the deterrence strategy a success? Just because Saddam Hussein did not invade Saudi Arabia does not prove that he was deterred. He may have had no intention of doing so. In fact, all agree that in the first weeks after the invasion of Kuwait before U.S. forces arrived in large numbers he could have successfully done so. Yet, he did not. General Powell believed that Saddam Hussein never intended to invade Saudi Arabia because of the larger geopolitical consequences of that move. These were consequences that existed quite apart from any display of U.S. force.

It is also possible to identify several shortcomings in the U.S. deterrent strategy that might have encouraged a calculating opponent to conclude that further aggression might still pay. First, the Bush administration was not completely clear why U.S. forces were being sent to the Persian Gulf. Defending Saudi Arabia was only one of several explanations put forward. Among the others were restoring the rulers of Kuwait, protecting American jobs, protecting the world order, dealing with Iraq's growing nuclear threat, and stopping a "mad dictator" who wanted to control "the economic well-being of every country in the world." Second, Saudi Arabia's resolve in the face of a possible Iraqi attack was in doubt at the very time the United States was searching for a military option. Should Saudi misgivings have been recognized by Iraq they could only have served to embolden it. These shortcomings may not have been crippling even if Saddam Hussein had been considering an invasion of Saudi Arabia. Studies show that secrecy does not have to be complete for strategic surprise to succeed (for example, Japan's attack on Pearl Harbor and Hitler's attack on the Soviet Union). The same may be true of deterrence. Credibility and capability gaps may arise but the overall policy may still succeed.

Compellence.   Where deterrence seeks to prevent an unwanted action from taking place, compellence seeks to reverse an unwanted situation. It does so using the same underlying logic as deterrence and with the same set of strategic requirements. A credible compellent force must be created and a willingness to use it must be communicated to the enemy. Once again, the enemy is assumed to base its actions on cost-benefit calculations arrived at in a rational manner. With the shift from Desert Shield to Desert Storm, the United States moved from deterrence to compellence. The goal now became bringing about an Iraqi withdrawal from Kuwait. Compellence failed. Iraqi forces did not leave Kuwait on their own accord but were forced out through military combat. As was the case with the deterrence failure, the root causes may have rested either with the concept of compellence or how it was implemented.

Where American policy makers had not thought it necessary to commit deterrence forces to the Middle East prior to Iraq's invasion of Kuwait, none quarreled with the need for a large compellence force. General Powell outlined these requirements in the days prior to the November 8 decision to move from Desert Shield to Desert Storm. The size of his request surprised many of those who heard it, but no one tried to reduce it. President Bush commented: "If that's what you need, we'll do it." The United States also went to great lengths to communicate its commitment. Diplomatic efforts by other states to bring about something less than a full withdrawal from Kuwait were resisted; UN authorization for the use of force was obtained; a clear deadline was established; and Congress had come on board with its December vote.

Why then did compellence fail? One possibility is that, as in the case of the deterrence failure, Saddam Hussein was not basing his decisions on the type of cost-benefit calculation that displays of force and commitment could influence. A second possibility is that he was engaged in the very type of cost-benefit calculation expected by compellence theorists but that he came up with the "wrong" answer. Instead of calculating that he would be defeated, Saddam Hussein may have concluded that Iraq could win. Stein identifies a series of miscalculations that he could have made: (1) the UN coalition would not hold together; (2) the United States would not use massive force because of domestic opposition; (3) air power would not eliminate the need for a bloody ground war; (4) the United States would not tolerate large numbers of American casualties; (5) Israel would retaliate if attacked, splitting the Arab world; and (6) even in military defeat there would be a political victory. All were plausible and represented concerns voiced by U.S. policy makers.[52]

SUMMARY

The cold war, Vietnam, and the Persian Gulf War show that learning from the past is not easily done. Not only are the events tremendously complex, but the question of learning from them hides a host of less visible preliminary questions: What is it about the event you wish to learn? What phase of the event are you concerned with? Whose views are you concerned with? What set of values are you going to bring to your analysis? In looking at Vietnam and the cold war, we have the luxury of time and distance from the event itself. This is not always the case, and when it is not, the task of learning from the past becomes even more complex. This comes through quite clearly in studying the Persian Gulf War. Whether near or distant, the past challenges us to learn from it. In the next chapters we examine how the traditional American approach to world politics, our domestic politics, and our political institutions complicate the task of learning lessons from the past.

NOTES

1. Richard K. Betts, *Surprise Attack, Lessons for Defense Planning* (Washington, D.C.: Brookings, 1982), p. 8.
2. Richard Ned Lebow, *Between Peace and War: The Nature of International Crisis Behavior* (Baltimore, Md.: Johns Hopkins University Press, 1981), p. 199.
3. Roberta Wohlstetter, *Pearl Harbor: Warning and Decision* (Stanford, Calif.: Stanford University Press, 1962), p. 70.
4. Ibid., p. 388.
5. On cognitive consistency and its application to world politics, see Robert Jervis, *Perception and Misperception in International Politics* (Princeton, N.J.: Princeton University Press, 1976); John D. Steinbruner, *The Cybernetic Theory of Decision: New Dimensions of Political Analysis* (Princeton, N.J.: Princeton University Press, 1974); and Lebow, *Between Peace and War.*
6. Ole Holsti, "The Belief System and National Images: A Case Study," *Journal of Conflict Resolution,* 6 (1972), 244–52.
7. *The Washington Post,* December 23, 1984, p. 11.
8. These points are discussed in George Quester, *Nuclear Diplomacy, The First Twenty-Five Years* (New York: Dunellen, 1970); and Michael Mandelbaum, *The Nuclear Question: The United States and Nuclear Weapons, 1946–1976* (New York: Cambridge University Press, 1979).
9. Jervis, *Perception and Misperception,* pp. 249–50.
10. Henry Kissinger, *The White House Years* (Boston: Little, Brown, 1979), p. 54.
11. Betts, *Surprise Attack,* p. 8.
12. Abraham Lowenthal, "The Dominican Intervention in Retrospect," *Public Policy,* 18 (1969), 133–48.
13. Betts, *Surprise Attack.*
14. John Lovell, "Lessons of U.S. Military Involvement: Preliminary Conceptualization," in Donald A. Sylvan and Steve Chan (eds.), *Foreign Policy Decision Making: Perception, Cognition, and Artificial Intelligence* (New York: Praeger, 1984).
15. Kennan's comments were made in testimony before the Senate Foreign Relations Committee. They are reported in *The Washington Post,* April 5, 1989.
16. Norman Graebner, "Cold War Origins and the Continuing Debate: A Review of the Literature," in Erik Hoffman and Frederick Fleron, Jr. (eds.), *The Conduct of Soviet Foreign Policy,* expanded 2nd ed. (New York: Aldine, 1980), p. 217.
17. See, for example, D. F. Flemming, *The Cold War and Its Origins, 1917–1950* (Garden City, N.Y.: Doubleday, 1961).
18. On this period see Adam Ulam, *Expansion and Coexistence, Soviet Foreign Policy, 1917–1973* (New York: Praeger, 1974); and John Lewis Gaddis, *Russia, the Soviet Union, and the United States, an Interpretive History* (New York: Wiley & Sons, 1978).

19. John Spanier, *American Foreign Policy Since World War II,* 9th ed. (New York: Holt, Rinehart & Winston, 1983), p. 16.

20. Gar Alperowitz, *Atomic Diplomacy, Hiroshima, and Potsdam* (New York: Viking, 1965), p. 229.

21. On the existence of multiple cold wars, see John Lewis Gaddis, "Containment: Its Past and Future," *International Security,* 5 (1981), 74–101.

22. For an orthodox perspective see Herbert Feis, *Between War and Peace: The Potsdam Conference* (Princeton, N.J.: Princeton University Press, 1960).

23. For a revisionist perspective see William A. Williams, *The Tragedy of American Diplomacy,* rev. ed. (New York: World, 1962).

24. Louis Halle, *The Cold War as History* (New York: Harper & Row, 1967), p. 2.

25. On the role of perceptions, see Uri Bronfenbrenner, "The Mirror Image in Soviet–American Relations," *Journal of Social Issues,* 17 (1961), 45–56.

26. John P. Lovell, *Foreign Policy in Perspective* (New York: Holt, Rinehart & Winston, 1970), p. 134.

27. Charles Learche, Jr., *The Cold War . . . and After* (Englewood Cliffs, N.J.: Prentice-Hall, 1965), Chap. 2.

28. See John Lewis Gaddis, "International Relations Theory and the End of the Cold War, *International Security,* 17 (1992/93), 5–58; Ted Hopf and John Lewis Gaddis, "Correspondence: Getting the End of the Cold War Wrong," *International Security,* 18 (1993), 202–15.

29. Beth Fischer, "Toeing the Hardline? The Reagan Administration and the Ending of the Cold War," *Political Science Quarterly,* 112 (1997), 477–96.

30. See Thomas Risse-Kappen, "Did 'Peace Through Strength' End the Cold War?" *International Security,* 16 (1991), 162–88.

31. Raymond L. Garthoff, "Looking Back: The Cold War in Retrospect," *The Brookings Review,* 12 (Summer 1994), 10–13.

32. Janice Gross Stein, "Political Learning by Doing: Gorbachev as Uncommitted Thinker and Motivated Learner," *International Organization,* 48 (1994), 155–83.

33. Thomas Risse-Kappen, "Ideas Do not Float Freely: Transnational Coalitions, Domestic Structures, and the End of the Cold War," *International Organization,* 48 (1994), 185–214.

34. Results of the public opinion poll are found in *The New York Times,* March 31, 1985, Sec. 6, p. 34. Reagan's comments can be found in the *Weekly Compilation of Presidential Documents,* 18 (February 18, 1982), p. 185.

35. John Stoessinger, *Why Nations Go to War,* 3rd ed. (New York: St. Martin's, 1982), p. 101.

36. *The Pentagon Papers* as published by *The New York Times* (New York: Quadrangle, 1971), p. 263.

37. David Halberstam, *The Best and the Brightest* (Greenwich, Conn.: Fawcett, 1972), p. 433.

38. On this point see Richard Barnett, *The Roots of War* (New York: Penguin, 1973), Chaps. 4 and 5.

39. Ernest May makes this point in his treatment of Vietnam in *"Lessons" of the Past: The Use and Misuse of History in American Foreign Policy* (New York: Oxford University Press, 1978).

40. Robert Gallucci, *Neither Peace nor Honor, the Politics of American Military Policy in Vietnam* (Baltimore, Md.: Johns Hopkins University Press, 1975), p. 33.

41. May, *"Lessons" of the Past,* p. 94.

42. Halberstam, *The Best and the Brightest,* p. 119.

43. May, *"Lessons" of the Past,* pp. 98–99.

44. Halberstam, *The Best and the Brightest,* p. 304.

45. Ibid., p. 212.

46. Ibid., p. 356.

47. Ibid., p. 643.

48. Ole Holsti and James N. Rosenau, "Vietnam, Consensus, and the Belief Systems of American Leaders," *World Politics,* 32 (1979), 1–56.

49. Material for this section is drawn from Michael Mazarr, Don M. Snider, and James A. Blackwell, Jr., *Desert Storm: The Gulf War and What We Learned* (Boulder, Colo.: Westview, 1993); Bob Woodward, *The Commanders* (New York: Simon & Schuster, 1991); and Janice Gross Stein,

"Deterrence and Compellence in the Gulf, 1990–91: A Failed or Impossible Task?" *International Security,* 17 (1992), 147–79.

50. The following perspectives are presented in Mazarr, Snider, and Blackwell, *Desert Storm,* 72–73.

51. Stein, "Deterrence and Compellence in the Gulf, 1990–91," 167.

52. Ibid., pp. 173–76.

6 The Domestic Context of American Foreign Policy

The end of the cold war did more than present American foreign policy with a new set of challenges and opportunities. It also has helped change the way in which foreign policy is made. Echoing what is now the conventional wisdom, one commentator observes:

> There is every indication of a new dynamic at work, one that redefines the relative roles of the public and leadership in the formulation of foreign policy, with the public assuming a larger role than some leaders may be comfortable with.[1]

The interplay of leaders and the public is of pivotal importance because a successful foreign policy must combine a well-crafted response to the challenges and opportunities of the international system with public support. Achieving public support is not always easily realized, and many questions surround how the public voice should be injected into the policy process. Should it come through the active participation of the public in making foreign policy decisions? If so, how should the public voice be expressed? Should it be through public opinion polls, elections, or interest group activity? Should it come early in the formulation of policy alternatives or only exist as a type of yes–no statement of support after policy makers have applied their expertise to the problem? Or should the public be largely passive, allowing policy makers a great deal of freedom of action in formulating foreign policy initiatives? James Billington argues the case for an active and involved public. "International affairs cannot be a spectator sport any more than policymaking can be the preserve of a small group of elites. Many must be involved; many more persuaded."[2] Walter Lippmann presents the opposite position.

> The people have imposed a veto upon the judgement of the informed and responsible officials. They have compelled the governments, which usually knew what would have been wiser, was necessary, or was more expedient, to be too late with too little, or too long with too much, too pacifist in peace and too bellicose in war, too neutralist or too appeasing in negotiation or too intransigent. Mass opinion . . . has shown itself to be a dangerous master of decisions when the stakes are life and death.[3]

In this chapter we examine the major avenues available to the public in exercising its voice on foreign policy matters: public opinion, elections, and interest group activity. We also discuss how policy makers view the public voice in making foreign policy decisions and the role of the media.

Before examining these avenues of influence, preliminary questions must be asked: Who is the public? How does one go about making distinctions among a population as diverse as that in the United States? The organizing principle found to be most helpful is the individual's level of awareness on foreign policy matters. Approached from this perspective, the American public is composed of four groups that have remained relatively consistent in size over time. Writing in 1950, Gabriel Almond broke the American public into three categories: a large mass public made up of 75 to 90 percent of the adult population which is largely disinterested in and unattentive to foreign affairs; a smaller, attentive public made up of 10 percent of the adult population which is informed and interested and listens to the ideas and policies put forward by the policy and opinion elite; and another group made up of 1 to 2 percent of the adult population which also includes the last group made up of the official policy leadership: legislators, bureaucrats, and office holders in the executive branch.[4]

In 1978 Barry Hughes outlined a quite similar profile of the American public.[5] First, he found a large group comprising 30 percent of the public which was unaware of all but the most significant international events. Members of this group had at best vague and weak opinions. Second, there existed a large group comprising 45 percent of the public which was aware of many major international events but was not deeply informed about them. Hughes characterized the remaining 25 percent as being generally knowledgeable about foreign issues and holding relatively firm convictions. He labeled this group the opinion holders. Within it he identified a smaller group of activists (1 to 2 percent) who served as opinion mobilizers for the other segments of the public.

Recent evidence suggests that this picture of the American public as being largely ill-informed and inattentive to foreign policy issues is somewhat out of focus. According to Catherine M. Kelleher "almost every general foreign policy survey . . . [now] shows that the American public is increasingly well-informed about global issues, devotes attention to evolving international events, and has opinions on most major foreign and defense policy questions."[6] This is not to say that the public necessarily favors the "correct" policy or the one best suited to protect American interests. But evidence does point to an American public that knows which policies it favors and which it opposes and that is consistent in its preferences.

THE MEDIA AND AMERICAN FOREIGN POLICY

Not unexpectedly, it is the mass media—especially television—that many commentators point to as a major reason for this change. It is only recently that television has emerged from the shadows of the print media to become a major force in the foreign policy process. As recently as the early 1980s there were no international television networks. There now are several global and regional news services.[7] The first transcontinental news broadcast in the United States took place in 1951 and it was only in 1954 that over 50 percent of American households reported owning a television set. It was only in the mid-1970s, with the launching of the Satcom I satellite, that 24-hour cable programming became possible in the continental United States. CNN first began transmitting via satellite to Japan in 1980, and CNN Europe started broadcasting in 1985. Its broadcasts are now available live in over 120 countries.

Consider how differently the October 1962 Cuban missile crisis might have been played out had it occurred in the 1990s.[8] Robert McNamara, President Kennedy's Secretary of Defense, observed, "I don't think that I turned on a television set during the whole two weeks of that crisis." During the 1990 Persian Gulf War, CNN was monitored regularly by government officials. Bush's Secretary of Defense Dick Cheney followed CNN in the period leading up to the air war for the first sign of leaks. CIA Director William Webster told National Security Adviser Brent Scowcroft to turn on CNN to find out where Iraqi missiles were landing. A similarly stark contrast exists among the viewing habits of the American people. In 1962 only 29 percent of Americans considered television news to be the most credible source of information, and the network evening news broadcasts on the major networks were only 15 minutes long and relied heavily on 16-millimeter black-and-white footage of international events that were at least a day old due to the need to develop, edit, and transport the film to the United States. By 1980, 51 percent of Americans found television news to be their most credible news source, and that same year CNN came on the air with its 24-hour news format.

During the Cuban missile crisis the Kennedy administration knew about the missiles in Cuba for six days before the information was broadcast to the American people. By contrast, President Bush was expected to respond almost instantly to Iraq's invasion of Kuwait and to pictures of starving people in Somalia. Today, it is not unreasonable to suspect that American television satellites might have discovered the presence of Russian missiles in Cuba at about the same time; that they would have run this story on *Nightline* or some other news program in which the pictures of Russian missiles were displayed along with recordings of Kennedy's September statement that there were no missiles in Cuba. Republican congressional leaders would have been invited to comment—and some would have demanded military action. Administration spokespeople would be inundated with questions about what they planned to do about the missiles and asked to explain how such a policy failure could have come about. Using military force was the option first embraced by the Kennedy administration, but it was abandoned as the week progressed in favor of the blockade. McNamara is uncertain that in such an altered decision-making environment the same decisions would have been reached.

To cope with the ability of the media to place administration foreign policy decisions under a telescope, it has become necessary for presidents to develop a television policy to accompany their foreign policy. The Bush administration succeeded in doing so during the Gulf War but failed with its Haitian, Bosnian, and Somalian policies, failures shared by the Clinton administration. In the former, the Bush administration was able to frame the policy issue in its own terms and control the media's coverage of it.[9] In the Gulf War a "pool system" was put in place which served to limit the scope and depth of media reporting (such as denying permission to go to a bombed Iraqi nuclear facility for security reasons). This allowed the administration to place its "spin" on unfolding events. The Pentagon also initiated a Hometown News Project which flew over 900 members of the press to Saudi Arabia to write stories about local servicepeople stationed in the Gulf. Not surprisingly, these human interest stories tended to be positive and served administration interests well.

Uncertain over how to proceed in Haiti, Bosnia, and Somalia, the Bush and Clinton administrations found the media far more troublesome.[10] Efforts to orchestrate coverage of Somalia failed. One Yugoslav commentator noted about coverage of the Balkans conflict, "confronted by the confusing new complexities of the post–cold war world, the world media had no clear guidance from their governments on how to view events." He continued, "in the absence of defined national interest, the U.S. media reported from the human side." The inability of U.S. administrations to respond to these images led to a chorus of congressional demands to "do something" and reinforced the view that American foreign policy had lost its sense of vision and competence. A similar failure to frame the issue on its own terms was evident on Haiti where the media gave extensive coverage to a hunger strike by Randall Robinson, executive director of TransAfrica, who was protesting Clinton administration policy.

Many in the media, responding to administration complaints that they are not fairly portraying American foreign policy or that they are hampering its conduct, make two points. First, very often administrations have developed television policies but not foreign policies. They are only showing the American public what is happening. If that does not correspond to declaratory statements of American foreign policy, it is not the media's fault. Second, the clearest way to limit the influence of the media is to enunciate a clear policy. The media's foreign policy influence is directly tied to the absence of a clear policy and the absence of contextual information to evaluate what they are seeing or reading about. Drawing upon his experience as a historian and CNN commentator, Michael Beschloss offers 16 lessons to future presidents as they make foreign policy in the television age. They are found in Table 6–1.

The influence of the media extends beyond that of serving as a catalyst and accelerator of the decision-making process in Washington. It also affects the diplomatic dialogue between states.[11] In 1962 it took six to eight hours for classified communications to go from Moscow to Washington. This time gap was a major concern as both sides sought to end the crisis. McNamara states that it was because of Khrushchev's interest in closing this gap that his message of October 28 was sent in the clear over Radio Moscow.

The pace and restricted nature of international communications also gave added weight to the intelligence reports and views put forward by government sources such as the KGB and defense ministry. Bush administration officials note that they tried to use television to communicate directly with Saddam Hussein and provide him with "the bad news" they felt his aides tried to hide from him. It could even be argued that under the glare of today's media coverage Khrushchev might not have tried to put Soviet missiles in Cuba, or that he might have proceeded differently. Only in places that the U.S. media "does not care about" might Khrushchev's strategy work today.

TABLE 6–1   Media Lessons for Modern-Day Presidents

1. Television offers presidents a superior weapon for framing issues and selling policy in crisis.
2. Television also amplifies public opposition; most presidents forget it, but this can improve and strengthen policy.
3. Television can encourage presidents to favor crisis management over long-term planning.
4. Television can drastically reduce the time, secrecy, and calm available to a president for deliberating with advisers on an urgent foreign policy problem.
5. Presidents cannot presume that they can maintain a monopoly on information for long.
6. Television allows presidents to communicate with adversary leaders and populations.
7. Television can seriously affect relations with allies.
8. LBJ's notion that Vietnam was lost on television is questionable.
9. Nonetheless, experience suggests that it is in a president's interest to design U.S. military ventures to be as brief and telegenic as possible.
10. Presidents shouldn't be obsessed in public over hostages.
11. Unexpected events shown on television can have inordinate influence on the public's perception of a foreign crisis.
12. When appearing on television during a crisis, a president and his high officials must be absolutely honest with the public.
13. Censorship can risk a damaging backlash.
14. During the use of force, there is no such thing as too much military success.
15. Television can help create an unexpected agenda, especially during the run-up or endgame of a war.
16. Presidents who fail to craft an implicit or explicit television strategy while dealing with a foreign crisis do so at their own peril.

Source: Hearings, Committee on Foreign Affairs, House of Representatives, 103rd Congress, April 26, 1994 (Washington, D.C.: U.S. Government Printing Office, 1994), pp. 52–53.

The media has had a similar impact on the relationship between diplomats and battlefield commanders and their respective superiors in Washington. During the Cuban missile crisis a great deal of concern was expressed that military action might be initiated in Cuba against the wishes of Khrushchev and that once begun their effect would be difficult to assess. The modern media and its associated technologies provides a direct link between decision makers in Washington and events abroad. The American media offered policy makers and citizens live broadcasts of incoming SCUD missiles and the Patriot antimissile defense system in operation. CNN provided live accounts of the effect of American bombing of Baghdad. It was not reports from the American embassy in Moscow that persuaded Bush that Yeltsin would survive the 1991 coup attempt but television images of him sitting atop a tank addressing his supporters.

That the American media does not care equally about all areas of the world or types of international relations problems is seen as a major source of bias in its impact on American foreign policy. Coverage decisions are based on three factors: "sizzle," parochial self-interest, and cost. Sizzle refers to a story's ability to stir emotions. It directs the media's attention to short-run, highly visual events and away from long-term stories which cannot be captured readily on film. Coups, civil war, demonstrations, and earthquakes are more visual and hence more likely to hold the audience's attention than are stories about grain production, trade in semiconductors, international debt, or rural development projects. But even graphic pictures are not enough to guarantee coverage. Footage of widespread famine in Ethiopia was first rejected by American television networks because it was not visual enough. When finally run, it was the last item on the national news broadcast for the evening.

Parochial self-interest deals with the perceived American stake in an issue. Typically, this is seen as involving areas where the United States has historically had close economic or cultural ties (Latin America, Israel, Western Europe) or where American troops are stationed (Korea, Vietnam). In other instances, parochial self-interest is largely defined by the White House. Presidential travel, presidential policy statements, and presidential agreements serve to drive the media's definition of what is important. The U.S. media is not unique in this regard. The French media tend to do a more thorough job covering Northern Africa and Francophone Africa than do the U.S. or British media. For its part, the British provides better coverage of events in the old British commonwealth than do the other two media.

Cost considerations have always played a prominent role in decisions about international news coverage. One of the first challenges facing Ted Turner in setting up CNN was making it cost-effective. To hold down costs, CNN developed exchange agreements with other states that would be conducted over satellites. For the same reason it decided to go with a newswire format that emphasized live programming and to go live with breaking stories wherever possible. The initial costs were estimated at about $15 to $22 million per year. At this time, ABC, CBS, and NBC were spending $110 to $150 million per year on news. These costs became prohibitive in the late 1980s as the new owners of these networks began to look to the news divisions as sources of revenue rather than as sources of prestige. By 1991 CBS had closed bureaus in Hong Kong, Rome, and Frankfurt, leaving it with nine. NBC had ten and CBS seven. The consequence was felt almost immediately. In 1992 they covered less international news than in any of the previous three years, and the number of long pieces they presented was also down from earlier years.

The Media and the Gulf War

One of the most hotly debated aspects of television's coverage of foreign policy is the role it plays in shaping public opinion. Is it a window that policy makers can use to judge the temper of public opinion on a policy issue, a device that policy makers can use to manipulate public attitudes, an instrument that the politically active can use to pressure policy makers, or a little bit of each? A particularly revealing case is the role that the media played shaping and sustaining public support for the Persian Gulf War.

American public opinion about the wisdom of using military force against Iraq underwent several abrupt shifts during the period between the August 1990 Iraqi invasion of Kuwait and the conclusion of hostilities in July 1991. Initially, the American public was sharply divided on the issue, with support for the war hovering around the 50 percent mark until President Bush's January 16, 1991, speech announcing the beginning of the bombing campaign. Support then shot up to 72 percent. Support surged again in February, this time to a high of 80 percent, when Bush announced the beginning of the ground war, and it remained high for the remainder of the conflict. One explanation for this pattern is the "rally-around-the-flag" argument, which pictures the public as being very responsive to cues from policy makers and as predisposed to support the president in times of international crisis. Looked at from this perspective, the media becomes little more than a transmission belt for the exchange of one-sided supportive messages.

While not denying the impact of the rally-around-the-flag effect in the first surge in public support for the war, Barbara Allen and her colleagues assert that a much more complex picture emerges if the entire crisis is examined.[12] They center their analysis on a "spiral of silence" hypothesis. According to it, when individuals hold opinions that they do not hear voiced by others they exercise self-censorship as a way of protecting themselves from criticism. The opposite reaction takes place among those who receive positive reinforcement for their views. They become even more vocal and confident in their beliefs, leading the dissenters to exercise even more self-censorship. The media plays a key role in this process by the way in which it frames issues through the use of symbols and causes individuals to access and use particular attitudes in evaluating an issue.

In the case of the Gulf War, where the media in its selection of stories portrayed a growing American consensus in favor of military action, actual polling data pointed to the existence of an American public that was closely divided on the question at the start of the conflict. The networks all but ignored antiwar stories. Of 2,855 minutes of network news coverage of the war between August 8 and January 3, only 29 minutes showed popular opposition to the American military buildup. Once military activities designed to liberate Kuwait began, network stories on opinion in the United States were framed in terms of patriotism, militarism, and nationalism. Film clips of war protesters were paired with scenes of Americans praying in churches. The views of congresspeople opposing the war were defined as "atypical" and the media declared that "of course, the political leaders are falling in behind the President."

Reporting from the Middle East also served to further the spiral of silence by its heavy reliance on such military jargon as "collateral damage," "smart bombs," and "decapitate the leadership and command and control facilities." Not only did this language frame the war effort in reassuring and antiseptic terms, but it was language that few Americans were familiar with, making it necessary for them to rely on the 38 "expert" commentators employed by the networks. The authors of this study conclude that "the continuous, repetitious, redundant, and unbalanced nature of media coverage contributed to the framing and priming of the war, reinforcing the potential for a spiral of silence to operate once the initial rally phenomenon dissipated."

PUBLIC OPINION

Public opinion polls provide a first avenue open to the public for expressing its views on foreign policy. But interpreting public opinion polls is complicated by a number of factors, foremost among which is the public's sensitivity to the phrasing of a question. This is illustrated by the polling results presented in Table 6–2. It presents responses to four questions about the desirability of foreign aid. Note how for both years the pro-aid and anti-aid positions change dramatically with changes in the wording of the question. In 1964 one question produced 52 percent in favor of foreign aid; the second produced 59 percent opposed to it. In 1966 the change is even more pronounced with the insertion of a reference to Vietnam. The more neutrally worded question shows 53 percent in favor of foreign aid. The emotionally loaded question shows 75 percent opposed to it.

The same sensitivity to wording is evident in questions about support of President Bush's decision to use force against Iraq.[13] Table 6–3 presents four different questions, all asked between November 14 and 18, 1990. The first question, asked by *ABC News/Washington Post*, produced the highest level of support for using force (65 percent). The other three questions produce far less support for the use of force, with the last question showing only 28 percent in favor of doing so. But notice that the question is worded quite differently. Where the

TABLE 6–2   **Public Attitudes on Foreign Aid**

Question	Opinion Distributions (In Percent)		
	Pro-Aid	Anti-Aid	No Opinion, Other
(1964) Should we give aid to other countries if they need help?	52	19	29
(1966) In general, how do you feel about foreign aid—are you for it or against it?	53	35	12
(1964) And now, what about economic aid to foreign countries? Do you think government spending for this purpose should be kept at least at the present level, or reduced or ended altogether?	32	59	9
(1966) Suppose another country—which is receiving aid from the United States—fails to support the United States in a major foreign policy decision, such as Vietnam. Do you think the United States should continue giving aid to that country, reduce aid, or cut off aid completely?	16	75	9

Source: Robert S. Erickson, Norman R. Luttbeg, and Kent L. Tedin, *American Public Opinion: Its Origins, Content, and Impact,* 2nd ed. (New York: John Wiley, 1980), p. 43. © 1980 John Wiley.

TABLE 6-3   Asking about Going to War

1. *ABC News/Washington Post,* November 14–15, 1990: Do you agree or disagree that the United States should take all action necessary, including the use of military force, to make sure that Iraq withdraws its forces from Kuwait?

Agree, Use Force	Disagree	Don't Know	N
65	26	8	(515)

2. *Gallup,* November 15–16, 1990: Now that the U.S. (United States) forces have been sent to Saudi Arabia and other areas of the Middle East, do you think they should engage in combat if . . . Iraq refuses to leave Kuwait and restore its former government?

Engage in Combat	Do Not Engage in Combat	Don't Know	N
46	40	14	(754)

3. *Los Angeles Times,* November 14, 1990: Overall, taking into consideration everything you heard or read about the Mideast crisis, do you think the United States should go to war against Iraq, or not?

Go to War	Do Not Go to War	Don't Know	N
38	53	9	(1,031)

4. *Gallup,* November 15–18, 1990: All in all, which of these courses of action do you agree with:

"The U.S. should keep troops, planes and ships in and around Saudi Arabia as long as is necessary to prevent Iraq from invading Saudi Arabia, but without initiating a war."

"The U.S. should initiate a war against Iraq in order to drive Iraq out of Kuwait and bring the situation to a close."

Initiate War	No War	Don't Know	N
28	65	7	(1,018)

Source: John Mueller, "The Polls—A Review," *Public Opinion Quarterly,* 57 (1993), 86–87. ©1993 University of Chicago.

ABC News/Washington Post question only asked if the respondent agreed or disagreed with the United States taking "all action necessary, including the use of military force, to make sure that Iraq withdraws its forces from Kuwait," the Gallup question ends by asking about whether "the United States should initiate a war against Iraq."

Trends and Content

Given these types of problems, analysts conclude that when taken out of context, answers to foreign policy questions seldom provide an accurate reading of public opinion. Far more valuable is trend analysis where responses to questions are traced over time for their content and stability. Approached this way, public opinion polls have captured several clearly identifiable changes in the structure of American public opinion about foreign affairs issues. The pivotal event for the first change was World War II. Public opinion polls prior to World War II suggested a strongly isolationist outlook. In 1939 70 percent of opinion holders said that the American entry into World War I was a mistake, and 94 percent of those with opinions felt that the United States should "do everything possible to stay out of foreign wars" rather than try to prevent one. The outbreak of fighting in Europe had little impact on U.S. attitudes. Public support for war against Germany only rose from 13 percent to 32 percent between late 1939 and late 1941.[14] Following the attack on Pearl Harbor, this situation changed dramatically. Internationalist sentiment came to dominate public perceptions about the proper U.S. role in the world. Between 1949 and 1969, 60 to 80 percent of the American public consistently favored an active U.S. participation in world affairs.[15]

Prior to Vietnam virtually all internationalists were in fundamental agreement on the nature of the international system and the makeup of U.S. foreign policy. Ole Holsti and James Rosenau suggest that eight axioms, or universally recognized truths, made up the foundation of this consensus. They were:

1. The United States has both the responsibility and capabilities to be actively involved in undertakings to create a just and stable world order.

2. Peace and security are indivisible.

3. The primary threat to a stable world order stems from Soviet or Soviet-sponsored efforts to alter the status quo by force.

4. Containment, rather than rollback or preventive war (or a retreat into isolation), represents the most effective means for meeting the challenge of Soviet expansion.

5. The United States should not only join but take a lead in creating peacetime alliances.

6. The United States should be actively involved in a broad range of international organizations.

7. Liberalization of foreign trade is necessary to avoid destructive trade wars that will damage all nations, while also contributing to political instability.

8. Foreign aid programs, both economic and military, are not only an obligation for the richest nation but also a hardheaded expression of the national interest.[16]

Foreign policy based on these axioms could expect to receive the support of the American people. When disagreements arose, they tended to be over the process of making foreign policy rather than over its substance.

Vietnam was the next pivotal event shaping the direction of public attitudes. Lloyd Free and William Watts have traced the shifting fortunes of internationalism from the time of the U.S. involvement in Vietnam.[17] Beginning with 1964 data, they have classified responses to public opinion polls along an internationalist–isolationist continuum. Their findings from 1964 to 1980 are presented in Table 6–4. What emerges from their study is a steady and precipitous erosion of internationalist sentiment from 1964 to 1974 and its reemergence as the majority perspective in 1980. In 1964, 65 percent of the public was defined as internationalist. This fell to 59 percent in 1968, 56 percent in 1972, and 41 percent in 1974. That year also saw a dramatic increase in the number of isolationist responses from 9 percent in 1972 to 21 percent. While isolationist sentiment would build to a high of 23 percent in 1976, 1974 was the low point for internationalism. Those supporting an active U.S. role rose in number to 61 percent in 1980. By that time isolationist sentiment had fallen back to 13 percent. No single, pivotal event seems to be associated with this rebirth of internationalism, although the 1972–1973 oil crisis is closely linked with it in terms of time. Instead, the American public gradually came to see the international system as threatening and out of control and had a renewed willingness to use U.S. power and influence to protect U.S. national interests.

What type of impact has the end of the cold war had on American public opinion? Many had speculated that because only an event as traumatic as Vietnam could shatter the cold war consensus, it would require an event of equal magnitude to unify the American public around a new set of principles. Was the end of the cold war such an event? Yes and no. The answer depends on what it is that you are concerned with: views on specific issues or the underlying structure of attitudes among the American public.

There is no doubting the fact that the end of the cold war has changed the way in which Americans look at the world.[18] Where in 1980 a public opinion poll found 84 percent of those surveyed citing the Soviet Union as a threat to American security, in 1990, the American public rated the Soviet Union fourth in favorability on a "feeling thermometer." Other polls showed that between 1990 and 1993 the percentage of Americans seeing Russia as threatening fell from 32 percent to 8 percent, and that in 1990 Russia fell out of the "top ten" security threats to the United States when four years earlier it had been ranked number one.

Even more pronounced have been changes in Americans' self-image and the types of foreign policy problems they worry most about. The 1990 poll showed that increasingly Americans were defining national security in economic terms. Two-thirds of those polled felt the United States could no longer solve its own economic problems. Japan had emerged in the public's mind as a more serious threat than Russia. By 1994 this had changed. The public's sense of economic vulnerability had diminished as had feelings of intimidation by Japan and Europe.[19] By mid-decade the biggest foreign policy problems the public sees as facing the United States, according to the Chicago Council on

TABLE 6–4   The Changing Fortunes of Internationalism

	1964	1968	1972	1974	1976	1980
Total Internationalist	65%	59%	56%	41%	44%	61%
Mixed	27%	32%	35%	38%	33%	26%
Total Isolationist	8%	9%	9%	21%	23%	13%

Source: Lloyd Free and William Watts, "Internationalism Comes of Age . . . Again," Public Opinion, 3 (1980). Reprinted with permission of American Enterprise Institute.

Foreign Relations, were stopping the flow of illegal drugs (85 percent), protecting jobs (83 percent), stopping the spread of nuclear weapons (82 percent), and dealing with immigration (72 percent). The poll found that support for humanitarian operations among both the public and American leaders was at a two-decade low. There was a 33-point drop in the public's willingness to protect weaker states against foreign aggression, a 24-point drop in its willingness to defend human rights, and a 19-point drop in its interest in promoting third world development. For all of this, the poll did not find most Americans to be isolationist. Almost two-thirds of the public and almost all of the leaders surveyed expected America to continue to play an active role in world politics. Looking ten years into the future, the public identified nuclear proliferation, immigration; terrorism, and economic competition from Japan as the leading problems facing the United States. Table 6–5 presents a comparison of public and leader responses to questions regarding the makeup of current and future threats to U.S. interests.

TABLE 6–5   How the Public and Leaders Rate Foreign Policy Problems

Problem	Public	Leaders
1994		
Stopping the flow of illegal drugs into the United States	89%	57%
Protecting the jobs of American workers	83%	50%
Preventing the spread of nuclear weapons	82%	90%
Controlling and reducing illegal immigration	72%	28%
Securing adequate supplies of energy	62%	67%
Reducing our trade deficit with foreign countries	59%	49%
Improving the global environment	58%	49%
Combating world hunger	56%	41%
2004		
The possibility of unfriendly countries becoming nuclear powers	72%	61%
Large numbers of immigrants and refugees coming into the United States	72%	31%
International terrorism	69%	33%
Economic competition from Japan	62%	21%
The development of China as a world power	57%	46%
The possible expansion of Islamic fundamentalism	33%	39%
The military power of Russia	32%	16%
Economic competition from Europe	27%	11%

Source: John E. Rielly, "The Public Mood at Mid-Decade," *Foreign Policy,* 82 (1995), adapted from tables on pages 82 and 87. Reprinted with permission from *Foreign Policy,* 98 (Spring 1995). Copyright 1995 by the Carnegie Endowment for International Peace.

The end of the cold war does not seem to have had as great an impact on changing the underlying structure of foreign policy attitudes. A 1992 study conducted by Ole Holsti found that it continued to be possible to place American opinion leaders into one of four categories that were developed by Eugene Wittkopf in the mid-1980s.[20] They are hard-liners, accommodationists, internationalists, and isolationists. Holsti's study found little support among opinion leaders for a return to across-the-board isolationism as the cornerstone of American foreign policy. Only 9 percent of respondents were classified in this manner. 53 percent were accommoaationists, 33 percent internationalists, and 9 percent hard-liners. Even more important than the distribution of opinion leaders across categories is that knowing where individuals fit continues to allow one to predict with great confidence their positions on issues involving the use of force, strengthening the United Nations, and the nature of future security threats facing the United States. One important policy area which does not fit into the framework (that is, one could not make accurate predictions about a respondent's policy position) is trade and protectionism.

Public Opinion and the Use of Force

Of particular interest to policy makers is divining how much public support they can expect to obtain for using military force in places such as Bosnia, Haiti, Somalia, the Persian Gulf, and Korea. The Chicago Poll found that the public was skeptical about using force to protect American allies.[21] Only 39 percent favored using force to protect South Korea from an attack by North Korea, while only 42 percent favored coming to the aid of Israel should it be attacked by Arab states. Important gender and race distinctions were found on questions regarding the use of force. By as much as 20 percentage points, men were more likely to favor the use of force than women. Whites were more willing than nonwhites to use force to defend Western Europe, South Korea, Saudi Arabia, and Israel. The only hypothetical conflict situation in which nonwhites were more willing to use force was in a South African civil war.

Another recent study suggests that the answer can be readily calculated because the public is not moody or volatile in how it views foreign events but reacts in a predictable fashion depending upon the specific characteristics of the undertaking. According to Bruce Jentleson the key determining factor is the principal foreign policy objective that the use of force is designed to achieve.[22] Based on his study of nine cases when the United States used military force in the 1980s, Jentleson argues that the American public is most likely to use military force when the purpose is to restrain the foreign policy actions of a hostile state and least likely to do so when the purpose is to bring about internal political change. A summary of his findings is presented in Table 6–6. This shows that all five uses of force which involved attempts to curb the foreign policy activities of another state ranked higher than any effort to use military force to bring about internal political change. Public support for the war against Iraq bears out Jentleson's argument. Support was highest for Operation Desert Shield and Operation Desert Storm, which were designed primarily to curb Iraqi foreign policy adventurism by defending Saudi Arabia and liberating Kuwait. The American public was distinctly less interested in using American military power to protect the Kurds or Shi'ites in southern Iraq after President Bush announced the ceasefire. A similar pattern of public support emerged in 1999 for NATO's bombing in Kosovo to stop Serb aggression. Miroslav Nincic also finds consistency in the public's outlook on foreign policy involvement.[23] In his study, he examines public perceptions of the domestic costs of foreign policy activism. He finds that the more serious the domestic problems relative to the external challenge the more powerful will be the public's isolationist impulse. Thus, the weaker the economy the less support a president is likely to find for an activist foreign policy.

Impact

The question of how much influence opinion has on American foreign policy can be answered two ways. One can look (1) to the type of impact it has and (2) to the conditions necessary for it to be heard. Public opinion can have three types of impact on the policy process and the nature of American foreign policy. It can serve as a constraint on policy innovation, a source of policy innovation, and a resource to be drawn upon by policy makers in implementing policy. Public opinion acts as a constraint by defining the limits to what is politically feasible. As we have just seen, many regard the existence of unstable moods as a powerful constraint on U.S. foreign policy. A case can also be made that the existence of too firm an outlook or too rigid a division of opinion is just as much a constraint. The deeply entrenched isolationist outlook of the American public during the 30s made it extremely difficult for Roosevelt to prepare the United States for World War II. A firm but divided opinion is cited by one major study as responsible for the prolonged U.S. presence in Vietnam.[24] Faced

TABLE 6–6   **Policy Objectives and Public Support**

Case	Principal Policy Objective	Public Support Score (re-ranking)*
Libya: antiterrorism	FPR	1
Persian Gulf reflagging	FPR	2
Lebanon	Mixed	3
Afghanistan	Mixed	4
Nicaragua: military exercises	FPR	5
Panama (preinvasion)	IPC	6
El Salvador	IPC	7
Libya: get Qaddafi	IPC	8
Nicaragua: overthrow Sandinistas	IPC	9

*Re-ranking excludes halo-effect cases

FPR = foreign policy restraint

IPC = internal political change

Source: Bruce W. Jentleson, "The Pretty Prudent Public," *International Studies Quarterly,* 36 (1990), 64.

by a damned-if-they-do-and-damned-if-they-don't dilemma, successive administrations are seen as having followed a strategy of perseverance until a public consensus developed for either a strategy of victory or withdrawal.

Observers are in general agreement that public opinion rarely serves as a stimulus to policy innovation. One commentator argues that "no major foreign policy decision in the U.S. has been made in response to a spontaneous public demand."[25] While this may be the case, public opinion today does appear to be capable of placing new items on the political agenda. The nuclear freeze movement demonstrates both the potential and the limitations of public opinion as a source of policy innovation. Springing spontaneously from the American public in winter 1982, the nuclear freeze movement did not produce a major breakthrough in arms control policy. It did, however, give renewed life to the arms control process which had stalled in the Reagan administration's first term. As an aide to Senator Edward Kennedy noted, Kennedy's legislative leadership on nuclear freeze matters was not a case of his mobilizing public opinion in opposition to Reagan's policies but one of Kennedy's trying to "catch up with the country."[26]

Four factors have been identified as playing a key role in determining how much influence public opinion will have on American foreign policy.[27] First, at least 50 percent of the American public must share the opinion. According to Thomas W. Graham, when 79 percent of the American public is of one mind the influence of public opinion will be nearly automatic. At 60 percent it should be enough to overcome strong bureaucratic opposition. Second, public opinion's influence is greatest if exercised at the agenda-building stage and ratification stages of the policy process. It will be indirect at best in the negotiation and implementation stages. Third, political elites must be open to public opinion and understand what they are being told. Historically, this inability to comprehend public opinion has been the primary determinant limiting its impact on policy. The final limiting factor is the ability (or, more commonly, inability) of political leaders to structure their policy positions in ways that allow them to turn existing public attitudes into a political resource.

ELECTIONS

Almost invariably, the winning candidate in an election cites the results as a mandate for his or her policy program. Yet is this really the case? Do elections serve as a mechanism for translating the public voice into policy? The evidence suggests that claims of popular mandates are overstated and are based on a flawed reading of election returns. A look back at the Lyndon Johnson–Barry Goldwater election of 1964 and the 1968 Democratic New Hampshire primary shows just how deceptive electoral outcomes can be. In each case Vietnam was the major issue. In 1964 Johnson won a landslide victory over Goldwater, who had campaigned on a platform of winning the war against communism in Vietnam "by any means necessary." The results were commonly interpreted as a mandate for restraint in the war effort. National surveys, however, revealed a far more complex picture: 82 percent of those who wanted to maintain the U.S. presence in Vietnam supported Johnson over Goldwater, as did 63 percent of those who favored withdrawal and 52 percent of those who favored a stronger stand such as invading North Vietnam.[28] In 1968 Eugene McCarthy "upset" Johnson in the New Hampshire primary even though Johnson received more votes than he did (49 to 41 percent). McCarthy's strong performance was widely interpreted as a repudiation of Johnson's handling of the war and an endorsement of McCarthy's dovish position. Analysis reveals that in terms of overall numbers, McCarthy received more votes from dissatisfied hawks than from doves. Quite simply, it often becomes difficult to tell whether people voted for candidates out of support for their policy stance or in spite of it.[29]

For elections to confer a mandate upon the winner, three demands are made of the voter:

1. Voters must be knowledgeable about the issues.
2. Voters must cast their ballots on the basis of their issue preferences.
3. Voters must be able to distinguish between parties or candidates.

Voter Knowledge and Issue Voting

Evidence on the first point is not encouraging. The large majority of citizens lack both a knowledge of foreign affairs and an interest in them. The lack of widespread public understanding about foreign affairs issues never ceases to amaze commentators. In 1996, Republican Presidential candidate Robert Dole sought to make President Clinton's refusal to build an antimissile system an issue in the campaign. It failed to catch on because many voters refused to believe the United States did not already have one. A participant in a focus group, when told no missile shield existed stated: "I don't believe you, you couldn't pay me enough to believe you . . . you see it in the movies." Other examples are equally telling:

1964: 38 percent know that Russia was not a member of NATO.

1964: 58 percent know that the United States was a member of NATO.

1966: Over 80 percent fail to properly identify the Vietcong.

1972: 63 percent could identify China as communist.

1979: 23 percent knew which countries were involved in the SALT talks.

1983: 8 percent knew that the United States supported the government in El Salvador and the insurgents in Nicaragua.

1987: Following the Reagan–Gorbachev summit in Washington, only 50 percent of the public correctly answered one or more of five questions regarding the basic provisions of the INF treaty.

1993: 43 percent could not identify which continent Somalia was on.[30]

Do candidates win because of their policy preferences or in spite of them? Much evidence supports the view that voters do not respond to issues when casting their ballots. Instead, they are heavily influenced by party affiliation, candidate image, incumbency, or some other nonissue factor. There are indications that this generalization may no longer be as true as it once was, but problems still remain. Historically, foreign policy has not been considered a good issue on which to base a campaign. In the 1956 and 1960 elections, foreign policy issues produced a ½ percent change in voting behavior from one election to the next. Voters polled in 1976 cited domestic issues over foreign policy ones by a 12-to-1 margin when questioned about which issues had the greatest impact on their vote.[31] The 1992 election presents somewhat of a mixed picture. On the surface it supports the notion that foreign policy issues do not sway voters. By a margin of 57–36 percent Americans felt that George Bush would do a better job handling American foreign policy than Bill Clinton but did not return him to office. Yet the influence of foreign policy issues cannot be completely dismissed. In 1992 the nine most widely cited issues by voters were domestic, and most voters chose Clinton when asked which presidential candidate was most likely to protect American jobs from foreign competition.

Charles Whalen, a six-term Republican from Ohio who retired in 1980, sees the sporadic interest and low information level of constituents on foreign policy matters as a point of vulnerability to incumbents.[32] Challengers attempt to create an image of having policy differences with the incumbent and to cast the incumbent in a negative light. They find a powerful weapon in foreign affairs voting records. These issues are often complex and when taken out of context can place the incumbent on the defensive and greatly increase the cost and uncertainty of a reelection campaign.

Morris Udall and Paul Findley are two prominent politicians who encountered electoral problems because of their vote on the Young Amendment to the FY1980 Foreign Aid Appropriations Bill. The original legislation would have barred any direct bilateral aid to Angola, Cambodia, the Central African Empire, Cuba, Laos, and Vietnam. During the floor debate Representative C. W. Young introduced an amendment to insert the phrase *or indirectly* to the sentence barring aid to those states. Indirect aid is channeled through international organizations such as the World Bank and the United Nations Development Program. The administration objected to these restrictions. While it had no intention of giving aid to any of these states, the Young Amendment would have had some serious negative side effects. It would have politicized these institutions, violated their charters (they cannot accept funds if limitations are placed on their use), and hurt the U.S. economy. For every $1.00 the United States contributes to the World Bank, $9.50 is returned to the U.S. economy by way of purchases and interest payments. Both Udall and Findley voted no on the Young Amendment, which passed the House by a vote of 281 to 117. Each then faced election campaign charges that they were in favor of aid for communist states.

Party and Candidate Differences

The third prerequisite for elections to serve as a mandate is that voters must be able to distinguish between party and candidate positions. Compared to their European counterparts, American political parties do not offer voters a clear and consistent choice. They are neither ideologically distinct nor internally cohesive. The essential sameness of the two parties is reinforced by bipartisanship and the nature of political campaigning in the United States. The objective of bipartisanship is to create a foreign policy consensus that will provide continuity and consistency for U.S. policy. The more bipartisanship succeeds, the less choice parties and candidates offer voters. Bipartisanship surfaced during the administration of Franklin Roosevelt and continued into the Eisenhower years. Throughout this period the general desire for a foreign policy consensus was reinforced by practical political considerations. These presidents needed the cooperation of the "opposition party" in order to get their foreign policy programs through Congress. As with so much else, Vietnam shattered bipartisan support for foreign policy to the point where the party's foreign policy stance has become a point of intraparty controversy.

Election campaigns generally find the two major parties on the same side of an issue. Both are for peace, opposed to corruption, and for a stronger defense. In 1980 both Carter and Reagan favored increasing U.S. military capabilities. In 1960 both Kennedy and Nixon presented themselves as being for a strong defense. In 1964 neither Johnson nor Goldwater advocated getting out of Vietnam, while in 1968 both Humphrey and Nixon did. Both Reagan and Walter Mondale claimed to be for peace, for a strong defense, and for arms control. The 1992 election found Clinton and Bush in general agreement on cutbacks in defense spending, NAFTA, and the conduct of the Persian Gulf War. Perhaps just as telling from the point of view of a voter trying to decide between two candidates is the fact that in two areas where Clinton did disagree with Bush and promised change—U.S. foreign policy toward Haiti and Bosnia—none was forthcoming after the election. William Schneider argues that candidates stress issues that find most people on the same side of the argument out of the need to form and hold together broad electoral coalitions. Issues where candidates may truly advocate competing policy positions are best suited to primary campaigns where the candidate is trying to stand out apart from other competitors. General elections thus turn out to be less a debate on the issues and more a contest in who the public feels is best capable of achieving the same goals.[33] This came through with great clarity in the 1984 and 1988 elections when public opinion polls repeatedly found that the electorate did not perceive either Mondale or Michael Dukakis as a strong leader.

Impact

What then is the impact of elections on U.S. foreign policy? Elections do serve to change leaders and thereby alter policies. They do not, however, appear capable of providing policy makers with a foreign affairs mandate. The preconditions for such a role go largely, although not entirely, unmet. Thus, while policies may change as the result of an election, the correspondence between this change and public attitudes is often tenuous. Many observers see one significant impact of elections on foreign policy that exists quite apart from its ability or inability to confer a mandate. "Foreign governments have long understood the difficulty of doing business with the U.S. in election years."[34] Foreign policy initiatives come to a halt as all sides await the outcome of the election, and U.S. foreign policy takes on a nationalistic and militant character. For example, in May 1988 the Senate by a vote of 83–6 voted to give the military a major new role in the war on drugs. In doing so the Senate was described as lining up in the election-year crusade against illegal drugs and critics were quoted as condemning the measure as election-year "posturing."[35] Candidates attempting to read the climate of opinion sense a general lack of interest in foreign policy initiatives. It is politically safer to restrict oneself to pledges of maintaining U.S. prestige and military strength than to advocate specific courses of action. Foreign policy initiatives always run the risk of failure and even in success can bring with them charges of having paid too high a price or of having let allies off too easily.

William Quandt believes that the influence of American elections on foreign policy extends well beyond the presidential election year.[36] He sees an electoral cycle existing that influences noncrisis foreign policy decisions during a president's entire term in office. The first year in office generally is characterized by policy experimentation, false starts, and overly zealous goals. This is due to the continued influence of overly simplistic campaign rhetoric that comes about because presidents are forced to take positions on issues before they have mastered the intricacies of managing the presidency. Instinctively, they return to the themes that served them so well during the campaign. During the second year in office pragmatism becomes more evident. This is due both to the increased knowledge and skill of the administration and the realization that a foreign policy mishap may lead to the loss of House and Senate seats in the mid-term election. In the third year Quandt suggests that foreign policy issues will largely be evaluated in terms of their impact on the reelection campaign. Potential successes will be pursued vigorously even if the price tag is high, while the administration will try and disengage itself from potential losses. As noted above, the final year brings stalemate to the foreign policy process. The most propitious time for foreign policy undertakings is the first year and one-half of a second term. Here one finds an experienced president who knows what he wants to do in foreign affairs operating under the halo effect of a reelection victory. By late in the second year of a president's second term, electoral considerations begin to overwhelm foreign policy as jockeying begins in both parties for their respective presidential nominations. At some point the president will come to be regarded at home and abroad as a "lame duck," which limits his or her ability to conduct foreign policy.

INTEREST GROUPS

The third avenue open to the public for expressing its outlook on foreign policy issues is interest group activity. Here the public communicates to policy makers through an intermediary rather than directly, as with public opinion and elections. To its advocates the interest group approach holds several advantages over the real or perceived limitations of the more direct mechanisms for expressing opinions about foreign policy. First, the informational demands on individuals are lessened. They need not stay up-to-date in their knowledge of foreign policy matters because they can rely on group leaders to look after their interests. Second, interest groups provide a more continuous and concrete form of input than do periodic elections and occasional public opinion polls. Third, this input brings with it more political clout than does the individual expression of an opinion or the anonymous act of voting.

Critics of the interest group approach raise two major, but quite different, objections to the utility of pressure group lobbying as a means of influencing policy. The first objection is that interest groups have little influence over foreign policy decision making. Two reasons are commonly given. Ineffective interest group activity is held to stem from the division of opinion within interest groups, the existence of competing interest groups within a policy area, and the very nature of lobbying. The first problem typically has plagued large business groups such as the Chamber of Commerce. Divisions within their ranks over the merits of protectionist legislation and restrictions on trade with communist states make it difficult for these groups to adopt a single policy position. The second problem is that interest groups and lobbyists typically are found on both sides of an issue. It was not the case that all interest groups opposed the SALT II treaty. Protreaty groups (the Federation of American Scientists and the Council for a Livable World) competed with those opposed to it (the Committee for the Present Danger and the Coalition for a Democratic Majority).

Two major lobbying campaigns in the first half of the Clinton administration illustrate these points. The first involved the successful effort of a united business community to get Clinton to reverse his campaign promise to tie most favored nation (MFN) status for China to improvements in its human rights record. Almost 800 major companies and trade associations wrote to Clinton calling on him to grant China unconditional MFN status, citing the loss of billions of dollars in business and tens of thousands of U.S. jobs. Only a handful of companies joined human rights groups in protesting the administration's decision to extend China's MFN status. The second lobbying campaign was fought over ratification of the North American Free Trade Agreement (NAFTA). It confirmed the challenges that interest groups face in affecting policy when they are divided over what that policy should look like. Among those lined up for NAFTA were AG for NAFTA (a coalition of 175 agricultural groups), the World Wildlife Fund, the National Wildlife Federation, the National Association of Manufacturers, the U.S. Chamber of Commerce, and Chase Manhattan Bank. Unsuccessful in their opposition to NAFTA were the AFL-CIO and the Sierra Club.

The second major objection to interest group activity is the reverse of the first. Interest group activity is too successful—but only for some. The resources needed for success (money, organizational infrastructure, leadership, access) are unevenly distributed. Instead of competition among groups to determine policy outcomes, there exists the permanent domination of a select group of interests against all the rest. "Iron triangles" are created in which interest groups, congressional committees, and bureaucrats are linked together, short-circuiting the open access of the policy process to domestic influences.

The most powerful statement of this point of view is expressed in the idea of a military industrial complex.[37] At the core of this argument is the assertion that there exists within U.S. policy-making circles a dominant force consisting of professional soldiers, industrialists, and government officials. Acting in unison, they determine policy on defense-related matters. The resulting policies are based on an ideology of international conflict which requires high levels of military spending, a large defense establishment, and a belligerent, interventionist foreign policy.

The idea of a military industrial complex is relatively recent in origin. The term was coined by C. Wright Mills in 1956 and given high visibility by President Eisenhower in his farewell address when he warned against its unwarranted influence and the dangers of misplaced power.[38] In the 1960s it became a major theme in writings of those who opposed the U.S. involvement in Vietnam. Concerns about its influence waned in the 1970s with the shift in emphasis from confrontation and containment to détente. Reagan's March 1983 "Star Wars" speech challenging the scientific community to develop a defense system that would make nuclear weapons "impotent and obsolete" has led to renewed interest in the idea of a military industrial complex. The Council on Economic Priorities estimated that in 1984 5,000 scientists, engineers, and technicians worked on SDI and that by 1987 this number would reach 10,600. In FY1985 the Defense Department's Strategic Defense Initiative Organization awarded 1,000 contracts with a value of over $1 billion to more than 260 companies and research laboratories. The largest share was awarded to Teledyne Brown ($237.1 million), followed by Boeing ($211.8), Rockwell International ($204.4), McDonnell Douglas ($199.0), Lockheed ($195.8), and TRW ($186.8).

The end of the cold war has not brought about an end to the military industrial complex although it has led to a series of mergers among defense contractors. One of the most significant is the consolidation of Lockheed and Martin Marietta into a single firm. Not only is it now the world's largest defense company, but as Figure 6–1 reveals, it may also be the most politically powerful because of how its workforce is distributed. In 1995 the five states with the most

FIGURE 6–1   Spreading the Work: Where Lockheed-Martin Jobs Would Be Concentrated.

Source: The Washington Post, December 6, 1994, from Martin Marietta Corp. © 1994 *The Washington Post.* Reprinted with permission.

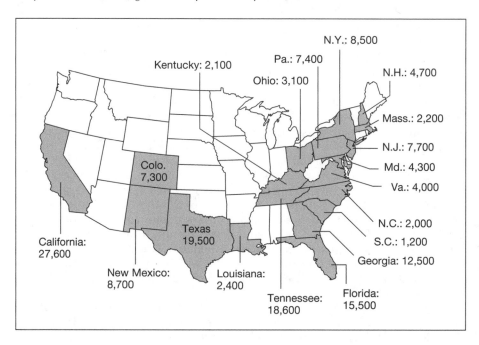

Lockheed-Martin Marietta workers were California (27,600), Texas (19,500), Tennessee (18,600), Florida (15,500), and Georgia (12,500). Another sign that the military industrial complex still exists is the Clinton administration's decision to help promote American arms makers at overseas trade shows. In February 1994 the Clinton administration spent approximately $575,000 to underwrite American firms at a Singapore show. The Pentagon sent 75 military personnel (including the commander of Pacific air forces and the Pacific fleet commander), 20 top-of-the-line fighters, and 13 different types of aircraft. Secretary of Defense Les Aspin stated that this type of participation by the Pentagon was "in the national security interests of the United States" and that "a strong U.S. presence at this event will demonstrate our commitment to the area."[39]

Efforts to establish the validity of assertions about the influence of the military industrial complex on U.S. foreign policy have produced mixed results. General agreement exists on the presence of a military industrial complex, but there is disagreement on how to interpret its influence. One observer suggests that the competing judgments can be reconciled if we make a distinction between the major political decisions, which set into motion high rates of defense spending, and the legislative and administrative decisions, which translate them into concrete programs.[40] The influence of the military industrial complex is greatest in the second area and far less in the first where it faces strong competition from ideological, economic, and other nonmilitary influences.

Types of Groups

A wide variety of groups are active in attempting to influence foreign policy decisions. Among the most prominent are business (Chamber of Commerce, National Association of Manufacturers), labor (AFL-CIO), agriculture (American Farm Bureau Federation), ideological-public interest groups (Heritage Foundation, Institute for Foreign Policy Studies), ethnic groups, and foreign governments and corporations. Here we limit our discussion to the last two interest groups we mentioned.[41]

Ethnic Groups. The most successful ethnic lobbies have relied on three ingredients to give them political clout: the threat of switching allegiances at election time either from one party to another or to another candidate in the same party, a strong and effective lobbying apparatus, and the ability to build their case around traditional American symbols and ideals.[42]

Currently, the Jewish-American lobby possesses the most formidable combination of these elements. The centerpiece of the Jewish lobbying effort for Israel is the highly organized, efficient, and well-financed American–Israel Public Affairs Committee (AIPAC), which serves as an umbrella organization for pro-Israeli groups. It "promptly and unfailingly provides all members [of Congress] with data and documentation, supplemented, as circumstances dictate, with telephone calls and personal visits on those issues touching upon Israeli national interests."[43] The successes of the Jewish lobby have been many. Beginning with the Truman administration's recognition of Israel in 1947 and later on matters of foreign aid and arms sales, successive administrations have privately acknowledged or publicly confronted its power.

While officially AIPAC does not endorse candidates and only provides voters with information about candidates' voting records and policy positions, evidence suggests that in the 1980s AIPAC became a much more active force in American electoral politics. During the 1986 election campaign it was estimated that 80 pro-Israeli PACs donated nearly $7 million to candidates. A 1986 memo that was obtained by *The Washington Post* from AIPAC to other pro-Israeli lobbies urged them to make donations to five specific Senate candidates that it wished to see reelected. In 1984 Senator Rudy Boschwitz, who chaired the Senate Foreign Relations Subcommittee on the Middle East, received more than one-third of the $4.25 million that pro-Israeli PACs gave to congressional candidates. Incumbents have also felt the wrath of AIPAC. Opponents of Representative Paul Finley, Senator Charles Percy, and Senator Jesse Helms all received hearty backing from pro-Israeli forces. (In Finley's case, 90 percent of his opponent's funds came from Jewish sources.) Finley and Percy were defeated and Helms became a strong supporter of Israel following his hard-fought reelection victory.

No Arab-American lobbying force equal to AIPAC has yet emerged, although steps in that direction are under way.[44] In 1972 a central organization, the National Association of Arab Americans (NAAA), was founded, and in the mid-80s it had field coordinators in every congressional district and a membership of some 100,000 Arab-American families. Also, in 1984 Arab-Americans were the top-ranked ethnic group in supplying volunteer workers to the Reagan-Bush campaign. Still, NAAA lags far behind AIPAC in political clout. In 1984, it founded a political action committee and provided $20,000 in campaign funding to 22 Democratic and 24 Republican candidates. This compares to the $2.8 million in funding provided by some 76 pro-Israeli political action committees. A major obstacle in the way of creating an effective Arab lobbying force is the ethnic diversity of Arab-Americans. Until 1948 most Arabs coming to the United States were Christians from Syria and Lebanon. Since 1978 most have been Muslims. The result is that no single political agenda exists for Arab-Americans. A consensus exists only on the broad issues of pursuing a comprehensive peace plan in the Middle East and establishing better U.S. relations with the Arab world. Of special concern in this regard are U.S. foreign aid and arms sales policies.

Blacks and Hispanics are frequently cited as potentially the next ethnic groups to be in a position of exerting major influence on U.S. foreign policy. In the mid-1970s both groups still had far to go in acquiring the necessary prerequisites for becoming a successful lobby. Neither group had yet demonstrated that African or Latin American affairs were of such importance to black and Hispanic Americans that they could sway votes. Similarly, there were few indications of African or Latin American interest in cultivating ties with their American counterparts for the purpose of establishing a strong lobbying presence. Black and Hispanic lobbying efforts were mainly directed at domestic rather than foreign issues. The great diversity of conditions in Africa and Latin America made it difficult to build sustained support for a policy program or to phrase arguments in terms of exporting American symbols and ideals. This last task is far easier to accomplish when the target is small in size or homogeneous in makeup such as Israel, Greece, Taiwan, or Eastern Europe.

By the mid-1980s black Americans had made great strides toward meeting two of the three prerequisites we listed. First, as the Reverend Jesse Jackson's 1984 bid for the presidency made clear, blacks make up an important constituency within the Democratic party. Second, an organizational base, TransAfrica, now exists. Founded in 1977, TransAfrica now has over 10,000 members and an annual budget of over $1.4 million. The major focus of black lobbying in the mid-1980s has been on reorienting U.S. policy toward South Africa. And while this effort has shown some success, an even greater challenge may lie ahead for black foreign policy lobbying. From now on, one commentator suggests, "the principal challenge before Blacks will be to influence U.S. policy toward the issues beyond Africa."[45] The change in perspective is necessary because of the continued Eurocentric focus of U.S. foreign policy.

In addressing this challenge one commentator has put forward a possible African-American lobbying agenda for the new world order. Recognizing that it will take time for African-Americans to formulate a well-defined vision of the future, Milton Morris argues that they should give special attention to three areas.[46] First is promoting economic policies that promise to improve U.S. competitiveness. This is important because agreements such as NAFTA may eliminate many low-wage jobs which historically have been held by African-American workers. Second is promoting policies that direct America's attention away from Europe. He suggests that African-Americans might especially look to the Caribbean as an area where natural bonds exist. Finally, Morris calls for a lobbying effort to revitalize the United Nations. This is important because African-Americans have been more skeptical about the benefits of using force than the rest of the American public. The United Nations represents an alternative to the use of force by the United States as a means of international conflict resolution.

Hispanic Americans have made fewer strides in establishing themselves as a lobbying force.[47] Ethnic diversity remains a problem. Mexican immigration has been motivated largely by economic considerations, is concentrated in the Southwest, and is largely Democratic. (In 1980 Carter got 72 percent of this vote.) Cuban immigration is concentrated on the East Coast, has been motivated largely by political concerns, and is politically conservative and Republican. (Reagan got 59 percent of Florida's Hispanic vote.) To this one must also add Puerto Ricans, who are concentrated largely in the Midwest and Northeast and who vote Democratic.

The most successful Hispanic lobby is the Cuban-American National Foundation.[48] Led by Jorge Mas Canosa, it vehemently opposes any change in American policy toward Cuba and has been charged with intimidating and harassing those members of the Cuban-American community in Florida who wish to open a dialogue with Castro. Former Reagan administration UN Ambassador Jeane Kirkpatrick and Florida Senators Bob Graham and Connie Mack have served on commissions that the foundation has established. Its Free Cuba Political Action Committee (PAC) made $114,000 in campaign contributions in the 1989–1990 elections. In mid-1992 it had contributed to 26 congressional candidates and "maxed out" on its contribution to Representative Robert Torricelli, who represents a large Cuban-American community in New Jersey and authored the 1992 Cuban Democracy Act. Passed by Congress in an election year and endorsed by both Bush and Clinton in an effort to gain the support of the Cuban-American community, this piece of legislation has been derided by its critics as an "economic declaration of war" against Castro and a violation of international free trade agreements. The act prohibits foreign affiliates of U.S. firms from doing business in Cuba. Jorge Mas Canosa flexed his muscles again in 1994. Over the objections of more moderate forces in the Cuban-American community, he succeeded in getting the Clinton administration to change its policy and prohibit Cuban-Americans from wiring money to relatives still in Cuba and end family reunification flights. The conservative leader hoped that doing so would bring further economic hardships to Cuba and speed Castro's departure from power. In 1995 an investigation by the United States Information Agency into the operation of its Radio Marti broadcasts into Cuba uncovered further evidence of Jorge Mas Canosa's influence on U.S. foreign policy.[49] It found that he had caused the station deliberately to misreport the content of U.S. policy toward Cuba and that in doing so he had seriously undermined U.S. immigration initiatives. The dynamics of Cuban-American lobbying changed dramatically in 1998 with Pope John Paul II's visit to Cuba and the death of Jorge Mas Canosa. Senator Jesse Helms, for example, endorsed a plan supported by anti-Castro forces that would leave the U.S. trade embargo in place but channel increased humanitarian aid through the Catholic Church and other nongovernmental organizations.

While ethnic groups have long been active in trying to influence U.S. foreign policy toward their homelands, the end of the cold war and the accompanying decline in influence of traditional foreign policy elites have ushered in a new era of activism and heightened influence. The 1996 senatorial race in South Dakota saw a battle in which the Democratic candidate raised over $150,000 from Pakistani-American groups while the Republican candidate (who authored legislation cutting U.S. foreign aid to Pakistan) raised approximately the same amount from Indian-American sources. Yossi Shain sees the leverage that these groups are gaining as presenting them with new challenges. Many ethnic diasporas are being galvanized into action by struggles for self-determination and democracy in their homelands.[50] If independence is realized without democracy, agonizing choices face these groups. Do they side with an oppressive government or support opposition forces? If they side with a nondemocratic regime, they risk undermining their standing in the American political system.

Foreign Lobbying.   Foreign lobbying has become big business in Washington. In 1990, with his capital under attack by rebel forces and the United States lukewarm in its support for him, Liberian President Samuel Doe paid a Washington lobbyist $800,000 to improve his image. One of the main objectives of Nelson Mandela's 1990 trip to the United States was to lobby Congress and mobilize public support for continued economic sanctions against South Africa. In 1993 Libya hired Abraham Stofaer to represent its interests in Washington. Stofaer had served in the State Department between 1985 and 1990 and was one of those who put together the 1986 economic sanctions directed at Libya for its role in the terrorist attack on Pan Am Flight 103, which exploded over Lockerbie, Scotland, killing 270 people. In 1988 alone, 152 Japanese firms and government agencies contracted with 113 Washington lobbying firms. And they were not alone. Canada had 61 organizations working on its behalf; Great Britain had 44. All told, there are now some 8,000 foreign agents registered with the Justice Department.[51] A virtual *Who's Who* of Washington "in-and-outers" and ex-legislators can be found in the employment of foreign concerns. Included among them are Walter Mondale, J. William Fulbright, Elliot Richardson, William Colby, Paul Warnke, and some 18 former senior presidential aides, 6 ex-senators, 10 ex-congressmen, and 4 retired top-level military officers. Clients include the governments of Saudi Arabia, South Africa, Indonesia, Haiti, and Nicaragua (under Anastasio Somoza). Corporations retaining the services of lobbyists include Zambian mining and metal companies, the United American Sugar Council, European Aerospace Corporation, and the Australian Meat and Livestock Corporation. Taiwan has been particularly active in cultivating ties with U.S. officials over the past several years. Defeated Republican presidential candidate Robert Dole registered as an agent for Taiwan with a $30,000 per month retainer. In 1996 at least 20 members of Congress and 124 congressional staffers took free trips to Taiwan at a cost in excess of $500,000. Among those who made this trip were the chairperson of the Republican Policy Committee and the ranking Democratic member of the Ways and Means Committee.

The most common concerns of foreign governments are foreign aid legislation and arms sales. The typical plan of attack involves two steps. First, one must secure the support of the executive branch. The Carter administration's reluctance to deal with oppressive third world governments often required lobbyists to work hard in supporting Defense Department and State Department bureaus favoring such ties. The second step is to lobby Congress. The goal here is to prevent resolutions of disapproval or amendments that would block the transfer of aid or weapons. The effort involved is often considerable. Charles Goodell, a former Republican senator and representative from New York, reported having a total of 253 meetings, lunches, and phone calls in his successful lobbying effort to get approval for a Moroccan arms sales package.

The primary concern of foreign firms is their ability to conduct business in the United States. Accordingly, their lobbying activities are directed at all levels of the American political system. Of particular concern at state and local levels are taxation, zoning, and labor laws. SONY threatened not to go ahead with plans to build new plants in California and Florida unless those states repealed that portion of the state tax code that would have taxed their earnings based on worldwide sales rather than just on what was produced within the state. Both states succumbed to the foreign lobbying campaign. The most intense and successful foreign lobbying campaign to date is that conducted by Toshiba in 1987–1988. In July 1987 the Senate, angered at the news that Toshiba had illegally sold sensitive technology to the Soviet Union, voted to ban it from the U.S. market, a move that would cost Toshiba $10 billion per year. By May 1988 that legislation had been amended so that Toshiba only lost its U.S. government contracts (which were valued at $100 million annually) for a period of three years. In the intervening months Toshiba unleashed what Senator Jake Garn labeled the most intense lobbying campaign he had seen in his 14 years in Washington. The total cost has been placed at over $9 million dollars. One Washington,

D.C. law firm alone was paid $4.3 million for its services. The message sent out by the lobbyists was that punishing Toshiba would cost 100,000 American jobs. Moreover, U.S. electronic firms such as AT&T and IBM argued that their products would suffer if they could not get Toshiba parts. The Reagan administration also voiced opposition to the measure, saying it was counterproductive to its efforts to get Japan to limit its sales of technology to the Soviet bloc. A last point on this case is worth noting: Because Toshiba America is considered a U.S. corporation, its lobbyists were not required to register as foreign agents.

Impact

Establishing the influence of an interest group on a specific policy is difficult. More is required than revealing the presence of group activity. A concrete link must be established between the group's actions and the actions taken by those who were influenced. "Koreagate," the influence-peddling activities of South Korean businessman Tongsun Park, made headlines and led to House and Senate investigations in 1978. Significant breaches in law and ethics were uncovered, but no policy change or votes were found tied to his efforts. "Foreign Money" also became a major issue after the 1996 presidential campaign, with evidence being produced that the Democratic National Committee illegally received funds from a network of Asian sources in Indonesia, Taiwan, Korea, Vietnam, and China.

Success is also not an all-or-nothing condition, and this further complicates the problem of establishing influence. Consider three examples.[52] The first involves the activities of the Eastern European ethnic lobby. Its actions never led to the stated goal of the Assembly of Captive European Nations: freedom and full independence for those states. Did their efforts therefore fail? Not necessarily. In the early 1960s their obstructionist tactics prevented Johnson from "building bridges" to Eastern Europe. They successfully lobbied to delay extending most favored nation (MFN) status to Yugoslavia, to organize boycotts of Eastern European products, and to cancel a 1964 contract between Firestone and Romania.

The second example involves the Jewish lobby and its efforts on behalf of the Jackson–Vanik Amendment. At the time, passage of this amendment was viewed as a major success and a show of strength. It is now seen by many as a hollow victory that brought with it ruinous costs. The Jackson–Vanik Amendment made freedom to emigrate from the Soviet Union a prerequisite for the granting of MFN status to Soviet goods. It did not have its intended impact. The amendment strained détente and embroiled the emigration issue in the larger context of rising U.S.–Soviet competition. Human rights remained largely an illusion within the Soviet Union, and emigration quickly became more difficult. From its high of 35,000 in 1973, emigration fell to a low of 13,000 in 1975. It would then climb up again with the signing of SALT II, only to fall once more with the Soviet invasion of Afghanistan.

The third example involves the strategy followed by defense industry political action committees (PACs) in distributing money to election campaigns. A 1980 review of the reports of 10 defense industry PACs, all of whom were among the top 20 military contractors and relied on government contracts for at least 25 percent of their sales, revealed the following. Of the nine PACs that contributed to the 1980 presidential election, all gave money to the Carter campaign, and seven also gave to the Reagan campaign. In the primaries Grumman Aerospace gave at least $2,000 to seven candidates. It also contributed to the 1980 New York senatorial campaigns of all three major candidates. Why this hedging of bets? One lobbyist gave this answer: "If they don't win this time, they may be back later. Money's not going to buy anyone, but you get their attention and you get the door open."

POLICY MAKER RESPONSE

Policy makers do not tend to share the view that the public voice on foreign policy is an important influence on policy—or that it should be. The prevailing view among policy makers holds that foreign policy is too important to be left to the uninformed and unstable flow of public perceptions of world affairs. It should be made by that small group of public officials who are informed about international problems. Public attitudes are something to be formed and shaped by the policy makers rather than followed by them. On one level of activity, this perspective takes the form of a preoccupation with educating the public. On another level it takes the form of a manipulative attitude toward public perceptions. In either case the objective is to secure the widest possible area of freedom for the policy maker to practice his or her craft.

This attitude (often associated with the realist school of thought on international relations) is very much in evidence in each of the avenues we identified as open to the public for influencing policy. In elections it takes the form of claiming mandates where none may exist. Policy makers respond to interest group pressure either by playing groups against one another or by attempting to manipulate perceptions of group self-interest. In the case of public opinion, it appears in the tendency to discount it. Elected policy makers define leadership as the process of getting all the necessary facts required for making a decision, making that decision, and then getting the public to follow. Professionals see their job as one of applying their expertise to a problem and not one of listening to the public. The State Department presents a clear example of this attitude.[53] Its Bureau of Public Affairs gradually changed from an office concerned with measuring public opinion to a public relations bureau.

The tendency of policy makers to discount the positive contribution of the public voice to foreign policy making also shows up in where they look to uncover the public voice. Our discussion has stressed public opinion polls, election results, and interest group activity. State Department officials emphasize public attitudes as interpreted by personal contacts, other institutions, and the working press. Especially important for the State Department is the view Congress has of public opinion. As one State Department official observed, "If a given viewpoint different from our own does not have congressional expression, forget it."[54] The inevitable result of this perspective is to narrow greatly the range of public attitudes taken into account in making policy.

An Example: U.S. Policy toward El Salvador

The Reagan administration's handling of intelligence on El Salvador illustrates both the range of ways in which policy makers can attempt to lead the public and the difficulties of doing so in an era that lacks a foreign policy consensus.[55] The Reagan administration entered office determined to change the course of U.S. foreign policy toward Central America from one emphasizing human rights violations to one centered on the growing communist threat in the region. El Salvador became the first test case for this policy reversal. The first effort to set the language of the national security debate came in 1981 with the preparation of a State Department White Paper that stated that documents considered to be authoritative indicated that in late 1980 the Soviet Union and Cuba had agreed to deliver tons of weapons to the Marxist-led guerrillas in El Salvador. In his public comments Secretary of State Alexander Haig echoed this theme by remarking about the unprecedented risk taking by the Soviet Union in support of revolutionary groups and defining El Salvador as a test case for relations with U.S. allies and the Soviet Union.

The White Paper did not have the desired result; instead of producing unity, it only sparked controversy. On March 6, *The New York Times* columnist Flora Lewis reported on the existence of a 29-page dissent paper drawn up in November 1980 by the National Security Council, the State Department, the Defense Department, and CIA personnel. The paper's major contention was that U.S. involvement in El Salvador would spread to other states and that intelligence reports contradicting the U.S. justification for increased involvement were being suppressed. In June *The Washington Post* and *The Wall Street Journal* published articles criticizing the White Paper for questionable translations and misidentifying authorship on various articles. Most serious was the questioning of the Soviet Union's role in supporting the guerrillas. Critics argued that the evidence did not support Haig's charge of "unprecedented risk taking." U.S. officials then acknowledged that the administration had "overreached" the evidence in blaming the Soviet Union, but they defended the correctness of the main conclusions of the White Paper: Cuba and Nicaragua did give aid to El Salvadoran guerrillas in November and December 1980.

Large sectors of the public remained unconvinced, and as the March 1982 El Salvadoran elections approached, the decision was made to try once again to mobilize public support for the administration's policy. As part of this effort, Reagan agreed to make public some classified intelligence reports. Citing reports not made public, Haig told the House Foreign Affairs Committee that evidence of foreign control over the Salvadoran guerrillas was "overwhelming and unrefutable," and Director of Central Intelligence William Casey outlined Nicaraguan support for Salvadoran rebels to the Senate Intelligence Committee. These statements were followed by the announcement that a Nicaraguan rebel leader (who had since escaped) had been captured in El Salvador, proving the administration's contention of foreign control. Later, the State Department held a press conference in which a second alleged Nicaraguan rebel leader operating in El Salvador was presented for questioning. Much to the embarrassment of State Department officials, the Nicaraguan recanted his story.

A few days before this press conference and after a long internal debate, the Reagan administration decided to release intelligence photos in an effort to substantiate Haig's charges. The photos showed (1) new military bases constructed along Cuban designs, (2) tanks and armored personnel carriers identified as Soviet types, (3) four airfields being enlarged to the point that they could receive heavy military aircraft, and (4) leveled Miskito Indian villages reportedly in preparation for a thrust into Honduras. The Nicaraguans countered that the buildup was exclusively defensive and that the airport extensions had been recommended by the United States and begun under the old Somoza regime. Again the administration's effort failed. Most problematic for the administration was the fact that the photos could not establish intentions or that El Salvadoran forces were being controlled from the outside. Such intelligence reportedly was available through electronic intercepts, but the CIA objected to making them public.

When the administration's focus shifted to Nicaragua, so too did its efforts to mold public perceptions. As revealed in the Iran–Contra investigations, the Reagan administration set up a special unit under the direction of the National Security Council that was staffed by CIA experts and Army psychological warfare specialists whose job it was to manipulate U.S. public opinion. One of its tasks was to prepare daily summaries of exploitable information, highlight areas of concern, and suggest themes for use in speeches and in the media. For example, after a public opinion poll found that many Americans feared an influx of refugees, Reagan made a speech in which he stated that only by crushing leftist movements could such a "tidal wave" of "feet-people" be stopped from "swarming into our country."

SUMMARY AND FUTURE ISSUES

In order to respond to the public's voice, policy makers must first know what is being said. Our discussion of public opinion, elections, and interest groups shows that the public's voice does get through but that it does so imperfectly. Problems exist in measuring it, in the mechanisms by which it is transmitted, and in the manipulative attitudes policy makers have toward it. Where does this leave us? Billington's vision of active public involvement is far from being realized, yet Lippmann's fears have not been borne out. The public remains on the fringes of the policy process but with a demonstrated capacity for injecting itself into that process when policy makers fail to address its concerns (nuclear freeze, South Africa) or when it believes that policy makers have betrayed its trust (the Iranian hostage crisis, the Iran–Contra affair).

What can we say of the future? We can expect the impact of public attitudes to vary from issue area to issue area. This is the case today, and there is no reason to expect it to change. The public's influence is the greatest today on issues where economic and security concerns are present and when the decision time is long. As these conditions are removed, the public's influence progressively lessens.[56] Table 6–7 presents in overview form the issues on which we might currently expect public opinion, elections, competitive interest groups,

TABLE 6–7   Identification of Issues Where Societal Influences Exert Influence on Nature of U.S. Foreign Policy

ECONOMIC CONSIDERATIONS IMPORTANT			
Security Issue		Nonsecurity Issue	
Decision Time Long	Decision Time Short	Decision Time Long	Decision Time Short
Public opinion/ Elections/ Competitive interest groups	Public opinion/ Elections/ Domineering interest groups	Competitive interest groups	

ECONOMIC CONSIDERATIONS RELATIVELY UNIMPORTANT			
Security Issue		Nonsecurity Issue	
Decision Time Long	Decision Time Short	Decision Time Long	Decision Time Short
Domineering interest groups	Domineering interest groups	Competitive interest groups	

Source: Adapted with permission from Barry Hughes, *The Domestic Context of American Foreign Policy* (San Francisco: Freeman, 1978), p. 225. Copyright 1978 W. H. Freeman and Company.

and domineering interest groups to have their greatest impact. Note that in some instances more than one of these avenues for exercising the public voice appears to be open while in others they all appear to be closed.

The divided public voice may also affect how foreign policy decisions are arrived at and implemented. Bold and self-contained foreign policy initiatives that allow the president to control the flow of information, such as the Reykjavik summit, the invasion of Grenada, air attacks on Libya, and the invasion of Panama, have been viewed quite favorably by the public regardless of the actual merits of the policy initiative or its concrete accomplishments. In contrast, the longer the issue remains in the public's eye and the less able the president is to control the information flow, as was the case with the Iranian hostage crisis and the Iran–Contra scandal, the more critical the public's assessment of the president's performance becomes. It is not unrealistic to expect that presidents will be tempted to seek out opportunities for the former and avoid the latter.

We might also expect to see changes in the way in which political elites interact with the public in order to gain their support for policy initiatives. As Daniel Yankelovich and John Immerwahr note:

In the past foreign policy leaders may have been reluctant to go to the trouble of engaging the public in complex foreign policy issues. But they never doubted their ability to do so. Yet the sad truth is that the foreign policy community has little or no idea how to go about engaging the public under these new post–cold war conditions.[57]

Uncertainty over the role of the media in making foreign policy is a major contributing factor to this confusion over how to engage the public. Take for example Somalia. Most commentators cite it as a textbook case of the media driving foreign policy decisions.[58] First, images of starving infants pushed the Bush administration to take action, and then images of a dead American soldier being dragged through the streets compelled the Clinton administration to leave. Jonathan Mermin paints a more complex picture.[59] He argues that for the most part the media only "discovered" Somalia after it had already become a major concern for key policy makers in Washington. Furthermore, the media followed the lead of policy makers in how they framed the story. None of this lessens the media's ability to influence American foreign policy, but it does point to a two-way flow of influence between the media and policy makers and the reality of collaboration as well as conflict.

One indication that much of the standard wisdom is no longer relevant (if it ever was) comes from a study of foreign policy and presidential popularity.[60] Particularly interesting was the finding that presidential "drama" (speeches, travel, forceful actions) if properly carried out can produce a short-term increase in public support for a president but that there are no guarantees attached. Increased support can be expected to follow from a prime time speech or sending large numbers of U.S. forces into a region of major concern to Americans. However, sending U.S. forces to regions that the American public does not consider important and presidential travel are not likely to improve a president's rating with the public and may even hurt it. Consistent with other recent studies, the public is seen as informed and willing to hold presidents accountable for the way in which international events unfold. Rather than advocating a plan of going to the public only after a policy has been agreed upon by elites, Yankelovich and Immerwahr call for a strategy in which leaders work to affect the public's position as it makes the passage from "raw opinion to public judgment." At the outset this means alerting the public to the existence of a problem and then convincing the public of its urgency. Later it means helping the public move from unstable and instinctive responses to making choices. At the end of the engagement process, elites must work to get the public to accept the decision and the commitments that come with it.

Finally, if some observers are correct, we may even see fundamental changes in the way in which American politics are conducted in the future because the cold war has ended. More may be involved than restructuring the federal budget, reorganizing departments, or finding new themes around which Democratic and Republic party candidates can campaign. The cold war "made it necessary and possible for the United States to build a strong state, manage an industrial economy, reduce social inequalities, and foster national cohesion."[61] Without this glue that served both to hold political institutions together and promote social unity, some fear that the United States may return to the political and social stalemate of the 1920s and 1930s. Averting this fate, they argue, will require (1) the forging of a new social bargain and (2) discovering new ways for presidents to use and harness political power.

NOTES

1. Daniel Sharp, "Preamble," in Daniel Yankelovich and I. M. Destler (eds.), *Beyond the Beltway: Engaging the Public in U.S. Foreign Policy* (New York: Norton, 1994), p. 13.
2. James Billington, "Realism and Vision in Foreign Policy," *Foreign Affairs*, 65 (1987), 630.
3. Walter Lippmann, quoted in Amos Jordan and William J. Taylor, Jr., *American National Security Policy and Process* (Baltimore, Md.: Johns Hopkins University Press, 1981), p. 43.
4. Gabriel Almond, *The American People and Foreign Policy* (New York: Praeger, 1961).
5. Barry Hughes, *The Domestic Context of American Foreign Policy* (San Francisco: Freeman, 1978), pp. 23–24.
6. Catherine M. Kelleher, "U.S. Public Opinion on the Use of Force," *The Brookings Review*, 12 (Spring 1994), 26–29.
7. Lewis A. Friedland, *Covering the World: International Television News* (New York: Twentieth Century Fund, 1992).
8. See prepared statement by Michael R. Beschloss, "Impact of Television on U.S. Foreign Policy," *Hearing before the Committee on Foreign Affairs, House of Representatives*, 103rd Congress, 2nd session, April 26, 1994.
9. Trevor Thrall, "The Gulf in Reporting the Gulf War," *Breakthroughs*, 2 (1992), 9–13.
10. Jacqueline Sharkey, "When Pictures Drive Foreign Policy," *American Journalism Review*, 15 (December 1993), 14–19.
11. Timothy J. McNulty, "Television's Impact on Executive Decisionmaking and Diplomacy," *Fletcher Forum*, 17 (Winter 1993), 67–83.
12. Barbara Allen, Paula O'Loughlin, Amy Jasperson, and John L. Sullivan, "The Media and the Gulf War: Framing, Priming, and the Spiral of Silence," *Polity*, 37 (1994), 255–84.
13. See John Mueller, "The Polls—A Review," *Public Opinion Quarterly*, 57 (1993), 80–91.
14. Robert S. Erickson, Norman R. Luttbeg, and Kent L. Tedin, *American Public Opinion: Its Origins, Content, and Impact*, 2nd ed. (New York: Wiley & Sons, 1980), p. 44.
15. Hughes, *The Domestic Context of American Foreign Policy*, p. 31.
16. Ole R. Holsti and James N. Rosenau, *American Leadership in World Affairs, Vietnam and the Breakdown of Consensus* (Winchester, Mass.: Allen & Unwin, 1984), pp. 218–20.
17. Lloyd Free and William Watts, "Internationalism Comes of Age . . . Again," *Public Opinion*, 3 (1980), 46–50.
18. See John E. Rielly, "Public Opinion: The Pulse of the 90's," *Foreign Policy*, 82 (1991), 79–96.
19. John E. Rielly, "The Public Mood at Mid-Decade," *Foreign Policy*, 82 (1995), 76–93.
20. Ole R. Holsti, "Public Opinion and Foreign Policy: Attitude Structures of Opinion Leaders After the Cold War," in Eugene R. Wittkopf (ed.), *Domestic Sources of American Foreign Policy: Insights and Evidence*, 2nd ed. (New York: St. Martin's, 1994), 36–56.
21. Rielly, "The Public Mood at Mid-Decade," *Foreign Policy*, 98 (1995), 76–95.
22. Bruce W. Jentleson, "The Pretty Prudent Public: Post-Vietnam American Opinion on the Use of Military Force," *International Studies Quarterly*, 36 (1990), 49–74.
23. Miroslav Nincic, "Domestic Costs, the U.S. Public, and the Isolationist Calculus," *International Studies Quarterly*, 41 (1997), 593–610.
24. Leslie Gelb and Richard K. Betts, *The Irony of Vietnam: The System Worked* (Washington, D.C.: Brookings, 1979).
25. Richard J. Barnett, *The Roots of War* (New York: Penguin, 1977), p. 243.

26. Quoted in William Schneider, "Conservatism, Not Interventionism: Trends in Foreign Policy Opinion, 1974–1982," in Kenneth A. Oye, Robert J. Lieber, and Donald Rothchild (eds.), *Eagle Defiant: United States Foreign Policy in the 1980s* (Boston: Little, Brown, 1983), p. 138.

27. Thomas W. Graham, "Public Opinion and U.S. Foreign Policy Decision Making," in David A. Deese (ed.), *The New Politics of American Foreign Policy* (New York: St. Martin's, 1994), pp. 190–215.

28. Gerald M. Pomper, *Elections in America: Control and Influence in Democratic Politics* (New York: Dodd, Mead, 1968), p. 251.

29. Erickson, Luttbeg, and Tedin, *American Public Opinion*, p. 216.

30. The figures for 1983 are reported in *The New York Times*, July 1, 1983, p. 1. The remaining figures are discussed in ibid., p. 19; and Hughes, *Domestic Context of American Foreign Policy*, p. 91. The 1987 figure is from William Galston and Christopher Makins, "Campaign '88 and Foreign Policy," *Foreign Policy*, 71 (1988), 9. The 1993 data is from *Time* (October 4, 1993).

31. Warren E. Miller, "Voting and Foreign Policy," in James N. Rosenau (ed.), *Domestic Sources of Foreign Policy* (New York: Free Press, 1967), pp. 213–30.

32. Charles Whalen, *The House and Foreign Policy* (Chapel Hill: University of North Carolina Press, 1982).

33. Schneider, "Conservatism, Not Interventionism."

34. Laurence Radway, "The Curse of Free Elections," *Foreign Policy*, 40 (1980), 61–73.

35. *The Washington Post*, May 13, 1988, p. 4.

36. William B. Quandt, "The Electoral Cycle and the Conduct of American Foreign Policy," *Political Science Quarterly*, 101 (1986), 825–37.

37. See Steven Rosen (ed.), *Testing the Theory of the Military Industrial Complex* (Lexington, Ky.: Heath, 1973).

38. C. W. Mills, *The Power Elite* (New York: Oxford University Press, 1956).

39. *The Washington Post*, February 28, 1994.

40. Patrick Morgan, "Politics, Policy and the Military Industrial Complex," in Douglas M. Fox (ed.), *The Politics of U.S. Foreign Policy Making* (Santa Monica, Calif.: Goodyear, 1971), pp. 232–37.

41. For accounts of interest groups not discussed here, see Bruce Russett and Elizabeth Hansen, *Interest and Ideology: The Foreign Policy Beliefs of American Businessmen* (San Francisco: Freeman, 1975); and Hughes, *The Domestic Context of American Foreign Policy*, pp. 156–71.

42. Martin Weil, "Can the Blacks Do for Africa What the Jews Did for Israel?" *Foreign Policy*, 15 (1974), 109–29.

43. Charles McMathias, Jr., "Ethnic Groups and Foreign Affairs," *Foreign Affairs*, 59 (1981), 975–99.

44. David J. Sadd and G. Neal Lendenmann, "Arab American Grievances," *Foreign Policy*, 60 (1985), 17–29.

45. Kenneth Longmyer, "Black American Demands," *Foreign Policy*, 60 (1985), 3–16.

46. Milton D. Morris, "African Americans and the New World Order," *The Washington Quarterly*, 15 (1992), 5–21.

47. Bill Richardson, "Hispanic American Concerns," *Foreign Policy*, 60 (1985), 30–39.

48. See Shawn Miller, "Trade Winds Stir Miami Storm," *Insight*, June 7, 1993; and Carla Anne Robins, "Dateline Washington: Cuban-American Clout," *Foreign Policy* 88 (1992), 165–182.

49. Guy Gugliotta, "USIA Probes Activist's Role at Radio Marti," *The Washington Post*, July 22, 1995, A12.

50. Yossi Shain, "Multicultural Foreign Policy," *Foreign Policy*, 100 (1995), 69–87; and "Ethnic Diasporas and U.S. Foreign Policy," *Political Science Quarterly*, 109 (1994–95), 811–41.

51. Congressional Quarterly, *The Washington Lobby*, 4th ed. (Washington, D.C.: Congressional Quarterly, 1982), pp. 155–62; and *The Washington Post*, June 19, 1988.

52. The first two examples are cited in McMathias, "Ethnic Groups and Foreign Affairs." The last example is from *The Washington Lobby*.

53. Bernard Cohen, *The Public's Impact on Foreign Policy* (Boston: Little, Brown, 1973).

54. Ibid., p. 117.

55. The case study is drawn from Glenn Hastedt, "The New Context of Intelligence Estimating," in Stephen Cimbala (ed.), *The Vulnerable Labyrinth* (Ardsley-on-Hudson, N.Y.: Transnational, 1987).

56. On the matter of issue areas, see Hughes, *The Domestic Context of American Foreign Policy*, Chap. 7.

57. Daniel Yankelovich and John Immerwahr, "The Rules of Public Engagement," in Daniel Yankelovich and I. M. Destler (eds.), *Beyond the Beltway: Engaging the Public in U.S. Foreign Policy* (New York: Norton, 1994), 43–78. The quote is on p. 45.

58. Frank J. Stech, "Winning CNN Wars," *Parameters,* 24 (1994), 37–56.

59. Jonathan Mermin, "Television News and American Intervention in Somalia: The Myth of a Media-Driven Foreign Policy," *Political Science Quarterly,* 112 (1997), 385–403.

60. Robin F. Marra, Charles W. Ostrom, Jr., and Dennis M. Simon, "Foreign Policy and Presidential Popularity," *Journal of Conflict Resolution,* 34 (1990), 568–623.

61. Daniel Deudney and G. John Ikenberry, "After the Long War," *Foreign Policy,* 94 (1994), 21–35.

7 The Constitution and Foreign Affairs

On February 16, 1990, President Bush signed into law a bill that provided operating funds for the State Department. In doing so he stated that "many provisions of this act could be read to violate fundamental constitutional principles by using legislation to direct . . . the conduct of negotiations with foreign nations" and that therefore he did not consider himself bound by all of its provisions.[1] Among the points he objected to were:

- The denial of funding to the U.S. delegation to the Conference on European Security and Cooperation unless a congressional representative is included in the delegation.
- The denial of funds to carry out the current Middle East peace process with the PLO if the president knows and advises Congress that the PLO has directly participated in the planning or execution of terrorist acts.
- The denial of permission to the Soviet Union to occupy a consulate facility in New York until the United States is certified to occupy an interim facility in Kiev.

Bush was not the first president to do battle with Congress over the proper division of authority in the conduct of U.S. foreign policy. In its very first pages the Tower Commission, which President Reagan established to produce a study of the Iran–Contra policy initiative, stated:

> The Constitution places the President and Congress in dynamic tension. They both cooperate and compete in the making of national policy. National Security is no exception. The Constitution gives both the President and the Congress an important role. . . .[2]

In this chapter we examine the constitutional basis for presidential and congressional interaction in making U.S. foreign policy. Four powers are discussed: treaty making, appointments, war, and commerce. In the following chapters we examine how each of these two institutions has built on these powers to exercise its foreign policy powers.

TREATY-MAKING POWERS

Senatorial Advice and Consent

The Constitution states that the president, by and with the advice and consent of the Senate, has the power to make treaties. The president's role in the treaty-making process has not been a source of serious controversy. He nominates the negotiators, issues instructions to them, submits the treaty to the Senate for its advice and consent, and if its consent is given, he makes a decision on whether or not to ratify the treaty and make it law. Far more controversial have been the nature of senatorial advice and consent, the topics to be covered by treaties, and the role of the House of Representatives in the treaty-making process.

Virtually from the start senatorial advice and consent have been given at the same time. The Constitution does not require that it be done this way. Louis Henkin argues that the Senate was originally intended to be a kind of advisory council, making recommendations to the president throughout the treaty-making process and on all aspects of the negotiations.[3] He also notes that neither the president nor the Senate ever accepted this model. In the place of formal Senate input into the negotiating process, presidents have developed a number of informal means for obtaining senatorial advice. A frequently used method is to include key members of the Senate in the delegation to the negotiations as observers. The impetus for this move can be found in Woodrow Wilson's experience with the League of Nations Treaty. Wilson went to Versailles to negotiate the treaty personally and did not include any senators or important Republicans in the American Peace Commission. On July 10, 1919, Wilson presented the 264-page Treaty of Paris to the Senate. Wilson indicated that he would accept no reservations to the treaty. This was not to be the case. The Senate split into four groups, only one of which supported the treaty without reservation. After a series of preliminary votes, all of which went against Wilson, in March 1920 a final vote was taken and the treaty was rejected 49 to 35.

On the basis of quantitative measures, the use of informal means of consultation has proven to be quite successful. The Senate has been a most compliant partner, failing to give its consent to only 11 treaties while approving over 1,200. In the postwar era alone, it has consented to over 450 treaties while rejecting 1.[4] These figures, however, do not tell the full story. They tell us nothing of the importance of the treaties accepted or rejected. Also omitted in this counting are treaties negotiated by presidents but never voted on by the Senate or those the Senate consented to only after prolonged delays. President Carter's withdrawal of the SALT II Treaty is only one example of major Senate "nonrejections." President Truman negotiated a treaty establishing an International Trade Organization that was to be part of the Bretton Woods system along with the World Bank and the International Monetary Fund. Because of certain Senate opposition, Truman never submitted the treaty for advice and consent, and the interim General Agreement on Tariffs and Trade (GATT) became the formal international vehicle for lowering tariffs. In 1988 the Senate gave its consent by a vote of 83 to 11 to a Convention on the Prevention and Punishment of Genocide that was signed by the United States in 1948 and first submitted to the Senate by Truman in 1949.

Finally, a tally such as we introduce on page 166 makes no mention of senatorial attempts to change the treaties. Between 1789 and 1963 the Senate made changes in 69 percent of the treaties that came before it. In the heated debate over the Panama Canal Treaties, 145 amendments, 76 reservations, 18 understandings, and 3 declarations were proposed. Senatorial changes are often designed to improve a treaty. But this need not be the case. In the debate over the SALT II Treaty, "killer amendments" were introduced in order to ensure its nonacceptance by the Soviet Union. Changes have also created serious problems for the president in his dealings with other states. Senatorial changes in a Treaty of Friendship and Cooperation with Spain brought forward changes of interference in Spanish domestic affairs and almost resulted in Spain's refusal to ratify the treaty.[5]

A significant presidential–congressional clash over the language of a treaty came in 1988. The centerpiece of the dispute was whether a president could reinterpret the language of a treaty (in this particular case the INF Treaty) without congressional approval. President Reagan had done so with the 1972 ABM Treaty, and on the basis of this new interpretation his administration asserted that it could legally test elements of his SDI shield. Here, the focus of concern was unclear language over how laser weapons and other futuristic technologies were to be dealt with. The Senate position prevailed and language was written into the INF Treaty banning any reinterpretation of it without Senate approval.[6] At the same time, the Senate beat back efforts by Senators Jesse Helms and Larry Pressler to "kill" the treaty by attaching amendments to it that the Soviet Union would find totally unacceptable. Helms wanted a ban on noncruise missiles included in the treaty and Pressler wanted its implementation tied to the achievement of parity in conventional military forces.

Presidents and the Senate have already clashed several times in the post–cold war period over the content and advisability of treaties. On the whole, the lines of conflict have been quite predictable and point to the continued weight of traditional congressional concerns for protecting its prerogatives. One frequently expressed concern has been the possibility that a treaty might infringe on U.S. sovereignty. Opponents of the GATT treaty pointed to a 1991 GATT ruling that the U.S. ban on tuna from Mexico and other states whose fishing fleets killed large numbers of dolphins was illegal. They used this as evidence that by signing the treaty U.S. environmental laws would be weakened. Similar fears were expressed regarding the possibility that GATT might consistently rule against the United States on economic matters. The Clinton administration argued that no loss of sovereignty was at stake in the treaty, but it took a last-minute deal struck between Clinton and Senate Minority Leader Robert Dole allowing the United States to leave GATT should this happen to secure its passage. A similar concern for protecting U.S. sovereignty prevented the United States from signing the Law of the Sea Treaty for over a quarter of a century. The United States ratified the treaty in 1994 only after amendments were added which gave it a virtual veto over decisions over the mining and allocation of deep ocean resources. Finally, conservative groups have long objected to provisions of the UN Children's Rights Treaty because they argue it would weaken the role of parents. The United States remains one of the few countries not to have ratified this 1989 convention.

A second familiar problem confronting presidents in the post–cold war period has been that of securing a political majority in the Senate to support the treaty. The GATT treaty ratified by a wide bipartisan margin in a special post-1994 session of Congress is a case in point. The Clinton administration hoped to have the Senate give its consent to the treaty prior to the November elections but was unable to do so because of Republican opposition. With many key Democratic leaders opposing the treaty, Clinton needed Republican votes to gain approval. A particularly troublesome point was the need to get at least 60 votes in the Senate to waive a requirement written into recent budgetary legislation that any revenues lost by a tariff agreement be offset with equal spending reductions. Part of the price that Clinton was forced to pay to get Republican support for the GATT treaty was dropping his request for "fast track" authority to negotiate trade agreements. Under the terms of a "fast track" agreement, Congress is presented with a "take-it-or-leave-it" vote. No amendments are permitted.

Finally, we find the president and Congress in continued conflict over who has the power to interpret treaty language. The primary area of controversy here involves arms control agreements. The Bush administration and Congress sparred over who had the power to interpret language in the Conventional Forces in Europe (CFE) Treaty and Strategic Arms Reduction Treaty (START). Both treaties were negotiated before the collapse of the Warsaw Pact and the disintegration of the Soviet Union. The Bush administration argued that it should be allowed to make any necessary adjustments without legislative consent. A diverse group of senators including Jesse Helms and Joseph Biden argued that any adjustments had to be approved by the Senate. The Clinton administration also found itself at odds with the Senate over the ABM Treaty. It approached Russia about modifying the language of the treaty in order to permit the deployment of mobile defensive systems against intermediate missiles. The Clinton administration said its proposal was only intended to clear up ambiguities in the treaty. Senate leaders responded that the administration should not try to put any change into effect without Senate approval.

The Clinton administration ultimately conceded this point in 1997. It recognized the Senate's right to review the revised treaty language as part of a deal that allowed the global treaty on banning the production and use of chemical weapons to come up for a vote. Action on the treaty had been held up for four years, largely due to the opposition of Senate Foreign Relations Committee chairperson Jesse Helms. In return for permitting a vote, Helms was promised that the administration would move forward on a foreign affairs bureaucratic reorganization that he favored. The Clinton administration also sent letters to Senate Majority Leader Trent Lott promising to withdraw from the treaty if others exploited its provisions and promising to submit for Senate ratification two existing treaties that it had previously maintained did not require Senate action.

It is important to note that not all treaty votes are controversial. During the Clinton administration, NATO enlargement and the START II Treaty received overwhelming support in the Senate in spite of the presence of serious disagreements within the academic and policy communities about their merits.

Executive Agreements

The Constitution specifies that the Senate should give its advice and consent to treaties, but it does not define what a treaty is or what international agreements are to be made in this form. From the outset presidents have claimed the constitutional authority to engage in international agreements by means other than treaties. This alternative is known as the *executive agreement,* and over time it had become the favored presidential method for entering into understandings with other states.

Unlike a treaty, an executive agreement does not require the consent of the Senate before coming into force. The Supreme Court has ruled that it carries the same legal force as a treaty. The principal limit on its use is political, not legal. This came through quite clearly in the dispute between Bush and Congress over how best to protect Chinese students in the United States following the Tiananmen Square Massacre. Bush promised to issue an executive order while Congress passed legislation. Each viewed the other's action as misguided. Congress felt the president's action did not make enough of a symbolic statement, and Bush argued that the congressional action was unnecessary and complicated his foreign policy dealings with China. Bush vetoed the legislation and, while the House voted to override it, the Senate sustained Bush's position.

Between 1946 and 1977 presidents entered into over 7,200 executive agreements, compared to 451 treaties.[7] At first glance these figures point to the increasing irrelevance of the Senate in the making of international agreements, but once again these numbers are somewhat misleading because 87 percent of these agreements were statutory agreements. When a president enters into a statutory agreement, he is acting with prior congressional approval. Tariff reductions are an example of a policy area where statutory executive agreements have been used with great regularity. Beginning with the 1934 Trade Agreements Act, Congress has periodically authorized the president to engage in negotiations to reduce tariff levels.

More serious questions about the involvement of the Senate in the treaty-making process center on the types of issues dealt with in treaties, statutory executive agreements, and pure executive agreements (ones made by the president without any prior congressional authorization). Table 7–1 lists the distribution of these agreement forms by policy area. In all five areas statutory agreements have been the dominant means for reaching an understanding with foreign governments, followed by executive agreements and the treaties. A closer look at military agreements reveals both the continued importance of treaties and the extent to which presidents have turned to executive agreements.[8] Of the 42 treaties signed in this time period, 32 dealt with major defense obligations such as security agreements with Japan, arms control accords, and the 1963 Nuclear Test Ban. Another nine treaties dealt with administrative aspects of major military pacts such as NATO. However, throughout this period every president relied more heavily on executive agreements than treaties for making major military commitments. Numbered among the 99 agreements are establishing military bases in the Philippines (1947), a military security agreement with South Korea (1949), a U.S. military mission in El Salvador (1957), security pledges to Turkey, Iran, and Pakistan (1959), and the military use of Bahrain (1971).

On a number of occasions, the Senate has attempted to curb the president's use of executive agreements. Three efforts have been particularly noteworthy. The first was the Bricker Amendment. It would have required that executive agreements receive the same two-thirds vote of approval from the

TABLE 7–1   Form of U.S. Foreign Agreements by Content Areas, 1946–1972

			Content		
Form	Military	Economic	Transportation-Communication	Cultural-Technical	Diplomatic
Executive agreements	12.4%[a]	4.6%	5.9%	3.7%	26.7%
Statutory agreements	84.0%	88.6%	84.6%	93.2%	60.1%
Treaties	3.6%	6.8%	9.5%	3.2%	13.2%
(N)	(1,146)	(2,229)	(630)	(1,580)	(371)

[a]Entries are percentages based on column N shown at the bottom. Thirty-five agreements, representing 0.6% of the total, were classified as "Other" for content and are not shown in the table.

Source: Loch Johnson, The Making of International Agreements: Congress Confronts the Executive (New York: New York University Press, 1984), p. 19.

Senate that treaties must get. In 1954 it failed by one vote to get the necessary two-thirds majority in the Senate needed to set into motion the amendment ratification process at the state level.

The second effort by Congress to reclaim a role in making international agreements was the 1969 National Commitments Resolution declaring that it was now the sense of the Senate that no future national commitments be made without affirmative action by Congress. It defined a national commitment as the use of the armed forces of the United States on foreign territory, the promise to use them, or the granting of financial aid. In making this statement, Congress was trying to undo what had become standard practice for two decades: recognizing in advance the president's authority to use force to protect American interests. The vehicle used for this purpose was the area resolution. The first area resolution came in 1955 and recognized U.S. interests in protecting Taiwan from China. Later resolutions dealt with the Middle East (1957), Latin America (1962), Berlin (1964), and Southeast Asia (1964). Known as the Gulf of Tonkin Resolution, this last resolution was cited by presidents Johnson and Nixon whenever they were challenged on the legality of U.S. involvement in Vietnam.

The most recent effort by Congress to reassert itself was the 1972 Case–Zablocki Act, which required that Congress be informed of all executive agreements. The goal was to give Congress the opportunity to take action blocking these agreements if it saw fit. According to Senator Clifford Case, this act was needed because there were at least 4,000 executive agreements in effect in the early 70s that Congress knew nothing about.[9] The Case–Zablocki Act did not end the practice of secret executive agreements. In part the problem is definitional. In 1975 Representative Les Aspin estimated that 400 to 600 agreements had not yet been reported to Congress because the White House claimed that they were either understandings, verbal promises, or statements of political intent.[10] Included among these were a 1973 secret message that Nixon had sent to North Vietnam promising them reconstruction aid in return for a peace agreement, Kissinger's 1975 understanding with Israel and Egypt that U.S. personnel would be stationed in the Sinai as part of the disengagement process, and the 1975 Helsinki Accords which were referred to as a statement of political intent. The problem is also bureaucratic. In 1976 the U.S. General Accounting Office reported that over 30 secret agreements existed with South Korea that the State Department had not been informed of.

Documents uncovered in the National Archives after the Persian Gulf War revealed a lengthy history of secret presidential agreements with Saudi Arabia.[11] In 1947, President Truman entered into an agreement with King Ibn Saud that stated that "one of the basic policies of [the] United States in [the] Near East is unqualifiedly to support [the] territorial integrity and political independence of Saudi Arabia." The document continued, "If Saudi Arabia should therefore be attacked by another power or be under threat of attack, the United States through medium of [the] United Nations would take energetic measures to ward off such aggression." In 1950 the king asked the Truman administration for a formal military treaty that would bind the United States to protect Saudi borders. The Truman administration replied that it could not do so, but a State Department official promised he "would suggest certain other measures which should achieve virtually the same end." He also told the king that the United States would "take most immediate action at any time that the integrity and independence of Saudi Arabia is threatened." The Truman administration was not alone in making secret commitments to Saudi Arabia. In 1963 President Kennedy also entered into a secret agreement with Saudi Arabia. On the heels of an Egyptian-inspired coup and the assassination of a member of the Saudi royal family, Kennedy sent a U.S. fighter squadron to train in Saudi Arabia as a public show of support for that government. What was not made public was that Kennedy had authorized these units to use force against Egypt if provoked.

The Role of the House and the Panama Canal Treaties

The third and most recent area of controversy involving treaty-making powers involves the role of the House of Representatives. The Constitution gives the House no formal role in the treaty-making process, and traditionally it has played the part of a spectator. This has begun to change as the House has seized upon its budgetary powers as the vehicle for making its will known to both the Senate and the president. Treaties are not always self-executing. They typically require enabling legislation and the expenditure of funds before their provisions take effect. In exercising its budgetary and legislative powers, the House possesses the ability to undo what the Senate and president have agreed upon. According to one observer, the House came quite close to destroying the Panama Canal Treaties by inserting into the implementing legislation language that disagreed with and contradicted parts of the treaty just approved by the Senate.[12] The need for House approval of implementing legislation is not unique to the Panama Canal Treaties. The House also voted on implementing legislation for the 1994 GATT treaty. It did so by a bipartisan vote of 288–146 in favor of the necessary legislation. The GATT treaty then went to the Senate where the final ratification vote took place.

On September 16, 1977, President Carter submitted one document containing two treaties defining the future status of the Panama Canal to the Senate for its consideration.[13] The Panama Canal Treaty abolished the Panama Canal Zone by terminating the 1903 treaty that established it. The United States would retain the right to manage and operate it until December 31, 1999, through a newly created Panama Canal Commission. At that time Panama would get complete control. Until then the United States would have military base rights and the primary responsibility for defending the canal, and a Neutrality Treaty established the permanent neutrality of the canal and guaranteed that it would always remain open. Furthermore, U.S. and Panamanian warships were to be allowed to pass through the canal "expeditiously." On March 16, 1978, by a vote of 68 to 32, the Senate gave its consent to the Neutrality Treaty. On April 18, it consented to the Panama Canal Treaty by a similar vote.

The Senate debate on the merits of the two treaties consumed more time than had any treaty debate since that on the Treaty of Versailles: 192 changes were offered during the course of the debate, and 88 were voted on. In the end the Senate made three major changes in the two treaties. Two points of controversy arose in the debate over the Neutrality Treaty. In his testimony Secretary of State Cyrus Vance stated that nothing in the treaties limited the freedom of the United States to intervene in order to guarantee the neutrality of the canal. Panama dissented on this interpretation. It also disagreed with the U.S. view that "expeditiously" meant "go to the head of the line." A hastily arranged meeting between Carter and General Omar Torrijos produced a statement of understanding designed to put the conflict to rest. It accepted the basic elements of the U.S. position on these two points as the correct interpretation of the treaty. Senate opposition continued. The impasse was finally broken when Senate Majority Leader Howard Baker met General Torrijos in Panama and convinced him to accept changes in the language of the treaty. The most important change was to insert into the treaty the language of the statement of understanding.

A more difficult problem was presented by an amendment introduced by freshman Senator Dennis DeConcini allowing the United States "to use military force in Panama" and to take other necessary actions to keep the canal open after the year 2000. Carter gave his support to the amendment, and it was adopted by a vote of 75 to 23 and attached to the Neutrality Treaty as a condition. Not surprisingly, Panama took strong objection to it. After 1999 the Panama Canal was to become Panamanian property, and this condition gave the United States the right to intervene in Panama's internal affairs. Action on the Neutrality Treaty had been completed, but the entire treaty package was now in jeopardy. If the DeConcini condition was not modified, Panama would not ratify the treaties. If it was taken out, the Senate was unlikely to consent to the Panama Canal Treaty, and without it the Neutrality Treaty was of little significance. The Panama Canal Treaty now became the object of intense bargaining among the Senate, the executive branch, and Panama. The issue was resolved by inserting a condition into the Panama Canal Treaty that omitted any reference to the use of force and stated that the United States' right to keep the Panama Canal open was not to be taken as a right to intervene in Panamanian affairs.

The controversy did not end here. It merely shifted to the House where the required implementing legislation now had to be passed. The administration bill was assigned to four committees. Primary jurisdiction was held by the Merchant Marine and Fisheries Committee whose chair, Representative John Murphy, opposed the treaty. He proposed his own version of the implementing legislation. Instead of creating a government corporation to run the canal which would pay its expenses out of tolls as the Carter administration proposed, Murphy's bill would create a government agency whose budget would be voted on annually by Congress. The administration's bill would also have transferred property to Panama automatically; Murphy's bill required a vote on each transfer. A third bill would have required Panama to pay the cost of implementing the treaties and to reimburse the United States for the net cost of building the canal.

Eventually, the Carter administration abandoned its own bill in favor of the Murphy bill. After a series of extremely close votes, the House accepted the Murphy bill by a vote of 224 to 202. The result angered Panama. President Aristides Royo cited almost 30 articles of the House bill that violated provisions of the treaty. The Senate passed implementing legislation more in line with the administration's original proposal, and because the two bills disagreed, the matter was sent to a conference committee. By a vote of 308 to 90, the House instructed its conferees to insist on the House language regarding the transfer of property and the status of the Panama Canal Commission. The House rejected the first conference report by a vote of 192 to 203 and finally gave its acceptance by a vote of 232 to 188 only four days before the treaty was scheduled to take effect and 60 percent of the Panama Canal Zone was to be transferred to Panama.

APPOINTMENT POWERS

As originally envisioned, the power to approve or reject presidential appointments was closely related to the power to give advice and consent to treaties. By exercising a voice in who negotiated the treaty, the Senate would be able to influence its content. In practice this linkage was never fully put into place, and it had long since unraveled. The Senate has failed to actively or systematically exercise its confirmation powers. Frequently, it has not hesitated to approve ambassadors appointed solely for political purposes and without any other apparent qualifications for the post. In 1956 a contribution of $22,000 to the Eisenhower campaign "bought" the ambassadorship to Sri Lanka. During the Nixon administration the ambassadors to Switzerland, Austria, and France all made contributions in excess of $100,000 to the Republican party. The Carter administration's ambassador to Singapore had not heard of Gandhi, Nehru, Sukarno, Chiang Kai-shek, or Deng Xiao-ping. His major qualifications were that he was a former Democratic governor of South Dakota and head of the Midwest Governors' Conference.

As did Reagan before him, President Bush continued the practice of converting political IOUs into ambassadorships, although not all of his nominees emerged unscathed from the confirmation process. Fred Bush (no relation to the president), who was a key figure in Bush's presidential campaign, was unable to win confirmation as ambassador to Luxembourg, and Joy Silverstein, who along with her husband gave some $300,000 to Republican causes in the 1988 election campaign, encountered strong senatorial opposition to her nomination as ambassador to Barbados. At the end of President Bush's term in office, 20 percent of the ambassador corps was made up of political or noncareer appointments. About 30 percent of Clinton's ambassadorial appointments could be classified as political in nature. In his first term, major campaign contributors were rewarded with ambassadorships to Luxembourg, Switzerland, Singapore, and Sweden. Early in his second term, campaign contributors were nominated for posts in Chile, the Bahamas, Barbados, and the Dominican Republic.

Senator Joseph Lieberman (D-Conn.), speaking in defense of Robert Gates's second nomination to serve as head of the CIA, stated that the confirmation question before the Senate was "not is he the best person to fill the job, but having been nominated by the president, is he qualified?" Typically, however, when the Senate has raised its voice, concern has been directed more at making a policy statement than questioning the qualifications of the nominee. Three recent nominees to head the CIA, Theodore Sorensen (by Carter), Robert Gates (by Reagan), and Anthony Lake (by Clinton) were "defeated." Reagan's nomination of Ernest Lefever as Assistant Secretary of State for Human Rights and Kenneth Adelman as director of the Arms Control and Disarmament Agency; Bush's nomination of John Tower as Secretary of Defense; and Clinton's nominations of Robert Pastor as ambassador to Panama and Morton Halperin for the proposed position of Assistant Secretary of Defense for Democracy and Peacekeeping all brought forward politically inspired opposition.

The resolution of these cases again points to the need for caution in making judgments about the Senate's use of its constitutional powers. Halperin, Sorensen, and Gates all withdrew their names from consideration before a vote was taken. Gates would later be nominated again by Bush and win confirmation as head of the CIA. Pastor's nomination was withdrawn after it had been approved by the Senate Foreign Relations Committee. This approval came prior to the 1994 election but was vigorously opposed by Senator Jesse Helms, who became chairperson of that committee after the Republicans won control of the Senate. Helms blamed Pastor, a Latin American expert who served on Carter's National Security Council, for the Panama Canal Treaties. Lefever's nomination was rejected by the Senate Foreign Relations Committee and then withdrawn, Adelman was approved, and Tower was rejected by a vote of the full Senate.

Presidents have also turned the confirmation powers into something less than what was originally intended by using personal representatives as negotiators. Franklin Roosevelt relied heavily on Harry Hopkins in making international agreements, leaving Secretary of State Cordell Hull to administer over "diplomatic trivia." Carter used Hamilton Jordan to conduct secret negotiations during the Iranian hostage crisis, and in the Reagan administration NSC staffers and private citizens were relied on to carry out the Iran–Contra initiative. A similar problem confronts the Senate if it wishes to influence the type of advice that the president gets. Presidents are free to listen to whom they please. Under Woodrow Wilson, Colonel House, a friend and confidant, was more influential than Secretaries of State William Jennings Bryan and William Lansing. Today it is widely recognized that the National Security Advisor often has more influence on presidential thinking than does the Secretary of Sate. Yet the former's appointment is not subject to Senate approval.

WAR POWERS

The war powers of the Constitution are split into three basic parts. Congress is given the power to declare war and the power to raise and maintain an army and navy, while the president is designated as commander in chief of the armed forces. In the abstract these powers fit together very nicely, but in practice a far different picture prevails. A problem immediately arises over defining when a state of war exists. Is it any instance where U.S. troops are placed into combat, or must a war be declared into existence? In its Prize Cases decision of 1862, the Supreme Court ruled that the existence of a war was found in the prevailing conditions and not in a formal congressional declaration. U.S. practice has borne this out. Congress has declared only 5 of the over 125 "wars" that the United States has fought: the War of 1812, the Spanish–American War, the Mexican War, World War I, and World War II.

In addition, no state today can wait until a war has broken out or has been declared to begin mobilizing its armed forces. Successful military action requires forces in being. The dilemma facing Congress is that once it has created a standing military establishment capable of going into combat without further mobilization, it has lost control over the president. The Cuban missile crisis and the Bay of Pigs invasion were played out without a declaration of war. Carter presented Congress with a *fait accompli* with the Iranian hostage rescue effort; Reagan acted unilaterally in invading Grenada and bombing Libya; Bush did the same in invading Panama and sending troops to Somalia.

President Clinton did not seek congressional authorization for his use of troops to return President Jean-Bertrand Aristide to power in Haiti. In fact, the Clinton administration asserted that the War Powers Resolution should be interpreted as recognizing and presupposing "the existence of a unilateral Presidential authority to deploy armed force." Neither the Clinton administration nor anyone in Congress mentioned the War Powers Resolution in February 1998, when President Clinton was contemplating air strikes against Iraq for its refusal to permit UN inspectors to search weapons sites.

Presidents have defended such uses of force, citing their commander in chief powers. The exact meaning of these powers is unclear. Alexander Hamilton saw it as a symbolic grant of power with the actual power to decide military strategy and tactics being held by professional soldiers. Yet many presidents have taken this grant of power quite literally. Franklin Roosevelt actively participated in formulating military strategy and tactics during World War II, and Lyndon Johnson actively participated in selecting bombing targets during Vietnam. According to constitutional scholar Louis Henkin, the president's repeated ability to commit U.S. troops to combat situations without effective congressional opposition has firmly established his authority to do so.[14] Not settled is the matter of the constitutional foundations or limits of this authority. Congress directly raised the question of limits in 1973 by passing the War Powers Resolution over President Nixon's veto.[15] The War Powers Resolution requires the president to do the following:

1. "In every possible instance" consult with Congress before committing U.S. troops in "hostilities or into situations where imminent involvement in hostilities" is likely

2. Inform Congress within 48 hours after the introduction of troops if there has been no declaration of war

3. Remove U.S. troops within 60 days (or 90 days in special circumstances) if Congress does not either declare war or adopt a joint resolution approving the action

Congress also can terminate the U.S. military involvement before the 60-day limit by passing a concurrent resolution. Such a resolution does not require the president's signature and, therefore, cannot be vetoed. From the outset the War Powers Resolution has been controversial. Senator Jacob Javits saw in it the basis for a new foreign policy compact between the president and Congress. Senator Thomas Eagleton, an original supporter of the legislation with Javits, voted against it because he claimed that it gave the president powers he never had: the power to commit U.S. troops abroad without prior congressional approval.

Presidents have argued that the act was unconstitutional. The particular object of presidential hostility is the provision granting Congress the right to terminate hostilities through the use of a legislative veto. The legislative veto is a device that Congress has relied on to reinsert its voice into foreign affairs decision making. It allows the Congress to approve or disapprove executive branch actions after the fact in a form short of legislation. In addition to the War Powers Resolution, Congress has inserted legislative vetoes into a wide range of foreign policy legislation, including arms sales, the export of nuclear fuel and facilities, presidential decisions not to grant relief to industries injured by imports, the continuation of most favored nation status of communist states, the stationing of U.S. personnel in the Sinai, presidential declarations of emergency, and national defense contracts in excess of $25 million.[16]

Presidents have maintained that only congressional action that has been approved by the president or is passed by Congress over his veto is legally binding. On January 23, 1983, in a landmark case, the Supreme Court agreed with the presidential interpretation in making its ruling in *U.S. v. Chadha.* The case centered on the exercise of a legislative veto by the House of Representatives of the Attorney General's decision to allow Chadha, an East Indian student holding a British passport, to stay in the United States. The Supreme Court reaffirmed this position 13 days later in a second case and explicitly linked its ruling to the legislative veto provisions of the War Powers Resolution. It should be noted that a foreign affairs legislative veto has never been exercised. The closest it came to being used was with the transfer of nuclear material to India in 1980 and the sale of an AWACS (Airborne Warning and Control Systems Aircraft) and F-15 enhancement package to Saudi Arabia in 1981.

Another sore point with presidents is the 60-day time limit imposed by the act. From the very outset presidents have challenged the time limit on constitutional and practical grounds while at the same time they have acted in accordance with its reporting provisions. Of interest is the language used by presidents in making their reports.[17] In some cases (the transportation of refugees from Da Nang in April 1975, the evacuation of U.S. nationals from Cambodia and Vietnam in April 1975, and the evacuation of U.S. nationals from Lebanon in 1976) the president reported his action in a perfunctory manner. In reporting the *Mayaguez* rescue operation in 1975, President Ford stated that he was "taking note" of the War Powers Resolution but asserted that he acted on the basis of his commander in chief powers. In this case it is also unclear whether the advance consulting provisions were met. Senator Hugh Scott, deputy minority leader and a member of the Senate Foreign Relations Committee, stated: "We were informed. We were alerted. We were advised. We were notified. . . . I don't know whether that's consultation or not."

Carter did not engage in advance consultations with Congress in carrying out the hostage rescue effort. He claimed that as a humanitarian action it was outside the scope of the War Powers Resolution, and in reporting to Congress, he stated that he was acting "consistent with" its reporting provisions. The invasion of Grenada was also defined by the Reagan administration as a humanitarian action and therefore beyond the scope of the War Powers Resolution. Still, the Reagan administration withdrew U.S. forces before the 60-day limit was reached. Bush also chose not to invoke the War Powers Resolution in his first opportunity to use it—the 1989 invasion of Panama. He limited his actions to consulting informally with congressional leaders just prior to the invasion. When questioned by a reporter if he would send the required notification to Congress, Bush responded that "the notification of the Congress will be in accordance with our policy."

The first real test of the War Powers Resolution came in 1982 with the sending of Marines to Lebanon as part of the Multinational Peacekeeping Force. The Reagan administration's original position was that because the Marines were invited in by the Lebanese government, they were not being sent into a combat situation, and the War Powers Resolution did not apply. Reagan adopted the Carter phrase *consistent with* the War Powers Resolution in reporting the deployment of troops in Lebanon and stressed it was being done "pursuant to the president's constitutional authority with respect to the conduct of foreign relations as Commander in Chief." These troops were withdrawn within a month and then were redeployed after Lebanese president Bashir Gemayel was assassinated and hundreds of Palestinian refugees were massacred in camps theoretically under Israeli control. Rising tensions and a rapidly deteriorating situation in Lebanon led the Reagan administration to begin exploring the possibility of getting congressional authorization for the presence of the Marines in Lebanon. In mid-October a compromise was reached that allowed both sides to claim victory. Citing the War Powers Resolution, Congress authorized the president to keep the Marines in Lebanon for 18 months. In signing the resolution, however, Reagan stated that he was not acknowledging the validity of the War Powers Resolution.

Reagan's actions were consistent with what appeared to be an uneasy truce on the part of Congress and the president over the constitutionality of the War Powers Resolution. One of the immediate effects of the end of the cold war was to unleash a series of regional conflicts and crises that tempted American presidents to respond with the use of military force. This new military agenda injected new life into the debate over the merits of presidential compliance with the War Powers Resolution. The first dispute came with the Persian Gulf War. President Bush only sought congressional approval for using American military forces to liberate Kuwait as the UN-mandated deadline approached. In reporting to Congress his August 1990 decision to send American forces to the Middle East to protect Saudi Arabia as part of Operation Desert Shield, Bush made no mention of the War Powers Resolution. This silence largely went unchallenged in Congress until November when he announced that additional U.S. forces would be sent to the region in order to establish an offensive capability. With this apparent change in mission, many in Congress now asserted that the War Powers Resolution was relevant and that its permission must be secured prior to the use of force. In the face of Bush's continued claim that he possessed the necessary authority to act without congressional approval, several members of Congress unsuccessfully brought suit in court to block any unilateral use of force by the president. Some members of Congress who supported Bush's interpretation of his constitutional powers were angered by his request of the United Nations that it grant him the authority to use force against Iraq. The UN Security Council voted him that authority in November 1990.

Bush went to Congress for a vote of support only in January when he believed that he had the votes to win what everyone expected to be a close vote. Both the debate and final vote reflected how deeply split America was on the wisdom of using force against Iraq. Rejecting a Democratic proposal that Bush be required to give economic sanctions and diplomatic initiatives more time, on January 12, the Senate voted 52–47 to grant Bush the authority to enforce the January 15 deadline established by the United Nations. The House followed with a 250–181 supporting vote. The congressional resolution referred to the War Powers Resolution and required that Bush inform congressional leaders before beginning offensive operations. Bush signed the resolution without mentioning the War Powers Resolution. Later, the Bush administration would reject the relevance of the War Powers Resolution in sending troops to Somalia, declaring it to be a humanitarian operation. More recently, President Clinton did not seek congressional authorization for his use of troops to return President Jean-Bertrand Aristide to power in Haiti or to use force in Kosovo to stop Serb aggression.

Once U.S. forces were in Haiti (1994), Congress struggled with the question of how to reassert its authority. One option favored by those most opposed to the Haitian undertaking was to set a binding deadline, at which point U.S. forces would have to be withdrawn. In the end the Senate avoided a direct confrontation with the administration by passing a nonbinding resolution calling for the "prompt and orderly withdrawal" of U.S. forces from Haiti, but it did not set a deadline at which this had to take place. The resolution also called for detailed reports to Congress on the progress of the operation.

COMMERCE POWERS

The Constitution gives Congress the power to regulate commerce with foreign nations. In theory this power belongs exclusively to Congress. No parallel statement exists laying out presidential powers. In practice power sharing between the two branches has been necessary. Congress may have the power to regulate foreign commerce, but only the president has the power to negotiate treaties, and it is the president whom the Supreme Court has designated as the "sole organ of the government in the field of foreign affairs." Power sharing in international economics has not produced the same level of conflict between the two branches as it has in other areas. Instead, it has produced a series of innovations that have brought a high degree of continuity and consistency to U.S. policy. The first innovative power-sharing arrangement is found in the 1934 Trade Agreements Act by which Congress delegated to the president the authority to "implement into domestic law the results of trade agreements as they relate to tariffs." This procedure greatly enhanced the president's power position in multilateral trade negotiations by removing the threat of congressional obstructionism in the formal approval and implementation of the negotiated agreement. Congress periodically renewed this grant of authority for a succession of presidents, changing only the time frame involved and the value of the reduction permitted and inserting legislative veto provisions. This procedure worked well until the Kennedy Round negotiations (1964 to 1967), when for the first time nontariff barriers to trade became the major points of contention. Changes in U.S. law and the congressional delegation of authority were now widely seen as necessary before the United States could effectively engage in another round of international trade negotiations.

The Trade Reform Act of 1974 introduced the second major innovative power-sharing arrangement. It created a "fast track" reporting procedure. The president would be able to send a draft bill containing the necessary implementing legislation to Congress, which would be required to vote yes or no within 90 days and which was prohibited from adding any amendments. The 1974 Trade Reform Act also created an elaborate set of advisory committees and targets to guide the negotiating process. These procedures were used with great success in the Tokyo Round negotiations (1973 to 1979). The president's representatives negotiated, and Congress quickly approved, an incredibly complex series of agreements with very little acrimony at a time when the two branches could agree upon little else.[18]

I. M. Destler suggests that these types of legislative innovations have allowed Congress to insulate itself from domestic pressures for protectionist trade legislation. The result is that congresspeople can "advocate, even threaten, trade restrictions, while nicely relieving them of the need to deliver on their threats." Such protection for Congress was necessary because congressional tariffs invariably meant high tariffs, and after the experience of the 1930s and the Smoot–Hawley Tariff, all agreed that this had to be avoided.

Congress freed itself from the protection that "fast track" had offered it from interest group pressures to amend trade legislation. In fact, Congress gave in to interest group pressures in insisting that President Clinton forgo his request for fast track authority as a price for its support of the GATT treaty. Business groups feared that if given this authority Clinton would use it to add environmental and labor safeguards to agreements that they would then be unable to block. Organized labor wanted to deny Clinton fast track authority out of fear that he would not include these provisions in a trade agreement; they wanted the opportunity to add protective amendments. Congressional opposition to fast track authority crossed party lines and was not directed only against Clinton. Having allowed his fast track authority to lapse in 1994, Clinton sought to regain it in 1997 after his reelection. He sought to obtain fast track authority until at least October 1, 2001 in order to facilitate the creation of Free Trade Area of the Americas. Facing the continued opposition of labor and environmental groups, Clinton was unable to unite congressional Democrats behind him or bring enough Republicans over to his side.

FEDERALISM AND THE STATES

The past several decades have seen an explosion in the foreign policy activity of states and local governments. They have surfaced as visible and active lobbyists on important foreign policy issues. State government associations spoke out vehemently against what they saw as a GATT treaty that discriminated against states.[19] They objected to provisions that in their view would reduce state and local taxes paid by foreign companies and transfer authority to determine state and local tax policies away from U.S. courts to international trade panels. States were also active in their opposition to certain facets of U.S. refugee policy. In 1994, Florida sued the federal government to recover millions of dollars state and local governments spent providing social services and law enforcement for illegal immigrants. California, Illinois, and Texas had voiced similar complaints. Later that year Florida Governor Lawton Chiles followed this up by "declaring a state of emergency" and calling on the Clinton administration to change its policy of allowing Cuban boat people to enter the United States.

Even more significant from a constitutional perspective is the emergence of state and local foreign policies. The range of these foreign policy initiatives is great.[20] At the local level, 86 communities formed linkages with Nicaragua and provided its people with humanitarian assistance. Twenty-nine communities provided sanctuary for Guatemalan and Salvadoran refugees. The U.S. Conference of Mayors demanded cuts in military spending and 120 localities refused to cooperate with the Federal Emergency Management Agency's nuclear war exercises. In addition, over 900 communities passed resolutions supporting a freeze in the arms race.

States have become particularly prominent actors in international economic transactions.[21] Raw economic figures point to their potential for global influence. Ten states would rank among the world's top 25 economies. All 50 states would rank in the top 75. This economic strength has become the foundation for an overseas economic presence. In 1970, only four states had offices abroad, but, in 1990, 43 states were operating 163 offices around the world. All 50 states now offer export assistance programs and many provide investment incentive packages in order to attract foreign investors. Increasingly states and localities have flexed their economic power in an effort to influence events abroad. In 1998, cities in California, Colorado, Wisconsin, Michigan, North Carolina, Rhode Island, New York, Florida, and Massachusetts had imposed investment or purchasing sanctions (or had them pending) against Burma, Nigeria, Cuba, Indonesia, and Tibet. Also in 1998, a committee representing about 800 municipal and state financial officers decided to go ahead with sanctions against Switzerland's three largest banks in an effort to force a settlement of claims from Holocaust survivors. In doing so, it rejected a warning from the State Department that their actions would worsen U.S.–Swiss relations and damage the reputation of the United States in international financial markets.

The U.S. Constitution established a federal system of government in which some powers were given exclusively to the national government, some to the states, and others shared among them. Among those granted exclusively to the national government are the powers "to conduct foreign relations" and "to regulate commerce with foreign nations and among states." As states and localities become more active in these areas and pursue policies at variance with those advocated by the federal government, the potential for conflict grows. For example, in 1989 Texas shipped hormone-fed beef to Great Britain over the objections of the federal government, and the Department of Agriculture at first refused to certify that the meat was drug-free. In 1991, only days after President Bush lifted U.S. economic sanctions against South Africa, New York City moved to tighten its restrictions on trade with that country. The Reagan and Bush administrations began taking limited action against what they viewed as local interference in American foreign policy. A Bush administration official in the Justice Department stated that it was contemplating a lawsuit over the "legal implications of states and local governments carrying out their own foreign policy with regard to South Africa."

Three recent court cases have touched upon the propriety of state and local foreign policies, and in each case the rulings have supported the principle of federal supremacy. In 1990 a federal district judge ruled that Oakland's nuclear free zone was illegal because it was "so comprehensive, so complete, so all-encompassing that it cannot help but conflict with the rights and authority of the federal government." Unlike most local nuclear free zones, which were largely nonbinding resolutions, this one had teeth. It banned firms from engaging in any contracting or subcontracting of missile production projects within the city limits. Also in 1990 the Supreme Court ruled that the governor of Minnesota (and, by extension, the governor of Massachusetts) could not stop their National Guard units from participating in exercises in Honduras. They had claimed such authority on the basis of Article I of the Constitution, which gives states authority to train the militia. The last case occurred in 1989 when the Maryland Supreme Court upheld Baltimore's policy of not investing in firms doing business in South Africa. While on the surface this decision supported local foreign policy initiatives, the logic behind the court's ruling pointed in the opposite direction. The court found in favor of Baltimore only because "the effect . . . on South Africa is minimal and indirect."

The question of where states and localities fit into the overall scheme of American foreign policy is sure to remain unanswered for the foreseeable future. Beyond the legal issues involved, the debate promises to center on three concerns.[22] First, can the United States have an effective foreign policy if it speaks with more than one voice? Second, since foreign policy decisions affect everyone, should they be made by state and local groups? Third, do states and local governments have the expertise to engage in foreign policy making? The traditional answer to all three questions is no. Defenders of state foreign policy making argue that the United States has never spoken with one voice in foreign policy; that there is a great deal of local- and state-level expertise on environmental, economic, and human rights issues; and that municipal and state foreign policies that affect voters' lives are more readily controlled by voters than is decision making in Washington.

SUMMARY AND FUTURE ISSUES

In this chapter we have reviewed the constitutional distribution of powers in foreign affairs as they exist in the areas of treaty making, appointments, war making, and commerce. This distribution of powers is not exhaustive. Gaps exist. No mention is made of the power to terminate a treaty, declare neutrality, make peace, or break diplomatic relations. The constitutional distribution of powers establishes only a starting point for foreign policy decision making. In the words of Edward Corwin, it is an "invitation to the president and Congress to struggle over the privilege of directing U.S. foreign policy."[23]

Attempts to change the balance of power between the Congress and president in this struggle take place frequently. Looking to the future we can identify two relatively new policy areas where conflict is likely. Both are a product of the emerging post–cold war international system and the blurring of the distinction between domestic and foreign policy. The first involves questions of global environmental protection. The Kyoto Summit in 1997 addressed the problem of global warming and committed the United States and other industrialized states to the first binding limits on heat-trapping gases. Citing its economic costs to the United States and the absence of any binding targets for the developing world, Republican leaders labeled the treaty "dead on arrival." Even those Democrats that supported the treaty agreed that it could not receive approval in its current form and urged President Clinton to delay in sending the treaty to the Senate. The second policy problem centers on a proposed treaty creating a standing International Criminal Court (ICC).[24] Where the existing International Court of Justice has jurisdiction over states, the ICC would have jurisdiction over individuals who violate international humanitarian laws. At issue are such complex matters as jurisdiction (the United States opposes including drug trafficking, terrorism, or actions growing out of humanitarian military operations) and whether it is constitutional (critics claim that many of the fundamental safeguards contained in the Bill of Rights would not be available to an American appearing before it).

If we look beyond specific issues, we can see that most of the time the struggle between the two branches takes the form of imposing (and resisting) specific restrictions on the exercise of presidential power. The perennial focus of attention is the War Powers Resolution. Recently Louis Fisher and David Gray Adler have argued that after twenty five years of experience, it would be better for both branches—and for constitutional government—to repeal the War Powers Resolution and rely upon traditional political pressures and the regular system of checks and balances, including impeachment. Over the long term, outright repeal would be less risky than continuing along the present path.[25]

More frequently heard than calls for its repeal are proposals for the revision of the War Powers Resolution. Congressional leaders in both parties have proposed that the section requiring that the president notify Congress be repealed and replaced by provisions allowing for (1) the expedited consideration of legislation to terminate any troop deployments that Congress objects to and (2) the establishment of a permanent congressional consulting group that the administration would be in touch with before and during military operations. Failing this, observers such as Destler believe that we will see congressional–presidential dealings in this area beginning to move on two separate tracks.[26] On big issues such as the war powers question, the president may gain additional leeway. On more routine issues such as arms sales and economic policy, the president will lose flexibility. In these areas Congress will develop more cumbersome means of regulating executive branch behavior.

After watching U.S. forces serve in international peacekeeping efforts in Somalia and Haiti, and fearing that the same thing might happen in places like Bosnia, Senate Majority Leader Robert Dole started off the 104th Congress by introducing a "peace powers act" that would place restraints on a president's ability to send U.S. troops and spend U.S. dollars policing post–cold war trouble spots. Dole's resolution would repeal that part of the War Powers Resolution which required a president to withdraw troops from hostile situations in 60 days unless Congress gave its approval. The notification and reporting requirements would be retained. With regard to peacekeeping operations, Dole's resolution would prevent the president from moving to initiate, expand, or extend peacekeeping operations without detailing in advance how they would be paid for. A second Republican bid to repeal the War Powers Resolution was turned back in the House in 1995 by a vote of 217–201. A letter from Clinton supporting the repeal was held back when it became clear that the move would fail.

The emergence of divided government in the post–cold war era has also produced calls for a more fundamental reexamination of the balance of power between the two branches. Most often cited as proof positive of the need for these changes are the inability to pass foreign policy legislation in a timely fashion and the transformation of "advise and consent" into "harass and maim." Reforms have also been sought at a much more fundamental level. William Fulbright, former chairman of the Senate Foreign Relations Committee, was among the first to speak out for such a reform, questioning whether "our constitutional machinery, admirably suited for the needs of a remote 18th century agrarian republic" was "adequate to the formulations and conduct of foreign policy of a 20th century nation."[27] In Fulbright's view modern foreign policy required the ability to act quickly, decisively, and persistently. Congress possessed none of these attributes. Lloyd Cutler, a former counsel to President Carter, argues that the separation-of-powers system all but guarantees a foreign policy stalemate. It is impossible today to "form a government."[28] The Constitution prevents presidents from being able to put their programs into effect. Cutler compares the U.S. separation-of-powers system with a parliamentary system and finds it lacking. Cutler does not expect to see a truly parliamentary system established in the United States. He does want to create a relationship between the two branches so that the president is able to carry out a program and can legitimately be held answerable for what the government does or does not do during his or her stay in office.

NOTES

1. Quoted in *The Washington Post,* February 17, 1990, p. 23.
2. The President's Special Review Board, *The Tower Commission Report* (New York: Bantam, 1987), p. 6.
3. Louis Henkin, *Foreign Affairs and the Constitution* (Mineola, N.Y.: Foundation Press, 1972), p. 131.
4. Thomas L. Brewer, *American Foreign Policy: A Contemporary Introduction,* 2nd ed. (Englewood Cliffs, N.J.: Prentice-Hall, 1986), p. 113.
5. Theodor Meron, "The Treaty Power: The International Legal Effect of Changes in Obligations Initiated by the Congress," in Thomas M. Franck (ed.), *The Tethered Presidency* (New York: New York University Press, 1981), pp. 103–40.
6. For a discussion of the Reagan administration's tendency to unilaterally reinterpret laws, see David Scheffer, "Nouveau Law and Foreign Policy," *Foreign Policy,* 76 (1989), 44–65.
7. Loch Johnson and James M. McCormick, "Foreign Policy by Executive Fiat," *Foreign Policy,* 28 (1977), 117–38.
8. Ibid.
9. James A Nathan and Richard K. Oliver, *Foreign Policy Making and the American Political System* (Boston: Little, Brown, 1983), p. 115.
10. Charles W. Kegley, Jr., and Eugene R. Wittkopf, *American Foreign Policy: Pattern and Process.* 2nd ed. (New York: St. Martin's, 1982), p. 418.
11. *The Washington Post,* February 9, 1992.
12. William L. Furlong, "Negotiations and Ratification of the Panama Canal Treaty," in John Spanier and Joseph Nogee (eds.), *Congress, the Presidency, and American Foreign Policy* (Elmsford, N.Y.: Pergamon, 1981), pp. 77–107.
13. The material in this section is drawn from the accounts by Furlong; and Cecil Crabb, Jr., and Pat M. Holt, *Invitation to Struggle: Congress, the President, and Foreign Policy,* 2nd ed. (Washington D.C.: Congressional Quarterly, 1984).
14. Henkin, *Foreign Affairs and the Constitution,* pp. 100–1.
15. Robert F. Turner, *The War Powers Resolution: Its Implementation in Theory and Practice* (Philadelphia: Foreign Policy Research Institute, 1983), presents a thorough and critical review of the cases to which the War Powers Resolution has been and could have been applied.
16. Congressional Research Service, *Foreign Policy Effects of the Supreme Court's Legislative Veto Decision* (Washington, D.C.: Congressional Research Service, February 23, 1984).
17. House Committee on Foreign Affairs, *The War Powers Resolution: Relevant Documents, Correspondence, and Reports* (Washington, D.C.: U.S. Government Printing Office, 1983); Reagan's actions are examined in Charles Madden, "Foreign Policy Report," *National Journal,* May 19, 1984, pp. 989–93.
18. I. M. Destler and Thomas R. Graham, "United States Congress and the Tokyo Round: Lessons of a Success Story," *The World Economy,* 3 (1980), 53–70.
19. Dan R. Bucks, "Trade Trouble Ahead," *State Government News,* May 1994, 6–9.
20. Michael H. Shuman, "Dateline Main Street: Courts v. Local Foreign Policies," *Foreign Policy,* 86 (1992), 158–77.
21. Earl H. Fry, "States in the International Economy: An American Overview," in Douglas M. Brown and Earl H. Fry (eds.), *States and Provinces in the International Political Economy* (Berkeley, Calif.: Institute of Governmental Studies Press, 1993), 45–64.
22. Shuman, "Dateline Mainstreet."
23. Edward S. Corwin, *The President: Office and Powers* (New York: New York University Press, 1957), p. 171.

24. Lee A. Casey and David B. Rivkin, Jr., "Against an International Criminal Court," *Commentary*, 105 (May, 1998), 56–8; and David Sheffer, "International Judicial Intervention," *Foreign Policy*, 102 (1996), 34–51.

25. Louis Fisher and David Gray Adler, "The War Powers Resolution: Time to Say Goodbye," *Political Science Quarterly*, 113 (1998), 1–18.

26. I. M. Destler, "Dateline Washington: Life After the Veto," *Foreign Policy*, 52 (1983), pp. 181–86.

27. William J. Fulbright, "American Foreign Policy in the 20th Century Under an 18th Century Constitution," *Cornell Law Quarterly*, 47 (1961), 1–13. A similar argument is made by John G. Tower, "Congress Versus the President," *Foreign Affairs*, 60 (1981/82), 229–46.

28. Lloyd N. Cutler, "To Form a Government," *Foreign Affairs*, 59 (1980), 126–43.

8 The Presidency

In the public's eye it is the president who makes U.S. foreign policy. Memoir accounts by recent presidents reinforce this image. In the following excerpt, President Nixon recounts his decision to send U.S. and South Vietnamese troops into the Parrot's Beak and Fishhook areas of Cambodia. The starting point for this policy debate is the overthrow of Cambodian head of state Prince Sihanouk by General Lon Nol, an anticommunist.

> My immediate reaction was to do everything possible to help Lon Nol, but [Secretary of State] Rogers, and [Secretary of Defense] Laird strongly recommended that we hold back. . . . By the end of April . . . it was clear that Lon Nol needed help to survive. . . . Support for Lon Nol was discussed at an NSC meeting on April 22. I woke up early that morning and dictated a memorandum to [National Security Adviser] Kissinger: Assuming that I feel the way today at our meeting as I feel this morning . . . I think we need a bold move in Cambodia to show that we stand with Lon Nol. . . . On Monday morning I met with Rogers, Laird, and Kissinger. It was a tense meeting, because even though Rogers and Laird had by now given up hope of dissuading me from taking some action in Cambodia, they still thought they could convince me not to involve American troops. . . . That night I sat alone going over the decision one last time. . . . I took a pad and began to make a list of the pluses and minuses of both operations.[1]

Carter gives this account of how he came to his decision to hold the Camp David summit conference between Israeli prime minister Begin and Egyptian president Sadat. He begins the account with a diary entry from February 3, 1978.

> We had quite an argument at breakfast with me on one side and Fritz [Vice-President Mondale], Cy [Secretary of State Vance], Zbig [National Security Adviser Brzezinski], and Ham [presidential aide Jordan] on the other. I think we ought to move much more aggressively on the Middle East question than any of them seem to. . . . Late in June, I called in a small group of Democratic "wisemen"—senior leaders who were experienced in political affairs. Their advice was to "stay as aloof as possible from direct involvement in the Middle East negotiations; this is a losing proposition." At the time, I could not think of any reason to disagree with them, but there was just no way I could abandon such an important commitment. . . . At our regular Friday morning foreign-affairs breakfast we spent much of our time talking about the Middle East. . . . I discussed the situation with Rosalynn, who was thoroughly familiar with the issues involved in the

Middle East dispute and understood what was at stake. . . . There was only one thing to do. . . . I would try to bring Sadat and Begin together for an extensive negotiating session with me. . . . I asked Mondale, Vance, [Secretary of Defense], Brown, Brzezinski, and Jordan to come to Camp David for a special meeting on the Middle East. There I described what I had in mind. None of us thought we had much chance of success but we could not think of a better alternative.[2]

Not all presidents are as deeply involved in making foreign policy decisions. In his videotaped testimony for the trial of one of his former national security advisers, John Poindexter, President Reagan made many comments that were at variance with the documentary evidence amassed by the Tower Commission and the testimony of other participants. The following is his response to a question regarding his recollection of a 1986 briefing by Poindexter on sending HAWK missile spare parts to Iran.

The only thing that I am aware of, and I cannot remember any meeting on this or not, was I do have a memory of learning or hearing that the Israelis, prior to these other things, had sent some of their HAWK missiles to Iran evidently in that sale. . . . And the thing that makes me remember this is that, apparently, the understanding was that this was going to be in return for some, perhaps, hostages of their own or the people that were held. That if these individuals had not been released by the time the plane of delivery had reached a certain point, the plane would turn around and come back without continuing the delivery.[3]

Reagan's strength as president (at least until the Iran–Contra affair became public) was seen as his ability to paint and communicate the "big picture," and his "hands-off" management style. Personal initiative and organizational design are two different strategies presidents use to move the rest of the government in the direction of presidential policy initiatives. Many see the challenge here as immense.

Hugh Heclo suggests that "far from being in charge of, or running the government, the president must struggle even to comprehend what is going on."[4] Information does not come to the president automatically. Nor can presidents count on speed and secrecy in making and carrying out decisions. Theirs is often the power to persuade rather than the power to command.[5] In this chapter we examine both of these solutions (personal initiative and organization) to the problem of presidential foreign policy leadership.

PRESIDENTIAL PERSONALITY

Textbooks and newspaper accounts of U.S. foreign policy are dominated by references to policies that bear a president's name: the Monroe Doctrine, the Truman Doctrine, the Nixon Doctrine, the Carter Doctrine, the Reagan Doctrine. Personalizing the presidency this way suggests that the identity of the president matters greatly and that if a different person had been president, U.S. foreign policy would look different. A Mondale Doctrine would be very different from the Reagan Doctrine, and a McGovern Doctrine would have been very different from the Nixon Doctrine. Yet is this necessarily the case?

How important is the personality of the president to the process and substance of U.S. foreign policy? A persuasive case can be made that situational factors, role variables, and the common socioeconomic backgrounds of policy makers place severe constraints on the impact of personality on policy. In this section we first look at a leading effort to capture presidential personality and then examine under what conditions we should expect presidential personality to make a difference.

The most famous effort to classify presidential personality and explore its implications for policy is by James David Barber, who defines personality in terms of three elements.[6] The first is world view, which Barber defines as an individual's politically relevant beliefs. The second element is style, which refers to an individual's habitual ways of responding to political opportunities and challenges through "rhetoric, personal relations, and homework." They are both heavily influenced by the third and most important component of personality: character, which develops in childhood. Character is the way the individual orients himself or herself toward life and involves two dimensions. The first is the amount of energy put into the presidency. Presidents are classified as either passive or active. The second dimension is whether the president derives personal satisfaction from the job. A president who does is classified as positive, and one who gets no personal satisfaction from being president is classified as negative. Together these two dimensions produce four presidential personalities. Table 8–1 present Barber's typology and his placement of presidents.

Active-positives put a great deal of energy into being president and derive great satisfaction from doing so. They are achievement oriented, value productivity, and enjoy meeting new challenges. Active-negatives are compulsive individuals who are driven to acquire power as a means of compensating for low self-esteem. Active-negatives adopt a domineering posture toward those around them and have difficulty managing their aggressive feelings. Passive-

TABLE 8–1 Barber's Classification of Presidents' Character

Active-Positive	Active-Negative	Passive-Positive	Passive-Negative
F. Roosevelt	Hoover	Taft	Coolidge
Truman	Wilson	Harding	Eisenhower
Kennedy	Johnson	Reagan	
Ford	Nixon		
Carter			
Bush			
Clinton			

Source: James David Barber, *The Presidential Character*, 4th ed. (Englewood Cliffs, N.J.: Prentice-Hall, 1992); updated with Fred I. Greenstein, "The Presidential Leadership Style of Bill Clinton: An Early Appraisal," (reprinted with permission from *Political Science Quarterly*, 108 (1993/94): 589–601.

positives are directed individuals who seek affection as a reward for being agreeable. Passive-positive presidents do not make full use of the powers of the presidency but feel satisfied with the job as they define it. Passive-negatives get little satisfaction from the job and use few of the powers available to them. They are only in politics because others have sought them out, and they feel a responsibility to meet these expectations. Their actions are plagued by low self-esteem and feelings of uselessness. They do not enjoy the game of politics. Rather than bargain and compromise, they seek to avoid confrontation by emphasizing vague principles and procedural arrangements.

Barber argues that his typology can be used to predict presidential performance. In Barber's original presentation he argued for the active-positive character as the one best suited for the modern presidency. A preferable approach is to recognize that each type of presidential character has different implications for U.S. foreign policy. Barber favored the active-positive personality (among whom he numbered Franklin Roosevelt, Truman, Kennedy, Ford, and Carter) for its flexibility and emphasis on the rational mastery of problems. Carter's handling of the Panama Canal Treaties illustrates the ability of active-positives to productively engage in coalition-building efforts and to accept the compromises necessary to get a policy measure passed. Carter's presidency also illustrates the problem with active-positive presidents. They may overreach themselves by pursuing too many goals at once and be insensitive to the fact that the irrationalities of politics can frustrate even the best laid plans. Carter was roundly criticized for being too flexible in the search for results and for trying to do too many things at the outset of his administration: negotiate a SALT II Treaty, negotiate a Panama Canal Treaty, and reorder U.S. foreign policy priorities by emphasizing human rights and economic problems over the Soviet threat.

The great danger of active-negatives is that they will rigidly adhere to a disastrous foreign policy. Woodrow Wilson did so in the League of Nations controversy; John Adams, with the Alien and Sedition Act; Lyndon Johnson, with Vietnam; and Richard Nixon, with his actions in the Watergate scandal and the impeachment proceedings. Both passive-negatives and passive-positives will rarely challenge the status quo. In each case the dangers are twofold. First, there is the problem of policy drift as issues go unexamined and challenges are not met. Second, there is the problem of accountability. Passive presidents are likely to delegate much of their authority, which raises the issue of how does one hold nonelected officials accountable for policy decisions. A major benefit of passive presidents, as Barber sees it, is their ability to offer the country a breathing spell after periods of activism.

Placing a president in one of Barber's categories involves a great deal of subjective judgment. Consider the case of Eisenhower. Fred Greenstein suggests that Eisenhower was not a passive-negative president as he is defined by Barber.[7] Based on previously unavailable materials, Greenstein concludes that Eisenhower deliberately cultivated the image of not being involved in policy making in order to deflect political pressures away from him. Eisenhower's "hidden hand leadership" employed a behind-the-scenes activism combined with a low profile in public.

Categorizing presidents in terms of shared qualities is useful because it allows us to move beyond making a series of singular observations. Bush, for example, has been characterized as an American "Tory." That is, he was "skeptical of grand ideologies and ambitious plans of action. Problems find you, in the Tory view; there is little reason to seek them out."[8] This is an insightful observation but still leaves us wondering how Reagan or Clinton compares to Bush. We must remember, however, that placing presidents in categories is only the beginning step in an analysis of their presidency and not the end. Attributes alone do not tell us what to expect from a president in terms of either policy or leadership style. Few would have predicted that Ronald Reagan, the arch anticommunist, would end his administration as an advocate of arms control or bring about a major improvement in U.S.–Soviet relations.[9] Bill Clinton is a second example. Clinton is a perfect fit for classification as an active-positive president. He is a supremely political animal who enjoys the game of politics; when defeated he bounces back; and he displays a fundamental pragmatism in approaching policy problems. Yet Clinton's performance as president has not produced a consistent pattern. He has displayed both the desirable qualities of an active-positive (an ability to be focused and accommodating) and the undesirable ones (a tendency to be undisciplined and to overreach).[10]

When Does the Individual Matter?

In a recent study of twentieth-century U.S. foreign policy, John Stoessinger was struck by how few individuals made crucial decisions shaping its direction.[11] He found that "movers" (exceptional individuals who for better or worse not only find turning points in history but help create them) have been far outnumbered by "players" (individuals caught up in the flow of events who respond in a standard and predictable fashion). One explanation for this imbalance is that there may exist relatively few situations where the personal characteristics of the policy maker are important for explaining policy.

A useful distinction can be made between action indispensability and actor indispensability.[12] Action indispensability refers to situations in which a specific action is critical to the success or failure of a policy. The identity of the actor is not necessarily a critical factor in explaining the action. It is possible that any individual (player) in that situation would have acted in the same manner. Actor indispensability refers to those situations where the personal characteristics of the involved are critical to explaining the action taken. In Stoessinger's terms the individual involved is a mover. "He increases the odds of success or failure . . . by virtue of the extraordinary qualities he brings to bear upon it."

A crucial element of action indispensability is the degree to which the situation permits restructuring. Some situations are so intractable or unstable that it is unreasonable to expect the actions of an individual policy maker to have much of an impact. The most favorable condition for individual actions to have an impact is when a "precarious equilibrium" exists and events are primed to move in any number of directions. This is seldom the case. Many of the foreign policy problems that a president confronts are either highly intractable situations or very unstable ones. Consider such intractable problems as the U.S. balance-of-payments deficit, energy policy, and illegal immigration and such unstable ones as the situation in Iran during the hostage crisis and the situation in Lebanon following the fall of the Gemayel government in 1983. In all of these areas, it is difficult to envision a single presidential action or set of actions having a dramatic and long-lasting impact. Presidents do not ignore these policy problems. Peace initiatives in the Middle East have become a common feature of U.S. foreign policy. Economic summit conferences bringing together the leaders of the advanced industrial states now occur at regular intervals. It is just that either the instability of the situation overtakes policy initiatives or its persistent features dilute the policy initiative perpetuating the status quo.

When, then, does personality matter? A 1969 survey suggests that the impact of personal characteristics will be especially crucial under certain conditions. Numbered among them are the following:

Completely new situations in which there are no familiar clues
Complex situations in which there are a great many clues
Contradictory situations in which different elements suggest different clues
Issues which are salient to the policy maker
Acts which are more demanding of the policy maker
Fewer constraints on the individual making the decision[13]

In concrete terms we can suggest that the president's personality will have its greatest impact on policy under these conditions. First is when the issue is new on the agenda. Carter's involvement in human rights policy and Reagan's championing of the strategic defense initiative are cases in point. Second is when the issue is addressed early in the administration. Carter's decision not to simply wrap up the SALT II package left him by Ford but to negotiate his own treaty illustrates this point. Clinton's handling of Somalia is another example. Third are those ongoing issues where the president is deeply involved. Vietnam was such an issue for Johnson and Nixon. Release of the American hostages in Lebanon was such an issue for Reagan. Finally, we can expect presidential personality to matter when the issue is in a state of precarious equilibrium. Recent issues which could be classified this way are arms control, the Middle East peace process, Bosnia, and the democratization movement in Russia.

PRESIDENTIAL BUREAUCRACY

Presidents have discovered that the strength of their personality alone is not enough to get others to follow. Leadership also requires an organizational foundation, and experience has taught them that the executive branch bureaucracy is not that organization. The bureaucrat's time frame is different from that of the president. Presidents have only four years (eight if they are lucky) to implement their agenda. Bureaucrats know that they will be there long after the current administration leaves office and the next one, claiming a new mandate, arrives. The result is that presidents have been forced to look elsewhere to create an organization that will allow them to lead. The central foreign policy structure that presidents have grown to rely on is the National Security Council (NSC). Before reviewing its history, it is important to recognize that a prerequisite for effectively using the presidential bureaucracy to exercise foreign policy leadership is presidential control over it. How this is done is up to the president and varies from president to president.

Three basic options exist.[14] None is by definition superior to another. All have contributed to foreign policy successes and failures. The first is a competitive model in which a great deal of emphasis is placed on the free and open expression of ideas. Jurisdictions and grants of authority overlap as individuals and departments compete for the president's attention in putting forward ideas and programs. Franklin Roosevelt is the only president who successfully employed such a model. Lyndon Johnson is seen as having tried and failed to emulate him. A second leadership style involves setting up a formalistic system in which the president establishes orderly routines and procedures for organizing the administration's policy deliberations. The system is hierarchically structured with the president deeply involved as the final arbitrator in defining strategy and policy choices. Truman, Eisenhower, Nixon, Ford, and Reagan set up formalistic systems. The third management style centers on the creation of a collegial system in which presidents try to bring together a group of advisers to operate as a problem-solving team. The Secretary of State may serve as the center of the team, although this need not be the case. Kennedy, Carter, Bush, and Clinton set up this type of system.

One way to anticipate which of these outcomes is likely to occur is by seeing if a president has laid the proper foundation for the system to work correctly.[15] Because only the formalistic and collegial systems have been tried with regularity, we will only look at their prerequisites. For a collegial system to work one of two conditions must be met. Either the team players must share a common world view or the president must be able to articulate a clear vision to keep the team focused. For a formalistic system to succeed, one of three conditions must be met. A firm guiding hand is needed at the top, strong coordinating leadership must be present below the presidential level, or a common world view must unite those involved in the decision-making process.

THE NATIONAL SECURITY COUNCIL

The history of the National Security Council (NSC) system can be broken down into four phases, each of which introduced distortions into the operation of the system that ultimately hindered the pursuit of foreign policy goals and its ultimate purpose. According to the 1947 National Security Act, this was to advise the president "with respect to the integration of domestic, foreign, and military policies relating to national security."[16] The first phase of the NSC's history runs from 1947 to 1960. During this period the NSC became overly institutionalized. Truman was the first president to have the NSC, and he was cautious in using it. He particularly wanted to avoid setting any precedents that would give it the power to supervise executive branch agencies or establish a norm of group responsibility for foreign policy decisions as some had hoped when the establishment of the NSC was being debated. For Truman foreign policy was the responsibility of the president alone. The NSC was to be an advisory body and nothing more. To emphasize this point, Truman did not attend early NSC meetings, and he relied heavily on his Secretary of State and personal contacts for foreign policy advice.

The NSC staff was modest in size, numbering only about 20 employees compared to the 50 staffers who worked there under Kennedy, the 75 who worked there under Nixon, and the 62 who worked there in 1982 under the Reagan administration.[17] Truman's NSC was directed by Sidney Souers, whose title was executive secretary and who acted as a manager rather than as a policy advocate. In 1949 the NSC staff began preparing policy review statements, the most significant of which was NSC-68. This report presented a grim picture of U.S. capabilities and the Soviet threat and called for a rapid buildup of the political, economic, and military strength of the free world. Truman sent the report back to the NSC with instructions that its budgetary implications be examined in more detail. Believing that national security required both a strong military posture and a strong economy, the Truman administration had placed a $15 billion ceiling on military expenditures, and Truman was not favorably predisposed to increasing defense spending. The outbreak of the Korean War changed Truman's approach to the NSC. He started to use it more systematically and began attending its regularly scheduled meetings. Organizational changes also took place. All national security issues were now to be brought to his attention through the NSC system, the NSC staff was reorganized, and the emphasis on outside consultants was replaced by a senior staff served by staff assistants.

Institutionalization continued under Eisenhower, who transformed the NSC system into a two-part unit that would be actively involved in making policy. A Planning Board was created to develop policy recommendations for the president, and an Operations Coordinating Board was established to oversee the implementation of national security decisions. Eisenhower also established the post of Assistant for National Security Affairs (commonly known as the president's National Security Adviser) to more forcefully coordinate the national security decision-making process. By all accounts the NSC system never really functioned as envisioned. Instead of producing high-quality policy recommendations, the concern for touching all the bureaucratic bases produced decisions made on the basis of the lowest common denominator. Rather than increasing presidential options, it limited them. Policy implementation continued to be governed by departmental objectives and definitions of the problem rather than by presidential goals and perspectives.[18]

The second phase of the NSC's history, in which it became overly personalized, began with the Kennedy administration and lasted until 1980. Under Kennedy the formal and hierarchically structured system that Eisenhower had created declined in importance. Kennedy adopted an activist approach to national security management grounded on informal operating procedures. Stress was placed on multiple lines of communication, direct presidential contacts with second- and third-level officials, and securing outside expert advice. Ad hoc interagency task forces replaced the formal NSC system as the primary decision-making unit for dealing with such international problems as the Cuban missile crisis, Berlin, and Laos. Within the NSC system, emphasis switched from the council itself to the NSC staff. The staff came to be viewed less as a body of professionals who would stay on from administration to administration and more as a group that closely identified with the current administration and was loyal to it. The NSC staff became the vehicle by which Kennedy could serve as his own Secretary of State.

In the revamped management system, the National Security Adviser played a key role. This person was responsible for ensuring that the staff operated from a presidential perspective and obtained the needed information and seeing to it that administration policy was being properly implemented. McGeorge Bundy held this post under Kennedy and in the first part of the Johnson administration. He was replaced by Walt Rostow in 1966. The change in advisers brought with it a change in operating style. Bundy saw his role as a facilitator whose job it was to encourage the airing of ideas and policy alternatives. Rostow was more of an ideologue concerned with policy advocacy over process management.

Like Kennedy, Johnson took an activist stance and favored small, informal policy-making settings over the formal NSC system. Major Vietnam decisions were made at the Tuesday lunch group which brought together Johnson and his key foreign policy advisers. The NSC staff became demoralized and felt little loyalty to Johnson or his policies. The Tuesday lunch group was a "procedural abomination" lacking a formal agenda and clearly stated conclusions, wearing on participants, and confusing to those at the working levels.[19] The NSC coordinating system was overwhelmed by the pressures of Vietnam, was often bypassed due to the tendency to make key policy decisions in the White House, and never received the enthusiastic support of either senior policy makers or foreign policy professionals in the bureaucracy.

Nixon began his presidency with a pledge to place the NSC system back at the center of the foreign policy decision-making process.[20] This was achieved by first selecting Henry Kissinger as his National Security Adviser and William Rogers as his Secretary of State. The combination of a strong, opinionated, and activist National Security Adviser and a Secretary of State with little foreign policy experience guaranteed that foreign policy would be made in the White House. Second, Nixon created an elaborate NSC committee and staff system. Separate bodies were created to deal with SALT-related verification issues, Vietnam, intelligence programs, covert action, crisis management, and defense programs. There also existed an Under Secretaries Committee and interdepartmental groups.

Positioned at the center of this elaborate system, Kissinger was able to direct the flow of paper in the direction he wanted, bringing the NSC system into play on certain issues and cutting it out of others. By the end of the Nixon administration, the NSC was largely on the outside looking in. It met only 3 times in 1973, compared to 37 times in 1969. Such important decisions as the invasion of Cambodia, Kissinger's trip to China, the Paris Peace Negotiations, bombing in Vietnam, and putting U.S. troops on worldwide alert in the Yom Kippur War were made outside the NSC system.

The formal structure of the NSC system changed little under Ford. What did change was Kissinger's position in it. He was forced to step down as chairperson of all but the Verification Panel (which dealt with arms control matters) and the Washington Special Action Group (which dealt with crisis management).[21]

Carter dismantled the elaborate Nixon–Ford–Kissinger committee system in favor of two committees. The Policy Review Committee was charged with handling long-term projects, and its chair rotated depending on the topic assigned to it. A Special Coordinating Committee (SCC) was created to deal with short-term problems, crisis situations, and covert action. It was chaired by Brzezinski. Originally, these two committees were to be equally important, but over time the SCC dominated. This was especially true with the advent of the Iranian hostage crisis and the Soviet invasion of Afghanistan. Collegiality was evident in the prominent policy-making roles played by the Friday foreign policy breakfasts (attended by Carter and his key foreign policy advisers) and the Thursday lunch meetings (at which these advisers met to prepare for the Friday meeting).

Carter's activism often overloaded the foreign policy agenda and created a number of problems for his NSC system. Many of them centered on the workings of the Friday foreign policy breakfasts, which became substitutes for full NSC meetings. The problem was that decisions arrived at here were not always fully integrated into the NSC system, nor did they necessarily produce clearly articulated positions.[22] In 1980 these problems produced a major foreign policy embarrassment. In the United Nations Security Council, the United States voted with 14 other states to rebuke Israel for increasing the number of Jewish settlements on Arab territory that it seized in the 1967 war. The next day an embarrassed Carter said that this had been a mistake and that the United States meant to abstain on the vote. The mistake was attributed to a failure to properly communicate a decision reached at the breakfast meeting to the NSC system.

During the Reagan administration, the NSC entered a third phase. Pledging to depersonalize the system, Reagan pushed too far in the opposite direction, causing it to go into decline. The National Security Adviser became a nonperson with little foreign policy influence or stature. And, as a direct consequence, the NSC staff ceased to function as either a policy-making or policy-coordinating body. With no force able to coordinate foreign policy, an unprecedented degree of bureaucratic infighting and fragmentation came to characterize (and paralyze) Reagan's foreign policy. Only with the arrival of General Powell as National Security Adviser and the passage from the Cabinet of such powerful and highly opinionated figures as Secretary of Defense Caspar Weinberger and Director of Central Intelligence William Casey did a coherent foreign policy agenda appear.[23] While this was happening the NSC staff moved in two different directions. On the one hand it became preoccupied with bureaucratic trivia. (There were 25 committees, 55 mid-level committees, and some 100 task forces and working groups.) On the other hand it became involved in the actual conduct of foreign policy in the Iran–Contra initiative.

With the Bush and Clinton administrations, decision making in the NSC system was transformed a fourth time. It has become collegial in nature. In Brent Scowcroft and Anthony Lake, both presidents selected low-key National Security Advisers who could be expected to avoid the excesses of Kissinger or the turf battles that were commonplace between Brzezinski and Vance. On the surface, a move to collegiality is an appropriate remedy for many of the past excesses found in the operation of the NSC system. The problem, as some see it, is that collegiality is ill-suited for an era in which world politics is engaged in a transition from the predictability of the cold war to the unpredictability of the post–cold war era. What may be needed is a system which fosters unconventional thinking and leads policy makers to explore policy options and goals that have not previously been considered as realistic or in the American national interest. The Bush administration's collegial system was unable to do so because all of its participants, including the president, were confident that they understood the world and were slow to adapt to the reality that this world was disappearing before their eyes. As one pair of commentators have noted, "in more stable times, the Bush policy-making team almost certainly would have been a striking success."[24] Clinton also has failed to make the collegial system work. Confident of his political skills and intellect, he has placed himself at the center of a collegial system of policy making in which most of the key players are tacticians rather than visionaries. The problem is that Clinton has neither been able to provide a consistent vision to guide his team nor to construct a division of labor among team members that produces a coherent policy. The Clinton White House constantly reinvents itself, lurching from issue to issue.[25] As with Bush, the result has been a largely reactive foreign policy and one that seems to be caught in the same "quagmire of caution" that engulfed the Bush administration.[26]

PRESIDENTIAL DECISION MAKING

The Iran–Contra Initiative

The twin influences of presidential personality and organization on U.S. foreign policy come together quite clearly in the Iran–Contra initiative by the Reagan administration. As best determined by the Tower Commission, events unfolded in the following manner.[27] In early 1984 members of the NSC staff system became concerned about the future of U.S. foreign policy in regard to Iran in the post-Khomeini era. One option raised and objected to by Secretary of State Shultz and Secretary of Defense Weinberger was to permit and encourage Western arms transfers to Iran. In July 1985 the United States received inquiries from Israel on U.S. attitudes toward a political dialogue with Iran. This inquiry followed a meeting a few months earlier between an NSC staffer and top Israeli leaders. The transfer of weapons to Iran and the release of American hostages in Lebanon became permanent agenda items in these discussions. At the outset it was thought by some that the sale of weapons to Iran would establish the United States' "bona fides" and that in return Iran would show its good faith by arranging for the release of the U.S. hostages. Very quickly the arms-for-hostages equation came to drive U.S. decision making, and the original goal of establishing a dialogue with Iranian leaders became a lesser concern.

It is the conclusion of the Tower Commission that in August President Reagan authorized the shipment of weapons to Israel which, in turn, delivered U.S.-made weapons in their possession to Iran. On September 15, 1985, the Reverend Benjamin Weir was released by his Lebanese kidnappers. Israeli arms shipments to Iran took place in August and September. In the following months the United States adopted a much more direct role in the process with

NSC staffer Lieutenant Colonel Oliver North and National Security Adviser John Poindexter playing the key roles. In January 1986 a Presidential Finding was signed allowing the CIA to purchase TOW missiles from the Defense Department and arrange for their transfer to Iran after receiving payment for them from the arms merchant intermediaries that the administration was using to coordinate the sale. Operating through this unofficial, private channel, the NSC managed four arms sales in 1986 in February, May, August, and October.

The process of buying and selling weapons generated large sums of money, much of which could not be accounted for. Evidence uncovered by the Tower Commission strongly suggests that some of this money was diverted to support the Contras in Nicaragua in their struggle against the U.S.-opposed Sandinista government. Such funding, while consistent with the Reagan administration's position of support for the Contras, was in violation of congressional statutes. In October 1984 Congress cut off all U.S. funding for the Contras unless specifically authorized by Congress.

The Reagan administration did not consider the NSC staff covered by this prohibition, and as early as September 1984, Lieutenant Colonel North became involved in garnering support for the Contras from private U.S. sources, aiding them in their operational activities through the provision of intelligence and the resupply of weapons. The Tower Commission concluded that the NSC staff role in supporting the Contras set the stage for its subsequent role in the Iran affair but that it was unclear whether North sought or received the formal authority to manage this diversion.

Bosnia

Policy vacillation is a characteristic routinely applied to President Clinton's foreign policy. Clinton's personality is held to be the primary contributing factor bringing about this condition. Yet, the Clinton administration's early decisions on Bosnia also show the influence of presidential organization.[28] During the presidential campaign, Clinton attacked the Bush administration for its Bosnia policy as "turning its back on violations of human rights" and "being slow on the uptake." He promised to "make the United States the catalyst for a collective stand against aggression."

Richard Holbrooke, who would later become a prime architect of the Dayton Peace Accords, was one of those who advised Clinton on foreign policy during his campaign. One week before Clinton's inauguration he wrote a memo to incoming Secretary of State Warren Christopher and National Security Advisor Anthony Lake about the importance of Bosnia and the need for action. He received no response. Holbrooke was told by associates that the Clinton team was deeply immersed in its own discussions over Bosnia and did not want to hear anyone else's views.

The question that preoccupied the Clinton team was whether or not to support the Vance-Owen Peace Plan. Bush had supported it and in a January 13, 1993 interview, so did Clinton. Repeated criticisms of the Vance-Owen Peace Plan, however, emanated from the Democratic Transition Office in the weeks leading up to the inauguration. Aspin wanted as little to do with Bosnia as possible; Lake favored strong action; and Christopher "was on different sides at different times." Many on Clinton's foreign policy team also opposed the Vance-Owen Peace Plan as part of a general desire to distance itself from the Carter administration in which Vance served as Secretary of State. According to Owen, this evolving debate over the merits of the peace plan proceeded without a firm understanding of its details.

The Clinton administration's first major decision on Bosnia was made on February 5, 1993, and was arrived at in a rather casual fashion. Policy making on Bosnia was the province of the Principals Committee, whose core members were Lake, Aspin, Christopher, Colin Powell, CIA Director James Woolsey, and UN Ambassador Madeleine Albright. This was the third long Principals Committee meeting that dealt with Bosnia. At the conclusion of the discussions Lake invited Clinton and Vice President Al Gore to join the group. Clinton stated that if for no other than humanitarian reasons the United States should take the lead on Bosnia and ordered a series of actions including asking the UN to authorize a no fly zone and trying to get economic sanctions tightened.

The administration's bold rhetoric announcing these policy initiatives did not match their impact on the ground and, on March 25, Lake called another Principals Meeting to inform the group that Bosnia was about to enter a new phase and that ideas were needed. In April a series of meetings were held with the President at which options were formulated but with Clinton repeatedly deferring action. In the words of one participant, they ceased serving as policy making meetings and became "group therapy—an existential debate over what is the role of America, etc."

On the weekend of April 16–17 the Principals agreed upon two options: (1) lifting the arms embargo and bombing strikes against the Serbs and (2) a cease-fire to protect Muslim enclaves. No decision was reached, yet in his public statements, Clinton repeatedly said that the United States had to act and that a policy would soon be announced. Aides expected the decision to come the weekend of April 24–25 but it did not. Meetings followed with congressional leaders, the Joint Chiefs of Staff, and key advisors. Finally, on May 1 a decision to adopt the "lift and strike" option was endorsed and Christopher was sent to Europe to sell the plan to America's allies. During his trip, Clinton read Robert Kaplan's best-selling account of the region, *Balkan Ghosts*, and began to have second thoughts about U.S. involvement in Bosnia.

Aspin walked away from a meeting with Clinton and telephoned Lake saying: "He's gone south on this policy. His heart isn't in it . . . We have a serious problem here. We're out there pushing a policy that the President is not comfortable with. He's not on board." Aspin then called Deputy Under-Secretary of Defense Walter Slocombe and stated, "Walt, we are going to pull the plug on it." With the administration's policy in shambles, Christopher returned from Europe and moved systematically to move Bosnia off the front pages.

SUMMARY AND FUTURE ISSUES

As the Iran–Contra and Bosnia cases show, personality and organization both exert an influence on presidential policy making. President Reagan's concern for the release of the hostages drove the process forward and his management style allowed the process to take place without supervision. President Clinton's public rhetoric over the need to take firm action on Bosnia was not matched by his own ability to stay focused on the problem or commit himself to a course of action. The collegial decision-making style of the Principals Committee exacerbated these tendencies by creating an atmosphere that did not impose discipline on the discussions or produce action-forcing decisions.

In the future as in the past, presidents will turn to the NSC and other organizations to establish leadership in foreign policy. No one organizational structure will be the "right" one for a president to select. As the Tower Commission stressed, "There is no magic formula which can be applied to the NSC structure and process. . . . It must adapt to each individual president's style and management philosophy." It goes on to note that this does not mean that guidelines cannot be put forward. In the eyes of some, such guidelines are desperately needed. In criticizing past presidential choices, Destler argues that the evolution and pattern of White House staffing has served the illusion of presidential power rather than its reality.[29]

Looking at specific choices, Philip Odeen suggests that foremost among the decisions a president must make in setting up an NSC system are (1) which issues demand presidential attention, (2) how to develop policy options, (3) how to coordinate bureaucratic input, and (4) how to oversee policy implementation.[30] Among the Tower Commission's recommendations were the following:

1. No substantive changes be made in the provisions of the National Security Act dealing with the structure and operation of the NSC system.
2. The National Security Adviser chair the senior-level committees of the NSC system.
3. Congress consider replacing the existing Intelligence Committees with a new joint committee.
4. Private individuals assisting the U.S. diplomatic initiatives, and covert action be limited and placed under close supervision.
5. Congress not require Senate confirmation of the National Security Adviser.
6. Each administration formulate precise procedures for restricted consideration of covert action and strictly adhere to these.

I. M. Destler points to what may be an even greater challenge that will face future presidents in organizing their foreign policy bureaucracy.[31] He observes that over time two semiautonomous subgovernments have come into being: a security complex and an economic complex. Historically, security concerns have either monopolized the foreign policy agenda or they have represented separate but unequal sets of foreign policy goals. With the greater importance of economic issues in the post–cold war era, presidents must find a mechanism for more fully integrating the two into a coherent foreign policy program. They may even need to go further and construct a mechanism in which economic concerns can dominate security ones. Clinton may have taken a first step in this direction by establishing a National Economic Council (NEC) to parallel the NSC, but this move still falls far short of that advocated by those calling for a true integration of economic and security issues.

NOTES

1. Richard M. Nixon, *RN: The Memoirs of Richard Nixon* (New York: Grosset & Dunlap, 1978), pp. 447–50.

2. Jimmy Carter, *Keeping Faith: Memoirs of a President* (New York: Bantam, 1982), pp. 305–16.

3. Excerpts from Reagan's videotaped testimony can be found in *The Washington Post,* February 23, 1990, pp. 10–11.

4. Hugh Heclo, "Introduction: The Presidential Illusion," in Hugh Heclo and Lester M. Salamon (eds.), *The Illusion of Presidential Government* (Boulder, Colo.: Westview, 1981), p. 1.

5. Richard Neustadt, *Presidential Power: The Politics of Leadership* (New York: Wiley & Sons, 1960).

6. James David Barber, *The Presidential Character: Predicting Performance in the White House,* 3rd ed. (Englewood Cliffs, N.J.: Prentice-Hall, 1985). Also see Alexander George, "Assessing Presidential Character," *World Politics,* 26 (1974), 234–82. For other formulations of presidential personality, see Lloyd S. Etheridge, "Personality Effects on American Foreign Policy, 1898–1968: A Test of Interpersonal Generalization Theory," *American Political Science Review,* 72 (1978), 434–51; and John Stoessinger, *Crusaders and Pragmatists: Movers of Modern American Foreign Policy* (New York: Norton, 1979).

7. Fred I. Greenstein, *The Hidden Hand Presidency: Eisenhower as Leader* (New York: Basic, 1982).

8. Bert A. Rockman, "The Leadership Style of George Bush," in Colin Campbell and Bert A. Rockman (eds.), *The Bush Presidency: First Appraisals* (Chatham, N.J.: Chatham House, 1991), p. 26.

9. John Lewis Gaddis, "The Unexpected Ronald Reagan," in John Lewis Gaddis (ed.), *The United States and the End of the Cold War: Implications, Reconsiderations, Provocations* (New York: Oxford University Press, 1992), pp. 119–32.

10. Fred I. Greenstein, "The Presidential Leadership Style of Bill Clinton: An Early Appraisal," *Political Science Quarterly,* 108 (1993/94), pp. 589–601.

11. Stoessinger, *Crusaders and Pragmatists.*

12. Fred I. Greenstein, *Personality and Politics* (Chicago: Markham, 1969).

13. This is a partial list taken from ibid., pp. 50–61.

14. Donald M. Snow and Eugene Brown, *Puzzle Palaces and Foggy Bottom: U.S. Foreign and Defense Policy-Making in the 1990s* (New York: St. Martin's, 1994), pp. 44–70.

15. Ibid., pp. 55 and 59.

16. Zbigniew Brzezinski, "The NSC's Midlife Crisis," *Foreign Policy,* 69 (1987/88), pp. 80–99.

17. James M. McCormick, *American Foreign Policy and Values* (Itasca, Ill.: Peacock, 1985), p. 179.

18. Greenstein, *The Hidden Hand Presidency.*

19. William P. Bundy, "The National Security Process: Plus Change . . . ," *International Security,* 7 (1982/83), pp. 94–109.

20. On the Nixon NSC system, see John P. Leacacos, "Kissinger's Apparat," *Foreign Policy,* 5 (1971), pp. 2–27.

21. Charles W. Kegley, Jr., and Eugene R. Wittkopf, *American Foreign Policy: Patterns and Process,* 2nd ed. (New York: St. Martin's, 1982) p. 340.

22. Robert E. Hunter, *Presidential Control of Foreign Policy: Management or Mishap,* Washington Paper #91 (New York: Praeger, 1982), pp. 35–36.

23. Terry Diehl, "Reagan's Mixed Legacy," *Foreign Policy,* 75 (1989), pp. 34–55.

24. Snow and Brown, *Puzzle Palaces and Foggy Bottom,* p. 61.

25. Ann Devroy, "Loops of Power Snarl in Clinton White House," *The Washington Post,* April 3, 1994, p. 1.

26. The term is used by John Steinbruner in a commentary on the Clinton foreign policy toward Bosnia: "The Quagmire of Caution," *The Washington Post,* April 25, 1993, p. C1.

27. The President's Special Review Board, *The Tower Commission Report.*

28. Elizabeth Drew, *On the Edge: The Clinton Presidency* (New York: Simon & Schuster, 1994); Richard Holbrooke, *To End a War* (New York: Random House, 1998); and David Owen, *Balkan Odyssey* (New York: Harcourt, Brace, 1995).

29. I. M. Destler, "National Security II: The Rise of the Assistant," in Heclo and Salamon (eds.), *The Illusion of Presidential Government,* p. 278.

30. Philip Odeen, "Organizing for National Security," *International Security,* 5 (1980), pp. 111–29.

31. I. M. Destler, "Foreign Policy Making with the Economy at Center Stage," in Daniel Yankelovich and I. M. Destler (eds.), *Beyond the Beltway: Engaging the Public in U.S. Foreign Policy* (New York: Norton, 1994), pp. 26–42.

CHAPTER

9 Congress and Foreign Policy

Whether it is aid to the Contras, consent to the SALT II Treaty, trade legislation, or a new weapons system, to a president Congress often appears to be an obstacle course through which his foreign policy proposals must first pass. It is an obstacle course made up of two parts: the constitutional distribution of powers between the Congress and the president that we examined in Chapter 7 and Congress's internal structure and operating procedures. These internal obstacles are every bit as formidable as those obstacles rooted in the constitutional separation of powers, and they are our focus in this chapter.

Before proceeding two points need to be stressed. First, just as the structure of the presidency has changed, so too has that of Congress. This is important because it means that the obstacles we will discuss in this chapter have been grafted onto one another over time and that as Congress continues to evolve new ones may be added to this list and old ones shed. Second, not everyone regards congressional participation in foreign policy making as an evil to be avoided. Congressional participation raises the public's awareness about issues, provides additional information to policy makers, and, in the long run, may improve the quality of U.S. foreign policy.[1] Former Director of Central Intelligence Stansfield Turner makes the same point regarding congressional oversight of the CIA. "It forces the DCI and his subordinates to exercise greater judiciousness in making decisions . . . it helps keep them [CIA people] in touch with national views."[2]

CONGRESSIONAL STRUCTURE AND FOREIGN POLICY

Blunt Foreign Policy Tools

Foremost among the tools Congress relies upon to influence policy are its general legislative, budgetary, and oversight powers. While they are formidable powers, Congress often finds itself frustrated in its efforts to fine-tune U.S. foreign policy or give it a new sense of direction due to their bluntness and essentially negative character.

Four basic forms of congressional action exist. Included are the simple resolution, which is a statement made by one house; the concurrent resolution, a statement passed by both houses; and the joint resolution, a statement made by both houses which is signed by the president. None of these carry the force of law; they are simply statements of opinion by Congress. Last, there is the legislative bill, which is passed by both houses and is signed by the president (or passed over the president's veto) and becomes law. In an early postwar study of Congress, James Robinson found that while presidential policy proposals were primarily phrased as bills, congressionally initiated actions tended to be expressed as simple resolutions.[3] He also found that of twenty-one major foreign policy initiatives between the 1930s and 1961 only three were initiated by Congress and that congressional influence was dominant in only six.

The situation today is much the same with one major exception. Congress still relies heavily upon resolutions to express its will. For example, in 1997 Congress passed a nonbinding resolution stating that all U.S. ground combat troops should be withdrawn from Bosnia by June 30, 1998. It went on to state that Clinton should consult with Congress before agreeing to any extension beyond that date but did not require that he receive congressional approval if he elected to keep them there. What has become more pronounced in the intervening years is the amount of legislation that has a bearing on U.S. foreign policy and Congress's use of its legislative powers to limit or amend presidentially initiated foreign policy legislation. The 1960 edition of *Legislation on Foreign Relations* ran 519 pages. The 1975 edition had 1,856 pages, and the 1985 edition was divided into two volumes with a total of 2,698 pages. The 1979 decision to normalize relations with the People's Republic of China required the United States to recast its relations with Taiwan from government-to-government relations to government-to-people relations. Thirty-four pages of statutes were affected by this simple change in language.[4]

Congress also has sought to make its voice heard by attaching amendments or "barnacles" to foreign policy legislation sought by the president.[5] One type of barnacle is to earmark or designate funds contained within a piece of legislation for a specific country. For example, in passing the fiscal year 1990 foreign aid bill, Congress earmarked $4 billion in aid for traditional U.S. ally Israel ($1.2 billion in economic aid and $1.8 billion in military aid). Other big winners included Egypt ($815 million in economic aid and $1.3 billion in military aid); Turkey ($500 million in military aid); Pakistan ($230 million each in military and economic aid); Greece ($350 million in military aid); and Poland ($251 million in economic aid). All totaled, $2.8 billion out of $3.2 billion from the Economic Support Fund was earmarked for specific countries. This figure is up dramatically from the mid-1980s when only about 50 percent of security assistance funds were earmarked.

Most barnacles contain escape clauses which allow the president to get around them. Some of the most prominent barnacles lie in the areas of human rights (the State Department's 1989 Human Rights Report ran 1,641 pages) and drug trafficking. A 1986 law requires that the State Department annually certify that recipients of U.S. foreign aid are "fully cooperating" in eradication efforts and the worldwide fight against drugs. Congress then votes to support or reject the State Department's judgment. If a country fails to win certification it loses American military and economic aid and trade preferences. In 1988, "national interests" were cited in the certification of Panama and Mexico. The Bahamas, Colombia, and Bolivia were also certified. Five states, Afghanistan, Laos, Paraguay, Syria, and Iran, were decertified. The Senate voted 63–27 to decertify Mexico but the House refused to do so and Mexico was able to continue receiving U.S. aid. In 1989 the Bush administration again certified Panama and Mexico and decertified Iran, Syria, and Laos. Because of the constant controversy surrounding the certification process a move was made to suspend it for two years as part of the 1998 foreign aid spending bill. The move was rejected by the Senate with many Senators fearing that a yes vote would portray them as soft on drugs. The underlying reality thus remains the same. Congress's general legislative powers are not easily used.

Members of Congress are not unaware of these problems. They recognize that foreign policy demands speed, flexibility, and subtlety. Yet they also feel a need—a right—to have a voice in policy making. The legislative veto was a response to this dilemma. It recognized the president's need to act unilaterally and gave the president the right to do so while ensuring congressional input into the policy process through the threat of a veto of his or her action. As we discussed earlier, the Supreme Court decided in the Chada case that the congressional veto was unconstitutional, thus forcing Congress into the position of either acquiescing to presidential foreign policy initiatives or making fuller use of the limited instruments at its disposal.

Congress's budget powers are equally blunt and difficult to use. In part this is because doing so involves three different sets of decisions. Congress must decide upon an overall authorization level for the budget under consideration, authorize the expenditure of funds for the programs contained in the budget, and then allocate funds for those programs. These decisions are made in different settings, at different times, and by individuals and committees that are responding to different sets of outside pressures. The decision on the overall budget ceiling is made by Congress as a whole and takes the form of a budget resolution. Authorization decisions are made separately by the committees with legislative jurisdiction over the policy area. Appropriation decisions are made by the House and Senate Appropriations Committee and their subcommittees.

An additional problem with using the budget as an instrument to shape the direction of U.S. foreign policy is that programs cost money but "policies" may not. What policies are able to do is raise expectations, place U.S. prestige on the line, or commit the United States to a course of action in the eyes of other states. When this occurs, Congress tends to find that it has little choice but to support—fund—the policy initiative at least on a cosmetic basis. The Nixon and Carter doctrines created such expectations. The Nixon Doctrine stated that the United States would no longer fight our allies' war for them. Instead, the United States would act as an arm supplier for those allies willing and capable of defending themselves. The Carter Doctrine defined the Persian Gulf as an area of vital interest to U.S. national security. Senator John Kerry (D-Mass) spoke to this same point in expressing his opposition to the congressional resolution supporting the Persian Gulf War. He noted:

> I hear it from one person after another—"I do not want the President to look bad. . . . The President got us in this position. I am uncomfortable—but I cannot go against him. . . . Are we supposed to go to war because one man—the President—makes a series of unilateral decisions that put us in a box. . . . Are we supposed to go to war because once the President has announced publicly, to reverse or question him is somehow detrimental to the Nation. . . ."[6]

Similar problems confront Congress in attempting to cut off funding for overseas military action. During the Reagan administration votes on cutting off aid to the Contras continually reappeared, and none was decisive. This continued hesitancy to use its budgetary powers is not new. Efforts to cut off funding for Vietnam routinely failed, and the vote which actually ended U.S. involvement in Vietnam came on a procedural vote to table the legislation before Congress. A notable exception to this pattern is the Clark Amendment to the 1976 appropriations bill, which forbade the use of funds for "any activities involving Angola directly or indirectly." This measure was passed at a time when the Nixon administration was already involved in the Angolan civil war and was engaged in planning for additional undertakings.[7]

There is a problem with presidential implementation of congressional budgetary decisions. In 1971, Congress appropriated $700 million for a manned bomber. The funds went unspent by the Nixon administration because it opposed the project. During Vietnam the Pentagon transferred several million dollars appropriated as military aid for Taiwan for the war effort. It then went back to Congress and asked for supplemental appropriations to cover these funds. Unless it was willing to offend Taiwan, Congress had little choice but to grant the request. Congress has taken steps to control presidential evasions of its will—the most noteworthy one is the Budget and Impoundment Act of 1974—but problems still remain. For example, prior to the Persian Gulf War Congress appropriated $600 million for the purchase of four fast sea lift vessels. The Navy was not interested in acquiring these ships and Secretary of Defense Dick Cheney agreed to divert some of this money to other projects and not spend the rest. When the Gulf War broke out, the Navy was forced to activate old sea lift vessels because it lacked a sufficient number of vessels to transport troops and supplies to the Middle East.

Oversight refers to the actions of Congress regarding the bureaucratic implementation of policy. Congress was long accused of shunning its oversight responsibilities in favor of looking after state and district interests and passing legislation. The mood changed markedly in the late 1970s and early 1980s as a new interest in oversight gripped Congress. At the same time the nature of oversight also began to change; the traditional investigatory approach to oversight was replaced by a desire to be informed in advance of how policy was going to be implemented.[8] Congress has been especially vigorous in using "reporting requirements" as a tool of oversight. Few policy areas have escaped the reach of congressional reporting requirements initiatives. In addition to the example of drug certification which was just discussed, Congress has required the executive branch to certify such practices as the human rights records of states, their stance on the nonproliferation or nuclear weapons, and their willingness to comply with trade agreements.

Ruth Collier has identified three major types of reporting requirements that Congress has used.[9] Periodic reports are produced in a policy area on a regular basis. For example, each year the State Department is required to submit a country report on human rights practices. A second type is the notification that a particular type of foreign policy action has been taken or will be taken. From Congress's point of view, the absence of presidential notifications of covert action was a major issue in the Iran–Contra affair. Most of these reports, however, are far less politically charged and involve changes in the distribution of foreign aid funds, arms sales, and arms control initiatives. In the mid-1980s an average of over 700 notifications were sent to Congress. The third type of reporting requirement is a one-time report where Congress is seeking a particular piece of information from the executive branch. In the 1986 Anti-Apartheid Act, Congress identified ten issues on which it wanted the president to furnish it with information.

The changing nature of oversight and the additional effort devoted to it have not necessarily produced the desired results. Members of the Senate Select Intelligence Committee expressed extreme disappointment with the CIA over the mining of Nicaraguan harbors. Senators Barry Goldwater and Daniel Moynihan, the ranking Republican and Democrat on the committee, both asserted that the committee had not been informed in advance of these actions and demanded changes in CIA reporting procedures. Morris Ogul suggests that such incidents are inevitable because "the seldom acknowledged fact is that systemic all inclusive oversight is simply impossible to perform."[10] Others have cautioned that the primary product of increased oversight may not be the exposure of misconduct but irresponsible meddling.[11]

Decentralization

Traditionally, the work of Congress was done in committees. It was here that the political deals were made and the technical details of legislation were worked out. Congress as a whole was expected to quietly and expeditiously give its consent to committee decisions, and more often than not, it did. Beginning in the early 1970s, all this began to change, and the focus of decision making shifted from the full committee to the subcommittee. The result has been an even greater decentralization of Congress, which is visible in a number of ways. First, there is the increased attention that the executive branch must give to the foreign policy views of all members of Congress. As one State Department official put it, "It used to be that all one had to do was contact the chairman and a few ranking members of a committee, now all 435 members plus 100 senators have to be contacted."[12] The Defense Department has experienced a similar change in its dealings with Congress. In 1964 Defense Department representatives spent 1,575 witness hours before Congress. In 1976 that number increased to 7,746.[13]

Second, there is the growing tendency for prospective pieces of legislation to be referred to more than one committee. Multiple referrals are necessary because of the lack of fit between the jurisdictions of congressional committees and policy areas. Thomas Brewer found a dozen Senate committees involved in foreign economic policy and nearly 50 subcommittees involved in foreign policy toward the third world.[14] Another study found that the House Armed Services Committee had jurisdiction over 13 agencies and departments and 12 legislative areas while its Senate counterpart had jurisdiction over 10 agencies and 11 legislative areas.[15]

Third, the impact of subcommittee government can be seen in the changed operating procedures of certain committees. One committee that has been especially affected is the House Armed Services Committee. In the Ninety-first Congress (1969–1970) the House Armed Services Committee reported only 12 percent of its legislation to subcommittees. By the Ninety-sixth Congress (1979–1980) 99 percent of its legislation was first referred to a subcommittee for action.[16]

Fourth, in combination with other trends, decentralization has brought about a change in the relative influence of committees on foreign affairs.[17] The biggest loser appears to be the Senate Foreign Relations Committee, which has seen its influence decline relative to that of other committees. James McCormick sees this as a result of a high membership turnover rate, an increased ideological polarization among committee members, and weak leadership.[18] The Armed Services committees of the two houses have stepped into this void and become more prominent players in determining the direction of American foreign policy. Not only did it have jurisdiction over many of the most contentious issues of the last decade (arms control, the size of the defense budget, the Persian Gulf), but it also had skilled leadership, with Senator Sam Nunn (D-Ga) and Representative Les Aspin (D-Wis) at the helm for much of this time. Also emerging with new-found influence were the House and Senate Appropriations Committees. In the 1980s only two foreign aid bills received congressional approval. In the absence of such legislation (which originates in the two foreign relations committees), foreign aid monies were made available largely through the action of these committees as they approved ad hoc funding measures.

Policy Entrepreneurship

A change in attitude has accompanied the trend toward increasing decentralization. Policy individualism has replaced party loyalty as the motivation behind much congressional action. As a result the long-standing congressional norms of deference and apprenticeship have been replaced by expectations of power sharing and policy input. *Entrepreneurship* is the label frequently attached to this new outlook. David Price defines a policy entrepreneur as someone who is committed to a continuing search for policy gaps and opportunities.[19] The entrepreneur is different from the traditional foreign policy "gadfly" who raises issues in order to influence the terms of the policy debate and is concerned with long-term policy gains.[20] Conservatives such as senators Jake Garn, Malcolm Wallop, Gordon Humphrey, and Jesse Helms dominate the current crop of gadflies. In the recent past, liberals such as George McGovern, William Proxmire, and Mark Hatfield were the most active gadflies attacking the basic premises of U.S. foreign policy. The policy entrepreneur is largely motivated by short-term considerations. The primary one is reelection and the belief that the likelihood of being reelected is enhanced if one can claim credit for authoring or amending important bills or publicly exposing a major problem or scandal. As I. M. Destler notes, the problem with credit taking, position taking, and self-advertising is that all three are concerned with the public's image of a piece of legislation and not with how it actually turns out.[21]

Foreign policy has always been a major area of entrepreneurial activity. The Senate Foreign Relations Committee long has been a focal point of media attention and a breeding ground for presidential candidates who used its visibility to their political advantage. International economic issues have also attracted the attention to congresspeople. "Japan bashing" in the form of harshly worded congressional resolutions has become a common staple of U.S. international economic policy. In 1995 many in Congress moved aggressively to promote retaliatory trade legislation against those who trade with Cuba and Iran. Senator Jesse Helms and Representative Dan Burton sought to bar sugar imports to the United States from anyone purchasing or renting property in Cuba that was confiscated after Castro seized power in 1959. Canada saw itself as the target of this legislation and sent a sharply worded protest to the United States stating that Helms–Burton violated NAFTA and World Trade Organization obligations entered into by the United States. At the same time that this legislation was being debated, the Clinton administration and Congress were engaged in a race to see who could propose the toughest actions against Iran. The administration barred Texas-based Conoco Oil Company from developing oil and gas fields with Iran, but Republicans in Congress wanted to go even further. Senator Alfonse D'Amato and Representative Peter King introduced a bill that according to D'Amato would force a foreign corporation or individual to "choose between trade with the United States or trade with Iran."

Individual activity, whether done as a policy entrepreneur or as a gadfly, has left a distinct mark on the conduct of American foreign policy by forcing foreign dignitaries to expand their negotiating agendas. Seeking to gain congressional support for the Clinton administration's plan to pay off a portion of its UN debt, Secretary General Kofi Annan met with Senate Foreign Relations Committee Chairperson Jesse Helms. Annan agreed to the meeting only after President Clinton told him it was essential to gain Helms's support if he hoped to see the United States pay its back dues. An even more vivid example of the expanded congressional role in American foreign policy came at the 1997 Kyoto Summit that examined the question of global warming. Four senators were present as part of a bipartisan observers' group chosen by the Senate leadership. One, Chuck Hagel (R-Neb.), made it clear that he opposed any agreement that set binding emission targets. Another, Joseph Lieberman (D-Conn.), made it quite clear he felt binding targets were necessary and hoped that the U.S. delegation could gain a global agreement on this problem.

Staff Aides

Information has always been a problem for Congress when it comes to making foreign policy. Thomas Brewer identified more than 100 House roll call votes on foreign policy issues in just one year.[22] Few members can hope to acquire the background and expertise to understand and stay on top of such a wide range of issues as Defense Department appropriations, export controls, world hunger, and recognizing the Transkei territory in South Africa. The emergence of a large and well-informed number of staff aides has given the problem a new focus.[23] The problem is no longer one of acquiring needed information from the executive branch or party leaders. It is now also one of using information in a controlled and coherent fashion. Concerns have been expressed over whether (1) the staffer is serving Congress or just leading willing congresspeople from issue to issue as they build their own reputations, and (2) an activist staff might not be overloading Congress with new issues, thereby robbing it of the time needed for debate and deliberation.

The tremendous increase in staff size is visible throughout Congress. In 1947 there existed roughly 500 committee and 2,000 personal staffers. In 1979 these numbers had jumped to 3,000 committee staff aides and over 10,000 personal staff aides. Congress as a whole has also increased its information-gathering and processing capabilities by establishing or increasing the size of the Congressional Research Service (established in 1914), the Congressional Accounting Office (1921), the Office of Technology Assessment (1972), and the Congressional Budget Office (1974). In 1976 the Office of Technology Assessment supervised a study for the Senate Foreign Relations Committee which estimated the number of American casualties in a nuclear war. Its findings challenged Defense Department assumptions and methodology. It has also studied questions relating to nuclear terrorism and energy policy.

In addition to being able to draw upon vast amounts of information from their staffs and congressional research services, congresspeople and senators can also draw upon the products of private nonprofit research institutes and think tanks such as the Brookings Institute, the Cato Institute, and the Heritage Foundation.[24] Until the 1970s, think tanks were relatively few in number. Today they are prominent fixtures on the Washington, D.C., political landscape, providing a base of operations for policy-oriented academics, defeated and would-be elected officials, and foreign policy experts who hope to enter or reenter government service in a future administration. Think tanks provide policy makers with a wide array of products, ranging from scholarly papers and conferences to serving as informal "talent banks" that can be drawn upon in debating policy choices.

THE INFLUENCE OF PARTY AND REGION

From what we have seen so far, it is clear that Congress has great difficulty speaking with one voice on foreign policy matters. We can bring this difficulty into even greater focus by examining the influence of party and region on foreign policy decisions. Current evidence suggests that the ability of party identification to unite individuals around a policy choice is not as great as we might expect, while the pull of regionalism is greater than commonly believed.

We need to look no further than the problems the Republican Party in Congress was having in formulating a unified foreign policy position in the late 1990s to see splits beneath the surface of party unity on foreign policy matters. Where senior Republican leaders embrace an internationalist outlook rooted in cold war foreign policy triumphs, those elected for the first time in the 1990s have a different world view. It is one which places budget deficits and eroding values at center stage. Junior Republicans have opposed supporting loan guarantees to Mexico, favor privitization of foreign aid, oppose expensive new weapons systems, and show little interest in bipartisan resolutions supporting the President in Bosnia or elsewhere. Past accomplishments mean little to them. As one second term Republican stated in the debate over Bosnia,

"I'm not the least bit interested in the prestige of NATO." The Democratic Party is not immune from the problems growing out of internal disunity. Led by organized labor, a protectionist wing of the Democratic Party has gained in influence at the expense of the more liberal free-traders. The combined result of these divisions was the inability of President Clinton and House Speaker Newt Gingrich working together to deliver enough votes to gain passage of legislation which would have granted Clinton fast track authority in trade negotiations.

It is commonly accepted by students of world politics that the globalization of the world's economy creates winners and losers. This is equally true for regions of a country as it is for countries as a whole. Peter Trubowitz asserts that today as in the 1890s and 1930s the changing nature of the global economy and the uneven impact it has on different areas of the United States has produced regional conflict over how to define the American national interest.[25] He sees U.S. foreign policy as being driven by a coalition of the South and the West, regions which benefit from a foreign policy designed to promote free trade and assure international stability. Opposed to it is the Northeast, which while once benefiting from such policies now sees itself as economically disadvantaged by them and favors protectionism and cuts in defense spending. This regional alignment of forces, rather than a Republican-Democratic divide, is what steered the Reagan build-up through Congress.

Foreign Policy Impact

Blunt foreign policy tools, decentralization, entrepreneurship, and large staffs combine to place a heavy burden on congressional participation in foreign policy making. First, congressional participation is sluggish. In large measure this is by design. James Sundquist asserts that "from the beginning, the Congress has shown that its most deep-seated fear is not obstructionism but quick majoritarian decisions."[26] Second, Congress's participation is parochial and unpredictable at both the institutional and individual levels. In 1978, for example, Carter won five major foreign policy victories: the Panama Canal Treaties, an arms sales package to the Middle East, energy legislation, lifting the Turkish arms embargo, and a foreign assistance bill. Only 11 senators voted yes on all five; only 1 voted no to all of them.[27] Parochialism is present regardless of which party is in control of Congress. Senator Henry "Scoop" Jackson, a conservative Democrat from Washington and long-time fixture on the Armed Services Committee, was known as the "Senator from Boeing" for his ability to steer contracts to Boeing aircraft, which was headquartered in Washington. In 1995 the Republican-controlled Senate Armed Services Committee added $5 billion in funds for weapons spending on to Clinton's request. Eighty-one percent of these funds were to go to states represented by committee members. A similar pattern took place in the area of military construction, where $345 million was added. Of the 44 projects added, 32 were in states represented on the committee. Parochialism extends beyond the committee system. The B-1 bomber, for example, had 400 subcontracts in over 400 of the 435 districts of the House.

When Congress acts, it acts with blunt instruments that often seem to produce overkill or make the problem worse. A compelling example occurred in May 1994 when on back-to-back votes of 50 to 49 the Senate first instructed Clinton to obtain allied support for lifting a multilateral weapons embargo against Bosnia and then voted to force him to do so unilaterally and immediately. Senator John Glenn summarized the votes this way: "We give clear guidance except when we change our minds."

The picture is not entirely negative. Robert Pastor argues that Congress actually possesses some comparative advantages over the White House in setting the direction of American foreign policy.[28] An assertive Congress helps the United States "adapt its means and its goals to changes within and outside itself" and provides skillful negotiators with a powerful bargaining lever in dealings with other countries. Congress is also able to provide a corrective for narrow presidential definitions of foreign policy problems. Pastor contends that this often has been the case with regard to Latin America. Under Carter, Congress insisted that long-standing American security concerns not be abandoned in the signing of the Panama Canal Treaty, and under Reagan it exerted pressure to make sure that human rights concerns were not ignored.

A more complicated and nuanced picture of Congress's impact on foreign policy emerges when we direct our attention to specific policy areas. Stephen Cohen identifies eight principles that are central to understanding congressional activity in international economic policy.[29] By collapsing some of his arguments, we can summarize his main findings as follows:

1. Congress is not equally concerned with all aspects of international economic policy. Simply put, some things matter more than others. Most important is international trade, followed by foreign assistance. International monetary, investment, and energy policy are far less important.

2. Extremely important for understanding congressional influence is the relationship between key congressional and administration officials. Good working relations can do a lot to defuse congressional anger and give the White House room to maneuver.

3. Congress is willing to take the lead, it is not simply a reactive body. But Congress deals with international economic issues at a slow, deliberate speed. Quick decisive actions are rare.

4. Congress has a two-tiered trade philosophy. On the one hand, it believes that free trade is important. On the other it believes that exceptions must be made due to economic or political considerations. Over time it has developed a finely tuned set of expectations regarding how the White House is supposed to manage these two sets of concerns in its dealings with other countries.

5. The dominant factors explaining a congressperson's position on international economic policy is geography (for trade policy) and committee assignments, not party affiliation or political philosophy.

A very different set of principles has guided congressional participation in making U.S. arms policy, an area that encompasses arms control and arms procurement legislation. According to Paul Stockton, historically arms control and arms procurement policies have moved forward in tandem.[30] This was because by themselves neither arms controllers nor those advocating the acquisition of new weapons systems had sufficient votes to realize their policy goals. Success was possible only by forming an alliance in which progress on one came at the price of advances in the other. For example, support for SALT I was "purchased" in part with an agreement to accelerate the Trident submarine program, and the chairman of the Joint Chiefs of Staff only supported SALT II after the Carter administration agreed to continue funding the MX missile program.

Stockton believes that the congressional politics of arms control are undergoing a fundamental change because of two factors. First, the demise of the Soviet Union severed the connection between arms control and forced modernization. Arms control can now be pursued without great fears of weakening American defenses against the Soviet Union. Second, budgetary pressures have split prodefense advocates with some remaining military hawks while others have become deficit hawks who are willing to cut defense spending. Table 9–1 summarizes the changing pattern of congressional coalition building in this area.

TABLE 9–1   Patterns of Congressional Coalition Building on Strategic Force Modernization and Arms Control

Priority of Congressmember	Cold War–Era Goals, Tactics, and Results in Congress	Post–Cold War Era
Force Modernizers	Want modernization programs to bolster deterrence, but often need the support of arms controllers to get programs adopted	With the decline of the Soviet threat, many now consider bolstering deterrence less important than cutting the defense budget
Arms Controllers	Want arms control to reduce the risk of war, etc., but always need the support of force modernizers to ratify treaties	Still want arms control (in part to cut modernization spending); less need and desire to logroll with force modernizers
Middle-of-the-Roaders	Believe that both arms control and force modernization are needed; want to avoid being called either weak on defense or too hard-line	Less fear of being called weak on defense; recognize new opportunities to negotiate arms control without requiring force modernization
Dominant Coalition-Building Process	Logrolling	Bipartisan budget-cutting of new stratgic programs (B-2, mobile MX, etc.)
Policy Impact	U.S. arms control policy in SALT I, SALT II and (until recently) START tied to continued offensive force modernization	Arms control no longer sells force modernization; possible to ratify agreements that impose much far-reaching constraints on the arms race

Source: Paul N. Stockton, "The New Game on the Hill: The Politics of Arms Control and Strategic Force Modernization," *International Security,* 16, 2 (1991), 165. © 1991 by the President and Fellows of Harvard College and the Massachusetts Institute of Technology.

CONGRESS AND THE PRESIDENT:
THE CHANGING RELATIONSHIP

Not only can we find variation in how Congress approaches foreign policy issues but we can also find differences in how Congress and the president interact in making foreign policy. These differences are apparent both over time and between policy areas.

Changes over Time

Viewed over time, congressional-presidential relations have moved from a long period of presidential dominance to one where Congress has emerged as an important player fully capable of frustrating presidential initiatives.[31] Congressional-presidential relations from 1945 to 1970 were essentially harmonious in nature. Congress adopted a largely passive role which often took on a plebiscitary character. The president was the acknowledged architect of U.S. foreign policy and Congress's role was to reaffirm his policy initiatives and provide him with the flexibility and means necessary to act. It reaffirmed his authority in a series of area resolutions covering Laos, Berlin, Cuba, the Middle East, and Vietnam. Congress provided flexibility by avoiding constitutional confrontations on the presidential exercise of war-making and treaty-making powers. Beneath the surface there did exist points of tension. President Truman felt compelled for political reasons to consult with Congress on many key foreign policy matters. His principal point of contact was Republican Senator Arthur Vandenberg, who had been an isolationist in the pre–World War II period. Mutual accommodation between the two branches produced bipartisan support for such foreign policy initiatives as the Marshall Plan, NATO, and the United Nations. Still, Vandenberg and others often felt left out of the policy process. As Vandenberg put it, "We want to be in on the take offs as well as the crash landings."

Pockets of antagonism became more visible in the early 1950s. Disenchanted with presidential activism in foreign affairs and to some extent fearful of presidential incursions into states' rights, a group of senators supported the Bricker Amendment, which would have limited a president's authority to enter into executive agreements. The 1950s also gave rise to McCarthyism. In 1951 Senator Joseph McCarthy charged that the State Department's Foreign Service Officer Corps harbored communist sympathizers and that because of this the United States had "lost" China. By the mid-1950s, harmony had been restored and a basic cold war consensus on both ends of Pennsylvania Avenue was in place that guided American foreign policy into Vietnam. As this conflict escalated cracks began to appear in this consensus. First, it was found in the opposition to the war of individual congresspeople such as William Fulbright and Eugene McCarthy. Later, it would take the form of an often adversarial Congress.

The end of the Vietnam War did not bring about the return of a passive Congress. Instead, Congress began to demonstrate a sustained interest in shaping specific policy decisions and placing limits on the powers of the president. Neither Carter, Reagan, nor Bush found Congress to be a fully compliant partner. Hard bargaining and a large expenditure of political resources were often necessary to secure congressional approval. And often this was not enough, as the ill-fated SALT II treaty and aid for the Contras in Nicaragua made clear. President Clinton has not fared much better. His administration's handling of foreign policy has come under constant criticism, and he was unable to prevent both houses of Congress from voting to lift the arms embargo to Croatia by veto-proof margins.

We can look to internal and external factors to explain why congressional-executive relations have become increasingly combative in nature. First, as we have already noted, structural and organizational changes in Congress have expanded the number of viewpoints that are brought to bear on foreign policy problems. And, just as important, Congress now expects to participate in foreign policy decisions. A second factor is the altered nature of the foreign policy agenda. Gone are the centerpiece cold war issues of deterring the Soviet Union and stopping the spread of communism. In their place are questions involving jobs, economic competitiveness, human rights, budget deficits, and the environment. From the congressional perspective the case for deferring to presidential leadership on these issues is far less compelling than it was for the old foreign policy agenda. Third, congressional activism and the potential for conflict with the executive branch have been heightened by the inability of post–cold war administrations to author a coherent foreign policy.

Changes by Policy Area

In addition to tracing changes in the nature of congressional-presidential relations over time, we can also make distinctions between policy areas. Bruce Jentleson studied the Reagan administration and found four patterns.[32] The first was outright confrontation, which characterized congressional-executive relations on such issues as Nicaragua, South Africa, and Middle East arms sales. All of these issues involved deep disagreements about the content of U.S. foreign policy and in them were found high levels of interest group activity. The second pattern was institutional competition. The most vivid examples here involved charges by the Reagan administration that Congress was micromanaging foreign policy in its handling of State Department authorization requests and foreign aid bills. Eighty-six amendments were added to the 1987 State Department Authorization Act. Included among them were provisions for protecting human rights in Tibet, establishing an ambassador at large for Afghanistan, limits on U.S. contributions to the United Nations, sanctions against Toshiba, and a new drug and lie detector program for some State Department personnel. The third pattern Jentleson found was constructive compromise. He cites military aid to El Salvador and the resignation of Philippine President Ferdinand Marcos as examples where congressional-presidential conflict was constructive because it led to a more sensible U.S. foreign policy. The final pattern was bipartisan cooperation. Often overlooked, Jentleson found three policy areas where the Reagan administration and Congress worked together in relative harmony: relations with the Soviet Union; relations with China; and the use of military force in selected regional conflicts, most notably against Libya and Afghanistan, and in the Persian Gulf. While the frequency with which these three types appear will vary over time, they do alert us to be sensitive to variations in congressional-presidential foreign policy interactions.

SUMMARY AND FUTURE ISSUES

The fundamental problem facing Congress in exercising its foreign policy voice in the future will be the one that we have outlined in this chapter: to establish its right to participate in making decisions and to manage the contradictory pressures for efficiency and participation. The optimal mix has yet to be found, and as we have seen, the nature of the relationship between Congress and the president has varied greatly. Blunt policy instruments, decentralization, entrepreneurship, and the role played by the congressional staff all make congressional participation inefficient (at least from the point of view of the president), yet the Constitution mandates its participation in the policy process.

Symbolic of both its intent to be more involved in making foreign policy and the evolving nature of world politics, the Republican-controlled Congress changed the names of the two long-established committees that dealt with foreign policy problems. The Armed Services Committee became the Committee on National Security and the Foreign Affairs Committee became the House Committee on International Relations. Congressional reformers argue that bolder steps are necessary if Congress is to fully participate in foreign policy making. One suggestion is to create a joint committee on national security.[33] It would oversee the workings of the National Security Council and act as a central foreign policy information repository for Congress. A variation on this idea is to expand the jurisdiction of the Senate Foreign Relations Committee and the House Foreign Affairs Committee to cover trade policy and give them sequential or concurrent jurisdiction over other foreign policy areas. Still another proposal calls for creating a committee on interdependence in each house. One of its primary responsibilities would be to react to and prepare the congressional response to a biannual comprehensive presidential statement on the purposes of U.S. foreign policy and the nature of existing commitments.

Another approach to improving congressional-presidential relations is to change the operating styles of the two branches. Presidents continue to operate on the basis of what James MacGregor Burns refers to as a presidential style of leadership.[34] According to this model, leadership requires that presidents guard and protect their power, especially from congressional encroachments. The cold war served as a catalyst and source of support for this style of presidential leadership. Its passing has robbed recent presidents of an important political pillar on which their preeminent position in the policy process was anchored.

The problem is that presidents have not changed their leadership style. Rather they have engaged in foreign policy "ad hocism" in which periodic understandings with Congress on how to conduct foreign policy are interspersed with presidential attempts to reassert primacy. The Bush administration is an excellent example. It reached a quick accommodation with Congress on Nicaragua but was unable to use the accord as a point of departure for other foreign policy initiatives. The most notable failing was with regard to its China policy. Even its greatest success, the Persian Gulf War, did not provide Bush with relief from the need to practice ad hocism. U.S. foreign policy toward Yugoslavia proceeded in fits and starts; while the humanitarian mission to Somalia was opposed by few, there was much disagreement about its scope and broader implications.

Some argue that what is needed is a collaborative model of leadership based upon Madison's notion of separate institutions sharing power. Thus each branch, while mindful of its own powers, would construct mechanisms or tools to aid interbranch collaboration.[35] Possible building blocks on which this leadership might be based are already in place or have been tried on an experimental basis. In the area of arms control the Carter administration established the practice of appointing congressional advisers to the SALT II Geneva negotiations. These advisers were involved in both formal and informal treaty discussions and reviewed the draft of the SALT II agreement.[36] The congressional advisory group continued under the Reagan administration despite its very different approach to arms control.

Other examples of collaborative arrangements include bipartisan congressional representatives within the executive's summit team or ensuring congressional participation in arms control verification bodies.[37] Another possibility is suggested by the National Academy of Public Administration in their report *Beyond Distrust: Building Bridges Between Congress and the Executive*. It advocates the establishment of executive and congressional staff-to-staff working groups to "facilitate interbranch communications during policy development and program implementation."[38]

NOTES

1. Douglas Bennett, Jr., "Congress in Foreign Policy: Who Needs It," *Foreign Affairs,* 57 (1978), 40–50.
2. Stansfield Turner, *Secrecy and Democracy* (Boston: Houghton Mifflin, 1985), pp. 150–51.
3. James A. Robinson, *Congress and Foreign Policy Making: A Study in Legislative Influence and Initiative* (Homewood, Ill.: Dorsey, 1962), p. 110.
4. Lee R. Marks, "Legislating and the Conduct of Diplomacy: The Constitution's Inconsistent Functions," in Thomas M. Franck (ed.), *The Tethered Presidency: Congressional Restraints on Executive Power* (New York: New York University Press, 1981), p. 201.
5. I. M. Destler, "Dateline Washington: Congress as Boss," *Foreign Policy,* 42 (1981), 161–80.
6. *The Congressional Record,* January 11, 1991, pp. S250–51.
7. This point and others about the budgetary powers of Congress are discussed by Charles W. Kegley, Jr., and Eugene R. Wittkopf, *American Foreign Policy: Pattern and Process,* 2nd ed. (New York: St. Martin's, 1982), pp. 417–29.
8. Abner J. Mikva and Patti B. Solis, *The American Congress: The First Branch* (New York: Watts, 1983), pp. 302–7.
9. Ruth Collier, "Foreign Policy by Reporting Requirement," *The Washington Quarterly,* 11 (1988), 74–84.
10. Morris Ogul, "Congressional Oversight: Structures and Incentives," in Lawrence C. Dodd and Bruce I. Oppenheimer (eds.), *Congress Reconsidered,* 2nd ed. (Washington, D.C.: Congressional Quarterly, 1981), p. 318.

11. James L. Sundquist, *The Decline and Resurgence of Congress* (Washington, D.C.: Brookings, 1981), pp. 315–43.

12. Roger H. Davidson, "Subcommittee Government: New Channels for Policy Making," in Thomas E. Mann and Norman J. Ornstein (eds.), *The New Congress* (Washington D.C.: American Enterprise Institute, 1981), p. 130.

13. Amos A. Jordon and William J. Taylor, Jr., *American National Security: Policy and Process* (Baltimore, Md.: Johns Hopkins University Press, 1981), p. 121.

14. Thomas L. Brewer, *American Foreign Policy: A Contemporary Introduction*, 2nd ed. (Englewood Cliffs, N.J.: Prentice-Hall, 1986), p. 119.

15. Steven S. Smith and Christopher J. Deering, *Committees in Congress* (Washington, D.C.: Congressional Quarterly, 1984), p. 276.

16. Ibid., p. 134.

17. John T. Tierney, "Congressional Activism in Foreign Policy: Its Varied Forms and Stimuli," in David A. Deese (ed.), *The New Politics of American Foreign Policy* (New York: St. Martin's, 1994). 102–31.

18. James McCormick, "Decision Making in the Foreign Affairs and Foreign Relations Committees," in Randall B. Ripley and James M. Lindsey (eds.), *Congress Resurgent: Foreign and Defense Policy on Capital Hill* (Ann Arbor: University of Michigan Press, 1993).

19. David Price, *Who Makes the Laws?* (Cambridge, Mass: Schenkman, 1972), p. 330.

20. Joshua Muravchik, *The Senate and National Security: A New Mood*, Washington Paper #80 (Beverly Hills: Sage, 1980), pp. 57–60.

21. I. M. Destler, "Executive–Congressional Conflict in Foreign Policy: Explaining It: Coping With It," in Dodd and Oppenheimer (eds.), *Congress Reconsidered*, p. 301.

22. Brewer, *American Foreign Policy*, p. 119.

23. For a discussion of congressional staffs, see Michael J. Malbin, "Delegation, Deliberation, and the New Role of Congressional Staff," in Mann and Ornstein (eds.), *The New Congress*, pp. 134–77; and Muravchik, *The Senate and National Security*.

24. James A. Smith, *The Idea Brokers: Think Tanks and the Rise of the New Policy Elite* (New York: Free Press, 1991, and David Newsom, *The Public and Foreign Policy* (Bloomington, Ind.: Indiana University Press, 1996).

25. Peter Trubowitz, *Defining the National Interest* (Chicago: University of Chicago Press, 1998).

26. Sundquist, *Decline and Resurgence of Congress*, p. 156.

27. Destler, "Executive–Congressional Conflict in Foreign Policy," pp. 296–316.

28. Robert Pastor, "Congress and U.S. Foreign Policy: Comparative Advantage or Disadvantage?" *The Washington Quarterly*, 14 (1991), 101–14. Pastor writes in rebuttal to the argument put forward by Aaron L. Friedberg, "Is the United States Capable of Acting Strategically?" *The Washington Quarterly*, 14 (1990), 5–23.

29. Stephen D. Cohen, *The Making of United States International Economic Policy*, 3rd ed. (New York: Praeger, 1994).

30. Paul N. Stockton, "The New Game on the Hill: The Politics of Arms Control and Strategic Force Modernization," *International Security*, 16 (1991), 146–70.

31. For examples of how various authors have broken down the relationship between the Congress and the president into different periods, see Francis R. Bax, "The Legislative–Executive Relationship in Foreign Policy: New Partnership or New Competition." *Orbis*, 20 (1977), 881–904; and John P. Lovell, *The Challenge of American Foreign Policy: Purpose and Adaptation* (New York: Macmillan, 1985), pp. 250–63. The discussion here also draws on comments made by I. M. Destler and others at a Project 87 Seminar on "The Constitution and Foreign Affairs," 1984.

32. Bruce Jentleson, "American Diplomacy: Around the World and Along Pennsylvania Avenue," in Thomas E. Mann (ed.), *A Question of Balance: The President, the Congress and Foreign Policy* (Washington, D.C.: Brookings, 1990), 146–200.

33. Destler, "Executive–Congressional Conflict in Foreign Policy," pp. 296–316.

34. James MacGregor Burns, *Presidential Government: The Crucible of Leadership* (Boston: Houghton Mifflin, 1973).

35. For essays on this theme see Thomas Mann (ed.), *A Question of Balance: The President, the Congress, and Foreign Policy;* also see Barry Blechman, "The Congressional Role in U.S. Military Policy," *Political Science Quarterly,* 106 (Spring 1991), pp. 17–32.

36. Stephen Flanagan, "The Domestic Politics of SALT II," in John Spanier and John Nogee (eds.), *Congress and the Presidency* (New York: Pergamon Press, 1981), 44–76.

37. Glenn Hastedt and Anthony Eksterowicz, "Congress, the President, and Conventional Arms Control," *Southeastern Political Review,* 18 (1990), 40–41.

38. The National Academy of Public Administration, *Beyond Distrust: Building Bridges Between Congress and the Executive* (Washington, D.C.: The National Academy of Public Administration, 1992).

10 The Foreign Affairs Bureaucracy

According to Henry Kissinger, "The purpose of bureaucracy is to devise a standard operating procedure which can cope effectively with most problems."[1] In doing so it frees high-level policy makers to concentrate on the unexpected and exceptional and to pursue policy innovations. When it fails to identify options or when those options prove to be irrelevant, bureaucracy becomes a hindrance, forcing policy makers to redirect their efforts away from problem solving to forging a bureaucratic consensus. The critical problem identified by Kissinger is integrating the roles of the professional expert and the political generalist. From one perspective this is a management problem solvable by identifying organizational tasks, establishing lines of communication and accountability, and carefully selecting personnel.

Viewed from another perspective, this tension reflects the fundamentally dual nature of all organizations, and it defies a managerial solution. Organizations can be divided into formal and informal subsystems.[2] The formal system is built around the legal lines of authority, rules, and regulations that make up the organization. It is embodied in organizational charts that reveal the tasks that the organization is charged with and lines of accountability. It is a goal-oriented system whose logic and coherence are derived from the tasks assigned to it by forces outside the organization. In the case of public bureaucracies, Congress, the president, and interest groups all participate in defining official organizational goals. The informal system springs up spontaneously around the formal system and consists of the unwritten rules of conduct and fundamental assumptions that guide the day-to-day behavior of those employed in the organization. The two systems frequently collide: Where the formal system is concerned with goal achievement, the informal system is concerned with the survival of organizational members. But no formal system can survive for long without an effectively operating system of unwritten rules and redundancy that allow it to cope with contingencies and problems that were not anticipated when the organization was set up. At the same time it also confronts policy makers with a challenge. As a spontaneous structure the informal system defies total control, and attempts to manipulate it will fail.

Our concern in this chapter is with the foreign affairs bureaucracy. The management dilemmas and the basic organizational realities sketched above are very much present here. Three organizations dominate the foreign affairs bureaucracy: the State Department, the Defense Department, and the Central Intelligence Agency (CIA). We examine their formal structure and informal value systems in order to understand better how they influence U.S. foreign policy. We also take a brief look at some organizational newcomers to the foreign affairs bureaucracy: the Treasury Department, the Commerce Department, and the Agriculture Department. Traditionally, they have been classified as domestic bureaucracies, but over the past few decades their foreign policy role has grown dramatically, and their foreign policy orientation is often quite different from that of the traditional foreign affairs bureaucracies.

THE STATE DEPARTMENT

Structure and Growth

According to the *U.S. Government Manual,* "It is to the State Department that the president looks for his primary advice in the formulation and execution of foreign policy." The State Department must serve as a transmission belt for information between the United States and foreign governments and as a resource for senior policy makers to draw upon as needed. Both of these tasks have become increasingly difficult to accomplish with the ever expanding agenda of American foreign policy. Annually, the State Department represents the United States in over 50 major international organizations and at over 800 international conferences. The volume of information that it must process has grown at a staggering rate. In the late 1960s and early 1970s, an average of over 4,000 messages were processed each day. Over one-half were classified. In 1975 the State Department processed approximately 1 million cables, a number that is increasing at the rate of approximately 15 percent per year. By the mid-1980s, approximately 10,000 messages, reports, and instructions were sent and received by the State Department each day. Two hundred of these are likely to require some kind of action or attention by policy makers. The Secretary of State is likely to be involved in only a small percentage of these decisions. Secretary of State Dean Rusk estimated that he saw only 6 of every 1,000 cables sent to the State Department each day and that the president saw only one or two. Rusk also estimated that he read only 20 to 30 of the 1,300 cables sent out each day.[3] In 1997, the State Department processed some 3 million cables.

Management challenges also lie in the number of non–State Department personnel that can be found in American embassies. In 1994 only 38 percent of U.S. government personnel in embassies worked for the State Department; 36 percent worked for the Defense Department; 5 percent for the Justice Department; 3 percent for the Transportation Department; and 18 percent for the Treasury, Commerce, and Agriculture Departments. The concept of a country team has been developed to bring coherence to the welter of agencies and programs now found represented at an embassy.

As chief of mission, the ambassador heads the country team. In practice ambassadors have found it quite difficult to exercise enough authority to transform a set of independent and often competing policies into a coordinated and coherent program. They have been frustrated by the scope and complexity of the programs being carried out, the access of non-State Department personnel to independent reporting channels, and the need of these individuals to meet the performance and promotion standards set by their own bureaucracies. Also complicating the problem is the background of the ambasssador. Frequently, the ambassador is not a career diplomat. Under Carter 75 percent of all ambassadors were career diplomats. This was up from 40 percent in 1955 and 68 percent in 1962, but under Reagan it fell back to 60 percent.[4] Approximately 30 percent of President Clinton's appointments were non-career diplomats.

In a move that mimicked those made by earlier administrations, the Clinton administration designated certain posts as "White House picks" and off limits to the State Department. In Latin America these included Uruguay, Brazil, Costa Rica, and Mexico. The presence of a political ambassador is often justified by the need to repay political supporters and the very real financial costs involved with being an ambassador in certain countries. A frequently cited problem that arises, however, is that politically appointed ambassadors often have little interest in managing the embassy or in foreign policy. Quite to the contrary, they see their role as being visible and public representatives of the United States.

The State Department's basic structure remained largely unchanged for the duration of the cold war. Beneath the Secretary of State were a small number of Deputy Secretaries of State with responsibility for political, economic, international security, and management affairs. The remainder of the State Department was organized around geographical areas and functional tasks. While the number and identity of the regional areas remained steady, the functional bureaus showed considerable change over time. An inspection of organizational charts dating back to 1960 would show the continued presence of bureaus responsible for intelligence and research, international organizations, economic and business affairs, and political-military affairs. It would also reveal the disappearance of the education and culture bureau and the addition of the refugee bureau and a bureau responsible for human rights and humanitarian affairs. Bureaus were also transformed as the international agenda changed. For example, the International Scientific and Technical Bureau to the Oceans became the International Environment and Science Bureau.

In part, organizational stability was realized by setting up semiautonomous organizations to deal with three of the more pressing problem areas of cold war diplomacy: foreign aid, arms control, and dispersal of information. Their emergence reflects a trend begun in World War II when rather than incorporate new foreign policy tasks into the State Department system, separate organizations operating under White House control were established. The Agency for International Development was established in 1961 and is responsible for administering the U.S. foreign economic aid program. The Arms Control and Disarmament Agency (ACDA) was also established in 1961 and is responsible for conducting studies on arms control and disarmament policies, managing U.S. arms control and disarmament negotiations, overseeing U.S. participation in arms control agreements, and advising the president, NSC, and Secretary of State on arms control and disarmament matters. The United States Information Agency (USIA) was established in 1953 and is charged with promoting a better understanding of the United States in other countries. The "Voice of America" is one of its best known undertakings.

All of this is changing. Along with the other principal cold war bureaucracies, the missions and structure of the State Department have come under close scrutiny as policy makers look to the next century. *State 2000: A New Model for*

Managing Foreign Affairs was the product of an internal State Department Task Force commissioned by Secretary of State James Baker. Its chair noted that "the State Department needs a new way of doing business" if it is to help the United States "meet the challenges presented by a dramatically altered international environment." Among its 39 reform proposals were the creation of an Undersecretary for Global Programs; establishing a new bureau for Democracy, Human Rights, and Labor Affairs and one for Narcotics, Terrorism, and Crime Affairs; setting up a new office for International Business Development; and merging ACDA back into the State Department.

Today, the State Department is undergoing two profound changes. One change involves the State Department's "shrinking presence" overseas. Between 1993 and 1996, the State Department cut more than 2,000 employees and closed five embassies, 23 AID missions, and 26 consulates, consulate generals, and State Department branch offices. This reduction is a by-product of a reduction in the international affairs budget from $37.5 billion in 1984 to $18.6 billion in 1996.

The second change involves the formal integration of USIA and ACDA into the State Department and an end to their status as semi-autonomous agencies. AID is to retain its independent status, but its director will report to the Secretary of State rather than to the president. This reorganization is the by-product of reform initiatives within the executive branch and the insistence of Senate Foreign Relations Committee chair Jesse Helms that streamlining the foreign affairs bureaucracy was the price to be paid for his willingness to allow the Chemical Weapons Convention come up for a vote.

Concerns have been expressed in many quarters about the pace of the reorganization, with congressional Republicans calling for rapid action, and possible problems brought on by mixing organizational cultures. For example, some USIA and ACDA personnel fear that the a focus on short-term political gains and maintaining good relations with other countries on the part of State Department officials will mean that less attention will be paid to their efforts at long-term program development.

These changes may not mark the end of efforts at reorganization. Former Secretary of State Lawrence Eagleburger advocates the changes mentioned and others.[5] He sees the proliferation of assistant secretaries as creating a balkanized administrative structure at the upper levels of the State Department. Eagleburger calls for reducing their number and returning to a system in which policy coordination occurred at the level of the regional assistant secretaries. He also advocates creating a freestanding International Trade Agency that would merge the Office of the U.S. Trade Representative and the International Trade Administration from the Commerce Department.

The State Department's Value System

The Secretary of State.   Capturing the essence of the State Department's value system is best done by looking at how secretaries of state have defined their role and how the Foreign Service Officer (FSO) corps approaches its job. The job of Secretary of State is not an easy one. Cecil Crabb suggests that "almost without exception, every post war Secretary of State has left under a cloud of criticism." Lack of leadership (James Byrnes, Dean Rusk), aloofness and arrogance

(Dean Acheson), and overly zealous attempts to dominate foreign policy making (John Foster Dulles, Henry Kissinger, Alexander Haig) are among the charges that have been leveled.

Secretaries of state have also found themselves excluded from key decisions. Cyrus Vance resigned from the Carter administration partly in protest over his exclusion from decision making on the Iranian hostage rescue effort. Edmund Muskie, his successor, suffered the embarrassment of not being informed about PD-59, the presidential directive that shifted U.S. strategic thought away from a strictly second-strike posture to one emphasizing nuclear flexibility and limited strategic options. George Shultz claimed that he was only marginally informed of the NSC plan to sell U.S. weapons to Iran and secure the release of U.S. hostages in Lebanon. James Baker, Bush's Secretary of State, was regarded as a key member of the president's inner circle and he was widely regarded as the most politically expert individual to hold that post. At the same time, career diplomats repeatedly criticized him for leaving the State Department in the dark on key foreign policy initiatives and surrounding himself with aides who worked with him at the White House when he was Chief of Staff and at the Treasury Department.

In practice, secretaries of state have had to make a choice: either become advocates of the State Department perspective or serve as the loyal allies of the president.[6] Adopting the first perspective makes one suspect in the White House. The second perspective requires disassociating oneself from the State Department and letting it drift for lack of leadership. Neither perspective is dominant. Haig adopted the first role orientation; Rusk, Dulles, and Shultz adopted the second; and Vance sought to combine elements of both in his approach to the job, as did Warren Christopher under Clinton. Neither of these perspectives succeeded. In large measure Vance failed because of the presence of a strong bureaucratic rival who possessed a different world view, National Security Adviser Zbigniew Brzezinski. Christopher's failings lay elsewhere. First, he served a president who was elected on a domestic politics agenda, who freely injected himself in the policy process, and who regularly changed policy positions. Christopher had little success selling the State Department position in such an environment. Second, Christopher was by nature cautious and approached controversial issues with an eye toward compromise and avoiding the spotlight. Madeleine Albright replaced Christopher as Secretary of State in Clinton's second term. Her selection was widely interpreted as a signal by Clinton that the United States needed to take a more active leadership role in world affairs. Albright routinely favored a more assertive role for the United States in Clinton's first term and was a strong voice in support of NATO's bombing of Kosovo.

Foreign Service Officers.   At the heart of the State Department system is its 3,700 FSO corps. The foreign service was created in 1924 by the Rogers Act. Foreign service officers were intended to be generalists, "trained to perform almost any task at any post in the world."[7] The principal organizational device for producing such individuals is to rotate them frequently among functional tasks and geographic areas. The civil service, which existed apart from the FSO corps, was relied on to perform the State Department's "lesser" technical and administrative tasks. In 1954 a reorganization proposal developed by Harry

Wriston led to the merger of these two personnel systems. Provisions were also made for widespread lateral entry into the restructured FSO system. "Wristonization" was not a complete success. Integrating the two career tracks did not bridge the differences in outlook that had arisen between them. Some had hoped that lateral entry would "Americanize" the foreign service by bringing into the FSO individuals with pasts different from the eastern, Ivy League, and upper-class backgrounds associated with it. Wristonization also created new problems. It created resentment in the ranks of the FSOs who felt that the corps was being diluted by the addition of outsiders, which caused an over-crowding at the top of the FSO career pyramid because while the number of FSOs had increased, there was no increase in the number of highly desirable positions. Further reform of the FSO system took place in 1980 with the passage of the Foreign Service Officer Act. It too trimmed the number of positions available for senior FSOs. From 1986 to 1990 between 350 and 450 upper-grade FSOs were forced to retire. The American Foreign Service Association contends that the negative impact of the 1980 reforms goes deeper than number cuts and extends to the quality of U.S. foreign policy:

> No one wants to serve as the political or economic counselor at overseas embassies because these are not management jobs. No one is going to be willing to spend two or three years learning Chinese or Japanese, because it's likely to be regarded as dead time when you come before a promotion board. The word in the corridors now is get a job managing something and forget everything else, or you're dead.[8]

For different reasons, FSO misgivings about their place in the making of American foreign policy grew in the Reagan, Bush, and Clinton administrations. Under Reagan and Bush, the concern was "political creep." By this FSOs meant the tendency for political appointees to be appointed to assistant secretary and deputy assistant secretary positions. In the 1950s few political appointees could be found at these levels. In 1973 only 11 of 63 deputy assistant secretaries of state were political appointees. In 1984 almost one-half (59 of 136) were political appointees. Beyond the loss of job opportunities, FSOs complained that the presence of this "new blood" made it difficult to have frank discussions of thorny issues.[9] Under Clinton, the problem is the potential outright elimination of these positions as part of the effort to hold down costs. The administration's initial reorganization plan called for cutting as many as 40 deputy assistant secretary positions. Many FSOs have responded to these challenges by becoming more politically active.

The representativeness of the FSO corps continues to be a major problem. Minorities and women are particularly underrepresented. In late 1993, 56 percent of the FSO corps was white male, 24 percent white female, 7 percent minority male, and 4 percent minority female. The distribution is even more skewed if attention is paid only to the senior ranks of the FSO Corps, from which ambassadors and policy makers are selected. At this same time, 84 percent were white male, 9 percent white female, 5 percent minority male, and 1 percent minority female.[10] Over one 11-year period, 586 appointments were made to the post of deputy chief of mission. Women received only nine of them.

At the same time, women were appointed to consular positions (which deal largely with passport and visa matters) as opposed to political posts (where one is likely to be involved in policy making) so much more frequently than men that the odds of its happening were 1 to 1 million. These revelations came about as part of a lawsuit filed against the State Department in 1976. In 1989 the State Department finally admitted that discrimination did exist and began taking steps to address the problem.

The controversy surrounding the State Department's hiring, promotion, and posting policies has intensified even further in the 1990s. With the discrimination case brought by women still not resolved, the president of the American Foreign Service Association wrote in 1994: "Many male officers have complained of their perceived inability to compete fairly against women and minority officers for attractive positions."[11] Black FSOs, who brought their own still-pending discrimination suit in the mid-1980s, continue to assert that they are being "ghettoized" by being posted primarily to Africa and Latin America instead of the more prestigious areas such as Europe, the Middle East, and Asia. In 1996, the State Department agreed to pay 3.8 million to compensate black FSOs and to grant retroactive promotions to 17 individuals.

The State Department is not alone in facing charges of discrimination. In 1993 "Jane Doe Thompson," a CIA professional with over 20 years experience in the clandestine service and who had once served as station chief, sued the CIA because of sex discrimination. In a separate legal action, over 100 female officers in the clandestine division, almost one-third of all female case officers, joined in a class action lawsuit alleging discrimination. The CIA settled both matters out of court. In the class action suit, it agreed to pay $990,000 in back salaries and to make 25 retroactive promotions. For its part, the military came under heavy criticism for its handling of the Tailhook investigation. It has also struggled to find answers to such broader issues as gays in the military and the role of women in combat.

The heart of the FSO corps is its value system. The subject of repeated studies, the FSO value system consists of a clearly identifiable world outlook and set of guidelines for survival within the State Department bureaucracy.[12] Agreement also exists in the belief that these qualities are not conducive to the formulation and administration of U.S. foreign policy and that they are one reason for the State Department's declining influence on foreign affairs. Central to the belief system of the FSO is the dual conviction that the only career experience relevant to the work of the State Department is that gained in the foreign service and that the core of this work lies in the areas of political reporting, negotiating, and representing U.S. interests abroad. The FSO is empirical, intuitive, and cautious. John Harr concludes that the "systematic and methodological approach associated with planning is largely alien to the FSO."[13] Risk taking in the preparation of analysis or processing of information is avoided. As many as 27 signatures have been required before instructions were sent regarding the Food for Peace program. As I. M. Destler put it, the "desk officer 'inherits' a policy toward country X, he regards it as his function to keep that policy intact."[14]

From the perspective of the FSO, the key to survival (and promotion) within the State Department is winning the respect of one's colleagues. On the one hand, this is a logical position to take because promotion in the foreign service is by peer review. On the other hand, an excessive concern for how one is viewed by one's peers stifles thinking and produces conformity in thought and action. Chris Argyris identified four norms operating within the FSO corps that inhibit open confrontation on difficult issues and penalize risk takers.[15] They are the following:

1. Withdrawal from interpersonal difficulties and conflict
2. Minimum interpersonal openness, leveling, and trust
3. Mistrust of others' aggressiveness and fighting
4. Withdrawal from aggressiveness and fighting

Foreign Policy Impact

Once the centerpiece of the foreign affairs bureaucracy, the State Department has seen its power and influence steadily erode. It has gone from being the leading force behind such policies as the Marshall Plan, NATO, and containment to largely playing the role of the critic who finds fault with the proposals of others. It has become defensive and protective in interdepartment dealings, unable to centralize and coordinate the activities of the foreign affairs bureaucracy. Two complaints frequently are voiced about the State Department's performance. First, its recommendations are too predictable. Regardless of the problem, the State Department can be counted on to advocate minimizing risks, avoiding quick action, and adopting a long-term perspective on the problem. Second, its recommendations are insensitive to the presidential perspective on foreign policy matters. It fails to frame proposals in ways that will produce political support or at least minimize the political costs to the president. The combined result is that State Department recommendations are easily dismissed. In the eyes of many, it has become more of a spokesperson for foreign viewpoints within the U.S. government than an advocate of U.S. national interests. This situation is not condemned by all. To some it is the role the State Department should play (and a role it plays well), and they believe it should stop trying to perform functions it is no longer suited for.[16]

Another factor contributing to the State Department's decline is the changing foreign policy agenda and the inability or unwillingness of the FSO corps to acquire the skills necessary to maintain a position of leadership.[17] Military instruments assumed a central role in the policy of containment, and with this the Defense Department's voice on foreign policy grew. In the 80s, the Treasury Department's foreign policy voice grew in importance.

Another problem confronting policy makers in their efforts to use the foreign affairs bureaucracy to its greatest potential is how to improve the skills and expertise of those working in it. A comparison of the U.S. foreign affairs bureaucracy with its Japanese counterpart illustrates some of the problems here.[18] While the Japanese place great importance on having a corps of diplomats well trained in the analysis of U.S. political, military, and economic affairs, Asian specialists in the U.S. foreign affairs bureaucracy tend to rank China as the more important area and view Japanese affairs from a paternalistic and outdated occupation-era mentality. These perceptual problems are reinforced by organizational ones: The Assistant Secretary of State for East Asian and Pacific Affairs is usually a China specialist or a generalist; one FSO handles economic affairs at the Japanese desk, and few staffers speak Japanese; of the 300 American professionals in the Tokyo embassy, only six are commercial officers, and only eight are economic officers. Similar problems exist in the Defense Department, CIA, Treasury Department, and Commerce Department.

Last, the State Department's ability to exert leadership within the foreign affairs bureaucracy has been hampered by the absence of a strong domestic constituency supporting its actions. The elitism fostered by the FSO corps has long made it suspect with prominent political forces. In the 1950s the State Department was the prime target of the McCarthy investigations into un-American activities. In 1953 alone, some 70 to 80 percent of the highest-ranking FSOs were dismissed or resigned, or were reassigned to politically safe positions.[19] Most recently, in the Reagan administration the State Department encountered stiff domestic opposition from Jesse Helms, who was concerned about the political outlook of many nominees who came before the Senate Foreign Relations Committee.

THE DEFENSE DEPARTMENT

Structure and Growth

For most of its history, the military security of the United States was provided by forces under the command of the War Department and the Department of the Navy. No political or military authority other than the president existed above these two departments to coordinate and direct their affairs. During World War II the ineffectiveness of this system became apparent and led U.S. policy makers to take a series of ad hoc steps to bring greater coherence to the U.S. war effort. In 1947 the National Security Act formalized many of these arrangements by establishing a Department of the Air Force and giving legal standing to the Joint Chiefs of Staff (JCS). It also created a National Military Establishment and the position of Secretary of Defense. Further changes were made in 1949 when the National Military Establishment was redesignated as the Defense Department. As part of the reorganization, the Army, Navy, and Air Force departments were made military departments within the Department of Defense and were dropped from the cabinet and the NSC. In addition, a chairperson was added to the JCS, and the office of Secretary of Defense was created. The objective of these reforms was to place the military services more fully under civilian control and to provide for greater coordination of their activities. These same motivations guided Defense Department reorganizations in 1953 and 1958. Since 1958 only minor changes have been made in the formal structure of the military establishment.

The dominant reform issue of the early 1980s within the defense establishment was improving the operational efficiency of the armed forces. The failed 1979 hostage rescue effort, the 1983 terrorist attack on the Marines in Beirut, and problems encountered in the 1983 invasion of Grenada were cited by many military reformers as proof that reforms were needed beginning at the very top.[20]

Congress shared the concerns of defense reformers. Over the objections of the executive branch and many in the military, in 1986 it passed two pieces of legislation designed to remedy perceived shortcomings in the performance of the U.S. military. The Goldwater–Nichols Act strengthened the position of the JCS relative to that of the individual services. It also gave added weight to those parts of the Pentagon that had an interservice perspective. In particular, it gave the commanders in chief of the eight unified commands the authority to make budgetary requests directly to the Secretary of Defense rather than go through the separate services. The second piece of legislation, the Cohen–Nunn Act, dealt with a more narrowly defined problem: U.S. difficulties in engaging in low-intensity conflict and special operations. It established a unified command for special operations and created an Assistant Secretary of Defense for special operations and low-intensity conflict.

Today the primary focal point of most military reformers is the size of the U.S. military establishment. This concern predates the end of the cold war but has become intensified with its passing. From a financial perspective the problems center around the constraints brought on by the budget deficit and gross overruns in weapons procurement costs. The overall magnitude of the problem can be seen by comparing the costs of specific weapons systems. For example, as originally planned the Air Force was going to obtain 132 B-2 stealth bombers at a cost of $500 million each. In April 1991 that figure was reduced to 75 planes with the per-plane cost now pegged at over $2 billion.[21]

A second dimension of the cost problem is how to restructure the Pentagon, given the expected cutback in available funds and the changed strategic environment. Les Aspin, Clinton's first Secretary of Defense, took two highly publicized steps in this direction, neither of which proved to be very successful. The first was a reorganization of the Secretary of Defense's office. Aspin sought to strengthen the office by having it take control over personnel, technology, and readiness functions performed throughout the Defense Department. He also reorganized it along lines comparable to those found in the State Department, creating such positions as assistant secretaries of defense for economic and environmental security, and for democracy and human rights. The logic was to make the Defense Department a more effective player in the policy-making process. In doing so, Aspin also eliminated some of the more important posts found in the Secretary's office: the assistant secretaries for international security policy and international security affairs. Terming this new structure as "ineffective," Aspin's successor, William Perry, moved quickly to return the office to its former shape.

The second was the "Bottom Up Review." Billed as a comprehensive review of U.S. military policy in the post–cold war era, its results disappointed many.[22] As a congressperson, Aspin had advocated a "win-hold-win" strategy in which the United States would possess an armed force capable of defeating an aggressor in one setting while simultaneously using air power to hold another aggressor at bay. Once the first aggressor was defeated, the United States would turn its full resources to bear against the second and defeat it as well. Instead of embracing this strategy, the Bottom Up Review reaffirmed the "two-war" strategy which had been guiding U.S. force decisions. Under this policy, the United States needs the simultaneous ability to fight and win two wars.

Reaffirmation of the two-war strategy leaves unresolved the question of how to structure U.S. forces to accomplish this task. This debate finds the political coalition that supported high levels of defense spending during the cold war split into two camps. On the one hand are military hawks who continue to argue the need for relatively high levels of spending for defense. They are opposed by deficit hawks who, while they agree that the world remains a dangerous place and that the United States needs a strong military to protect its national security interests, see a greater danger in uncontrolled federal spending and large budget deficits. From their point of view, defense dollars cannot be left untouched in the drive to cut government spending. Joining the side of the deficit hawks are those who have long opposed high levels of military spending. They see the two-war strategy as one which fits U.S. enemies to the existing force structure rather than tailoring U.S. forces to meet future threats. Moreover, they see the Bottom Up Review as offering little in the way of a peace dividend. One author has calculated that it would cut defense spending by only 7 percent over the five-year period of the base plan, reducing it from $1.33 trillion to $91 billion.[23]

More is involved than deciding how much to cut. Also at issue is what to cut. Reducing spending on new weapons may not be enough. It may also be necessary to do something that the Bottom Up Review did not really do: make major cuts in the size of the military forces themselves.[24] The fear expressed by analysts such as Caroline Ziemke and Joseph Romm is that when this happens the United States will return to the cost-cutting practices of the 1970s post-Vietnam era.[25] Rather than cut back on the overall size of the military establishment, cuts were made in such invisible areas as spare parts, ammunition, training, and maintenance. The result was "hollow forces," a military establishment that looked robust on paper but was sorely lacking in readiness and could not be sustained over a long period of time.

The Defense Department's Value System

Secretary of Defense.   Secretaries of defense generally have adopted one of two roles.[26] The first is that of the generalist. According to James Roherty, the generalist recognizes and defers to military expertise. He is concerned with coordinating and integrating the judgments he receives from the military professionals. He sees himself as being the Defense Department's representative in the policy process. In contrast, the functionalist is concerned with consolidating management and policy control in the office of the Secretary of Defense. The functionalist rejects the notion that there exists a unique area of military expertise, and he sees himself as first among equals in defense policy decision making. Above all else, the functionalist seeks to efficiently manage the system in accordance with presidential policy objectives.

Among the early secretaries of defense, James Forrestal adopted the generalist perspective while Robert McNamara was a functionalist. McNamara's tenure was significant for his efforts to expand the range of issues that the Secretary of Defense had control over and the methodology used in making decisions. Until McNamara, even functionalist-oriented secretaries of defense largely restricted themselves to managing the budgetary process and mediating between interservice rivalries. McNamara sought and acquired a voice in designing defense policy. In doing so he brought Planning, Programming, and Budgetary Systems (PPBS) analysis to the Defense Department. As was commonplace in other government bureaucracies, the Defense Department's budget was organized by department (Army, Navy, Air Force) and broken down into such traditional categories as personnel, maintenance, and construction. Under PPBS "all military forces and systems were grouped into output-oriented programs according to their principal missions [conventional defense of Europe, nuclear deterrence], even though missions cut across traditional service boundaries categories."[27] Cost–benefit calculations were then made on whether or not to acquire a new system. Based on this type of decision calculus, the B-70 manned bomber, the Skybolt missile, and nuclear naval vessels were rejected while the Poseidon submarine, F-111 fighter, and the Minuteman III missile were accepted.

Not all of his successors have followed in McNamara's footsteps. Melvin Laird, Secretary of Defense under Nixon, adopted a generalist role orientation. He saw his role as that of an institutional spokesperson, serving as a buffer between the military and the rest of the political system. Cheney, who like Laird served in the House, followed in his footsteps. Both of Clinton's first two secretaries of defense were defense experts, but they adopted very different role orientations. Building on his experience as chair of the House Armed Services Committee, Aspin adopted a functionalist role orientation as Secretary of Defense that often placed him in conflict with the military. Perry's expertise lies in the area of high-technology programs. He is considered by some to be the father of the stealth technology that has become an integral part of many weapons systems. Perry adopted a role orientation that is both functionalist and generalist in nature. He pushed the military to make changes in the way it acquires items, urging it to rely as much as possible on the open marketplace rather than making highly detailed specification documents and going through defense-specific suppliers. At the same time, he demonstrated ability to manage Pentagon programs in a noncontroversial fashion, something which requires a willingness to embrace military expertise. It was this trait that led the Clinton administration to nominate him for the post.

Professional Military.   To understand the system of values operating inside the Defense Department, we must also look at the outlook that the professional military has on policy making. Two different general sets of perspectives exist.[28] The traditional view sees the professional soldier as being above partisan politics. A clear line separates military and political affairs, and professional soldiers are expected to restrict themselves to speaking out only on those subjects falling within their sphere of expertise. In the fusionist perspective the professional soldier must acquire and use political skills if he or she is to exercise an effective voice on military matters. Moreover, the line separating military decisions from political ones is blurred. No pure area of military expertise exists wherein the professional soldier can expect to find his or her opinion accepted without challenge by civilian policy makers. To the fusionist, military involvement in traditional nonmilitary areas is all but guaranteed by the increasing use of the military as an instrument of foreign policy and by problems of re-source scarcity.

Problems exist regardless of which perspective is adopted by the professional soldier. While the traditional view still has its advocates, most believe that it is no longer practical. Korea and Vietnam brought an end to whatever separation may have existed between politics and the military. The fusionist perspective, however, is not easily translated into practice, a point brought home most vividly by the actions of National Security Adviser Vice Admiral John Poindexter and his aide, Lieutenant Colonel Oliver North, in the Iran–Contra affair.

Differences in outlook also exist among the military services. They each have different "personalities."[29] The Navy, it is said, worships at the altar of tradition, the Air Force at the altar of technology, and the Army at that of country and duty. They also have different views of their own identities. The Navy sees itself above all else as an institution whose stature and independence must be protected. The Air Force sees itself as the embodiment of the idea that air power is the key guarantor of national security in the modern age. The Army views itself as artisans of warfare, whose members are divided into mutually supportive guilds—infantry, artillery, and armor (cavalry). These traits combined with still other differences give each service a distinct outlook on questions of war and peace and the use of force as an instrument of U.S. foreign policy.

Foreign Policy Impact

The professional military's foreign policy impact is a subject often discussed with great emotion. Some believe that military professionals are more aggressive than their civilian counterparts. Richard Betts rejects this argument.[30] Where the military professional and the civilian policy maker part company is over how and when to use force, not over whether to use it. The military prefers to use force quickly, massively, and decisively, and it is skeptical of making bluffs that involve the threatened use of force. Diplomats, on the other hand, prefer to avoid using force as long as possible because they see its use as an indication of a failure in policy, but they are positively predisposed to making military threats. Betts also found divisions within the military on advocating the use of force. Since World War II the most bellicose recommendations have come from the Chiefs of Naval Operations and field commanders. The Army Chiefs of Staff have been the most cautious in advocating the use of force.

Betts argues that military influence can operate on four levels in the decision making on military intervention and escalation.[31] The highest level of influence is when the military participates directly in the policy process and makes a negative recommendation against the use of force. Clinton did just this in ordering NATO bombing against Serbia in 1999. The next highest level is when the military participates indirectly in the policy process and opposes the use of force. In these cases the military does not make explicit recommendations against the use of force but presents alternatives or gives only conditional endorsement to the plan. One step below this is when the military participates indirectly in the policy process and favors the use of force. At this level the military's advice is not necessarily accepted, but it still influences the decision to use force through its presentation of data and policy alternatives. At the lowest level of influence, the military's participation is direct, and it supports the use of force. Betts finds that in these cases the military's recommendations are either superfluous (a civilian consensus already exists on the use of force) or rejected. For example, in the Cuban missile crisis, Kennedy rejected a nearly unanimous military recommendation for an armed attack.

Betts concludes that the military's real policy influence comes not through its direct participation in the policy process but through its indirect influence: its ability to get the context of a decision through the presentation of information, capabilities, and tactics. Bob Woodward, author of *The Commanders*, similarly reflects on how variable the influence of the military is on decisions regarding the use of force.[32] The Pentagon, he notes, "is not always the center of military decision making." It was in the months before the Bush administration's invasion of Panama when the attention of the White House was on other matters. In the case of the Persian Gulf War the White House paid attention to little else. "When the President and his advisors are engaged, they run the show." One recent case where the nature of the advice given by professional military officers to the president appears to have made a difference is the Clinton administration. Robert Worth writes that Colin Powell, who chaired the JCS during Clinton's first nine months in office, sharply disagreed with the president on the use of force and often "won the argument every time."[33] He was replaced by John Shalikasvili, who was much more sympathetic to Clinton's interventionist tendencies.

THE CIA AND THE INTELLIGENCE COMMUNITY

Structure and Growth

Created in 1947, the CIA is not the first effort to centralize intelligence within the government. In 1939, Roosevelt established an Interdepartmental Intelligence Committee to coordinate the activities of the FBI, the Office of Naval Intelligence, and the Military Intelligence Division of the War Department.[34] This arrangement proved unsatisfactory, and after experimenting with another organizational arrangement, Roosevelt assigned the task to the Office of Strategic Services (OSS). The OSS was to "collect and analyze strategic information" as directed by the JCS and to "plan and operate such special services" as instructed by it. The OSS, in turn, became a victim of postwar demobilization.

The breakup of the OSS did not end the ongoing dispute over whether a central or federal intelligence system was best suited for the postwar era. In the end the federal principle prevailed when, in 1946, Truman established a National Intelligence Authority (NIA) and a Central Intelligence Group (CIG). The NIA was to plan, develop, and coordinate intelligence. The CIG operated under the direction of the NIA and was headed by a director of Central Intelligence (DCI). Its job was to coordinate, plan, and disseminate intelligence and to carry out covert action. One of the considerable handicaps that the DCI labored under was that all of the people working under him in the CIG were still formally part of other intelligence organizations and, in a sense, were only on loan to him. Both the NIA and CIG were dissolved by the 1947 National Security Act when they were replaced by the NSC and CIA respectively.

Three points need to be stressed before outlining the makeup of the intelligence community. First, the concept of a community implies similarity and likeness, and it suggests the existence of a group of actors who share common goals and possess a common outlook on events. In these terms the U.S. intelligence community is a community only in the loosest sense. More accurately, it is a federation of units existing with varying degrees of institutional autonomy in their contribution to the intelligence function. Second, the concept of an intelligence community is not inherent in the definition of intelligence or in the common practice among states. The National Security Act of 1947, which created the CIA and assigned it the task of coordinating the activities of other departments, did not use the term *community* or identify those departments whose activities were to be coordinated. Third, the intelligence community is not a static entity. Its composition, as well as the relative importance of its members, has changed over time as new technologies have been developed, the international setting has changed, and bureaucratic wars have been won and lost.

The status of charter member is best conferred upon the CIA; the State Department's intelligence unit, the Bureau of Intelligence and Research (INR); and the intelligence units of the armed forces. All of these were given institutional representation on the NSC at the time of its creation. Three institutions that have a long-standing but lesser presence in the intelligence community are the FBI, the Treasury Department, and the Atomic Energy Commission (AEC). While the FBI's counterintelligence role has remained constant, significant changes have occurred with regard to the other two. Early accounts of the Treasury Department's role in the intelligence community stressed its drug enforcement mission. By the Ford administration the Treasury Department was responsible for the overt collection of foreign financial, monetary, and general economic information, and its drug enforcement role had been dropped. The fate of the AEC is somewhat different. The task of collecting, evaluating, and providing technical information on the nuclear power programs of other states still is very much alive. It is the organization that no longer exists. The AEC gave way to the Energy Research and Development Administration in the Ford administration and this, in turn, has given way to the Energy Department.

The first major addition to the intelligence community occurred in 1952 when Truman issued a presidential directive transforming the recently created Armed Forces Security Agency into the National Security Agency (NSA).[35] This operates as a semiautonomous agency of the Defense Department and is charged with (1) maintaining the security of U.S. message traffic and (2) interpreting traffic, analyzing, and cryptanalyzing the messages of all other states. In 1961 the Defense Intelligence Agency (DIA) joined the intelligence community as its newest major member. The Defense Intelligence Agency emerged as part of the centralization process then occurring within the Defense Department. The major objectives behind its creation were to unify the overall intelligence efforts of the Defense Department and to more effectively collect, produce, and disseminate military intelligence. Over the years DIA has emerged as the principal challenger to the CIA in the preparation of intelligence estimates. The Defense Intelligence Agency's challenge to the CIA's status as first among equals reached a new height in the Reagan administration. Both the Reagan transition team and the Senate Select Committee on Intelligence called for upgrading DIA's estimating capabilities so that it might more effectively challenge the estimates produced by the CIA.

Organizationally, the CIA is divided into five operational components. Each is headed by a deputy director who reports to the DCI.[36] The Directorate of Administration is responsible for recruitment, training, support activities, communications, and the physical security of CIA buildings. The Directorate of Science and Technology (DS&T) is the newest major directorate. It was established in the early 60s out of the conviction that technology had begun to change the nature of the intelligence function and that the CIA had to stay on top of this trend. The results of these efforts have been considerable. The U-2 and SR-71 spy planes and satellite reconnaisance systems all owe much to the efforts of this directorate.

The third operating unit of the CIA is the Directorate of Intelligence (DI). It was created in 1952 through a reorganization of the CIA's intelligence-producing units and is the largest of the CIA's directorates. Three major offices exist within DI. They are the Office of Strategic Research, which deals with the war-making plans of other states, especially those with nuclear capabilities; the Office of Economic Research, which provides reports and analyses on such subjects as Soviet grain production, OPEC oil production, the economic impact of weather patterns, and the strength of major foreign currencies; and the Office of Political Research, which addresses topics such as terrorism, governmental stability, the link between foreign and domestic policies, and the impact of culture and religion on politics.

The DI is the primary producer of government intelligence documents which range in frequency from daily briefs (at varying levels of secrecy) to weekly, quarterly, and yearly summaries, to occasional special reports. The best known of these reports are the National Intelligence Estimates (NIEs). Until 1973 they were produced by the Office of National Estimates, which was part of the DI. At that time the office was replaced by a National Intelligence Officer system that currently operates out of the DCI's office. The change was made in order to increase the responsiveness of the intelligence community to policy maker needs and to improve the overall quality of the product. The purpose of an NIE remains the same: to present the intelligence community's best judgment on a given topic. Using 1982 as an example, 67 NIEs were produced; the DCI requested 21 of them, and approximately that same number were done on a routine basis; 58 percent of them were drafted in DI while another 24 percent were drafted by the National Intelligence Center, which supervises the work of the National Intelligence Officers. The Soviet Union is typically the most frequent subject of an NIE. Europe, the Near East, and Latin America are also frequent subjects. The time required to put together an NIE varies widely. In 1982 31 of the 67 NIEs were "time urgent" and produced under a tight deadline.

The fourth directorate is the Directorate for Operations (DO). This is the most controversial component within the CIA's system and one frequently recommended for splitting off or outright abolition. Like the DI, it was created in 1952. The Directorate for Operations has three basic missions: the clandestine collection of information, counterintelligence, and covert action. Within DO there exists a staff for each mission. The Foreign Intelligence Service monitors, assesses, and directs the clandestine collection of information; the counter-intelligence staff is concerned with protecting the CIA from foreign penetrations; and the covert action staff plans and carries out covert action. The actual operations of DO are grouped on regional lines and subdivided into stations. Each station is headed by a station chief and is generally housed in the U.S. embassy. Their size varies from that of only a few individuals to several hundred. The last directorate, for planning and coordination, was set up in 1990. It is to focus on identifying the changing requirements for intelligence in today's world.

The mid-1990s found the CIA an institution under siege. Not only was its level of performance criticized but the need for its continued existence was called into question. Angered by its failure to predict the fall of communism in the Soviet Union, Daniel Patrick Moynihan, who once served on the Senate Intelligence Committee, called for abolishing the CIA and transferring its intelligence functions to the State Department. David Boren, a past chair of that committee, called for significant budgetary cuts and the creation of a new director of national intelligence who would be responsible for preparing, submitting, and overseeing a single budget for the entire intelligence community. Post–cold war DCIs Robert Gates and R. James Woolsey have commented publicly on the need for the CIA to undertake institutional changes and reexamine its intelligence priorities if it is to make a continuing contribution to American foreign policy. Former CIA analysts have drawn upon their experiences to suggest ways of "shaking up the CIA," and "reinventing" it.[37]

Perhaps most damaging to the CIA was its failure to detect that the Soviet Union had planted a spy in their midst. Aldrich Ames, who joined the CIA in 1962 and worked on Soviet counterintelligence operations, had been on the Soviet payroll since 1985 and received more than $1.5 million to serve as a mole. He exposed over 100 spy operations and the identities of at least ten key agents, all of whom were executed. Compounding the problem was the CIA's reluctance to take strong action against those responsible. Rather than fire or demote those who failed to recognize that Ames was a Soviet spy, DCI James Woolsey chose only to reprimand them, with the most severe reprimands going to CIA officials already in retirement or about to retire. Congress reacted more forcefully. It established the Aspin Commission to study the CIA's future.

Concern over the future direction of the CIA also has been present in the executive branch. Sufficient uncertainty existed within the Bush administration over where and how the CIA fit into American foreign policy that the president issued National Security Directive 29 in November 1991 calling for a "top to bottom examination of the mission, role, and priorities of the intelligence community" and directing the intelligence community to identify intelligence priorities for the post–cold war era. At virtually the same time he nominated John Deutch to be his second Director of Central Intelligence, President Clinton issued a classified executive order that for the first time established formal White House priorities for intelligence agencies. At the top of the list are renegade states such as North Korea, Iraq, and Iran. Also receiving high priority are weapons proliferation and transnational forces such as Muslim fundamentalism. Economic issues occupy the middle rank, and environmental and health issues are at the bottom.

The Intelligence Community's Value System

Director of Central Intelligence.   The DCI simultaneously is head of the intelligence community and the CIA. Because of this dual position, DCIs have many role orientations available to choose from. Few have sought, and none have achieved, real managerial control over the intelligence community. The most recent to try was Stansfield Turner, Carter's DCI, who ran into stiff and successful resistance from Secretary of Defense Brown. The DCIs have not given priority to their role as head of the intelligence community because significant weaknesses lie beneath their formal position. Of all the members of the intelligence community, only the CIA exists as a separate organizational entity; all the others are parts of larger departments, most often the Defense Department. Consequently, the other members of the intelligence community look with only one eye to what the DCI demands while keeping the other eye firmly fixed on departmental positions and priorities. As a result the DCI's budgetary authority over the other members of the intelligence community remains largely unrealized, and his ability to direct their collection efforts is imperfect.

When defining their role as head of the CIA, three outlooks have been dominant: managerial, covert action, and estimating. Only John McCone gave primacy to the intelligence estimating role, and he was largely an outsider to the intelligence process before his appointment. Allen Dulles and Richard Helms, the two men who have headed the CIA longer than any others, both stressed the covert action side of the agency's mission. Since the replacement of Helms by James Schlesinger, DCIs have tended to adopt a managerial orientation. Although their particular operating styles have varied, a common theme to these managerial efforts is to increase White House control over the CIA. Turner came to the intelligence community as an outsider and left it as an outsider. William Casey came to the post of DCI with a well-developed set of ideas about what was wrong with U.S. intelligence. Casey brought to his managerial role orientation a much more positive attitude to covert operations than his recent predecessors did.

Controversy has surrounded the managerial orientations of recent DCIs. A criticism directed at both Robert Gates and R. James Woolsey was that they were ill-suited to managing the CIA's transition to the post–cold war world: Gates because he was too much of a cold warrior and Woolsey because he was an outsider to the intelligence community with no internal base of support to build on. Gates, a protégé of Casey, encountered unprecedented public opposition from active and retired intelligence professionals when nominated for the post by Bush.[38] At the heart of their critique was the charge that as Director of Intelligence under Casey, Gates had politicized the intelligence process. By this they meant that he had tightened managerial control over the intelligence product to the point that its conclusions were being driven by the policy concerns and values of senior management. If Gates embodied the dangers inherent in an overly intrusive managerial style, Woolsey came to symbolize the problems that arise when an outsider DCI tries to manage change without the support of the White House. Clinton frequently did not attend the CIA's daily White House briefing, and Woolsey's access to the president reportedly was blocked by National Security Adviser Anthony Lake. John Deutch, still another outsider to intelligence, replaced Woolsey in 1995. By his own admission, he was uncomfortable with the CIA's culture and was frustrated by his inability to bring about meaningful reform. He resigned fifteen months later. Deutch was replaced by George Tenet, who earlier in his career had served as staff director for the Senate Intelligence Committee. Tenet was described as the "ultimate staff guy," and his appointment was seen as proof of "the rewards of being a loyal and obedient servant of one's boss."[39]

Intelligence Professionals.   In order to understand how the intelligence professional thinks about intelligence, we first need to note how the consumers of intelligence think about it because it is their demands and inquiries that the intelligence professional responds to.[40] First is the conviction that analysts should furnish information and nothing more. Analysts are not expected to explore alternatives or come to conclusions—this is the responsibility of the consumer. The underlying assumption is that the facts contain self-evident implications and that if all the facts are known, then any question can be answered. Second is the assumption that experience rather than the application of analytical techniques to a problem provides the most insight into the meaning of raw data. Third is an emphasis on current events. The perceived need is for up-to-the-minute information to solve an ongoing problem. Long-range planning is too academic an exercise and too far removed from the policy maker's most immediate concerns to be highly valued. A final shared attitude toward intelligence is the tendency to treat it as a free good. Intelligence is seen as something "on tap" and always on call.

The views on intelligence existing within the intelligence community are far from uniform. Differences exist both between and within organizations.[41] With this qualification in mind, it is possible to identify four tendencies in the approach to intelligence adopted by members of the intelligence community.[42] One tendency is to be current events-oriented, to be a "butcher," cutting up the latest information and presenting the choicest pieces to the consumer. This perspective appears to be adopted only grudgingly by analysts out of a desire to participate in the policy process. Analysts see their most important role as that of giving warning, but to stick to this role orientation in the face of policy maker disinterest condemns them to working on the fringe of the policy process. A second tendency is for analysts to adopt a "jigsaw theory" of intelligence. The analyst here acts like a "baker"; everything and anything is sought after, classified, and stored on the assumption that at some point in time it may be the missing ingredient to solving a riddle. Like the butcher, the baker's role orientation is consistent with the policy maker's notion of intelligence as a free good and the assumption that the ambiguity of data can be overcome by collecting more data.

A third tendency is for the production of "intelligence to please" or "backstopping." Often when consumers of intelligence stress current data, they combine it with known policy preferences. The analyst is then placed in a very difficult position. Efforts at providing anything but supportive evidence will be ignored. Decisions on troop strength in Vietnam and target selection for bombing and rescue raids reveal the extent to which pressures to produce "intelligence to please" can be felt and the detrimental effect this can have on the intelligence function. The final role orientation is that of the "intelligent maker" who acts as an organizational broker forging a consensus on the issue at hand. Because a consensus is needed for action, this role orientation is valuable, but a danger exists in that the consensus does not have to be based on an accurate reading of events. Facts bargained into existence provide an equally suitable basis for a consensus.

Foreign Policy Impact

The purpose of intelligence is to provide policy makers with enough warning to allow them to act in the face of a challenge to national security. This is not easily done. Surprise is a fundamental reality of international politics, and no foreign policy or defense establishment can expect to escape completely from its negative consequences. Yet intelligence is not easily integrated into the policy process.[43] The conventional wisdom holds that policy and analysis must be kept separate, or policy will corrupt analysis. The alternative view holds that analysis cannot be kept value free or separate from policy making. The position holds that analysts must articulate and evaluate policy options as well as force policy makers to confront alternatives.

The relationship between the CIA and the president is the key determinant of its impact on the policy process. This relationship is marked by a series of tensions that often serve to make the impact of intelligence on policy less than what it could be under optimum circumstances. The first tension is between the logic of intelligence and the logic of policy making.[44] The logic of intelligence is to reduce policy options by clarifying issues, assumptions, and consequences. The logic of policy making is to keep options open for as long as possible. One way to do this is to keep secrets from intelligence agencies. The second tension is between the type of information the president wants to receive and the type of information that the intelligence community is predisposed to collect and disseminate. Commenting on his experience at INR, Thomas Hughes states that policy makers were most eager to get information that would help them convince Congress or the public about the merits of a policy. They were most frustrated with information that was politically impossible to use and generally skeptical about the incremental value of added information for policy-making purposes.[45] Third, intelligence produced by the intelligence community is not the only source of information available to policy makers. Interest groups, lobbyists, the media, and personal acquaintances all compete with it, and presidents are free to choose which intelligence they wish to listen to. No one can make a policy maker accept or act on a piece of intelligence.

THE DOMESTIC BUREAUCRACIES: TREASURY, COMMERCE, AND AGRICULTURE

The most recent additions to the foreign affairs bureaucracy are organizations that have been classified traditionally as domestic in their concerns and areas of operation. Raymond Hopkins argues that the foreign policy involvement of these agencies parallels a process that happened earlier with the Defense Department. After World War II the Defense Department was instrumental in shaping global arms development programs and international security arrangements.[46] A similar process is at work in the areas of food, energy, and raw material production. The responsibility for the international management of these commodities has fallen on the U.S. government and, more specifically, non-State Department agencies. Hopkins cautions that there is nothing irreversible in this trend to greater involvement in international affairs. There is no reason why in the future the domestic bureaucracies might not once again have only a minor foreign policy role.

Integrating these newcomers into the foreign affairs bureaucracy has not been an easy task. At the core of the problem is finding an agreed-upon balance between foreign policy and domestic concerns. In the early postwar period, the foreign policy goal of containing communism dominated over private economic goals, but more recently, domestic goals have become dominant and are often pursued at the cost of broad foreign policy objectives.

Foremost among the domestic bureaucracies are the Treasury, Commerce, and Agriculture departments. By the mid-70s the State Department had become more of a participant than a leader in the field of international economic policy. Its chief bureaucratic challenger is the Treasury Department, and the two approach international economic policy from quite different perspectives. Like the other domestic bureaucracies, the Treasury Department takes an "America first" perspective and places the needs of its clients at the center of its concerns. One author describes it as having an "undifferentiating adversary attitude" toward world affairs.[47] This is in contrast to the State Department's tendency to adopt a long-range perspective on international economic problems and one sensitive to the position of other states. A type of standoff currently exists between the State Department and Treasury Department for influence in the policy process. Each exercises a virtual veto over intragovernmental agreements on international economic policy. When disagreements arise, the issue gets kicked up the bureaucratic ladder for a decision by higher authorities. However, it now takes a strong Secretary of State to neutralize the influence of the Treasury Department and its domestic allies.[48]

The Commerce Department has also emerged as a major foreign affairs bureaucracy, but its influence is not on the level of the Treasury Department's. It still functions as somewhat of a junior partner and is more involved in operating issues than in policy ones. Until 1969 the Commerce Department's primary foreign policy involvement stemmed from its job of overseeing U.S. export control policy. These controls were largely aimed at restricting the direct or indirect sale of strategic goods to communist states. In 1969 its mandate was expanded to include encouraging "peaceful trade with the East" while at the same time "vigilantly protecting" U.S. national security interests. Since 1980 the Commerce Department has become the primary implementor of nonagricultural trade policy and the chief administrator of U.S. export and import programs. As part of this task, it supervises the enforcement of antidumping regulations and the distribution of assistance to those industries injured because of lower-priced imports. Through its Foreign Commercial Service, the Commerce Department has representatives stationed in 66 countries and has become active in export promotion activities. The Commerce Department is not without its own challengers for influence on trade policy. The Office of the Special Trade Representative (OTR) has also benefited at the expense of the State Department and enjoys a great deal of congressional support for its activities.

The Agriculture Department also remains a junior partner in the foreign affairs bureaucracy. It is active in administering U.S. food export programs throughout the world and has representatives in approximately 40 embassies. Its best known foreign policy role is as the administrator of P.L. 480, the Food for Peace program which provides for the free export of government-owned agricultural commodities for humanitarian and developmental purposes. In 1982 $1.3 billion worth of farm products were shipped abroad. While the Food for Peace program is primarily oriented to the third world, the Agriculture Department is also keenly concerned with Europe, and this concern has often brought it into conflict with the State Department. The long-standing object of this dispute is the Common Market's Common Agricultural Plan (CAP). Its purpose is to protect the politically powerful, small European farmers from foreign competition through a system of subsidies and price supports. Both the State Department and the Defense Department have been supporters of CAP because it is seen as contributing to European unity and security. The Agricultural Department has been hostile to it because it discriminates against American farmers by denying them access to the European market. In the third world the Agriculture Department has clashed with the State Department in the war on drugs. The State Department has supported programs designed to encourage the production of crops other than coca which is used for cocaine. The Agriculture Department has objected, citing the potentially harmful impact that this would have on U.S. farm exports.

Just as with State, Defense, and the CIA, structural reorganization has also become a prominent theme in thinking about the future of these domestic bureaucracies. A main focus of concern is on improving the coordination of U.S. international economic policy. Policy coordination occurs through a variety of mediums. Informal though they may be, breakfast or luncheon meetings, telephone calls, and the exchange of memos are commonly used means for coordinating policy. Interagency working groups, joint staff meetings, and task forces represent more formal responses to the problem of coordinating policy.

SUMMARY AND FUTURE ISSUES

Viewed solely in terms of lines on an organizational chart, the foreign affairs bureaucracy offers presidents a powerful set of organizations to use in pursuit of their foreign policy agendas. Looked at from the perspective of values and roles, a more challenging picture emerges. The bureaucracy cannot be used as freely as would be liked. Not only must coordination be achieved between and within organizations, but the way in which bureaucrats approach their jobs must also be addressed. The problem of forging a consensus is a real and enduring one because different bureaucratic units see different sides of an issue.

In looking to the future, we see that the greatest challenge in each of the bureaucratic areas we highlighted will be creating what Paul Bracken refers to as "the military after next."[49] Bracken observes that it will not be very hard to anticipate the shape of the next U.S. military. It will be a product of trends and pressures either already in place or that are very visible. Much of this military is already in place. Where creative thinking needs to take place is in looking beyond the next decade to the military after it, that we must soon begin to create and that will be in place 30 years from now. Bracken argues that the next military, the one whose structure, roles, and missions we are presently debating, will be all but blind to fundamental changes in the international system as it struggles to find solutions for the immediate problems confronting it. He asserts that in thinking about the "military after next" we must reexamine such fundamental concepts as hierarchy, span of control, and response time. Even more fundamentally, Bracken states that we must rethink the competitive environment in which the United States operates, find new ways to distinguish among military competitors, and devise strategies to deal with each. Extending Bracken's arguments, the need also exists to begin thinking about the "CIA after next," the "State Department after next," and the "Treasury Department after next."

We conclude by noting one of the classic defenses of the State Department's performance. When asked by President Kennedy what was wrong with the State Department, career diplomat Charles Bohlen replied, "You are."[50] George Ball, also a career diplomat, seconds this observation by suggesting that the State Department is being used by presidents as a scapegoat for foreign policy failures. Presidents claim all of the successes but none of the failures.[51] Diplomats are not alone in this view that much of what is wrong with the foreign affairs bureaucracy is the doing of elected officials. The professional military view was that escalation in Vietnam would fail. They also believed that when the war ended and the civilians who championed escalation were no longer in office, the professional military would be left to shoulder the blame for what went wrong.[52]

NOTES

1. Henry Kissinger, "Conditions of World Order," *Daedalus,* 95 (1966), 503–29.

2. Victor A. Thompson, *Modern Organization* (New York: Knopf, 1961).

3. On the volume of State Department message traffic, see Werner Feld, *American Foreign Policy: Aspirations and Reality* (New York: Wiley & Sons, 1984), p. 61; and Gene Rainey, *Patterns of American Foreign Policy* (Boston: Allyn & Bacon, 1975), p. 175.

4. Henry T. Nash, *American Foreign Policy: A Search for Security,* 3rd ed. (Homewood, Ill.: Dorsey, 1985), pp. 134–35.

5. Lawrence Eagleburger and Robert L. Barry, "Dollars and Sense Diplomacy," *Foreign Affairs,* 75 (1996), 2–8.

6. Leslie H. Gelb, "Why Not the State Department," in Charles W. Kegley, Jr., and Eugene R. Wittkopf (eds.), *Perspectives on American Foreign Policy: Selected Readings* (New York: St. Martin's, 1983), p. 286.

7. Donald P. Warwick, *A Theory of Public Bureaucracy: Politics, Personality and Organization in the State Department* (Cambridge, Mass.: Harvard University Press, 1975), pp. 29–30.

8. *The Washington Post,* March 28, 1986, p. 13.

9. David Corn, "At the Foggy Bottom of the Barrel, Political Hacks," *The Washington Post,* January 10, 1993, p. C3.

10. John M. Goshko, "Foreign Service's Painful Passage to Looking More Like America," *The Washington Post,* April 21, 1994, p. 29.

11. Ibid.

12. In addition to other studies cited in this chapter, see Andrew Scott, "The Department of State: Formal Organization and Informal Culture," *International Studies Quarterly,* 13 (1969), 1–18; and his "Environmental Change and Organizational Adaptation: The Problem of the State Department," *International Studies Quarterly,* 14 (1970), 85–94.

13. John Harr, *The Professional Diplomat* (Princeton, N.J.: Princeton University Press, 1969), pp. 197–98.

14. I. M. Destler, *Presidents, Bureaucrats, and Foreign Policy: The Politics of Organizational Reform* (Princeton, N.J.: Princeton University Press, 1972), p. 158.

15. Cited in Harr, *The Professional Diplomat,* p. 230.

16. Robert Pringle, "Creeping Irrelevance at Foggy Bottom," *Foreign Policy,* 29 (1977/78). 128–39; and Warwick, *A Theory of Public Bureaucracy,* p. 72.

17. Pringle, "Creeping Irrelevance at Foggy Bottom," p. 135.

18. Ronald A. Morse and Edward A. Olsen, "Japan's Bureaucratic Edge," *Foreign Policy,* 52 (1983/84), 167–80.

19. Nash, *American Foreign Policy,* p. 141.

20. For a discussion on the pros and cons of reorganizing the JCS system, see William J. Lynn and Barry R. Posen, "The Case for JCS Reform," *International Security,* 10 (1985/86), 69–97; Mac-Kubin Thomas Owen, "The Hollow Promise of JCS Reform," *International Security,* 10 (1985/86), 98–111; and Edward Luttwak, *The Pentagon and the Art of War* (New York: Touchstone, 1985).

21. Joseph J. Romm, "Laid Waste by Weapons Lust," *The Bulletin of the Atomic Scientists,* 48 (October 1992), 15–23.

22. For alternative plans and their corresponding military force requirements, see David Callahan, "Saving Defense Dollars," *Foreign Policy,* 96 (1994), 94–112; and William Kaufmann, "Some Small Change for Defense," *The Brookings Review,* 8 (Summer 1990) 26–33.

23. Robert L. Borosage, "Inventing the Threat: Clinton's Defense Budget," *World Policy Journal,* 10 (1993), 7–15.

24. For contrasting views see F. Andy Messing, Jr., "No Time for Defense Downsizing," *The World & I,* 21 (March 1994), 94–99; and Christopher A. Preble, "Shrink, Shrink, Shrink the Navy," *USA Today,* 122 (May 1994), 12–16.

25. Romm, "Laid Waste by Weapons Lust," and Caroline Ziemke, "Rethinking the Mistakes of the Past: History's Message to the Clinton Defense Department," *The Washington Quarterly,* 16 (1993), 47–60.

26. James Roherty, "The Office of the Secretary of Defense," in John E. Endicott and Roy W. Stafford (eds.), *American Defense Policy,* 4th ed. (Baltimore, Md.: Johns Hopkins University Press, 1977), pp. 286–96.

27. Amos A. Jordon and William J. Taylor, Jr., *American National Security: Policy and Process* (Baltimore, Md.: Johns Hopkins University Press, 1981), p. 185.

28. John H. Garrison, "The Political Dimension of Military Professionalism," in Endicott and Stafford (eds.), *American Defense Policy,* pp. 578–87.

29. Carl Builder, *The Masks of War* (Baltimore, Md.: Johns Hopkins University Press, 1989).

30. Richard K. Betts, *Soldiers, Statesmen, and Cold War Crises* (Cambridge, Mass.: Harvard University Press, 1977), pp. 4–5.

31. Ibid., pp. 11–12.

32. Bob Woodward, *The Commanders* (New York: Simon and Schuster, 1991), p. 33.

33. Robert Worth, "Clinton's Warriors," *World Policy Journal,* 15 (1998), 43–48.

34. Mark M. Lowenthal, *U.S. Intelligence: Evolution and Anatomy,* Washington Paper #105 (New York: Praeger, 1984), pp. 5–15.

35. James Bamford, *The Puzzle Palace: Inside the National Security Agency* (Baltimore, Md.: Penguin, 1982).

36. Lowenthal, *U.S. Intelligence,* pp. 89–92; and Stafford Thomas, *The U.S. Intelligence Community* (Latham, Md.: University of America Press, 1983), pp. 45–63.

37. See for example Herbert Meyer, "Reinventing the CIA," *Global Affairs,* 7 (1992), 1–13; and Marvin Ott, "Shaking Up the CIA," *Foreign Policy,* 93 (1993), 132–51.

38. See for example the comments made by Harold Ford and Jennifer Glaudemans in *Hearings Before the Select Committee on Intelligence of the United States Senate on the Nomination of Robert M. Gates to be Director of Central Intelligence,* vol. II (Washington, D.C.: U.S. Government Printing Office, 1991).

39. Tim Weiner, "For the 'Ultimate Staff Guy,' a Time to Reap the Rewards of Being Loyal," *The New York Times,* national edition, March 26, 1997, p. A14.

40. Roger Hilsman, *Strategic Intelligence and National Defense* (Glencoe, Ill.: Free Press, 1956), pp. 37–56.

41. For a discussion of these points, see Patrick J. McGarvey, *The CIA: The Myth and the Madness* (Baltimore, Md.: Penguin, 1973), pp. 148–59; and Victor Marchetti and John D. Marks, *The CIA and the Cult of Intelligence* (New York: Dell, 1974), pp. 235–77.

42. Hilsman, *Strategic Intelligence and National Defense,* pp. 199–222; and Thomas L. Hughes, *The Fate of Facts in a World of Men* (New York: Foreign Policy Association, Headline Series #233, 1976), pp. 36–60.

43. Sherman Kent, *Strategic Intelligence for American World Policy* (Princeton, N.J.: Princeton University Press, 1966); and Willmoore Kendall, "The Functions of Intelligence," *World Politics,* 2 (1949), 542–52.

44. Hughes, *Fate of Facts in a World of Men,* p. 47.

45. Thomas Hughes, "The Power to Speak and the Power to Listen: Reflections on Bureaucratic Politics and a Recommendation on Information Flows," in Thomas M. Franck and Edward Weisband (eds.), *Secrecy and Foreign Policy* (New York: Oxford University Press, 1974), p. 18.

46. Raymond Hopkins, "The International Role of 'Domestic Bureaucracies,'" *International Organization,* 30 (1976), p. 411.

47. Stephen D. Cohen, *The Making of United States International Economic Policy: Principles, Problems, and Proposals for Reform,* 2nd ed. (New York: Praeger, 1981), p. 40.

48. Ibid., p. 41.

49. Paul Bracken, "The Military After Next," *The Washington Quarterly,* 16 (1993), 157–74.

50. Quoted in Destler, *Presidents, Bureaucrats, and Foreign Policy,* p. 155.

51. Quoted in Cecil Crabb, Jr., *American Foreign Policy in the Nuclear Age,* 4th ed. (New York: Harper & Row, 1983), p. 102.

52. Betts, *Soldiers, Statesmen, and Cold War Crises,* p. 11.

11 Models of Policy Making: Overview

Roger Hilsman, a former policy maker and the author of many pieces on U.S. foreign policy, states that "the business of Washington is making decisions."[1] President Bush's first major foreign policy initiative came in late May 1989 when he broke with long-standing U.S. policy and agreed to proposals for troop level and air force reductions at a May 1989 NATO meeting in Brussels. Only the month before, a four-month policy by review had concluded that the United States should not undertake any major new initiatives toward the Soviet Union or Europe. As the NATO meeting approached and Gorbachev's diplomatic arms control offensive drew ever-increasing amounts of praise in Europe, Bush decided to change course. He informed his staff that he wanted "creative" ideas. In less than two weeks a small group of senior advisers and their staffs came up with new proposals and rewrote most of the speeches Bush was scheduled to give.

Our purpose in this chapter is to get a better understanding of how policy makers come together to make foreign policy decisions. For a number of reasons, this is easier said than done. First, no single decision-making process exists. Decisions are arrived at in a number of ways. They may be made by an individual, a small group, an organization, or some combination of them. In each case the procedures followed and the methods used to make the decision may vary. Second, the notion of *a decision* is itself somewhat misleading. It suggests the existence of a specific point in time at which a conscious judgment is made on what to do about a problem. Reality is often far less organized. Decisions are seldom final or decisive; they tend to lack concrete beginning and end points; and they often amount to only temporary breathing spells or truces before the issue is raised again. Decisions are also often made with far less attention to their full meaning and consequences than is commonly recognized. "A government does not decide to inaugurate the nuclear age, but only to try and build the bomb before its enemy does."[2]

A final factor complicating efforts to understand how policy is made is the relationship of the policy process to policy outcomes. Our intuitive sense is that if the policy process can be made to work properly, then the policy outcome should also work. Accordingly, bad policy can be attributed, at least in part, to bad policy making. Unfortunately, the link between the two is imperfect. Good policy making does not ensure good policy. In a provocative account of the U.S. experience in Vietnam, Leslie Gelb and Richard Betts argue that the irony of Vietnam is that while U.S. policy has been roundly criticized, the policy-making system worked.[3] It achieved its basic purpose of preventing a communist victory until domestic political opinion coalesced around either a strategy of victory or withdrawal. The political system produced policies responsive to the wishes of the majority and near the political center while at the same time allowing virtually all views to be aired. The bureaucracy selected and implemented measures designed to accomplish these ends, and these policies were undertaken without illusion about their ultimate chances of success.

In an effort to make sense out of the complicated business of making decisions, models have been developed to help explain, describe, predict, and evaluate how U.S. foreign policy is made. Models are analytical tools that are designed to serve as a simplified representation of reality. As a simplification they leave out much of the detail and texture of what goes on in the policy-making process in an effort to isolate and highlight what are felt to be the most salient features. Models can be distinguished from one another in terms of how they seek to capture and depict reality. The critical task for the foreign policy analyst is deciding how to select from the range of models available and combine them in an insightful fashion.

In this chapter we survey five of the most frequently used models of U.S. foreign policy making.[4] The next chapter presents case studies that illustrate how these models can be used to gain insight into how U.S. foreign policy is made. Before turning our attention to the models, two final caveats need to be raised. First, we are not arguing that policy makers consciously choose one of these models and act accordingly. We are only arguing that these models can help us understand what is happening in the policy-making process. Policy makers are not ignorant of the existence of these models, but their actions are far more likely to be governed by the complexities, uncertainties, and time constraints inherent in the policy-making process. Second, these models should not be judged in terms of being right or wrong. A more useful standard is how helpful the model is for explaining, describing, or evaluating the workings of the foreign policy process for the policy you are studying.

THE RATIONAL ACTOR MODEL

The most frequently employed policy-making model is the rational actor model. At its core is an action-reaction process. Foreign policy is viewed as a calculated response to the actions of another actor. This action then produces a calculated response that in turn causes the state to reevaluate and readjust its own foreign policy. In carrying out these calculations, the state is seen as being unitary and rational. By unitary it is meant that the state can be viewed as calculating and responding to external events as if it were a single entity. There is no need for the analyst to delve into the intricacies of governmental organization, domestic politics, or personalities in trying to understand why a policy was selected. The state can be treated as a "black box," responding with one voice to the challenges and opportunities confronting it. We implicitly employ this model when we speak of Israeli goals, Argentine national interests, or Soviet adventurism.

The calculations by which a foreign policy is selected are assumed to be rational. The basic elements of a rational decision process are (1) goals are clearly stated and ranked in order of preference, (2) all options are considered, (3) the consequences of each option are assessed, and (4) a value-maximizing choice is made. Broadly speaking, there are two ways of carrying out a rational actor analysis of policy making. The first is inductive. It is frequently employed in diplomatic histories. The analyst tries to understand the foreign policy decision by placing himself or herself in the position of the government taking the action. The objective is to appreciate the situation as the government sees it and to understand the logic of the situation. The second approach is deductive. It is best exemplified by game theory and is frequently employed by military strategists and deterrence theorists. Here it is assumed that "a certain kind of conduct is inherent in a particular situation or relationship."[5] Rather than relying on actual events to support its analysis, the deductive approach relies on logical and mathematical formulations of how states should (rationally) behave under given conditions.

The rational actor model is attractive because it places relatively few informational demands upon the observer. It is also frequently criticized for essentially the same reason: It understates the complexity of foreign affairs and the reality of the policy process. Foreign policy is not just made in response to external events, but also is heavily influenced by domestic political calculations, personalities, and organizational factors. Additionally, the rational actor model assumes that "important events have important causes." By doing so, it downgrades the importance of chance, accidents, and coincidence in foreign affairs. Critics also contend that the model's information-processing demands exceed human capabilities. Goals are seldom stated clearly or rank ordered. The full range of policy options and their consequences are rarely evaluated. And in making decisions the need for value trade-offs is denied more than it is faced up to. In place of the assumption of rationality, many critics advance a model based on an incremental decision-making process in which goals are only loosely stated, a limited range of options is examined, and the policy selected is one that "satisfies" (from *satisfactory* and *sufficient*) rather than optimizes.[6]

A final challenge to the rational actor model centers on its methodology. Carried out either inductively or deductively, the rational actor model relies heavily on intuition and personal judgment in interpreting actions or placing weights on policy payoffs. Graham Allison has captured this criticism in his "rationality theorem."[7] He states that there isn't a pattern of activity for which an imaginative analyst cannot find objectives that are maximized by a given course of action.

BUREAUCRATIC POLITICS

Bureaucratic politics is the "process by which people inside government bargain with one another on complex public policy questions."[8] As this definition suggests, the bureaucratic politics model approaches policy making in a completely different way from the rational actor model. Policy making is seen as a political process dominated by conflict resolution and not problem solving. Politics dominates the decision-making process because no individual is in a position to decide on matters alone. Power is shared, and the individuals who share power disagree on what should be done because they are located at different places within the government and see different faces of the problem. Using military force to punish terrorists looks different to a secretary of state who must balance the diplomatic pluses and minuses of such a move than it does to the military chiefs of staff whose forces would be used or to a presidential aide who is perhaps most sensitive to the domestic implications of the success or failure of such a mission.

Not everyone in the government is a participant in a particular policy-making "game." The political bargaining process is constrained by the organizational context within which policy makers operate. Fixed organizational routines define the issue, produce the information on which policy decisions are made, link institutions and individuals together, and place limits on the type of policy options that can be implemented. Furthermore, the players in the game are not equal in their ability to influence the outcome of the bargaining process. Deadlines, the rules of the game, and action channels confer power to some and deny it to others. Rules determine what kind of behavior is permitted and by whom. Can unilateral statements be made, or must the decision be cleared by a committee? Can information be leaked? Action channels link policy makers together and determine who is in the best position to leak information, make a unilateral statement, or be included in a committee that approves action. Deadlines force issues by accelerating the tempo of the decision-making process and creating pressure for an agreement. Deadlines come in many forms: a meeting with a foreign head of state, a presidential press conference or speech, the adjournment of Congress, and the beginning of a fiscal year. Congress may also establish deadlines. It did so in 1981 when in passing a defense appropriations bill it ordered the president to select a basing mode for the MX by July 1983. It established a reoccurring deadline in 1977 when it required that the Secretary of State report annually to Congress on human rights conditions in every state receiving U.S. development assistance.

Rarely do policy problems enter or leave the policy process in a clearly definable manner. More frequently, they flow through it in a fragmented state and become entangled in other ongoing policy issues. The result is that policy is not formulated with respect to any underlying conception of the U.S. national interest. Instead, its content is heavily influenced by the way in which the problem first surfaces and how it interacts with the other issues on the policy agenda. For example, from the bureaucratic politics perspective, the 1981 sale of Airborne Warning and Control Systems Aircraft (AWACs) to Saudi Arabia should not be approached in terms of U.S. national security calculations. Instead, the analyst needs to know what facet of the issue dominated the attention of policy makers and what other issues were on the agenda.

Doing so would reveal that, not wanting to be identified in any way with the outgoing Carter administration's foreign policy, the incoming Reagan administration turned down its offer to present the sales proposal to Congress.[9] It would also reveal that the Reagan administration long lacked any coherent political strategy to sell the arms package to Congress. The reason for this disarray lay not in conditions within the Middle East but with internal conflicts inside the executive branch. Secretary of State Alexander Haig favored pushing the F-15 sale through Congress as quickly as possible and deferring any decision on selling Saudi Arabia an unspecified airborne warning system. Secretary of Defense Caspar Weinberger and the Pentagon openly pushed for an immediate sale of the entire arms package and specifically backed selling AWACs to Saudi Arabia. In April 1981, Reagan publicly supported Weinberger's approach. Little headway, however, was made in getting congressional approval, and for a while it appeared that Reagan might become the first president to have Congress veto an arms sale. Reagan's inner circle was preoccupied with tax and budgetary issues, and it did not trust Haig to act without close White House supervision on this issue. As a result, foreign policy officials were barred from presenting the administration's position to Congress, and when lobbying did begin, it was not coordinated with the White House Congressional Relations Staff. In the end, the Reagan administration received Senate support for the sale of AWACs to Saudi Arabia by a vote of 52 to 48. It won not because it had convinced the Senate that the arms package was in the U.S. national interest but because the Senate was unwilling to repudiate Reagan in his first year in office on an issue that he had made the litmus test of his foreign policy credibility.

In putting all of the foregoing together, advocates of the bureaucratic politics model argue that policy is not, and cannot, be a product of deliberate choice. Instead, policy is either a result of a political bargaining process or the product of organizational standard operating procedures.[10] In either case the new policy arrived at is not likely to differ greatly from the existing policy. This is because bargaining is a time-consuming and expensive process. Not only do policy makers disagree, but they are often quite deeply committed to their positions. The need for agreement pushes policy makers toward accepting a minimal decision, one that is not radically different from the existing compromise and one that will allow all sides to claim partial victory. The inflexible and blunt nature of organizational routines and procedures reinforces the tendency for policy to change only at the margins. Administrative feasibility is a constant check on the ability of policy makers to tailor policy options to meet specific problems. In sum, from the bureaucratic politics perspective, the best predictor of future policy is not the policy that maximizes U.S. national interests but that which is only incrementally different from current policy.

The bureaucratic politics model makes important contributions to understanding U.S. foreign policy by highlighting the political and organizational nature of policy making. However, it has also been the subject of extensive criticisms. First, by emphasizing compromise, bargaining, and standard operating procedures, the bureaucratic model makes it very difficult to assign responsibility for the decisions being made.[11] Second, it misrepresents the workings of the bargaining process by overstating the extent to which policy simply emerges from the policy process.[12] Third, the bureaucratic politics model is chastised for artificially separating the executive branch bargaining process from the broader social and political context. In this view Congress and domestic political forces cannot be treated as outside interlopers in the policy process. Attention must also be given to the values of policy makers and not just the policy-making games they play. Finally, it is criticized for being too complex, a virtual "analytic kitchen sink" into which almost anything can be thrown that might be related to how an issue is resolved.[13] The result is a story which may make for interesting reading but which violates one of the most fundamental rules of explanation. All things being equal, simple explanations are better than complex ones.

SMALL GROUP DECISION MAKING

A third policy-making model focuses on the dynamics of small group decision making. Advocates of this perspective hold that many critical foreign policy decisions are made neither by an individual policy maker nor by large bureaucratic forces. From a policy maker's perspective, small group decision making offers a number of advantages over its bureaucratic counterpart. Among its perceived advantages are the following:

> The absence of significant conflict because there will be few viewpoints to reconcile
>
> A free and open interchange of opinion among members because there will be no organizational interests to protect
>
> Swift and decisive action
>
> Possible innovation and experimentation
>
> The possibility of maintaining secrecy[14]

Three different types of small groups can be identified.[15] First is the informal small group which meets regularly but lacks a formal institutional base. The Tuesday lunch group in the Johnson administration and the Friday breakfast and Thursday lunch groups of the Carter administration are prominent recent examples. Second is the ad hoc group that is created to deal with a specific problem and then ceases to function once its task is completed. In the first week of the 1950 Korean crisis, six small group meetings were held. During the Cuban missile crisis, the key decisions were made by ExCom, an ad hoc group of about 15 individuals brought together by Kennedy specifically for the purpose of dealing with this problem. The third type of small group is permanent in nature, possesses an institutional base, and is created to perform a series of specified functions. The subcommittees of the National Security Council (NSC) fall into this category. During the Carter administration two subcommittees were established. One, the Special Coordinating Committee (SCC), was set up to deal with crisis situations when they arose. During the Iranian hostage crisis, Robert Hunter, an NSC official in the Carter administration, reported that:

> Throughout the hostage crisis, the SCC met at 9:00 a.m.—at first daily and later less frequently—with an agenda coordinated with the government by the NSC staff in the early hours of the morning. Discussion was brisk, options were presented crisply, and recommendations were rapidly and concisely formulated for presidential decision. . . . The crisis team, with nearly three years' experience of working together, did its job efficiently and with dispatch. . . . Subcommittees of the SCC worked on specialized parts of the problem. The State Department Iranian Working Group worked around the clock all 444 days and fed information back and forth. . . . The results of the days' labors were reported back; new wrinkles in the crisis were assessed; and the SCC was ready to act again the next morning.[16]

In spite of its advantages, small group decision making often results in policy decisions that are anything but rational or effective. Pearl Harbor, the Bay of Pigs invasion, and key decisions in Korea and Vietnam have all been analyzed from a small group decision-making perspective.[17] The Iranian hostage rescue mission and the Iran–Contra initiative can easily be added to this list.

These policy failures are held to result from the presence of strong in-group pressures on members to concur in the group's decision. This pressure produces a "deterioration of mental efficiency, reality testing, and moral judgment" that increases the likelihood of the group's making a potentially defective decision.[18] Irving Janis coined the term *groupthink* to capture this phenomenon. He also identified eight symptoms that indicate its presence. He divides them into three categories: overestimation of the group's power and morality, closed-mindedness, and pressures toward conformity. The full list of these symptoms is found in Box 11–1. Janis argues that the more symptoms that are present, the more likely it is that concurrence-seeking behavior will result and that defective decisions will be made. Table 11–1 presents a series of observations made by the Tower Commission report about the decision making on the Iran–Contra affair with the symptoms mentioned by Janis.

BOX 11–1   The Groupthink Syndrome

Type 1: Overestimations of the Group—Its Power and Morality

1. An illusion of invulnerability, shared by most or all the members, which creates excessive optimism and encourages taking extreme risks
2. An unquestioned belief in the group's inherent morality, inclining the members to ignore the ethical or moral consequences of their decisions

Type II: Closed-Mindedness

3. Collective efforts to rationalize in order to discount warnings or other information that might lead the members to reconsider their assumptions before they recommit themselves to their past policy decisions
4. Stereotyped views of enemy leaders as too evil to warrant genuine attempts to negotiate, or as too weak and stupid to counter whatever risky attempts are made to defeat their purposes

Type III: Pressures toward Uniformity

5. Self-censorship of deviations from the apparent group consensus, reflecting each member's inclination to minimize to himself the importance of his doubts and counterarguments
6. A shared illusion of unanimity concerning judgments conforming to the majority view (partly resulting from self-censorship of deviations, augmented by the false assumption that silence means consent)
7. Direct pressure on any member who expresses strong arguments against any of the group's stereotypes, illusions, or commitments, making clear that this type of dissent is contrary to what is expected of all loyal members
8. The emergence of self-appointed mindguards—members who protect the group from adverse information that might shatter their shared complacency about the effectiveness and morality of their decisions

Source: Irving L. Janis, *Groupthink: Psychological Studies of Policy Decisions and Fiascos,* 2nd ed. (Boston: Houghton Mifflin, 1982), pp. 174–75. Copyright © 1982 by Houghton Mifflin Company. Reprinted by permission.

TABLE 11–1   Groupthink and the Iran–Contra Affair

Elements of Groupthink	Findings of The Tower Commission Report
Illusion of invulnerability	The president "was all for letting the Israelis do anything they wanted at the very first briefing." McFarlane, p. 131.
Unquestioned belief in group's morality	The president distinguished between selling to someone believed able to exert influence with respect to the hostages and dealing directly with the kidnappers, p. 39.
	The administration continued to pressure U.S. allies not to sell arms to Iran and not to make concessions to terrorists, p. 65.
Collective efforts to discount warnings	"There is a high degree of risk in pursuing the course we have started, we are now so far down the road that stopping . . . could have even more serious repercussions. We all view the next step as confidence building." North, p. 167.
Stereotyping the enemy	Release of the hostages would require influence with the Hezballah which could involve the most radical elements of the Iranian regime. The kind of strategy sought by the United States, however, involved what were regarded as more moderate elements, p. 64.
Self-censorship	Evidence suggests that he [Casey] received information about the possible divergence of funds to the Contras almost a month before the story broke. He, too, did not move promptly to raise the matter with the president, p. 81.
	Secretary Shultz and Secretary Weinberger, in particular, distanced themselves from the march of events, p. 82.
Illusion of unanimity (presidential support)	"I felt in the meeting that there were views opposed, some in favor, and the President didn't really take a position, but he seemed to, he was in favor of this project somehow or other." Shultz, p. 183.
	"As the meeting broke up, I had the idea the President had not entirely given up on encouraging the Israelis." Casey, p. 198.
Direct pressure against dissenters	"Casey's view is that Cap will continue to create roadblocks until he is told by you that the President wants this move NOW." North to Poindexter, p. 232.
Emergence of mindguards	"I don't want a meeting with RR, Shultz, and Weinberger." Poindexter, p. 45.
	North directed that dissemination be limited to Secretary Weinberger, DCI Casey, McFarlane, and himself. North said McFarlane had directed that no copy be sent to the secretary of state and that he, McFarlane, would keep Secretary Shultz advised orally on the NSC project, p. 149.

Source: President's Special Review Panel, *The Tower Commission Report* (New York: Bantam, 1987).

While the match is not perfect (for example, illusion of unanimity is better seen as an illusion of presidential support), the parallels are striking.

Groupthink is a phenomenon that occurs irrespective of the personality traits of group members. It is not an inevitable product of a tight-knit decision group, nor is it necessarily the cause of a policy fiasco. Poor implementation, changed circumstances, or accidental factors also produce policy failures. Groupthink exists as a tendency that is made more or less likely by three sets of antecedent conditions: the coherence of the decision-making group, structural faults of the organization, and the nature of the decision context. At its core is the assumption that concurrence-seeking behavior is an attempt on the part of group members to cope with stress by developing a mutual support base. The source of the stress may be internal or external to the group. External stress is conducive to groupthink when it stems from a threat for which there appears to be little hope of finding a better solution than the one put forward by the leader. Internal stress tends to come from feelings of low self-esteem such that "participating in a unanimous consensus along with respected fellow members of a congenial group will bolster the decision maker's self-esteem."[19]

Because groupthink is a tendency and not a condition, it can be avoided. Recognizing that each proposed solution has its own drawbacks, Janis puts forward several measures that he feels would improve the quality of small group decision making.[20] They include modifying leadership strategies so that impartial and wide-ranging discussions of alternatives will take place, establishing multiple groups for the same task, multiple advocacy, establishing a devil's advocate, and having a "second chance" meeting where decisions might be reconsidered one final time.

Three general lines of criticism have been directed at the groupthink approach to small-group decision making. First, the proposed solutions probably will not work. Consider the idea of multiple advocacy which attempts to ensure that all views "however unpopular" will receive serious attention.[21] Two dangers exist here. In each case they are brought on by overloading the intellectual capabilities of policy makers and by highlighting the ambiguity of the evidence before them. One outcome is that policy makers will simply choose whatever policy option is in accord with their preexisting biases. If a wide range of options are all made to appear respectable and doubts exist about the effectiveness of each, why not "let Reagan be Reagan" or "Bush be Bush" and select the one that best fits his image of the world. The other equally undesirable outcome is paralysis. Confronted with too many policy options, all of which appear to have problems, policy makers may end up doing nothing.

Second, criticism is directed at the criteria used to establish a good decision.[22] The standard used (vigilant appraisal) virtually duplicates the functional steps involved in making a rational decision that we presented in our discussion of the rational actor model. The point remains: If the rational actor model is an unrealistic benchmark against which to judge decision making, isn't the same true for groupthink? A final point is more theoretical in nature. The groupthink approach is grounded in a conflict model of individual decision making. According to this model, individuals often confront decision-making situations in which they feel "simultaneous opposing tendencies to accept and reject a given course of action."[23] Vigilant appraisal is realized when individuals successfully address this stress, and groupthink occurs when they do not. The cybernetic approach to policy making suggests an alternative starting point to understanding individual decision making. According to this perspective, individuals do not even attempt to resolve the value conflict and tensions involved in making such a decision. Instead, "the decision process is organized around the problem of controlling inherent uncertainty by means of highly focused attention and highly programmed responses."[24] Based on this line of argument, John Steinbruner suggests that in place of the calculating policy maker we focus our attention on three types of thinkers, each of whom avoids the need for making value trade-offs.[25] Any individual may exhibit these patterns of thinking or switch between them as time constraints and issues change. The uncommitted thinker has difficulty making up his or her mind on an issue and is very susceptible to the arguments and positions of others; the theoretical thinker approaches an issue from an ideological perspective; and the grooved thinker deals with a problem by placing it into a limited number of preexisting categories.

ELITE THEORY AND PLURALISM

We have already encountered the final two perspectives on policy making that we will examine, elite theory and pluralism. During the 1960s and early 1970s, these two models served as the focal point for an intense debate that raged within political science over how best to understand the process by which public policy was made. While no longer the center of attention, elite theory and pluralism remain important approaches for understanding how U.S. foreign policy is made, and we briefly summarize the arguments that they make.

Elite theory represents a quite different perspective on foreign policy making than do the three approaches that we have examined so far. It is not concerned with the details of the action taking place inside the policy process, but it also does not ignore what goes on inside of the state. Elite theory is vitally concerned with the identity of those individuals making foreign policy and the underlying dynamics of national power, social myth, and class interests. From this perspective foreign policy is formulated as a response to demands generated by the economic and political system. But not all demands receive equal attention, and those that receive the most attention serve the interests of only a small sector of society. These special interests are transformed into national interests through the pattern of office holding and the structure of influence that exists within the United States. Those who hold office are seen as being a stable and relatively cohesive group that share common goals, interests, and values. Disagreements exist only at the margins and surface most frequently as disputes over how to implement policy and not over the ends of that policy. Those outside the elite group are held to be relatively powerless, reacting to the policy initiatives of the elite rather than prompting them. Furthermore, public reactions are often "orchestrated" by the elite rather than being expressions of independent thinking on policy matters. This explains why certain policy proposals routinely fail to attract serious attention: Ideas that do not build upon the relatively narrow range of value assumptions shared by the elite and rooted in the underlying dynamics of the socioeconomic structure will be rejected as unworkable, fundamentally flawed, or fatally naive. It also suggests that the basic directions of U.S. foreign policy will change slowly, if at all.

Within this broad consensus, elite theorists disagree on a number of points. First, disagreement exists over the constraints on elite behavior. Some see few, if any, constraints on the type of policies elites can pursue. Others see a more open policy process that is subject to periodic "short circuiting" by the public, as perhaps was the case with the nuclear freeze movement. Disagreement also exists over how conspiratorial the elite is. Some elite theorists pay great attention to the social backgrounds and linkages between members of the elite class while others deemphasize these features in favor of an attention to the broader and more enduring forces of a capitalistic economic system that drives U.S. foreign policy to be expansionist, aggressive, and exploitive.[26]

Both the Reagan and Carter administrations were the subject of conspiratorial-style elite analyses. In the case of the Carter administration, the object of attention was the presence of large numbers of Trilateral Commission members in high policy-making positions. The Trilateral Commission was organized in 1973 to foster closer cooperation between the United States, West Europe, and Japan on policy problems. Nineteen of its 65 members served in the Carter administration, including Carter, National Security Assistant Zbigniew Brzezinski, Secretary of State Cyrus Vance, Secretary of Defense Harold Brown, and Vice President Walter Mondale.[27] In the Reagan administration the object of attention was on the links between Reagan appointees and the Committee on the Present Danger, a group established in the 1970s to heighten the public's concern about the continuing threat to U.S. national security posed by the military power of the Soviet Union. Among committee members who served in the Reagan administration are Reagan, Secretary of State George Shultz, National Security Assistant Richard Allen, Director of Central Intelligence William Casey and Representative to the United Nations Jeane Kirkpatrick.[28]

Elite theorists see in the Clinton administration confirmation of their views regarding the circumscribed and linked nature of the backgrounds of those operating at the highest levels of policy making. In 1994, in addition to President Clinton, eight members of the cabinet were members of the Council of Foreign Relations, a New York–based foreign policy think tank which has long been synonymous with East Coast establishment thinking on foreign policy matters. Moreover, almost every important foreign policy voice in the Clinton administration has been a member of the Aspin Group: Vice President Al Gore, former Secretary of Defense Les Aspin, Secretary of Defense William Perry, Bobby Inman, who was nominated to replace Aspin, Director of the CIA James Woolsey, his successor John Deutch, and Chairman of the National Intelligence Council Joseph Nye. Formed in 1993 to study arms control problems, it has sought to rebuild a bipartisan, centrist foreign policy elite that existed in the early cold war period.[29]

In sum, elite theory is a valuable source of insight into U.S. foreign policy making because it stresses the ties that bind policy makers together rather than the issues that separate them. In contrast to elite theory, pluralism is regarded as the orthodox interpretation of how the U.S. policy making system works. Just as with elite theory, no single comprehensive statement of the argument exists. Still, six common themes can be identified:

1. Power in society is fragmented and diffused.
2. Many groups in society have power to participate in policy making.
3. No one group is powerful enough to dictate policy.
4. An equilibrium among groups is the natural state of affairs.
5. Policy is the product of bargaining between groups and reflects the interests of the dominant group(s).
6. The government acts as an umpire supervising the competition and sometimes compels a settlement.

Pluralists acknowledge that power resources are not evenly distributed throughout society. However, they hold that merely possessing the attributes of power (wealth, status, etc.) is not equal to actually possessing power itself.[30] This is because the economic and political sectors of society are held to be separate. In addition, power resources may be substituted for one another. Large numbers may offset wealth; leadership may offset large numbers; and commitment may overcome poor leadership. Pluralists would point to the grass-roots movement within the United States to force South Africa to end apartheid as evidence of the validity of their case. What began as a movement on college campuses to force companies to disinvest from South Africa and later took the form of daily, peaceful demonstrations at the South African embassy gradually succeeded in sensitizing policy makers and the American public to the problem, with the result that in 1985 U.S. policy toward South Africa began to show signs of change. More recently, the change in U.S. policy on Cambodia, in which support for the rebel forces (including the Khmer Rouge) was dropped in favor of talks with Vietnam, can also be linked to shifting political power of domestic political forces on this issue.

Theodore Lowi has suggested a major flaw in the pluralists' argument.[31] Pluralists assume that competition between groups produces policy makers who compete over the content of policy. What happens when policy makers do not compete over policy but instead are so fragmented that they rule over separate and self-contained policy areas? Lowi suggests that these conditions better describe the operation of the U.S. government than does the pluralist model and that when this happens the government is not an umpire but a holding company. Pluralism then exists without competition as interest groups capture different pieces of the government and shape its policies to suit their needs. New groups or the poorly organized are effectively shut out of the decision-making process. Just as important, interest group liberalism reduces the capacity of the government to plan because it is unable to speak with one voice or examine problems from a national perspective.

SUMMARY: INTEGRATING MODELS

The scope of activity involved in making U.S. foreign policy is so vast that no single model can hope to capture all of it, and few models try.[32] Instead, models draw our attention to a select set of assumptions about what is central to the policy-making process. Simplifying the policy process in this way inevitably creates problems, and, as we have seen, each model has certain inherent limitations. The task facing the student of foreign policy making is to blend these models together to produce a picture containing the maximum amount of insight and a minimal amount of distortion on the nature of the policy-making process without overwhelming him or her with data demands. Typically, there are four ways that this integration can be attempted. The first is to shift from model to model as the focus of the analysis changes. For example, from the rational actor perspective, the decision to send U.S. troops to Korea in 1950 is a single decision. From the bureaucratic or small group perspective, a number of separate decisions can be identified.[33] A distinction can also be made between the sociopolitical aspects of policy making and the intellectual task of choosing a response.[34] The pluralist and bureaucratic politics models help us understand why policy makers act as they do once they are "in place," but they tell us little about how they got there or the values they bring to bear in addressing a problem. To answer these questions, we might want to turn to insights from elite theory or the rational actor model.

A second way to integrate policy-making models is to recognize that some models are more appropriate for analyzing some problems, or issue areas, than they are for others. For example, some authors distinguish between structural, strategic, and crises decisions.[35] Structural decisions center on procurement, personnel, and organizational matters. Strategic issues involve decisions about matters such as military force postures, foreign trade quotas, and arms sales. Crises decisions involve responses to situations that are highly threatening, demand a quick response, and take policy makers by surprise. The general argument is that the more open the policy process and the longer the issue is on the policy agenda (such as is typically the case for structural and strategic issues), the more useful will be the bureaucratic and pluralist models. The more closed the process and the quicker the response, the more useful will be the rational actor, elite theory, or small group model.

A third way to integrate these models is to shift from one to another as the policy problem develops over time. Thus, the elite or rational actor model might be especially helpful for understanding how the United States got involved in Vietnam; the small group or bureaucratic politics model might be most helpful for understanding key decisions during the course of the war; and the pluralist or bureaucratic politics model might be most helpful for understanding the actual process by which the United States withdrew from Vietnam. A similar longitudinal analysis could be carried out for the Iranian hostage crisis. A full examination of the policy-making process during those 444 days might best be accomplished by shifting from model to model.

A final way of integrating these models is based on the values guiding one's analysis. We have already suggested that while the rational actor model may be deficient as a description of the policy-making process, it is still valuable if your purpose is to evaluate the policy process. One must be careful in using models in this way, for embedded in each are assumptions about how policy should be made that are not always readily apparent. For example, implicit in the rational actor model is a belief in the desirability of a strong president and the ability to act quickly. The model does not place great value on widespread participation in decision making or in a system of checks and balances. These latter qualities are very much consistent with the bureaucratic politics model which, as we noted, is often criticized for its normative short-comings.[36]

NOTES

1. Roger Hilsman, "Policy Making Is Politics," in Charles W. Kegley, Jr., and Eugene R. Wittkopf (eds.), *Perspectives on American Foreign Policy: Selected Readings* (New York: St. Martin's, 1983), p. 250.

2. Ibid., p. 251.

3. Leslie H. Gelb with Richard K. Betts, *The Irony of Vietnam: The System Worked* (Washington, D.C.: Brookings, 1979).

4. A short summary of additional models can be found in Thomas L. Brewer, *American Foreign Policy: A Contemporary Introduction,* 2nd ed. (Englewood Cliffs, N.J.: Prentice-Hall, 1986), pp. 26–54.

5. Patrick Morgan, *Theories and Approaches to International Politics: What Are We to Think,* 3rd ed. (New Brunswick, N.J.: Transaction, 1981), p. 110.

6. Herbert A. Simon, *Administrative Behavior: A Study of Decision Making Processes in Administrative Organization,* 3rd ed. (New York: Free Press, 1976).

7. Graham T. Allison, *Essence of Decision: Explaining the Cuban Missile Crisis* (Boston: Little, Brown, 1971), p. 35.

8. I. M. Destler, *Presidents, Bureaucrats, and Foreign Policy: The Politics of Organizational Reform* (Princeton, N.J.: Princeton University Press, 1974), p. 52.

9. This account is drawn from I. M. Destler, "Congress and Foreign Policy Operations: The AWACS Sale to Saudi Arabia" (paper presented for the Executive–Legislative Relations Project, Center for Strategic and International Studies, Georgetown University, June 1984).

10. As originally presented by Allison in his *Essence of Decision,* two separate models were used to explain foreign policy making through organizational routines and governmental politics. Subsequently, Allison combined them into one model as is being done here. See Graham T. Allison and Morton H. Halperin, "Bureaucratic Politics: A Paradigm and Some Policy Implications," *World Politics,* 24 (1982), 40–79.

11. Robert L. Gallucci, *Neither Peace nor Honor: The Politics of American Military Policy in Vietnam* (Baltimore, Md.: Johns Hopkins University Press, 1975), p. 153.

12. Robert J. Art, "Bureaucratic Politics and American Foreign Policy: A Critique," in Robert J. Art and Robert Jervis (eds.), *International Politics: Anarchy, Force, Political Economy, and Decision Making,* 2nd ed. (Boston: Little, Brown, 1985), p. 471; Stephen D. Krasner, "Are Bureaucrats Important? (Or Allison Wonderland)," *Foreign Policy,* 7 (1972), 159–79; and Jerel Rosati, "Developing a Systematic Decision Making Framework: Bureaucratic Politics in Perspective," *World Politics,* 33 (1981), 234–51.

13. Jonathan Bendor and Thomas H. Hammand, "Rethinking Allison's Models," *American Political Science Review,* 86 (1992), 301–22.

14. Robert L. Wendzel, *International Politics: Policymakers & Policymaking* (New York: Wiley & Sons, 1981), p. 439.

15. Ibid., p. 438.

16. Robert E. Hunter, *Presidential Control of Foreign Policy: Management or Mishap?* Washington Paper #191 (New York: Praeger, 1982), pp. 35–46.

17. Irving L. Janis, *Groupthink: Psychological Studies of Policy Decisions and Fiascos,* 2nd ed. (Boston: Houghton Mifflin, 1982).

18. Ibid., p. 9.

19. Ibid., p. 256.

20. Ibid., pp. 172, 262–71.

21. Richard K. Betts, "Analysis, War, and Decision: Why Intelligence Failures Are Inevitable," *World Politics,* 31 (1978), 61–89.

22. Carol Barner-Barry and Robert Rosenwein, *Psychological Perspectives on Politics* (Englewood Cliffs, N.J.: Prentice-Hall, 1985), p. 247.

23. Irving L. Janis and Leon Mann, *Decision Making: A Psychological Analysis of Conflict, Choice, and Commitment* (New York: Free Press, 1977).

24. John D. Steinbruner, *The Cybernetic Theory of Decision: New Dimensions of Political Analysis* (Princeton, N.J.: Princeton University Press, 1974), pp. 66–67.

25. Ibid., pp. 125–36.

26. Compare Gabriel Kolko, *The Roots of American Foreign Policy* (Boston: Beacon, 1969), with C. Wright Mills, *The Power Elite* (New York: Oxford University Press, 1956).

27. Charles W. Kegley, Jr., and Eugene R. Wittkopf, *American Foreign Policy: Pattern and Process*, 2nd ed. (New York: St. Martin's, 1982), p. 252.

28. John Spanier and Eric Uslaner, *American Foreign Policy and the Democratic Dilemmas*, 4th ed. (New York: Holt, Rinehart & Winston, 1985), p. 143.

29. David Ignatius, "The Curse of the Merit Class," *The Washington Post*, February 27, 1994, p. C1.

30. Robert A. Dahl, "A Critique of the Ruling Elite Model," in G. William Domhoff and Hoyt B. Ballard (eds.), *C. Wright Mills and the Power Elite* (Boston: Beacon, 1968), p. 31.

31. Theodore J. Lowi, *The End of Liberalism: Ideology, Policy, and the Crisis of Public Authority* (New York: Norton, 1969).

32. One model that does try is the decision-making model presented by Richard Snyder, H. W. Bruck, and Burton Sapin in "Decision Making as an Approach to the Study of International Politics," in Richard Snyder, H. W. Bruck, and Burton Sapin (eds.), *Foreign Policy Decision Making* (New York: Free Press, 1963).

33. See, for example, Glenn D. Paige, *The Korean Decision, June 24–30, 1950* (New York: Free Press, 1968).

34. Glenn H. Snyder and Paul Diesing, *Conflict Among Nations: Bargaining, Decision-Making, and System Structure in International Crises* (Princeton, N.J.: Princeton University Press, 1977), p. 355.

35. Randall B. Ripley and Grace A. Franklin, *Congress, the Bureaucracy and Public Policy*, rev. ed. (Homewood, Ill.: Dorsey, 1980), pp. 26–28.

36. Spanier and Uslaner, *American Foreign Policy and the Democratic Dilemmas*, p. 175.

12 Decision Making: Case Studies

We draw on the models presented in Chapter 11 in order to gain insight into some important post–World War II U.S. foreign policy decisions and the ways in which policy-making models help us understand the policy-making process. The first is the Cuban missile crisis. We look at it from three perspectives: rational actor, bureaucratic politics, and small-group decision making. Our discussion shows how different models provide different explanations of an event. Decision making on the MX missile is the second case study. Here we show how two models can be combined to provide a more complete explanation of an event than could either model if used alone. The MX decision making is divided into two stages. The first stage involves decisions about the need for a new missile and the characteristics that it should possess, and it is organized around the bureaucratic politics model. The second stage is organized around the pluralist model and involves decisions about whether or not to build the missile and how to deploy it. The third case study employs the elite model and examines U.S. decision making on foreign aid to Latin America. It compares Kennedy's Alliance for Progress with Reagan's Caribbean Basin Initiative. The case study is structured to show how models of foreign policy decision making can be used not only to describe policy but also to critique it. Lastly, we examine NAFTA with an eye toward unlocking the interaction between domestic and international bargaining.

THE CUBAN MISSILE CRISIS

The Crisis: An Overview

Taking place over 13 days (October 16–28, 1962), the Cuban missile crisis is widely regarded as a major turning point in the cold war.[1] Never before and never since have the United States and Soviet Union appeared to be on the brink of nuclear war. At the time of the crisis, President Kennedy estimated the odds of averting such an outcome were between one out of three and even.[2]

Soviet weapons shipments to Cuba had been taking place since the summer of 1960. A slowdown in these shipments occurred in early 1962, but the pace quickened again in late July. By September 1, the inventory of Soviet equipment in Cuba included surface-to-air missiles (SAMs), cruise missiles, patrol boats, over 5,000 technicians and other military personnel, and large quantities of transportation, electrical, and construction equipment.[3] The first strategic missiles secretly arrived in Cuba on September 8. They were medium range ballistic missiles (MRBMs) possessing a range of 1,100 nautical miles. Forty-two of these missiles would reach Cuba before the crisis was resolved. Equipment also began arriving for the construction of intermediate range ballistic missiles (IRBMs) and IRBM sites although no IRBMs would reach Cuba. Finally, Soviet September shipments included IL-28 jet bombers, MIG-21 jet fighters, plus additional SAMs, cruise missiles, and patrol boats.

Intelligence on the exact dimensions of the Soviet buildup in Cuba came from a number of different sources: refugee reports, CIA agents operating in Cuba, analyses of Soviet shipping patterns, and U-2 overflights. Not all of the information from these sources was equally reliable, nor did it all come together at the same time and place for analysis. For example, refugees were reporting the presence of Soviet missiles in Cuba before Cuba began receiving weapons of any kind from the Soviet Union, and great care had to be taken in processing reports from agents operating inside Cuba. The United States Intelligence Board met on September 19 and approved an intelligence estimate stating that the Soviet Union would not introduce offensive missiles into Cuba.

This conclusion was not uniformly shared within the administration. In late August Director of Central Intelligence John McCone told Kennedy, Secretary of Defense Robert McNamara, and Secretary of State Dean Rusk that he believed the Soviet Union was preparing to place offensive missiles in Cuba. In late September others began to agree with McCone, and, on October 4 the Committee on Overhead Reconnaissance (COMOR) approved a U-2 overflight over western Cuba. No U-2 overflights had been authorized over this area since September 5 because of recent mishaps with U-2 overflights in Asia. Fearful that all U-2 flights might be canceled if another incident were to occur, COMOR had decided not to send any U-2s over western Cuba where SAM sites were known to be under construction. A jurisdictional dispute between the Defense Department and CIA over who would fly such a mission led to an unsuccessful flight on October 9, and it was not until October 14 that a successful U-2 flight took place. Its pictures firmly established the presence of Soviet offensive missiles in Cuba. On October 22, President Kennedy went on national television announcing their discovery.

Kennedy called together a special ad hoc advisory group known as the Executive Committee of the National Security Council (ExCom) to deal with the crisis. ExCom's initial meeting took place on October 16, and it began to identify the options open to the United States. Six major options surfaced: (1) no action, (2) diplomatic pressures either at the United Nations or at the Soviet Union, (3) a secret approach to Castro with the option of "split or fall," (4) invasion, (5) surgical air strike, and (6) a naval blockade.[4] The first option seized upon was the surgical air strike.[5] The blockade was not lobbied for strongly until the end of the day, and Kennedy's initial response to this option was one of skepticism because he was not sure how the blockade itself would get Soviet missiles out of Cuba.

By the end of the first day, Kennedy identified three options. Participant accounts suggest that attention focused primarily on two of these, the surgical air strike and the blockade. (The third option appears to have been the invasion.) In his October 22 statement, Kennedy also announced that on October

24 a naval quarantine would be imposed on Cuba and threatened future action if the missiles were not taken out. The blockade was chosen for what it did and did not do. It was a visible, forceful, military response, but it did not put the Soviet Union into a position where it had no choice but to fight. In fact, it placed responsibility for the next move back on Khrushchev. A number of additional measures were publicly taken to impress upon the Soviets the depth of U.S. resolve and to make credible Kennedy's threat of additional action: Squadrons of U.S. tactical fighters were moved to points where they could attack Cuba; an invasion force of 200,000 troops was readied in Florida; some 14,000 air force reserves were called up; and U.S. forces around the world were put on alert.[6]

The air strike remained a live option. An air strike had tentatively been scheduled for October 20 but was postponed in favor of the blockade. On October 27, one day before Krushchev offered to remove the missiles, Kennedy approved plans for an October 29 air strike on Soviet missile silos, air bases, and Cuban and Soviet antiaircraft installations. At that same meeting ExCom also concluded that an invasion would follow. McNamara held that an "invasion had become almost inevitable," and he felt that at least one missile would be successfully launched at the United States.[7]

The blockade did bring an end to Soviet military shipments to Cuba, but it did not bring a stop to the construction of Soviet missiles and missile sites in Cuba. SAM missiles became operational during the crisis and shot down a U-2 on October 23. Kennedy's original orders were that if this happened the United States would destroy the site that had launched the missile. However, when the incident occurred, Kennedy delayed retaliation in an effort to allow quiet diplomacy some additional time to bring about the withdrawal of the Soviet missiles.

Recent accounts of the Cuban missile crisis suggest that Kennedy would not have ordered an air strike had Khrushchev not responded favorably to U.S. demands, and that he was prepared to pursue additional negotiations—perhaps through the United Nations—to resolve the crisis.[8] These accounts also argue that U.S. policy makers felt a sense of urgency in their deliberations not out of a fear that Soviet missiles might soon become operational, but that the longer they remained in Cuba the more legitimate they would come to be seen by the other states.

On October 28, Khrushchev publicly agreed to remove Soviet missiles in Cuba in return for a U.S. pledge of nonintervention into Cuba. This allowed both sides to achieve their publicly stated goals. The United States got the missiles out of Cuba, and the Soviet Union could claim it had succeeded in protecting Cuba from U.S. aggression (the justification it gave for having placed the missiles in Cuba when confronted by Kennedy). Recently released documents reveal the existence of a secret agreement between Kennedy and Khrushchev with terms different from those that officially ended the crisis. In order to entice Khrushchev into removing the missiles from Cuba, Kennedy promised to remove U.S. missiles from Turkey. The secret offer was made by Robert Kennedy to Dobrynin on October 27. Dobrynin was also told that a commitment was needed from the Soviets the next day if the crisis was to be ended on these terms. For reasons of domestic politics and international prestige, Kennedy had refused to publicly accept this trade-off which had been repeatedly called for by the Soviets and suggested to him by some members of ExCom.

Implementation of the U.S. part of the agreement was made conditional on the Soviets' keeping the agreement secret.

While October 28 marks the conventional point for ending the Cuban missile crisis, it in fact continued for several more weeks as both sides struggled with the question of how to implement the agreement. Particularly troublesome issues involved defining what was meant by "offensive" weapons—the United States insisted that the IL-28s must be removed—and establishing a date for ending the blockade—the Soviets wanted the blockade ended and a no-invasion pledge issued before they took out the bombers. Within the U.S. government there occurred a repeat of the earlier debate on how to proceed: Take unilateral military action to resolve the issue, tighten the blockade, or concede the point and go on to other matters. Diplomacy again came to the rescue when on November 20 Kennedy announced that the Soviet Union had agreed to remove the IL-28s and that the blockade was being ended.

Three Views of the Cuban Missile Crisis

The account of the Cuban missile crisis presented above is largely consistent with a rational actor interpretation of U.S. foreign policy making. It emphasizes the thorough canvassing of alternatives once a problem has been identified and the selection of a value-maximizing choice. For U.S. policy makers the goal directing the search for policy options was clear: Get Soviet missiles out of Cuba without the appearance of having appeased the Soviets and without starting a war. A hard-line stance was in part dictated by domestic political considerations. Cuba had become an important emotional and reoccurring issue in American electoral politics since Castro had come to power in 1959, and Kennedy was vulnerable on Cuba. The Bay of Pigs fiasco had made Cuba Kennedy's political Achilles' heel, raising questions about his judgment and leadership. The Republican Senate and Congressional Campaign Committees had already identified Cuba as the major issue in the upcoming 1962 election. Inaction (a possibility suggested at one point by McNamara) and quiet diplomacy, therefore, were not policy options capable of achieving both the removal of the missiles and the demonstration of political resolve. The air strike was rejected because the Air Force could not give Kennedy a 100 percent guarantee that the missiles would be knocked out. Similar problems confronted the selection of an invasion. Coupled with highly visible signals of further military action, the blockade was selected as the option offering the greatest likelihood of getting the missiles out and demonstrating U.S. resolve without running a high risk of setting off a war between the United States and Soviet Union.

As the rational actor model would suggest, the blockade itself was structured to fit the needs of U.S. policy makers. It was not implemented until U.S. officials were sure that Soviet leaders had been able to communicate with Soviet ship captains, and the blockade was placed closer to Cuba than was militarily prudent in order to give the Soviet leadership the maximum amount of time to formulate a peaceful response. The first ship stopped was also carefully selected to minimize the possibility of a hostile Soviet response. Two ships that clearly did not carry missiles were allowed to pass through the blockade. The first ship stopped also did not carry missiles. It was a U.S.-built World War II Liberty ship, registered in Lebanon, owned by a Panamanian firm, and under lease to the Soviet Union.

A similar analysis of policy options and consequences late in the crisis would identify Kennedy's secret offer to remove U.S. missiles from Turkey as the logical follow-up move. The blockade did buy time and show U.S. resolve, but, in and of itself, it could not remove the missiles. Domestic political considerations again limited Kennedy's options as did the continued inability of the military to guarantee that the air strike/invasion would not result in one or more Soviet missiles reaching the United States. Kennedy's publicly announced deadline ensured that the military option with all of its drawbacks would be used unless Khrushchev could be convinced to take the missiles out of Cuba. The key was to find a face-saving way out for the Soviets that was also true to Kennedy's stated objectives. The combined secret agreement and public pledge of Soviet missiles out of Cuba in return for a nonintervention pledge by the United States accomplished this.

The bureaucratic perspective on decision making during the Cuban missile crisis points to a quite different picture of what transpired. Rather than emphasizing the logic of policy making, it stresses the politics and organizational context of policy making. Politics is evident first in the discovery of missiles in Cuba. Consider the following: As early as August, DCI McCone voiced concern about Soviet offensive missiles being placed in Cuba, but he was overruled by McNamara and Rusk; no U-2 flights were directed over the area most likely to have Soviet missiles from September 5 until October 14; the October 14 flight had been authorized October 4, but a jurisdictional dispute between the Defense Department and CIA over who would fly the aircraft and which aircraft would be used delayed it. (The solution agreed to was that an Air Force officer in uniform would fly a CIA plane.) Moreover, evidence now points to the fact that the United States underestimated by one-half how many troops (42,000) the Soviet Union had sent to Cuba. Had this figure been known or had the United States discovered the missiles at an earlier date, the nature of policy options considered, reading of Soviet goals, and U.S. objectives might have been quite different.

The "logic" of the blockade also suffers when the air strike option is examined in closer detail. First, the Air Force did not specifically design an option to meet ExCom's goal of removing the Soviet missiles. Instead, it merely dusted off an existing contingency plan that also called for air strikes against arms depots, airports, and artillery batteries opposite the U.S. naval base at Guantánamo Bay. Second, Air Force calculations on its ability to destroy the Soviet missiles were based on an incorrect labeling of the missiles as mobile field type missiles when they were actually movable missiles that required six days to be switched from one location to another. Because the Air Force believed that the Soviet missiles might be moved between the time when the last reconnaissance mission was flown and the time of the air strike, it was only able to offer Kennedy a 90 percent guarantee that it could knock out all of the missiles. The limits of rational choice are also revealed in the implementation of the blockade. Like the Air Force, the Navy did not tailor its plans to meet ExCom's needs. After-the-fact reconstructions of the timing of ship stoppings show that contrary to

Kennedy's orders the Navy did not move the blockade closer to Cuba but placed it where they had originally proposed.

The bureaucratic politics model would also raise a number of troubling questions about the logic of the agreement that ended the crisis. One point centers on the nature of Soviet goals. No one in ExCom gave serious consideration to the possibility that the Soviet Union was genuinely concerned with deterring a U.S. invasion of Cuba. Evidence now suggests that along with balance-of-power considerations, this was one of Khrushchev's goals. Moreover, it appears that it was not the threat of nuclear retaliation but the possibility that the United States might use the crisis as a pretext for invading Cuba that led to the decision to remove the missiles. The formal ending of the crisis on the Soviet side also raises troubling questions. Early accounts suggested that Khrushchev wasn't in full control of the Politburo and for this reason contradictory messages were being received in Washington concerning the terms for ending the crisis. Evidence now suggests that this may not have been the case but that faulty intelligence may have been responsible. The first and more conciliatory note was sent when Soviet intelligence was indicating an imminent U.S. attack on Cuba. The second and more stringent communiqué was sent once it became clear that there would not be an invasion.

Early accounts of Cuban missile crisis decision making from the small group perspective praised ExCom for not falling victim to groupthink. Janis credits ExCom with not stereotyping the Soviets but actively trying to understand what led them to try to secretly place missiles in Cuba.[9] He cites Robert Kennedy's concern about a Pearl Harbor in reverse as evidence of a sensitivity to the moral dilemmas involved in the air strike option. Janis also notes that members of ExCom frequently changed their minds and came to the conclusions that there were no good policy options at their disposal. President Kennedy is credited with having learned from the Bay of Pigs and practicing a leadership style that maximized the possibility that ExCom would produce quality decisions. To encourage free debate, he did not attend all of its meetings, and he split ExCom into smaller groups to debate the issues and reexamine the conclusions reached by other participants.

More recent accounts of ExCom's deliberations suggest that its escape from groupthink was far less complete than was originally believed.[10] At least three decision-making defects surfaced which are fully consistent with the groupthink syndrome. First, ExCom operated with a very narrow mandate: It was to consider the pros and cons of a variety of coercive measures. Kennedy had declared off limits any consideration of either acquiescence to the Soviet move or diplomacy. ExCom was true to that mandate; 90 percent of its time was spent studying alternative uses of troops, bombers, and warships. Thus, ExCom did not engage in a full search for policy options or operate as an open decision-making forum.

Second, those who sought to expand the list of options under consideration and break out of the group consensus were ostracized. U.S. Ambassador to the United Nations Adlai Stevenson initially opposed the use of force and wrote Kennedy a note cautioning him on the dangers of this option. Kennedy was annoyed by the note and blocked efforts by McNamara and Stevenson to include diplomacy on the options list. Stevenson also suggested a trade of

Soviet missiles for U.S. missiles in Turkey or for the Guantánamo Bay Naval Base. For these suggestions he came under sharp personal attack by Kennedy and was frozen out of the core decision-making group.

Third, Sorensen and Robert Kennedy acted as surrogate leaders for Kennedy, reporting back to the president on the discussion and pushing group members to reach a consensus. Here too the impact was to limit the choice of policy alternatives and to stifle discussion. Stevenson observed that "we knew little brother was watching and keeping a little list where everyone stood." On Friday night, October 25, President Kennedy informed ExCom that he had chosen the blockade. The very next day the consensus within ExCom for the blockade began to unravel. At that point Kennedy told his brother to "pull the group together quickly." Sorensen would tell the group that they were "not serving the president well," and Robert Kennedy would tell them that the president could not possibly order an air strike.

THE MX

At 71 feet in height, 92 inches in diameter, and 190,000 pounds at launch, the MX (missile experimental) is the largest missile in the U.S. inventory. It possesses the ability to send 10 separately targeted nuclear warheads over 8,000 miles and deliver them within 200 feet of their target. For all of this the MX has been a troubled missile program. The central problems have to do with the strategic rationale for the missile and where to put it.

The MX has been a missile in search of a home and rationale. At least 37 different plans have been considered for deploying it. Originally, it was presented as the answer to the increased vulnerability of U.S. land-based intercontinental ballistic missile (ICBM) minuteman missiles (MM) to a Soviet attack. Yet the MX was placed in the same refitted silos that were originally held to be indefensible. Originally, President Carter sought to deploy 200 MX missiles; now it appears that no more than 50 will ever be deployed. At the beginning of Reagan's first term, the MX was widely pictured as the centerpiece of the U.S. rearmament program. By its end the MX was defined as a temporary move until a new, smaller single warhead missile—the midgetman—was ready for service.

By the end of Reagan's second term it had been decided that rather than place the MX in underground silos, they should be placed on trains, and under President Bush a plan was developed to deploy the 50 existing MX missiles on 25 trains in 10 locations in six states on over 120,000 miles of track. At the same time, as part of the administration's budget-cutting efforts Secretary of Defense Cheney announced that the midgetman program would be terminated. Congress did not accept this decision and included money for both missiles in the budget it approved in 1989. The tenuous compromises on the MX began to unravel in 1990. The past three chairmen of the Joint Chiefs of Staff testified that both weapons systems were not needed; leading congressional figures indicated that they were not predisposed to continue funding for both weapons as requested by the administration in its FY1991 budget given developments in the Soviet Union and Eastern Europe; and National

Security Adviser Brent Scowcroft (a supporter of the midgetman missile) advocated including a ban on land-based multiple warhead missiles in an arms control deal with the Soviet Union.

The perspective most frequently used to study the way in which the United States goes about acquiring new weapons systems is the bureaucratic politics model.[11] We also employ this perspective, but only for the initial stages of the decision-making process: the origins of the idea, the specification of requirements, and the research and development tasks. When we examine the decisions to acquire and deploy the MX, we employ the pluralist model. A change in models is necessary because at this point in the decision-making process the number of participants involved, the factors being considered, and the places where these decisions are being made all are incompatible with the central thrust of the bureaucratic politics model. The point at which one should abandon the bureaucratic politics model for the pluralist one cannot be marked out clearly. There exists a transition zone in the decision-making process centering on the testing and development of the MX where both models provide much insight into how policy is made.

First Stages: A Bureaucratic Perspective

Policy-making activity in the early stages of the MX decision is readily understandable from the bureaucratic politics perspective. Few actors were involved in the decision. Among the most influential were the Strategic Air Command (SAC) and other subunits of the Air Force, engineering groups within the Department of Defense, and defense contractors. Technical feasibility and organizational self-interest guided their behavior. The prominence of these concerns over national and strategic interests at the beginning of the weapons procurement process is due to two factors. First, research decisions are frequently made 10 to 15 years before the development of strategic doctrine and the identification of Soviet weapons systems capable of threatening the United States while design and development decisions are often made 5 to 10 years in advance.[12] The technical uncertainties involved in developing a new weapons system and the hundreds of separate research decisions involved create a situation where bargaining rather than logic dictates the weapons system selected.

Second, there is the inevitable lack of attention by high-ranking policy makers to activity several layers down in the bureaucracy. This creates an environment in which organizational self-interest can assert itself. In the field of weapons procurement, this takes the form of a constant effort to improve the quality of the weapons central to its major areas of responsibility. The MX is such a missile. It is the Air Force's attempt to develop a follow-on missile to the minuteman. Along with the manned bomber and submarine-launched missiles, the minuteman is part of the U.S. nuclear triad designed to deter a Soviet attack on the United States. One thousand MM-Is were deployed in the early 60s as part of the U.S. effort to close the "missile gap," and since then they have been regularly upgraded. In the late 60s, long before any concrete threat to the minuteman had been identified, the Air Force's Advanced ICBM Technology Program was already beginning a research program that would prove to be the basis for the MX. The laboratories involved in this early work were the same ones that had developed earlier missiles, and they directed their efforts at improving upon their previous design.[13] In missile technology the most important areas of improvement are in precision (guiding the missile to its target) and payload (the size of the warhead[s] that it can carry). Once research showed that it was possible to build a more accurate missile capable of carrying a larger payload, the Air Force became convinced that it needed just such a weapon to accomplish its mission.

The Strategic Air Command, the organizational subunit of the Air Force in charge of the B-52 and minuteman forces, defined its mission needs in terms of its ability to destroy Soviet missiles. In 1971 (one year after the first squadron of MM-IIIs became militarily active in North Dakota), SAC took two steps that started to move the MX missile from being a technically feasible idea to an actual missile system. First, it formally requested that the Defense Department carry out a Required Operational Capability study on the need for a new, larger, and more accurate missile to replace the minuteman. Second, in November 1971 it formally detailed the technical features it wanted to see embodied in a follow-on missile to the minuteman: (1) the ability to carry more reentry vehicles, (2) the ability to carry a heavy payload with sufficient accuracy so that it could destroy a Soviet missile site, and (3) a survivable basing mode. The first two points served as a way of integrating the many separate ongoing research and development programs and focusing them on a single weapon. The last requirement reflected the growing fear that U.S. land-based ICBMs were becoming vulnerable to Soviet missiles.

The term *MX* first appeared in the March 1973 issue of the Air Force magazine *Air Force* where it was described as an air-launched missile.[14] The Air Force then spoke of it as only being a possibility, but that changed quickly. In 1974 the Air Force formally requested and Congress approved research and development funding for a new generation of mobile ICBMs. Over the next three years, the Air Force went ahead with research and development on the MX, and by 1975 it had successfully tested an air-launched version of the missile.

During these years the Air Force continued to be the dominant actor on MX decision making, but the circle of participants began to expand. The Office of the Secretary of Defense, the National Security Council, and Congress all became more active as the MX became a more visible weapons system with more clearly defined policy implications. The Air Force and SAC concentrated their attention on the performance criteria to be assigned to the new missile. The basing mode was of secondary interest to them. From SAC's perspective a mobile MX per se was of little value if it lacked a hard target-kill capability. The greater concern was that because of the vulnerability problem faced by land-based missiles, the MX might be rejected in favor of a greater reliance on submarine-launched missiles or the production of a missile for use by both the Navy and Air Force. The primary need was seen as gaining approval for a missile that did not fit into the proposed Trident submarine but might be placed into a refitted minuteman silo.

The Strategic Air Command and the Air Force were able to concentrate on the performance characteristics of the MX rather than its basing mode because of how the MX linked up to the concerns of Secretary of Defense James Schlesinger. Along with many others, Schlesinger had become concerned about the growing ability of the Soviet Union to threaten the United States with its nuclear weapons and the lack of response options in U.S. strategic plans. These fears gained credence in 1974 with the appearance of a new generation of Soviet missiles: the SS-16, SS-17, SS-18, and SS-19. To redress his imbalance, Schlesinger urged the adoption of a new strategic posture, one that would emphasize strategic options calling for the controlled use of nuclear weapons during a war. For this to be credible, the United States needed to possess a missile capable of knocking out Soviet missile silos. None of the weapons currently in the U.S. strategic inventory were capable of carrying out such a mission, but the Air Force's plans for a large, highly accurate missile did fit this requirement. Because he was anxious to get such a missile moving as quickly as possible, Schlesinger recommended that the MX be temporarily housed in refitted minuteman silos until a mobile basing mode could be identified. In 1975 the Air Force reversed itself and now advocated a silo-launched MX instead of the mobile version it had requested funding for only the year before.

Congress entered the MX decision-making process with a very different set of priorities. It focused on the survivability problem, and the Air Force's new proposal to place the MX into minuteman silos did not calm these concerns. The matter of selecting a basing mode also embroiled the MX in the highly political debate over the merits of the Strategic Arms Limitations Talks (SALT). Whereas the link between MX and a doctrine of flexible response had proven to be helpful from the Air Force's perspective, the link between MX and SALT worked against Air Force priorities. The question of survivability was one the Air Force and others had been examining since the late 50s. The possibility of a mobile ICBM was first explored in 1966 when Secretary of Defense Robert McNamara directed the Pentagon's Institute for Defense Analysis to explore ways of meeting this Soviet threat. Its report, the STRAT-X Report, was an exhaustive study of future basing concepts and missile performance characteristics. It examined virtually all of the more than three dozen basing schemes that have been considered for the MX. The basic alternatives are hardening, mobile launch, concealment, deception, and active defense. In more concrete terms this translates into plans for launching the MX from bombers, placing them on small submarines, dropping them overboard from surface ships and launching them by remote control, placing them on trucks and moving them around the U.S. highway system or a military reservation, constructing a series of protective shelters and launch points for them and secretly shuttling the MX from one point to another in a version of the shell game, and constructing an antiballistic missile (ABM) defense system for the MX.[15]

At first research on the MX was grounded in the assumption that it could be protected by an ABM system. By prohibiting the deployment of more than two ABM systems (only one of which could protect a missile site), SALT I led the Air Force to search for other means of protecting the MX. In 1971 the Air Force decided that its new generation of ICBMs would be mobile, and it began work on air mobile and land mobile basing options. The problem was that since these options relied on concealment and deception, they both were counter to the spirit of the SALT process. In fact, the United States had tried to get the Soviet Union to agree to a ban on mobile missiles. Having failed at this, the United

States issued a unilateral statement indicating that it would consider the deployment of a mobile missile (the SS-16) to be inconsistent with the spirit of SALT I.

So long as the MX remained only an idea deep within the Air Force bureaucracy, the conflict between the Air Force's long-term goal of making the MX mobile and the Nixon–Ford administrations' desire to ban such missiles could be ignored. When the MX came before Congress for funding, this was no longer the case. One way to overcome this contradiction was to identify long-term MX mobility as a bargaining chip for SALT II. Schlesinger supported this approach, but his successor as Secretary of Defense, Donald Rumsfeld, did not. To him MX mobility was too valuable to bargain away, and he lobbied within the Ford administration for the United States to modify its position on SALT II so that certain types of mobility (those being studied by the Air Force for the MX) would be permissible. Ford agreed. Electoral considerations as well as strategic ones influenced Ford's decision. He was challenged by Ronald Reagan for the Republican nomination, and a pro-defense spending, hard-line bargaining position was a political imperative.

Later Stages: A Pluralist Perspective

Since it is the way in which a missile is deployed that makes it vulnerable and not the characteristics of the missile itself, it is not surprising that in 1976 many in Congress were skeptical about the Air Force's claims that the MX could be placed temporarily in minuteman silos. This skepticism plus the long-range incompatibility between MX and the SALT process led Congress to approve funding for continued research on the MX but forbade the Air Force from spending any funds for hardened silo deployment. This compromise was engineered by Senator Thomas McIntyre, who chaired the Armed Services Research and Development Subcommittee. He opposed the MX because of the verification problems it raised for the SALT process. He opposed the sea-launched cruise missile for the same reason. In 1976 these two weapons systems plus the B-1 bomber came up before his subcommittee for funding. Senator Barry Goldwater was among the strongest supporters of B-1, but he too was skeptical about the merits of the sea-launched cruise missile. In a classic compromise McIntyre and Goldwater agreed to fund the B-1, kill the sea-launched cruise missile, and fund the MX but prevent any money from being spent for hardened silo deployment.[16]

At this point MX decision making was breaking out of the pattern suggested by the bureaucratic politics model and moving in the direction pictured by pluralists. The number of participants was increasing, and the arena of decision making was moving both up the bureaucratic ladder and out of the bureaucracy into the White House and Congress. In the process, decision making was increasingly dominated by the interplay of larger domestic and strategic considerations. Foremost among these were electoral concerns, widespread interest group opposition from the Great Basin region where the MX was to be installed, and disagreement over the value of arms control agreements with the Soviet Union. The influence of bureaucratic factors, however, did not totally disappear. Its pull was repeatedly evident as attempt after attempt was made to find an acceptable basing mode for the MX. The ideas debated in the late 1970s and early 1980s were essentially the same as those explored in the 1960s.

Had Ford been reelected, he was prepared to authorize the full-scale deployment of the MX in a mobile land-based mode. The Air Force's plan called for moving the MX back and forth in shallow, underground tunnels. They would be launched by breaking through the earth covering that was protecting them. Carter entered office skeptical about the MX and ordered the White House, Defense Department, and Air Force to undertake a thorough review of the research and development work done on the MX by the Ford administration. All three studies rejected the trench-basing concept favored by the Ford administration but agreed on the need for a follow-on missile to the MM-III. In November 1977, the Air Force formally abandoned this plan as well.

Carter initially treated the MX as a SALT II bargaining chip and played it in March 1977 when he presented the Soviet Union with a comprehensive arms reduction package. At its core was a trade-off of the MX for large-scale reductions in Soviet land-based ICBMs. The Soviet Union rejected this proposal, and gradually a change in outlook took place in the Carter administration. The very logic of the bargaining-chip approach to the MX began to make it difficult to abandon it. A bargaining chip is worth more the closer it is to completion. To promise not to build "star wars" or an ABM system does not get you nearly as much as the agreement to dismantle it. At the same time, the closer to completion a weapons system gets, the more uses can be found for it and the more difficult it becomes to bargain it away.

With a mobile MX gaining favor within an administration committed to the SALT process, the search began to find some way of making the MX compatible with SALT II. Both the character of the missile and its basing mode were examined. Once again the Air Force successfully pushed for a large missile over one small enough also to fit in the Trident submarine. Political rather than strategic considerations were central to determining the MX's exact specifications. Pentagon studies showed that the MX would be most effective with six to eight warheads. Instead, it was agreed that ten warheads were to be placed atop the MX. This matched the number of warheads that the Soviet Union had on its largest existing ICBM (the SS-18). The MX itself was to be approximately the size of the Soviet Union's SS-19, which was the largest replacement missile allowed by SALT II. All of this was done in an effort to gain JCS and Senate consent to the SALT II Treaty. Mobility was made compatible with SALT II through an agreement that allowed each side to develop one replacement missile system.

In June 1979 Carter approved the full-scale deployment of the MX but did not select a basing mode. The first option to be embraced was a vertical shelter multiple aimpoint system (MAP). In this scheme several hundred MX missiles would be secretly placed in several thousand hardened silos. Therefore, in order to knock out all of the MX missiles, the Soviets would have to destroy all of the possible launch sites. Problems with maintaining secrecy over the exact location of the missiles, the nonverifiability of the system, and its incompatibility with SALT II's limit on the number of launchers (in this case, silos) that each side could have crippled this option. In the end a variation of this plan, the multiple protective shelter (MPS) system, was selected by the Carter administration in

August 1979. Versions of the MPS system had been circulating since the mid-1960s. The Carter administration selected a "race track" MPS in which each MX would be housed in one of 200 separate oval race tracks, each of which would have 23 shelters. A transporter would shuttle the MX from shelter to shelter. The MPS system would be verifiable because each silo could be opened for satellite inspection to show that only one missile was on each race track. Also, SALT II placed a limit on Soviet launchers and warheads, thereby guaranteeing that the Soviets could not simply try to blow up all 23 launch sites per race track.

The formal selection of a basing mode for the MX set off a new wave of political problems. Widespread opposition arose in those states where the MX was to be placed. The MX was originally viewed positively by westerners who saw the project as a windfall for their economies. But as the dimensions of the project became clear (10,000 miles of heavy-duty roads alone would have to be built across the Great Basin), support turned to opposition. United in opposition to the MX were such diverse groups as antinuclear organizations, the Mormon Church, cattle ranchers, local government councils, and wheat growers. The region's elected representatives both in their respective state houses and Washington, D.C., came out strongly against the deployment plans. Opponents had a potentially strong weapon at their disposal. Constructing the MPS system would have required the Air Force to meet the conditions of at least 38 different federal laws, state and local regulations, permit procedures, and executive orders.[17] Legal challenges to Air Force compliance with these requirements could have delayed MX deployment considerably and worked against the concerns of those who supported the MX out of a fear of growing Soviet strength.

Carter withdrew the race track system in May 1980. In its place he proposed a linear MPS system which would save land (20 percent), money ($2 billion), and manpower (15 to 20 percent) over the race track scheme. Along with local opposition, the demise of SALT II and the upcoming election were behind this move. Without SALT II the Soviets were free to try to overwhelm any basing system. Moreover, liberals who had supported the MX largely in hopes of gaining conservative votes for the SALT II Treaty now felt free to challenge it on the grounds that it was a provocative missile which invited a Soviet attack instead of deterring one.

In his campaign for the presidency, Reagan criticized both the pace of Carter's MX program and its details as unworkable and unduly complex. In October 1981 Reagan announced that he was abandoning Carter's plan and would place the MX in hardened minuteman silos as an interim measure until a permanent basing mode could be identified. This effectively put the MX back where it was before Carter took office: in hardened minuteman silos and in search of a permanent basing mode. Reagan's announcement caught the Air Force by surprise; it was still convinced that some form of mobile basing was essential to the survivability of the MX. Once again Congress reacted without enthusiasm to plans to put the MX in minuteman silos. In December it passed an appropriations bill that funded the MX but severely restricted the use of research and development funds to harden silos. It also instructed the Reagan administration to select a permanent basing mode by July 1983, and not 1984 as announced by the Reagan administration.

The search for a new basing mode had actually begun in March 1981, when a committee was established under the chairmanship of Charles Townes. Political considerations were as important as strategic ones in setting up the Townes Panel. Anti-MX pressure continued to build in the West with the release of a draft environmental impact statement that confirmed the region's worst fears about the impact of the MX on the Great Basin. Conservatives were pressing Reagan to introduce his plan quickly. Since he had no alternative, establishing a study group allowed him to deflect these pressures while at the same time appearing receptive to their concerns. The Townes Panel was free to examine all forms of basing, but it was restricted to using existing data. The result is that the committee became "vulnerable to ideas proposed . . . thoroughly reviewed, and rejected during the previous 11 years."[18] The panel was unable to agree upon an effective alternative to the Carter scheme. However, it did suggest that an airborne MX might be the most promising option to pursue.

Events moved quickly in 1982. In February the Reagan administration abandoned the idea of placing the MX in hardened minuteman silos; in June the Pentagon rejected the Townes Panel's proposal to deploy an airborne MX; and in November the Reagan administration unveiled its MX basing plan to Congress. One hundred MX missiles (half of the total proposed by Carter) would be placed in hardened silos 1,800 feet apart in a column 14 miles long at Warren AFB near Cheyenne, Wyoming. Officially known as the Closely Spacing Basing plan, it quickly became dubbed "densepack." It was not a new idea. Densepack can be traced back to the 1970s and had been considered and rejected by the Carter administration because of its technical uncertainties. Politically, densepack was very appealing. It was less expensive than Carter's plan, and it calmed the concerns of many in the West about MX's impact on their way of life. Densepack would be constructed on an existing military base and would not require that great amounts of public lands be taken out of service. The problem was that densepack rested on a controversial and unproven principle: fratricide. In theory the MX missiles were positioned so close to one another that the blast produced by the first attacking Soviet missile would lessen the effectiveness of the others, thereby "saving" the bulk of the MX force.

The Reagan administration had not formulated any plans to sell dense-pack to Congress in part because it had assumed that the MX issue would not be taken up again until the beginning of the next session. To its surprise, the House moved quickly to include MX funding in the appropriations bill then under consideration in the lame-duck session. The Air Force engaged in a massive effort to sell densepack, conducting over 200 personal briefings as well as briefings for the House and Senate Armed Services committees. Secretary of State Shultz and Secretary of Defense Weinberger lobbied by phone from overseas. President Reagan linked MX to arms control in a letter that he sent to all members of Congress. The administration's case was badly damaged when the chairman of the Joint Chiefs of Staff testified that the Army had reservations about the validity of fratricide and that the Navy questioned the idea of hardening silos. Congress took a middle course of action. It refused to kill the MX but prohibited the president from spending money on it as he pleased. Research and development funds were "fenced in" until Congress approved an MX basing mode through a concurrent resolution.

In January 1983, in an effort to break the deadlock on the MX, Reagan established a bipartisan commission to study MX basing. The committee was chaired by Lieutenant General Brent Scowcroft, who had been President Ford's National Security Adviser, and it included among its members four former secretaries of defense and two former secretaries of state. In its report the Scowcroft Commission called for developing a new, smaller single warhead missile (the midgetman) to replace the MX. It also came out in support of placing the MX in hardened minuteman silos as an interim measure. In general, the Scowcraft Commission depicted the MX more as a bargaining chip than as a permanent addition to the U.S. strategic arsenal.

President Reagan endorsed the commission's proposals and sent them on to Congress. From that point forward the MX became the subject of a seemingly endless and bewildering series of votes. The Senate alone has voted on the MX over 12 times. By terms of the MX legislation passed in 1982, Congress only had until mid-June to pass a resolution approving funds for the MX basing. While the measure passed handily, congressional speeches emphasized a link between continued support for the MX and progress on arms control. Support turned to opposition in 1984. The House Armed Services Committee reduced Reagan's request for an additional 40 MX missiles to 30 which was then cut to 15 on the House floor. Furthermore, the House stipulated that no money could be spent until April 1985, by which time it would be clear whether or not the Soviet Union intended to return to the arms control bargaining table at Geneva. The Senate was less hostile to the MX, but the House–Senate compromise essentially followed the House's position: Both chambers would vote twice on the MX in April 1985. Opponents would have to win only one vote to block the MX. If all four votes were positive, then 15 more MX missiles could be built.

To the surprise of most observers, the MX survived all four votes. Once more political realities rather than strategic concerns were crucial. Democrats were fearful of being labeled as weak on defense, and Reagan continued to successfully link the MX to arms control. Political considerations, however, quickly turned against the MX. The issue was Reagan's request for an additional 48 MX missiles in the FY1986 budget. To those who viewed the MX as a bargaining chip, the request made little sense. To those who saw it as a valuable military asset, it was an essential move. The Senate cut the number down to 21 while House Democrats indicated a desire to limit total MX deployment to 40 instead of the 100 called for in the Reagan plan. In May 1985, after much bargaining between the White House and Congress, a compromise was worked out establishing a 50-MX limit for the next fiscal year. At the end of 1994, 50 MX missiles were in the U.S. nuclear arsenal. They are scheduled to be retired when the START II treaty takes effect.

THE ALLIANCE FOR PROGRESS
AND THE CARIBBEAN BASIN INITIATIVE

Two decades separate the Caribbean Basin Initiative (CBI) from the Alliance for Progress. Introduced by President Kennedy in 1961, the Alliance for Progress was widely hailed as a bold, new foreign policy initiative, the beginning of a ten-year effort to bring economic growth and social reform to Latin America. The CBI was put forward by President Reagan in 1982. It too was characterized as a major departure in U.S. foreign aid policy that would bring economic growth to that portion of the Western Hemisphere. The Alliance for Progress must be judged a failure as economic growth and development remain scarce commodities throughout Latin America, and although it is too early to pronounce the CBI a failure, the prognosis is not good. Real economic development continues to elude the Caribbean states. Moreover, the United States decreased its economic aid to the region in order to provide funds for Eastern Europe. Aid originally budgeted at $60 million for fiscal year 1990 was cut back to zero before approximately one-third of it was restored. In yet another attempt to spur economic growth, attention has now turned to the creation of a regional free trade zone.

Any number of factors can be cited for the inability for these two programs to bring about economic growth. Some would point to the lack of support they received in Congress and the opposition of important domestic interest groups. Others would point to conflicts within the bureaucracy on their content and implementation. Still others would point to the nature of the economic crisis that these programs were designed to address and the political conditions within Latin American states.

To those who bring an elite theory perspective to the study of U.S. foreign policy, these explanations miss the point. An elite theory analysis begins by challenging the very premise on which these explanations are offered. The Alliance for Progress and the CBI are united not by their commitment to bring about economic growth in Latin America but by their commitment to forestall social developments that might adversely affect America's security and business interests in the area. For elite theorists these two programs, the first proposed by a liberal Democratic president and the second by a conservative Republican president, demonstrate how widespread and enduring is the ideological bias that guides the formulation of U.S. foreign policy. They see the Alliance for Progress and the CBI not as new foreign policy initiatives but only as the latest in a series of tactical adjustments by U.S. policy makers to preserve the American empire.

Alliance for Progress

The Alliance for Progress was first officially proposed by Kennedy in March 1961.[19] It formally came into existence on August 17, 1961, when the United States and other Latin American states met at Punta del Este to sign its charter. The Alliance for Progress was to be an alliance of free governments dedicated to eliminating tyranny and poverty from the hemisphere. Its central feature was to be a massive influx of capital to help generate peaceful social and economic reforms. A ten-year plan called for combining $20 billion in foreign capital with $80 billion in capital from the Latin American states themselves to produce a growth rate of 2.5 percent. Of the $20 billion in foreign capital, $10 billion would come from the U.S. government and $300 million annually from private U.S.-based investors. Economic and social reform were crucial to the success of the plan because without these reforms the Latin

American economies would not be able to generate sufficient capital to meet the Alliance's ambitious objectives.

Neither the stated goals nor the spirit of the Alliance for Progress was truly realized. Two years after it began, the United States pointed to the presence of land-reform legislation in ten Latin American states. The figure is doubly deceptive. First, little substantial progress followed from these laws. Second, in five cases these laws predated the Alliance for Progress, dating back in one case to 1917. Furthermore, during the early years of the Alliance for Progress, U.S. private investments actually declined, as did the growth rate in several states. The commitment to democracy proved to be as illusive as the goal of achieving economic growth. Alliance funds went to military dictatorships in Paraguay, Nicaragua, Haiti, Argentina, Peru, Ecuador, El Salvador, and Guatemala. The Kennedy administration also recognized and supported five of the seven military coups against democratic governments, and the Johnson administration recognized the other two. In 1966, Assistant Secretary of State and Alliance for Progress Coordinator Thomas Mann stated the obvious when he announced that no preference would be shown for representative democratic institutions in distributing Alliance funds.[20]

From the elite theorist point of view this reading of the Alliance's record is both accurate and superficial because it conceals the success of the Alliance for Progress in meeting its hidden agenda. The key elements of its true agenda only become clear once one looks beyond the rhetoric of the alliance to its details and implementation. A first objective was heading off social revolution. Only economic development goals and social reforms held to be compatible with U.S. national security interests and private investment opportunities for U.S. firms were encouraged. The primary danger to be avoided was a Castro-type movement in which the government became openly hostile to the U.S. government and U.S. private investors. Also of concern were reactionary policies by the political right which might serve as a catalyst for leftist revolutionary movements. The Hickenlooper Amendment to the 1962 Foreign Assistance Act revealed the true U.S. thinking on this problem. U.S. foreign aid was to be suspended to any country that nationalized the property of U.S. citizens without prompt and just compensation or placed excessive taxes on them. In 1962 Honduras attempted to undertake a program of land reform.[21] As part of this effort, it nationalized some of the land owned by the United Fruit Company. Short on cash, Honduras proposed to compensate United Fruit Company through interest bonds. The United Fruit Company and Congress found this to be unacceptable, and the State Department informed Honduras about the terms of the Hickenlooper Amendment. Honduras then reversed its position on land reform.

The practical result of these amendments was to prevent far-reaching social change. Given the level of U.S. private investment in Latin America, virtually any large-scale reform effort had to come at the expense of U.S. firms. No Latin American state could easily afford to promptly compensate U.S. firms in hard currency. The very purpose of land reform is to raise the scarce capital needed for investment. To take this money and transfer it to the multinational corporation defeats the purpose of the reform effort.

A second objective revealed in practice was to create or maintain a positive-investment climate. Translated into specifics, this meant that Latin American states were expected not only to pursue nonthreatening reform programs but also to operate on a balanced budget. This had two consequences. It ruled out the use of deficit financing to promote economic reforms and economic growth, and it served as a check on inflation. Both these features encouraged the inflow of private foreign investments. Government spending was to be directed at building an infrastructure that would permit economic development, and private investment was assigned the profitable task of building on this base. Aid to Mexico in the first two years of the Alliance for Progress vividly illustrates this concern for the climate of investment. Of the $700 million committed, $345 million was in standby credits to bolster the peso; $266 million was for development projects; $80 million was extended as credit to U.S. exporters; and $14 million was extended to private borrowers through the Export–Import Bank. Overall, 25 to 40 percent of the Alliance for Progress's first-year spending went for debt repayment.[22]

The third objective was to promote and subsidize specific U.S. investments. In the eyes of some, this made the Alliance for Progress a government-administered welfare program for U.S. corporations. The 1961 Foreign Assistance Act, passed the same year that the Alliance for Progress was established, stipulated that U.S. aid had to be used to favor the U.S. economy. Of the $1.5 billion distributed in the first two years of the Alliance for Progress, $600 million was in Export–Import Bank loans for the purpose of buying U.S.-made goods, and $150 million was provided as surplus food under the P.L.-480 (the Food for Peace) program.

Perhaps most damaging to the prospects for growth in Latin America was the repeated pattern of using Alliance for Progress funds to expropriate unprofitable U.S. firms at above-market prices. Elite theorists see this practice as enriching U.S. corporations by freeing them from an unprofitable business and providing them with funds to invest elsewhere while denying Latin American states funds that could be used for development projects. The classic case is Brazil. In early 1962 the foreign ownership of public utilities became a major political issue. The center of the controversy came to settle on an ITT-owned company valued at $6 million which had been nationalized by the local state government. The crisis was resolved when the State Department got Brazil to pay ITT the amount it claimed was owed to it and then reimbursed Brazil for the cost of the settlement out of Alliance for Progress funds.[23]

The driving force behind these policies was the U.S. business community. At the outset business was highly skeptical of the Alliance for Progress. Its novelty and scope worried the heads of many U.S.-based corporations. Their primary concerns were with bringing an end to the nationalization of their subsidiaries, abolishing restrictions on profit remittances, and expanding the insurance available for investment guarantees. The rhetoric of the Alliance for Progress was vague or silent on these points. Leaders of the U.S. business community were not invited to attend the meeting at Punta del Este until three days before it began. At that time the Kennedy administration called the Rockefeller-owned International Basic Economy Corporation (IBEC) in an effort to line up observers. Ford, Standard Oil of New Jersey (now Exxon), and IBEC were among those in attendance. This group left the conference feeling that private investment targets set were unrealistic and that business concerns had not been adequately addressed.

The strength of these concerns and the scope of business influence became clear as the bold rhetoric of the Alliance for Progress was translated into action. No countervailing interest groups existed to lobby against its views. It was Harold Geneen, president of ITT, who urged Hickenlooper to introduce his amendment. Collectively, some 20 to 30 chief executive officers of companies with holdings in Latin America formed the Business Group for Latin America.[24] Under the direction of David Rockefeller, it advised the U.S. government on the Alliance for Progress. In 1965 this group was expanded into the Council for Latin America (CLA). Still led by Rockefeller, its members represented 224 corporations, including Chase Manhattan, Caterpillar, Standard Oil of New Jersey, and DuPont. Together, they made up approximately 85 percent of all U.S. corporations doing business in Latin America. The CLA held meetings with State Department, World Bank, and AID officials. The CLA also established subcommittees corresponding to State Department and AID country desks. These subcommittees met informally with their bureaucratic counterparts two or three times a year to exchange views on the political, economic, and investment climate of the region.

As a final observation on the Alliance for Progress, the elite theory perspective would challenge the novelty of the program. Elite theory presumes continuity in foreign policy due to the underlying value consensus (bias) that guides policy and the alignment of political forces behind it. To some the Alliance for Progress was nothing but a "dressed up version" of Truman's Point Four Program.[25] Others cite the similarity between the Alliance for Progress and aid packages proposed for Cuba by the Foreign Policy Association in 1935, the World Bank in 1950, and the Department of Commerce in 1956.[26] Elite theorists thus see in the Alliance for Progress not an abandonment of traditional goals but only a modification of technique.

Caribbean Basin Initiative

From their vantage point elite theorists also find little new and innovative in the Caribbean Basin Initiative (CBI). It is just the latest tactical adjustment designed to maintain the subservience of Latin America to U.S. national security and private economic interests. Its impetus was not the continuing poverty in the region but the emergence of governments and political conditions hostile to traditional U.S. concerns.

The CBI was announced by President Reagan in a speech to the Organization of American States on February 24, 1982. It was made up of six essential elements.[27] First, and most important, a one-way free trade zone would be created so that Caribbean goods (with certain exceptions) would enter the United States duty free. Second, a system of tax incentives would be established to encourage the flow of private investment capital to the Caribbean Basin. Third, increased emergency financial and military assistance would be made available. Emphasis was to be placed on increasing the amount of Economic Support Funds (ESF) available to those states especially hard hit by economic problems for financing private-sector imports. Fourth, technical assistance and training would be offered to help the private sector of the Caribbean Basin states in such areas as investment planning, export marketing, and technology transfer.

Fifth, a pledge was made to work closely with other lending states to coordinate development assistance in the region. Finally, promises were made to Puerto Rico that its economic development efforts would not be adversely affected by the CBI aid package.

Just as with the Alliance for Progress, the true intent of the CBI is revealed not by its rhetoric but by how it is put into practice. A first indication of the true purpose of the CBI lies in how the Caribbean Basin is defined and the criteria for eligibility. Geopolitics is the common thread uniting the CBI. Central America and the Caribbean islands differ in culture, economic structure, and political institutions. Moreover, within the Caribbean Basin only those states that are not designated by the president as communist and that do not discriminate against U.S. exports or expropriate U.S. property without compensation are eligible. Also cited as being of importance in making eligibility decisions are the would-be recipients' attitudes toward foreign investments and the policies they take to advance their own economic development.

Further evidence of the dominance of national security and investment concerns over economic development ones comes from how CBI funds were initially distributed. The CBI's best chance for economic development success lay with some of the Caribbean states and Panama where the necessary political stability for economic growth was already in place. Yet $243 million of the proposed $359 million package of ESF money included in the CBI was targeted at Central America. El Salvador alone originally was in line to receive 36 percent of the $350 million. (Congressional action reduced this figure by placing a $75 million limit on the amount of funds that could be given to any one state.) Other major recipients included Jamaica, which had just recently voted out of office a socialist government in favor of a pro-Western government, 14 percent; the Dominican Republic, a state into whose internal affairs the United States had repeatedly intervened, 11.4 percent; Costa Rica, 20 percent; and Honduras, 10 percent. These last two states are central actors in the U.S. policy of opposition to the government of Nicaragua. The eastern Caribbean islands which are in the most serious need of money for infrastructure development were in line for less than 3 percent of the funds. Haiti, for example, was to get 1.4 percent.

A closer look at some of the details of the CBI and Congress's reaction to them provides further insight into the relative priorities of promoting foreign economic growth versus promoting the growth of the U.S. economy.[28] Under trade arrangements in place at the time the CBI was announced, 87 percent of Caribbean Basin exports came into the United States duty free. Excluded from eligibility were sugar and textile and apparel products. In terms of the volume of Caribbean Basin exports to the United States, the major beneficiaries of the free trade area would be beef and veal, electronic tubes, capacitors, cigars, benzenoid drugs, and analgesics. Still, the proposed one-way free trade zone encountered strong opposition. Congress added leather and footwear products to the list of ineligible products. By one account this reduced the value of the free trade zone to Caribbean Basin states by 15 to 20 percent.[29]

The volume of textiles entering the United States from the Caribbean Basin was to be increased by giving this area part of the quota set aside for Far Eastern textile imports. Sugar imports were to be increased by raising the quotas for the leading sugar exporters (the Dominican Republic, Guatemala, and Panama). A likely negative consequence of this move is that it would reduce the sugar exports of other Latin American states, which would hurt their economies. It must also be noted that the CBI left in place the nontariff barriers to trade that have been a major limiting factor in the ability of third world states to export their products to advanced industrial states.

The investment incentives proposed by Reagan encountered heavy opposition from the House Ways and Means Committee and were dropped from the legislation. Opposition came from business groups that felt that they would be placed at a competitive disadvantage if these incentives were offered to overseas investors and from those who feared a further loss of jobs within the United States. Many felt that this element of the CBI was poorly conceived in the first place if the goal was to promote economic growth. Critics held that at best these funds would be used for the minimal purpose of keeping an existing plant in operation rather than for expanding production or setting up a new venture. The most effective way of meeting these goals was held to be through a multilateral approach. Yet the Reagan administration acted unilaterally in proposing the CBI. Prior to Reagan's speech, discussions were under way with Canada, Mexico, and Venezuela on a multilateral strategy. According to one observer, other donor states are "proceeding as if the Caribbean Basin Initiative had never been announced."[30]

When it was passed in 1983, the plan was that the CBI was to be reviewed after 12 years of operation. An interim assessment published in 1990 found that while the CBI did help U.S. corporations, "it is fairly clear that greater U.S. economic involvement in the Caribbean has done little to solve the economic problems of the region or enhance the standard of living of the majority of Caribbean people."[31] The study found that the vulnerability of Caribbean economies to the "dictates of profit maximization by international capital" has been increased due to several factors. Three stand out as particularly important. First, Congress has amended the CBI several times in response to protectionist pressures, and each time Caribbean states have suffered. The Tax Reform Act of 1986 eliminated ethanol from eligibility. This has idled firms in Costa Rica, Jamaica, and the Virgin Islands. Costa Rica also hosted one of the early successes of the CBI, a cut-flower industry. It has been hurt severely by new countervailing duties placed on its exports that grew out of charges that it was engaged in dumping. Second, the CBI has allowed firms to play off Caribbean states against each other in the pursuit of their business. Before the CBI, Barbados was a leading regional exporter of manufactured goods. Since CBI its exports to the United States have fallen from $202 million to $51 million in 1988 as manufacturers have sought out—and found—cheaper labor costs. In 1988 a worker in Barbados made $2.16 per hour while a worker in the Dominican Republic made 55 cents per hour. Finally, because so many of the manufacturing industries are located in free trade zones and are geared for export sales, there has been little effort to create backward linkages into the local economies. Moreover, these manufacturing firms earned their host states relatively little by way of foreign capital compared to traditional agricultural exports. The Dominican Republic is a case in point. The total value of its exports to the United States increased 43 percent between 1980 and 1988, from $117.1 million to $516.8 million. Yet, where the Central Bank received 45 percent of the value of those early exports, it received only 25 percent of those in 1988.

From the elite perspective, then, there is little to distinguish the Alliance for Progress from the CBI. Both are merely the latest in a series of tactical adjustments in the ongoing U.S. concern with keeping the Western Hemisphere subservient to U.S. national security and private economic interests. Both efforts are politically motivated. Both are economically flawed—at least from the point of view of producing economic growth in the Western Hemisphere.[32] Elite theorists would also confidently predict that the Alliance for Progress and the CBI will not be the last of such efforts.

NEGOTIATING THE NORTH AMERICAN FREE TRADE AGREEMENT (NAFTA)[33]

Traditionally, when we studied international negotiations such as those surrounding the SALT talks, GATT, or the Rio Earth Summit, our focus was on the interaction of diplomats. The study of diplomacy was what these individuals did. Only recently have we begun to appreciate the ways in which domestic politics enters into the negotiating process (and conversely, the extent to which international negotiations can shape domestic politics). Robert Putnam suggests that we can think of negotiators as simultaneously occupying positions in two linked games: one to conclude an international agreement, the other to secure domestic approval for it.[34] Success in one means little without success in the other. Thus, policy makers are forced to engage in an interactive double-edged negotiating process in which "deals at the international level change the character of domestic constraints, while the movement of domestic politics opens up new possibilities for international accords."[35] In this final case study we examine the NAFTA agreement for insight into how the two linked bargaining games that were being played out. Following Putnam, we divide the negotiation process into a bargaining phase and a ratification phase. Because our interest is in activity that bridges the two bargaining games, we will not chronicle in detail the negotiations themselves but will focus instead on the international-domestic linkages that influenced the talks.

The Bargaining Phase

In the 1960s, Mexico pegged its development hopes on an import substitution strategy. Growth could come about by protecting domestic industries from foreign competition. Over time, firms now too weak to compete with foreign multinationals would become vibrant enterprises providing Mexicans with jobs and lessening its dependence on foreign states. By the 1990s it was clear to many in Mexico that this strategy had not been able to produce sustained growth. From an economic perspective the most attractive alternative was integration into the larger markets of its industrialized trading partners. And the most logical market was that of the United States. Politically, however, this was an unattractive option given nationalistic sentiments against closer economic ties with the United States and fears that such ties would only lead to Mexican dependence on the American economy. Given these considerations, it is not surprising that Mexican President Carlos Salinas de Gortari embraced the idea of a North American free trade zone only after exploring other options. In early 1990, Salinas had tried unsuccessfully to broaden Mexico's economic ties with Japan and Western Europe. On the heels of this failure he turned his attention to securing a free trade agreement with the United States, an idea that he had virtually dismissed out of hand when inaugurated. In the United States, the idea of a continental free trade pact had emerged as early as the 1980 presidential campaign, when Ronald Reagan, Jerry Brown, and John Connally all endorsed the idea. President Bush had embraced it in the 1988 campaign. Salinas now telephoned Bush to determine if interest still existed and the answer was positive. After months of exploratory talks, in August 1990 Salinas formally notified the United States of Mexico's interest in negotiating a bilateral free trade area.

The Bush administration was divided over the wisdom of entering into talks with Mexico. The National Security Council, the Commerce Department, and the States Department supported the idea. The Department of Agriculture and the Office of the Special Trade Representative (USTR) were less enthusiastic. The USTR's misgivings centered on the difficulties experienced in concluding the 1989 U.S.–Canada Free Trade Agreement (CFTA) and the fact that the Uruguay Round GATT negotiations had not yet been completed. By spring, the USTR had put these reservations behind it and joined with other agencies in recommending to Bush that the United States officially move ahead with these talks. Doing so meant informing Congress. This was done by a letter sent on September 25, 1990 to Representative Dan Rostenkowski, chair of the House Ways and Means Committee, and Senator Lloyd Bentsen, chair of the Senate Finance Committee. The letter also indicated that Canada wished to join the negotiations. In a March 1, 1991 communiqué to Congress, Bush asked for "fast track" authority to negotiate a continental free trade agreement and bring the Uruguay Round talks to a conclusion.

Fast track authority is a procedure by which Congress agrees in advance to accept or reject a trade agreement as a single package. Without fast track authority Congress would have the right to make whatever changes it feels prudent when a trade agreement is put before it for approval. The problem is that by doing so Congress might undo delicate compromises reached by negotiators and in the process raise questions about the reliability of U.S. promises. Although Senate approval of fast track authority seemed assured, it was a different matter in the House, where the administration appeared to be some 80 votes shy of the number it needed. In May, after the conclusion of the Persian Gulf War, President Bush began a fervent lobbying campaign on behalf of the fast track. He played upon his new-found popularity and defined the vote as one of free trade versus protectionism. Bush also enlisted the support of key legislators such as House Speaker Thomas Foley, House Majority Leader Richard Gephardt, and Rostenkowski, and major business leaders; and entered into agreements with labor and environmental groups. Labor Secretary Lynn Martin signed a memorandum with Mexican officials dealing with such matters as worker health and safety standards, collective bargaining, and working conditions. Efforts to placate environmental groups included the announcement of an Integrated Environmental Plan for the border, and a promise that environmental groups would serve on bodies advising U.S. Trade Representative Carla

Hills. These efforts were successful, and in May both houses defeated motions denying Bush fast track authority.

NAFTA talks began in Toronto on June 12, 1991. On October 7, 1992, the 2,000-page agreement was signed in San Antonio. In between, there were countless hours of formal negotiating sessions, informal working groups, faxes, and telephone calls. Little of substance was accomplished at the first several meetings. A first attempt at producing a composite treaty was taken at the end of 1991 and amounted to nothing more than listing in sequential order the Mexican, American, and Canadian position on each topic. For some topics (agriculture, energy, textiles, automobiles, and trade remedies) it was not even possible to do this.

With this "run-on" text in place, U.S. negotiators pressed hard for concessions in early 1992 as attention turned to finding common language for each section. In part, they were motivated by the realization that at this stage the agreement was not a very good one. As one participant noted, settling for a "half-assed agreement . . . would have cost us badly needed support within the business community at a time of intense labor union opposition." Steady confirmation of the need to get real concessions from Mexico on its protectionist trade policies came in the form of a constant flow of communication from Capitol Hill.

Several factors came together to give birth to this stream of political discourse. First, angered by the Reagan administration's lack of candor in informing it about the progress of talks with Canada on the CFTA, Congress was determined to make its voice heard on NAFTA. Second, very real concerns continued to exist in many districts over the contents of any agreement, and the golden rule for most congresspeople is that "all politics is local" and foreign policy is no exception. Finally, exception was taken by some to the "five noes" put forward by Mexico's Commerce Secretary Jaime Serra Puche. Mexico would say no to diminishing its control over the exploration, development, and refinement of primary petrochemicals; guaranteeing oil supplies to other states; relinquishing its monopoly over commerce, transportation, storage, and distribution of energy; permitting high-risk contracts in exploration and production; and allowing foreign gasoline stations. In mid-March 1992, seven energy state senators proposed a set of "guiding principles" for negotiations in this area which were at odds with each of these five noes. In fact, the United States and Canada also entered the talks with their list of unnegotiable items. For the United States they included Mexican immigration to the United States; "set asides" and other preferences given to minorities, veterans, and small businesses in government contracting; and the requirement that goods shipped between U.S. ports must be carried on ships built and registered in the United States and staffed by American crews.

Progress continued to be slow, and U.S. hopes of concluding an agreement in time for congressional action before the upcoming presidential election faded. All of this changed with the February 1992 Dallas meeting. This was the first session at which all 19 working groups were present. It also witnessed an explosion by U.S. chief negotiator Julius Katz, who charged Mexico with holding an unacceptable position on the question of trade barriers. With the Mexican negotiator acknowledging that because its economy was the most closed of the three Mexico would have to make the most concessions, the talks became energized. By late winter the 1,200 contested or bracketed portions of the Dallas Composite Text had been reduced to a few hundred.

The endgame to the NAFTA negotiations began in July at the Watergate Hotel in Washington. The Bush administration wanted to announce that an agreement had been reached prior to the start of the Republican national convention. It looked upon the NAFTA agreement as a vehicle for generating Republican votes in Texas and California. Together these states led the United States in exports to Mexico and possessed 86 of the 270 electoral votes needed to win the presidency. Marathon sessions produced enough progress that such an announcement was made by Bush on August 12. NAFTA was mentioned frequently at the convention and USTR Carla Hills addressed the delegates extolling its virtues. The NAFTA agreement was not, however, complete. Almost round-the-clock negotiations continued for three weeks into late August as points of disagreement were resolved so that the treaty could be submitted to the Senate in September.

The Ratification Phase

In a political sense the NAFTA ratification debate began with Bush's signing of the agreement. And the battleground was not Congress but the political campaign trail. Bush hoped that the NAFTA agreement would cement his place in the eyes of the American public as a world leader. Instead, it became a central issue in what would become a referendum on the state of the American economy. Leading the early charge against NAFTA was a one-time supporter of it, Ross Perot. Proclaiming it the product of a conspiracy among Washington insiders, foreign lobbyists, PAC-influenced congresspeople, and huge corporations, Perot asserted that NAFTA would cost American workers their jobs, homes, and savings. In mid-July, during the Democratic convention, Perot ended his presidential bid.

With that the focus of attention shifted to the views of the Democratic party and its nominee. Bill Clinton had straddled the fence on NAFTA during the primaries and would repeat this strategy during the general election. A long-standing advocate of free trade, Clinton softened his endorsement of NAFTA in order not to offend organized labor, whose voice carried a great deal of weight in many of the Democratic primaries, as it had traditionally supported Democratic candidates. After securing the nomination Clinton used the fact that all of the details of the NAFTA agreement had not been worked out as his rationale for not moving to endorse the agreement quickly. In late September the Clinton campaign team was still split on whether to back the NAFTA agreement. When Clinton finally announced his support for NAFTA in October, he conditioned it on the stipulation that the text be improved through the addition of supplemental agreements to cover "serious" omissions. Election results and exit polls showed that the Bush campaign had misread the mood of the American public. By November, only 21 percent of the voters supported NAFTA and a majority opposed it in Texas and southern California.

The three side deals required as necessary by candidate Clinton involved "surges," or the sudden inflow of large amounts of foreign goods into the U.S. market; the environment; and labor. The issues involved in the environmental side deal were sufficiently complex that it took the U.S. delegation several months to agree upon a unified position. For example, the question of whether trade sanctions should be used against polluters found the USTR, the Environmental Protection Agency (EPA), and the Treasury Department supporting the idea and the State Department opposing it. Environmental groups strongly supported the use of trade sanctions and expressed their views to a wide range of officials in the Clinton administration, including Vice President Gore's office; the White House's Office of Environmental Policy; the EPA; the National Security Council; and the offices of likeminded legislators. These multiple contact points not only reflected the reality of policy making in Washington but a decision by the Clinton administration to encourage environmental groups to submit recommendations on key issues.

As to the negotiations, it was clear that the United States was at odds with Mexico and Canada over many of the key points to be resolved. Clinton's initial response was to allow the negotiations to drift. This reflected the reality that presidents only have so much political capital to invest and that priorities must be established. Health care and the budget came far ahead of NAFTA for most in the Clinton administration. Only in later summer did the Clinton administration decide on a position with regard to sanctions. At a meeting of the National Economic Council, Clinton asked Secretary of State Warren Christopher and USTR Mickey Kantor to lay out the pros and cons of sanctions. When Secretary of the Treasury Lloyd Bentsen, a known opponent of sanctions, endorsed the concept as politically necessary for securing approval of NAFTA, Clinton came on board. Mexico continued to oppose the idea and reportedly only dropped its objections after Majority Leader Richard Gephardt informed Serra Puche that without sanctions NAFTA would not pass the House.

Formally the side deals were treated as executive agreements and not parts of the treaty to be voted on by Congress. The side deals allowed the Clinton administration to achieve three important political goals: (1) they fulfilled a campaign promise; (2) they demonstrated that the administration was capable of successfully addressing important policy problems; and (3) they laid the foundation for a pro-NAFTA lobby on Capitol Hill that would be needed for the ratification vote.

As the ratification vote neared, the Clinton administration was convinced it had won the scholarly argument over the merits of NAFTA. Support came from across the ideological spectrum. Conservatives (James Buchanan and Milton Friedman) and liberals (Paul Samuelson and James Tobin) joined with political moderates in endorsing it, as did all eight living Nobel prize winners in economics. The problem facing the Clinton administration was that the political argument was far from won. The AFL-CIO remained steadfast in its opposition as did political figures inside and outside of Congress. Gephardt and Majority Whip David Bonior were prominent members of the first group while Ralph Nader, Ross Perot, Pat Buchanan, and Jerry Brown were vocal members of the second. Dissatisfaction with the environmental side deal negotiated by the Clinton administration led many environmental groups to continue their opposition to NAFTA. Also lobbying against NAFTA were groups that condemned ongoing electoral fraud and human rights abuses in Mexico.

Within the Clinton administration, NAFTA continued to compete with other policies, most notably health care, for the president's attention. Convinced that NAFTA would only be ratified if President Clinton actively became involved in the lobbying effort, Kantor arranged for William M. Daley to be appointed as special counselor to the president for NAFTA. His job was to raise the stakes of the NAFTA vote so high that Clinton would have no choice but to direct his energies toward securing its passage. A three-pronged effort was organized. First, Howard Pastor, the Presidential Assistant for Legislative Affairs, began building links with Capitol Hill by setting up briefing sessions and arranging for personal communications between Clinton and wavering legislators. Second, Daley mobilized the cabinet to lobby for NAFTA. Alone, the State Department produced 216 speeches and 116 media interviews on NAFTA as well as conducting 63 briefings for congresspeople. Laura D'Andrea Tyson, chair of the Council of Economic Advisers, called or visited almost every female legislator. Daley also arranged for major media events highlighting support for NAFTA. The first took place on September 16 when Clinton signed the three side deal agreements in the presence of former presidents Bush, Carter, and Ford.

The final element of the administration's strategy to win approval for NAFTA involved yet another round of side deals designed to gain the final votes needed. This effort was led by Kantor, who met with dozens of undecided congresspeople. Among the bargains struck: Florida legislators were assured that the administration would put in place safeguards for sugar, citrus, tomato, sweet pepper, and asparagus growers as tariffs were reduced and increasing amounts of Mexico produce entered the U.S. market; legislators from southern textile-producing states were promised that textile quotas would be phased out over 15 years instead of 10; a Texas congressperson received an assurance that a Center for the Study of Trade in the Western Hemisphere would be located in his district; and another Texas congressperson got the administration's pledge to construct two C-17 military cargo planes. Many of these deals required Kantor to contact his Mexican counterparts and gain their approval. Reportedly, these last-minute deals angered Mexican leaders who nevertheless felt that they had no choice but to go along with them in order to get NAFTA ratified.

Congress voted on NAFTA on November 17, 1993. The Senate gave its approval by a vote of 61–38 while the House voted 234–200 in favor of it. As this case study shows, the Bush and Clinton administrations found themselves in two sets of negotiating games. The first involved getting agreement from Mexico and Canada on the details of a continental free trade pact. The second involved securing a domestic political consensus for the agreement. The two games often proceeded at the same time and agreements reached in one had major consequences for how the other was played.

SUMMARY

In this chapter we used policy-making models to help make sense of four complex and important sets of foreign policy decisions: the Cuban missile crisis, the decision to build the MX, the giving of U.S. foreign aid, and negotiating NAFTA. To repeat a point made at the end of the previous chapter, no one perspective is able to provide us with insight into all foreign policy decisions. Different models must be used at different times, and the challenge to the student of U.S. foreign policy is to decide which model(s) will be most helpful. In the next several chapters, our attention shifts from how policy is made to the range of instruments available to policy makers to achieve their goals.

NOTES

1. For discussion of Cuban missile crisis decision making, see Graham T. Allison, *The Essence of Decision: Explaining the Cuban Missile Crisis* (Boston: Little, Brown, 1971); Theodore Sorensen, *Kennedy* (New York: Harper & Row, 1965); and Richard Ned Lebow, *Between Peace and War: The Nature of International Crisis* (Baltimore, Md.: Johns Hopkins University Press, 1981).

2. James A. Nathan and James K. Oliver, *United States Foreign Policy and World Order*, 3rd ed. (Boston: Little, Brown, 1985), p. 275.

3. Allison, *The Essence of Decision*, p. 103.

4. Ibid., pp. 58–61.

5. *The Washington Post*, July 25, 1985, Sec. A, p. 10.

6. Allison, *The Essence of Decision*, p. 64.

7. *The Washington Post*, Sec. A, p. 1.

8. The most important of these is Raymond Garthoff, *Reflections on the Cuban Missile Crisis*, rev. ed. (Washington, D.C.: Brookings, 1989). The revised edition contains insights into the crisis that came out of a joint U.S.–Soviet conference on the Cuban missile crisis held in 1987.

9. Irving Janis, *Groupthink*, 2nd ed. (Boston: Houghton Mifflin, 1982), pp. 132–58.

10. Lebow, *Between Peace and War*, especially Chap. 8.

11. The analysis presented here follows the general argument made by Lauren H. Holland and Robert A. Hoover, *The MX Decision: A New Direction in U.S. Weapons Procurement Policy* (Boulder, Colo.: Westview, 1985). They too cite the increasing inadequacy of the bureaucratic politics model for explaining MX decision making in the later stages, though they fall short of switching to an explicitly pluralist model. Other key works on the MX are Herbert Scoville, Jr., *MX: Prescription for Disaster* (Cambridge, Mass.: M.I.T. Press, 1981); Paul N. Stockton, "Arms Development and Arms Control: The Strange Case of the MX Missile," in Allan P. Sindler (ed.), *American Politics and Public Policy: Seven Case Studies* (Washington, D.C.: Congressional Quarterly, 1982); Congressional Quarterly, *U.S. Defense Policy*, 3rd ed. (Washington, D.C.: Congressional Quarterly, 1983), pp. 82–98; and John Edwards, *Super Weapon: The Making of the MX* (New York: Norton, 1982).

12. Graham T. Allison and Frederic A. Morris, "Armaments and Arms Control: Exploring the Determinants of Military Weapons," *Daedalus*, 104 (1975), 99–130.

13. Holland and Hoover, *The MX Decision*, Chap. 6.

14. Edward Ulsamer, "M-X: The Missile System for the Year 2000," *Air Force*, 56 (1973), 38–44.

15. Congressional Quarterly, *U.S. Defense Policy*, pp. 86–90; and Holland and Hoover, *The MX Decision*, Chap. 3.

16. Edwards, *Super Weapon*, p. 119.

17. Holland and Hoover, *The MX Decision*, p. 101.

18. Ibid., p. 172.

19. For discussions of the Alliance for Progress, see David Horowitz, "The Alliance for Progress," in Robert I. Rhodes (ed.), *Imperialism and Underdevelopment* (New York: Monthly Review Press, 1970), pp. 45–61; James Petras, "U.S. Wealth and Power in Latin America," in Michael Parenti (ed.), *Trends and Tragedies in American Foreign Policy* (Boston: Little, Brown, 1971), pp. 90–140; Abraham Lowenthal, "U.S. Policy Toward Latin America: 'Liberal,' 'Radical,' and 'Bureaucratic' Perspectives," *Latin American Research Review*, 8, (1973), 3–25; Jose Levinson and Juan de Onis, *The Alliance That Lost Its Way* (Chicago: Quadrangle, 1970); and Christopher Mitchell, "Dominance and Fragmentation in U.S. Latin American Policy," in Julio Cotter and

Richard E. Fagan (eds.), *Latin America and the U.S.: The Changing Political Realities* (Stanford, Calif.: Stanford University Press, 1974). The Lowenthal essay is also reprinted in the Cotter and Fagan volume.

20. Mitchell, "Dominance and Fragmentation," p. 190.

21. Horowitz, "The Alliance for Progress," p. 54.

22. Ibid., p. 57; and Petras, "U.S. Wealth and Power," p. 99.

23. Levinson and de Onis, *The Alliance That Lost Its Way;* and Petras, "U.S. Wealth and Power," p. 98.

24. Levinson and de Onis, *The Alliance That Lost Its Way,* pp. 71, 159–61.

25. Stephen E. Ambrose, *Rise to Globalism,* 2nd ed. (New York: Penguin, 1980), pp. 254–55.

26. David Horowitz, *The Free World Colossus: A Critique of American Foreign Policy in the Cold War,* rev. ed. (New York: Hill & Wang, 1971), pp. 216–17.

27. For discussions of the Caribbean Basin Initiative, see Abraham Lowenthal, "Caribbean Basin Initiative: Misplaced Emphasis," *Foreign Policy,* 47 (1982), 114–18; Peter Johnson, "Caribbean Basin Initiative: A Positive Departure," *Foreign Policy,* 47 (1982), 118–22; Richard E. Feinberg and Richard Newfarmer, "The Caribbean Basin Initiative: Bold Plan or Empty Promise," in Richard Newfarmer (ed.), *From Gunboats to Diplomacy: New U.S. Policies for Latin America* (Baltimore, Md.: Johns Hopkins University Press, 1984), pp. 210–17; and Ramesch Ramsaran, "The U.S. Caribbean Basin Initiative," in Suzanne P. Ogden (ed.), *World Politics 83/84* (Guilford, Conn.: Dushkin, 1983), pp. 182–85.

28. Feinberg and Newfarmer, "The Caribbean Basin Initiative," pp. 213–24.

29. Ibid., p. 226.

30. Ibid., p. 212.

31. Carmen Diaian Deere (coordinator), *In the Shadows of the Sun: Caribbean Development Alternatives and U.S. Policy* (Boulder, Colo.: Westview, 1990), p. 182.

32. This argument is made by the dependency school. For examples, see Susanne Bodeheimer, "Dependency and Imperialism: The Roots of Latin American Underdevelopment," in K. T. Fann and Donald C. Hodges (eds.), *Readings in U.S. Imperialism* (Boston: Porter Sargent, 1971), pp. 155–82.

33. The material in this section is taken from George W. Grayson, *The North American Free Trade Agreement: Regional Community and the New World Order,* Volume III, the Miller Center Series on a New World Order (Latham, Md.: University of America Press, 1995).

34. Robert D. Putnam, "Diplomacy and Domestic Politics: The Logic of Two-Level Games," *International Organization,* 42 (1988), 427–60.

35. Peter B. Evans, "Building an Integrative Approach to International and Domestic Politics," in Peter B. Evans, Harold K. Jacobson, and Robert D. Putnam (eds.), *Double-Edged Diplomacy: International Bargaining and Domestic Politics* (Berkeley: University of California Press, 1993), p. 397.

CHAPTER

13 Diplomacy

SELECTING A POLICY INSTRUMENT

Policy makers must decide not only what goals to pursue but how to pursue them. Depending on the specifics of the situation and a state's power resources, the range of instruments available to it may be large or quite restricted. The choice is an important one because an improperly chosen policy tool can do as much harm to U.S. national interests as can misguided policy objectives.[1] The most basic consideration to be kept in mind is that all choices are costly. No instrument frees policy makers from having to decide what risks they are willing to take and what values and goals they are willing to sacrifice. More problematic is how to measure these costs. The temptation is to ignore costs altogether. This danger is especially great when the options appear to be few and the need to act great. Confronted with this situation, policy makers are apt to place too great a value on the options still open to them by refusing to recognize their limitations and liabilities.

A second basic consideration is that measuring effectiveness is a complicated undertaking. Success and failure are often treated as absolute categories, yet this is seldom the case. Far more typical are situations where success and failure are both present in varying degrees. Also, a state rarely has only one goal when it undertakes a course of action, and the reality of multiple goals further complicates the calculations of costs and benefits. Estimates of success and failure also depend on one's time frame. Economic sanctions work slowly, but that does not mean that they are any less effective than fast-acting ones. They might even be preferable because they minimize the risk of miscalculation that accompanies crisis situations.

A third consideration to be kept in mind in selecting a policy instrument is the context within which it will operate. Economic strategies that worked well in an era when the United States was a hegemonic or predominant economic power may prove less useful in an era of economic decline or parity. Similarly, policy tools that were effective in a cold war international system will not necessarily be as effective in a post–cold war system. International crisis management techniques, military alliance systems, covert action, and arms transfer, to name only a few, derived their underlying rationale from the existence of global U.S.–Soviet rivalry. Today, it is argued that "soft" or intangible sources of power are fast becoming the primary means of influence which states must rely upon to achieve their goals. If this is the case then future American foreign policy instruments will have to be based less on military power and the ability to coerce others and more on the control of information and the ability to set agendas and structure situations in such a way that others will be coopted and accept U.S. leadership.

Our focus in this chapter is on diplomacy. As an instrument of foreign policy, diplomacy is closely identified with bargaining and negotiation. For many it remains the classic policy instrument and the one best suited to producing lasting and workable solutions to foreign policy problems. Others point out that the use of diplomacy is not without its dangers. Negotiations also hold the potential for exacerbating hostilities, strengthening an aggressor, preparing the way for an attack, and eroding the moral and legal foundations of peace.[2] They do so because in addition to solving problems, negotiations can also be used to stall for time, obtain information, and make propaganda.

The twentieth century has been a period of great change in the practice of diplomacy. Prior to World War I diplomacy was largely European centered and dealt with a fairly restricted range of issues. Diplomacy was also the preserve of the Great Powers. Negotiations were confidential with the outcome largely rooted in a quid pro quo spirit of compromise. The diplomacy of the 1990s and beyond promises to look far different. It will be a hybrid characterized by secret discussions and public declarations; and it will be carried out in an international environment in which nonstate actors often play a prominent role.

A case in point is American human rights policy. Holly Burkhalter, the Washington director of Human Rights Watch, observes that "constructing a successful human rights policy in the 1990s is a vastly different proposition than it was in the late 1970s or early 1980s."[3] Compared to today, the issues were relatively uncomplicated and problems could be addressed by holding American policy makers responsible for the human rights violations of their client states and counseling them to "first, do no harm." Few of today's human rights problems can be directly tied to the actions of American or Russian allies, and a "do no harm" strategy offers little prospect of alleviating many of the human rights violations chronicled in the press. The complexity of today's human rights policy is evident at all levels of U.S. diplomacy.

Since 1977 the State Department has submitted annual human rights reports to Congress. That year, 82 countries, all of which received American foreign aid, were reported on. In 1993, 193 reports were compiled. This figure far exceeded not only the number of states receiving foreign aid but also the total membership of the United Nations.[4] The initial drafts were prepared by U.S. embassies and then sent to Washington where they were reviewed by the Bureau of Human Rights and Humanitarian Affairs. At both stages, diplomats were in contact with officials from other parts of the State Department, nongovernmental organizations (NGOs), and international organizations (IGOs). Along with Amnesty International, the Human Rights Watch is one of the many NGOs that have come to play a prominent role in human rights foreign policy issues as agenda setters, mobilizers of public and elite opinion, and compliance monitors.[5] They target not only governments but international organizations (where they often meet in "shadow" or parallel international forums that preceed major international conferences) and multinational corporations investing in states such as South Africa or China whose human rights policies they oppose.

In addition to being carried out on a bilateral basis, American human rights policy is also conducted in multilateral settings such as in the United Nations system and at global conferences. This aspect of American foreign policy has come under heavy criticism in the 1990s. But according to Margaret Karns and Karen Mingst, on the whole multilateral institutions have not placed real constraints on U.S. strategic choices although they often have necessitated changes in strategies and tactics and influenced the makeup of the policy agenda.[6] Human rights is no exception to the rule.[7] American involvement in UN human rights policy making went through several distinct stages during the cold war: (1) a period of limited support (1945–1953); (2) a period of neglect (1954–1974); (3) a period of renewed interest (1974–1981); and (4) a period of renewed anticommunism (1981–1990). More so than changes in the nature of human rights as a problem or the makeup of the United Nations, it was changes in the nature of American domestic politics that produced this pattern.

BILATERAL DIPLOMACY

The most common form of diplomacy is bilateral diplomacy in which two states interact directly with one another. These relations occur at varying levels from the head of government and ambassador down to the most junior foreign service officer. They also can cover a wide array of subjects ranging from sensitive security and economic issues to the routine issuing of passports. The full range of contacts that are possible can be grasped from an inspection of the list of those accompanying President Clinton on his trip to China in 1998. They are listed in Table 13–1 and include representatives from the State Department, Commerce, Treasury, Defense Department, National Security Council, Peace Corps, the Office of Special Trade Representative, and members of Congress.

Bilateral relations are assuming a new prominence today. In part this is due to the end of the cold war, the disappearance of the cold war alliance systems, and the emergence of a series of new states out of the breakup of the Soviet Union and Yugoslavia. Its increased visibility is also a product of the absence of any overarching strategic framework for guiding American foreign policy. Without it, decisions will be heavily influenced by country-specific considerations.

We can identify three different types of bilateral relationships, each of which has its own unique set of characteristics: allies, friends, adversaries. Dealings with allies are marked by high levels of commitment to the negotiation process, a recognition that a wide area of common interests exists, and a willingness to address the specific issues involved in a dispute. Relations with adversaries also are marked by a high degree of commitment and attention but lack any sense of shared interests. Instead there is an underlying sense of conflict and distrust. As a result, much of the bilateral dialogue centers on finding formula-based solutions for problems. Finally, there are bilateral relations among friends. These are relations between states that are on good terms but lack extensive dealings with one another. As a result, it is often difficult to strike a deal as each side advances its own particular interest in the absence of widely perceived common interests.

TABLE 13-1   Clinton's Trip to China

U.S. Official Delegation to China, 1998

President Clinton

First Lady Hillary Rodham Clinton

James Sasser, U.S. ambassador to China

Madeleine K. Albright, secretary of state

Robert E. Rubin, secretary of the treasury

Dan Glickman, secretary of agriculture

William Daley, secretary of commerce

Janet Yellen, chair, Council of Economic Advisers

Ambassador Charlene Barshefsky, U.S. trade representative

Erskine B. Bowles, chief of staff to the president

Sen. Max Baucus (D-Mont.)

Sen. John D. "Jay" Rockefeller IV (D-W.Va.)

Sen. Daniel K. Akaka (D-Hawaii)

Rep. John D. Dingell (D-Mich.)

Rep. Lee H. Hamilton (D-Ind.)

Rep. Edward J. Markey (D-Mass.)

John Podesta, deputy chief of staff to the president

Samuel R. "Sandy" Berger, assistant to the president for national security affairs

Gene Sperling, assistant to the president for economic policy and director, National Economic Council

Phillip Caplan, staff secretary

Bruce R. Lindsey, deputy counsel

Michael McCurry, White House press secretary

Doug Sosnik, counselor to the president

Melanne Verveer, chief of staff to the first lady

David Lipton, undersecretary of treasury

Elaine Shocas, chief of staff to the secretary of state

Michael Froman, chief of staff, Treasury Department

Mark Gearan, director, Peace Corps

Mary Mel French, chief of protocol

Andrew Pincus, general counsel, Commerce Department

John Shattuck, assistant secretary of state for democracy, human rights and labor

Stanley Roth, assistant secretary of state for East Asian affairs

Linda Robertson, assistant treasury secretary

Howard Schloss, assistant treasury secretary

John Schroeder, assistant agriculture secretary

Robert Cassidy, assistant U.S. trade representative

Jay Ziegler, assistant U.S. trade representative

Marsha Berry, director of communications

Nancy Hernreich, director of Oval Office operations

Capricia Marshall, social secretary

Doris Matsul, deputy director of public liaison

Dan Rosenthal, director of advance

James Steinberg, deputy assistant to the president for national security affairs

Barry Toiv, deputy press secretary

Adm. Joseph Prueher, CINCPAC

Glyn Davies, executive secretary, National Security Council

Lael Brainard, special assistant to the president for international economic policy

Sandra Kristoff, NSC senior director for Asian affairs

Jeff Bader, director for Asian affairs, National Security Council

Source: The Washington Post, June 24, 1998, p A24.

SUMMIT DIPLOMACY

The most visible of all the forms of diplomacy today is summit diplomacy in which the heads of state meet personally with one another. The most important cold war summit conferences involved meetings of U.S. and Soviet leaders. Western leaders have also begun to meet annually in summits in an effort to deal with economic problems. Summit conferences perform a number of valuable services.[8] Foremost among them is establishing a personal relationship between leaders that sensitizes each to the domestic constraints operating in the other's political system. A second valuable service performed by a summit is that it energizes the bureaucracy and sets a deadline for decision making. The benefit here is not so much the summit itself but the preparations for the summit. The SALT I negotiations and the U.S.–Japanese agreement over the status of Okinawa were both carried out under the deadline of an approaching summit conference.

Aligned against these positive virtues of summit diplomacy are a number of potentially negative consequences.[9] First, the personal contacts established may result in an inaccurate reading of the adversary's character and the constraints the adversary operates under. This appears to have happened at the 1961 Kennedy–Khrushchev summit in Vienna. Khrushchev reportedly came away from it with the impression that Kennedy could be intimidated, and many link the Soviet attempt to place missiles in Cuba to this meeting. Another prime example is Roosevelt's belief that he could establish a personal working relationship with Stalin as a result of the World War II summit conferences in Tehran and Yalta.

Energizing the bureaucracy does not necessarily guarantee the emergence of a coherent policy. It may only intensify the ongoing bureaucratic struggle so that only a lowest-common-denominator position is taken to the summit. Summit deadlines may also politicize or impede decision making. This point is most forcefully raised with reference to annual economic summitry, but as the many accounts of U.S.–Soviet arms control talks reveal, it is equally applicable to other forms of international diplomacy.[10] Other commentators suggest that periodic meetings are a questionable device for addressing a continuously evolving problem. Agreements reached in April become obsolete in November, but the next summit is still months away. Inaction rather than adaptive problem solving is likely to characterize the bureaucratic process for most of the intervening months. Additionally, summit deadlines offer the recalcitrant state a golden opportunity to exploit the other's eagerness for the summit. One observer suggests that this may have happened with the Carter–Brezhnev summit. Carter's desire for a summit is seen as partly responsible for his supporting a Soviet initiative to reconvene the Geneva talks on the Middle East. The result, had this actually happened, would have been to give the Soviet Union a voice in the Middle East peace process that was denied to it as long as U.S. peace initiatives dominated the agenda.[11]

Summit conferences have also been criticized for unfairly raising public expectations about the potential for a meaningful agreement. Should no positive benefits be forthcoming, the resulting public disillusionment can greatly complicate the conduct of future diplomatic ventures. The SALT agreements were negotiated as part of the process of détente, and when détente began to unravel, arms control efforts were one of the main casualties. To deal with many of these shortcomings, former President Richard Nixon advocated regular summit conferences as a way of keeping the pressure on the Soviet Union, curbing its behavior, and taking the pressure off getting a major agreement at any one summit.[12]

East–West Superpower Summits[13]

East–West summit conferences became a frequent, if irregularly spaced, feature of the cold war. Several points about the evolution of East–West summitry bear special mention. A first phase lasted from 1955 to 1967. The United States and Soviet Union approached each other as antagonists in these meetings. European security issues dominated the agenda and over time they became bilateral affairs, with the French and British forced to watch on the sidelines.

With the Glassboro Summit nuclear issues became firmly established as the central concern of superpower summitry. The Glassboro Summit presents an interesting point of comparison with the Reagan–Gorbachev summits. At Glassboro the United States tried to convince the Soviet Union to abandon its defensive antiballistic missile (ABM) system because it was a destabilizing factor in the nuclear balance and threatened to set off an expensive arms race. The Soviet Union replied that because the ABM was a defensive system it should be unobjectionable to all concerned.

The next five summits were part of an effort to institutionalize détente. All told they produced more than 24 agreements, including SALT I, SALT II, and the ABM Treaty. The sequence began with the 1972 Nixon–Brezhnev summit in Moscow and culminated in the 1979 Carter–Brezhnev summit with the signing of the ill-fated SALT II Treaty. The Reagan–Gorbachev summits marked the beginning of a third phase of East–West summitry. They were "postdétente" summits, and took place against a backdrop of renewed U.S.–Soviet rivalry and heightened public concerns about the specter of nuclear war. To the surprise of most observers, this sequence of summits ended with the signing of an arms control treaty on intermediate range nuclear weapons and progress on a treaty controlling strategic nuclear weapons.

The most controversial of the Reagan–Gorbachev summits for both the apparent absence of preparation and the proposals put forward took place at Reykjavik in 1986. The Reykjavik Summit took place with little more than one week's notice and began without an agreed-upon agenda or well-established backup negotiating positions. At one point Reagan proposed the abolition of all ballistic missiles. Gorbachev countered with a proposal to eliminate all strategic arms, a proposal Reagan may have agreed to. Reagan's one sticking point was permitting SDI testing outside of the laboratory, and in the end this prevented an agreement from being reached. Even so, the willingness to sacrifice the U.S. nuclear deterrent capability in order to protect SDI and the highly informal manner in which U.S. proposals were generated caused alarm throughout the policy community, among U.S. allies in Europe, and with the public at large.

A fourth, post–cold war, phase of East–West summitry began when President Bush met with Gorbachev off the coast of Malta in December 1989. While little of substance came out of the meeting, a notable change in tone had taken place. As one observer put it, the two leaders had exorcised the ghost of Reagan. Issues that had divided the two sides in the past (such as SDI) received little attention. Instead, much of the meeting was devoted to discussion of cooperative measures and expressions of a willingness to work together for stability in a rapidly changing world. The second Bush–Gorbachev summit took place in Washington in 1990. It produced an unexpected agreement on an economic aid package for Russia.

A fifth phase in East–West summitry began in July 1991 when a third Bush–Gorbachev summit took place in Moscow after the Persian Gulf War, amid the disintegration of the Soviet Union. For the first time, arms control issues did not occupy a prominent place on the summit's agenda. Here and at the Clinton–Yeltsin summits at Vancouver (1993) and Moscow (1995) primary attention would be given to the economic and political problems that often seemed on the very brink of overwhelming Russia. At Vancouver an aid package was unveiled that included credits for grain sales and trade guarantees; funds for dismantling Russian missiles; money for medical supplies, food, and housing; and a program to spur the development of new businesses. The Moscow summit produced few successes.

Western Economic Summits

Beginning in 1975, the heads of state of the major Western economies have met at an annual summit conference. With the end of the cold war, the passing of the Soviet threat, and the emergence of economic issues as paramount foreign policy concerns, economic summits have replaced "military" summits as the primary meeting place for world leaders. Two different models exist for how these meetings should be conducted.[14] The library group model stresses flexible, private, and periodic (not annual) discussions involving a minimum of participants (few or no bureaucratic aides). This was the concept that French president Giscard d'Estaing had in mind in proposing the first economic summit. The model draws its name and inspiration from the periodic and informal meetings of U.S. and Western European finance ministers that took place between 1973 and 1975. The Atlantic council model emphasizes the need for the formal international coordination of economic policy making. Regularly scheduled and fully staffed summits would serve the dual purpose of directing national bureaucracies and educating the public about the nature of the economic problems facing advanced industrial societies.

Considerable changes took place in the nature of the Western economic summits during the first decade of their existence, and neither model has been fully put into practice.[15] Meetings have been more formal than the library group model calls for and more ad hoc than stipulated by the Atlantic council model. The early summits came close to approximating the library group model. They were designed to energize policy making and to help the heads of state overcome bureaucratic resistance to policy changes. There was no expectation that a second conference would be held in 1976. In fact, the second summit was called for by President Ford only one month before it took place. It reflected the pressures of electoral considerations more than economic ones. Summits moved considerably closer to the Atlantic council model under Carter as he sought to use them as a means of institutionalizing international collaboration.

Western economic summits deal with more than Western economic issues. For much of the Reagan era Soviet expansionism, arms control and defense policies, and terrorism were also on the agenda. One observer suggested that during Reagan's term in office economic summits took on the character of an "international jousting match" as leaders adopted more nationalistic outlooks and U.S. economic policies came under increasing attack. In 1989, the first meeting attended by Bush, much of the discussion focused on aid for Eastern Europe, but international environmental issues, drug trafficking, and aid and debt relief for the third world were also dominant issues on the agenda. In 1990 prior to that year's economic summit, the United States and the European Community (EC) agreed to hold twice-yearly summits. This move was regarded as significant in many quarters because it signaled a willingness on the part of the United States to treat the EC as an economic partner and not a protectionist-minded rival.

Recent economic summits have followed this pattern of addressing economic and noneconomic concerns. In 1996, at President Clinton's urging the summit's agenda was broadened to include terrorism and international crime. Considerable time at the 1997 summit was spent on global warming as well as the situation in Bosnia and the wisdom of the U.S. pledge to withdraw its peacekeeping forces in June 1998. At the 1998 summit, the heads of state expressed their frustration over India's detonation of a nuclear device, urged the Israelis and Palestinians to resume negotiations, and called for political and economic reform in Indonesia. The willingness to address a broad agenda has not been matched by an ability to reach a consensus on what action to take. For example, in 1996 Clinton was able to get support for a crackdown on terrorism but not for punishing firms that do business with countries that sponsor terrorism, and in 1998 the heads of state were unable to agree on whether to apply sanctions against India. The 1998 summit was significant because it marked the formal entrance of Russia into the summit process and for its renaming from the annual meeting of the Group of Seven (G-7) to the Group of Eight (G-8).

CONFERENCE DIPLOMACY

GATT

In addition to summitry, the United States also has relied heavily on international conferences to accomplish U.S. foreign policy objectives. Particularly important for the U.S. economy have been the GATT talks, the most recent of which has been the Uruguay Round. Begun in 1986 with a scheduled adjournment date of 1990, this conference did not end until 1994 when 125 states signed an agreement that would further liberalize international trade.

A far-ranging and complex set of issues was on the negotiating agenda. Trade in agriculture proved to be a particularly difficult problem area with which to deal. The controversy pitted both the rich countries against the poor and the United States against Western Europe. At the heart of the problem was the need for more markets for agricultural goods, the widespread presence of subsidies and quotas that protected farmers from foreign competition, and the unwillingness of leaders to antagonize the politically powerful agricultural interests within their states. For its part, the United States was unwilling to stop subsidizing sugar growers and expose them to competition from third world producers. But at the same time it demanded that France stop subsidizing its soybean farmers and open European markets to American soybean producers. A second area of concern to the United States was international protection for intellectual property. American firms charged that third world states routinely disregarded copyrights and patents in the production of such items as books, compact disks, and computer software. A third area of controversy centered on the demands of the United States and Europe for setting international labor standards with regard to child labor, convict labor, minimum wages, and unions. The United States and Europe also pressed, against third world objections, for the establishment of a body to examine the environmental impact of the GATT agreement.

A key element in the Uruguay Round agreement was the creation of a new international body, the World Trade Organization (WTO), that would supervise international trade law and formally bring the GATT process to an end. From its first meeting in Geneva in 1947, GATT had been seen as a transitional body that would deal with international trade matters only until an international trade organization (ITO) was set up. Because of political opposition within the United States to the broad powers which were to be given the ITO, President Truman never submitted the treaty creating it to Congress for approval. Similar concerns about the loss of U.S. sovereignty were expressed when the WTO was proposed. Only a last-minute compromise between President Clinton and Senate majority leader Robert Dole, which reserved the right of the United States to leave the WTO should it consistently rule against the United States, cleared the way for the treaty's approval by the Senate.

Two earlier important rounds of GATT trade negotiations were the Kennedy Round (1964 to 1967) and the Tokyo Round (1973 to 1977). The Kennedy Round sought to reduce barriers to international free trade, and marked the high point of international trade cooperation. By the late 1970s tariffs averaged less than 10 percent. This compared to 25 percent in 1945 and 60 percent in 1934. The second prolonged negotiating session, the Tokyo Round, was not as successful. Much had changed in the intervening years that made duplicating its success an impossible task. Not only was the United States no longer the totally domineering economic giant it had been in the 1960s, but tariffs were no longer the major impediment to international trade. The new focus of concern was nontariff barriers to trade (NTBs). The Tokyo Round made some progress on NTBs. Agreements were reached on such practices as subsidies, dumping, countervailing duties, product standards, and government purchases. The principal failings of the Tokyo Round were that little headway was reached on liberalizing agricultural trade, and that questions of trade in services were not addressed. The Uruguay Round took up these issues.

Helsinki Accords

The results of conference diplomacy have often proved to be quite controversial politically in the United States. One such agreement is popularly known as the Helsinki Accords, which was the product of negotiations at the Conference on Security and Cooperation in Europe (CSCE). The controversy centers on just what the United States got from the Soviet Union in making the agreement. The origins of the conference go back to 1954 when the Soviet Union began calling for an all-European conference to settle the problem of what to do about postwar Germany. The first positive response from the West came in 1969. At the 1972 Nixon–Brezhnev summit, President Nixon formally endorsed the idea if the Soviet Union would agree to simultaneous negotiations on reducing troop levels in Europe. The conference began in June 1973 with 35 states present. The final declaration was signed in August 1975. It was divided into three "baskets." Basket I dealt with security and confidence-building measures. Basket II dealt with measures to increase trade, economic, scientific, and environmental cooperation among European states. Basket III dealt with humanitarian affairs. It was also agreed that periodic follow-up meetings would be held to review and evaluate progress in these three areas.

Critics of the agreement argued that in signing the Helsinki Accords the West officially recognized the division of Europe and the Soviet sphere of influence in Eastern Europe. In particular, they objected to a reference to the inviability of international frontiers included in basket I. Defenders of the agreement argued that this wording was nothing more than a reaffirmation of the language of the UN charter. They also argued that the Soviet Union paid a high price for getting the West to sign the Helsinki Accords when it agreed to having basket III included in the agreement. Soviet and Eastern European noncompliance were major issues at the Belgrade and Madrid follow-up meetings.

The Helsinki Process today is in an anomalous position. On the one hand it has achieved far more than many had expected and its follow-up meetings have become an established fixture on the European political landscape. The following were among the activities mandated by a 1992 Helsinki follow-up meeting: seminars on the democratic process, a Forum for Security Cooperation, a seminar on the Mediterranean, a seminar on migration, an Implementation Review Meeting, an Economic Forum, and a Review Conference. At the same time, there is a growing sense that the CSCE must move beyond its present role if it is to remain relevant, and there is no doubt that it is capable of doing so. The problem from this perspective is that the CSCE process was set up to deal with one type of problem, East–West competition in Europe, and that a very different type of problem exists today.[16] Instead of a vehicle for moderating superpower conflict, Europe needs an instrument for enforcing peace in places such as Bosnia, Georgia, and Chechnia. As CSCE critics note, the Helsinki Accords did little to prevent the widespread violence in these places. One of the most ambitious proposals is to transform the CSCE into the centerpiece of a European collective security system.

Environmental Conferences

For each of the past several administrations, conference diplomacy also has become a central vehicle for international environmental policy making. However, just as with international economic conference diplomacy, the complexity of these issues, coupled with the imperatives of American domestic politics, has made it difficult for the United States to exert leadership and has often placed it at odds with the rest of the world. This was very much the case during the first Reagan administration, which sought both to weaken domestic environmental standards and limit U.S. support for international environmental programs. The convergence of many factors brought about a policy shift in Reagan's second term as the United States assumed a leadership position in international negotiations that led to the signing of the 1987 Montreal Protocol on Substances That Deplete the Ozone Layer. Foremost among these factors were changes in personnel at the Environmental Protection Agency and the State Department; the commitment of leading American firms such as Dupont to support a ban on CFC emissions; growing global concern about the environment spurred by the Chernobyl nuclear reactor accident; and mounting scientific evidence regarding ozone depletion and global warming.[17]

The Montreal Protocol was hailed widely for the real cuts it was able to make in the production and consumption of ozone-depleting materials and for its procedural approach to the problem. Rather than seek a definitive and comprehensive statement about levels of reduction, funding, and the obligations of signatory states as had commonly been done in the past, negotiators at Montreal established a framework for addressing the problem and committed themselves to periodic review conferences where target figures and timetables could be adjusted.

The Bush administration's principal foray into international environmental conference diplomacy was the United Nations Conference on Environment and Development. Better known as the "Earth Summit," it took place June 3–14, 1992, in Rio de Janeiro, Brazil. The product of almost two years of advance negotiations and attended by about 35,000 accredited delegates representing over 178 countries, the Earth Summit ended with the signing of seven major pacts and initiatives. It also found the United States on the defensive and the only major state not to sign a biodiversity treaty. The Bush administration objected to the treaty's provisions calling for all states to protect endangered animal and plant species, on the grounds that it did not provide patent protection to U.S. biotechnology firms. This was later signed by the Clinton administration. The United States was also virtually alone in its objections to a treaty for protection against global warming. It only agreed to support it after references to binding targets and timetables were dropped in favor of a more general pledge to reduce the emissions of gases that cause global warming.

After the conference concluded, Environmental Protection Agency head William Reilly criticized the Bush administration for assigning the Earth Summit a low priority and committing few resources to it. Others criticized the Bush administration for allowing reelection concerns to dominate policy. The head of the Australian delegation commented, "The big shame is that the conference is being held during an election year . . . when you're negotiating the future of the earth, it puts pressure on negotiations if your preoccupation is here and now."[18]

One area in which very little progress was made at the Earth Summit was overpopulation. Pressure from the Vatican, conservative Catholic states, and Muslim states led to a deemphasis on population control strategies in summit documents. The Clinton administration found itself at the center of controversy on population matters with these same forces two years later at the United Nations' Third International Conference on Population and Development in Cairo. This 1994 meeting brought together representatives from 180 states and produced a 113-page "Program of Action." At issue was the conference's stand on abortion. The Vatican opposed abortion on moral grounds and successfully maneuvered to soften the language used in final conference documents. The United States' position stopped short of asserting that abortions should be an international right. Rather, it argued that abortions must be legal, safe, and voluntary and that they should be part of a wide range of health services available to women.

A major international environmental conference took place in Kyoto in 1997. It was agreed that industrialized states would reduce "greenhouse" gas emissions of six gases from 1990 levels by more than 5 percent between 2008–2012. In hopes of encouraging the adoption of cost-effective strategies, it was agreed that countries that did not meet their targets could make deals with those that exceeded them and "buy" the excess quota. Kyoto was significant because it was the first legally binding environmental agreement even though no compliance mechanisms were established. Third world states such as China and India would be asked to set up voluntary targets.

The Kyoto Protocol is binding on a state only after its government has ratified the agreement. In the case of the United States this promises to be a politically charged undertaking. Not only is there considerable opposition from conservative groups to the general outline of the agreement (most pointedly to the mandated reduction levels and the voluntary nature of third world targets), but there is also debate over the specific measures that will be needed to bring about the necessary reductions. Few expect quick Senate ratification unless changes are made in the agreement.

THE POLITICAL USE OF FORCE

American military power serves as an instrument of diplomacy by its very existence. Without ever having to be used or even referred to, it heightens U.S. prestige and gives importance to U.S. proposals and expressions of concern. The knowledge that it exists influences both how U.S. policy makers approach problems and the positions adopted by other states. Barry Blechman and Stephen Kaplan identified 218 incidents between 1946 and 1975 in which the United States used military forces for political purposes.[19] To qualify as a political use of force, the military action had to involve a physical change in the disposition of U.S. forces and be consciously done to achieve a political objective without going to war or trying to physically impose the U.S. position on the target state. Acts excluded by this definition are Korean- and Vietnam-type wars, in which success or failure was due to actions on the battlefield; the use of force to protect U.S. property or military positions such as evacuating U.S. citizens or placing troops into the Korean demilitarized zone; the continuous presence of U.S. forces in an area; foreign military aid; and routine military exercise for the purpose of maintaining or improving combat readiness.

On average, the political use of force has lasted 90 days, with U.S. military forces staying at their maximum force level for 56 days. The actions ranged from a port visit by a single warship to the deployment of major land, sea, and air units in conjunction with a strategic alert and reserve mobilizations. As many as 20 incidents and as few as 3 have taken place in one year with the average number of incidents being 8. The greatest number of incidents occurred between 1958 and 1965 when an average of 12 incidents per year took place. In terms of geography, the 218 incidents are spread relatively evenly across the Northern Hemisphere although the points of emphasis changed over time. Between 1946 and 1948, Western Europe was the primary area where the United States sought to use military power for political purposes and Southeast Asia and East Asia were the predominant areas of activity between 1949 and 1955. Between 1966 and 1975, U.S. attempts to use military power for political purposes were divided relatively evenly between Southeast Asia and East Asia and the Middle East and North Africa. Only South Asia and sub-Saharan Africa have been consistently neglected.

In the post–cold war era, air power emerged as the tool of choice in attempting to influence the decisions of leaders in other states. Typically the results have been disappointing. Periodic bombing of Iraq for its violations of "no fly zones" and other aggressive acts have had little impact on Saddam Hussein's overall foreign policy. The use and threatened use of air strikes in Bosnia, Serbia, and Kosovo did not end the fighting and also created discord among U.S. allies.

The utility of using military power in the pursuit of political objectives was found to depend on four factors. First was the nature of the U.S. objective. Favorable outcomes were most often realized when the objective was to maintain the authority of a specific regime. They were least likely to be achieved when the goal concerned third-party support for someone. The success rate of efforts to offset the use of force by another state fell in between these two extremes. Second, negative outcomes often found the Soviet Union to be involved militarily and/or politically. Third, favorable outcomes were most likely to be realized if the issue was domestic rather than international in scope. In the case of international conflicts, a favorable outcome was most likely if the United States was present from the outset of the conflict. Fourth, it was found that the firmer the commitment, the more often a favorable outcome was achieved. In concrete terms this meant that troops actually doing something were preferable to troops displaying a potential for action; troops on foreign soil were preferable to naval forces; and forces with a place in U.S. nuclear war plans were especially effective in realizing positive results. The authors found that the utility of force as an instrument of political influence decreased over time. Only when the objective was to reinforce regime behavior was a success rate of over 50 percent maintained in the long run (two and one-half years). Significantly, while the more direct commitment of military force was highly correlated with success in the short run (six months), success in the long run for this type of involvement declined dramatically.

As a counterpoint to this broad overview of the political use of military power, we briefly examine one political use of military power that has become especially important in the postwar era. It is the use of conventional forces for deterring communist aggression. Case study analysis of U.S. attempts to practice deterrence below the nuclear level suggests that it is a complex and demanding task. Demonstrating commitment and resolve is difficult. States seeking to change the status quo have many ways of proceeding. The status quo power, therefore, must deter a wide range of actions, something it is not likely to be able to do effectively across the board. Even when resolve and commitment are displayed, deterrence is not guaranteed. Alexander George and Richard Smoke identify three patterns of failure.[20]

In one, deterrence fails through a *fait accompli*. Communist policy makers detect no U.S. commitment and feel that they can control their risks. The June 1950 Northern Korean attack on South Korea is an example of deterrence failing through a *fait accompli*. The thirty-eighth parallel divided North and South Korea as a result of a World War II decision to have Soviet forces accept the surrender of Japanese troops north at that point. George and Smoke argue that the *fait accompli* strategy was rational because no clear U.S. commitment existed and the risks appeared to be controllable. Public statements by leading U.S. diplomats (Secretary of State Dean Acheson) and military figures (the JCS) had placed South Korea outside of the U.S. "defense perimeter" and referred to it as a "liability" in the event of war in the Far East. Reinserting U.S. forces into Korea was not expected to be an easy task, so the most likely response to an attack would be diplomatic protest or a minimal military action.

Deterrence can also fail as a result of a limited probe where the challenging action is easily reversed or expanded depending on the nature of the U.S. response. In these cases the U.S. commitment is unclear, and the risks still seem to be controllable. The Berlin Wall crisis of 1961 illustrates how deterrence can fail through a limited probe. A succession of Berlin crises in 1948, 1958, and earlier in 1961 had demonstrated the existence of a U.S. commitment to Berlin. Yet they had also demonstrated a U.S. desire to avoid a direct military confrontation and had brought home the military reality that East Berlin was over 100 miles into communist territory, making Western military operations difficult but not impossible. From the perspective of the East German leadership, the situation in Berlin had become intolerable. An average of over 1,000 people were fleeing to West Berlin each day. Included among them were many professionals whose skills would be needed to build up the East German economy. The Soviet Union and East Germany moved at midnight on May 12 to close the border by constructing a barbed wire wall on East Berlin territory. Only when the minimal nature of the U.S. response was clear (the Western powers did not make a protest for four days) did they move to construct a more substantial and permanent wall with only a few highly guarded openings.

Finally, deterrence can fail as a result of controllable pressure where the U.S. commitment is seen as unequivocal but "soft" and where the risks are considered to be controllable. George and Smoke do not identify any situation where controlled pressure was found to operate alone. Rather, it tends to be the second phase of a deterrence failure, occurring after a *fait accompli* or limited probe has failed and when the challenging state has decided to continue to press ahead. They suggest that the second phase of the Cuban missile crisis fits this pattern. In September Kennedy made a series of public statements in which he underlined the U.S. opposition to offensive missiles in Cuba. At this point George and Smoke argue that the U.S. commitment had to be seen as unequivocal. But rather than abandon its plans or engage in a more limited probe, the Soviet Union sought to get around the U.S. commitment or negate it by secretly placing missiles in Cuba. Khrushchev may have judged the risks to be controllable because of the secrecy of the operation and his apparent belief that Kennedy could be intimidated.

ARMS TRANSFERS

Arms transfers have established themselves quickly as a favorite instrument of policy makers.[21] In 1980, one observer noted that the United States annually receives nearly 10,000 requests from foreign governments for military equipment and services and over 20,000 applications from private firms for export licenses.[22] The Arms Export Control Act of 1976 requires that all arms transfer valued at $25 million or more or those involving the transfer of significant combat equipment be reported to Congress. This same study found that over 100 cases have been reported each year. States sell and buy weapons for a number of different reasons, and the relationship between them has been compared to a reciprocal bargaining process in which each tries to use the other to accomplish goals that are often incompatible.[23] The potential tensions are most clearly evident when each side is driven by strategic imperatives.

For arms sellers three strategic rationales are most often advanced. First, arms transfers can provide influence and leverage abroad by serving as a symbolic statement of support for a regime and providing access to elites. Second, they can be used to protect specific security interests abroad and further regional stability. Third, they can be used as barter in acquiring access to overseas bases. None of these rationales are without their problems. Leverage tends to be a transitory phenomenon in world politics, and an arms transfer relationship can promote friction just as much as it can cement ties. It can also produce a situation of reverse leverage where the recipient state, rather than the seller, exercises the most influence. Iran provides a useful example of influence gone awry. The United States sold sophisticated weapons to the Shah of Iran in the hopes that he would use them to contain the spread of communism in the Persian Gulf, while the Shah saw these weapons as a way of realizing his dream of making Iran into a regional superpower. Not only was he quite willing to work with the Soviet Union when it suited his interests, but in the last years of his rule, the large volume of U.S. weapons in Iran created hostility among the people toward the United States. Efforts designed to improve regional stability can be easily interpreted as an attempt to alter the regional balance of power. The result can be a competitive situation that takes on all of the characteristics of an arms race such as has become commonplace in the Middle East. Like political leverage, access to bases has proven to be transitory. It can also be an increasingly costly proposition as the host state raises the economic, political, and military favors that must be granted for continued access. The Reagan administration found this to be the case in its negotiations to renew basing rights with a number of states. In 1985 Turkey publicly stated that the price for renewing U.S. basing rights would be an increase in the value of future Turkish exports to the United States from their 1984 level of $433 million to $3 billion.

There have been five major turning points in the development of U.S. arms transfer policy. The first came in the early 1960s when the Kennedy administration made a distinction between arms sales and arms transferred abroad as foreign aid. Kennedy turned to arms sales in an effort to counter the growing U.S. balance-of-payments problem that was brought about in part by the high cost of stationing U.S. troops in Europe. The second turning point came during the Nixon administration. Arms transfers now became an important instrument of foreign policy and a cornerstone of the Nixon Doctrine which stressed the need for U.S. third world allies to assume the primary responsibility for their own defense. To that end the United States was prepared to channel aid and assistance, but it would not readily intervene into the conflict itself. Other changes also took place. Sales replaced aid as the primary vehicle for transferring arms, the Middle East became the primary area of U.S. arms transfers, and the quality of the weapons transferred increased dramatically. No longer were arms transfers dominated by obsolete weapons in the U.S. inventory. Now they regularly involved the most sophisticated weapons that it possessed. A number of statistics vividly capture these changes. Measured in constant dollars, U.S. arms transfers increased 150 percent between 1968 and 1977. In FY1971 FMS (foreign military sales) orders were valued at $1.4 billion, in FY1973 they reached $5.3 billion, and in FY1975 they had jumped to $15.5 billion. In 1970 sales to Iran were valued at $13.3 million. In 1974 they were valued at $3.9 billion.

The third turning point in the evolution of U.S. arms transfer policy came with the Carter administration. It represented a turning point for what it sought to do rather than for what it accomplished. Carter sought to replace the Nixon–Ford–Kissinger view of arms transfers as a normal instrument of foreign policy with one seeing it as an "exceptional tool."[24] The Carter policy had an immediate impact. In the first 15 months after it was announced, 614 requests from 92 states for over $1 billion worth of arms were turned down. The Carter administration refused to sell F-18L fighters and F-4G fighter-bombers to Iran; A-7 bombers to Pakistan; and F-4 phantom jets to Taiwan. Israel was denied permission to export its Kfir fighter to Ecuador. The United States had a veto because the plane in question contained U.S.-built components, and as a condition of its sale the United States reserved the right to veto its reexport.

Gradually, however, the Carter administration found it difficult to work within its own guidelines. The dollar ceiling became a numbers game in which creative accounting procedures and loopholes were used to maximum advantage—to the point where total U.S. arms sales increased from $12.8 billion in 1977 to $17.1 billion in 1980. The first major exception to its own rules was the sale of seven AWACs to Iran for $1.8 billion. The Carter administration also agreed to a $1.8 billion arms package for South Korea in compensation for the reduction in U.S. ground forces to be stationed there. In March 1980 the Carter administration all but abandoned its policy of restraint. This move appears to have been prompted by the perceived need to continue sweetening the Camp David Accords and to cement ties with Saudi Arabia now that the Shah had fallen and the Soviet Union had invaded Afghanistan. After Camp David, Israel was given $2.2 billion in new arms credits while Egypt was advanced $1.5 billion in credits.

The fourth turning point in U.S. arms transfer policy came with the arrival of the Reagan administration. When the Carter administration came to an end, negotiations were under way with Saudi Arabia on a new arms package. It would be up to the Reagan administration to complete these negotiations. The arms transfer package announced by the Reagan administration stunned Washington. Not only were enhanced F-15s to be made available to Saudi Arabia, but 5 AWACs, 7 KC-135 tankers, and 22 ground radar stations were also included in the $8.5 billion package, the largest ever in U.S. history. The Reagan administration moved quickly to use arms transfers as a tool in its global struggle against communism. In its first three months in office, it offered approximately $15 billion in weapons and other forms of military assistance to other states. The Bush administration proposed making $30 billion available in foreign military sales in 1990. Among the major intended recipients of these weapons were Egypt (which was to get 700 surplus tanks from U.S. forces in Europe); Colombia (a $7 million radar command center for drug trafficking); Kuwait (200 M-1A2 tanks valued at $1 billion); and Israel, Japan, Norway, South Korea, and Spain (which were to get varying numbers of shoulder-fired Stinger missiles).

The most recent phase began after the Persian Gulf War with the United States and other states calling for an end to arms shipments to the Middle East and the establishment of an international registrar of arms. A reversal of direction, however, quickly ensued. By 1993, the United States, France, and Great Britain had arranged for almost $50 billion in new orders from the Middle East.[25] The 1992 election played a pivotal role in this turnaround. In the course of a six-week period in September and October, President Bush authorized $20 billion in new arms sales, with the announcement coming at arms plants in key electoral states like Texas and Missouri. The Clinton administration also embraced arms transfers as an instrument of foreign policy to the point that in 1993 the United States became the world's leading arms supplier, selling over $31 billion worth of weapons to over 140 states. In 1995 it opposed a draft congressional plan that would have established a code of conduct for arms sales. Only states with democratically elected governments that protect basic freedoms and that are not engaged in "gross violations of internationally recognized human rights" would be eligible to receive U.S. weapons. The Clinton administration argued that rigid rules governing the sale of weapons would intrude on the president's authority to conduct foreign policy and that no single criterion should take precedence over all others in determining whether an arms sale should be made.

The net result of these decisions is that, since 1990, the U.S. has exported over $96 billions of weapons, with yearly amounts ranging between $11.5 billion

(FY94) and $15.3 billion (FY95). The range of weapons transferred has also been great, ranging from highly sophisticated weapons systems to "recycled" weapons. Between 1990–1995, for example, the Pentagon transferred $7 billion of surplus weapons abroad including some 4,000 tanks, 125 attack helicopters, 500 bombers, and 200,000 pistols and rifles. A particularly controversial issue involving arms transfers is NATO expansion. Critics of arms transfers argue that a majority of new arms transfers programs have been targeted at potential NATO members and that with NATO expansion now a reality we can expect to see a significant increase in arms transfers to these states in the name of military preparedness and standardization.

SUMMARY AND THE FUTURE

Diplomacy as an instrument of foreign policy is a quite varied tool, encompassing such forms as summit and conference diplomacy, the political use of force, and arms transfers. None are without their problems. Some observers reach the conclusion that modern diplomacy, especially in its summit and conference forms, is not well suited to cope with the dilemmas of international politics. Reasons for this pessimism include the loss of flexibility and the ability to compromise, and the prominence given to the public side of international negotiations. This dissatisfaction is often accompanied by a desire to reestablish the central features of the old diplomacy. Others argue that while these problems do complicate matters, what is really needed is a change in focus. The principal problem in diplomatic negotiations has changed. It is no longer to outwit the adversaries and take more from them than they take from you, but to create a framework for resolving disputes.[26] Ideally, the framework would reduce the complexity of the issue and limit the range of variation permitted in the future so that the most undesirable developments would fall outside the range of permissible options.

We have already seen movement in this direction. The SALT process and the GATT talks have been less concerned with resolving specific points of dispute than with developing a common set of perceptions and expectations on how to move forward in dealing with the problem. GATT has sought to make certain classes of protectionist measures nonoptions, and to a certain extent it has succeeded. The United States, for example, has resisted imposing quotas on incoming goods and has instead relied on "voluntary agreements." The effect on the volume of goods coming into the United States is the same, but the impact on the international trading system is much different. Quotas would threaten to undermine the system while voluntary agreements can be accommodated by it. In much the same way, SALT I did not directly address the question of what type of nuclear relationship should exist between the United States and Soviet Union as much as it excluded certain ones—those premised on the existence of viable ABM systems.

The authors of the study on the political use of force also provide us with some important cautionary notes in looking to the future. First, their findings suggest that the political use of force can buy time, but that may be all it can do. The long-term success rate is not high. Achieving a durable success requires the effective integration of the political use of force with other policy instruments. Second, their study measures the utility of using force: Did it accomplish the goals officially put forward by U.S. policy makers? It did not address the wisdom of using force for political purposes. For each political use of force, the question of wisdom must be answered both for the ends sought and for the tactics used. Should the United States have sent peacekeeping troops to Lebanon? Should U.S. planes have been used to evacuate "Baby Doc" Duvalier from Haiti and Ferdinand Marcos from the Philippines? Should carriers be sent into the Gulf of Sidra? Should frequent large-scale training exercises be held with the Honduran army? Were the goals behind these actions legitimate? Could they have been accomplished more effectively by other means? And, looking to Kosovo, we might ask: When is the use of force counterproductive? Can air power alone achieve diplomatic goals?

Assessing the utility of arms transfers depends on the type of trade-offs that one is willing to make. A first set deals with one's time frame: Are the short-term economic, diplomatic, or military benefits of an arms transfer worth the possible negative long-term impact on regional stability or arms control efforts that might also result? A second trade-off involves prioritizing values. It is in this area that the Carter administration had its greatest failing. In its policy statements the Carter administration was a staunch advocate of human rights. Yet its policy decisions demonstrated a willingness to selectively sacrifice human rights in the name of national security.

NOTES

1. David Baldwin, *Economic Statecraft* (Princeton, N.J.: Princeton University Press, 1985), especially pp. 8–28.
2. Fred Ikle, *How Nations Negotiate* (New York: Harper & Row, 1964), p. ix.
3. Holly J. Burkhalter, "The 'Costs' of Human Rights," *The World Policy Journal*, 11 (1994), pp. 39–49.
4. "Oversight of the State Department's Country Reports on Human Rights Practices for 1993 and U.S. Human Rights Policy," *Hearings, Committee on Foreign Affairs, House of Representatives*, February 1 and May 10, 1994 (Washington, D.C.: U.S. Government Printing Office, 1994).
5. Peter J. Spiro, "New Global Communities: Nongovernmental Organizations in International Decision-Making Institutions," *The Washington Quarterly*, 18 (1994), 45–56.
6. Margaret P. Karns and Karen A. Mingst (eds.), *The United States and Multilateral Institutions: Patterns of Changing Instrumentality and Influence* (Boston: Unwin Hyman, 1990).
7. David P. Forsythe, "The United States, the United Nations, and Human Rights," in Karns and Mingst (eds.), *The United States and Multilateral Institutions*, pp. 261–86.
8. For references to the positive contributions of summitry, see Robert Putnam, "Summit Sense," *Foreign Policy*, 55 (1984), 73–91.
9. For a discussion of the negative contributions of summitry, see J. Robert Schaetzel and H. B. Malmgren, "Talking Heads," *Foreign Policy*, 39 (1980), 130–42.
10. Ibid., p. 138, for the case of economic summits; see the discussion in Strobe Talbot, *Deadly Gambits* (New York: Vintage, 1984), for examples from arms control talks.
11. Adam B. Ulam, *Dangerous Relations: The Soviet Union in World Politics, 1970–1982* (New York: Oxford University Press, 1983), p. 186.
12. Richard Nixon, "Superpower Summitry," *Foreign Affairs*, 64 (1985), 1–11.

13. For a review of U.S.-Soviet summit conferences, see the various references in James E. Dougherty and Robert L. Pfaltzgraff, *American Foreign Policy from FDR to Reagan* (New York: Harper & Row, 1985).

14. George de Menil, "The Process of Economic Summitry," in George de Menil and Anthony M. Solomon, (eds.), *Economic Summitry* (New York: Council on Foreign Relations, 1983), pp. 55–63.

15. Putnam, "Summit Sense."

16. Richard Schifter, "The Conference on Cooperation and Security in Europe: Ancient History or New Opportunities," *The Washington Quarterly,* 16 (1993), 121–29.

17. Richard Elliot Benedick, *Ozone Diplomacy: New Directions in Safeguarding the Planet* (Cambridge, Mass.: Harvard University Press, 1991).

18. Quoted in Michael Weisskopf, "Behind the Curve in Rio," *The Washington Post,* July 11, 1992, p. 1.

19. Barry M. Blechman and Stephen S. Kaplan, *Force Without War: U.S. Armed Forces as a Political Instrument* (Washington, D.C.: Brookings, 1978).

20. Alexander George and Richard Smoke, *Deterrence in American Foreign Policy: Theory and Practice* (New York: Columbia University Press, 1974).

21. For background data on arms transfers, their history, the policies of specific states, and a discussion of their rationale, see Stephanie G. Neuman and Robert E. Harkavy (eds.), *Arms Transfers in the Modern World* (New York: Praeger, 1980); Andrew J. Pierre, *The Global Politics of Arms Sales* (Princeton, N.J.: Princeton University Press, 1982); and Michael T. Klare, *American Arms Supermarket* (Austin: University of Texas Press, 1984).

22. Richard H. Wilcox, "Twixt Cup and Lip: Some Problems in Applying Arms Control," in Neuman and Harkavy, *Arms Transfers,* p. 32.

23. Edward Kolodiej, "Arms Transfers and International Politics: The Interdependence of Independence," in Newman and Harkavy, *Arms Transfer,* p. 3.

24. Klare, *American Arms Supermarket,* pp. 43–44.

25. William D. Hartung, "Welcome to the U.S. Arms Superstore," *The Bulletin of the Atomic Scientists,* 49 (September 1993), 20–26.

26. Gilbert R. Winham, "Negotiation as a Management Process," *World Politics,* 30 (1977), 87–114.

CHAPTER

14 Covert Action

Covert action seeks results by altering the internal balance of power in a foreign state. No instrument of foreign policy is more controversial or difficult to control. As the Tower Commission stated in its report, "Covert action places a great strain on the process of decision making in a free society."[1] Writing in a similar vein, two scholars who have studied the CIA extensively assert that there are only two legitimate reasons to carry out covert action: (1) when open knowledge of U.S. responsibility would make the operation infeasible and (2) to avoid retaliation or to control the potential for escalation.[2]

In popular usage covert action is all but synonymous with paramilitary undertakings. This is not the case. A number of different activities fall within its definitional boundaries. A list of key terms central to the techniques of covert action is presented in Table 14–1. Accompanying these definitions is a list of recent U.S. foreign policy initiatives in which they have been employed. In the next section we place these efforts in a broader historical context. The discussion of examples is not exhaustive but only meant to illustrate the range of situations in which covert action has been employed. Following that, congressional efforts to control the CIA are reviewed.

U.S. covert action predates the CIA but until recently official histories of U.S. foreign policy largely were silent on it. This has begun to change. In 1994 the State Department's official history of U.S.–Indonesian relations noted how President Eisenhower approved a covert operation to support anticommunist rebels in a plan that bore similarities to the later Bay of Pigs operation against Castro. When it became clear that the anticommunist rebels would fail, Eisenhower changed direction and threw U.S. support to the Indonesian military in an effort to lessen the power of the Indonesian communist party and President Sukarno. In 1995 the CIA organized a conference at which it made public previously secret material on its role in the 1954 overthrow of the Arbenz government in Guatemala. Material released in 1997 revealed that the CIA had considered assassinating President Jacobo Arbenz. It had a "hit list" of 58 targets and had trained individuals for the job. No assassinations were carried out.

The first forays into covert action were taken during World War II and were carried out by the Office of Strategic Services (OSS). They tended to be paramilitary in nature and were designed to bring the war to the enemy behind its front lines.[3] In the early postwar period, the rapidly deteriorating U.S.–Soviet relationship in Europe led to a renewed interest in covert action and the creation of a permanent covert action capability within the CIA. Roughly speaking,

TABLE 14–1   Types of Covert Action, with Recent Examples

Type of Covert Action	Recent Example
Clandestine support for individuals and organizations (training, financing, technical advice, etc.)	Anti-Khomeini exiles in France; pro-Western forces in El Salvador; training for Thai military for heroin raids
Propaganda involves making use of print media, radio, TV, news services to influence perceptions on events taking place	Misleading reports picked up in U.S. news media that Qaddafi was planning new round of terrorism and hinting at U.S. military action
Economic operations designed to disrupt economy of target state	Mining of Nicaraguan harbors
Paramilitary operations involve furnishing secret military assistance and guidance to unconventional and conventional foreign forces	Aid to Contras, Afghan rebels, pro-U.S. forces in Angola
Assassination	CIA production of psychological warfare manual in Nicaragua which contained passages that have been interpreted to call for assassination. Reported effort to target Qaddafi in Libyan bombing raid

the period of the Eisenhower administration coincides with the heyday of U.S. covert action.[4] In the 1960s covert action produced a mixed pattern of successes and failures. The Bay of Pigs was a disaster, but the CIA followed with successes in Laos, the Congo, and Chile. The 1970s saw a dramatic reversal in fortunes. Sparked by revelations before the Church Committee, a firestorm of opposition came down on the CIA. More efforts were made to tightly limit and control covert action undertakings. A former chief of the CIA's Covert Action Staff who is an advocate of its continued use lamented that during the 1970s covert action was rapidly becoming a "dying art form."[5] In the Carter administration, propaganda and media operations made up the bulk of covert action undertakings. Only one or two major covert action programs (that is, ones costing $5 to $7 million or designed to overthrow a government) were reported to the congressional intelligence committees. In the Reagan administration's first term, this number jumped to seven or eight per year. The increase in the number of paramilitary covert operations has its roots in the Reagan Doctrine, which calls for assisting groups fighting governments aligned with the Soviet Union. Undertakings in progress in 1985 included support for the Afghan rebels; the Contras in Nicaragua; and anti-Qaddafi forces; pro-Western forces in El Salvador; anti-Khomeini Iranian exiles in Turkey and France; training for Thai military forces for raids against heroin production and processing centers; a joint operation with China to supply arms to the forces of former Cambodian ruler Pol Pot in their struggle with the Hanoi-supported Cambodian government; and training, arming, and financing for military forces in Ethiopia, Angola, and the Sudan.[6] President Bush approved his first covert action campaign (a $10 million propaganda campaign directed at Noriega) in his second month in office. In 1990 the three most politically sensitive covert action programs were those in Cambodia ($10 million); Angola ($50 million); and Afghanistan ($300–400 million).

TECHNIQUES OF COVERT ACTION

The most common form of covert action is the clandestine support for individuals and organizations. This support takes many forms (financial, technical, training) and can be directed at many targets (politicians, labor leaders, journalists, unions, political parties, church groups, professional associations). This form of covert action was the major focus of CIA efforts in France, Italy, and West Germany in the immediate postwar era.[7] Between 1948 and 1968 the CIA spent over $65 million in Italy on these types of programs, and in 1976 President Ford approved $6 million in secret subsidies for anticommunist forces in the upcoming election. In his 1987 book, *VEIL, The Secret Wars of the CIA, 1981–1987,* Bob Woodward reveals that DCI William Casey arranged for Saudi Arabia to supply $2 million for the May 1985 Italian election. CIA clandestine support programs were so prevalent that a former CIA station chief testified to a Senate committee that "any aspiring politician would come to the CIA to see if we could help him get elected."[8]

A widely publicized case of CIA clandestine support involved efforts to block the election of Salvador Allende.[9] These efforts succeeded in 1958 and 1964 but failed in 1970. Between 1964 and 1969 the CIA spent almost $2 million on training anticommunist organizers among Chilean peasants and slum dwellers. It spent $3 million on the 1964 election and almost $1 million on the 1970 election. Allende won a plurality of the vote in 1970, and according to Chilean law and custom, he would be selected as the next president by the Chilean Congress. The United States unsuccessfully sought to block his selection through a two-track policy. Track I was approved by the 40 Committee, the NSC committee charged with oversight of CIA covert operations. Track II was kept secret from it. In track I the CIA was ordered to engage in political, economic, and propaganda tactics to influence political events. As part of this plan, $25,000 was authorized (but never spent) to bribe members of the Chilean Congress.

Another form of clandestine support is the provision of security assistance and intelligence training to foreign governments. Third world leaders are particularly responsive to offers of training and equipment to help them combat potential coups, terrorist attacks, and assassination attempts. These operations cost between $300,000 and $1 million and are often carried out by as few as three or four people. According to Woodward's book, 12 leaders received such assistance from the CIA in 1983. Numbered among them were President Hissene Habre of Chad, President Mohammed Zia ul-Haq of Pakistan, Samuel Doe of Liberia, Philippine President Ferdinand Marcos, and President Amin Gemayel of Lebanon. Another example of covert assistance was "Project X." This was a U.S. military training program in Latin America and elsewhere that included instruction on clandestine activity against domestic political adversaries. Documents indicate that the operation was probably shut down in the early 1980s.

A second category of covert action is propaganda. The CIA has used a number of techniques for dispensing its propaganda. One of the most primitive involved using balloons.[10] In an effort to exploit dissatisfaction and increase the internal unrest in China in the early cold-war era, the CIA loaded balloons with an assortment of leaflets, pamphlets, and newspapers. Reagan and Bush approved clandestine radio propaganda operations against Noriega. Neither effort was particularly successful. Press accounts characterized the former effort as "half-hearted" and the latter as "inept."

The best known covert radio broadcasting systems were Radio Free Europe (RFE—directed at Eastern Europe) and Radio Liberty (directed at the Soviet Union). During its early years both stations took a militant, anticommunist line. The tone of their broadcasts changed after the 1956 Hungarian invasion. Critics contended that RFE broadcasts gave the distinct and misleading impression that the United States would support the efforts of the freedom fighters when no such intention existed. Radio Free Asia, which broadcast to China from 1951 to 1955, and AIP, a radio news agency that produced programs and sent them free to over 100 small Latin American and Central American radio stations, are other notable radio systems that have been used for propaganda. At its peak the CIA's propaganda assets numbered over 800 news and public information organizations and individuals. This number reportedly included some 36 American newspaper people.[11]

A third category of covert action involves economic operations. As we have already seen, economic operations were an integral part of the CIA's efforts to stop Allende. The economy was a major target of track I activity. The general goal given to the CIA's economic program was "to make the economy scream." U.S. multinational corporations were approached and asked to cut off credits and the shipment of spare parts to Chile. Covert CIA economic and political activity did not stop with Allende's inauguration.

According to one account, comparatively few economic operations have been undertaken by the CIA, and they have not been very successful.[12] The available evidence suggests that the most persistent target of CIA covert economic operations has been Castro's Cuba. One of the most famous programs that has come to light is Operation Mongoose.[13] Authorized by President Kennedy in November 1961, it was designed to "use our available assets . . . to help Cuba overthrow the communist regime." The first act of covert economic sabotage was to have been the demolition of a railroad yard and bridge that would have been made to look like an inside job. This plan was called off when the saboteurs were spotted approaching Cuba by boat. The CIA did have its successes. It succeeded in getting European shippers to turn down Cuban delivery orders and a German firm to agree to send off-center bearings to Cuba, and British buses destined for Cuba were sabotaged on the docks. In 1962 the CIA successfully contaminated a shipment of Cuban sugar destined for the Soviet Union while the ship was docked for repairs in Puerto Rico.

Operation Mongoose was canceled in January 1963, but covert economic operations against Cuba continued. For example, CIA-financed commandos set fire to an 8,000-gallon oil tank and attacked a copper mine. In June 1963 Kennedy authorized a stepped-up program of sabotage, and in October 1963 13 sabotage operations were approved. They too were to be carried out by CIA-financed commandos. Included in the target list were an electric power plant and a sugar mill. In 1969 and 1970 the CIA directed a program of weather modification against Cuba's sugar crop with the hope of producing rain over nonagricultural areas, leaving the cane fields parched. The CIA has also been charged with infecting Cuban pig herds with an African swine flu virus. The result was a serious shortage of pork, which is a staple in the Cuban diet. The United Nations Food and Agricultural Organization labeled the outbreak the "most alarming event of the year" and had no explanation for why it happened.

The fourth category of covert action involves paramilitary undertakings. A former practitioner defines paramilitary operations as the furnishing of covert military assistance and guidance to unconventional and conventional foreign forces and organizations. He argues it represents a highly valuable "third option" between sending in the Marines and doing nothing.[14] Initially, these operations were targeted against the Soviet Union and its Eastern European satellite states.[15] Almost uniformly, they were failures. Numbered among them were efforts to support resistance fighters in the Ukraine (the program ended with their defeat by the Soviet army); an effort to establish an underground apparatus for espionage and revolution in Poland (only after several years did it become clear that the Polish secret service had coopted the network and was using it to acquire gold and capture anticommunist Poles); and an effort to overthrow the Albanian government (virtually every mission failed, and it later became known that Kim Philby, the British intelligence officer in charge of the mission, was a Soviet agent).

As the 1950s progressed, the more significant CIA paramilitary operations were taking place in the third world. In 1953, the United States and Great Britain undertook a joint venture, Operation AJAX, to bring down the government of Iranian Prime Minister Mohammed Mossadegh.[16] After coming into power in 1951, Mossadegh quickly established himself as the dominant figure in Iranian politics. By 1953, his power eclipsed that of the Shah, who fled into exile. The United States strongly objected to Mossadegh's antiwestern policies, and in particular it opposed the 1951 nationalization of the Anglo-Iranian Oil Company. When the Army proved unable to remove him from power, covert action was deemed necessary. The coup itself involved two stages. First, a propaganda campaign stressed the likelihood of communist takeover if Mossadegh remained in power. Second, the CIA organized pro-Shah street gangs and supported them with knives, clubs, and an occasional rifle. Mossadegh fled when his followers were unable to control the subsequent street demonstrations and rioting. With Mossadegh gone the Shah returned, his rule more dependent than ever on U.S. support.

In 1954 the CIA helped bring down the Arbenz government in Guatemala.[17] Jacobo Arbenz took office in 1950 and set out on the path of social reform and modernization. The Truman administration's initial response was one of moderate opposition that relied heavily on economic sanctions. By the end of Truman's administration, some were convinced that covert action in collaboration with neighboring pro-U.S. dictatorships was necessary. In 1953 Eisenhower approved such a plan (PB/SUCCESS). As was the case with Iran, the paramilitary operation itself was relatively small in scale, and it was preceded by a propaganda campaign. The acknowledged key to PB/SUCCESS was convincing Arbenz that the opposition forces would defeat his forces. Arbenz was to be frightened into accepting a *fait accompli*.

As the 1950s ended, so too did the string of CIA successes. In 1958 it supported an unsuccessful coup against President Sukarno of Indonesia. A still greater embarrassment came in 1961 with the Bay of Pigs invasion of Cuba. Originally conceived during the Eisenhower administration, the plan was approved by Kennedy in April 1961. Later that month a brigade of some 1,400 Cuban exiles was put ashore in Cuba where it was expected to link up with Cuban opposition forces and topple the Castro regime. Everything went wrong. On the first day of the invasion, two of the four supply and ammunition ships were sunk, and the other two fled. On the second day the brigade was surrounded by 20,000 well-armed and loyal Cuban soldiers. On the third day the 1,200 surviving members of the invasion force surrendered. Almost two years later most were released in exchange for $53 million in food and drugs.

The Bay of Pigs put a temporary dent into Washington's fascination with paramilitary covert action programs, but it did not put an end to them. By the mid-1970s a controversial covert paramilitary operation was under way in Angola.[18] A 1974 coup in Portugal signaled the beginning of the end of Portuguese colonial rule in Africa. In January 1975 agreement among the three rival independence movements in Angola led to the creation of a coalition transitional government that would rule Angola until elections were held in October. Angola's independence was to be officially realized in November. The United States threw its support to an alliance between the National Front for the Liberation of Angola (FLNA) under the leadership of Holden Roberto and the National Union for the Total Independence of Angola (UNITA) led by Jonas Savimbi.

Covert operations began almost immediately. Seven days after the agreement to establish a transitional government was reached, the CIA was authorized to pay $300,000 to the FNLA, traditionally the most aggressive and warlike of the independence movements. In February the FNLA was encouraged by the United States and President Mobutu of neighboring Zaire to move its forces from Zaire into Angola and attack the MPLA. Shortly thereafter, the Soviet Union reentered the picture. It had given aid to the MPLA in the early 70s but had stopped in 1973. Now, in March 1975, in response to Chinese and U.S. aid to the UNITA-FNLA alliance, it resumed shipments of aid to the MPLA. The CIA was informing U.S. policy makers that the MPLA would triumph unless there was a considerable escalation in the U.S. commitment. The reason for this pessimism was the arrival of a small number of Cuban advisers to aid the MPLA and the expectation that they would be followed by large numbers of well-trained Cuban regulars. As predicted, this occurred, and in November 2,800 Cubans arrived in Angola.

It was in the last stages of the fighting that the depth of the CIA's involvement became known. The CIA maintained that no U.S. personnel were directly involved in the fighting. The CIA pictured its role only as one of resupplying Mobutu and said it was he who was sending aid to the UNITA-FNLA forces. In reality funds were being sent directly to Angolan forces, and CIA personnel were in Angola to help manage the war. Many in Congress expressed concern over the escalating U.S. involvement in Angola. Congress as a whole reacted angrily to these disclosures. In December 1975 it passed the Tunney Amendment, which forbade spending funds from the FY1976 Defense Appropriations Bill on Angola. In 1976 it placed additional limitations on the CIA by passing the Clark Amendment, which forbade spending funds from any source "for any activities involving Angola directly or indirectly."

Pressures for a renewed U.S. involvement in Angola began to build as U.S.–Soviet relations deteriorated. For Secretary of State Alexander Haig and others in the new Reagan administration, the introduction of Cubans into Angola marked a major turning point in Soviet adventurism in the third world, and it required a U.S. response even at this late date. The first real opportunity to do so came in 1985 when Congress repealed the Clark Amendment. No immediate U.S. reinvolvement occurred because in spite of its rhetoric the Reagan administration initially was divided on how to proceed, and Congress was also unsure of what to do next.

In the 1980s, the most controversial of the CIA's paramilitary programs was its Nicaraguan operation. The impetus for CIA involvement in Nicaragua lay with evidence collected in the late 1970s that the Sandinista government was increasing its shipments of arms to El Salvadoran rebels, intensifying pressure on domestic opposition forces, and becoming the site of a substantial Cuban-backed military buildup. The Carter administration responded to these events with economic sanctions. They were continued by the Reagan administration but had little impact. In 1981 the Reagan administration authorized a $19.5 million program of covert action to stop the flow of arms to El Salvador. By November 1981 the program's goals expanded to include creating an anti-Sandinista force that might effectively challenge the "Cuban support structure in Nicaragua."[19] The CIA's paramilitary program has had its successes. It is credited with having slowed down the shipment of arms to El Salvador and with hampering Sandinista offenses in 1983 and 1984. It has also been the object of intense criticism. In particular, Congress became concerned with the scope of the CIA's program compared to the program of action that it had earlier agreed to fund. As a result, in 1982 it passed the Boland Amendment which forbade funding the Contras for the purpose of overthrowing the Nicaraguan government. In 1984 renewed questions were raised over the mining of Nicaraguan harbors and the CIA-sponsored production of a psychological warfare manual that could be interpreted as calling for assassination. This time Congress responded by cutting off all funding for the Contras. This measure was partially lifted in 1985 when Congress voted to allow sending humanitarian aid to the Contras, but it continued to forbid the spending of CIA funds. For 1986 these restrictions were further loosened when Congress allowed the CIA to supply communication and intelligence to the Contras, but it still prohibited direct or indirect military participation in the struggle. A new twist was added to the paramilitary operation when it became known that in spite of the 1985 and 1986 congressional bans on direct military assistance, NSC staffer Lieutenant Colonel Oliver North had been deeply involved in orchestrating Contra operations and in securing foreign and private funds for them.

The largest, and in some eyes the most successful, third world paramilitary covert operation program run by the CIA was in Afghanistan. In FY1985 the CIA spent about $250 million, or more than 80 percent of its covert action budget, helping the Afghan guerrillas evict Soviet forces. In FY1989, after the Soviet Union had withdrawn, the CIA was still spending $100 million on the Afghan operation. The Afghan paramilitary operation is also significant because for the first time, the CIA was authorized to send "made in America" weapons to forces it was supporting. Until then, adherence to the doctrine of "plausible denial" had blocked such transfers. This 1986 decision to send Stinger missiles to the Afghan guerrillas is widely credited with being a decisive turning point in that conflict. Those who question the wisdom of supporting the Afghan rebels point to the current problems produced by these very Stinger missile sales.[20] Concerned with the military problems these missiles create for any future deployment of U.S. forces in the Middle East, the United States has tried with little success to buy them back. An even broader problem exists. Many of the Afghan rebels are now fighting as volunteers in other conflicts involving the Islamic cause. Others have become members of terrorist groups such as that responsible for the bombing of the World Trade Center in New York. Moreover, the political and economic conditions inside Afghanistan remain oppressive, with the result that terrorist groups are likely to continue to find new recruits there.

A final form of covert action involves the assassination of foreign leaders. The existence of a unit for the planning of "special operations" can be traced back to the earliest days of the CIA.[21] By all accounts no actual assassination operations or planning was ever done by it, but suggestions for assassination were put forward. By 1961, another CIA unit had been established for "disabling" foreign leaders, including assassination as a last resort. A former CIA official has stated that between 1959 and 1962 the White House, NSC, and CIA all talked seriously of killing foreign leaders.[22] In 1972 following the kidnapping and assassination of Chilean General Rene Schneider, DCI Richard Helms issued a directive banning assassinations. This ban has since been included in the presidential executive orders setting forth guidelines for CIA behavior.

Controversy over the meaning of the prohibition on assassination has resurfaced recently. During the Reagan administration questions were raised about CIA sponsorship of a psychological warfare manual in Nicaragua that could be read as endorsing assassination and about the real purpose of the bombing raid on Libyan leader Qaddafi's headquarters.[23] In 1990 just prior to the invasion of Panama, President Bush authorized a $3 million covert action plan to overthrow Noriega. The plan was controversial because it acknowledged the possibility that Noriega might be killed "indirectly" because of the operation. At the time the Bush administration was under widespread criticism for its performance in a failed October coup. In defending itself, the administration argued that the existing ban on any involvement in actions that could lead to the assassination of a foreign leader had prevented it from acting in a decisive fashion.

The most thorough investigation into U.S. involvements in assassination plots was carried out by the Church Committee. It investigated five cases of alleged U.S. involvement:

Cuba	Fidel Castro
Congo (Zaire)	Patrice Lumumba
Dominican Republic	Rafael Trujillo
Chile	General Rene Schneider
South Vietnam	Ngo Dinh Diem

The committee concluded that only the Castro and Lumumba cases involved plots conceived by the United States to kill foreign leaders. In the

Trujillo case the United States did not initiate the plot, but it did aid dissidents whose aims were known to include assassinating Trujillo. In the Diem case some U.S. officials sought his removal from office, but there is no indication that these officials sought his death. General Schneider's death is linked to the track II policy of the Nixon administration, which was designed to spark an anti-Allende military coup. In the Congo it appears that events overtook U.S. policy and nullified U.S. plans to assassinate Lumumba. U.S. authorities had authorized Lumumba's assassination in the fall of 1960, and CIA officers in the Congo urged his "permanent disposal." Toxic substances had been selected as the method for Lumumba's assassination. CIA planning went so far as to send vials of poison to the CIA's Léopoldville station for an assassination attempt. Led by Lumumba and Joseph Kasavubu, the Congo declared its independence from Belgium in June 1960. Shortly thereafter, Lumumba threatened to invite Soviet forces to the Congo if Belgium did not speed up its withdrawal. By mid-September Soviet troops were present in that portion of the Congo under Lumumba's control. Later that month, Lumumba was the loser in a power struggle with Kasavubu and Joseph Mobuto. In December Lumumba was captured by Mobutu's forces and placed under the custody of local authorities known to be hostile to him. Several weeks later, his death was announced. It appears that the CIA knew the likely consequences of Lumumba's capture but was not involved in the assassination.

The Church Committee found concrete evidence of at least eight CIA plots to assassinate Castro between 1960 and 1965. One former CIA official characterized these efforts as ranging from "the vague to the weird."[24] Proposed assassination devices included arranging an "accident," poison cigars, poison pills, poison pens, placing deadly bacterial powder in Castro's scuba-diving suit, and rigging a seashell to explode while Castro was scuba-diving. While most of these approaches never went beyond the planning stage, some were attempted. Twice poison pills were sent to Cuba, and on another occasion weapons and other assassination devices were provided to a Cuban dissident.

Post–Cold War Covert Action

Covert action programs have not disappeared with the end of the cold war. Two of the most "public" covert actions have taken place in Bosnia and Iraq. Bosnia constitutes a gray-area case. In 1994 and 1995 the Bosnian government survived largely due to the illegal flow of weapons from Iran. In 1992 U.S. officials learned that this was occurring in defiance of a UN embargo on weapons shipments to Bosnia and Serbia but made no effort to stop it in spite of Clinton's public support for the UN arms embargo. According to the DCI, R. James Woolsey, the CIA was ready to undertake a covert operation of its own in support of the Muslim-led Bosnian government at the time. Congressional critics of Clinton's Bosnia policy were outraged that they had not been told of the arms shipments and claimed Clinton was legally required to do so. Woolsey, speaking after resigning as DCI and in opposition to the plan, asserted that permitting the arms shipments was unwise but not illegal and that Congress did not have to be informed. It could only be seen as a U.S. covert action if American personnel had actively participated in its planning or conduct.

The CIA ran a "cold war"–style operation against Saddam Hussein between 1992–1996. The goal was to remove him from power by encouraging a military coup and reducing his control over Iraq's outlying regions such as Iraqi Kurdistan. The cost of the program is estimated to have approached $100 million. Included in the funding was support for a clandestine radio station in Jordan that blanketed Iraq with anti-Saddam Hussein propaganda. Little was achieved. In June 1996 Saddam Hussein arrested and executed more than one hundred Iraqi dissidents and military officers associated with the CIA plan. Political infighting among Kurdish leaders further crippled CIA efforts to remove him from power.

CONGRESS AND THE CIA

A discussion of covert action as an instrument of foreign policy is incomplete without examining the problem of control. In this section we examine how Congress has interacted with the CIA. Not only do we follow the changing pattern of relations between the two institutions, but we also evaluate Congress's use of its legislative, budgetary, and oversight powers. Loch Johnson, who served as assistant to the chairperson of the Senate Intelligence Committee and as staff director of the Oversight Committee of the House Intelligence Committee, divides congressional–CIA relations into three periods.[25] From 1947 to 1974 there existed an Era of Trust. The second period, 1974 to 1976, was an Era of Skepticism. A third period, that of an Uneasy Partnership, existed from 1976 to 1989. We are now in a fourth period where Congress acts as an impatient overseer.

Era of Trust

During the Era of Trust, there was little, if any, meaningful congressional control over the CIA. Congressional reluctance to investigate the CIA had many roots. In part it was due to the climate of the times. A national consensus existed on the need to combat communism, and the CIA was an important tool in this effort. Many also felt that command of the CIA was exclusively an executive function and that congressional oversight ran against the principle of separation of powers. Finally, there was the feeling that Congress lacked the necessary information to exercise a voice in the area of intelligence oversight and that efforts to obtain the necessary information would jeopardize the secrecy vital to the success of intelligence operations.

According to the 1947 National Security Act which created it, the CIA is empowered to do the following:

1. Advise the National Security Council (NSC) on intelligence matters related to national security
2. Make recommendations to the NSC for coordinating the intelligence activities of government agencies and departments
3. Correlate, evaluate, and disseminate intelligence within the government

4. Perform additional services for existing intelligence agencies which the NSC believes can be done best by a central organization

5. Perform other functions and duties relating to national security intelligence as directed by the NSC

Commentators stress three points about this list of functions. First, nowhere is there a specific reference to covert action. The CIA was essentially seen as an intelligence-processing organization. Only by referring to the phrase *other functions and duties* can covert action be justified. Second, there is no reference to intelligence-collection activities, clandestine or otherwise. Third, by writing the legislation in this manner, Congress established only the broadest statement of permissible CIA activities. Statutory limits on the CIA were loosened even further with the passage of the 1949 amendments to the National Security Act. Among its provisions were exemptions from civil service regulations in the hiring and firing of personnel and permission for the director of Central Intelligence (DCI) to spend money from CIA appropriations on his own authority.

In place of detailed statutory guidelines, a body of "para laws" were developed to guide CIA activity. According to Robert Borosage, para laws are internal bureaucratic directives that give the appearance of providing legal regulations but are put into effect without the participation of Congress.[26] Collectively, these directives came to be known as the CIA's secret charter, and it was not until 1973 that Congress was given access to them. The CIA is not alone in its reliance on para laws. The National Security Agency was established and its duties laid out by a secret presidential directive, and the Defense Intelligence Agency was established on the authority of the Secretary of Defense.

During this period the congressional appropriations process served to protect the CIA more than restrain it. Beginning in 1949 congressional oversight committees were informed about CIA covert operations and regularly approved funding for them. The actual figures involved were not revealed to the whole Congress, and CIA funds were concealed in the budgets of other departments, especially that of the Defense Department. The fiction of congressional budgetary control came to the forefront in 1971. Senator Stuart Symington introduced an amendment placing a $4 billion limit on intelligence spending governmentwide. His proposal was defeated, but in the course of the debate, he asked Senator Alan Ellender, chairperson of the Senate Appropriations CIA Subcommittee, if the committee had approved funding a 36,000-man "secret" CIA army in Laos. Ellender replied, "I did not know anything about it. . . . I never asked. . . . It never dawned on me to ask about it. I did see it published in the newspaper some time ago."[27]

Oversight of the CIA formally fell upon subcommittees of the House and Senate Appropriations and Armed Services committees. In the 1960s the Senate combined its oversight committees into one body under the chairpersonship of Senator Richard Russell. Frequently, Russell was the only legislator whom the CIA reported to on intelligence matters. Significantly, the Senate Foreign Relations Committee and the House Foreign Affairs Committee were not involved in the oversight process. When oversight did occur, it took place largely on the CIA's terms. Ray Cline, formerly a deputy director for intelligence in the CIA, notes that the very terms used to describe these meetings captured the essence of what took place.[28] They were *briefings* and not *hearings*. Congressional overseers were there to *learn*, not to *restrict* or *monitor*.

Conflicting accounts are found about the quality of CIA oversight in this period. Allen Dulles, DCI from 1953 to 1961, stated that he never cut off a question with the response that "we don't want to talk about this." Yet at the same time comments by senators suggest less than thorough oversight. Leverett Saltonstall, a supporter of the CIA, observed: "It is not a question of reluctance on the part of CIA officials to speak to us. Instead it is a question of our reluctance . . . to seek information and knowledge on subjects which I personally . . . would rather not have."[29]

Not everyone in Congress was pleased with these arrangements. Between 1947 and 1975 over 200 resolutions were introduced for the purpose of improving congressional oversight. Few ever emerged from committee. The first significant attempt to reform the structure of congressional oversight came in 1956. Senator Mike Mansfield introduced a measure calling for the establishment of a joint committee on the CIA. The committee would be kept "fully and currently informed" by the CIA and would have a mandate to investigate the activities of the CIA, look into problems related to gathering intelligence, and examine the coordination and utilization of intelligence by all government departments. The bill was reported out of the Senate Foreign Relations Committee by a vote of 8 to 1 and was introduced on the floor of the Senate with 34 co-sponsors.

Supporters of the Mansfield proposal stressed four points.[30] First, oversight in the area of atomic energy by a joint committee had worked, and this proposal called for a committee along the same lines. Second, a special committee on intelligence would promote confidence between the CIA and Congress. Third, ad hoc studies of the CIA were not enough. Fourth, notwithstanding problems created by the need for secrecy, congressional oversight of intelligence was necessary. Opponents contended that the parallels being drawn between the CIA and the Atomic Energy Commission were flawed, that existing surveillance mechanisms were adequate, and that the proposal raised questions about the separation of powers. The Mansfield proposal was defeated 59 to 27, with 14 co-sponsors voting no. The Senate leadership and those serving on the existing oversight committees unanimously opposed the proposal.

The issue of congressional oversight did not become a major issue again until 1966 when Senator Eugene McCarthy introduced a resolution calling upon the Foreign Relations Committee, a committee on which he served, to undertake a "full and complete study with respect to the effects of the operations and actions of the CIA upon the foreign relations of the United States." Opposition came from members of the Senate Armed Services Committee who saw the proposal as an effort to "muscle in" on their jurisdiction. While this effort also failed, McCarthy's attempt to change the structure of CIA oversight was not without some impact. Beginning in 1967 Russell did "invite" three members of the Foreign Relations Committee to sit in on CIA oversight hearings. This practice continued under his successor, John Stennis. It ended, as did the oversight sessions themselves, when Fulbright and Symington, two of the three Foreign Relations Committee members sitting in on these briefings, became outspoken in their opposition to the war in Vietnam and CIA activities. No Senate oversight hearings at all were held in 1971 or 1972.

Era of Skepticism

Beginning in 1974 Congress's attitude toward the intelligence community began to change. One factor prompting the new outlook was a series of revelations about CIA wrongdoing and excess. The two most publicized ones implicated the CIA in a destabilization campaign directed at bringing down the Socialist government of Salvador Allende in Chile and allegations that the CIA had violated its charter by undertaking surveillance of U.S. citizens inside the United States.

The first indication of the changed congressional mood was passage of the Hughes–Ryan Amendment to the 1974 Foreign Assistance Act. It required that except under exceptional circumstances the CIA inform members of six congressional committees "in a timely fashion of the nature and scope of any CIA operation conducted for purposes other than obtaining information." According to the terms of the Hughes–Ryan Amendment, the president was also required to make a "finding" that each covert operation is important to national security. Presidential findings have included such information as the time and duration of the activity, the risks involved, funding restrictions, the relationship to prior NSC decisions, policy considerations, and the origin of the proposal.[31] This has not always meant that Congress has been well informed by the presidential finding. The presidential finding for the Iran arms transfers carried out by the NSC was signed after the operation began, and DCI Casey was instructed not to inform Congress. It is presented in Box 14–1. The 1975 presidential finding supporting U.S. activities in Angola was so vague that only Africa was identified as the location of the operation. The stated purpose was to provide "material, support, and advice to moderate nationalist movements for their use in creating a stable climate in order to allow genuine self determination."[32]

The House and Senate also created temporary select committees to investigate the intelligence community. The two committees adopted different operating styles and sets of concerns. The Senate Select Committee on Intelligence was chaired by Frank Church. Its investigations focused on unmasking illegal and questionable CIA activities. Among the subjects examined were CIA mail openings, CIA activity in Chile, illegal communication intercepts by the National Security Agency, covert action, and assassination attempts. In pursuing these subjects, the committee sought the cooperation of the executive branch, held most of its hearings in closed sessions, and relied on intensive staff investigations in reaching its conclusions. The House Select Committee on Intelligence, chaired by Otis Pike, focused its investigation on management and organizational issues. One topic it devoted considerable time to was intelligence failures.

Whereas the Church Committee concentrated on dealing with middle-level bureaucrats in conducting its investigation, the Pike Committee focused on senior-level policy makers, and instead of cooperation its relations with the executive branch were characterized by confrontation.[33] In the end the House committee's unruly behavior resulted in the House's refusal to publish its final report because it contained information still classified as secret. All told, the Church and Pike committees offered over 100 recommendations, and in spite of their different approaches, they tended to agree on many points. Most significantly, neither

BOX 14–1   Presidential Finding on CIA Involvement in Arms Shipments to Iran

I hereby find that the following operation in a foreign country (including all support necessary to such operation) is important to the national security of the United States, and due to its extreme sensitivity and security risks, I determine it is essential to limit prior notice, and direct the Director of Central Intelligence to refrain from reporting this Finding to the Congress as provided in Section 501 of the National Security Act of 1947, as amended, until I otherwise direct.

Scope

Iran

Description

[Assist selected friendly foreign liaison services, third countries, which have established relationships with Iranian elements, groups, and individuals] sympathetic to U.S. Government interests and which do not conduct or support terrorist actions directed against U.S. persons, property or interests for the purpose of: (1) establishing a more moderate government in Iran, and (2) obtaining from them significant intelligence not otherwise obtainable, to determine the current Iranian Government's intentions with respect to its neighbors and with respect to terrorist acts, [and (3) furthering the release of the American hostages held in Beirut and preventing additional terrorist acts by these groups.]ª Provide funds, intelligence, counterintelligence, training, guidance and communications, and other necessary assistance to these elements, groups, individuals, liaison services and third countries in support of these activities. The USG will act to facilitate efforts by third parties and third countries to establish contact with moderate elements within and outside the Government of Iran by providing these elements with arms, equipment and related material in order to enhance the credibility of these elements with arms, equipment and related material in order to enhance the credibility of these elements in their effort to achieve a more pro–U.S. government in Iran by demonstrating their ability to obtain requisite resources to defend their country against Iraq and intervention by the Soviet Union. This support will be discontinued if the U.S. Government learns that these elements have abandoned their goals of moderating their government and appropriated the material for purposes other than that [*sic*] provided by this Finding.

ªPoint (3) did not appear in the first draft.

Source: President's Special Review Board, *The Tower Commission Report* (New York: Bantam, 1987), pp. 217–18.

proposed a ban on covert action, but both wanted Congress to receive prior notice on any such undertakings.

Era of Uneasy Partnership

The Senate moved quickly and established a permanent bipartisan intelligence oversight committee in 1976. (The House was slower to act, creating its oversight committee in 1977.)[34] The Senate committee succeeded in establishing a working relationship with the CIA for overseeing covert action. The CIA agreed to provide it with 48 hours' notice before a plan approved by the president would be implemented. The agreement is important because while the committee cannot legally prevent a covert action plan from being executed, advance notice allows it to voice its disapproval and have input into the policy process. In summing up its first year of operations, the committee concluded that it had been "informed of every covert action requiring a presidential finding ... and that it had formally voted on all covert action projects in the new budget." Much of the traditional congressional aversion to any detailed control over the intelligence community was still present. For while the budget subcommittee had held 45 hours of hearings, asked 500 questions for the record, and examined 2,000 pages of justification material presented by the intelligence community, only three members of the Senate took up the committee's offer to read its classified report, which spelled out the money appropriated and described the projects whose funding it had cut or eliminated.

Based on his experience as a staffer with the House Intelligence Committee, Loch Johnson made several cogent observations about the actual monitoring of CIA activities by Congress.[35] First, oversight was carried out by a changing combination of committee members and staffers. Often it involved only a single committee member and one or two staffers who would hear a briefing, visit a site, or write a report. Second, oversight became more intense whenever members felt that the CIA was flouting the prerogatives of Congress. Third, members made little use of congressional information resources such as the GAO (General Accounting Office) or CRS (Congressional Research Service), preferring to rely instead on their own knowledge and sources. Fourth, several minority party staffers became overseers of the majority party staff instead of the CIA. Fifth, what the committee investigated depended on the interests of its members and the nature of the subject matter. For example, it once spent two hours questioning DCI Stansfield Turner on his personnel decisions (some of those he fired came from the districts of committee members) and then touched only briefly on a technically complex, expensive, and controversial hardware issue.

During much of the Carter administration, the task of writing a charter for the CIA dominated the intelligence agenda. The first congressional effort to write a charter emerged from the Senate Intelligence Committee and had over 200 pages spelling out detailed restrictions on CIA actions. Included among its controversial provisions were separating the post of DCI from that of head of the CIA, establishing rigorous guidelines governing the conduct of covert action and the clandestine collection of information, and formulating an extensive series of CIA reporting requirements. This bill was not approved by the Senate, and in 1980 a second attempt was made to pass a legislative charter for the CIA. It was trimmed down to 172 pages. Cut out were most of the more controversial provisions of the earlier proposal, including those establishing detailed reporting requirements and those placing elaborate restrictions on CIA covert action.

At the same time that this bill was being put forward, pressure was building within Congress to modify the reporting requirements of the Hughes–Ryan Amendment. The CIA's failure to anticipate the fall of the Shah, controversy over its Soviet missile estimates, the Soviet invasion of Afghanistan, and the growing threat of communism in Latin America caused many to argue that the problem with the CIA was not one of excessive and uncontrolled actions but one of inadequate resources and incompetence. In the course of the debate over the proposed CIA charter, the latter perspective won out. The Senate passed the Intelligence Oversight Act, which ran only three pages in length. It reduced the Hughes–Ryan reporting requirements to the two intelligence committees, mandated that the CIA keep these committees "fully and currently informed" of CIA operations including intelligence failures, and required that the committees be given all the information they request and that they receive reports from all members of the intelligence community, not just from the CIA.

In the Reagan administration relations between Congress and the CIA deteriorated markedly. The main point of contention also changed. It was no longer the question of intelligence charters but that of covert action, especially in Nicaragua. The CIA's behavior both in Nicaragua and before the committees brought about a major confrontation over the congressional control of intelligence and CIA reporting responsibilities.

The 1982 Boland Amendment provided the point of departure for Congress's oversight of the CIA's Nicaraguan operations.[36] The Boland Amendment grew out of congressional concern over the deepening U.S. involvement in Nicaragua and prohibited the use of CIA or Defense Department funds for purposes of overthrowing the Nicaraguan government or for provoking a war between Nicaragua and Honduras. In 1983, concerned with the level of the paramilitary program under way in Nicaragua and the clarity of U.S. goals, the Senate Intelligence Committee took the unusual step of requiring a new presidential finding before allocating any more funds to be spent in Nicaragua. After receiving the new presidential finding (which was revised to take into account the committee's views), the committee voted nearly unanimously to approve funds for the redefined program for FY1984. The Senate passed the measure by a voice vote. Because the House had voted to terminate all funds for the program, a conference committee was established, and a compromise figure of $24 million was agreed upon.

Then according to a Senate Intelligence Committee report, "without notifying Congress as required by the Intelligence Oversight Act, major changes [were] made in the program." Included among these changes was the mining of Nicaraguan harbors. Moreover, without going to the Senate Intelligence Committee first, the Reagan administration went to the Senate Appropriations Committee for an additional $21 million for its Nicaraguan program. The first action served to undermine the "strong majority of the committee" which had suppported the funding of CIA operations in Nicaragua. The second action angered the committee to the point where Secretary of State Shultz was moved to apologize to it for violating established procedures. In the end a deadlock with the House prevented any further funds from being allocated for the Nicaraguan program, although the Senate Intelligence Committee had recommended the additional funding contingent on CIA compliance with the notification provisions of the Intelligence Oversight Act.

In April 1984, shortly after it approved additional funds for CIA operations in Nicaragua, the Senate passed a resolution that no funds shall be obligated or spent for the purpose of planning, supporting, or directing the mining of Nicaraguan harbors. That same month, DCI Casey, with the approval of the president, signed a written agreement with the committee in order to better ensure "prior notice and adequate information concerning covert action programs including those in furtherance of ongoing covert action programs."

The involvement of the NSC in funding and running the covert action program in Nicaragua has further complicated the problem of controlling intelligence. Congressional legislation banned the spending of funds by the CIA, Defense Department, "or any other agency or entity of the United States involved in intelligence activities." Because it is not listed as a member of the intelligence community, Reagan administration officials concluded that the NSC was not prohibited from involving itself in the Nicaraguan operation by this restriction. Congress has rejected the validity of this interpretation. Also troubling to the Congress is the absence of notification by DCI Casey. Reagan directed Casey not to inform Congress, and he complied with those instructions in spite of his agreement with Congress. It should be stressed that the problem of notification is not unique to the Reagan administration. As DCI, Stansfield Turner did not inform Congress on three occasions about covert action programs approved by Carter and being undertaken by the CIA. All of them were preparatory to the failed hostage rescue mission. In an attempt to rectify this situation, Congress considered legislation that had it passed would have required presidents to inform Congress within 48 hours of the start of any covert action rather than in a "timely fashion," as the law now requires. The measure was dropped in return for a pledge from Bush who, while maintaining that he did not have to notify Congress, promised that he would try to do so "within a few days."

Congress as Impatient Overseer

The uneasy partnership of the third era was never placed on a firm foundation and broke down under the pressure of a series of incidents in the early years of the post–cold war era. The end of the cold war created special problems for the CIA in its relations with Congress. Unlike the State Department and the Defense Department, it was almost totally a creature of the cold war. Not only did it lack a significant organizational history that predated the conflict, which could be spotlighted in a time of global transition, but it was unable to highlight goals and missions that did not seem in some way linked to defeating communism. Added to this was the fact that the CIA had failed to predict the end of the cold war and the collapse of the Soviet Union. The net result was that from across the political spectrum congressional voices began to call for fundamental reform of the CIA. For example, Senator Daniel Patrick Moynihan, who once served on the Senate Intelligence Committee, called for abolishing the CIA and transferring its intelligence functions to the State Department. David Boren, a past chair of that committee, called for significant budgetary cuts and the creation of a new director of national intelligence. They were not alone in calling for change. Former CIA officials also called for reform, and DCIs Robert Gates and R. James Woolsey openly spoke of the need to redirect the CIA's efforts to meet the new security challenges facing the United States.

This consensus on the need for change in no way foreordained the collapse of the uneasy congressional-CIA partnership. Past behavior plus the great variety of proposals being aired suggested that Congress was more interested in raising issues in order to prompt internal reform efforts than it was in dictating changes to the CIA. Congress was transformed from an uneasy partner to an impatient overseer as a result of a series of incidents in the early 1990s. On several occasions the CIA angered many in Congress by its continued inability or unwillingness to keep intelligence committees fully abreast of its behavior. One incident did not actually involve the CIA but the National Reconnaissance Office (NRO), which is responsible for conducting American satellite spy operations. Members of the Senate Intelligence Committee had charged that they had not been adequately informed about the NRO's construction of a new headquarters complex costing $310 million. Congress also was angered by what it saw as CIA unwillingness to share with it information regarding the loss of agents in Eastern Europe in the 1980s. Acting director Admiral William O. Studeman was forced to acknowledge that the CIA had "not fulfilled its obligations to keep the committee fully informed" about the loss of at least ten agents.

Yet another point of tension involved the CIA's failure to disclose to Congress that it had paid a Guatemalan army colonel $44,000 in 1992 for information about that country's civil war, in spite of the fact that it knew him to be linked to a 1990 murder of a U.S. citizen. The incident was particularly heated because the information was made public by Representative Robert Torricelli, a Democratic member of the House Intelligence Committee. House Speaker Newt Gingrich labeled Torricelli's actions "totally unacceptable" because committee members are sworn to keep all classified information they receive secret. House Republicans demanded that Torricelli be removed from the committee, complaining that such actions made it difficult for the committee to earn the trust of the intelligence community. Torricelli defended his actions, saying he had a greater loyalty to the Constitution, and added that "I'm not going to earn their trust. . . . Their testimony is not a gift to the Congress. . . ."

Even more damaging to the health of the congressional-CIA partnership was the agency's handling of the Aldrich Ames spy affair. Ames was a 31-year veteran of the CIA who worked in counterintelligence and had spied for the Soviet Union for nine years. According to an internal CIA investigation, Ames had provided the Soviet Union with information that resulted in "the loss of virtually all of the CIA's human resources reporting on its primary target in the 1980s, the Soviet Union." All of this happened in spite of his possessing what Woolsey described as a record of "alcohol abuse, sloppy operational and financial accounting, undisciplined behavior, and poor judgment." Many in Congress felt that DCI Woolsey was being overly protective of the CIA in his approach to reorganization and far too lenient in his handling out of punishment for its failure to detect Ames. While he issued 11 reprimands, no one was fired or demoted. The four most severe reprimands went to three retired CIA officials and one who was days away from retirement.

The CIA's reluctance to take corrective action in the Ames case combined with the agency's perceived lack of candor in dealing with it prompted a Democratically controlled Congress to establish a presidential commission headed by long-time congressperson and former Secretary of Defense Les Aspin to study the post–cold war mission of the intelligence community. After the Republican landslide in the 1994 elections, Representative Larry Combest used his new post as head of the House Intelligence Committee to set up "IC21" to study what needs to be done to prepare the intelligence community for the 21st century. In keeping with his own penchant for action and recognizing Congress's interest in a "take-charge" DCI, John M. Deutch promised swift reform and less tolerance of mistakes in his 1995 confirmation hearings. He quickly moved to punish those responsible for mishandling intelligence reports on Guatemala that prevented Congress from being "fully and currently" informed of significant intelligence activities and failures. Deutch followed this with public criticism of CIA officers for their "inexcusable" handling of Soviet intelligence.

Deutch's actions alienated many intelligence professionals and did little to calm congressional concerns about the CIA's past or present performance. The Congressional Black Caucus called for federal investigations into allegations (since considered unfounded) that the CIA introduced crack cocaine into black communities in the 1980s as part of a plan to raise money to support the Contras in Nicaragua. The Chairman of the House Intelligence Committee, a former intelligence officer, asserted that the CIA's human intelligence espionage capacity was lacking. The CIA was roundly condemned for its failure to predict the Indian nuclear explosion and became embroiled in the political controversies over Clinton's approval of a missile deal and technology transfers to China.

SUMMARY AND THE FUTURE

More questions remain unanswered than have been resolved in Congress's attempts to exercise its powers over the CIA. While a return to the Era of Trust seems highly unlikely, a smoothly functioning partnership has yet to be created. Congress and the CIA and the executive branch are all engaged in a learning process about what each can and cannot do and what each can expect from the other. The passing of the cold war only promises to make this learning process more difficult for three reasons.

First, there is a great deal of uncertainty over the proper role of the CIA in the future conduct of American foreign policy. Changing roles call into question the relevance of old methods of oversight and control. For example, Senator Alan Specter and others have called upon the CIA to become more active in the area of economic intelligence. He wants the intelligence community to provide American businesses with information that affects their operations. Most intelligence professionals argue against such a role. They maintain that while it is proper for the CIA to provide government officials with intelligence about the economic activity of other states and even specific foreign firms, the intelligence community should not be put in a position of having to provide competing American firms with secret intelligence.

Second, in the final analysis CIA-congressional relations are congressional–executive relations. Changes in the balance of power between the two branches inevitably will become reflected in CIA oversight mechanisms. With so much of the growth in presidential power having been tied to the need for the United States to play an active role in international conflicts during the cold war, more than one observer has speculated that its end will lead to a dramatic reduction in the president's ability to gain congressional acquiescence for foreign policy initiatives. To a greater extent than in the past Congress may be positioned to play a leading role in setting America's foreign policy agenda. Should this prove to be the case, then Congress can be expected to push its views on the intelligence community with unprecedented vigor. For example, in 1995 the Clinton administration bowed to congressional pressure and approved a small-scale covert action program intended to moderate the radical Islamic regime in Iran.

Third, even if presidential–congressional relations remain constant, problems will continue to plague the relationship between Congress and the CIA because Congress has still not found an appropriate oversight mechanism. Even before the end of the cold war new problems surfaced in this area with the revelation of DCI Casey's willingness to employ foreign states to carry out covert action programs and his interest in the "off the books" intelligence capacity.

Congress has still to pass a legislative charter for the CIA and the other members of the intelligence community. Budgetary control has been exercised but only at the cost of a confrontation between the president and Congress. It remains a blunt instrument and one that must be wielded by the full Congress. A look back at the record of the Senate Intelligence Committee's handling of the Nicaraguan operation, for example, reveals a circular pattern of funding—reevaluation of wrongdoing or excess—plan revision—funding. A staffer on the Senate Foreign Relations Committee has observed that "the tools the textbooks tell us are available to the two branches . . . are largely irrelevant to the daily give and take of congressional intelligence oversight."[37] Congress's "big guns"—its subpoena power, appointment powers, etc.—are only brought out in the face of an absolute refusal to cooperate by the executive branch. In the daily "war of attrition" between the two branches, the executive is able to dominate through such devices as delaying, manipulating classification systems, wording the memorandums of understanding that set the conditions for the exchange of classified information, and claiming that it is only protecting intelligence sources and methods as it is required to do by law.

The fundamental question about congressional oversight of the CIA is whether revelations of wrongdoing, questionable activities, or incompetence constitute control. The primary obstacle in the way of moving from revelations to control is the lack of relevant information. At issue is the quality of the information available to Congress more than its quantity. The tension between Congress's right to know and the CIA's need for secrecy is real and enduring. Consider, for example, the following issues:

Must Congress be informed of contingency plans for covert operations?

Should Congress be informed about the sources of CIA information?

Should Congress have access to internal agency papers that went into the preparation of an estimate?

Should Congress be allowed to go into the field and inspect covert operations?

Should Congress be given access to CIA communications so that it can formulate its own intelligence estimates?

What makes the problem of control so important is that there is every reason to expect covert action to remain a frequently used tool of U.S. foreign policy. Too many situations arise where policy makers see threats to U.S. national interests and for which conventional policy instruments are judged to be inappropriate. The unresolved question is, how useful is it? Consider, for example, the following arguments about its use:

1. If action capabilities take time to develop, it is also important that, once in being, they be used or they will atrophy.[38]
2. The effectiveness of any intelligence service is directly proportional to the degree to which it is prepared to break the laws of its adversaries.[39]
3. Political assassination in times of peace . . . has no place in the American arsenal.[40]

We are beginning to pursue answers to these types of questions. Richard Immerman's account of U.S. involvement in Guatemala is particularly important for helping us think critically about covert action.[41] His study reveals that neither the CIA nor American policy makers held any illusions about the difficulty of the task they were attempting or the high risks it entailed. His work also reveals a capacity for clear thinking and an attention to detail on the part of U.S. officials in putting together the covert action plan. From the outset the operation was seen as psychological and political rather than military. In selecting a leader for the "revolution," an effort was made to avoid too close an identification with either the old rightist forces or the military. Efforts were carefully targeted at the group that Arbenz was most dependent on: the wealthy, urban class which made up most of the officer corps. Attention was given to establishing an international climate supportive of an anti-Arbenz coup. Finally, detailed control was exercised over all facets of the operation from gaining Eisenhower's approval for additional planes for bombing Guatemala City to the engineering of a series of juntas and resignations in order that the U.S. candidate would emerge as the victor in the wake of Arbenz's resignation.

From Immerman's account we can identify not only the reasons for success but also those for later failures. For all of their careful planning, U.S. policy makers made one fatal mistake. They confused the necessary and sufficient conditions for the success of the operation against Arbenz. The careful attention to details, the control exercised, and the appreciation of risks were necessary for the success of the plan, but they were not sufficient to guarantee its success. U.S. policy makers did not appreciate the extent to which their success was dependent on circumstances within Guatemala. In Immerman's words the CIA "reaped the harvest" of Arbenz's failure to institute real agricultural reforms that would have cemented ties between the regime and the oppressed Indian majority.

The United States paid a high price for confusing the necessary and sufficient conditions for success with the Bay of Pigs invasion. Immerman argues that the CIA plan failed not because of its deficiencies but because of Castro's reaction to it based on his reading of events in Guatemala. Castro and Che Guevara had both concluded that Arbenz's critical mistake was in not pursuing reform forcefully enough. This left him vulnerable to outside-generated pressure because he lacked a strong base of support from which to challenge CIA-sponsored revolutionaries. With such backing they were confident that the political and psychological impact of the CIA's operation would not have been sufficient to bring down his regime. Therefore, upon seizing power Castro set out to create a strong domestic base. He pursued a radical policy of economic reform and dismantled the remnants of Fulgencio Batista's army. Later, by reacting with speed and vigor to the Bay of Pigs invasion, Castro blunted any possibility of a psychological warfare campaign against him and at the same time destroyed the CIA's image of invulnerability.

NOTES

1. The President's Special Review Board, *The Tower Commission Report* (New York: Bantam, 1987), p. 15.

2. Bruce D. Berkowitz and Allan F. Goodman, "The Logic of Covert Action," *The National Interest*, 51 (1998), 38–46.

3. For comments on the OSS and covert action, see Victor Marchetti and John D. Marks, *The CIA and the Cult of Intelligence* (New York: Dell, 1975); and Richard Harris Smith, *OSS: The Secret History of America's First Central Intelligence Agency* (Berkeley: University of California Press, 1972).

4. The observation is made by B. Hugh Tovar in Roy Godson (ed.), *Intelligence Requirements for the 1980s: Covert Action* (Washington, D.C.: National Strategy Information Center, 1981), p. 195.

5. The observation is made by B. Hugh Tovar in Roy Godson (ed.), *Intelligence Requirements for the 1980s: Elements of Intelligence*, rev. ed. (Washington, D.C.: National Strategy Information Center, 1983), p. 71.

6. Jeffrey T. Richelson, *The U.S. Intelligence Community* (Cambridge, Mass.: Ballinger, 1985), p. 236.

7. Ibid., pp. 228–29.

8. Morton H. Halperin and others, *The Lawless State: The Crimes of the U.S. Intelligence Agencies* (New York: Penguin, 1976), p. 40.

9. Ibid., pp. 15–29.

10. Marchetti and Marks, *CIA and the Cult of Intelligence*, p. 167.

11. Richelson, *The U.S. Intelligence Community*, p. 235.

12. Marchetti and Marks, *CIA and the Cult of Intelligence*, p. 72; and Richelson, *The U.S. Intelligence Community*, pp. 230–31.

13. Warren Hinckle and William Turner, *The Fish Is Red: The Story of the Secret War Against Castro* (New York: Harper & Row, 1982).

14. Theodore G. Shackley, *The Third Option: An American View of Counterinsurgency Operations* (New York: Reader's Digest Press, 1981).

15. Trevor Barnes, "The Secret Cold War: The CIA and American Foreign Policy in Europe: 1946–1956," *Historical Journal*, 24, 25 (1981, 1982), 399–415, 649–70.

16. Ray S. Cline, *Secrets, Spies and Scholars: The Essential CIA* (Washington, D.C.: Acropolis, 1970), pp. 132–33; and Barry Rubin, *Paved with Good Intentions: The American Experience and Iran* (New York: Penguin, 1981), Chap. 3.

17. Richard H. Immerman, *The CIA in Guatemala: The Foreign Policy of Intervention* (Austin: University of Texas Press, 1982).

18. John Stockwell, *In Search of Enemies: A CIA Story* (New York: Norton, 1978).

19. Christopher Dickey, "Central America: From Quagmire to Cauldron," *Foreign Affairs*, 62 (1984), 669.

20. Ted Galen Carpenter, "The Unintended Consequences of Afghanistan," *World Policy Journal*, 11 (1994), 76–87.

21. U.S. Congress, Senate Select Committee to Study Government Operations with Respect to Intelligence Activities, *Alleged Assassination Plots Involving Foreign Leaders* (Washington, D.C.: U.S. Government Printing Office, 1976).

22. Cline, *Secrets, Spies and Scholars,* p. 187; Rositzke, *The CIA's Secret Operations,* p. 196.

23. Seymour Hersh, "Target Qaddafi," *New York Times Magazine,* February 22, 1987.

24. Rositzke, Harry, *The CIA's Secret Operations: Espionage, Counterespionage, and Covert Action* (New York: Reader's Digest Press, 1977), p. 197.

25. Loch Johnson, "Legislative Reform of Intelligence Policy," *Polity,* 17 (1985), 549–73.

26. Robert L. Borosage, "The Central Intelligence Agency: The King's Men and the Constitutional Order," in Robert L. Borosage and John D. Marks (eds.), *The CIA File* (New York: Grossman, 1976), pp. 125–41.

27. Quoted in Marchetti and Marks, *CIA and the Cult of Intelligence,* p. 324.

28. Cline, *Secrets, Spies, and Scholars,* p. 246.

29. Quoted in Harry H. Ransom, *The Intelligence Establishment* (Cambridge, Mass.: Harvard University Press, 1970), p. 169.

30. A discussion of the Mansfield and McCarthy reform proposals and how they fared in Congress can be found in Ransom, *The Intelligence Establishment,* pp. 157–79.

31. William Corson, *Armies of Ignorance: The Rise of the American Intelligence Empire* (New York: Dial, 1977), p. 472.

32. Stockwell, *In Search of Enemies,* p. 47.

33. Thomas M. Franck and Edward Weisband, *Foreign Policy by Congress* (New York: Oxford University Press, 1979), pp. 117–24.

34. Ibid., pp. 125–34.

35. Loch Johnson, "The U.S. Congress and the CIA: Monitoring the Dark Side of Government," *Legislative Studies Quarterly,* 4 (1980), 477–99.

36. For an overview of congressional oversight on the Nicaraguan program, see U.S. Senate, Select Committee on Intelligence, *Report, January 1, 1983–December 31, 1984* (Washington, D.C.: Government Printing Office, 1985), pp. 4–15. Hereafter cited as Senate Intelligence Committee, *Report.*

37. Michael J. Glennon, "Investigating Intelligence Affairs: The Process of Getting Information for Congress," in Thomas Franck (ed.), *The Tethered Presidency* (New York: New York University Press, 1981), pp. 141–52.

38. Tovar in Godson (ed.), *Elements of Intelligence,* p. 87.

39. Ladislav Bittman, "Soviet Bloc 'Disinformation' and Other Active Measures," in Robert Pfaltzgraff, Uri Ra'anan, and Warren Milberg (eds.), *Intelligence Policy and National Security* (Hamden, Conn.: Anchon [sic] 1981), p. 214.

40. Cord Meyer, *Facing Reality: From World Federalism to the CIA* (New York: Harper & Row, 1980), p. 219.

41. Immerman, *The CIA in Guatemala.*

CHAPTER

15 The Economic Instruments of Foreign Policy

Economic statecraft involves the deliberate manipulation of economic policy to promote the goals of the state. The United States is no stranger to the use of economic power in pursuing foreign policy objectives. A prime target of U.S. economic statecraft during the Reagan administration was the Sandinista government in Nicaragua. A list of actions taken would include the following. First, shortly after taking office Reagan terminated all foreign aid. Second, the administration pressured such international organizations as the World Bank and the Inter-American Development Bank (IDB) to stop lending Nicaragua funds. Beginning in 1982 the World Bank froze all loan applications and after 1983 the IDB did not give its approval to any Nicaraguan loan application, including a 1985 loan that was to go to private farmers. Third, and with considerably less success, it pressured U.S. allies to stop sending aid to Nicaragua. Fourth, in 1985 the United States put a trade embargo in place. This action followed a 1983 move that cut back by 90 percent the amount of Nicaraguan sugar that would be allowed to come into the United States. Finally, the United States through the CIA and Contras engaged in economic sabotage. Between September 1983 and April 1984 one source estimates that 21 attacks were carried out on economic targets in Nicaragua. The most controversial involved the mining of Nicaraguan harbors.

As this account suggests, the array of economic options at the disposal of policy makers is impressive. The range of uses also appears to be quite lengthy. A partial list would include modifying behavior, deterrence, punishment, demonstrating solidarity, and communicating resolve.[1] All of these objectives can be found in the Clinton administration's imposing of sanctions on Serbia for its expansion of the war into Kosovo, and against India and Pakistan for their detonation of nuclear devices.

From a policy maker's perspective, a very different picture emerges. Constraints and not opportunities dominate the scene. The first constraint is that foreign economic policy involves domestic and international concerns. The relative importance assigned to domestic concerns influences the degree to which trade, aid, and monetary relations can be manipulated to accomplish foreign policy goals.

Second, national wealth does not automatically translate into national economic power. Policy makers must be able to manipulate economic resources skillfully, and their potential for doing so is not the same everywhere. Traditionally, the concepts of mercantilism and liberalism have been employed to capture the different possibilities that exist.[2] Under liberalism the state has few claims on society's resources. A laissez-faire approach is held to be in the best interest of the state because there is no long-term conflict between private economic interests and the national interest. Mercantilists see a far greater potential for conflict between these two sets of interests and favor a policy of state intervention into the economy to ensure that private gain and political influence reinforce one another.

In this chapter we begin by introducing the more prominent economic instruments of foreign policy. A glossary of key terms is presented in Box 15–1. Next, we examine specific cases where economic instruments were used, and as part of that we take a more in-depth look at foreign aid. We conclude by raising questions about the future utility of economics as an instrument of foreign policy.

A SURVEY OF ECONOMIC INSTRUMENTS

The most overlooked of all economic instruments of foreign policy is *free trade*.[3] Contrary to common expectations, there is nothing inevitable or natural about free trade, nor does a policy of free trade mean the renunciation of eco-

---

BOX 15–1   Glossary: Key Terms of Economic Instruments of Foreign Policy

Boycott: A refusal to buy products from a particular country or group of countries.

Cartel: An agreement among firms or countries to restrict competition.

Dumping: Sales of goods in foreign markets at net unit prices below those charged to domestic consumers.

Embargo: A government edict prohibiting citizens from trading with one or several countries. It may apply to only certain types of products or a total prohibition of trade.

Export Control: Government restrictions on the sales of certain materials, commodities, products, or weapons in foreign trade.

Foreign Aid: Economic, social, or military assistance rendered to a country by another government or international institution.

Free Trade: The flow of trade based on supply and demand, free from governmental regulations, controls, and promotional activities.

GATT: General Agreement on Tariffs and Trade. An international organization that promotes trade by serving as a forum for negotiating agreements to reduce tariffs and other barriers.

Quota: A quantitative restriction established by a state to control the importation of certain commodities.

Tariff: A tax levied on imports or exports. Its primary purpose is to raise revenue or retaliate against the restrictive trade policies of other states.

Source: Jack C. Plano and Roy Olton, *The International Relations Dictionary*, 3rd ed. (Santa Barbara, Calif.: ABC-CLIO, 1982).

nomics as an instrument of foreign policy. International free trade systems exist because they are in the interests of the dominant power—Great Britain in the nineteenth century and the United States in the postwar era. From 1944 to 1962 free trade was the principal instrument of U.S. economic statecraft, and access to U.S. markets was used as an inducement to get other states to adopt policies favored by the United States. Among the goals pursued by the United States were strengthening military alliances, promoting the economic recovery of Western Europe, ensuring access to strategic raw materials, stimulating economic development in the third world, creating markets for U.S. exports, and creating an international system conducive to peace and security. U.S. policy makers were also sensitive to the limits of free trade as an instrument of foreign policy. On a selective basis discrimination against U.S. goods was permitted or encouraged to help countries experiencing severe balance-of-payments problems. Also, the creation of the European Common Market encouraged discrimination.

Recently, the United States has used free trade as an economic instrument both in bilateral and multilateral relations. A recent bilateral attempt to do so has met with little success. It involved efforts to get China to adjust its human rights and economic policies in return for continuing to grant it most favored nation (MFN) status. This designation allows Chinese goods to enter the American market at the most favorable tariff rate made available to any state. Access to the American market on equal terms with its competitors is important for China, but so too is American access to China's domestic market, considered to be the world's fastest growing economy. Confronted with Chinese defiance and under heavy pressure from American business interests (in 1995 an estimated 150,000 American jobs depended on American exports to China), President Clinton broke with a campaign pledge to get tough with China and continued President Bush's policy of granting China MFN status in spite of its lack of progress on human rights.

If the growing importance of the overseas markets to American firms has placed limits on the utility of free trade as a bilateral economic weapon, it continues to make it an attractive multilateral policy tool. Using what some have termed "the power of exclusion," the Clinton administration has been able to use the threat of denial to the American market as a weapon to get other states to embrace the concept of free trade areas. Canada found itself in this position once the Bush administration decided to go ahead with Mexico as a free trade area. Already a partner with the United States in a free trade zone agreed to in 1988, Canada was not enthusiastic about the prospects of a North American Free Trade Agreement to include Mexico but feared the economic consequences of not joining in such a venture. Further steps in the direction of multilateral free trade were taken in the Clinton administration after the GATT agreement was finally concluded. In late 1994 the United States entered into agreements in principle with both Latin American states and Pacific Basin states to form free trade zones early in the twenty-first century.

A second economic instrument that has gained prominence over the past two decades stands in sharp contrast to free trade. It is strategic or fair trade. The impetus behind strategic trade is the inability of American policy makers (and American industry) to put a dent in the U.S.–Japanese trade imbalance. Every president since Richard Nixon has tried and failed to reduce the size of the Japanese surplus. In 1971, Richard Nixon was moved to act when the imbalance reached $1.3 billion. In 1980, under Carter it had grown to $2.9 billion before skyrocketing to $21.6 billion in 1983 in the Reagan administration. In 1991 Bush was confronted with a $43.4 billion trade imbalance and in late 1993 it had grown to $54 billion.

In its efforts to deal with the problem, the Clinton administration entered into a series of intense trade negotiations, conducted under the backdrop of threats of an eminent trade war, that produced few tangible results. Events in 1993–1995 are illustrative of the pattern that these talks have taken. In July 1993 as a G-7 economic summit came to an end the United States and Japan agreed on a framework for future talks that would address the problems experienced by American firms in such areas as automobile parts, government procurement, medical and telecommunications equipment, and insurance. Hopes that the agreement might mark a change in U.S.–Japanese economic relations faded quickly, and in early 1994 an impasse had been reached and negotiators on both sides worked feverishly to produce a new agreement in time for a February summit meeting between Clinton and Japanese Prime Minister Morihiro Hosokawa. Their failure to do so led the Clinton administration to threaten trade sanctions against Japan. In August the United States formally accused Japan of discriminatory trade practices, setting in motion a 60-day deadline for resolving the dispute, after which sanctions automatically would go into effect. After 15 months of negotiations the United States and Japan announced a new agreement in early October to avert sanctions. Of the areas identified in the July 1993 agreement, the pact made progress in all areas but automobile parts, which account for two-thirds of the trade surplus. In May 1995 the battle over automobile parts was joined again when the United States charged Japan with discrimination before the newly established World Trade Organization. It also threatened to place 100 percent tariff increases on Japanese luxury cars coming into the United States. Once again open conflict was avoided as an agreement was reached, with both sides claiming victory and little of consequence accomplished. The United States was able to cite specific target figures in the agreement (1,000 new Japanese dealers and $2 billion in increased car part exports to Japan). Japanese officials stressed that compliance by Japanese auto makers was voluntary and that the government had no formal responsibility for meeting them.

The political basis for U.S.–Japanese trade talks is the 1988 Omnibus Trade and Competitiveness Act, especially Section 301. Commonly referred to as "Super 301," this section provides for retaliatory trade sanctions against states engaging in unfair trading practices against the United States. It requires that the president identify "priority countries" that are unfair traders and set a timetable for resolving the dispute, after which time sanctions will take effect. Japan, India, and Brazil are among the states that have been singled out as unfair traders. Under the pressure generated by Super 301, the United States and Japan began a series of negotiations in 1989 known as the Structural Impediments Initiative (SII). While technically these talks were designed to address the problems each state encountered in trading with the other, their real purpose was to open up the Japanese market to U.S. goods.

Strategic trade is championed over free trade by some out of the conviction that the comparative advantage enjoyed by states in international trade is not due to a country's resource base or historical factors, but to imperfections in markets that have been deliberately created by government policy. The only way for American firms to become competitive is for the U.S. government to target specific sectors for investment, subsidies, and protection. By not having a strategic trade policy, it is argued that the United States is allowing other states to set the international trade agenda and influence the structure of the American economy. Critics of the strategic trade argument concentrate on two points. First, they question whether the government is well suited in terms of either information or political will to identify sectors of the economy for this type of special attention. They charge that much of the demand for protection rests on old-fashioned interest group lobbying. Second, they question the relationship of international competitiveness with economic growth in the United States and the relationship between trade competitiveness.

Though it can be seen as part of a strategic trade policy, tariffs also deserve to be treated as a separate instrument of international economic policy. A tariff is a tax on foreign-made goods entering one's country. Typically, tariffs are applied in order to protect domestic industry against foreign competition or to raise revenue, but they can also be manipulated to serve foreign policy goals. Twice in the postwar era, the United States has made notable efforts to manipulate its tariff structure to accomplish foreign policy goals. First, the United States has used its tariff system as a lever in dealing with communist states. Historically the United States has excluded communist states from equal access to the U.S. market. Only Poland and Yugoslavia were granted special status out of the hope that higher levels of trade with the United States might to some extent offset Soviet domination. During détente the United States sought to use access to the U.S. market and MFN status as an inducement to the Soviets for cooperation in noneconomic areas such as the SALT talks. In the late 1970s and 1980s, equal access to the U.S. market was denied as punishment for what the United States defined as unacceptable Soviet behavior. The second attempt to use tariffs as an instrument of foreign policy came in 1971 when President Nixon placed a 10 percent "surcharge" on all imports not already under a quota. The primary objective behind this move was to force major changes in the trading practices of other states. It failed to do so and created foreign hostility toward the United States.

The primary danger inherent in the excessive use of tariffs is retaliation. Faint echoes of the past were heard in 1986. Within weeks of each other, the Reagan administration retaliated for EEC restrictions on U.S. farm sales to Portugal by placing quotas on the importation of white wine, chocolates, and other EEC products into the United States, and Canada retaliated for Reagan's decision to place a 35 percent tariff on cedar products from Canada by announcing a tariff on such U.S. items as books, magazines, and computer products. The major instance of retaliation took place in the early 1930s after the United States passed the Smoot–Hawley Tariff. The highest tariff in U.S. history, the Smoot–Hawley Tariff taxed imports at an average rate of 41.5 percent of their value. Retaliation by foreign governments led to a sudden and dramatic drop in U.S. exports, which only worsened the ongoing depression, something the Smoot–Hawley Tariff was intended to help solve. In the first half of 1929, U.S. exports exceeded $2.5 billion; by the first half of 1932, they were valued at less than $1 billion. The Trade Agreements Act of 1934 broke the spiral of raising tariffs that had begun in 1879 and set off a new downward spiral. It authorized the president to lower existing tariffs by as much as 50 percent to those states that made reciprocal concessions.

Manipulating nontariff barriers (NTBs) to trade is a modern variation on this theme. Taking forms ranging from labeling requirements, health and safety standards, and license controls to taxation policy, they have become powerful tools in the hands of policy makers who want to protect local firms from foreign competition or remedy a balance-of-payments problem. U.S. use of NTBs dates at least from the 1930s when the Buy America Act required the government to purchase goods and services from U.S. suppliers if their prices were not unreasonably higher than those of foreign competitors. Another piece of legislation in the 1930s gave preferential treatment to U.S. shipping interests. It required that goods purchased overseas with U.S. loans or guaranteed funds had to be transported whenever possible in U.S. vessels.

An *embargo* is a refusal to sell a commodity to another state, and it is a third economic instrument of foreign policy. Embargoes (and the more subtle concept of export controls) have long played a prominent role in U.S. cold war foreign policy. Building upon the Trading with the Enemy Act of 1917, the United States embargoed financial and commercial transactions with North Korea (1950), the People's Republic of China (1950), Cuba (1962), and North Vietnam (1964). Trade with communist states was also controlled by the Export Control Act of 1949 and the Battle Act of 1950. The Export Control Act denied export licenses for strategic goods intended for communist bloc states. At the outset practically every commodity that might be considered to have some military or strategic value was placed on the Department of Commerce's Commodity Control List. During the Korean War the list of restricted items reached 1,000 in number. The Battle Act was passed in an effort to overcome European resistance to U.S. export controls. It both prohibited the export of strategic goods and denied defense assistance to any state that reexported American goods on the restricted list. In a related effort to realize alliancewide cooperation in restricting the sale of strategic goods to communist bloc states, the United States helped create the Coordinating Committee for Export Controls (COCOM). Coordination was not easily achieved or ever fully realized. The United States has always had a broader definition of strategic goods than have the Europeans or the Japanese. U.S. allies have tended to restrict the label to those items with clear and direct military implications. Reagan sought to use COCOM as part of his strategy of denying high technology to the Soviet Union. With the tumultuous events in Eastern Europe, the Bush administration reversed course and sought to have COCOM relax some of its export restrictions.

In the post–cold war international system embargoes have become a prominent instrument of American foreign policy. They have also been an especially controversial instrument: Experts have debated their impact and President Clinton and a Republican Congress have battled over whether they should be used. Bolstered by support in Congress for the move, in 1994 the Clinton administration lifted the American trade embargo on Vietnam. That embargo was first imposed in May 1964 in response to North Vietnamese attacks on the south. Progress toward lifting the embargo was slow because of questions regarding Vietnam's cooperation in helping locate American POWs and MIAs. A first concrete step in the direction of lifting the embargo came in 1992 when Bush allowed U.S. firms to participate in humanitarian projects. At the same time, congressional opposition continued to block lifting the embargo against Cuba. In fact, as the 1992 presidential election approached Congress actually tightened the embargo by passing the Cuban Democracy Act, which asked the president to encourage other states to join the embargo and placed heavy penalties on U.S. firms engaging in trade with Cuba through a foreign subsidiary. Confronted with a mounting number of Cuban refugees coming to the United States, the Clinton administration sought to tighten the embargo yet again by banning cash gifts from exiles in the United States to family members still in Cuba. An embargo also played a central role in American efforts to bring down the Haitian military junta and return deposed president Jean-Bertrand Aristide to power. In June 1993, the UN voted to impose an oil and arms embargo on Haiti. The ease with which oil and other goods reached the military through the Dominican Republic blunted its effectiveness, and in 1993 Clinton got the United Nations to impose a near total embargo on Haiti. Only food and humanitarian supplies were exempt.

Perhaps most controversial have been two post–cold war embargoes in different parts of the world that have been linked politically in Washington. They are the arms embargo against the Bosnian Muslims and the near total embargo against Iraq. Both were instituted on a multilateral basis and pressure repeatedly surfaced that they be lifted. An embargo on trade with Iraq was put into place in April 1991. It was to be lifted only when Iraq met the United Nations' terms for dealing with its nuclear program. By 1994, France and Russia were arguing that these terms had been met because Iraq was beginning to cooperate with UN monitors. The United States considered Iraq's action insufficient and continued to view Saddam Hussein as a regional threat to be contained. It argued that Iraq still had not met all of the conditions of UN Resolution 687 regarding its invasion of Kuwait and that until it did the embargo should remain in place. About the same time that the Iraqi embargo went into effect the United Nations also put into place an arms embargo in Yugoslavia. While neutral in its language, the embargo had a far more serious impact on the military capabilities of the Bosnian Muslims than it did on the Bosnian Serbs. The Serbs were able to draw upon the military resources of the old Yugoslav army now in the possession of the neighboring Serbian government. As Serb atrocities mounted and the Bosnian Muslims suffered greater and greater losses, Republicans in Congress demanded that Clinton lift the arms embargo and finally succeeded in passing a resolution to the effect in 1995. The Clinton administration argued against doing so in part because it would make it easier for other states to break with the United States on the embargo against Iraq.

A *boycott* is a refusal to buy a product(s) from another state, and it represents a fourth economic instrument available to policy makers. One of the most recent and visible uses of a boycott involved U.S. participation in UN-sponsored sanctions against Rhodesia (Zimbabwe).[4] Off and on, these sanctions lasted for over a decade. They were first imposed by President Johnson in a 1968 executive order, and they were finally lifted in 1979. International sanctions were first requested by Great Britain in 1966 in response to the unilateral declaration of independence by the white minority government of Rhodesia. The purpose of the sanctions was to force the Rhodesian government into accepting the principle of majority rule. The U.S. commitment to the boycott was never firm. Congress amended the boycott in 1971 to allow the import of raw chromium and other critical materials. It closed this loophole in 1977 when the same groups that lobbied for the exemption objected to the flood of low-priced Rhodesian-processed chromium into the U.S. market. Throughout 1979 the Carter administration fought a holding action against moves by the Senate to lift the boycott until such time as the British were able to mediate the changeover to majority rule.

In 1995, the Clinton administration instituted a boycott against Iran in response to evidence that it was seeking to acquire nuclear technology and expertise from Russia. Clinton publicly labeled Iran a threat to peace in the Middle East and a sponsor of terrorism. The move came on the heels of an administration ban on trade between Iran and U.S. oil companies and their subsidiaries. Political pressures played a major role in these decisions as Congress had been pressing the administration for even tougher action against Iran. Republican Senator Alfonse D'Amato, chair of the Senate Banking Committee, termed it "a good first step." Analysts, however, expected it to have only a minimal impact on Iran unless other states joined in the boycott, and this appeared unlikely. France, Britain, and Germany opposed the boycott while Japan only agreed to put the issue under consideration. Part of the American difficulty in gaining multilateral support was the fact that under the provisions of the Non-Proliferation Treaty, the Russian sale technically was legal.

The fifth policy tool we examine in our survey is the *quota,* which is a quantitative restriction on goods coming from another state. In addition to serving as an instrument of economic warfare, quotas are often used to supplement tariffs as a means of protecting domestic firms from foreign competition and correcting balance-of-payments problems. Because of GATT quotas have not played a large role in foreign economic policy making for most of the postwar era. This began to change as the U.S. balance-of-payments situation continued to deteriorate and as concerns grew over the international competitiveness of American-made products. One recent notable use of quotas came in 1994 when the Clinton administration threatened to limit the amount of Canadian grain entering the United States. The move was a response both to a surge in the amount of Canadian grain exports, which caused political problems in wheat-growing states, and an attempt to gain bargaining leverage with Canada in a broader dispute over trade in agriculture.

ECONOMIC INSTRUMENTS: THREE CASE STUDIES

We began this chapter by reviewing how the United States manipulated its economic instruments against Nicaragua. In this section we look more closely at three other attempts to use economic power in order to place this example into perspective: the imposition of economic sanctions against Cuba and Iran, the grain embargo against the Soviet Union, and sanctions against Iraq.

Economic Warfare: Cuba and Iran

Castro's Cuba was a major irritant to U.S. policy makers in the 1960s, and economic pressure was only one of several policy instruments brought into play. In 1959, the year Castro came to power, Cuba was heavily dependent on the United States: 67 percent of its exports went to the United States; 70 percent of its imports came from the United States; and under the terms of legislation passed in 1934, the United States purchased the bulk of Cuban sugar at prices substantially above world market rates. Relations between the United States and Castro were tense from the very beginning. In February 1960 Castro concluded a barter deal with the Soviet Union involving an exchange of Cuban sugar for Soviet crude oil. After U.S.-owned oil refineries refused to process the Soviet oil, Castro took them over. The U.S. response was to terminate all remaining foreign aid programs and to cancel all purchases of Cuban sugar for the remainder of the year. Castro retaliated with additional nationalizations of U.S. property. Next, the United States imposed an embargo on all exports to Castro except for food and medicine. With this move Cuba entered into more economic agreements with the Soviet Union, and, in turn, the United States broke diplomatic relations. Even after the Cuban missile crisis and the Bay of Pigs invasion, the United States continued to apply economic sanctions. The Foreign Aid Act of 1963 required the president to stop U.S. aid to states that refused to restrict their trade with Cuba unless he felt that it was in the U.S. national interest not to do so. The United States also succeeded in getting the Organization of American States first to expel Cuba and then to sever commercial relations with it.

The United States also resorted to broad-based economic warfare in an effort to free the 52 hostages taken in Iran in 1979. Three days into the crisis, Carter placed a boycott on Iranian oil. Ten days after the hostages were taken, Carter froze all Iranian government assets in the United States and those under the control of U.S. banks, businesses, and individuals abroad. This move was the largest blocking of assets in U.S. history. It was also highly controversial because never before had overseas deposits been blocked. They were left untouched in similar moves against China (1952), Cuba (1962), and North Vietnam (1970). The Carter administration also cut off most export transactions with Iran but failed in its efforts to get the United Nations to vote similar sanctions due to a Soviet veto. All told, Carter's actions deprived Iran of access to over $12 billion. They also deprived Iran of critical supplies and spare parts, forcing it to turn to unreliable and expensive middlemen in an effort to obtain these materials. Iran appeared to be highly vulnerable to these sanctions because of its dependence on U.S. military equipment and oil and gas technology. Fourteen months later, the hostages were released.

How do we evaluate these two efforts? The conventional wisdom is that sanctions against Cuba were a failure.[5] Cuba's economy clearly suffered as a result of these sanctions, but few, if any, of the U.S. foreign policy goals were realized. Cuba not only remained communist but became heavily dependent on the Soviet Union. The sanctions were also costly because they provoked a series of confrontations between the United States and its allies. Overlooked by this line of reasoning are two points.[6] First, if the U.S. economic sanctions are judged a failure, then economic aid must be judged a success for the Soviet

Union. Its economic aid allowed Cuba to weather the storm of U.S. sanctions. Second, while they did not succeed in bringing down Castro (something not even covert action was able to do), economic sanctions may have made a positive contribution to a series of secondary objectives at very little cost to the United States. They delivered a clear message to the Soviet Union that "a threshold had been crossed and that no further action would be tolerated"; they demonstrated to Latin American states the intensity of U.S. hostility to communism; and they limited Cuba's capability to promote subversion abroad.

Judgments about the effectiveness of sanctions against Iran are equally difficult to make. The sanctions themselves appear to have had little direct impact.[7] They became effective only after Iran became bogged down in a costly war of attrition with Iraq. Just as important, economic sanctions were seen as ineffective and insufficient by the American public. As the crisis wore on, Carter's foreign policy leadership and the policy instruments he relied on (SALT, the grain embargo, and sanctions against Iran) became increasingly questioned. However, not all share in this negative assessment. The costs of the sanctions to the United States were quite small, and the United States did achieve its fundamental objective—getting the hostages back alive. *The Economist* put forward a compelling case in defending Carter's use of economic sanctions.

> The United States had succeeded in peacefully prying its embassy staff from the hands of a government-turned-gangster for a ransom siphoned off from Iran's own bank account. . . . He avoided making a settlement which might have encouraged further blackmail. . . . The Iranians first demanded the extradition of the Shah; he never returned. They sought an American admission of past responsibility for meddling in Iran; none was forthcoming. They sought the return of the Shah's wealth; it has not come. . . . The Iranians secured an end to the freeze of their assets and to western economic sanctions. But there would have been no freeze or sanctions, had the hostages never been taken. . . . But the main test for any hostage deal was whether it might encourage another government of would-be America-bashers to grab another embassy. The answer, almost certainly, is no.[8]

Food Power: Grain

In 1980, the Carter administration implemented a grain embargo in response to the Soviet Union's December 1979 invasion of Afghanistan. The potential appeared to exist for a grain embargo to have its intended impact. In 1979 Soviet grain production fell 21 percent below the figure set by planners and 25 percent below the level of the record 1978 harvest. To cope with this shortfall, the Soviet Union planned to import a record amount of grain. Approximately 70 percent of it would come from the United States. In addition, since this grain was destined to feed livestock, cutting it off would threaten Soviet meat production.

In announcing the embargo, Carter went against his 1976 campaign promise of no more embargoes and created a storm of controversy. Opposition to it came first from the International Longshoremen's Association. It wanted a total embargo on grain shipped to the Soviet Union. Carter's plan allowed the shipment of 8 million tons of grain contracted for in a 1975 agreement. A few months later, the American Farm Bureau spoke out against the embargo, charging that in spite of his promise Carter was not protecting the American farmer from the negative financial consequences of the embargo. Next, Congress questioned the wisdom of the embargo. During his 1980 campaign Reagan echoed Carter's 1976 theme of no more embargoes. Once elected president, Reagan moved to end it. Significantly, he made no move to reinstate the grain embargo in the wake of events in Poland or to couple a grain embargo to his embargo of pipeline technology to the Soviet Union. In fact, Reagan moved in the opposite direction by signing a new agreement with the Soviet Union to sell them between 9 and 12 million tons of grain annually. Political fallout followed from Reagan's decision not to use grain power just as it had followed Carter's decision to use it. Conservatives in the United States objected to the administration's passive response to the evolving crisis in Poland, and U.S. allies objected to the double standard on grain and technology sales to the Soviet Union.

Judging the grain embargo a success or failure hinges largely on one's definitions of goals. Carter's stated goal was to punish the Soviet Union, not to get its troops out of Afghanistan or to deter further aggression. On this score the embargo would appear to have failed. The U.S. Department of Agriculture concluded in a 1987 report that the embargo did not diminish the Soviet Union's supply of grain. In large part this is because the embargo did not affect the overall volume of world trade in grain and because other grain-producing states refused to support the embargo.[9] The Agriculture Department study also concludes, however, that the embargo was not the cause of the recent hardships that have befallen the American farmer. If we shift the terms of the debate a little, the grain embargo does not appear to be such an unwarranted act. For example, one author states that the principal purpose of the grain embargo was to send a message—to demonstrate toughness—and that economic sanctions did this far better than could quiet diplomacy or propaganda and far more safely than could military action.[10] According to this line of thought, the U.S. concern was not Afghanistan but with influencing Soviet perceptions of future U.S. intentions and resolve. The grain embargo accomplished this by being highly visible and by demonstrating a willingness to act even when it was clear that there would be political and economic costs to the United States. Were there no costs involved to the grain embargo, then it could be dismissed as posturing.

Economic Sanctions in the Persian Gulf War

The final case of economic sanctions we will examine centers on the role that sanctions played in the Persian Gulf War. In late 1990, the House Armed Services Committee held hearings on the eve of that war. After they were concluded Les Aspin, then chair of that committee, summarized its findings in a series of papers. In one, he took up the question of whether the sanctions were working.[11] Aspin concluded that the question yielded different answers depending upon whether one was interested in their technical ability to inflict harm on Iraq's economy or their political ability to induce Iraq to withdraw from Kuwait. From a technical perspective, Aspin viewed the sanctions as an unprecedented success.

The embargo on Iraq's trade was nearly total, with more than 90 percent of its imports and 97 percent of its exports shut off. Aspin found no evidence that Iraq anticipated the imposition of economic sanctions by stockpiling crucial supplies or spare parts. Estimates suggested that by spring 1991 Iraq would have depleted most of its available foreign reserves and that it would be forced to shut down growing numbers of facilities. To this point, the sanctions' impact on Iraq's military capability was judged to be only marginal. This was because Iraq had succeeded in developing an indigenous arms industry and possessed large inventories of basic military supplies. Of the two, the Iraqi air force was seen as more vulnerable to the long-term effects of the sanctions than was the Iraqi army.

Politically, the picture was quite different. Aspin identified two scenarios through which sanctions might produce the desired outcome: Saddam could decide to withdraw from Kuwait or he could be overthrown and the new leadership would make this decision. Based on testimony from the CIA, he concluded that as 1990 ended there were no signs that the sanctions were working politically and that it was far from certain that they would ever work. CIA Director William Webster testified that the Iraqi people had suffered greater hardships during the Iran-Iraq War and showed no signs of turning on Saddam Hussein. Other testimony suggested that Saddam's psychological profile was such that the suffering of the Iraqi people was not likely to move him to make the decision to evacuate Iraq. Only "the peril of imminent military attack" that threatened his political survival would bring this about.

Aspin then turned his attention to the future. Noting that the economic sanctions may take a year or two to have their full effect, he identified advantages and risks of continuing to rely upon them. Three advantages stood out: Sanctions might avoid a war, they could attract a broader domestic consensus in the United States and elsewhere on the need to defeat Iraq, and they might reduce its military capability. As to risks, Aspin identified three. First, could the anti-Iraq coalition be maintained over such a long period of time? Second, sanctions left the initiative with Iraq. Third, because the Bush administration had established an early 1991 deadline for Iraq's withdrawal from Kuwait, to change policy and allow sanctions time to work might call into question American leadership. Finally, Aspin asked the question: If sanctions work, what have they achieved? He noted that with Iraq's withdrawal from Kuwait, the immediate threat to oil and peace in the Middle East would have passed, but that nothing would have been done to eradicate Iraq's growing military might or its pursuit of weapons of mass destruction.

Economic Sanctions Evaluated

How typical are these three cases of economic warfare? An answer can be found by examining a recent study of 115 instances of economic sanctions over 75 years.[12] The investigators found that economic sanctions succeeded in their stated objectives only 34 percent of the time. The greatest success (52 percent) was enjoyed by sanctions designed to destabilize a government, while those designed to put a major dent in the target country's military capabilities were least likely to succeed (20 percent). The success rate for economic sanctions also showed a marked decrease over time. Almost one-half of those imposed prior to 1973 succeeded and the success rate dropped to approximately 25 percent after that date. Measuring success and failure was complicated by the fact that in some cases multiple or changing goals were present. In others, the sanctions were imposed in such a way as to fail or have little impact on the target state. The study suggests that this was the case in Bush's economic sanctions imposed on China after the Tiananmen Square incident.

Overall, the study concluded that sanctions succeed only under a restricted set of circumstances. The U.S.-led operation against Iraq is not seen as a model for the future but something likely to be the exception to the rule. A more relevant experience for judging the utility of economic sanctions is held to be the UN-led effort to bring about an end to apartheid in South Africa. Post 1985 UN sanctions were judged to have cost South Africa less than 1 percent of its gross national product. The most effective sanctions were imposed by private business and banking firms. In recognition of the difficulty of constructing an effective set of economic sanctions, the study put forward nine "commandments" to guide policy makers. We can paraphrase them as follows:

1. Don't have inflated expectations about what sanctions can accomplish.
2. The more countries you need to make sanctions work, the less likely they will succeed. More is not better.
3. Countries in economic distress are far more likely to succumb to coercion than those with healthy economies.
4. Attack your allies, not your friends. Allies are more willing to make concessions than enemies.
5. Sanctions imposed slowly or incrementally are more likely to fail than those imposed swiftly.
6. To be effective sanctions must hurt the target state.
7. Sanctions will be costly to the sender states. The greater these costs the greater will be the domestic opposition to them.
8. Economic sanctions often work best in combination with other policy tools.
9. "Look before you leap." Sanctions, even those done for symbolic purposes, should be thought out in advance.

Even this relatively stringent set of limiting conditions is seen as overly optimistic in tone by some. A reexamination of the case studies used to generate these commandments asserted that the original study was too optimistic in classifying something as a success and did not give enough credit to the role of military force when success was achieved.[13] Regardless of the potential for success, it appears that economic sanctions are becoming the United States' "policy tool of choice" since between 1993 and 1996, 35 countries were targeted for economic sanctions.[14]

FOREIGN AID

The FY1997 foreign operations funding bill totaled $12.2 billion, down from the $12.9 billion that President Clinton had requested. The bill provided $385 million to international family-planning organizations and did not contain language that denied aid to those that provided abortion services. Among other notable features of this legislation was funding for the Korean Peninsula Energy Development Organization, which would help pay for U.S. shipments of heavy fuel to North Korea, and authorization (but no funds) to participate in a Middle East Development Bank. Bowing to administration objections, the bill did not bar aid to Turkey unless it ended its blockade against Armenia and admitted to participating in genocide against Armenians between 1915–1923.

The FY1998 foreign aid appropriation approved by Congress was $13.1 billion for economic and military aid including $3.2 billion for Israel, $2.1 billion for Egypt, and $770 million for the states that emerged out of the Soviet Union's collapse. The bill did not contain two provisions sought by the Clinton administration. Removed were monies for paying most of the back UN dues owed by the United States and for contributing to a new International Monetary Fund emergency fund to prevent economic crises in developing countries. Congressional efforts to deny funding to family-planning organizations were again defeated.

Types of Foreign Aid

Three categories of foreign aid can be identified. First is humanitarian aid. It is said by some to be the only nonpolitical form of foreign aid. Others counter that the humanitarian impulse to give foreign aid is inseparable from the more obvious political and security ones.[15] The most visible U.S. humanitarian aid program is the Food for Peace Program (PL480). It makes surplus U.S. agricultural goods available to third world states in need of food in local currency and at concessional prices. A look at the disbursement of PL480 funds reveals the tension between the humanitarian and political purposes of foreign aid. In 1973, only two of the top 20 recipients of PL480 funds as measured by per capita income (South Vietnam and Burundi) were among the top 40 poorest states. The situation was little different in the mid-1980s. The state slated to receive the largest amount of PL480 funding in the Reagan administration's FY1986 budget request was Egypt with $222.1 million. Next came India with $93.5 million. Third and fourth were El Salvador ($50.8 million) and the Sudan ($50.7 million).

A second category of aid is economic development aid. Economic development aid has become the "ideology" by which foreign aid must be rationalized and justified.[16] It is valued so highly because of the presumed link running from economic growth to political stability, to the resistance of communist appeals, culminating in U.S. security. The validity of this ideology was called into question by Alan Woods, the administrator of the Agency for International Development, in a report presented to Congress in 1989.[17] He argued that U.S. foreign economic aid had lost sight of its original rationale: providing transitional help to third world states in meeting their own developmental needs. Not only has it become permanent, but in most cases "dependency seems to have won out over development." Part of the problem is seen as lying with an overemphasis on third world ruling elites as the chief source of progress and a neglect of individual citizens working to improve their own lot.

A particularly troublesome area of economic foreign aid in the 1980s and 1990s is debt relief. The sums involved were staggering. In 1988, Brazil's outstanding debt was $120.1 billion, Mexico's was $107.4 billion, and Argentina's was $59.6 billion. At first the Reagan administration approached the problem as one solvable through a combination of austerity measures by third world states and more prudent (i.e., private sector) lending policies by international agencies such as the World Bank, International Monetary Fund (IMF), and the Inter-American Development Bank. This definition of the problem changed somewhat in 1985 with the Baker Plan, which sought to increase the level of international funding available for third world states if they followed more conservative fiscal policies. Under the Bush administration thinking about how to deal with the international debt problem changed again. Instead of piling "old debts on top of new ones" as critics of the Baker Plan claimed it would do, the Brady Plan called upon private banks to voluntarily forgive a portion of the debt and interest owed to them by third world countries in return for World Bank and IMF guarantees of the remaining sums.

Beginning in 1997, a new problem area moved into the forefront that demanded economic aid: global economic distress due to collapsing financial markets in Asia. Once before, in 1995, the Clinton administration had been forced to act to protect a falling national currency. It provided Mexico with $12 billion in loans to stabilize the value of the peso. The Asian crisis, however, was far greater in scope. Initially, the Clinton administration worked with the International Monetary Fund (IMF) in putting together ad hoc solutions to individual country problems. By late 1998, this response was seen as inadequate, and calls were heard for developing a global strategy for regulating international financial flows. In October 1998, the United States met with a group of states known as the Group of 22 in an attempt to construct a new architecture for global monetary transactions. A key proposal was to shift international policy away from trying to bail out private creditors who made unwise investments and to support the idea of "debt suspension" to aid countries faced with massive capital outflows.

A third type of aid is security assistance. The U.S. security assistance program can be divided into four areas. Foreign Military Sales (FMS) make up the largest portion of this aid. Through it the United States provides loans for the purchase of U.S. military equipment. A second form of security assistance involves grants which have long been relied on as the primary means for financing arms transfers. A third category is Economic Support Funds (ESF). These are grants and loans to states that are not eligible for development assistance but are held to be of strategic importance to the United States and in need of aid. Finally, there is the grant military training assistance program which funds the training of foreign military personnel in U.S. service schools and sends U.S. training teams and equipment abroad. Long a mainstay of U.S. foreign aid programs, security assistance was especially favored by the Reagan administration, which carefully targeted this aid. Security assistance for Egypt increased 136 percent from 1981 to 1984 ($550 million to $1.3 billion). Even larger increases went to Tunisia (800 percent), Morocco (200 percent), Sudan (220 percent), and Spain (230 percent).

U.S. Foreign Aid: A Historical Overview

The relative importance of these three types of foreign aid has varied in the postwar period. This changing pattern is summarized in Figure 15–1. The

Truman administration's foreign aid program was dominated by such economic development initiatives as the 1947 Marshall Plan, which made $17 billion in loans and grants available for European recovery, and the 1949 Point Four Program, whose goal was to bring economic development and modernization to the third world through the transfer of U.S. technical assistance. All told, 96 percent of Truman's foreign aid fell into this category. In the early 1950s the situation was largely reversed, primarily due to the Korean War and the view among policy makers that foreign aid should be seen as an instrument of mutual security: It should provide defense for the state to which it is given and help the United States protect its global interests. More than 60 percent of U.S. foreign aid was now military in nature. The focus of U.S. aid also underwent a change reflecting the shift in U.S.–Soviet competition from Europe to the third world. Between 1949 and 1952 Europe received 86 percent of U.S. foreign aid. Between 1953 and 1957 its share dropped to 25 percent and then to 6 percent between 1958 and 1961. While this was happening, the third world's share of U.S. foreign aid rose to 64 percent and then to 68 percent.

A number of major changes in the U.S. foreign aid program took place during the Kennedy administration. Most visible was the change in the relationship between military and economic aid. In the mid-1960s, economic aid was once again dominant, accounting for 75 percent of all U.S. foreign aid disbursements. Within the economic aid category, a shift took place from grants to loans, and a greater emphasis was placed on providing incentives for private investment. The legal and institutional basis for the U.S. foreign aid program also changed in the Kennedy administration. The 1961 Foreign Assistance Act

FIGURE 15–1   Economic Assistance as a Percentage of Total Foreign Assistance, FY1946–85

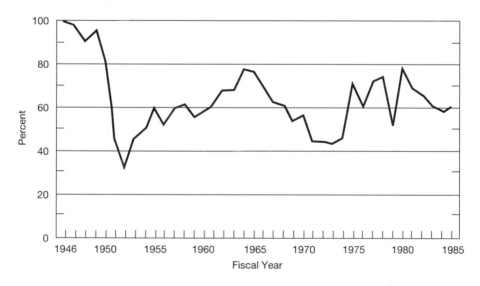

replaced the 1953 Mutual Security Act, and the Agency for International Development was set up to administer U.S. foreign aid programs.

The military component began to rise once again with the growing U.S. involvement in Vietnam and the shipment of weapons to the Middle East following the 1973 war. By the mid-1970s, it had risen to nearly 60 percent of U.S. foreign aid outlays. By 1980 economic aid was again preeminent, accounting for almost 80 percent of the total. The Reagan administration's first term saw a gradual erosion of this dominance with economic aid declining to 60 percent of the total. From 1980 to 1985 U.S. economic aid rose a modest amount from some $7.5 billion to nearly $10 billion while military aid virtually tripled in size from $2 billion to almost $6 billion.

Post–Cold War Foreign Aid

Controversy over the makeup of the U.S. foreign aid program has continued in the post–cold war era. Three topics have dominated the debate. The first involves aid for Russia. The United States has targeted two areas in giving Russia foreign aid. One is economic development assistance. Both the amount of money provided for this task and the speed with which it has been made available have been controversial. Russia has requested as much as $50 billion in aid. This figure dwarfs that produced or under consideration by the West. In his FY1995 budget request, Clinton sought $887 million for aid to Russia and the other members of the former Soviet Union. This was up from the $635 million appropriated in FY1994. Critics also argue that, as epitomized by the Bush administration's decision-making style in 1991, the United States has been slow to respond to the opportunity presented by democratization in Russia. In June, the Bush administration approved up to $1.5 billion in loan guarantees for grain purchases, but only after an extensive review of Russia's creditworthiness. In April, Bush had said that Russia was not creditworthy. Later, at a G-7 meeting, Bush was publicly cool toward Gorbachev's requests for aid, stating that the United States was not going to pull the rug out from underneath him, but that there were limits to what the United States could do. After the August coup the Bush administration relaxed the requirement that Russia undertake sweeping market reforms as a precondition for aid and replaced it with the requirement that it need only be committed to taking such steps. Still, in October, Bush turned down Gorbachev's request for economic aid, citing the lack of sufficient economic cooperation among the Russian republics.

The United States has also provided aid to help Russia denuclearize.[18] In 1991 Congress approved a program sponsored by Senators Sam Nunn and Richard Lugar that would provide Russia with funds to transport and destroy nuclear and chemical weapons, establish safeguards against the proliferation of such weapons, and assess the potential environmental damage of nuclear waste. In concrete terms this has meant furnishing Russia with armored blankets to ensure the safety of warheads during transit, modifying Russian railcars, providing Russia with protective clothing, and designing long-term storage facilities for plutonium. Here too critics argue that not enough money is being spent and that it is being spent too slowly. In 1993 of the $800 million appropriated by Congress only $31 million had actually been obligated. Furthermore, the Nunn–Lugar money was not "new" money but represented funds reprogrammed by the Defense Department from existing accounts. Supporters of the plan argue that the slow pace with which the program moved forward was due in part to the unwillingness of the Bush administration to support a program it had no role in putting together. The Clinton administration embraced the Nunn–Lugar plan on coming into office, requesting $400 million in new money for FY1994 to expand the program.

A second area of foreign aid controversy centers on the role that foreign aid can play in protecting the global environment. Spurred by the public attention brought to environmental issues by the Rio Earth Summit, many observers have called for giving greater emphasis to environmental concerns in America's foreign aid program. This does not necessarily mean giving more money. As Robin Broad and John Cavanagh note, one of the enduring myths about international environmental problems is that what is needed is a Marshall Plan for the environment.[19] They maintain that not only do large aid flows not solve the problem but much of the evidence suggests that it only makes the problem worse. What is needed is "less and better aid." James Speth suggests that at the heart of a proenvironment aid program should be the concept of sustainable development.[20] It would include such features as effective family planning, meeting food and agricultural needs without damaging the natural resource base, providing increased supplies of energy without aggravating problems of urban pollution and global warming, conserving biodiversity while at the same time providing forest resources for economic development, and promoting public health by protecting air and water resources. Controversy surrounds these proposals for two reasons. The first is cost. The foreign aid budget has always been an inviting target for those interested in cutting federal spending, and even reduced foreign aid programs cost money. Second, not all agree that foreign aid should be used for this purpose. Those that would exclude it argue that in addition to furthering U.S. security interests foreign aid should be restricted to stimulating private trade and investment.[21] Senator David Boren stated: "Only by giving the American taxpayer a return on our foreign aid investment can we build a broad-based constituency for foreign aid."[22]

A final and continuing area of foreign aid controversy surrounds the problem of structuring foreign aid programs so that they will produce economic growth. With many studies finding no relationship between foreign aid and economic growth there are increasing calls for abandoning conditionality. Currently, borrowing countries must meet specific conditions or requirements in order to receive loan aid. Often they involve undertaking politically painful domestic economic adjustment programs. According to World Bank statistics, only 60 percent of the agreed-upon conditions are usually met, yet the second phase of a loan is almost always approved. Carol Graham and Michael O'Hanlon argue for a twofold change in policy.[23] First, stop demanding the adoption of a detailed set of economic reforms and press borrowers to agree to a more general policy package. They contend that "aid is most beneficial when it influences policy at the level of ideas." Second, foreign aid should be more selective to the point of withdrawing aid because "withdrawing aid could bring genuine reform in many countries."

SUMMARY AND THE FUTURE

As our survey has revealed, U.S. policy makers have used a great variety of economic instruments in order to further U.S. foreign policy goals. It is less clear that any agreement exists on what mixture of economic tools is most desirable or when they will be most effective. Disagreement even exists over the very utility of economic statecraft. David Baldwin, one of its defenders, argues that four shortcomings in the standard approach to thinking about economic power tend to produce overly negative assessments of its usefulness.[24]

First, day-to-day economic exchanges are generally defined to be outside the scope of economic power. As we have already noted, free trade is typically not considered to be an economic instrument of foreign policy. Second, economic sanctions are often said to fail when they do not produce a change in policy in the target state. Underappreciated is the added cost that economic sanctions place on the target state even if it does not change its policies. This is somewhat surprising since the ability to inflict pain is generally recognized as a valuable component of military power. Part of the problem here is not recognizing that economic sanctions have political, psychological, and military consequences even when the economic impact appears to be negligible. Third, economic power has often been judged a failure because it is examined out of context. Policy makers often turn to it when no other instruments are available or to accomplish the almost impossible. Consider the following "failures" of U.S. economic statecraft:

Getting Castro to step down
Getting Rhodesian whites to accept majority rule
Getting the Soviet Union to change its political system[25]

It is hard to imagine any mixture of policy instruments that would have accomplished these goals. Used more judiciously, economic statecraft is capable of producing successes. A recent study of economic sanctions against third world states suggests that when relatively subtle economic sanctions are employed (delaying the delivery of spare parts, snags in licensing technology transfers, shutting off or reducing bilateral loans and grants, refusing to refinance debts), political objectives can be realized even when there is only a moderate economic effect.[26]

Fourth, economic statecraft suffers because writers on world politics underestimate how important symbolic actions are to policy makers and to domestic pressure groups. For example, all of the Reagan administration's 1985 and 1986 uses of economic sanctions were widely acknowledged to be symbolic acts. White House–announced sanctions against South Africa were taken to head off congressionally imposed sanctions and keep policy making on South Africa in the executive branch. Included among the sanctions were bans on the sale of computers, most nuclear technology, most new loans to South African government agencies, and the sale of the Krugerrand in the United States. The U.S. sanctions also mandated that U.S. multinational corporations operating in South Africa treat black and white employees equally. These sanctions were put forward more as a statement of political necessity and/or moral outrage over apartheid than as part of a specific agenda to bring about its end.

In looking to the future, three broad trends can be identified that promise to hold considerable influence over how policy makers wield America's economic power. The first involves a projected increase in the demand for humanitarian aid. In 1994, the CIA reported that the increase in ethnic and religious conflict in Africa and Asia would lead to a skyrocketing demand for relief assistance.[27] Most at risk, according to the CIA report, is sub-Saharan Africa. Described as "the most strife-torn region in the world," it forecast that approximately 30 million people would be at risk of malnutrition or death in 1995. Another 10 million would face similar prospects in Central and South Asia. Not since the 1960s has the scale of the humanitarian relief effort reached these proportions and there is little evidence that the trend is subsiding.

The second significant trend involves efforts to target U.S. overseas investments and economic activity in countries that hold the greatest promise for profitability and maximizing America's global influence. The Clinton administration already has taken the first step in this direction by identifying a group of states as "Big Emerging Markets" (BEMs) and working to strengthen the American economic presence in those states.[28] A strong U.S. presence in BEMs is seen as essential to creating jobs, limiting inflation, reducing deficits, and ensuring the competitiveness of the American economy. The original list of BEM states included China (including Taiwan and Hong Kong), India, Indonesia, Brazil, Mexico, Turkey, South Korea, South Africa, Poland, and Argentina. Collectively these countries were projected as accounting for 44 percent of the non-U.S. growth in world imports by 2010. This list has already been expanded to include Vietnam, Thailand, Malaysia, the Philippines, Brunei, and Singapore. As the United States concentrates its attention on BEM states, the resources available for other states and other policy objectives will of necessity decrease.

The third trend is the centrality of domestic politics to the use or non-use of economic instruments of foreign policy. This connection had always existed but has become more prominent of late as cold war security concerns have receded into the background and national security threats have become less direct. Controversial economic sanctions were imposed on Cuba in 1996 in the context of a presidential election, over the objections of Canada and many European allies. After winning re-election, Clinton suspended indefinitely its most offensive provisions. Efforts to impose economic sanctions against China for human rights violations and the sale of nuclear weapons–related equipment to Pakistan were blocked largely through the lobbying efforts of firms, such as Boeing and Westinghouse, eager to invest in China. Finally, in an effort to depoliticize the economic instrument, the term "most favored nation status" has been replaced in legislation with that of "normal trade."

NOTES

1. Daniel J. Kaufman, Jeffrey S. McKitrick, and Thomas J. Leney (eds.), *U.S. National Security: A Framework for Analysis* (Lexington, Mass.: Lexington, 1985), p. 346.
2. This account of mercantilism and liberalism is based on David Baldwin, *Economic Statecraft* (Princeton, N.J.: Princeton University Press, 1985), pp. 83–87. For a contrasting discussion see

Robert Gilpin, "Economic Interdependence and National Security in Historical Perspective," in Klaus Knorr and Frank N. Trager (eds.), *Economic Issues and National Security* (Lawrence: University of Kansas Press, 1977), pp. 19–66.

3. Baldwin, *Economic Statecraft,* pp. 44–47, 207–9.

4. Stephen R. Weissman and Johnnie Carson, "Economic Sanctions Against Rhodesia," in John Spanier and Joseph Nogee (eds.), *Congress, the Presidency, and American Foreign Policy* (New York: Pergamon, 1981), pp. 132–60.

5. K. J. Holsti, *International Politics: A Framework for Analysis,* 4th ed. (Englewood Cliffs, N.J.: Prentice-Hall, 1983), pp. 220–22; and Knorr, *Power and Wealth,* pp. 146–48.

6. Baldwin, *Economic Statecraft,* pp. 174–89.

7. Robert Carswell, "Economic Sanctions and Iran," *Foreign Affairs,* 60 (1981), 247–65.

8. Quoted in Baldwin, *Economic Statecraft,* p. 256.

9. Robert L. Paarlberg, "Lessons of the Grain Embargo," *Foreign Affairs,* 59 (1980), 144–62.

10. Baldwin, *Economic Statecraft,* pp. 262–75.

11. Les Aspin, *The Aspin Papers: Sanctions, Diplomacy, and War in the Persian Gulf* (Washington, D.C.: The Center for Strategic and International Studies, Significant Issues Series, Volume 13, Number 2, 1991).

12. Gary Hufbauer, Jeffrey Schott, and Kimberly Ann Elliott, *Economic Sanctions Reconsidered* (Washington, D.C.: Brookings, 1990).

13. Robert A. Pope, "Why Economic Sanctions Still Do Not Work," *International Security,* 41 (1997) 90–136.

14. Richard Haass, "Sanctioning Madness," *Foreign Affairs,* 76 (1997), 74–85.

15. See the views expressed in Hans J. Morgenthau, "A Political Theory of Foreign Aid," *American Political Science Review,* 56 (1962), 301; and Robert C. Johansen, *The National Interest and the Human Interest: An Analysis of U.S. Foreign Policy* (Princeton, N.J.: Princeton University Press, 1980), pp. 126–95.

16. Morgenthau, "Political Theory of Foreign Aid."

17. *Development and the National Interest* (Washington, D.C.: Agency for International Development, 1988).

18. Dunbar Lockwood, "Dribbling Aid to Russia," *The Bulletin of the Atomic Scientists,* 49 (July 1993), 39–42.

19. Robin Broad and John Cavanagh, "Beyond the Myths of Rio," *World Policy Journal,* 10 (1993), 65–72.

20. James Speth, "A Post-Rio Compact," *Foreign Policy,* 88 (1992), 145–61.

21. Ernest Preeg II, "The Aid for Trade Debate," *The Washington Quarterly,* 16 (1993), 90–114.

22. Quoted in Ernest Graves, "Restructuring Foreign Assistance," *The Washington Quarterly,* 16 (1993), 192.

23. Carol Graham and Michael O'Hanlon, "Making Foreign Aid work," *Foreign Affairs,* 76 (1997), 96–104.

24. Baldwin, *Economic Statecraft,* makes this point throughout this work. The statement is found on p. 115.

25. Ibid., p. 133.

26. Richard Olson, "Economic Coercion in World Politics: With a Focus on North–South Relations," *World Politics,* 31 (1979), 471–94.

27. Jeffrey Smith, "Demand for Humanitarian Aid May Skyrocket," *The Washington Post,* December 17, 1994.

28. John Strenlau, "Clinton's Dollar Diplomacy," *Foreign Policy,* 97 (1994), 18–35.

CHAPTER

16 Military Power

During the height of the cold war, American defense planners often thought in terms of a 2½ war capacity: the simultaneous ability to fight major wars in Europe and Asia plus a smaller conflict elsewhere. The principal antagonist in this drama was well known: the Soviet Union. The stakes were clear. Communism represented a global threat to American political democracy and economic prosperity. It was a conflict in which both sides publicly proclaimed that there could be but one winner. The means for deterring and fighting such challenges included strategic, tactical, and battlefield nuclear weapons; large numbers of conventional forces; alliance systems; arms transfers; and the development of a guerrilla war capability.

In the initial euphoria that followed the demise of communism and the breakup of the Soviet Union, there seemed little need for the United States to possess such a highly structured military strategy. The enemy had been defeated and attention could now be focused on pressing domestic issues. Many spoke of a peace dividend that would come about by the radical reduction in the size of America's armed forces. Others spoke of the "end of history" and the obsolescence of war as a means of solving disputes now that the world would be populated by democratic states. This optimism was reinforced by the almost breakneck speed with which the United States and the Soviet Union unilaterally reduced their conventional and nuclear inventories to levels that arms control negotiators never dreamed of approaching.

By the mid-1990s it had become apparent that while the post–cold war world might mark the beginning of a new era of world politics, it would not be an era in which military power was irrelevant. Less evident than the continued need for military power was how to respond to the post–cold war challenges of Iraq, Somalia, Bosnia, and North Korea. For some, cold war strategic concepts still provide the most sturdy base on which to construct American national security policy. Others have come to believe that this new international order requires rethinking basic premises and assumptions. In this chapter we will review traditional methods of thinking about the use of American military power and the contemporary debate over the structure and purposes of American military power. We begin by examining American nuclear strategy, because of the central role that it played in American cold war defense policy, and then turn to strategies for the use of conventional weapons.

DEVELOPMENT OF U.S. AND SOVIET NUCLEAR ARSENALS

At 5:30 A.M. on July 16, 1945, in the New Mexican desert, the first atomic bomb was detonated. On August 6, Hiroshima was destroyed by an atomic bomb. On August 9, Nagasaki was similarly destroyed by a plutonium bomb. These two attacks effectively depleted the U.S. (and, therefore, the global) inventory of atomic weapons. The U.S. nuclear arsenal grew slowly. Only 2 weapons were stockpiled at the end of 1945, 9 in July 1946, 13 in July 1947, and 50 in July 1948.[1] None of these weapons were preassembled; it took 39 men over two days to put them together. The year 1949 marked the end of the U.S. nuclear monopoly as the Soviet Union detonated its first atomic bomb. Estimates suggest that by 1949 the U.S. arsenal had only 100 to 200 weapons. Part of the U.S. response was to develop a more powerful weapon, the hydrogen bomb. The United States successfully tested an H-bomb in November 1952, and the Soviet Union duplicated the feat in August 1953. Until then nuclear bombs were produced by fission. They drew their explosive power by splitting the atom, and their destruction was measured in equivalents to thousands of tons of TNT (kilotons, or kt.). The bomb dropped on Hiroshima was a 13 kt. weapon, and the one dropped on Nagasaki was a 22 kt. bomb. With the advent of the hydrogen bomb, a new era began. These weapons draw their power by fusing atoms together, and their destructiveness is measured in equivalents to millions of tons of TNT (megatons, or mt.). While there is an inherent upper limit to how much power can be generated by fission, no upper limit exists with fusion. It is estimated that by 1957 the United States probably had 2,000 nuclear bombs and the Soviet Union possessed a few hundred.[2] Reinforcing this U.S. numerical advantage in bombs was a marked superiority in delivery systems. The Soviet bomber fleet was small and could only reach the United States on a one-way mission. The United States did not face a similar handicap because it was able to use bases in Western Europe to deliver attacks on the Soviet Union.

The year 1957 was pivotal in the development of the U.S. and Soviet nuclear arsenals. In August the Soviet Union successfully tested an ICBM, and in October it launched Sputnik into orbit. With these two actions the Soviet Union demonstrated the theoretical capability to deliver a nuclear attack on U.S. cities and its overseas military bases. Moreover, the United States was not positioned to counter these moves. Together, these concerns gave rise to the concept of a "missile gap" and the fear that the Soviet Union might attempt to exploit its advantage by boldly challenging U.S. security interests around the world. The United States took a number of measures to counter this perceived Soviet advantage. It stepped up production of its own ballistic missile force: the first-generation Titan and Atlas missiles and the second-generation Minuteman and Polaris missiles. It also constructed new early warning radar systems and placed the Strategic Air Command (SAC) on a heightened alert status so that almost half of its planes could take off on 15 minutes' notice.

As it turns out, no missile gap existed. While the Soviet Union gave the appearance of moving ahead with the full-scale deployment of its ICBMs, it actually deployed only about 50 of them, choosing instead to focus on research and development of a second-generation ICBM. This decision only became known to U.S. policy makers in 1961. The combined result of the Soviet decision to forgo the large-scale production of ICBMs and the U.S. decision to accelerate its ICBM program produced a situation of overwhelming U.S. nuclear superiority. At the time of the Cuban missile crisis in October 1962 the United States had an ICBM advantage of 226–75 and 144 Polaris missiles to zero SLBMs for the Soviet Union. It also had a lead of 1,350 to 190 in the area of long-range bombers.

Just as important as the overall imbalance in forces is the imbalance within categories. The United States enjoyed great leads in the numbers of SLBMs and ICBMs. The U.S. buildup continued through the mid-1960s before leveling off in 1967. By the mid-1960s the long-predicted Soviet buildup got under way, and for several years the pace of this buildup exceeded the worst-case scenarios painted by the U.S. intelligence community. Between 1966 and 1970 the Soviet Union increased the number of its ICBMs from 292 to 1,300 with 300 more under construction. By the end of the decade, rough parity had arrived. Because of the influence of the unratified but observed SALT II Treaty, U.S. and Soviet nuclear inventories remained stable in the 1980s. In 1985 the Soviet Union possessed 1,398 ICBMs and 979 SLBMs in 77 submarines with a total of 9,207 warheads. The United States countered with 1,018 ICBMs and 616 SLBMs on 37 submarines and 7,654 warheads. When long-range bombers and cruise missiles were added to these figures, the United States emerged with a small lead over the Soviet Union in the total numbers of strategic warheads: 10,174 to 9,987. The term *parity* is used because the two arsenals still did not mirror one another. Instead, they were marked by compensatory advantages. The Soviet Union's lead in ICBM launchers (1,200 to 1,054) was offset by the U.S. advantage in SLBMs and long-range bombers (380 to 1,196). Approximately 5,800 strategic nuclear warheads now existed: 4,000 for the United States and 1,800 for the Soviet Union.

In the 1970s the United States began to replace many of its single warheaded ICBM and SLBM missiles with multiple independently targeted reentry vehicles (MIRVs). The United States pursued MIRV technology for three reasons. First, the Soviet Union was about to equal the United States in the total numbers of launchers it possessed. Second, the Soviet Union was working on an antiballistic missile system that could threaten the United States' ability to retaliate against Soviet targets. Third, it was a relatively inexpensive way to rapidly increase U.S. nuclear strength. During the 1970s the United States MIRVed 550 Minuteman III ICBMs, giving them 3 warheads instead of 1, and the Poseidon SLBM with approximately 10 warheads replaced the unMIRVed Polaris. The upshot of the United States' MIRV program was to increase the number of strategic nuclear warheads possessed by the United States from 4,000 in 1970 to 8,500 in 1977. The Soviet Union followed the U.S. lead, and by 1977 it was MIRVing its land-based launchers at a faster rate than was the United States. By 1975 it had a 1,618 to 1,054 advantage over the United States in ICBMs.

Much of the Soviet buildup in the 1970s was predictable, based on the need to modernize its nuclear forces. What became disturbing about the buildup was that once again it exceeded Western expectations. This larger-than-expected growth plus the aging of the U.S. nuclear inventory gave rise to pressures within the United States to embark upon a nuclear revitalization campaign of its own. Four weapons systems have dominated the U.S. research and development agenda in this game of catchup: the B-1 bomber, the cruise missile, the MX, and the Trident submarine. The United States also continued to modernize its existing nuclear forces. Large numbers of Minuteman IIIs were fitted with new warheads and guidance systems which doubled their yield and improved their accuracy.

WHAT DOES IT ALL MEAN?

What do all of these numbers mean? The bombings of Hiroshima and Nagasaki killed an estimated 170,000 people, yet these figures do not really offer us very much insight into the amount of devastation and destruction that would follow from a nuclear war today. Today's nuclear weapons are typically 3 to 50 times as powerful as those dropped in 1945. We approach the question of consequences two ways. First, we outline the destructive processes that a nuclear explosion sets in motion. Second, we make use of a standard scenario for measuring the destruction produced by a nuclear weapon: the dropping of a single 1 mt. bomb, a bomb 80 times more powerful than that dropped on Hiroshima. It needs to be stressed that any effort to illustrate the consequences of a nuclear attack rests on a series of arbitrary assumptions about such factors as the height of the explosion, weather conditions, wind velocity, and the nature of the target. Change the assumptions and the consequences change.

A nuclear explosion has three major components and one lesser consequence.[3] The first component is thermal radiation. Fifty percent of the energy released by a nuclear weapon is emitted as thermal radiation (heat) within 10 milliseconds of the explosion. This produces flash burns caused by radiation striking directly on the skin and secondary burns caused by ignited clothing or other fires. A 1 mt. blast would produce second- and third-degree burns over an area of seven to eight miles on a clear day and ignite clothing for five miles. It could cause retinal burns up to 13 miles away on a cloudy day or 53 miles on a clear day. Third-degree burns over 25 percent of the body and second-degree burns over 30 percent of the body are generally considered to be fatal. Under certain conditions (such as those that took place at Hiroshima, Tokyo, and Dresden), individual fires might merge into large firestorms. If this happened, people in fallout shelters would be killed by heat, suffocation, or carbon monoxide poisoning.

The second major component of a nuclear explosion is a shock wave that travels at supersonic speed outward from the blast site. The Department of Defense calculates that 10 seconds after a 1 mt. bomb is exploded, the shock wave is three miles away. At 50 seconds it is about 12 miles ahead and is moving at a speed slightly faster than the speed of sound at sea level. It is the overpressure produced by the blast effect that the military counts on most heavily to achieve its goals. The hardness of a target (its ability to withstand overpressure) determines the altitude at which the bomb(s) must be detonated. Destroying a hard target such as a Minuteman silo requires a near-to-the-surface blast while destroying a soft target such as an unprotected city can best be accomplished when the bomb is detonated higher in the atmosphere. A single 1 mt. weapon detonated at 6,000 feet would destroy every structure within a 2.7-mile radius. Almost no one within this circle would survive who was not in a blast shelter. From 2.7 to 4 miles from the blast site, individual residences would be destroyed and about one-half of the population killed, largely as a result of falling buildings and flying debris. Almost all who survived would be injured. From four to seven miles from the blast site, there would be widespread damage to buildings and many personal injuries. The greatest damage here would be from fires which could be expected to spread for at least 24 hours and consume one-half of all buildings. Finally, 7 to 10 miles from the blast site, there would be only light damage to commercial structures and moderate fatalities largely due to the secondary effects of the explosion. The Office of Technology Assessment (OTA) estimates that a 1 mt. bomb detonated at night at a height of 6,000 feet over Detroit would produce 470,000 immediate deaths and 630,000 injuries. Flash burns and fires would result in anywhere between 1,000 and 190,000 additional fatalities depending on the physical situation at the time of the blast. A similar attack on St. Petersburg would produce some 900,000 deaths and over 1 million injuries. The OTA also made estimates of the consequences of larger nuclear exchanges between the United States and Soviet Union. These included attacks on oil refineries that were limited to 10 missiles, a counterforce attack limited to ICBM silos, and an attack on a range of military and economic targets that would involve a large fraction of each side's existing nuclear arsenal. Its findings are summarized in Table 16–1.

The third major component of a nuclear explosion is nuclear radiation. Of concern here is the damaging effect that ionization causes on cells exposed to large dosages of radiation. Severe illness sets in at about 200 rems, and a dose of 300 rems could be expected to kill about 10 percent of its victims. Exposures in the range of 600 rems within a short period of time (six to seven days) are fatal to 90 percent of those exposed. A distinction is made between prompt radiation and residual radiation, with prompt radiation being that given off within the first minute. Smaller dosages of radiation also have significant consequences for human health when measured over time. While a dose of 50 rems generally has no short-term effects, over the long run 0.4 to 2.5 percent of those persons exposed to it will die of cancer, and serious genetic effects can also be expected.

The amount of residual radiation emitted depends on the nature of the explosion. The closer the explosion is to the surface of the earth, the greater is the amount of residual radiation produced due to the large amount of debris sucked up into the atmosphere by the explosion, which returns to earth as fallout. A 1 mt. surface explosion can excavate a crater hundreds of meters in diameter and eject between 100,000 and 600,000 tons of soil into the atmosphere. A 1 mt. surface blast when there was a constant 15-mph wind and no precipitation would expose 1,000 square miles to a total dose of 900 rems. Approximately 4,000 square miles would receive over 100 rems. A 15 mt. explosion at Bikini Atoll in 1954 sent fallout with a substantial amount of contamination over an area in excess of 7,000 square miles.

A fourth component of a nuclear explosion is an electromagnetic pulse (EMP). It poses no direct threat to humans, but it is capable of destroying the communication systems that would be so important should a nuclear war ever

TABLE 16–1 OTA Nuclear War Scenarios and Their Consequences

Case	Description	Main Causes of Civilian Damage	Immediate Deaths	Middle-Term Effects	Long-Term Effects
1	Attack on single city (e.g., Detroit or Leningrad); 1 weapon or 10 small weapons.	Blast, fire, and loss of infrastructure; fallout is elsewhere.	200,000– 2,000,000	Many deaths from injuries; center of city difficult to rebuild.	Relatively minor.
2	Attack on oil refineries, limited to 10 missiles.	Blast, fire, secondary fires, fallout. Extensive economic problems from loss of refined petroleum.	1,000,000– 5,000,000	Many deaths from injuries; great economic hardship for some years; particular problems for Soviet agriculture and for U.S. socioeconomic organization.	Cancer deaths in millions only if attack involves surface bursts.
3	Counterforce attack; includes attack only on ICBM silos as a variant.	Some blast damage if bomber and missile submarine bases attacked.	1,000,000– 20,000,000	Economic impact of deaths; possible large psychological impact.	Cancer deaths and genetic effects in millions; further millions of effects outside attacked countries.
4	Attack on range of military and economic targets using large fraction of existing arsenal.	Blast and fallout; subsequent economic disruption; possible lack of resources to support surviving population or economic recovery. Possible breakdown of social order. Possible incapacitating psychological trauma.	20,000,000– 160,000,000	Enormous economic destruction and disruption. If immediate deaths are in low range, more tens of millions may die subsequently because economy is unable to support them. Major question about whether economic viability can be restored—key variables may be those of political and economic organization. Unpredictable psychological effects.	Cancer deaths and genetic damage in the millions; relatively insignificant in attacked areas, but quite significant elsewhere in the world. Possibility of ecological damage.

Source: Office of Technology Assessment, *The Effects of Nuclear War* (Montclair, N.J.: Allanheld, Osmun, 1980), p. 10.

begin. Virtually everything that relies on solid state electronics and that is not protected by an electromagnetic shield would be rendered useless. This would include automobile ignition systems, the control systems on airplanes, and the electric guidance systems of missiles. An EMP is a pulse of energy producing an electronic field up to 50,000 volts per meter. It is estimated that a 1 mt. bomb exploded 500 kilometers over Nebraska would bathe the entire continental United States in EMP sufficient to shut down the entire electrical grid. There is only one recorded case of an EMP resulting from a high-altitude explosion: an early 1960s test of a 1.4 mt. bomb exploded over Johnson Island set off burglar alarms and streetlights on Oahu, some 800 miles away.

During the cold war, the consequences of nuclear war were discussed as if they would be restricted to the main participants or at most felt on a regional basis (Europe or North America). Today, a new concern has been added: the global climatic impact of a nuclear war. The great fear is that even a limited nuclear war could trigger climatic changes due to the sunlight-blocking action of the dust particles raised by a nuclear explosion and the smoke from the urban fires it would cause. The resulting drop in temperatures could produce a "nuclear winter," threatening all survivors with cold, starvation, and a shortage of fresh water.[4] A study by the National Academy of Sciences concluded that a nuclear exchange involving only half the world's inventory of nuclear weapons would produce a temperature drop of 18 to 55 degrees Fahrenheit throughout most of North America and Eurasia depending on whether the attack occurred in April or July. It also concluded that more than 99 percent of the sun's light would be blocked out for a period of days or weeks. If war occurred just prior to or during the growing season, virtually all land plants in the Northern Hemisphere would be killed or damaged. Continued cold weather and the loss of sunlight would seriously impair productivity and growth in the next planting season. Tropical and Southern Hemisphere food production could also be seriously reduced.

A HISTORICAL SURVEY OF U.S. NUCLEAR STRATEGY

Once only a topic of debate among experts, the elements and assumptions of U.S. nuclear strategy have become widely debated in public circles. In the process the "nuclear priesthood" has been defrocked, and people are no longer as willing to defer to the nuclear expertise of policy makers or the professional military.[5] We make use of two concepts in organizing our discussion: declaratory policy and action policy.[6] Involved here is a distinction between what policy makers say their strategy is and what is actually called for in their plans for using nuclear weapons. The former is known as declaratory policy, and the latter is known as action policy. Analysis has shown that there have been persistent gaps between the two and that changes in declaratory policy do not necessarily lead to changes in action policy.

It is not much of an exaggeration to suggest that for the first eight years of the nuclear age there existed no such thing as nuclear strategy per se at either the declaratory or action level. The uniqueness of nuclear weapons was not yet appreciated. They were simply treated as the largest explosive device yet created, and it was expected that the next war would be fought just along the lines of World War II. Long-range bombers would deliver these weapons against Soviet cities, industries, and military support facilities. When the small stockpile of atomic bombs was exhausted, plans called for using conventional bombs and a general mobilization of U.S. forces.[7] Throughout the 1945 to 1953 period, a number of specific war plans were drawn up. The first war plan to identify atomic bomb target lists was BROILER in the fall of 1947. It called for 34 bombs to be dropped on 24 cities. TROJAN, approved in December 1948, anticipated using 133 atomic bombs on 70 Soviet cities over a 30-day period.

There was a certain degree of unreality to these war plans. We have already noted the limited nature of the U.S. stockpile. To this can be added limited delivery systems. In 1948 SAC had only 30 modified B-29 bombers. A more fundamental critique of U.S. policy was presented by Bernard Brodie.[8] He questioned whether nuclear weapons could be used in the same way as other weapons or if deterrence rather than war fighting was not their sole credible use. Moreover, if deterrence was to be the principal purpose to which nuclear weapons were put, then some thought was necessary on how to accomplish it. Deterrence could not simply be assumed to exist.

The first formal statement of nuclear strategy was put forward by the Eisenhower administration as part of its new-look defense posture. The nuclear component of this strategy was massive retaliation. Massive retaliation was intended to deter a wide spectrum of Soviet attacks, guaranteeing not only the security of the United States but also that of its European and third world allies. It would accomplish this by threatening the Soviet Union with massive destruction in retaliation for aggressive behavior. No details were given as to what type of Soviet aggression would bring about massive retaliation or what would be attacked. All that was promised was "retaliation instantly, by means and places of our own choosing." The lack of specificity was intentional. The Eisenhower administration felt that the Truman administration's pledge of help for any country threatened by communism had given the initiative to the Soviet Union. Massive retaliation was designed to give it back to the United States.

Two recurrent lines of criticism were leveled against massive retaliation. The first concerned its credibility. Critics asserted that deterrence required more than just the capability to inflict damage. The threat also had to be credible. To threaten the Soviet Union with massive destruction for an attack on the United States was one thing, but to make the same threat for attacks on third world states was quite another. Soviet leaders would find the former credible but not the latter, and therefore, they would not be deterred. The United States would then be left with the distasteful choice of having to implement its threat or do nothing. To prevent being placed in this position, critics argued that the United States must abandon massive retaliation for a policy containing more strategic options. The second line of criticism was that massive retaliation was ill-suited to the changing nuclear relationship between the United States and Soviet Union. Massive retaliation assumed the existence of an invulnerable retaliatory force, and this was no longer the case because of the growth in the Soviet nuclear arsenal and its development of ICBM technology. The growing vulnerability of nuclear forces to attack transformed deterrence from a certainty into one based on a "delicate balance of terror."[9]

Massive retaliation was U.S. declaratory policy. Action policy was reflected in U.S. war plans. Evidence suggests that U.S. war plans were not being tailored to meet the two primary contingencies spoken of by policy makers: retaliation and preemption (striking first in self-defense). Instead, U.S. war plans had become capability plans. They were constructed in such a way as to employ all of the nuclear weapons in the U.S. inventory and provide a rationale for acquiring additional weapons.[10] The gap between what the war plans would produce and what policy makers wanted was often quite glaring. For example, in 1955 a SAC officer stated that its plan would leave the Soviet Union "a smoking, radiating, ruin at the end of two hours." At the same time others in the administration, including Eisenhower, favored concentrating solely on military targets.[11]

In the 1950s, each military command developed plans for using the nuclear weapons under its control. SAC came to dominate this process to the point where it was selecting targets with virtually no supervision from above. In 1956 the SAC target list stood at 2,997. By the end of the 1950s SAC had examined over 20,000 potential Soviet bloc targets. War games carried out by the Eisenhower administration in the late 1950s indicated that over 300 duplicate targets existed. A clearly stated and prioritized target list and war plan seemed to offer the best hope for escaping from this situation of constantly escalating target lists and larger and larger war plans. In 1960, Eisenhower took the first steps to create order out of this chaos by approving the establishment of a National Strategy Target List (NSTL) and a Single Integrated Operational Plan (SIOP) for using nuclear weapons.

The results staggered Eisenhower. Planners selected 2,600 separate installations for attack out of an overall list of 4,100 targets.[12] This translated into approximately 1,050 designated ground zeros (DGZs), 151 of which were urban-industrial targets. Plans called for launching all 3,500 nuclear warheads if sufficient warning time existed. If not, an alert force of 800 bombers and missiles would attack approximately 650 DGZs with over 1,400 weapons and a total of 2,100 mt. By directing multiple attacks against targets, the first SIOP sought to achieve a 97 percent assured delivery rate against the first 200 DGZs and a 93 percent rate against the next 400 targets. According to one calculation, the SIOP assigned 300 to 500 kt. of weapons to accomplish the level of destruction done by a single bomb on Hiroshima. Officially known as SIOP-62, this is the war plan inherited by the Kennedy administration.

The Kennedy administration shared its predecessors' conviction that deterrence was the proper role for nuclear weapons. It differed in how to structure deterrence, and it gave attention to a problem never fully addressed in the 1950s: how to fight a nuclear war. Kennedy replaced massive retaliation with the concept of flexible response under which the United States would have a range of options to choose from in deterring and responding to Soviet aggression, running the gamut from unconventional forces (Green Berets) to conventional forces to nuclear weapons. Controlled response was the initial statement of how nuclear weapons would be employed in this strategy. It emphasized the measured and restrained use of nuclear weapons to accomplish political objectives. To that end the Kennedy administration officially incorporated three new features into U.S. nuclear thinking.

First, prominence was given to the use of tactical nuclear weapons in the hope that because of their less destructive nature they might be more manageable. Second, a new targeting policy was adopted that emphasized attacks on military forces and avoidance of population centers. In McNamara's own words the counterforce strategy sought to use nuclear weapons "in much the same way that more conventional military operations have been regarded in the past." Third, the Kennedy administration looked into two measures that might limit the damage done to the United States in case of a nuclear war: civil defense and damage limitation.[13] Political and technical problems plagued both of these initiatives and they were abandoned.

The value of these changes in nuclear strategy was called into question by the Cuban missile crisis. The way in which the crisis was played out suggested that "deterrence, in practice was less graduated and more absolute than had been imagined."[14] Attention now shifted back to formulating a nuclear posture built less on war fighting and more on the ability to inflict widespread devastation on the enemy. To be credible, McNamara estimated that U.S. forces must have the assured capability to destroy 25 to 30 percent of the Soviet population and 66 percent of its industrial capacity. Later he lowered these levels to 20 to 25 percent of the Soviet population and 50 percent of its industry. Assured destruction, as this policy came to be known, was not a return to massive retaliation. Massive retaliation rested on U.S. nuclear supremacy and was ambiguous as to where and when the United States would strike. Assured destruction recognized the difficulty—if not impossibility—of defending the United States against Soviet missiles and guaranteed retaliation for a Soviet attack on the United States.

Movement from massive retaliation to controlled response and then to assured destruction implied a parallel set of changes in U.S. targeting policy. Changes in the SIOP did occur, but not necessarily on the scale implied by the change in declaratory policy. Prepared under McNamara's direction, SIOP-63 relied on the same three target schemes established in the 1950s (nuclear capable targets, other military, and urban-industrial) and combined them into five attack options:

1. Soviet strategic nuclear delivery forces
2. Other elements of Soviet military forces and military resources located away from cities
3. Soviet military forces and military resources near cities
4. Soviet command and control centers and systems
5. If necessary, all-out "spasm" attack[15]

In spite of this effort to restructure the SIOP, one observer noted that "the basic patterns of nuclear strategy it [the SIOP] embodied proved resistant to change." The SIOP remained a capabilities plan rather than an objectives plan. In spite of the change in declaratory policy, attacks on Soviet population centers remained a target of last resort.[16]

Major changes in U.S. strategic thought began to occur in the Nixon administration. And while the names given to the ideas developed here have changed and the concepts have been refined, they continued to guide U.S. thinking in the 1980s. The first change came in U.S. declaratory policy. In 1970 the Nixon administration introduced the principle of "sufficiency." It required that (1) the United States must possess an assured destruction capability (in a statement reminiscent of McNamara's calculations, Carter's Secretary of Defense, Harold Brown, defined assured destruction as the ability to destroy a minimum of 200 major Soviet cities, or about 33 percent of its population, and 65 percent of its industry); (2) the United States must have flexible options; (3) there must be strategic equality between the United States and Soviet nuclear forces (assured destruction was concerned only with maintaining a minimum level of retaliatory threat while sufficiency added a concern for the relative destructive capabilities of the two nuclear forces); (4) the two sides must be seen as equal by both sides; and (5) the strategic balance must provide for crisis stability so that neither side has an incentive to go first with its nuclear weapons in a crisis.[17]

The Nixon administration also undertook a review of U.S. action policy. The impetus for change was strategic parity. The existence of a large Soviet nuclear force made it unwise to carry out a retaliatory attack on Soviet population centers because of the Soviet ability to retaliate against U.S. cities. Work on changing the SIOP began in 1974. The NSDM-242 authorized the drafting of a Nuclear Weapons Employment Policy (NUWEP) to establish planning assumptions, attack options, targeting objectives, and damage levels. The NUWEP emphasized the destruction of Soviet economic recovery assets as the primary objective of U.S. nuclear forces. It stipulated that under all circumstances the United States must be able to destroy 70 percent of the Soviet industrial capacity needed for postwar economic recovery. Together with NSDM-242, NUWEP laid out the foundations for SIOP-5 which officially took effect in 1976.

Neither Carter, Reagan, nor Bush formally broke away from the concepts laid out in the Nixon years. At most there were refinements in thinking, changes in priorities, and alterations in rhetoric. Carter's countervailing strategy called for possessing "strategic options such that at a variety of levels of exchange, aggression would either be defeated or would result in unacceptable costs that exceed gains." Along with recasting U.S. declaratory strategy, the Carter administration also undertook a restructuring of the SIOP. The document setting this reassessment in motion was Presidential Directive (PD) 59 which authorized production of a new NUWEP.

Three changes lay at the heart of the Carter administration's NUWEP. First, the emphasis was shifted away from economic recovery targets to military and political targets, including the targeting of Soviet leadership. The requirement that 70 percent of Soviet industry be destroyed was now formally lifted. According to one report, the four primary target sets now were:

1. 700 underground shelters for key Soviet officials
2. 2,000 strategic targets
3. 3,000 other military targets
4. 200 to 400 key factories[18]

Second, the SIOP incorporated a capacity to engage in a protracted nuclear conflict, one lasting months instead of days. Third, the target list grew in length. It went from 25,000 potential targets to 40,000. The list reportedly included over 20,000 military targets, 2,000 leadership and control targets, and some 15,000 industrial targets.

The major notable and controversial addition by the Reagan administration to Carter's policy was the requirement that the United States be able to "prevail" and "force the Soviet Union to seek the earliest termination of hostilities on terms favorable to the U.S." SIOP-6, which went into effect in October 1983, represented the Reagan administration's attempt to translate this goal into reality. The two broad aims that guided the identification of targets were (1) to deny the Soviet Union the ability to achieve essential military objectives by holding their war-making capabilities at risk, and (2) to place at risk Soviet political leadership assets. Planning for a new SIOP (SIOP-6F) began in the last year of the Reagan administration. Work on it was continued by the Bush administration. It replaced the Reagan emphasis on prevailing in a nuclear conflict with a more ambiguous goal of being prepared for an "extended conflict involving the survival of the nation" and placed even greater emphasis than previous SIOPs on the ability to paralyze Soviet war-making and leadership assets in the opening hours of a nuclear conflict.

POST–COLD WAR NUCLEAR STRATEGY

The U.S. Strategic Nuclear Arsenal

In 1998, the United States had more than 2,300 warheads on alert at any given time. Taken together they could deliver the equivalent of 44,000 Hiroshimas or about 550 megatons of TNT. They are aimed at some 3,000 targets, down from the 12,500 targets of the cold war SIOPs.[19]

The START II Treaty sets a 2003 ceiling of 3,000–3,500 nuclear warheads for the United States. Each of the component parts of the nuclear triad are undergoing changes.[20] The number of ICBMs has been reduced from 1,000 missiles armed with 2,550 warheads to a force of 550 missiles with 2,050 warheads. With the retirement of the MX missile as part of the START II Treaty, this number will shrink to 500 Minuteman III missiles that will be upgraded with MX warheads. The ballistic submarine force has been reduced from 32 submarines armed with 584 missiles and 5,024 warheads to 18 submarines armed with 432 missiles and 3,456 warheads. In the process older submarines have been retired and Trident II missiles capable of destroying all enemy targets are being introduced. Finally, the bomber force now consists of 92 aircraft armed with 1,800 warheads and cruise missiles. Table 16–2 presents the size of the U.S. nuclear weapons stockpile as of July/August 1997.

Accompanying this reduction in the size of the U.S. strategic arsenal have been several attempts to redefine American nuclear strategy. The first presidential statement of U.S. post–cold war policy came in 1997 with Clinton's 1997 Presidential Decision Directive 60 (PDD-60). This directive formally replaced PDD-13 issued by President Reagan in 1981. One impetus for the plan was the view held by key military advisors that PDD-13 could no longer be carried out under the constraints of a 3,000–3,500 warhead nuclear force. Another was President Clinton's offer to Russian President Boris Yeltsin to further reduce the U.S. inventory to 2,000–2,500 warheads as part of the evolving START process.

According to PDD-60, the U.S. military should no longer prepare to win a protracted nuclear war as was required by PDD-13. The military aim of the

TABLE 16–2   **U.S. Nuclear Weapons Stockpile, Operational Forces**
                (July/August 1997)

Warhead/ Weapon	First Produced (lab)	Yield (kilotons)	User	Number (war- heads)	Status
Bombs					
B61–7	10/66 (LA)	sub to 350	AF	300	The Mod–7 is a converted Mod–1 with a Cat D PAL IHE and several yield options up to 350 Kt.; Weighs 763 lbs. Another 310 in storage.
B61–11	1996 (LA)	sub to 350	AF	50	Earth penetrator, modified B61 Mod–7 weighing an additional 450 lbs.
B83	6/83 (LL)	low to 1,200	AF	480	Strategic megaton-range bomb. Another 120 in storage.
Submarine-launched ballistic missiles					
W76/ Trident I C4	6/78 (LA)	100	N	3,200	Over 1,500 W76 warheads from retired Trident I SSBNs have been used to arm Atlantic Fleet Trident II SSBNs.
W88/ Trident II D5	9/88 (LA)	475	N	400	Warheads supplement the W76 and arm Atlantic Fleet Trident II SSBNs.
Intercontinental ballistic missiles					
W62/ Minuteman III	3/70 (LL)	170	AF	610	In a reversal from the Nuclear Posture Review, W62 warheads will be retained.
W78/ Minuteman III	8/79 (LA)	335	AF	915	Some may be used to arm single-warhead Minuteman IIIs.
W87–0/MX	4/86 (LL)	300	AF	525	Missile will be retired and most W87 used for single-warhead Minuteman III if START II is implemented.
Air-launched cruise missiles					
W80–1/ ALCM	12/81 (LA)	5 and 150	AF	400	Several hundred have been modified to conventional versions (CALCMs). Some 940 ALCMs are in storage with their warheads removed. W80s are used to arm ACMs.
W80–1/ ACM	1990 (LA)	5 and 150	AF	400	Operational in 1991. Original program of 1,461 ACMs was cut to 460. Uses W80 warheads from ALCMs.

**TABLE 16–2   U.S. Nuclear Weapons Stockpile, Operational Forces
(July/August 1997) (*continued*)**

Warhead/ Weapon	First Produced (lab)	Yield (kilotons)	User	Number (war- heads)	Status
Non-strategic forces					
B61 Tactical Bomb	3/75 (LA)	0.3 to 170	AF, NATO	750	Mods-3, -4, -10. The Mod-10 is a converted W85 Pershing II warhead. All three Mods have Cat F PALs and IHE. Each Mod has four yield options: The B61-3 (0.3, 1.5, 60, and 170 Kt), the B61-4 (0.3, 1.5, 10, and 45 Kt), and the B61-10 (0.3, 5, 10, and 80 Kt).
W80–0/SLCM	12/83 (LA)	5 and 150	N	320	Nuclear SLCMs now stored ashore. Original program of 758 for 200 ships and submarines reduced to 367 SLCMs for 25 *Sturgeon*-class, 62 *Los Angeles*-class and 3 *Seawolf*-class attack submarines.

AF: Air Force; N: Navy; NATO: non-U.S. delivery system; LA: Los Alamos; LL: Lawrence Livermore; ACM—advanced cruise missile; ALCM—air-launched cruise missile; IHE—insensitive high explosive; PAL—permissive action link; SLBM—submarine-launched ballistic missile; SLCM—sea-launched cruise missile; SSBN—nuclear-powered ballistic missile submarine. In weapons nomenclature B stands for "bomb" and W for "warhead." The number following the letter indicates the order in which it was introduced into the stockpile; for example W88 followed W87.

Source: The Bulletin of the Atomic Scientists (July/August 1998), p. 70. Reprinted by permission of *The Bulletin of the Atomic Scientists,* © 1999 by the Educational Foundation for Nuclear Science, 6042 South Kimbark, Chicago, IL 60637. A one-year subscription is $28.

nuclear arsenal was defined as one of deterring the use of nuclear weapons against the United States and its allies. PDD-60 continues to call for the existence of a wide range of nuclear strike options against Russian nuclear forces and its civilian and military leadership. It also contains a requirement for planning for nuclear strikes against states that have "prospective access" to nuclear weapons or that may become hostile to the United States.

U.S. Nuclear Strategy

Revisions in U.S. nuclear strategy have largely been made at the margins and reflect the continued influence of cold war deterrence thinking. For example, the Clinton administration's 1994 Nuclear Posture Review envisioned American nuclear forces being used for two purposes: (1) to counter Russian strategic forces and (2) as a retaliatory force against "hostile and irresponsible" states that would use nuclear weapons against the United States.

Michael Mazarr suggests that at least in its early stages the debate over how to think about nuclear weapons after the cold war is still very much under the influence of cold war concepts.[21] He divides the contending forces into two broad groups: maximalists and minimalists.

The Nuclear Posture Review captures many aspects of maximalist thinking about the role of nuclear weapons in American foreign policy after the cold war. Maximalists expect the United States to play an active—and often unilateral—role in world affairs. Accordingly, they perceive the continued need for a robust nuclear force that is capable of deterring a renewed Russian nuclear threat against the United States, protecting American allies, and countering the nuclear ambitions of would-be regional hegemonies such as Iran and Iraq. The target set for U.S. nuclear forces would also largely remain unchanged. It would continue to emphasize counterforce targeting and contain a war-fighting capability. Carrying out these tasks requires that the United States retain a sizable inventory of nuclear weapons. Few maximalists are comfortable with a nuclear force of less than 3,000 strategic warheads, and some argue for retaining as many as 5,000. The Nuclear Posture Review adopts similar reasoning. It embraces the START II ceiling of 3,500 warheads as the long-term goal of U.S. strategic policy but calls for preserving the ability to reconstitute the U.S. nuclear arsenal should Russia emerge as a threat. This would be accomplished by holding large numbers of weapons in reserve and "uploading" them onto ICBMs, SLBMs, and B-1b bombers. One informed estimate places the future size of the U.S. nuclear reserve at 8,500 warheads.

Minimalists assert, just as they did during the cold war, that the United States does not need large numbers of nuclear weapons. At that time they based their argument on the belief that the Soviet Union was not as aggressive as pictured by cold war hawks. Now, they see the post–cold war era as presenting the United States with the opportunity to adopt a more measured role in world affairs, one that does not require it to be an overshadowing presence around the globe. The exact extent to which the United States should be involved in world affairs is a point of dispute among minimalists. Some are isolationists while others are multilateralists. Both agree, however, that the only legitimate role for nuclear weapons is to defend the United States from a direct nuclear attack. Minimalists see no need for the United States to engage in an arms race to do this. It can be accomplished through a policy of finite deterrence built around a nuclear arsenal containing fewer than 3,000 warheads. Some minimalists suggest that as few as 100 warheads may be sufficient. Finally, minimalists also take issue with the maximalist emphasis on counterforce targeting. From their view, targeting an enemy's nuclear weapons forces only adds to the state of tension and increases the likelihood of war by creating a "use it or lose it" mentality.

Current Issues

Because the debate over post–cold war U.S. nuclear strategy is in its early stages, many issues have yet to be resolved. Here we will highlight three issues which already have sparked controversy or suggested the need for a fundamental rethinking of U.S. strategy. The first is *extended deterrence*. During the cold war strategists were concerned with deterring attacks both on the United States and on its allies. The former was defined as direct deterrence while the latter was termed extended deterrence. American strategists held few doubts about their ability to construct a credible direct deterrence strategy. It was taken as a given that any nuclear attack on the United States would be met in kind. Extended deterrence, however, presented problems. How could the United States convince its allies and the Soviet Union that it would fight a nuclear war to protect them? French leaders concluded that formal treaty commitments and personal assurances from presidents were not sufficient to guarantee the promised American response and used this as a justification for acquiring France's own nuclear capability. In the end, the United States sought to lend credibility to its extended deterrence strategy by establishing a series of "trip wires" that once broken would bring an immediate U.S. response. These trip wires took the form of U.S. forces stationed in Germany and South Korea that of necessity would be engaged by any attacking communist forces.

Two problems confront a policy of extended deterrence in the post–cold war era. One involves continued reliance on trip wires built around American overseas forces as the primary means to initiate an American commitment. Budgetary pressures plus the desire to avoid becoming involved in future Bosnias and Somalias have led many commentators to call for stationing fewer troops abroad and for avoiding involvement in regional conflicts. A second problem centers on the continued reliance on nuclear weapons in extended deterrence strategies.[22] Those who support a continued policy of nuclear deterrence base their case on three major points: (1) The great destructiveness of nuclear weapons makes it easy to communicate their effect to opponents; (2) with the retrenchment of U.S. forces, nuclear weapons will be essential to discouraging the proliferation of weapons of mass destruction (WMD); and (3) nuclear weapons are essential for reassuring regional allies against WMD threats. Those who argue that conventional weapons ought to be made the centerpieces of U.S. deterrence strategies counter that nuclear deterrence is not credible, that the increased lethality and effectiveness of conventional weapons now is recognized widely, and that if the nuclear threshold is crossed it will only result in increased nuclear proliferation and security challenges to the United States.

The second issue set involves the closely related concepts of *no first use* and *preemptive strikes*.[23] Dating back to the Carter administration, it has been U.S. policy not to be the first state to use nuclear weapons in a conflict. President Bush went so far as to refer to them as weapons of last resort. Some analysts now argue that a blanket no-first-use pledge does not make sense in the post–cold war international system. During the cold war the primary concern of crisis managers was to make sure that a conflict did not escalate into U.S.–Soviet confrontation where either side felt it necessary to use its nuclear weapons. No-first-use pledges were an important restraining force under such conditions. Today, however, the strategic problem is more complex. It includes the challenge of responding to renegade states engaging in nuclear blackmail or attempting to establish themselves as regional hegemonies. These types of security challenges, it is argued, may require a preemptive strike to prevent these states from acquiring the necessary nuclear capacity to carry out their plans. Israel's 1981 attack on Iraq's nuclear facilities is often cited as an example of such a strategy.

If the logic of preemptive strikes is accepted, two further questions arise. First, should nuclear weapons be used? Those in favor of doing so argue that in dealing with these types of states only the specter of a nuclear attack on their homelands may deter them from pursuing aggressive foreign policies. Those who argue against using nuclear weapons point to both the increased effectiveness of conventional weapons and the importance of maintaining the international taboo against using nuclear weapons. They call for a policy of "assured nonnuclear retaliation." The second issue centers around the question of authority. Should the United States act unilaterally in making the determination that a preemptive strike is necessary or should the decision be made in consultation with the United Nations? Military effectiveness points to the first option while political legitimacy suggests that the second is preferable.

The third issue set centers on the problem of *deterrence failures*. Civil defense systems and damage-limiting systems such as the Anti-Ballistic Missile (ABM) system and the Strategic Defense Initiative (SDI or "Star Wars") were highly controversial elements in cold war nuclear strategic thought. Advocates argued that they were necessary in order to deny the Soviet Union any hope of victory in a nuclear war and to limit the damage inflicted on American society should a war occur. Opponents countered that such systems were destabilizing and that, in the final analysis, there was no such thing as an effective defense against nuclear weapons on the scale envisioned in a U.S.–Soviet war.

Once again, the emerging strategic problem is different. Rather than deliberately launched massive exchanges of nuclear weapons on an intercontinental scale directed at the United States, future challenges are likely to involve accidents and the existence of comparatively small nuclear forces on the part of states such as Iran, Iraq, and North Korea. The possible sources of deterrence failures here are many. They include miscalculations based on poorly designed strategies or cultural barriers, ineptitude, technical command failures, or deliberate provocations. Given this changed setting, some strategists argue that it is time to revisit damage-limitation and defense programs to see if they might not be able to offer American leaders a valuable insurance policy should deterrence fail. Others add that the possibility of deterrence failures against such states also requires that the United States must begin to plan for conducting military operations against nuclear-armed states. As we will discuss shortly, the Clinton administration's 1993 "Bottom-Up" defense review did not include this possibility in its war-gaming of a future conflict with North Korea and Iraq.

STRATEGIES FOR THE USE
OF CONVENTIONAL MILITARY FORCE

In Korea, Vietnam, Grenada, and Panama, policy makers sent troops into combat situations in an attempt to realize U.S. political objectives through military victory using conventional military force. Throughout the postwar era policy makers have taken it as a given that the United States must have enough conventional military power to protect its interests abroad from communist challenges and domestic insurgencies. Where administrations have differed is in defining the contingencies that U.S. forces must be prepared to deal with. The most vivid statement of needs lies in calculations about how many wars the United States must be prepared to fight simultaneously. Under Kennedy the United States possessed a 2½ war strategy in which U.S. forces were to be prepared to fight two major wars (one in Europe and the other in Asia) and one limited war simultaneously. In the Nixon administration the 2½ war strategy was replaced by a 1½ war strategy; the Reagan administration embraced a 3½ war strategy. According to Secretary of Defense Weinberger, U.S. forces must be capable of simultaneous "reinforcement of Europe, deployment to South West Asia, the Pacific, and support for other areas."

The most frequent use of conventional military power in the postwar period has been for containing communism. In practicing containment, the United States has vacillated between two approaches.[24] The first strategy is based on a symmetrical response. In it the United States responds to threats where and when they occur and with force proportionate to that threat. The second strategy is an asymmetrical response in which the United States responds to a specific threat in a place other than where it occurs and with whatever level of force it feels is necessary. Ideally, the point of retaliation is one better suited to U.S. strengths and that maximizes as much as possible Soviet weaknesses. Korea and Vietnam are examples of symmetrical response. Massive retaliation and the Nixon–Kissinger strategy of linkage are examples of asymmetrical retaliation.

In putting forward the Carter Doctrine and warning the Soviet Union to stay out of the Persian Gulf, the Carter administration adopted a policy of symmetrical response. The Reagan administration opted for an asymmetrical response strategy. Known as horizontal escalation, it assumed that the Soviet Union could be deterred from attacking vulnerable U.S. positions through threats of retaliation against equally valued and vulnerable Soviet positions elsewhere in the world. In advocating a strategy of horizontal escalation, Weinberger argued that "our deterrent capability in the Persian Gulf is linked with our ability and willingness to shift or widen the war to other areas." Cuba, Libya, Vietnam, and Asiatic Russia were frequently mentioned as potential pressure points.[25]

Post–Cold War Scenarios and Threat Assessments

Just as with American nuclear strategy, the end of the cold war has necessitated a reevaluation of the purposes and structure of American conventional military power. The first steps in this direction were taken during the Bush administration when General Colin Powell, then chairman of the Joint Chiefs of Staff, observed that no longer could U.S. defense planners think in terms of a single threat. American military capabilities now had to be evaluated against an array of threats.[26] To that end, the Bush administration put forward the notion of a Base Force which would provide for military forces "focused on the Atlantic region, the Pacific region, contingencies in other regions and on continued nuclear deterrence." The primary danger that Powell and others warned against in setting up the Base Force was cutting back U.S. conventional forces to the point where they became "hollow." This occurred in the early

1970s after Vietnam when force reductions were pursued so vigorously that they created military units which, while impressive on paper, lacked trained people to use and maintain the weaponry.

The dilemma confronting the Bush administration was not a new one and it continues to frustrate defense strategists. A wide variety of threats can be identified against which American military forces would be needed. The problem begins with the recognition that the same military force is not equally effective against all threats. Units and weapons ideally suited to fight a jungle guerrilla war campaign are not the same one would use to defend Western Europe from an invading Russian army. It is aggravated by financial constraints which prevent defense strategists from purchasing a full array of capabilities. Choices must be made and trade-offs entered into in deciding how to structure a Base Force.

In 1991 the Bush administration released information from the "Military Net Assessment" constructed by the Joint Chiefs. It tried to provide guidance to policy makers and strategists by identifying conflict situations and classifying them in terms of their likelihood and degree of violence. The findings are presented in Figure 16–1. The most likely conflict situation expected to confront the United States involved counterinsurgency and counternarcotics operations. This was followed by a "major regional contingency-east," which

FIGURE 16–1   Future Conflicts: How Likely, How Violent?

This bar chart, based on information presented in the Joint Chiefs' 1991 "Military Net Assessment," lists potential conflicts and shows how likely they are to occur: the higher the bar, the more likely the occurrence. The chart also indicates the level of violence military strategists predict: Less violent incidents are depicted with narrower bars, more violent incidents with wider, darker bars.

Source: Peter Alsberg, *The Washington Post,* May 19, 1991. © 1991 *The Washington Post.* Reprinted with permission.

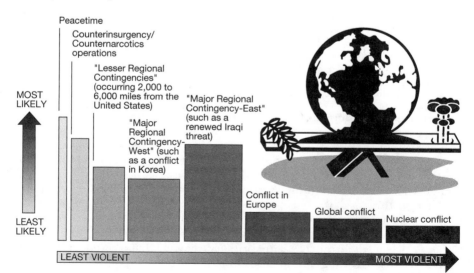

was identified as similar in scope to a renewed Iraqi threat, and lesser regional contingencies occurring 2,000–6,000 miles from the United States. The three least likely conflict situations expected to present themselves to the United States were also the most violent: conflict in Europe, global conflict, and a nuclear conflict.

Greater specificity was added the following year, with the February 1992 release of information from the "1994–99 Defense Planning Guidance Scenario Set." It identified seven paths to war which might occur over this five-year span and (in all but one instance) the amount of time needed for U.S. and allied forces to triumph. The document did not predict that these scenarios would come about. The seven scenarios are presented in Box 16–1. Most controversial was the seventh scenario, which centered on the emergence or reemergence of a hostile superpower. Depicted as "an authoritarian and strongly anti-democratic government . . . ready to begin a second cold war," the scenario was criticized for being overly alarmist in nature. This was especially true since no outcome was projected for the resulting global war and the earlier Bush planning document had discounted the possibility of such an occurrence.

Three other scenarios pointed to the continued need for a strong military capability. It was envisioned that it would take NATO forces 89 days of combat, including 21 days of "very high intensity counterattacks" to thwart a Russian invasion of Lithuania; 91 days for the United States and South Korea to repel a North Korean attack; and 54 days for a U.S.-led coalition to defeat an Iraqi invasion of Kuwait and Saudi Arabia. Controversy also existed over these last two scenarios because neither anticipated the use of nuclear weapons by the attacking state, although each is expected to possess deliverable nuclear devices. One other important observation has been made regarding these scenarios. Note how they are heavily influenced by cold war foreign policy priorities and experiences. Absent are any scenarios involving the use of U.S. forces in, or against, the Balkans, South Africa, India-Pakistan, China, Egypt-Israel-Syria, South America, or the Russian near abroad (the countries bordering Russia).

Thinking about future threats has continued in the Clinton administration. In 1993 it issued a "Bottom Up Review," and in 1997 it issued its "Quadrennial Defense Review." The Bottom Up Review drew attention to the potential threat to U.S. security posed by regional rogue states that possessed large numbers of armed vehicles and combat aircraft. Secretary of Defense Les Aspin had sought to remove the requirement that the United States be prepared to fight two regional wars at the same time from the Bottom Up Review's final report but failed to do so, and the two-war scenario became a central part of the Clinton administration's military policy during its first term. One of Aspin's successors, William Perry, defined a major regional contingency as one in which the enemy would possess an army of up to 1 million soldiers and have between 2,000–4,000 tanks.

The Quadrennial Defense Review outlined the anticipated strategic environment facing the United States between now and 2015. It anticipates that U.S. forces will be in high demand for peacekeeping, humanitarian assistance, and antidrug and other noncombatant operations. It continues to insist that

BOX 16–1   Seven Scenarios

The Pentagon's classified "1994–99 Defense Planning Guidance Scenario Set" describes seven potential paths to war by the end of the decade, though it does not predict that they will happen.

1. Russia Invades Lithuania

An expansionist authoritarian government resumes power in the former Russian Republic. Using rights of Russian minorities as a pretext, Moscow launches an attack with 18 Russian and 6 Belarussian divisions and seizes portions of Poland and Lithuania. Poland and Lithuania request assistance, and NATO sends its rapid reaction corps and reinforcements totalling 24 divisions, 70 fighter squadrons and 6 carrier battle groups. Russia has consolidated control over all former Soviet nuclear weapons, but is not expected to use them unless national survival is at stake.

NATO forces win in 89 days of combat, including 21 days of "very high intensity" NATO counterattack.

2. Iraq Invades Kuwait and Saudi Arabia

UN sanctions slacken by 1995, and oil revenues allow Iraq to rearm with top-of-the-line tanks and Russian aircraft. Baghdad sends 21 divisions, 450 combat aircraft and 2,200 tanks into Kuwait and northeastern Saudi Arabia. Iraq immediately takes all major sea and airports to prevent a repetition of easy U.S. reinforcement through Jubail, Dammam and Dhahran. The United States sends 4⅔ Army divisions, 15 fighter squadrons, 4 bomber squadrons, 3 aircraft carrier battle groups and a Marine expeditionary force. Iraq may have "a small number of nuclear explosive devices" but is not expected to use them.

U.S.-led coalition wins in 54 days of combat, including seven days of "very high intensity" counterattack.

3. North Korea Attacks South Korea

Under cover of a peace initiative, North Korea launches a surprise attack aimed at reunifying the peninsula by force. Three armies of 300,000 men armed with 5,000 tanks and 600 combat aircraft attack on two fronts, with capture of Seoul as an early objective. The United States rushes reinforcements and fights under overall command of the South Koreans. Altogether, more than 5 Army divisions, 16 fighter squadrons, 4 bomber squadrons, 5 carrier groups and 2 Marine expeditionary forces are required.

North Korea possesses 5 to 10 nuclear weapons "deliverable by aircraft or missiles" but is unlikely to use them. All U.S. nuclear weapons have been withdrawn from South Korea, but submarine-launched nuclear weapons would be available.

United States and South Korea win after 91 days of combat, including 28 days of very high intensity counterattack.

4. Iraq and North Korea Invade at Once

While the United States is preoccupied with fighting Iraq, "the North Korean leadership seizes the opportunity to strike against the Republic of Korea." The

United States tries to fight one war at a time, delivering the full required complement of forces to the Persian Gulf before shifting scarce cargo ships, planes, and medical supplies to Korea.

U.S.-led coalition wins against Iraq in 70 days of combat, 16 more than required without the concurrent Korea conflict. Defeating North Korea requires another 157 days.

5. Coup in Panama

Right-wing police in alliance with drug-dealing Panama Defense Force leaders and Colombian "narco-terrorists" stage a coup attempt with 3,000 men, threatening to close the Panama Canal unless the government turns over power. Thousands of American citizens are vulnerable to hostage-taking. The United States moves to protect the canal, free any hostages and evacuate 15,000 American and foreign nationals, employing simultaneous airborne and amphibious landings. U.S. forces include 2 airborne brigades, 2 Ranger battalions, an amphibious brigade, a carrier battle group to establish air superiority, a squadron of ground attack planes and special forces.

U.S. wins in 8 days of mid-intensity combat.

6. Coup in Philippines

In the aftermath of a major coup attempt, fighting continues among factions of the Philippine military and national police, with the insurgent New People's Army siding with an anti-American faction. Three hundred Americans working at the largely abandoned Subic Bay Naval Base are taken hostage.

U.S. forces make three simultaneous landings: an amphibious assault to free the hostages at Subic, an air drop of Army paratroops on Manila airport, and a Marine landing to secure the U.S. Embassy in Manila. Forces required include a Ranger regiment, an airborne infantry brigade, another brigade or more of light infantry, a squadron of ground attack jets, 2 aircraft carrier groups, an amphibious brigade and special forces.

U.S. wins in 7 days of low to mid-intensity combat.

7. A Hostile Superpower Reemerges

A "resurgent/emergent global threat," or REGT, becomes capable of threatening U.S. interests worldwide. According to national security sources, the scenario refers to Russia, with or without other former Soviet republics.

The REGT develops into an "authoritarian and strongly anti-democratic" government over about three years, beginning in 1994. After four or five years of military expansion, the REGT is ready to begin "a second Cold War" by the year 2001, or launch a major global war that could last for years. Pentagon planners assume that the United States would spend years of political debate before beginning a buildup in response to the REGT. "Reconstitution" of U.S. forces, as the Pentagon calls the buildup, would include expanded recruitment, weapons modernization and greatly increased production, and, if necessary, the draft.

No outcome is projected for a global war.

Source: The Washington Post, February 20, 1992. © 1992 The Washington Post. Reprinted with permission.

the United States must be capable of fighting two regional wars "in close succession." Overall, the report anticipates a period of "strategic pause" in which no new superpower emerges to challenge the United States. In 1997 Congress chartered a panel of defense experts, the National Defense Panel, to monitor and provide alternatives to the Quadrennial Defense Review. In its report, the National Defense Panel took exception to the Pentagon's two-war strategy and called for a greater emphasis on defending the United States from electronic sabotage, terrorist strikes, missile attacks, and chemical and biological warfare.

ISSUES IN THE POST–COLD WAR USE
OF CONVENTIONAL MILITARY POWER

The type of threat analysis that we have presented points to contingencies that might require U.S. military action. They do not necessitate an American military response. And, should a response be forthcoming, they do not speak to the important questions of how and when that military response should be carried out and what goals ought to govern it.

Up until the Persian Gulf War, the debate over how and when American military forces ought to be used largely centered on the way in which they were placed into combat. On one level the debate was between those who advocated the limited use of force and supported a policy of graduated escalation (the McNamara Doctrine) versus those who argued for the decisive deployment of American military power (the Powell Doctrine). On another level it involved a disagreement over the requirements for successful military action. During much of the Reagan administration advocates of both sides of this debate were represented in the cabinet. Secretary of Defense Caspar Weinberger argued that U.S. forces should only be engaged under strictly defined circumstances that included the presence of clearly defined goals, widespread public support, and the clear intention of winning. Secretary of State George Shultz argued for a more permissive set of operating conditions. He stated that the United States must be prepared to act "even without the assurance of victory or total public support."

Alliances and Coalitions

Attention today is directed at yet another dimension of this debate. It centers on whether U.S. forces ought to be used unilaterally or multilaterally. As we noted when discussing the American national style, traditionally the United States has acted in a unilateral fashion even if it was within a multilateral context. Perceived limits on American economic, political, and military resources combined with the loosening of cold war restraints on second tier powers and a resurgence in ethnic conflict have led many observers to conclude that in the future American military power will have to be exercised in truly multilateral frameworks. Two different versions of multilateral military operations exist: alliances and coalitions. As defined by the Defense Department, coalitions are "informal agreements for common action between two or more nations" and an alliance is a "more formal arrangement for broad, long-term objectives."[27]

Controversy surrounds both of these options due to a constant tension between the demands of coalition or alliance politics and the logic of military action. Typically, the former involve consensus-driven compromises and lengthy consultations and the latter place a premium on speed, expediency, and unity of command.

The most successful coalition effort of the post–cold war era was the 1990 Persian Gulf War, in which the United States led 37 states in a war against Iraq. The stunning military success of this campaign obscured many of the military and political problems associated with coalition warfare. It was only after the war ended that claims for the technical proficiency of the Patriot missile system and other "smart weapons" came in for careful scrutiny.[28] On the political side, a study of burden sharing in the Persian Gulf War found that "few countries other than the United States can lead international coalitions successfully, and even for the United States demanding conditions must be met." American leaders must be willing to take the initiative, solicit contributions from dependent allies, and deftly manage international and domestic pressures.[29]

These problems became even more apparent in subsequent coalition ventures that were also coordinated under UN auspices. On the political front, peacemaking efforts in Bosnia were hampered by disagreements between the United States, its major European allies, and other UN members over such fundamental questions as granting diplomatic recognition to Bosnia and Croatia, the use of economic sanctions, and the proper peace plan. On the military side, there was repeated friction over the wisdom of retaliatory bombings against the Bosnian Serbs and the reluctance of the United States to commit ground forces to the peacemaking process. In Somalia unexpected American casualties in the effort to capture Somali warlord Mohammed Aidid brought the UN-led operation under intense public scrutiny. What emerged was a sense that the United Nations was unprepared for such an extensive military operation and that its political agenda was ill-considered. The political backlash against multilateralism that grew from these negative experiences was a major force behind Clinton's September 1993 speech to the United Nations, in which he argued that it was now time for the United Nations to ask hard questions before sending in military forces. He stressed the limits of U.S. support for such efforts and spoke of the need to reform the UN structure.

The complexity involved in putting together international coalitions is one reason strategists continue to find alliances such as the North Atlantic Treaty Organization (NATO) to be valuable institutions. As William Odom, a former head of the National Security Agency, puts it, "NATO provides the single institution where the tedious, difficult, and highly technical details have been worked out."[30] While this may be true, NATO is in the midst of its own identity crisis. Established in 1949 as a collective defense organization designed to protect America's Western European allies against Soviet-led aggression and provide a rationale for an American military presence in Europe, NATO is an alliance in search of a mission. With the prospect of a Soviet-led invasion of Western Europe becoming increasingly implausible, attention has shifted to devising an institutional structure that will allow Europe to cope with regional crisis such as that in Bosnia, as well as provide its members with a sense of security against future aggressors.

The overarching mission of such an organization thus would be collective security rather than collective defense. Whereas collective defense systems are organized with a specific aggressor in mind, collective security systems offer their members protection from any aggressor. They do so by presenting a would-be aggressor with the prospect of having to defeat all members of the collective security organization. Then not only does collective security deter specific acts of aggression but it creates an international climate that fosters cooperation among states instead of competition. Collective security organizations can take a variety of forms, ranging from a universal collective security organization in which all states are members to an informal concert of power organized around a small group of states.[31]

In 1997, NATO expanded to include the former communist states of Poland, Hungary, and the Czech Republic. Romania and Slovenia are expected to join in a second wave of expansion in 1999. The challenge facing NATO is similar to that which existed prior to its expansion: Is it capable of serving as the centerpiece of a new European collective security system? Those who argue in favor of NATO's continued existence point to its ability to respond to new challenges, the residual presence of a Russian threat, and its important intra-alliance functions.[32]

For critics of NATO, the end of the cold war marked an end to an "era of simplicity" in U.S.–European relations, when intraalliance disagreements could be put aside in the desire to maintain unity in the face of a common enemy. Disagreements will become more commonplace and a new institution is needed where all facets of U.S.–European relations can be brought together. The most frequently suggested successor to NATO is the Conference on Security and Cooperation in Europe (CSCE). Established with an all-European membership in 1975, CSCE was a focal point of efforts to reduce East–West tensions in Europe. Over time it has developed specialized skills in such areas as arms control, confidence-building measures, conflict mediation, and human rights. What it lacks are effective decision-making procedures and an enforcement capability. Should these be put into place, the CSCE is envisioned as being a "one-stop" mediation and peacekeeping service that could be called upon to deal with problems in Bosnia and the Russian near abroad.

The Post–Cold War Purposes of American Military Power

As we noted, the second major set of issues confronting American strategists in the post–cold war international system center on the purposes to which American military power ought to be put.[33] It is not hard to construct a list of goals that American military power might be used to realize. Among the most prominent would be: (1) meet alliance obligations, (2) deter proliferation, (3) protect individual Americans, (4) support democracies, (5) interdict drugs, (6) combat terrorism, (7) conduct peacekeeping/peace enforcement operations, and (8) protect key allies threatened with internal disorder. The hard question is which of these goals actually warrant the use of force. One important way in which the use of American military power today is different from that in the cold war is that then it focused on producing acceptable foreign policies on the part of hostile states. Relatively little attention was paid to domestic issues. Today, American foreign policy increasingly is concerned with the internal behavior of governments. Two domestically oriented uses of American military power have received considerable attention.

The first involves building democracy. After the end of the cold war voices from across the political spectrum began to argue that American power ought to be used to promote democracy abroad. Harking back to Wilsonianism, they asserted that a democratic world would be a more peaceful and stable world. For example, in its 1992 report, *Changing Our Ways,* the Carnegie Endowment for International Peace identified four benefits to the United States that would accrue as a result of the spread of democracy.[34] They would have few illusions about the nature of modern warfare; they would be better trade and investment partners; they would pursue more rigorous environmental policies; and they would be more respectful of human rights. Can military power be used to further the spread of democracy? As we noted above, many advocates of extending NATO membership to the former members of the Warsaw Pact believe that it can be. They see NATO membership as providing a protective umbrella that will allow these states to pursue democracy. Others caution that by providing this protection it may actually slow down the movement toward democracy in these states as leaders feel less of a need to establish their domestic legitimacy.

Though it was domestic intervention of a very different type, cold war efforts to preempt revolutions against pro-U.S. dictators point to America's limited ability to promote democracy through the use of military power. Robert Pastor studied seven cases where the United States sought to prevent a pro-U.S. dictator from being removed from power.[35] Included among them were Cuba (Batista), Nicaragua (Somoza), Iran (the Shah), the Philippines (Marcos), and the Dominican Republic (Trujillo). What Pastor found was that the American response to the declining fortunes of these dictators followed a predictable pattern and that the United States pursued a consistent set of objectives. Most important, he found that the primary determinants of whether the dictatorship was replaced by a democracy, an anti-U.S. revolution, or a new dictatorship were domestic in nature. They had to do with whether or not the middle class allied itself with a guerrilla movement, whether the military abandoned the dictator, and whether there were free elections. American influence over the final outcome, Pastor concludes, was marginal and in each case military intervention to prop up the falling dictator was ruled out.

A second domestically oriented use of military power that has come under intense debate is peacekeeping and peacemaking operations. Peacekeeping operations came into being in the 1950s as part of the UN policy of preventive diplomacy. The goal was to prevent internal conflicts or border clashes from escalating into conflicts that would involve either of the two superpowers by inserting neutral peacekeeping forces into the struggle. As a practical matter, peacekeeping forces had to be invited in and only arrived after both sides had agreed to their presence, thereby signaling a willingness to end the fighting. Peacemaking, or peace enforcing, is a post–cold war phenomenon. It involves sending troops into ongoing conflicts such as Bosnia and Somalia and does not necessarily require the permission of the warring parties. Such was also the case when NATO considered sending ground forces to Kosovo to protect ethnic Albanians from continued Serb attacks.

Operation Restore Hope (Somalia), Operation Provide Comfort (Northern Iraq), and Operation Restore Democracy (Haiti) are prominent examples of post–cold war U.S. military interventions that at least in part can be classified as humanitarian in nature. Opposition to these undertakings has been expressed from across the political spectrum. In part, objections are directed at the multilateral nature of these operations. Deeper issues, however, have also been raised. Neo-isolationist commentators have questioned whether humanitarian interventions are really in the American national interest. Arguing that U.S. security interests were not involved in the Somalian operation, Ted Galen Carpenter states that "if the U.S. abandons its own security interests as the standards by which to decide whether to use military force, there is virtually no limit to the possible arenas in which American lives may be sacrificed."[36] He likens the Somalia intervention to bungee jumping. "A risky undertaking for which there is no compelling need."

During the cold war U.S. anticommunist military interventions were consistently opposed by those on the political left on the grounds that they represented unwarranted attempts to influence the internal affairs of other states. Humanitarian interventions, on the other hand, are often embraced as justified due to the stronger moral and legal case for such interventions and the more genuinely benign goals behind them. Richard Falk argues that this view is incorrect.[37] He asserts that while nonintervention is intolerable, intervention which (1) relies on military power, (2) seeks to bring about political restructuring, and (3) takes place without consent is never good foreign policy no matter how strong the case for action may appear. After examining the Somalian, Bosnian, and Haitian operations, Falk identifies several inherent weaknesses in U.S. military humanitarian interventions. One is insufficient political will, which leads policy makers to engage in the "politics of gesture." Enough is done to reassure the public that steps are being taken to deal with the crisis but not enough is done to change the situation. A second problem is that American military interventions still take place in the shadow of Vietnam, which gives them an imperialistic tinge. They are also carried out with a concern for minimizing American casualties and operating in a quick and decisive fashion. As a result, Falk argues, rather than being the beneficiaries of the intervention they are forced to bear a disproportionate amount of the burdens imposed by peacemaking operations.

Advocates of military humanitarian interventions reject the argument that American interests are not at stake in Somalia, Bosnia, or Haiti. They contend that definitions of American national interest that focus only on the physical security of the United States or the health of its economy are anachronistic. Just as important as these traditional foreign policy goals is the creation of an overall international environment that is supportive of American values. Humanitarian interventions are an important aspect of such a strategy. At the same time, it is recognized that military humanitarian operations are complex endeavors that are fraught with danger. If they are to succeed care must be taken that the mistakes made in Bosnia, Somalia, and Haiti are not repeated. Thomas Weiss suggests that three lessons can be learned from these experiences that will make humanitarian interventions more effective in the future.[38] First, international military interventions should be timely and robust. Second, because of serious shortcomings in the UN Secretary General's command and control system, U.S. forces should remain under U.S. or NATO command. And third, regional organizations are not viable alternatives to the United Nations for carrying out such missions.

The Nature of Post–Cold War Conflict

Not only are the purposes of American military power being debated but so too are the nature of the conflict situations into which it will be inserted. The concern here is not with the triggers of potential conflicts (that is, ethnic strife, falling governments, or control over natural resources) but the manner in which wars will be fought. A useful first cut is to distinguish between deliberate and inadvertent wars. Much of U.S. post–cold war military policy has been directed at dealing with deliberate acts of violence. Wallace Thies suggests that the lack of strategic depth, vulnerable command systems, the fast pace of modern warfare, and time pressures imposed by the geographic proximity of hostile states creates a situation where policy makers will "feel pressured to choose between war and peace without adequate reflection."[39] If he is correct, inadvertent wars will be on the rise in the future and will present military planners with significant operational challenges.

Looking more directly at the manner in which future wars may be fought, many analysts see a need for significant changes in the training American forces receive. Ralph Peters argues that "the future of modern warfare lies in the streets, sewers, high-rise buildings, industrial parks and the sprawl of houses, shacks, and shelters that form the broken cities of our world."[40] Rather than preparing to fight in jungles, deserts, or rolling plains, he believes that the American military must be ready to fight in urban environments. Edward Luttwak sees a change not so much in the setting of future wars as in the code according to which they will be fought.[41] According to Luttwak, the culture of war that existed during the cold war demanded controlled tension, discipline, and restraint. He sees a more sinister and less restrained culture of war emerging where catastrophic destruction and widespread atrocities are commonplace. The nature of fighting in Kosovo in 1999 lends support to Luttwack's agreement.

SUMMARY AND THE FUTURE

During the cold war the debate over the structure and purposes of American military power were encapsulated by two terms: nuclear deterrence and containment. This is no longer the case. Both in the conventional and nuclear areas a great deal of diversity of thought exists on how to move forward. Where some have sought to revitalize these concepts and their military embodiments to make them more relevant to the changed political and economic requirements of post–cold war international politics, others have called for replacing them with new ideas.

Janice Gross Stein recommends that in addition to thinking about military power in terms of deterrence and compellence we also ought to develop strategies of reassurance.[42] She notes that where deterrence tries to prevent an adversary from taking unwanted actions by threatening it with punishment or denying it any hope of victory, reassurance seeks to accomplish the same end by reducing the fears and insecurities of the would-be aggressor. Reassurance strategies are needed because deterrence is likely to succeed only against opportunistic states. For those states driven by fear it will have little impact.

The cost of the post–cold war military has become a point of growing concern, with pressures mounting for increases in defense spending. Advocates of increased defense spending argue that the frequency and duration of post–cold war peacekeeping operations have been underestimated. Not only are the costs greater than anticipated but these operations have siphoned off troops designated for meeting other contingencies, thereby reducing America's ability to fight a war if it had to. They are joined by those who point to the need for reinvesting in America's military technological base after years of budget cutting. Aligned against them are those who continue to favor cutbacks in defense spending as a means of reducing the overall level of government spending and those who see defense planners as inventing threats as a means of justifying new weapons requests.

Finally, there continues to be an ongoing debate over the fundamental morality and utility of nuclear weapons. Robert G. Joseph and John F. Reichart propose that three standards be used for evaluating the soundness of any proposed nuclear strategy.[43] First, the policy must be achievable. Second, it must take into account the full range of unintended consequences of its adoption. Third, the policy must point the United States toward a safer world. The adoption of such tests will not end the nuclear debate, but they will provide a common starting point for evaluating strategic policies and arms control initiatives.

NOTES

1. David Alan Rosenberg, "The Origins of Overkill: Nuclear Weapons and American Strategy, 1945–1960," *International Security*, 7 (1983), p. 124.

2. The Harvard Study Group, *Living with Nuclear Weapons* (New York: Bantam, 1983), p. 79.

3. Information in this section is drawn from Dietrich Schroeer, *Science, Technology, and the Nuclear Arms Race* (New York: Wiley & Sons, 1981); Office of Technology Assessment, *The Effects of Nuclear War* (Montclair, N.J.: Allanheld, Osmun, 1980); and Leo Sartori, "Effects of Nuclear Weapons," *Physics Today*, 36 (1983), 32–58.

4. For discussions of the concept of nuclear winter, see Paul R. Ehrlich and others, *The Cold and the Dark: The World After Nuclear War* (New York: Norton, 1984); Richard P. Turco and others, "The Climatic Effects of Nuclear War," *Scientific American*, 251 (1984), 33–43; and The Committee on the Atmospheric Effects of Nuclear Explosions, and others, *The Effects on the Atmosphere of a Major Nuclear Exchange* (Washington, D.C.: National Academy Press, 1985).

5. This is a theme of Michael Mandelbaum in his *The Nuclear Future* (Ithaca, N.Y.: Cornell University Press, 1983).

6. Desmond Ball, "U.S. Strategic Forces: How Would They Be Used?" *International Security*, 7 (1982/83), 32–33.

7. There are a number of excellent volumes dealing with the development of U.S. nuclear strategy. The major ones relied on in constructing this history are Rosenberg, "The Origins of Overkill"; Jerome H. Kahan, *Security in the Nuclear Age: Developing U.S. Arms Policy* (Washington, D.C.: Brookings, 1975); Michael Mandelbaum, *The Nuclear Question: The United States and Nuclear Weapons, 1946–1976* (Cambridge, Mass.: Cambridge University Press, 1979); and

Richard Smoke, *National Security and the Nuclear Dilemma: An Introduction to the American Experience* (Reading, Mass.: Addison-Wesley, 1984).

8. Bernard Brodie and others, *The Ultimate Weapon* (New York: Harcourt Brace, 1946).

9. Albert Wohlstetter, "The Delicate Balance of Terror," *Foreign Affairs*, 37 (1959), 211–56.

10. See Rosenberg, "The Origins of Overkill"; and Peter Pringle and William Arkin, *S.I.O.P.: The Secret U.S. Plan for Nuclear War* (New York: Norton, 1983).

11. See David Rosenberg, "A Smoking Radiating Ruin at the End of Two Hours: Documents of American Plans for Nuclear War with the Soviet Union, 1954–55," *International Security*, 6 (1982/83), 3–38.

12. Rosenberg, "The Origins of Overkill," pp. 116–17.

13. On the ABM decisions see Morton Halperin, *Bureaucratic Politics and Foreign Policy* (Washington, D.C.: Brookings, 1974).

14. Mandelbaum, *The Nuclear Question*, p. 134.

15. Rosenberg, "The Origins of Overkill," p. 178.

16. Ball, "U.S. Strategic Forces," p. 34.

17. Warner R. Schilling, "U.S. Strategic Nuclear Concepts in the 1970s: The Search for Sufficiently Equivalent Countervailing Parity," *International Security*, 6 (1981), 59.

18. Ball, "U.S. Strategic Forces," pp. 36–38.

19. Brian Hall, "Overkill is Not Dead," *New York Times Magazine*, March 15, 1998, 42–49+.

20. William M. Arkin and Hans Kristensen, "Dangerous Directions," *The Bulletin of the Atomic Scientists*, 54 (March/April 1998), 26–31.

21. Michael Mazarr, "Nuclear Weapons After the Cold War," *The Washington Quarterly*, 15 (1992), 185–201.

22. See Charles T. Allan, "Extended Conventional Deterrence: In From the Cold and Out of the Nuclear Fire?" *The Washington Quarterly*, 17 (1994), 203–33; and Seth Cropsey, "The Only Credible Deterrent," *Foreign Affairs*, 73 (1994), 14–20.

23. See George H. Quester and Victor A. Utgoff, "No-First-Use and Nonproliferation: Redefining Extended Deterrence," *The Washington Quarterly*, 17 (1994), 103–14.

24. John Lewis Gaddis, "Containment: Its Past and Future," *International Security*, 5 (1981), 73–102.

25. Joshua Epstein, "Horizontal Escalation: Sour Notes of a Recurrent Theme," *International Security*, 8 (1983/1984), 19–31.

26. Colin L. Powell, "U.S. Forces: Challenges Ahead," *Foreign Affairs*, 72 (1993), 32–45.

27. Wayne Silkett, "Alliance and Coalition Warfare," *Parameters*, 23 (1993), 75–85.

28. See Theodore A. Postol, "Lessons of the Gulf War Patriot Experience," *International Security*, 16 (1991), 119–71; and the correspondence between Postol and Robert M. Stein, *International Security*, 17 (1992), 199–240.

29. Andrew Bennett, Joseph Lepgold, and Danny Unger, "Burden Sharing in the Persian Gulf War," *International Organization*, 48 (1994), 39–75.

30. William E. Odom, "NATO's Expansion: Why the Critics Are Wrong," *The National Interest*, 39 (1995), 38–49.

31. Charles A. Kupchan and Clifford A. Kupchan, "Concerts, Collective Security, and the Future of Europe," *International Security*, 16 (1991), 114–61.

32. See John S. Duffield, "NATO's Functions After the Cold War," *Political Science Quarterly*, 109 (1994/95), 763–87.

33. See, for example, Richard N. Haass, *Intervention: The Use of American Military Force in the Post-Cold War World* (Washington, D.C.: Carnegie Endowment for International Peace, 1994); and David Wendt, "The Peacemakers: Lessons of Conflict Resolution for the Post-Cold War World," *The Washington Quarterly*, 17 (1994), 163–78.

34. Carnegie Endowment for International Peace, *Changing Our Ways, America and the New World* (Washington, D.C.: Brookings, 1992), p. 80.

35. Robert Pastor, "Preempting Revolutions: The Boundaries of U.S. Influence," *International Security*, 15 (1991), 54–86.

36. Ted Galen Carpenter, "Foreign Policy Peril: Somalia Set a Dangerous Precedent," *USA Today* (May 1993), 13.

37. Richard Falk, "Hard Choices and Tragic Dilemmas," *The Nation* (December 20, 1993), 755–64.

38. Thomas G. Weiss, "Triage: Humanitarian Interventions in a New Era," *World Policy Journal*, 11 (1994), 59–66.

39. Wallace Thies, "Deliberate and Inadvertent War in the Post Cold War World," *Strategic Review*, 25 (1997), 26–34.

40. Ralph Peters, "Our Soldiers, Their Cities," *Parameters*, 26 (1996), 43–50.

41. Edward Luttwak, "Toward Post-Heroic Warfare," *Foreign Affairs*, 74 (1995), 109–22.

42. Janice Gross Stein, "Deterrence and Reassurance," in Philip E. Tetlock et al. (eds.), *Behavior, Society, and Nuclear War, Volume 2* (New York: Oxford University Press, 1991), 8–72.

43. Robert G. Joseph and John F. Reichart, "The Case for Nuclear Deterrence Today," *Orbis*, 42 (1998), 7–19.

CHAPTER

17 Arms Control and Missile Defense

SUCCESS OR FAILURE?

Just as military forces and strategies that served the United States well during the cold war may now be outmoded, so too may be the strategies relied upon to stabilize military balances and prevent war. In this chapter we will examine the policy choices facing strategists and the historical context within which these choices are rooted.

During the cold war two general strategies were pursued: arms control and disarmament. Arms control seeks to place restraints on the use of weapons, while disarmament has as its ultimate goal the systematic elimination of weapons. A third strategy, defense, came into prominence late in the cold war with President Reagan's advocacy of the Strategic Defense Initiative (SDI).

Gauging the potential utility of these strategies in the post–cold war era is a complex undertaking for several reasons. First, evaluations of the effectiveness of cold war arms control and disarmament efforts vary widely and are influenced heavily by the political outlook of the observer. Proponents of arms control and disarmament see them as the only true way of ensuring America's security. Attempts at achieving either a preponderance of power vis-à-vis an enemy or balancing its power are seen as self-defeating. All that such policies produce are expensive arms races that raise the balance of terror. Critics argue that arms control and disarmament agreements have been largely unverifiable and have served only to weaken the United States while legitimizing Soviet buildups. Some supporters have even expressed displeasure over past agreements. Too often, they note, arms control negotiations legitimized and fueled the arms race rather than curtailed it. Negotiated weapons ceilings were placed so high that the two superpowers were able to go forward with their nuclear modernization and expansion programs. They also objected to the recurring practice of using arms control negotiations as a lever to get approval for new weapons and increased military spending by using the rationale that they were needed as bargaining chips.

The difficulty of coming up with a single overarching judgment about the utility of past arms control efforts is captured by Lewis A. Dunn in his detailed evaluation of the cold war nonproliferation efforts.[1] He divides the record into three categories: wins, losses, and draws. The decisions by Western European states not to acquire the nuclear weapons; the strengthening of the nonproliferation norm among third world states; the creation of a nuclear supply regime;

general acceptance of the nonproliferation treaty (NPT); and institutionalizing U.S.–Soviet nonproliferation talks are cited by Dunn as wins. He cites four losses: the failure to stop China, Israel, India and other countries from acquiring nuclear capabilities; the long-running holdout of some states against signing the NPT treaty; the widespread civilian use of plutonium; and failures of cooperation among nuclear suppliers. Finally, Dunn classifies some outcomes as draws because he judges them to have had positive and negative consequences. Here he lists the continuing openness and scope of nuclear weapons programs; the cessation of nuclear activities by some states because of U.S. pressure; the nonuse of nuclear weapons; and movement toward a nuclear free zone in Latin America.

A second factor that complicates efforts to judge the future utility of existing arms control and disarmament efforts is that they do not exist in isolation from one another. Arms control and disarmament efforts form a web of treaties, organizations, informal agreements, and principles that taken together serve to place restrictions on the behavior of states. This packaging is often referred to as a regime, and making judgments about the effectiveness of any one part of the regime in isolation from its other parts is fraught with uncertainty, as the 1995 debate over extending the NPT treaty revealed.[2] In this debate some argued that an indefinite extension of the NPT was essential if the proliferation of nuclear weapons was to be stopped while others argued that it outlived its usefulness. The NPT is an integral part of the nonproliferation regime, which also includes the International Atomic Energy Agency, the Nuclear Suppliers Group, nuclear free zones, test ban treaties, no-first-use declarations, the Missile Technology Control Regime, and the proposed Open Skies Treaty.[3]

Third, the factors that contributed to whatever success these efforts may have had may no longer be present.[4] Thus, even though existing arms control and disarmament programs may have prevented the use of nuclear weapons during the cold war they may no longer be able to do so. Foremost among those factors no longer present is the limited nature of the stakes fought over by the United States and the Soviet Union. Neither superpower sought the physical destruction of the other or was willing to run the risk of a nuclear attack on its homeland. Also now missing are strong domestic institutional restraints on the use of nuclear weapons and predictable foreign policy behavior on the part of the two superpowers.

Fourth, the problem has changed. Cold war arms control and disarmament agreements, as well as the first steps toward defensive systems, were engineered largely with one enemy (the Soviet Union) and one weapons system (nuclear weapons) in mind. Today the problem set is much more varied. Russia is no longer the only nuclear threat or even the primary one. Strategists must now also direct their attention to the activities of "second tier" states that seem bent on acquiring a nuclear capability. Moreover, nuclear weapons are not the only weapons systems of concern. Increasingly they are grouped with chemical and biological weapons under the common heading of weapons of mass destruction (WMD). The increased sophistication and spread of conventional weapons have emerged as still another important problem area that post–cold war policy makers must address.

A HISTORICAL SURVEY

We can better understand these evaluations if we look at the history of nuclear disarmament and arms control efforts and examine some of the major issues over how to proceed in trying to minimize the danger of war. For purposes of tracing the history of arms control and disarmament efforts, the cold war era can be divided into four periods. Activity in each is driven by a different set of priorities, guiding assumptions, and sense of urgency.

1946 to 1957

The first period extends from 1946 to 1957. Disarmament proposals dominated the international negotiating agenda in this first period. Little by way of significance was achieved, and nuclear diplomacy was not a high-priority item. Primary attention was given to the production of nuclear weapons and the formation of nuclear strategy. As a consequence proposals were put forward more with an eye to their propaganda and image-creating potential than to their substantive merits.

The first nuclear disarmament proposal to command global attention was the Baruch Plan. Presented by the United States at the United Nations in 1946, it sought to place all aspects of nuclear energy production and use under international control. As a first step in this direction, an International Atomic Development Authority (IADA) was to be created with the power to hand out "immediate, swift, and sure punishment" to states that sought to acquire atomic bombs. Under the Baruch Plan the IADA would report to the General Assembly and not to the Security Council, thus placing it out of the reach of the Soviet Union's veto power and under the jurisdiction of a body dominated by U.S. allies. Once the IADA was in place and functioning, the United States promised to destroy its atomic arsenal and make its atomic expertise available to the IADA, provided all other states pledged not to pursue atomic weapons. The Soviet Union rejected the Baruch Plan. In its place the Soviet Union called for a scheme in which the United States would first disarm and then an international organization, operating under a system of vetoes, would be created to disseminate scientific expertise and establish safeguards. Negotiations between the United States and Soviet Union proved unable to resolve these differences. In fact, it is unclear whether the United States would have been willing to implement the Baruch Plan. A general reluctance existed in Congress toward sharing U.S. nuclear secrets with other states, including U.S. allies.

Proposals for lessening the danger of nuclear war were not forthcoming again until the Eisenhower administration. Its first proposal was the 1953 Atoms for Peace Plan. This was followed in 1957 by the Open Skies Proposal. The Atoms for Peace Plan was only a disarmament plan in an indirect sense. It sought to get states to cooperate on the peaceful development and use of atomic power. Eisenhower's proposal led to the creation of the International Atomic Energy Agency, but it did not produce movement in the direction of disarmament. The proposed Open Skies Treaty focused on reducing the fear of surprise attack by exchanging blueprints of military installations and allowing each side to carry out aerial surveillance of each other's territory. It too failed to serve as a first step toward disarmament. Rather than accepting the plan as a way of side-stepping the question of on-site inspection, the Soviet Union interpreted it as a device of legitimizing U.S. spying.

1958 to 1972

According to Thomas Schelling, a founding theorist on arms control, the second phase of nuclear diplomacy began in 1958 with the unsuccessful multilateral East–West negotiations on the problem of surprise attack and ended in 1972 with the ABM Treaty.[5] This period saw the emergence of arms control on the international negotiating agenda and the disappearance of disarmament proposals. The Cuban missile crisis added an element of urgency and importance to these negotiations that until then had been lacking. According to Schelling and other early arms control theorists, nuclear diplomacy was not a competitive zero sum game in which the winnings of one side were equal to and came at the expense of the other, but one that had to be governed by the recognition of common interests and the possibility of cooperation between potential enemies. Attention needed to be directed away from a concern for reducing the destructive capacity of weapons and lowering the numbers of weapons in existence to ways of reducing the incentives to go to war and the destructiveness of war. Moreover, arms control agreements did not have to take the form of formal agreements or treaties. More flexible and informal "traffic rules" agreements were also valuable, the rationale being that the treaty itself did not produce arms control. Arms control was a product of mutual restraint, and that could be arrived at without explicit negotiations or formal treaties.

The first major breakthrough came in 1963 with the signing of the Limited Test Ban Treaty, which outlawed nuclear explosions (testing) in the atmosphere, under water, and in outer space. Unlike the Baruch Plan negotiations of the first period, negotiations on the Limited Test Ban Treaty were conducted on a bilateral basis, in private, and with a sense of resignation that comprehensive institution-building solutions were not feasible in the current international system.

A second milestone was reached in 1968 with the signing of the Nonproliferation Treaty (NPT). The United States and Soviet Union had a common interest in stopping the spread of nuclear weapons and in preserving their nuclear monopolies. For a long time action on this common interest was frustrated by the fact that the primary proliferation concerns of both sides were directed at Europe. This placed the United States in a difficult position. It was unsure that it could convince its European allies not to go nuclear without somehow giving them a voice in NATO decision making on nuclear weapons. A ban on proliferation would cut off the potential solutions the United States was looking for to solve this problem, some form of a multilateral nuclear force.[6] In the mid-1960s concern about European proliferation, and especially concern over a West German nuclear force, lessened, and attention shifted to the problem of third world proliferation. The NPT represented an agreement between nuclear and nonnuclear states. Those states possessing nuclear weapons promised not to provide them to nonnuclear states and to negotiate in good faith among themselves to reduce their nuclear stockpiles. They also pledged to help nonnuclear states develop nuclear energy for peaceful purposes. In return, the nonnuclear states agreed not to try to obtain nuclear weapons. The full potential of the NPT was not realized. States such as France, China, Israel, India, Pakistan, South Africa, and Saudi Arabia did not ratify the treaty. India has gone so far as to detonate a peaceful nuclear explosion, something permitted in the NPT. In the eyes of many nonnuclear states, the United States and Soviet Union have not lived up to their end of the bargain, especially their responsibility to negotiate arms reductions in good faith.

The third major arms control agreement reached in this period was the 1972 ABM Treaty and the SALT I agreement. The ABM Treaty, which is of unlimited duration and was modified by a 1975 agreement, now limits each side to one ABM deployment area, either around its national capital or an ICBM field. It also prohibits the development, testing, or deployment of ABM components, or the development of ABM components on exotic physical principles that are capable of substituting for ABM launchers. The SALT I agreement on offensive forces expired in 1977. It set limits on the number of fixed launchers for ICBMs (1,054 for the United States and 1,608 for the U.S.S.R.) and prohibited the conversion of launchers used for light ICBMs into launchers for heavy ICBMs. The agreement also set numerical limits for SLBMs (656 for the United States and 740 for the U.S.S.R.) and permitted some additional SLBM launchers to be substituted for older ICBM launchers.

1973 to 1988

In Schelling's eyes, the ABM Treaty marked the end point of successful arms control efforts. In the next period, he finds the United States' arms control program to be lacking in "any coherent theory of what arms control is supposed to accomplish." In place of arms control, Schelling sees a public exchange of accusations and a situation where arms control had become a driving force in the arms race instead of a restraint on it. Especially disturbing to him is the shift in interest away from the characteristics of weapons to a fixation with the numbers. He sees both the public and policy makers as having succumbed to this false view of what arms control is all about. Critics of arms control efforts speak of freezing the numbers while official policy in the Carter and Reagan administrations had emphasized matching numbers. One of the few exceptions to this trend was the Scowcroft Commission's endorsement of a small, single warhead missile (the midgetman) to replace the MIRVed MX.

A first step toward the SALT II agreement was reached in November 1974 with the signing of the Vladivostok Accords, which set ceilings on the total numbers of strategic launchers that each side could possess (2,400) and the number of vehicles that could be MIRVed (1,320). Negotiations had also established that SALT II restrictions would cover U.S. bombers but not U.S. forward-based systems. Building on the Vladivostok Accords, the SALT II agreement was to have been completed in the summer of 1973. Two new issues and a new administration caused the negotiations to drag on for almost five more years. The two new issues were the U.S. cruise missile and the Soviet Union's backfire bomber. The Soviet Union insisted that the cruise missile be counted as a strategic launch vehicle while the United States insisted that the backfire bomber be similarly counted. In the end the question of the backfire bomber was left unaddressed, and cruise missiles were only limited for a short time.

Many in the new Carter administration were sympathetic to the charges raised by critics of the Vladivostok agreement that the ceilings were set so high as not to be arms control. The overall limit was within 10 percent of the Soviet Union's limit in SALT I, and the MIRVed ceiling was very close to the number that the United States planned to deploy. The Carter administration put together two options for the Soviet Union to choose from. One would leave cruise missiles and the backfire bomber out of the SALT II agreement and use the numbers from the Vladivostok Accords as the basis for an agreement. The second would include these two systems but substantially reduce the number of launchers permitted. The Soviet Union rejected the Carter proposals. Advances in U.S. cruise missile technology made the Soviet Union insist on some form of controls over them, but the prospect of deep cuts was too novel to accept, and they objected to provisions of the second plan which called for cuts in heavy ICBMs since they were the only ones building this type of missile.

As it finally emerged, SALT II was a complicated multilayered document which the U.S. Senate has never given its consent to and which has now technically expired. An overall limit of 2,400 was placed on delivery vehicles. The ceiling was to be reduced to 2,250 by the end of 1981. A complex series of subceilings was also established: Only 820 ICBM launchers could be MIRVed; next, a maximum of 1,200 ballistic missile launchers could be MIRVed; finally, an overall ceiling of 1,320 was placed on all MIRVed launchers.

In his campaign for the presidency, Reagan attacked the SALT II Treaty as fatally flawed because it placed the Soviet Union in a position of military advantage. Accordingly, the first priority of his administration was not arms control but arms modernization and expansion. Only after restoring the nuclear balance and showing evidence of a willingness to match Soviet military advances could a meaningful arms control agreement be reached. Reagan's first concrete arms control proposal was directed at the problem of nuclear weapons in Europe. In November 1981 he unveiled his "zero option." The Soviet Union would eliminate its existing intermediate range ballistic missiles (IRBMs) targeted at Europe in return for a U.S. pledge not to deploy its Pershing II and ground-launched cruise missiles (GLCMs) in Europe. This deployment was set to begin in December 1983. The Reagan administration inherited a serious political and military problem in the area of European nuclear forces. In the 1950s NATO had begun relying on nuclear weapons as a way of offsetting the Warsaw Pact's superiority in conventional forces. In the late 1970s this supremacy was seriously challenged by the Soviet Union's introduction of the mobile SS-20. In 1979, after much debate, NATO agreed on a two-track policy of response to this development. First, it pledged itself to a nuclear modernization plan. Its key elements were the Pershing II and the GLCMs. Without them NATO would not have comparable weapons to the SS-20. Second, and simultaneously, it called for talks to limit the number of nuclear weapons in Europe.

The idea of a zero option was quickly rejected by the Soviet Union. Yuri Andropov's counteroffer was to reduce the number of Soviet IRBMs to that of the combined French and British nuclear forces. The Soviet IRBMs taken out of Europe would not be destroyed but moved to behind the Ural Mountains.

The United States found this offer unacceptable because it prevented the modernization of NATO's nuclear forces, reduced the U.S. presence in Europe, and did nothing about the SS-20 threat.

This deadlock was broken in dramatic fashion when, in September 1987, the United States and Soviet Union agreed in principle to an agreement covering intermediate range nuclear forces (INF). These are weapons with a range between 300 miles and 3,400 miles. Under terms of the proposed agreement the United States and Soviet Union would dismantle more than 1,000 weapons. The United States would dismantle 72 Pershing 1A, 108 Pershing 2, and 256 Cruise missiles. The Soviet Union would dismantle 20 SS-23, 110 SS-12, 441 SS-20, and 112 SS-4 missiles.

The Reagan administration's position on strategic arms control negotiations was even slower to take shape. In the same speech in which he unveiled his zero option, Reagan indicated that his administration was preparing proposals for a new round of strategic arms talks to be known as START (Strategic Arms Reduction Talks). Little visible movement was forthcoming, and public concern began to mount over the administration's commitment to arms control and its loose language about nuclear war. The nuclear freeze movement became a focal point for efforts to push the administration back to the arms control negotiating table.[7] In June 1982 over 500,000 people met in New York to protest the arms race. Calls for a nuclear freeze were approved by voters in 8 states, 11 state legislatures, and over 500 town meetings and city councils. Pressure also came from policy elites. The most notable statement was made by Robert McNamara (Secretary of Defense for Kennedy and Johnson), McGeorge Bundy (National Security Adviser to Kennedy), and Gerald Smith (chief negotiator at SALT I) in a *Foreign Affairs* article in which they called for a policy of no first use in Europe.[8] (Interestingly, this position was adopted by NATO under a different name, as an instrument of last resort, in 1990. The change was made at the urging of President Bush in response to the changes in Eastern Europe and the Soviet Union.)

To blunt this criticism and regain the political initiative on arms control, the Reagan administration presented a two-step START proposal in May 1982. In the first step a reduction in the number of warheads and launchers would be negotiated. Sublimits would be placed on ICBM warheads and the numbers of ICBMs and SLBMs. No ceilings were to be placed on bombers or cruise missiles. In the second step equal limits on throw weights would be sought. The Soviet Union found the START proposal unacceptable, but it did not reject it out of hand as it had done with the Carter proposals. In 1983, Reagan changed his approach to START. He embraced the concept of a nuclear "build-down."[9] At the heart of the build-down concept is the provision that each side should reduce the size of its nuclear forces as it proceeds with its own nuclear modernization plans. The build-down approach was dismissed by the Soviet Union as "old poison in new bottles." As a result of negotiations begun in 1985, the United States and Soviet Union were able to agree on a basic START framework by the time Reagan left office. It centered on a limit of 1,600 launchers; a limit of 6,000 warheads of certain types and sublimits on the number of permissible warheads on ballistic missiles and heavy missiles; and a reduction of about 50 percent in Soviet aggregate ballistic missile throw-weight.

1989 to 1992

The ascension into power of Gorbachev, the subsequent collapse of communism, and the end of the cold war provided the background against which the fourth and final period of cold war arms control took place. It witnessed both a broadening of the arms control agenda to include conventional forces and a flurry of unilateral arms cuts that produced unprecedented reductions in the levels of U.S. and Soviet nuclear forces.

The initial focal point for U.S.–Soviet arms control efforts in this period was the Negotiations on Conventional Armed Forces in Europe (CFE) talks begun in March 1989. In attendance were the 16 members of NATO and the 7 Warsaw Pact states. Also under way was the Negotiations on Confidence and Security Building Measures (CSBMs) talks where all 35 members of the Conference on Security and Cooperation in Europe (CSCE) were represented. Neither of these talks was without precedent.

Conventional arms control has become a familiar feature of the European political landscape. The CFE talks succeeded the Mutual and Balanced Force Reduction (MBFR) talks which focused on the military balance of forces in Central Europe but failed to produce an agreement. Begun in 1973, they were terminated by mutual consent in 1989 so that the CFE talks could begin. The MBFR talks were never able to move beyond disagreements over such issues as the size of the two alliance armies in Central Europe, the point to which reduction should be made and how to get there, and the meaning of such key terms as *parity* and *stability*. The CSBM talks were follow-on negotiations to the Conference on Security Building Measures (CDE) talks which began in 1984 under the auspices of the CSCE (also known as the Helsinki Accords). In 1986 the CDE talks produced the first post–World War II agreement on the use of conventional arms in Europe. Among the most significant provisions of the agreement are the requirements that (1) each state must give all other signatory states two years' notice in advance of any military exercise involving over 40,000 troops; (2) a yearly calendar of all out-of-garrison military activities of formations over a certain size must be produced; and (3) all signatories must be invited to observe such exercises. In the language of arms control, the CDE agreements were in the area of traffic rules and restraints in the use of force rather than force reductions.

Both the CFE and CSCE-sponsored talks produced agreements in 1992. Addressing only the "Atlantic to the Urals" region, CFE negotiators had reached agreement in 1990 on a complex set of reductions in the level of offensive military equipment that could be stationed in this area.[10] As would be the case with other arms control agreements negotiated in this period, the CFE accord was temporarily thrown into disarray by the breakup of the Soviet Union. All eight of the newly independent states that lie within this region now would have to agree to the CFE formula before the treaty could be implemented. Such agreement was reached and in June 1992 the CFE treaty was signed. The next month CSCE negotiators signed off on a nonbinding agreement to significantly reduce the number of military forces in the Atlantic to the Urals region.

Movement was also forthcoming in the area of nuclear weapons. At first this movement was quite predictable, taking the form of the official signing of a START I Treaty by President Bush and President Gorbachev at a summit conference in July 1991. It then proceeded in an unexpected fashion. Rather than engaging in a new round of protracted negotiations to further reduce the size of their nuclear arsenals, the United States and the Soviet Union entered into a series of unilateral cuts. In September 1991 Bush ordered that (1) all tactical nuclear weapons except those dropped from planes be removed from the U.S. arsenal; (2) all nuclear cruise missiles and bombs be taken off naval ships, attack submarines, and land-based naval aircraft; (3) all strategic bombers be taken off high-alert status; and (4) a halt take place in the development and deployment of mobile ICBMs. Gorbachev responded by calling for the elimination of all land-based tactical nuclear weapons and the removal of all nuclear arms from ships, submarines, and land-based naval aircraft. In his State of the Union address in 1992, Bush focused on strategic weapons and offered to reduce by one-third the number of U.S. SLBM warheads in return for Russia, Ukraine, and Kazakhstan agreeing to eliminate all of their heavy multiple warheaded ICBMs. Yeltsin responded with a call for even deeper cuts that would leave each side with some 2,500 warheads. These pronouncements led to the signing of a joint understanding by Bush and Yeltsin in June 1992 that in turn led to the January 1993 signing of START II. According to its terms both sides agreed to make deep cuts in their nuclear forces by 2003. The target figure for the United States was set at 3,500 bombs and warheads while that for the Soviet Union was 2,997. Moreover, each side agreed to eliminate all of its multiple-warhead ICBMs and sublimits favorable to the United States were set on the numbers of submarine-launched warheads and air-launched nuclear weapons.

Before the Clinton administration could move to bring the START II treaty to the Senate for its approval, it first had to deal with problems surrounding the ratification of START I. Here again, the problem was the breakup of the Soviet Union. Its dissolution had left four nuclear states in its wake: Russia, Ukraine, Belarus, and Kazakhstan. All expressed misgivings about giving up their nuclear weapons and sought compensation from the West in terms of security guarantees and foreign aid as a precondition for doing so. The last holdout was Ukraine, which formally did not give its approval to the START I treaty and the NPT treaty until November 1994.

DEFENSE

The Strategic Defense Initiative

According to one observer, "The great missing innovation in the nuclear age is the development of means to defend against nuclear attack."[11] If this capacity is lacking, it is impossible to protect one's population and territory without the cooperation of the enemy. Both parties must agree not to attack population centers. Strategists have established that such tacit cooperation between enemies is possible and often takes place during war.[12] Still, many are troubled that the defense of the United States in the nuclear age is possible only with the cooperation of an adversary. Reagan gave voice to these concerns in a March 1983 speech when he called upon the scientific community to find a way for the United States to escape from this situation.

> What if free people could live secure in the knowledge that their security did not rest upon the threat of instant U.S. retaliation to deter a Soviet attack; that we could intercept and destroy their strategic missiles before they reached our soil or that of our allies? . . . Is it not worth every investment necessary to free the world from the threat of nuclear war?[13]

As presented by Reagan, the Strategic Defense Initiative (SDI) was a long-term research and development program designed to identify viable policy options for creating a nuclear defense system. The decisions as to which system, if any, to pursue were scheduled to be made in the 1990s. However, in early 1987 the Reagan administration began examining the possibility of an early deployment of SDI. As envisioned by most observers, Reagan's SDI system involved a series of defensive systems layered together in such a way as to create a protective shield.

Each layer in this system was to perform the same tasks: It would search out and detect targets, track them, discriminate between real targets and dummy targets, and intercept and destroy the real targets. The layers in the SDI system would roughly correspond to the four major phases in the trajectory of an ICBM.[14] The boost phase occurs immediately following launch and lasts several hundred seconds. The major advantage in attacking incoming missiles in the boost phase is that the targets are relatively few in number, easily visible to space-based sensors, and relatively vulnerable. The major problems are the short length of time available to act and the exotic nature of the technologies needed to carry out a defensive strike. Next comes the postboost phase. It too lasts several hundred seconds. This is the deployment stage where the "bus" maneuvers to achieve a variety of trajectories and deploys its warheads, decoys, and other penetration aids. Defense is now complicated by the added number of targets that need to be tracked and the need to discriminate between real and diversionary targets. There is also a midcourse phase lasting approximately 1,000 seconds. The warheads are easily targeted in this stage because of the predictable free-fall trajectories of objects in the vacuum of space. Discrimination between real and diversionary targets is the major problem here. Finally, there is the reentry phase. It lasts 30 to 100 seconds. The atmosphere acts to filter out the decoys and penetration aids, making the warheads easy to identify. The major problem here is the shortness of time in which to act. Each target being defended has a "keep-out" distance beyond which incoming warheads must be intercepted if the target is to be protected. The greatest challenge lies in defending cities. Here, the keep-out distance is the greatest, and the consequences of even one missile getting through are catastrophic. Hardened missile sites have a short keep-out distance and can better withstand the consequences of missiles penetrating the defense. The goal is not to protect every missile but only to protect some fraction of them.

During the Reagan administration the scope and funding of a "star wars" system was progressively cut back, although the goal was never formally abandoned. In 1989, Secretary of Defense Dick Cheney declared that SDI had been "oversold" as a leak-proof umbrella (a possibility he described as "extremely remote"). Still, the Bush administration continued to seek funding for it under the guise of "brilliant pebbles." Under it, missiles sent into space would be sent into layered orbits and would possess the ability to detect the launch of enemy missiles at a distance of several thousand miles. Upon receiving orders to attack, the missiles would speed toward the enemy missiles and ram them at high speed, thereby destroying them.

SDI's short-lived existence formally came to an end in the Clinton administration. In May 1993, Secretary of Defense Les Aspin announced that the Strategic Defense Initiative Office was being closed. It would be replaced by a Ballistic Missile Defense Office whose mission would be to develop follow-on missiles to the Patriot system used against SCUD missiles in the Persian Gulf War. Instead of constructing a nuclear shield over the United States the new goal would be to prevent attacks by short-range ground-launched missiles.

In looking back at the rise and fall of Star Wars, Eugene Skolnikoff, a specialist in science policy and international relations, observes that SDI holds four cautionary lessons for policy makers intent upon using technology to solve policy problems.[15] First, there is a major difference between the development of a specific piece of technology and the creation of a complex technological system that draws upon and integrates many individual technologies. SDI was such a system and it presented policy makers with tremendous construction and implementation challenges. Second, technological achievements such as SDI are not one-time breakthroughs. They must be thought of as evolving systems that will become part of an ongoing game of move and countermove between the United States and its adversaries. Third, even when technology holds the promise of solving a policy problem (which Skolnikoff did not believe was the case with SDI), it will fail unless it is coupled with the necessary levels of political and financial commitments. These accompaniments were present for the Manhattan Project and Project Apollo but were lacking in the case of SDI. Fourth, in the final analysis, the success or failure of SDI-type projects does not rest on technological criteria but on whether it accomplishes its stated policy goal. Judgments on this score are political in nature and derive from the nature of the strategic relationship existing between the United States and other countries.

Missile Defense Systems

As it currently is envisioned, the U.S. missile defense system is made up of two parts. The first is a national defense system capable of protecting all fifty states against an attack by intercontinental ballistic missiles. The second is a theater missile defense system capable of protecting U.S. troops in the field. At least six different weapons programs have been studied for this purpose including an upgrading of the Army's Patriot missiles, a Navy Area Wide system located on cruisers and destroyers, and an Army Theater High-Altitude Area Defense system that would engage enemy missiles at higher altitudes and longer ranges than the Patriot or Navy system.

As with its predecessor, Star Wars, the development of missile defense systems continues to be marked by political controversy. A national missile defense system was part of Newt Gingrich's Contract With America in 1994 and was pushed for in 1996 by Republican presidential candidate Robert Dole. Republicans retreated when Congressional Budget Office figures put the short-term price tag at $10 billion, with costs escalating to as high as $60 billion by 2010. In 1998, a bipartisan Commission to Assess the Ballistic Threat to the United States challenged intelligence estimates that minimized the existence of such a missile threat to the United States. The intelligence community is on record as having stated that such a threat is unlikely to emerge until 2010; that the main threat is from North Korea; and that it could be detected well in advance. Development of theater defense systems was held up by concern that it would be a violation of the 1972 ABM Treaty. This stumbling block was removed in 1997 when at their summit conference Clinton and Yeltsin agreed to a formula that would allow the testing of theatre missile defense systems. Yet, in 1998, a key interceptor missile in the Army's Theater High-Altitude Area Defense system failed for the fifth time in a row. Missile interceptors designed to be part of a national defense system failed 13 times in 20 attempts between 1983–1997, with the last successful attempt coming in May, 1987.

The Clinton administration has sought to find a middle ground in these debates. In a 1996 deal with Congress, Clinton agreed to a "three-plus-three" deal. His administration would spend the next three years designing and testing a national defense system that could be deployed in another three years if it was determined wise to do so in 2000. The administration appears unwilling to choose among the different theater defense systems under development in large measure because both Army and Navy versions have strong supporters in Congress.

THE POST–COLD WAR AGENDA

The Proliferation Challenge

The central preoccupation of American arms controllers in the immediate post–cold war era no longer is the Soviet strategic threat. It is proliferation. This is not entirely new ground. A number of institutions, treaties, and principles are already in place and constitute a nonproliferation regime. Still, dealing with nonproliferation in the post–cold war era promises to be a very difficult undertaking. Not only are the problems different but many see America's early post–cold war nonproliferation policy as being outdated and plagued by shortcomings.[16] The first of these is an attempt to revitalize strategies based on denying would-be proliferators the needed weapons technology. Such strategies are seen as offering diminishing returns in the effort to stop proliferation. The second is a failure to create an international political climate conducive to new efforts at dealing with the proliferation problem. The absence of an international consensus on the need for new policies robs them of the legitimacy they need to be effective. The final shortcoming is the tendency to approach nonproliferation problems in an ad hoc and segmented manner. Where arms control is seen as a policy for managing East–West relations, proliferation policy is seen as a tool for managing North–South relations.

Why Proliferation?

With the detonation of nuclear devices by India and Pakistan in 1998, the problem of dealing with proliferation has taken on a new sense of urgency. It has led some analysts to revisit the most fundamental of all questions: Why does proliferation occur? According to Albert Wohlstetter, one of the first cold war nuclear theorists, the way to prevent nuclear proliferation was by providing potential nuclear states with a protective nuclear umbrella. Brad Roberts asserts that the proliferation problem has changed fundamentally since the 1950s.[17] Today, not only are some states opting to become the next nuclear state as did India and Pakistan but others are making the conscious decision to stop being nuclear powers as was the case with South Africa, Belarus, and Kazakhstan. The nuclear proliferation problem has also become complicated by the intersection of this problem with that of chemical and biological weapons proliferation, as well as the proliferation of associated technologies in the areas of ballistic missiles, cruise missiles, and other advanced weapons delivery systems.

The net result of these developments is that no single motive lies behind the decision to "go nuclear."[18] It may come about as a result of a strategic chain reaction in which the decision of one state to go nuclear prompts others to follow suit. It may come about as a result of domestic pressures in which the acquisition of a nuclear device is seen as a solution to an internal political problem. Finally, nuclear proliferation may be a result of shared international norms and beliefs about how to bolster a state's international standing and prestige. Many see the multiplicity of motivations as requiring the United States to rethink the goals it wishes to achieve and to reevaluate the policy tools it uses to prevent proliferation.

Policy Choices: Goals

Any discussion of policy choices must begin with an attention to goals. The problem confronting policy makers is how to frame their goals in a way that guides policy choices. First, policy makers will need to decide what weapons systems they are most worried about. The cold war focus of nonproliferation efforts was on nuclear weapons and this remains a serious problem. At present the number of declared nuclear states and covert nuclear states is relatively small. Five states (the United States, Russia, China, Great Britain, and France) officially possess nuclear weapons; one (South Africa) has announced that it has dismantled its nuclear weapons; and five (India, Israel, Pakistan, North Korea, and Iraq) are believed capable of producing nuclear arms. The proliferation concern is with keeping these numbers from growing. A 1988 study projected that by 2000, 40 countries will be capable of making nuclear weapons.[19] The situation becomes even more challenging if nuclear weapons are grouped with chemical and biological weapons under the heading of weapons of mass destruction (WMD). A 1993 treaty pledges signatory states to eliminate all chemical weapons by 2005 and open themselves to rigorous international inspections. Nevertheless, a 1994 report estimated that more than 25 states may be developing WMD capabilities and that more than 24 states have chemical warfare programs, some of which include stockpiling these weapons.[20] Just as troubling as the spread of these weapons is the increased availability of delivery systems. This same report stated that at least 15 states possess operational ballistic missiles and 66 have operational cruise missiles.

The possession of technological know-how does not translate into a decision to build a WMD, nor does the possession of such weapons automatically create the same type of security problems for the United States. Just as important as the number of new nuclear states is their identity and motive for developing these weapons. Michael Mandelbaum suggests that we think in terms of three types of states that have a motive to go nuclear.[21] The first group is made up of U.S. allies such as Japan and Germany who may feel that they no longer can rely on American security guarantees. The second group is composed of orphans, states who may feel that they have legitimate and pressing security concerns and that they cannot rely on others to protect them. Israel, Pakistan, and Ukraine fall into this category. Finally, there are the rogue states such as Iraq and North Korea who are openly hostile to neighbors and distrustful of the international community.

Nuclear weapons are not the only proliferation problem facing policy makers. Proliferation in conventional weapons is also a problem, and for some it is the major problem. Traditionally, efforts to curb conventional weapons proliferation have focused on restricting the sale or transfer of major weapons systems from one state to another. For a brief period of time it appeared that conventional arms transfers were becoming less pronounced in world politics. Between 1989 and 1991 worldwide sales fell 53 percent and U.S. sales fell almost 34 percent. This downward trend has since been reversed. In 1992, U.S. defense firms increased their foreign orders from $12 billion in 1991 to $28 billion. In 1993, U.S. arms transfers totaled more than $32 billion. Relatively little attention has been paid to the problem of curbing arms transfers. Conventional Arms Transfer Talks were held between 1977 and 1979 but ended with no agreement being reached.[22] The United States and Soviet Union entered these talks with conflicting agendas that prevented any agreement from being reached. In the aftermath of the Persian Gulf War, a new conventional arms control initiative has taken place in the form of a UN Arms Transfer Register.[23] The register identifies seven different categories of conventional weapons, and countries are requested to submit to the United Nations an annual statement of the number of these items it exported or imported during the previous year. The goal is to bring a heightened degree of transparency to the arms transfer process and thereby reduce the military advantages that arms transfers bring to states. The danger, according to one observer, is that because the system is a control mechanism, it may have the unintended effect of legitimizing those arms transfers that are registered.

Not all conventional arms controllers agree with the focus on major weapons systems. Aaron Karp argues that in the 1990s the purpose of conventional arms transfers has changed from that of maintaining or creating regional power balances to regulating the emergence of new states.[24] In his view, major weapons systems have become largely symbolic. If one looks at fighting in Bosnia, Rwanda, Liberia, and Chechnia it is small and light arms that are the weapons of choice. These are the weapons that upset strategic balances and inflict high levels of human misery.

Yet another dimension to the problem of curbing the proliferation of conventional weapons has also emerged. It involves the globalization of the arms production process. Cutbacks in defense spending and shrinking military establishments have led major arms producers to engage in a growing number of joint ventures, strategic alliances, and foreign acquisitions.[25] This is transforming the security environment facing the U.S. military by placing increasingly advanced military equipment in the hands of potential adversaries. It has also led to the development of sophisticated third world arms industries. Between 1986 and 1993, there were 27 joint ventures, 23 strategic alliances, and 78 mergers or acquisitions among defense firms around the world. Among others, the United States has entered into coproduction agreements on the F-16 fighter with Israel, South Korea, Singapore, Taiwan, Greece, and Indonesia. About 40 third world states now possess significant defense industries; almost 100 major conventional weapons systems have been licensed for coproduction in the third world; and seven third world states have the ability to produce land, sea, and air combat weapons.[26]

Having decided which weapons systems they wish to keep from proliferating, policy makers must decide on their ultimate objectives. One long-time advocate of nonproliferation argues that the American strategic community no longer embraces the traditional arms control objective of stopping proliferation. Leonard Spector argues that strategists are now more concerned with coping with the consequences of nuclear proliferation than they are with preventing it.[27] Representative of this thinking is the list of five policy objectives Joseph Nye has proposed for dealing with new nuclear states.[28] They are (1) slow the pace of vertical proliferation within their arsenals, (2) discourage these states from deploying their nuclear weapons, (3) discourage these states from actually using them, (4) prevent their transfer to other states, and (5) prevent them from falling into the hands of terrorists. Spector finds this loss of confidence in traditional arms control measures surprising because in his view the past several years have been characterized by some notable arms control successes. South Africa has eliminated its nuclear program; Belarus, Ukraine, and Kazakhstan have agreed to transfer their nuclear weapons to Russia; and Argentina and Brazil have ended their nuclear arms race.

Some analysts propose even more ambitious goals. Seeing the world at a historical turning point, they urge American policy makers to pursue a goal of nuclear disarmament.[29] In their view a fundamental contradiction exists between U.S. nonproliferation efforts and its continued reliance on nuclear weapons as part of its defense posture. This contradiction places severe limits on whatever nonproliferation policy goals it might realize. They concede that conditions do not permit the United States to disarm its nuclear arsenal unilaterally, but they argue that the time is ripe for taking steps that would move the world closer to this goal.

Strategies and Tactics

Along with identifying goals, policy makers also need to choose strategies and tactics for realizing them. A starting point for making such selections is to recognize that there are many pathways by which proliferation may take place. Strategies and tactics suitable for dealing with one contingency may be counterproductive in another setting. In the case of nuclear weapons we can identify at least three different proliferation scenarios, each of which has different consequences for American security interests. First, it is possible that nuclear proliferation will proceed in a gradual and evolutionary fashion so that the military balance of a region is not disturbed greatly and regional security organizations are able to adapt to its presence. A second possible outcome would see proliferation taking place at such a rapid pace that it revolutionizes the balance of power in the region and leads to political instability. In this scenario states are likely to forsake collective security efforts and rely increasingly on their own resources to counter the proliferation problem. Finally, nuclear proliferation might occur in a competitive setting but in such a way that neither state is able to realize any military advantage from gaining additional numbers or types of nuclear weapons. The end result here might be a situation in which both sides rediscover the value of cooperative measures as ways of realizing their national security interests and embrace arms control.

It is against this background of alternative futures and policy goals that strategic and tactical decisions will be made. The most basic of these is a choice between tactics fundamental to a strategy of nonproliferation and ones that support counterproliferation. As noted earlier, nonproliferation strategies are designed to stop the spread of nuclear weapons. Counterproliferation is a term coined by Secretary of Defense Aspin in 1993. It entails increased attention to developing counterforce capabilities against WMD and devising strategies for fighting adversaries who have WMD. According to Aspin, the two strategies are not incompatible because counterproliferation also embraces the traditional concerns of nonproliferation. Most strategists, however, see the two as being at odds with one another and hold that it is only possible to pursue one line of action at a time.

Nonproliferation.   Controversy has surrounded four central elements of a nonproliferation strategy since the end of the cold war. The first is the Nonproliferation Treaty (NPT). It prohibits nuclear states from transferring nuclear weapons and technology to nonnuclear states. Nonnuclear states promise not to "receive, manufacture or otherwise acquire nuclear weapons." While the NPT agreement has been signed by over 150 states since it was agreed to in 1968, it has operated under the stigma of being a discriminatory document because of the way in which it perpetuates the existence of an elite "nuclear club." Furthermore, some states thought to possess covert nuclear programs have not signed the agreement or have done so only recently. Numbered among them are Pakistan, India, China, South Africa, and Israel. Nonproliferation efforts received a boost in 1995 when the Clinton administration successfully negotiated an unlimited extension of the NPT. Serious doubts had been raised that this would be possible. Mexico and South Africa entered the negotiations on record as opposed to such an extension and became supporters through the diplomatic efforts of the American delegation.

The second point of controversy has surrounded the operation of the International Atomic Energy Agency (IAEA). The NPT provides for IAEA inspections of facilities in nonnuclear states in order to verify that nuclear material is not being diverted from peaceful uses to military ones. The IAEA came under heavy criticism for its failure to detect the Iraqi nuclear program before the Persian Gulf War and its subsequent difficulties in documenting the extent of nuclear programs in the Middle East and North Korea. Defenders of the IAEA assert that the problem is not with the logic of IAEA inspections or its ability to contribute to nonproliferation but the conditions under which they must be carried out. They note that by custom IAEA inspections were limited to declared nuclear facilities. Part of the reason that evidence about Iraq's nuclear capability was so slow to surface was the existence of undeclared facilities. Another part of the problem lies with the lack of political will on the part of the international community to make the IAEA process work. It was only after the Persian Gulf War that the international community was willing to back IAEA inspection efforts with the political clout necessary to take on would-be proliferators such as North Korea.

The third point of controversy has centered on nuclear testing.[30] Between 1945 and 1994 six states officially conducted nuclear tests. The United States leads the way with 942 tests followed by Russia (715), France (210), Great Britain (44), China (39), and India (1). Preventing nuclear testing is an important element in nonproliferation strategies, since few strategists are likely to have confidence in using a weapons system that has never been tested. Among the international agreements aimed at preventing nuclear testing are the 1963 Limited Test Ban Treaty, which prohibits testing above ground, under water, and in space; the 1974 Threshold Test Ban Treaty, which bans explosions of greater than 150 kiloton; and the NPT, which calls upon signatory states to discontinue all test explosions of nuclear weapons.

After the end of the cold war it appeared that a comprehensive ban on nuclear testing might be possible. In 1992 Russia announced that it would unilaterally stop testing and called for the United States to do the same. President Bush was reluctant to make such a pledge but Congress embraced the idea, attaching the Mitchell–Hatfield–Exon Amendment to the 1993 Energy and Water Development Appropriations Act. This amendment imposed an immediate nine-month moratorium on nuclear testing, permitted five tests per year until 1996, and required that all U.S. testing end by September 1996. While the Clinton administration entered office committed to the test ban moratorium, repeated pressures have arisen to resume testing. The Defense Department has requested permission to conduct all nine of the allowed tests. This permission was denied, but the Clinton administration did instruct the Energy Department to prepare for testing following an October 1994 Chinese test. A new round of Chinese tests in 1995, as well as the French announcement that it would resume testing prior to signing any comprehensive test ban agreement, placed further pressure on the Clinton administration to reverse its position.

The final point of controversy surrounds the cost of getting states to forgo the acquisition of nuclear weapons. The price tag to the United States for getting Ukraine to sign the START I agreement was an additional $200 million in foreign aid. The 1994 agreement between the United States and North Korea was even more expensive. Over a ten-year period North Korea will dismantle its most troublesome nuclear facilities and in return it will receive two 1,000-megawatt light-water nuclear power reactors. The first of these reactors is not expected to be operational for nine years. Until that time an international consortium will provide North Korea with heavy oil for heating and electricity. Questions have been raised as to whether the United States and the international community can or should pay such a high price for nonproliferation promises or whether this practice only encourages other states to engage in a form of nuclear blackmail.

Counterproliferation.   While a fully articulated strategy of counterproliferation has yet to be spelled out, two prominent features of such a strategy have emerged. The first involves the development of a military capability to operate against states that possess nuclear weapons or other WMD. The second is the development of a defensive capability to protect the United States and its forces from WMD attacks.

Developing a military capability to fight against a state possessing WMD is a complicated undertaking that must take a host of factors into account.[31] At the heart of the matter is a paradox: The more threatening a state's WMD threat becomes the less vulnerable it is to military action by an outsider. Attacking the nuclear reactors of an immature WMD state is quite different from attacking those of a mature WMD state. In the former a successful military operation may set back or stop WMD proliferation. Because it already possesses nuclear fuel, has a cadre of trained scientists and engineers, and may have a retaliatory capability, the same military attack is unlikely to be as successful in the latter case and may entail significantly higher risks.

With this realization in mind strategists have identified three sets of parameters that must be taken into account in planning military operations designed to eliminate or limit the dangers of WMD proliferation. The first involves the timing and political context for military action. Is the contemplated military action part of a prolonged crisis, an ongoing war, or a "bolt-from-the-blue" response in which the United States gives no warning? Unless it is the last case, one most analysts find highly unlikely, the primary implication to be drawn is that the targeted country is likely to have advance warning that an attack is being contemplated and will be able to prepare for that contingency. Second, what type of adversary is the United States dealing with? Unless the enemy is close to the United States (or its overseas military bases) and possesses few defensive and retaliatory capabilities, the United States will be in a position to act only after mobilizing and positioning large numbers of forces. Third, decisions must be made regarding what targets to attack. Possibilities range from the WMD themselves to air forces, ground forces, and the political leadership of the enemy state. The force-level implications of these parameters point to the probable need for large forces and discourage confidence in the ability to launch an undetected preemptive attack or disarm a WMD state with a single precision attacking operation.

The second most discussed feature of a counterproliferation strategy involves the construction of a defensive system against ballistic missiles. The most elaborate rendition of such a system was presented shortly after the Persian Gulf War when the Strategic Defense Initiative Office proposed a System for Global Protection Against Limited Strikes (GPALS). Congress has endorsed a much more modest proposal. All options currently under study for a BMD system fall somewhere between these two visions.

Much like the Star Wars system, GPALS was to be a layered system. The first stage to be implemented would be a theater missile defense (TMD) system that would be centered around an upgraded Patriot air defense system and longer-range ground-based missiles. A second stage would be designed to protect the United States. It would consist of mobile radar systems and some 750 ground-based interceptor missiles stationed in Alaska, Hawaii, and the continental United States. The final stage was to feature 1,000 space-based hit-to-kill interceptors that were being developed as part of President Bush's brilliant pebbles initiative. The estimated costs of the proposed GPALS system was placed at between $45 and $85 billion.

Congress endorsed the idea of a ballistic missile defense in passing the Missile Defense Act of 1991. According to its terms the United States would be defended by a missile system at a single site that would be consistent with the ABM Treaty. The limiting nature of this treaty has emerged as a point of controversy in the debate over a BMD system. The Missile Defense Act urges the president to negotiate modifications in the treaty should they be needed to deploy an effective BMD system. Critics claim that an altered ABM Treaty would give Russia the legal basis on which to build a much more robust system around its borders. Should U.S.–Russian relations sour, the presence of such a system would complicate the task facing U.S. military planners. Also at dispute is whether any changes in the language of the ABM Treaty would have to be approved by the Senate or if the treaty could be amended by executive agreement. In 1995 the House and Senate moved vigorously to support the construction of a BMD system. The House Republicans voted to increase 1996 spending on a BMD system by approximately 25 percent over what the Clinton administration had requested, contending that the increased efforts of Iraq, North Korea, Iran, and Libya to obtain nuclear weapons necessitated such a move. In the Senate Republicans voted funds to build a nationwide BMD system to protect American cities within the next eight years. As in 1991 supporters and critics of the proposed BMD system disagreed over whether it would violate the ABM Treaty and, if so, what the consequences would be.

Treaties and Agreements.   Going hand-in-hand with an interest in pursuing military solutions to the proliferation problem are continued attempts to fashion international agreements to stop the spread of deadly weapons. Three initiatives have moved to center stage. The first is an attempt to extend the START process. In 1997, Presidents Clinton and Yeltsin agreed in principle to negotiate a START III treaty that would restrict each state to a total of 2,000–2,500 warheads. START III would also be the first of the START treaties to call for the actual destruction of warheads rather than simply the destruction of the means to deliver them. The American initiative was seen as a necessary inducement to obtain Russian ratification of START II. A major Russian fear holding up ratification is that START II limits were too high for Russia to maintain nuclear parity with the United States. Taken together, the ailing Russian economy, aging missiles, and the START II agreement make it unlikely that Russia will possess 3,000 warheads in 2003 as permitted by START II.

A second international agreement of significance is the Chemical Weapons Convention. This agreement was negotiated by the Bush administration and signed by President Clinton in 1993, but the Clinton administration did little to push for its ratification by the Senate. The politics of ratification changed dramatically with the Republican triumph in the 1994 congressional elections. A 1996 attempt to secure its ratification floundered due to the opposition of Robert Dole and conservative Republicans. Ratification was secured in 1997 as part of a deal with Majority Leader Trent Lott and Senate Foreign Relations Committee chairperson Jesse Helms. The Clinton administration agreed to bring about the reorganization of the foreign affairs bureaucracy that had been championed by Helms and submit to the Senate for its approval language clarifying the 1972 ABM Treaty.

A third major international undertaking involved the negotiation of a Comprehensive Nuclear Test Ban Treaty that prohibits the explosion of nuclear weapons. This treaty was the result of three years of negotiation by a 61-country Conference on Disarmament. The agreement was signed by President Clinton in 1996 but as of late 1998 had not yet been ratified by the Senate. A Senate vote on funding for implementation of the agreement passed in September, 1998, but 44 senators voted against the measure, signaling that the treaty lacked the necessary 67 supporting votes for ratification. India's opposition to the agreement and its subsequent detonation of a nuclear device have proven to be a major impediment to its ratification.

SUMMARY AND THE FUTURE

Arms control, disarmament, and missile defense represent three attempts to escape from the dangers of nuclear war. Disarmament proposals never prospered or received serious attention. Arms control has had a checkered history. The Strategic Defense Initiative was put forward optimistically as a way of making nuclear weapons obsolete but was met with great skepticism. Of the three, it is arms control that has taken center stage in the efforts of policy makers to lessen the likelihood of war in the post–cold war era. Challenges to arms control can be found at two different policy levels. At the most basic level, Richard Betts questions the utility of pursuing arms control agreements in an age in which there is no clearly defined enemy.[32] He argues that the fundamental purpose of arms control agreements is to stabilize military relationships between adversaries. Negotiated arms control treaties make little sense between friends because the significance of an arms control agreement depends on what we believe would happen in the absence of that agreement. Until such time as an enemy reemerges, Betts advocates the pursuit of unilateral cuts in military equipment and expenditures as the best way of reducing the likelihood of war. A second set of challenges exist at an operational level. Regardless of whether arms control is accomplished through unilateral cuts or negotiated treaties, the management of arms control arrangements has received very little attention.[33] What has received attention is the problem of compliance. Are the terms of an agreement being lived up to? Management is more than compliance. It also involves such issues as anticipating problems, planning, and searching for and exploiting possible spillover effects of an arms control agreement. Without careful attention to the management of an agreement, second and third order problems may not be addressed in time and may become major points of dispute.

NOTES

1. Lewis A. Dunn, "Four Decades of Nuclear Nonproliferation: Some Lessons from Wins, Losses, and Draws," *The Washington Quarterly*, 13 (1990), 5–18.

2. See Alexander T. Lennon, "The 1995 NPT Extension Conference," *The Washington Quarterly*, 17 (1994), 205–27; and Ted Galen Carpenter, "Closing the Nuclear Umbrella," *Foreign Affairs*, 73 (1994), 8–13.

3. See David Albright and Kevin O'Neill, "Jury-Rigged, but Working," *The Bulletin of the Atomic Scientists*, 51 (1995), 20–29.

4. Lewis A. Dunn, "New Nuclear Threats to U.S. Security," in Robert D. Blackwill and Albert Carnesale (eds.), *New Nuclear Nations: Consequences for U.S. Policy* (New York: Council on Foreign Relations, 1993), pp. 20–52.

5. Thomas C. Schelling and Morton H. Halperin, *Strategy and Arms Control* (New York: Pergamon-Brassey Classic, 1985), originally published by the Twentieth Century Fund, 1961; and Thomas C. Schelling, "What Went Wrong with Arms Control," *Foreign Affairs*, 64 (1985/86), 219–33.

6. On the politics of the MNF, see John D. Steinbruner, *The Cybernetic Theory of Decision: New Dimensions of Political Analysis* (Princeton, N.J.: Princeton University Press, 1974).

7. For a statement of the nuclear freeze position, see Randall Forsberg, "Call a Halt to the Arms Race—Proposal for a Mutual U.S.-Soviet Nuclear Weapons Freeze," in Burns H. Weston (ed.), *Toward Nuclear Disarmament and Global Security: A Search for Alternatives* (Boulder, Colo.: Westview, 1984), pp. 384–89.

8. McGeorge Bundy and others, "Nuclear Weapons and the Atlantic Alliance," *Foreign Affairs*, 60 (1982), 753–68.

9. Alton Frye, "Strategic Build-Down: A Context for Restraint," in Charles Kegley, Jr., and Eugene Wittkopf (eds.), *The Nuclear Reader: Strategy, Weapons, and War* (New York: St. Martin's, 1985), pp. 174–86.

10. For a discussion, see Jonathan Dean and Randall Watson Forsberg, "CFE and Beyond: The Future of Conventional Arms Control," *International Security*, 17 (1992), 76–117.

11. Michael Mandelbaum, *The Nuclear Future* (Ithaca, N.Y.: Cornell University Press, 1983), p. 43.

12. Thomas C. Schelling, *The Strategy of Conflict* (New York: Oxford University Press, 1960).

13. Reagan's speech is reprinted in P. Edward Haley, David M. Kethly, and Jack Merritt (eds.), *Nuclear Strategy, Arms Control, and the Future* (Boulder, Colo.: Westview, 1985), pp. 311–12.

14. For a discussion of how a BMD system would work, see Stephen Weiner, "Systems and Technology," in Ashton Carter and David N. Schwartz (eds.), *Ballistic Missile Defense* (Washington, D.C.: Brookings, 1984), pp. 49–89; Sidney Drell, Philip J. Farley, and David Holloway, "Preserving the ABM Treaty: A Critique of the Reagan Strategic Defense Initiative," *International Security*, 9 (1984), 67–79.

15. Eugene Skolnikoff, "The Lessons of SDI," *Breakthroughs*, 5 (1995), 23–7.

16. Brad Roberts, "1995 and the End of the Post-Cold War Era," *The Washington Quarterly*, 18 (1994), 5–25.

17. Brad Roberts, "Rethinking N+1," *The National Interest*, 51 (1998), 75–80.

18. Scott R. Sagan, "The Causes of Nuclear Proliferation," *Current History*, 76 (April, 1997), 151–55.

19. Fred C. Ikle and Albert Wohlstetter, *Discriminate Deterrence: Report of the Commission on Integrated Long-Term Strategy* (Washington, D.C., U.S. Government Printing Office, 1988).

20. Quoted in Philip L. Ritcheson, "Proliferation and the Challenge to Deterrence," *Strategic Review*, 23 (1995), 38–48.

21. Michael Mandelbaum, "Lessons of the Next Nuclear War," *Foreign Affairs*, 74 (1995), 22–37.

22. Janne Nolan, "U.S.-Soviet Conventional Arms Transfer Negotiations," in Alexander George, Philip Farley, and Alexander Dallin (eds.), *U.S.-Soviet Security Cooperation* (New York: Oxford University Press, 1988), 27–36.

23. Edward J. Laurance, "Conventional Arms: Rationales and Prospects for Compliance and Effectiveness," *The Washington Quarterly*, 16 (1993), 163–72.

24. Aaron Karp, "The Arms Trade Revolution: The Major Impact of Small Arms," *The Washington Quarterly*, 17 (1994), 63–77.

25. Richard A. Bitizinger, "The Globalization of the Arms Industry," *International Security*, 19 (1994), 170–98.

26. Roberts, "1995 and the End of the Post-Cold War Era," p. 7.

27. Leonard S. Spector, "Neo-Nonproliferation," *Survival*, 37 (1995), 66–85.

28. Joseph S. Nye, Jr., "Diplomatic Measures," in *New Nuclear Nations* (New York: Council on Foreign Relations Press, 1993), pp. 77–96.

29. Barry M. Blechman and Cathleen S. Fisher, "Phase Out the Bomb," *Foreign Policy*, 97 (1994), 79–95. For the opposite view see Kathleen Bailey, "Why We Have to Keep the Bomb," *The Bulletin of the Atomic Scientists*, 51 (January/February, 1995), 30–7.

30. Matthew Stephenson, "Resisting Temptation: US Debates Resumption of Nuclear Testing," *Harvard International Review*, 16 (1994), 62–64 and 91–92.

31. Philip Zelikow, "Offensive Military Operations," in Blackwill and Carnesale (eds.), *New Nuclear Nations*, pp. 162–95.

32. Richard Betts, "Systems for Peace or Causes of War? Collective Security, Arms Control, and the New Europe," *International Security*, 17 (1992), 5–43. Also see the exchange between Betts and Michael Mazarr in the Winter 1992/93 issue.

33. James Goodby, "Can Arms Control Survive Peace?," *The Washington Quarterly*, 13 (1990), 93–104.

18 Alternative Futures

Beneath the coherence and unity implied by the phrases *U.S. foreign policy* and *the national interest* lies a complex array of individuals and institutions constantly competing for positions of prominence in the setting of values and priorities. To successfully confront the future—to meet the challenges and opportunities provided by the international system—requires that U.S. foreign policy be rooted in a firm understanding of the past. The past must be explored both for the answers it gives and for the questions it leads us to ask of the future. Policy makers must also come to accept the limitations of its lessons and the continued existence of conflicting interpretations of events. Within the boundaries set by the pull of the past and the structure of the international system, the identity of the participants in the policy process, the way they interact, and the instruments available to them combine to further refine the shape of U.S. foreign policy.

Today, the makers of American foreign policy occupy unfamiliar but not totally unprecedented territory. For the first time in over four decades the content and direction of U.S. foreign policy truly is open for debate and reshaping. Twice before in the twentieth century American policy makers were in analogous situations. The first time came after World War I when Woodrow Wilson's vision of an American foreign policy based on the principles of liberal internationalism collided with the conservative internationalism of Henry Cabot Lodge. The second time came after World War II when policy makers rejected proposals for a foreign policy of partnership with the Soviet Union for one that emphasized containing it.

Just as World War I and World War II called into question the value of existing images of American foreign policy, so too has the end of the cold war called into question the principles on which cold war U.S. foreign policy rested. As of yet, no new set of strategic principles have emerged to take the place of containment. The absence of a new strategic doctrine is not due to the absence of vision on the part of policy makers and commentators. A vibrant contest is well under way to control the language of the debate over the future of American foreign policy. It is a debate in which the number of alternative foreign policies put forward for consideration continues to grow rather than one which has winnowed the contenders down to a final few.

We close our treatment of U.S. foreign policy by introducing eight competing visions. The differences between them are many but there are also points of overlap. We ask three questions of each alternative future: (1) What is the primary threat to U.S. national security? (2) What responsibility does the United States have to other states? and (3) What responsibility does the United States have to the global community? The answers given reflect different views about the degree to which the United States should be involved in world politics, how much power it possesses, and the extent to which the post–cold war world will differ from its predecessor.

While the correctness of any foreign policy decision becomes clear only with 20–20 hindsight, two observations about the problem of selecting a course of action can be made with certainty. First, the values and goals open to U.S. foreign policy will be just as unlimited as in the past. Second, limitations on the resources at the disposal of policy makers will continue to be quite real, leaving a frustrating gap between what U.S. foreign policy can aspire to and what it can accomplish.

Before exploring the options that lie before the United States, some prefatory questions need to be raised. What is the larger context within which this choice will be made? Is there an unlimited amount of time available or does a "window of opportunity" exist? Must we act now or lose the ability to choose from a full menu of options? Or, is the entire notion of choice an illusion? Does the United States really have a choice or, as many realists would contend, will the future direction of American foreign policy be dictated by forces beyond our control?

ALTERNATIVE FUTURES

The United States as an Ordinary State

For some, the key to the future is realizing that foreign policy can no longer be conducted on the assumption of American uniqueness or that U.S. actions stand between anarchy and order. The American century is over, and the challenge facing policy makers is no longer that of managing alliances, deterring aggression, or ruling over the international system. It is now one of adjusting to a new role orientation, one in which the United States is an "ordinary state."[1] The change in outlook is necessary because international and domestic trends point to the declining utility of a formula-based response to foreign policy problems be they rooted in ideology, concepts of power politics, or some vision of regional orders. Governments ruling over internally divided societies and those ruling over unified populations are finding themselves forced to pursue narrowly defined national interests at the expense of international collaborative and cooperative efforts. In this altered environment flexibility, autonomy, and impartiality are to be valued over one-sided commitments, name calling, and efforts at the diplomatic, military, or economic isolation of states.

As an ordinary state the United States would not define its interests so rigidly that their defense would require unilateral American action. If the use of force is necessary, it should be a truly multilateral effort; and if others are unwilling to act, there is no need for the United States to assume the full burden of the commitment. Stated as a rule: "The United States should not be prepared, on its own, and supported solely by its own means, to perform tasks that most other states would not undertake."[2] Ordinariness does not, however, mean passivity, withdrawal, or a purely defensive approach to foreign policy problems. The quality of U.S. participation in truly multilateral efforts to solve international problems will be vital because the core ingredients to international influence in the future will be found in the fields where the United States is a leader: economics, diplomacy, and technology. The goal of these collaborative efforts should be to "create and maintain a world in which adversaries will remain in contact with one another and where compromises are still possible."[3] The three primary areas for such efforts (and thus for U.S. foreign policy) are to bring about a balance between Russia and the West, the Arab oil producers and the consuming states, and the rich and the poor states. To summarize, in the Ordinary State perspective:

1. The greatest threat to U.S. national security lies in trying to do too much and in having too expansive a definition of its national interest.
2. The United States' responsibility to other states must be proportionate and reciprocal to that which other states have to the United States.
3. The United States' responsibility to the global community is to try to keep the international system open and flexible.

The imagery advanced by the Ordinary State perspective is one most Americans find troubling. Its denial of American uniqueness; its lack of optimism; its focus on restraints rather than opportunities; and its admonition to not try to do too much all run against the traditional American approach to world politics. For that reason it is a perspective which is unlikely to be endorsed (at least by this name) by politicians. At the same time, it is a perspective on the future that cannot be dismissed. Political leaders must acknowledge it because it taps into a feeling shared by many Americans that while the United States should not retreat into isolationism it should not be the first to take risks in places such as Bosnia, Somalia, and Haiti. Its admonition not to undertake herculean tasks also resonates well in some portions of the scholarly community. Ronald W. Pruessen, for example, in comparing the 1950s with the 1990s notes that one reason for the failure of American foreign policy at the earlier time was the overly optimistic "game plan" that the Eisenhower administration sought to execute.[4]

Reformed America

According to proponents of the Reformed America perspective, U.S. foreign policy has traditionally been torn between pursuing democratic ideals and empire.[5] The United States wants peace—but only on its own terms; the United States supports human rights—but only if its definitions are used; the United States wants to promote third world economic growth—but only if it follows the U.S. model and does not undermine U.S. business interests abroad. Historically, the thrust toward empire (whether it is called containment, détente, or trilateralism) has won out, and democratic ideals have been sacrificed or only given lip service. Whether it is foreign aid, human rights, environmental protection, or arms control, U.S. policy makers have given highest priority to maintaining the United States' position of dominance in the international system and promoting the economic well-being of U.S. corporations.[6]

The need now exists to reverse this pattern. Democratic ideals must be given primary consideration in the formulation and execution of U.S. foreign policy. Not doing so invites future Vietnams and runs the risk of undermining the very democratic principles the United States stands for. Foreign policy and domestic policy are not seen as two separate categories. They are held to be inextricably linked together, and actions taken in one sphere have an impact on behavior and policies in the other. Bribery of foreign officials leads to bribery of U.S. officials; an unwillingness to challenge human rights violations abroad reinforces the acceptance of discrimination and violations of civil rights at home; and a lack of concern for the growing disparity in economic wealth on a global basis leads to an insensitivity to the problems of poverty in the United States.

The Reformed America perspective demands global activism from the United States. The much heralded decline in American power is not seen as being so great as to prevent the United States from exercising a predominant global influence. Moreover, the United States is held to have a moral and political responsibility to lead by virtue of its comparative wealth and power. The danger to be avoided is inaction brought on by the fear of failure. The United States cannot be permitted to crawl into a shell of isolationism or to let itself be "Europeanized" into believing that there are limits to its power and accepting the world "as it is." The power needed for success in creating what amounts to a new world order that is faithful to traditional American democratic values is not the ability to dominate others but to renew the American commitment to justice, opportunity, and liberty. In sum, the Reformed America perspective holds that:

1. The primary threat to U.S. national security is a continued fixation on military problems and an attachment to power-politics thinking.

2. The United States' responsibility to other states is great provided they are truly democratic, and the United States must seek to move those that are not in that direction.

3. The United States' responsibility to the global community is also great and centers on the creation of an international system conducive to the realization of traditional America values.

The values underlying this perspective were widely embraced in the immediate post–cold war period as many commentators urged the Bush and Clinton administrations to move aggressively toward a neo-Wilsonian foreign policy. At a declaratory or rhetorical level, this call was answered more positively by the Clinton administration than by that of Bush. In 1993, Anthony Lake, Clinton's National Security Adviser, asserted that enlargement would replace containment as the guiding thought behind American foreign policy. The United States would now focus on extending and enlarging the global reach of democracy and free markets. According to Lake such a strategy was possible and necessary. It was possible because the United States was still the world's dominant power. It possessed the strongest military, the largest economy, and the most dynamic society. It was necessary because the quickened pace of international change required the United States to become proactive if it was not to become a captive victim of unfolding trends.

The United States as a Global Manager

According to the Global Manager perspective, the key issues in world politics no longer revolve around cold war or power-politics concerns but focus on the dynamics of interdependence. When first put forward as an alternative organizing principle to power politics, interdependence tended to be treated as a uniformly positive force for international cooperation. As we have gained experience living with the political and economic realities of interdependence, it is now recognized that interdependence does not mean an end to conflict but only that conflict will take new forms. Interdependence does, however, require that adjustments be made in the nature of U.S. foreign policy. In addition to a switch in its substantive focus (away from military issues and toward economic ones), there must also be a change in the nature of U.S. leadership.

For the bulk of the cold war era, the United States was able to exercise a hegemonic leadership style, one in which it commanded others and orchestrated their behavior. Whether it is to impose an American empire on the world or American values on it, such a leadership style is ill-suited to an era of interdependence. By the same token, leadership by committee cannot and has not worked as a means of managing the international economic order. In the Global Manager perspective, the United States must develop a new style of leadership, one that emphasizes leading by example, exercising foresight and a long-term global perspective in addressing problems, and being the first to offer concessions.[7] Pragmatism alone is an inadequate guiding principle to bring to the international bargaining processes that will occupy the energies of this new style of leadership. A sense of direction must accompany it. The objective should be to organize and manage an international system tolerant of diversity yet fundamentally compatible with traditional U.S. values. Continued U.S. leadership in world politics is taken as a given. While U.S. power may have experienced a decline, the United States continues to be the only state with the power resources to overcome the vulnerabilities inherent in interdependence and to help others deal with theirs in a constructive fashion. In sum, the Global Manager perspective holds that:

1. The primary threats to U.S. national security are economic in nature and stem from the growing pace of global interdependence.
2. The United States has a responsibility to help other states deal with their economic problems, but it cannot solve these problems for them. Its first concern must be to position itself so that others will follow its lead.
3. The United States' responsibility to the world community is great because its economic well-being is inseparable from the well-being of all states.

The Global Manager orientation to American foreign policy comes through quite clearly in the effort to create a North American Free Trade Zone and to move with Asian states toward the creation of a Pacific Rim trade zone. A major challenge in the future from this perspective is to establish working relationships among the emerging regional trading blocs.[8] On the bilateral level the major challenge facing the United States as a Global Manager is to create a new architecture for U.S.–Japanese relations. Cold war deference by Japan to the United States has been replaced by a situation where Japan sees itself as being bullied by the United States and the United States sees Japan as a free rider.[9] Instead of solving problems, U.S. and Japanese negotiators seemingly have become hostages to a cycle of crisis-induced negotiations that produce little by the way of real progress. While economic issues have all but monopolized the attention of U.S. and Japanese policy makers in these sessions, security issues also hold the potential for dividing the two states. Thus, from a Global Manager perspective, the pressing need for American foreign policy in Asia (and elsewhere) is to "anchor itself in a web of overlapping regional institutions in order to enhance political and defense cooperation; serve as an early warning system for potential conflict; bolster market-oriented economic growth; mediate conflict; and build trust and confidence in America as a durable and reliable partner."[10]

Pragmatic America

The Pragmatic America perspective holds that the United States can no longer afford foreign policies that are on the extreme ends of the political spectrum. Neither crusades nor isolationism serve America well. In the words of long-time strategist and policy maker James Schlesinger, what is needed in U.S. foreign policy is "selectivity."[11] The United States, he argues, must avoid impulse and image in formulating foreign policy. What is needed is a strong dose of moderation in means and ends. Above all else, the end of the cold war is seen as vindicating a policy of moderation.[12] As to ends, some world problems require U.S. attention, but not all do. The United States must recognize that the American national interest is not identical to the global interest and that not all problems lend themselves to permanent resolution. The most pressing issue on the agenda is for the United States to develop a set of criteria for identifying these problems and then acting in moderation to protect American interests.

A certain amount of overlap exists between the Global Manager and Pragmatic America perspectives. Both emphasize a utilitarian outlook on world politics and recognize the lessened ability of military force to solve foreign policy problems. They differ in their view of what needs to be managed. Instead of economics, the Pragmatic America perspective sees military problems as continuing to be the most threatening ones facing the United States. The nature of these problems is not what it used to be and thus the remedies must also differ. President Clinton's first Director of Central Intelligence R. James Woolsey pointed out that while the cold war dragon represented by the Soviet Union has been slain, the world confronting the United States is now populated by large numbers of poisonous snakes. For many who embrace this view, the most effective means of countering those snakes deemed to be threatening to the United States is through some form of collective action instead of by unilateral or bloc-based moves.

In sum, the Pragmatic America perspective holds that:

1. The primary threats to U.S. national security continue to be military in nature.
2. The United States has a responsibility to other states on a selective basis and only to the extent that threats to the political order of those states would lessen American security.
3. The United States' responsibility to the global community is limited. More pressing is a sense of responsibility to key partners whose cooperation is necessary to manage a threatening international environment.

President Bush in his farewell foreign policy address argued for a position that is consistent with this view.[13] Warning against becoming isolationist, Bush asserted that the United States can influence the future but that "it need not respond to every outrage of violence." It cannot be the police officer of the world but must be prepared to act militarily. He went on to note that no formula exists that tells with precision when and where to intervene. "Each and every case is unique. To adopt rigid criteria would guarantee mistakes involving American interests and lives. . . . Similarly we cannot always decide in advance which interests will require our using military force." When force is used, Bush urged that the mission be clear and achievable, that a realistic plan exist, and that equally realistic criteria be established for withdrawing U.S. forces.

The Pragmatic America perspective is seen by some as well suited for an international system in a state of flux. Rigidly applied guiding principles such as containing communism or spreading democracy are held to be of little value in a world where change is the dominant condition. At the same time, its measured approach to solving foreign policy problems is also a fundamental weakness in the Pragmatic America perspective. Few would argue in theory with the points outlined by President Bush. Yet, as events in his administration and that of Clinton have made clear, these are rules of engagement that do not easily yield a coherent and enduring foreign policy. Because pragmatism can be interpreted differently by different people, the policy it produces tends to move forward in a series of disjointed steps. The result is that where defenders see it as producing flexibility and adaptability, detractors see in it a foreign policy by lottery in which the past provides little guidance for friends or enemies as they seek to anticipate America's position.

Neo-Containment

The Neo-Containment perspective takes issue with the assertion that a fundamental change has taken place in the nature of world politics.[14] Neither the overall stake of the United States in the makeup of the international system nor its underlying dynamics are different from those that confronted U.S. policy makers in the years immediately following World War II. World politics continues to be governed by considerations of (military) power politics, and Russia continues to be the primary national security threat to the United States. In the

words of Zbigniew Brzezinski, talk of an American-Russian partnership is premature.[15] It is based on flawed assumptions regarding the prospects for democracy
there and an incorrect reading of Russian strategic goals. As was the case with its
Soviet predecessor, Russian foreign policy continues to be governed by an imperial impulse. Moreover, it is an imperial impulse which extends beyond the near
abroad and encompasses central Europe. This region remains an area of special
Russian influence and interest. A premature and enthusiastic embrace of Russia
could cause the United States and its allies to squander all that has been accomplished in Europe since the end of the cold war.

Advocates of the Neo-Containment perspective see the primary goal of
U.S. foreign policy as ensuring that Russia, regardless of its domestic political
system, emerges as a "good neighbor" in Europe. This requires a policy built
upon the conceptual foundation that underlay the cold war doctrine of containment. Most pointedly this involves basing political relationships on power
and not on notions of transnational common interests. It also involves a recognition that international stability is best assured by a foreign policy which seeks
to establish a balance of power among states and to offset the military power of
potentially hegemonic states. Thus, a key point of similarity between the old
and new containment doctrines is the emphasis on delineating lines beyond
which Russian domination is not to extend. Attention has focused most clearly
on Ukraine. As one critic of neo-containment observed, its advocates believe
that "a Russia that absorbs the Ukraine is a great power in the heart of Europe;
without the Ukraine, Russia is a remote if still formidable presence on the European fringe."[16] Should Ukraine fall, Neo-Containment sees a new domino theory taking effect as one after another of the former members of the Soviet
Union are brought back under firm Russian domination. In practical terms,
Neo-Containment calls for a more balanced U.S. foreign policy toward Russia
and its neighbors with far more attention being given to the needs of the Central Asian republics as well as Ukraine, Belarus, and Kazakhstan. It also advocates expanding NATO's defensive shield eastward in order to fill the political
and security vacuum that exists there before Russia can move to do so.

In sum, Neo-Containment holds that:

1. The primary threats to U.S. national security continue to emanate from quite traditional sources and call for a buildup of U.S. military power to offset that possessed by a potentially hostile superpower.

2. The United States' responsibility to other states is real but limited to its
   European allies.

3. The United States' responsibility to the global community is minimal. A balance-
   of-power system is held to exist, and the primary responsibility of the United
   States is to act in a manner consistent with its basic principles.

Critics of Neo-Containment come from three quarters. Not unexpectedly, one set argues that Neo-Containment misreads both the extent to which
the international system has been transformed, making balance-of-power
thinking obsolete, and the potential for democracy to take root in Russia. A
second group of critics agrees with the concept of containment but disagrees
on the question of who is to be contained. It is not clear to all strategists that

Russia is the primary threat to the United States. Colin Gray speaks of the likely need for the United States to intervene in Europe in order to support Russia and Britain against a continental bloc led by Germany.[17] Others have identified Japan as the primary future national security threat to the United States. A final set of critics, those whose ideas we now will begin to examine, take exception with a Neo-Containment policy because they have different policy solutions for dealing with threats emanating from a hostile international system.

Triumphant America

Those who embrace the Triumphant America perspective on the future see the post–cold war world as a dangerous place and believe that a new strategic environment confronts the United States. But, unlike many, they see the world as having become unipolar rather than multipolar. The alternative to American unipolarity is held to be chaos, not an eighteenth-century balance of power among mature European states. The roots of today's chaos are found in the proliferation of weapons of mass destruction throughout the third world. Iraq represents the prototypical threat with North Korea and Libya not far behind.

From the Triumphant America perspective, the United States emerged from the cold war as the clear winner, and the end of the Persian Gulf War symbolized the beginning of a Pax Americana. It will take a generation before new power centers emerge that are capable of challenging the United States for preeminence. Only the United States possesses the military, economic, and diplomatic resources to intervene decisively in conflicts around the world. That the United States possesses this ability does not mean that it should involve itself in every conflict. As Charles Krauthammer, the leading exponent of this perspective, notes, primacy places great burdens on the United States. It must "make the connection between America's moral and geopolitical standing."[18] This connection is necessary because the American peace cannot rest on power alone. It must be acquiesced to by the nations of the world or the United States will find itself encountering the kind of resistance that marked the Soviet cold war rule of Eastern Europe. However, when the United States chooses to intervene it must do so in a "robust" fashion. It must act decisively and unashamedly. When possible it should act with allies in a multilateral setting, but it must not hesitate to act unilaterally if it is the right thing to do.

In sum, the Triumphant America perspective holds that:

1. The primary threats to U.S. national security stem from the proliferation of weapons of mass destruction. There are no states equal in power to the United States.
2. The United States' responsibility to other states is limited and determined by American values and interests as it defines them.
3. The United States has a responsibility to the world community that stems from its ability to lay down the rules of world order and enforce them.

Putting these principles into prescriptive policy advice, Krauthammer opposed the Clinton administration's policy in Somalia.[19] Referring to Somalia as a place for "Utopians," he argued that the United States is not in the business of nation-building. "It is bad enough playing cop to the world. Playing God is crazy." He went on to argue that with the passing of the immediate humanitarian crisis there were no U.S. interests at stake in Somalia. U.S. policy should be "to stay in Somalia just long enough to punish Aidid—preferably by killing him—to show one does not murder four American soldiers with impunity. Then get out."

America the Balancer

Some commentators agree that the United States is now a country without an enemy its equal, yet they maintain that any attempt to base a foreign policy on American unipolarity is doomed to failure. Because of this the United States cannot pursue its traditional foreign policy of attempting to create a condition of absolute security out of the conviction that "America must maintain what in essence is a military protectorate in economically critical regions to ensure that America's vital trade and financial relations will not be disrupted by political upheaval."[20] In this view, containing the cold war Soviet threat provided a rationale for America's interventionist policy but was quite incidental to its fundamental thrust. So long as U.S. interests are defined in global terms, "Bosnias will be like buses . . . there will always be another one coming down the street" to tempt the United States with intervention on the grounds that if an end is not put to regional instability, America's interests will be threatened.

The starting point of wisdom from this perspective is that not all problems are threatening to the United States or require its involvement. The end of the cold war has left the United States relatively secure. It possesses a considerable amount of freedom to define its interests. Additionally, the United States must recognize that one consequence of having put a global security umbrella in place is that it has discouraged other states and regional organizations from taking responsibility for preserving international stability. This must be reversed. The United States must really stop being the world's police officer. Others must be encouraged to act in defense of their own interests. Finally, the United States must learn to live with uncertainty. Absolute security is an unattainable objective and one that only produces imperial overstretch.

In sum, the America as Balancer perspective holds that:

1. The primary national security threats to the United States are self-inflicted. They take the form of a proliferation of security commitments designed to protect America's economic interests.

2. The United States has a limited responsibility to other states because the burden for protecting a state's national interests falls upon that state.

3. The United States' responsibility to the global community is limited. American national interests and the maintenance of global order are not identical.

Christopher Layne provides a rationale for the role of balancer as part of a strategy of strategic independence.[21] He argues that a return to multipolarity is inevitable. Trying to reassert or preserve American preeminence and suppress the emergence of new powers is held to be futile. There is thus little reason for the United States to become deeply involved in the affairs of other states on a routine basis. In spite of this inevitable move toward multipolarity, Layne sees no reason to change America's long-standing foreign policy concern with the rise of a hegemony in Europe. What is needed is a hedging strategy, one that will allow the United States to realize this goal without provoking others into uniting against it or accelerating their separate pursuits of power. Blessed by its geopolitical location, Layne believes that the answer lies in adopting the position of an offshore balancer. The United States is positioned to allow global and regional power balances to ensure its strategic independence. Only when others prove incapable of acting to block the ascent of a challenging hegemony should the United States step in to affect the balance of power. Given its continued power resources, such an intervention is held likely to be decisive.

Disengaged America

The final alternative future put forward here calls for the United States to selectively yet thoroughly withdraw from the world.[22] The Disengaged America perspective sees retrenchment as necessary because the international system is becoming increasingly inhospitable to U.S. values and unresponsive to efforts at management or domination. Increasingly, the choices facing U.S. foreign policy will be ones of choosing what kinds of losses to avoid. Optimal solutions to foreign policy problems will no longer present themselves to policy makers, and if they do, domestic constraints will prevent policy makers from pursuing such a path. In the Disengaged America perspective, foreign policy must become less of a lance—a tool for spreading values—and more of a shield—a minimum set of conditions behind which the United States can protect its values and political processes.[23]

Becoming disengaged means that the United States will have to learn to live in a "second-best world," one that is not totally of its liking but one in which it can get by. Allies will be fewer in number, and those that remain will have to do more to protect their own security and economic well-being. Nonintervention will be the rule for the United States and self-reliance the watchword for others. The United States must be prepared to "let" some states be dominated and to direct its efforts at placing space between the falling dominoes rather than trying to define a line of containment. In the realm of economics, the objective should be to move toward autarchy and self-sufficiency so that other states cannot manipulate or threaten the United States. If the United States cannot dominate the sources of supply, it must be prepared to "substitute, tide over, (and) ride out" efforts at resource manipulation.[24] World order concerns must also take a back seat in U.S. foreign policy. As George Kennan has said about the food-population problem, "We did not create it and it is beyond our power to solve it."[25] Kennan argues that the United States needs to divest itself of its guilt complex and accept the fact that there is really very little that the United States can do for the third world and very little that the third world can do for the United States. In sum, the Disengaged America perspective holds that:

1. The major threat to U.S. national security comes from an overactive foreign policy. Events beyond U.S. borders are not as crucial to U.S security as is commonly perceived, and moreover, the United States has little power to influence their outcome.

2. The United States' responsibility to other states is minimal. The primary responsibility of the United States is to its own economic and military security.

3. The United States' responsibility to the global community is also minimal. The issues on the global agenda, especially as they relate to the third world, are not the fault of the United States, and the United States can do little to solve them.

Consistent with the Disengaged America perspective, Earl Ravenal asserts that in a period of international nonalignment such as the one we are now in, traditional principles of defense planning are largely irrelevant.[26] Military power, for example, should no longer be employed to further human rights or economic principles beyond American borders. Rather than pursue military goals, American foreign policy must concentrate on protecting American lives and property, the territorial integrity of the United States, and the autonomy of its political system. Consistent with these priorities, American military power would only be used for three purposes: (1) defend the approaches to U.S. territory; (2) serve as second chance forces to be used if deterrence fails or unexpected threats arise; and (3) provide finite essential deterrence against the United States and its forces overseas.

Ravenal's assessment of how American foreign policy needs to be changed is shared by other analysts at the Cato Institute, a foreign policy think tank, with which he is affiliated. Doug Bandow urges the United States to remain culturally, economically, and politically engaged in the world, but insists that it curtail foreign aid programs and bring its troops home.[27] Ted Galen Carpenter, its director, asserts that the primary responsibility of American foreign policy is to "guard the security and liberty of the American people. Washington has neither a constitutional nor moral writ to play Don Quixote and attempt to rectify all the ills of the world."[28] Or, in the words of Pat Buchanan, "America First—and Second, and Third."[29]

THE FUTURE

Agreement cannot be expected on any of these (or other) visions of American foreign policy in the near future. Deciding which among them is best suited to protect and further American interests into a new century is only one of the challenges confronting the United States today. A second and equally important challenge is obtaining the leadership resources necessary to translate a desired strategic vision into policy.[30] This challenge operates at several different levels. At a structural level, it entails acquiring the power resources necessary to lead. Whether these resources primarily are military or economic in nature will depend on the vision selected, but traditional international relations theorizing suggests that little will be accomplished unless the United States has the power to get others to follow. Realizing many of these visions will demand more than just possessing the ability to dominate others, it will also depend upon the ability to get others to follow in multilateral settings. Leadership at the institutional level will require that the United States develop a capacity for fostering cooperation among states by framing issues so that joint action is possible and providing the resources needed to implement solutions.

Finally, leadership will be necessary at the situational level. Here, the challenge will be to find creative solutions to problems, to find "good people" with insight into human nature and the dynamics of world politics so that opportunities for action are not lost.

NOTES

1. Richard Rosecrance, "New Directions?" in Richard Rosecrance (ed.), *America as an Ordinary Country: U.S. Foreign Policy and the Future* (Ithaca, N.Y.: Cornell University Press, 1976), pp. 245–66; and reprinted in Jeffrey Salamon, James P. O'Leary, and Richard Shultz (eds.), *Power, Principles, and Interests* (Lexington, Mass.: Ginn, 1985), pp. 433–44.

2. Salamon, O'Leary, and Shultz (eds.), *Power, Principles, and Interests,* p. 443.

3. Ibid., p. 442.

4. Ronald W. Pruessen, "Beyond the Cold War—Again: 1955 and the 1990s," *Political Science Quarterly,* 108 (1993), 59–84.

5. On this theme, see Robert A. Isaak, *American Democracy and World Power* (New York: St. Martin's, 1977); and Robert C. Johansen, *The National Interest and the Human Interest: An Analysis of U.S. Foreign Policy* (Princeton, N.J.: Princeton University Press, 1980).

6. Johansen, *National Interest and the Human Interest.*

7. On this theme, see Robert O. Keohane and Joseph S. Nye, *Power and Interdependence: World Politics in Transition* (Boston: Little, Brown, 1977); and Stanley Hoffman, *Primacy or World Order: American Foreign Policy Since the Cold War* (New York: McGraw-Hill, 1978).

8. Robert D. Hormats, "Making Regionalism Safe," *Foreign Affairs,* 73 (1994), 97–108.

9. Kishore Mahbubani, "Japan Adrift," *Foreign Policy,* 88 (1992), 126–45.

10. Robert A. Manning, "The Asian Paradox: Toward a New Architecture," *World Policy Journal,* 10 (1993), 55–64.

11. James Schlesinger, "Quest for a Post Cold War Foreign Policy," *Foreign Affairs,* 72 (1992/93), 17–28.

12. Robert W. Tucker, "1989 and All That," in Nicholas X. Rizopoulos (ed.), *Sea-Changes: American Foreign Policy in a World Transformed* (New York: Council on Foreign Relations Press, 1990), 204–37.

13. George Bush, "Remarks at the United States Military Academy," *Public Papers of the President* (Washington, D.C.: U.S. Government Printing Office, 1993), 2230–31.

14. On this theme, see Robert W. Tucker, "The Purposes of American Power," *Foreign Affairs,* 59 (1980/81), 241–74.

15. Zbigniew Brzezinski, "The Premature Partnership," *Foreign Affairs,* 73 (1994), 67–82.

16. Walter Russell Mead, "No Cold War Two: The United States and the Russian Federation," *The World Policy Journal,* 11 (1994), 1–17.

17. Colin Gray, "Back to the Future: Russia and the Balance of Power," *Global Affairs,* 7 (1992), 41–52.

18. Charles Krauthammer, "The Unipolar Moment," *Foreign Affairs,* 70 (1990/91), 23–33.

19. Charles Krauthammer, "Playing God in Somalia," *The Washington Post,* August 13, 1993.

20. Christopher Layne and Benjamin Schwarz, "American Hegemony—Without an Enemy," *Foreign Policy,* 93 (1993/94), 5–23.

21. Christopher Layne, "The Unipolar Illusion: Why Great Powers Will Rise," *International Security,* 17 (1993), 5–51.

22. On this theme, see Earl C. Ravenal, *Never Again: Learning from America's Foreign Policy Failures* (Philadelphia: Temple University Press, 1978).

23. Ibid., p. 15.

24. Ibid., p. xv.

25. George Kennan, *Cloud of Danger: Current Realities of American Foreign Policy* (Boston: Little, Brown, 1977), p. 32.

26. Earl Ravenal, "The Case for Adjustment," *Foreign Policy,* 81 (1990/91), 3–19.

27. Doug Bandow, "Keeping the Troops and Money at Home," *Current History,* 579 (January 1994), 8–13.

28. Ted Galen Carpenter, "Foreign Policy Peril: Somalia Set a Dangerous Precedent," *USA Today,* 121 (May 1993), 10–13.

29. Patrick Buchanan, "America First—and Second, and Third," *The National Interest,* 19 (1990), 77–82.

30. G. John Ikenberry, "The Future of International Leadership," *Political Science Quarterly,* 111 (1996), 385–402.

Index

Powell, General Colin, 74, 117, 120, 121, 122, 365
  in Haiti, 77
  as National Security Advisor, 191, 194
Powell Doctrine, 370
Power:
  diffusion of, 4–6
  emergence of new forms of, 12
  inequalities in international system, 4
Pragmatic America perspective, 406–7
Preemptive strike, 363–64
Presidential Decision Directive 13, 359
Presidential Decision Directive 60, 359, 361
Presidential Findings, 193, 316, 317
Presidents:
  and bureaucracy, 187–92
  decision making, 192–94
  media lessons for, 130
  personality of, 183–86
  style of, 188
Pressler, Senator Larry, 163
Price, David, 203
Principals Committee under Clinton, 194, 195
Prize Cases decision of 1862, 171
Proliferation of conventional weapons, 392–93
Propaganda, as covert action, 306–7
Proxmire, Senator William, 203
Prussen, Ronald W., 403
Public opinion, 133–40
  changes in focus of, 134–38
  impact on foreign policy, 139–40
  impact of Vietnam on, 107–8
  and use of force, 138–39
Putnam, Robert, 276

Q

Qaddafi, Libyan Leader Moammar, 305, 311
Quandt, William, 144
Quota, 334

R

Radio Free Asia, 307
Radio Free Europe, 307
Radio Liberty, 307
Radio Marti, 150
Rally-around-the-flag effect, 132
Rational actor model, 241–42
  and Cuban missile crisis, 258–59
Ravenal, Earl, 412
Reagan, President Ronald, 4, 143, 183
  and ABM Treaty, 163
  and anti-nuclearism, 99
  and arms sales, 36, 243–44
  and Caribbean Basin Initiative, 273–75

and Congress, 210, 320
and Contras, 17, 25, 62–63
and diplomacy, 289
and embargoes, 332, 337
and end of cold war, 98–99
and Gorbachev, 37, 99
and Grenada, 171
and human rights, 28
and Iran-Contra, 18, 38, 161, 183, 192–93
and military force strategy, 365
and military industrial complex, 146
and MX missiles, 261, 267–69
and NAFTA, 273, 275
and National Security Council, 191
and nuclear strategy, 358, 359
personality of, 184, 186, 187
and SALT II, 384
and SDI, 146, 379, 387–88
style of, 44, 188
and Tower Commission, 183, 192
and trade imbalance, 330
and Vietnam, 100
Reagan Administration:
  activist foreign policy, 33
  and Angola, 310
  and arms control, 385
  and arms sales, 38, 243–44, 300–301
  and assassination, 311
  and CIA, 310, 319–20
  and COCOM, 332
  and covert action, 310
  and debt relief, 341
  and economic aid, 343
  and elite theory, 250
  and El Salvador, 154–55
  and environmental conferences, 294
  evaluation of foreign policy, 18, 65–66, 82
  and invasion of Grenada, 171
  and Iran–Contra, 18, 192–93
  and Lebanon, 20–21, 36
  and Nicaragua, 319–20
  and renewal of cold war, 59–65
  and Sandinistas, 38, 322
  and START, 37, 385
  and State Department, 220
  unilateralism, 36–37
Reagan Doctrine, 45, 63, 305
Reagan–Gorbachev Summit, 289
Reassurance, strategy of, 375
Reformed America perspective, 403–5
Refugee policy, 18
Regional diversity of international system, 9–10
Reichert, John, 376
Reilly, William, 294
Reykjavik Summit, 36, 289
Rhodesia, economic sanctions against, 333–34
Rio Earth Summit, 294